Ethnoarchaeology
of Shuwa-Arab Settlements

Ethnoarchaeology
of Shuwa-Arab Settlements

Augustin F. C. Holl

LEXINGTON BOOKS
Lanham • Boulder • New York • Oxford

LEXINGTON BOOKS

Published in the United States of America
by Lexington Books
A Member of the Rowman & Littlefield Publishing Group
4501 Forbes Boulevard, Suite 200, Lanham, Maryland 20706
www.rowmanlittlefield.com

P.O. Box 317, Oxford OX2 9RU, United Kingdom

British Library Cataloguing in Publication Information Available

Library of Congress Cataloging-in-Publication Data Available

ISBN 0-7391-0407-1 (cloth : alk. paper)

Printed in the United States of America

♾™ The paper used in this publication meets the minimum requirements of American
National Standard for Information Sciences—Permanence of Paper for Printed Library
Materials, ANSI/NISO Z39.48-1992.

This book is dedicated to Roy D'Andrade.

Contents

Figures

Tables

Acknowledgments

The project "ethnoarchaeology of Shuwa-Arab settlements" is part of a larger regional archaeological and ethnoarchaeological research program. Its fieldwork component lasted from 1982 to 1991, a period during which eleven field seasons took place with crews of students and workmen. This research was partially funded by Grant No. 3715-87 from the National Geographic Society Committee for Research and Exploration, and multiyear grants from the French Ministry of Foreign Affairs and Ministry of Cooperation.

In Cameroon, the Institute of Human Sciences has been extraordinarily supportive. Research permits have always been granted in a timely fashion, and logistical support was always available. P. A. de Labriffe, Francoise Lafage, and Alison Jones supervised task-units. Dr. Anne Bridault collected and analyzed part of the faunal remains; and Dr. T. E. Levy made the field season an unforgettable experience in scholarship and friendship. Thanks to Solomon Kuah, Margie Burton, Adolfo Muniz, and Stephen Dueppen, who, as research assistants, helped, processed, and organized the material published in this book at one stage or another.

Gratitude is extended to Mr. Mahamat Bahr Maarouf, Sultan of Logone-Birni, the late May Hassana, the last Sultan of Houlouf, the Galadima, other elders from the Kotoko town of Houlouf, and Bilama Harfi of Alaya I for their patience and teachings. Finally, O. Abdoulaye, Adoum, Mahamat Arouna, Arouna, O. Babawa, Z. Harfi, M. Mahamat, and J. Ngarba are acknowledged for their constant support and contribution to fieldwork.

Introduction

An Idea of Ethnoarchaeology

A Definition

Human imprint on landscape, the constant interaction with and modification of natural habitats, and the production, use, and discard of artifacts, all allow archaeologists to document pieces and bits of the human career. How this is done is another story, a story not only about worldviews and theories, but also about techniques and methods. The idea of ethnoarchaeology is one component of this unrelenting search for accurate knowledge about the world we live in.The idea of ethnoarchaeology is barely new; it is the level of conceptual, theoretical, and methodological systematization achieved in this subfield of anthropological research during the last few years that makes the difference (David and Kramer 2001).The definitional issues remain open and generally depend on the practice of the researchers involved (Agorsah1990; Atherton 1983; Binford 1978; David et al. 1988; Gallay et al. 1996; Gould 1978, 1980; Hodder 1982; Kramer 1979, 1982; MacEachern 1996; Miller 1985; Longacre and Skibo 1994; Yellen 1977).

Is ethnoarchaeology the handmaiden of archaeology? Is it a new sub-discipline of anthropological archaeology, or simply of anthropology? Or is it a component of cultural studies devoted to the investigation of the relationships between humans and things? Clark (1968: 280) on the one hand clearly favors the "handmaiden" situation as he spelled out his expectations: "The operation as I see it, is twofold: first obtain this ethnoarchaeological data by fieldwork, to apply it to the archaeological evidence with sufficient precision that a reasonable measure of accuracy in reconstruction is ensured." Hodder (1982) on the other hand advocates a bold move in the direction of cultural studies: "Each aspect of the material culture data, whether burial, settlement pattern, wall design or refuse distribution, can be interpreted in terms of common underlying schemes. These structures of meaning permeate all aspects of archaeological evidence. Each material item has significance in terms of its place in the whole" (Hodder 1982: 212). There are many possible combinations of and subtle variations around these themes ranging from narrowly focused technical research to broad-based regional investigations discussed at length

1

by N. David and C. Kramer in their new book *Ethnoarchaeology in Action.* Ethnoarchaeology is therefore not a theory. It is not a method either. It is the ethnographic study of living societies from archaeological perspectives. And to be more precise, it is "a research strategy embodying a range of approaches to understanding the relationships of material culture as a whole both in the living context and as it enters the archaeological record and to exploiting such understandings in order to inform archaeological concepts and improve interpretation" (David and Kramer 2001: 2).

Research Goals

The work presented in this book tries to make the best of all the ethnoarchaeology brands to generate what can be termed *general ethno-archaeology.* This approach is anchored on the search for patterns from the material record first, with very strict and selective reliance on informants. Such an approach is more easily implemented with the study of whole settlement systems. The study area, an ethnic mosaic, is particularly exciting. The Shuwa Arab, migrant minorities a few centuries ago, are today the largest and fastest growing population in the study area, and Northern Cameroon in general. What can be learned from their settlement location strategies; the shape, size, and layout of their settlements; the architecture and organization of their houses, the domestic equipment and furniture they manufacture or buy, use, and discard? Many if not all the issues raised here are equally relevant for a strictly archaeological research project, the Houlouf Archaeological project conducted in the same study area, following the same general guidelines.The study area appears to have been settled at the very beginning of the second millennium BC (ca. 1900 BC) and the project succeeded in documenting the formation of the Houlouf chiefdom and its annexation in the sixteenth-seventeenth centuries by the expanding state [kingdom] of Lagwan [Logone-Birni] (Holl 2002). This book is clearly an extension of the archaeological work and a companion volume to *The Land of Houlouf: Genesis of a Chadic Chiefdom (BC 1900–AD 1800).* It is a sort of ethnoarchaeology of political systems addressing issues of sociocultural evolution.What has been learned during this research was totally unexpected but not totally unpredictable. Podlewsky (1966), a demographer who studied the population dynamics of different ethnolinguistic groups from Northern Cameroon in the early 1960s, predicted political unrest within a thirty-year time-span. This issue is dealt with in the book. What this *Ethnoarchaeology of Shuwa-Arab Settlements* documents is surprisingly the final stage of the paradoxical collapse of the Houlouf chiefdom and the rise to primacy of a Shuwa-Arab Polity. The trend toward increasing sedentarization, craft specialization, occupational diversification, and population growth are predicated on the steady weakening of the Kotoko centralized political systems with, in the later and recent period, the backdrop of remote nation-state policy. The outcome is simply fascinating for students of social evolution, a dream case study of paradoxical collapse without violence, and an explosive surge to primacy.

About Field Methods

The methodology developed during the three field seasons of ethnoarchaeological research had a very simple and straightforward objective, that of recording the most accurate picture of the state of Shuwa-Arab settlements. Depending on the situation at the time of fieldwork, presence or absence of settlers, some adjustments had to be made. A general research tactic was adopted to deal with all the sites in a similar if not comparable manner. The research team, including students and workmen, was divided into three task-units. One task-unit dealt with the general mapping of the whole site and its immediate surroundings using a theodolite, a compass, and measuring tapes. Another task-unit dealt with the mapping of each individual architectural feature, with its in-situ artifactual content. And the remaining task-unit studied the artifact assemblages found in each house. This involved the drafting and systematic measurement of pottery, calabashes, and other vessels found, each reported on an individual card. Crucial house's furniture like beds and hearths were also described systematically.Within this research tactic however, abandoned settlements, de facto archaeological sites were investigated with a strict archaeological methodology: (1) cleaning the site if it was overgrown; (2) removing the collapsed house superstructures; (3) cleaning the exposed floors with all the represented features, furniture, and artifacts left in situ; (3) mapping, and taking photographs; (4) artifact recording; and (5) in few cases test-excavations were conducted.

At the end of the eleventh, and last, field season in the study area, two more formal evening sessions, involving the most senior among the elders and focused on local ethnohistory, were organized and audio-taped. One took place at Houlouf in the residence of the *Galadima* and the other one at Alaya I, in the house complex of the village headman, *Bilama* Harfi.

Organization of the Book

The book is divided into five parts. Part I includes two chapters and deals with the historical background and the presentation of the study area. History played a critical role in what made the Shuwa Arab of the study area remain Shuwa Arab. Sketching the complex migration of their ancestors from the eastern Nile Delta to their settlement in the Chad basin at the end of the fourteenth century AD and their later expansion in the Chadian Plain and Kotokoland is the purpose of chapter 1. Chapter 2 describes the major physical characteristics of the study area, the climate, vegetation, as well as key environmental features. It also outlines the ethnic diversity of the area, the distribution of population, and preferential locational patterns of the involved ethnic groups and their socioeconomic similarities and differences.

The tested settlements are first arranged according to their geographic location into more or less coherent subregional clusters: a classic step in the organization of survey data. Part II is devoted to semipermanent villages, inhabited for most of the year except for a few months during the dry season. It is divided into three chapters. Chapter 3 describes four villages from the S; chapter 4, six villages from the W and chapter 5, two northern sites. Part III provides the material from the 1990 dry-season camps in two chapters. The rainy-season was virtually nonexistent that year, and the usually flooded hinterland depression received a small amount of water. Chapter 6 deals with the Amachita camps' cluster and chapter 7 with the Agedipse one. In this case, informants were crucial in the identification of the origins of the camps' settlers. Part IV is comprised of four chapters dealing with permanent villages. These permanent settlements are, on average, larger in size, each being dealt with in a chapter. Chapter 8 for Abuzrega, chapters 9 and 10 for the Djidat I and II twin settlement complex, and finally, chapter 11 for Marafaine.

Part V looks at the evidence from a historical perspective and concentrates on general patterns and trends discernible from the body of data at hand. Based on a broad array of parameters, the investigated settlements are arranged into four chronological categories, the Early. Middle, and Late Groups, as well as the Dry-Season Camps settled in 1990. The discussion is structured around three major sets of issues dealt with in three chapters. Chapter 12 deals with the spatial dimension of the sampled Shuwa-Arab settlements. Chapter 13 sharply narrows the focus and discusses the range of sociocultural information to be extracted from a stringent analysis of the variability in the shape and decoration of hearths. And finally, chapter 14 considers the structure and variation in subsistence systems developed in each of the sites.

The short conclusion takes the debate farther from where it was left at the end of chapter 2. The studied material documents the continuation of Shuwa-Arab history, this time, a peaceful rise to regional primacy. It goes without saying that it is probably the overarching presence of the Cameroonian state that smoothed this phase's transition and kept any violent reaction at bay.

PART I

People, Land, and the Study Area

Chapter 1

A Brief History of Shuwa-Arab Expansion

Introduction

The Shuwa-Arab form a distinct ethnic group among the societies in the Lake Chad basin of West Africa. How they merged out in this region as a unique socio-economic unit represents a case study in the ethnogenesis of pastoral societies. Seen in this context, the history of the Shuwa-Arab not only provides many of the historical clues which help understand their unique process of settlement in the basin, but also provides a comparative historical mode useful for analyzing other pastoral societies around the globe. Arab and Muslim expansion was boosted during the second half of the first millennium AD by religious proselytism, trade, and extensive territorial conquest. In Northeastern Africa, the south and westward expansion of some Arab factions was a delayed and unpredictable consequence of the Muslim conquest of Egypt with its southward extension from AD 639 to 652. The Arab tribes moving on the southern and western frontiers of the expanding Muslim world belonged to several ethnic and sociopolitical groups. Their changing adaptation to local biomes, as well as differential and long-term interaction with local ethnic groups, generated the formation of new cultural entities. While being still identified as Arabs, they were nonetheless granted several ethnonyms, with those from the Chad basin later called *Shuwa-Arab* (Eastern Arabs) by the Kanuri from Bornu. As such, the Arab's south and westward expansion is a long-term migration and an extensive process of ethnogenesis linked to the vagaries of the balance of power between ranked and competing social groups (fig. 1). These processes probably operated through selective retention of significant patterns of pastoral Arab social organization-like kinship and preferential marriage (Conte 1991), the stochastic dynamic of fission and fusion among the involved tribal units, peaceful and/or conflictual relations with local polities, as well as absorption of different cultural identities.

In general, historical sources are selective and usually represent the views of members of the dominant sedentary group. During the early centuries of their settlement in Egypt and the Nile valley, the nomadic fractions of the expanding Arab

7

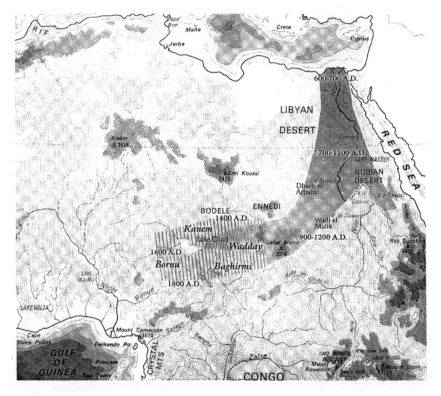

Figure 1: Map of Shuwa-Arab migrations from the Nile Delta to Lake Chad basin

groups did not fit into the newly emerging "Administrative-Commercial-City-dwellers" ethos. According to circumstances, their relations with dominant political authorities shifted back and forth from alliance to enmity, their territorial range expanding or contracting. Clearly, among the consulted historical sources, there is a neat prejudice against Arab nomadic tribes. They nonetheless provide useful evidence concerning Arab final expansion westward, toward the Chad basin. The portrait of Arab pastoral tribes painted by I. Hrbek (1977: 69) is significant of an epoch:

> "On the fringes of the cultivated lands and beyond them roamed Arab nomad tribes not yet assimilated to a settled life. Some of these tribes, coming from Arabia or Syria, used Egypt only as a corridor to the west or the south; others remained for a shorter or longer time. Being notoriously anarchic, turbulent and always in opposition to any outside control, they represented an element of danger and unrest, too often causing disruption of economic life by their raids on villages or by holding up caravans."

Arab Nomads in Early Muslim Egypt (ca. 650–1000)

To trace the genesis of Shuwa-Arab settlement in the Lake Chad basin it is necessary to look briefly to Egypt and the history of relations between the sedentary complex societies of Egyptians and Nubians and the nomadic pastoral Arab groups beginning in the seventh century AD. Arab and Muslim troops, lead by Amr ibn al 'As, entered the Byzantine province of Egypt in AD 639. Alexandria, the most important commercial and political center was captured in AD 642; and a fortress was later built at Fustat-Misr. After several unsuccessful attempts to conquer Nubia, the *Bakt*—a diplomatic and trade agreement—was signed between Nubians and Arabs in AD 652. According to this agreement, the Nubians accepted to provide Egypt with slaves in exchange of foodstuff and craft items (Bianquis 1990: 194). Muslim conquerors had to implement new governmental institutions and territorial administration, strengthen and consolidate their power bases, and raise funds to finance their new domain. From the seventh to the ninth century, the early Muslim Egyptian society was divided into several changing but ranked social groups within compatible and conflicting interests (Hrbek 1977; Bianquis 1990; Hiskett 1994; Insoll 1996). There were different cultural, linguistic, ethnic and occupational cleavages; between the conquerors and the conquered, Arab Muslims and Byzantine Christians, peasant farmers and citizens, pastoral-nomads and peasants. Numerous Arab nomadic groups organized along tribal lines were settled in *Qabilat* (allocated landed settlements) in the periphery of major towns. During the formative years of the Egyptian Muslim society, most of them were concentrated in Lower Egypt, in the Hawf and the Eastern Nile delta (fig. 1). Peasant and pastoral-nomad revolts were an endemic feature of Muslim Egypt for almost two centuries. From 767 to 868, during the *Abbassid Khalifate,* revolts are recorded to have occurred almost continuously for fifty years (785–832) in the eastern delta. Peace was restored in 832 and consolidated by the *Fatimids.* The reaction of central governmental authorities was a radical one, setting the stage for later widespread unrest and more troubles. Arab nomads lost their privileges: "Arabs were strikken out of the *diwan,* freed from military duties, they were no more entitled to benefit from pensions paid by the state" (Bianquis 1990: 198). The process of ethnogenesis was well under way; additional Arab and Berber tribes from Arabia, Syria, and the Maghrib entered Egypt from E and W. Large fractions of the former Christian peasantry were converted to Islam. Some Arab tribesmen shifted to sedentary agriculture. Others remained pastoral-nomads. Another part adopted city life style as merchants, bureaucrats, or craft specialists.

The social and political scenery was characterized by shifting alliances, palace intrigues, succession troubles, doctrinal intolerance, and the rise and fall of dynasties. Heavy taxes imposed on peasants and pastoral nomads generated long lasting revolts. At the end of the first millennium AD, the Arab conquest of Egypt had generated a situation in which descendants of the conquerors were divided into several ranked groups with a ruling aristocracy supported by wealthy merchants, high ranking state officials, scholars, and bureaucrats at top of the social hierarchy, free citizens with varying occupations, a dominated and exploited peasantry, and finally, large fractions of excluded pastoral-nomads living on the edge of cultivated land and desert steppes (Bianquis 1990). The seeds of conflict and ultimate ethnic movement were sown.

Arab Nomads' Southward Expansion (ca. 1000–1300)

The territorial range of Arab nomad tribes was not exclusively confined to Lower Egypt (fig. 1). "Already prior to the tenth century many Arab tribes, or part of them, had migrated southward to Upper Egypt and to the eastern desert between the Nile valley and the Red Sea littoral. Penetrating farther S along the Nile was for a long time made difficult by the relatively strong Christian kingdoms of Al-Maqurra in Northern Nubia, but even there, the Arabs were able to infiltrate gradually (Hrbek 1977: 69). The process of southward expansion was nonetheless a complex one, resulting from a combination of a few independent factors. The first factor was linked with Arab nomad attempts to escape from state control and heavy taxation. They usually managed to settle in desert steppes, moving from one place to another, beyond the reach of settled communities. The second was an artifact of a purposeful state military policy and can be divided into two components. During the Ayyubid period (1171–1250 AD), "some of the n nomadic and seminomadic Arabs from Upper Egypt were recruited into the Ayyubid army and later rewarded with lands" (Hrbek 1977: 75). This policy was implemented in parallel with more systematic attempt to definitely crush Arab nomad rebellions; the stronger pressure thus exerted on nomads resulted in sustained out-migrations (Bianquis 1990; Hrbek 1977; Kropacek 1985; Garcin 1985; Zeltner 1979). The third important factor revolves around the weakening of formerly strong Nubian Christian kingdoms, resulting from stronger pressures from Muslim Egypt, internal dissension, and sustained infiltration and raiding from Arab nomad tribes (Kropacek 1985). It is nonetheless "difficult if not impossible to discern the numerous migratory moves and to fix them chronologically, since the Arabs who penetrated into the Sudan came mainly in small groups of different tribal origin rather than in large tribal entities, and because their immigration was more akin to infiltration over centuries than a sudden invasion" (Hrbek 1977: 78). Thus, using existing historical documents it is impossible to pinpoint a specific event in time when Arab nomads migrated to the Lake Chad basin. Instead, their expansion in the Chadian plain is best characterized as a gradual, above all, "peaceful" process of infiltration.

There is a large body of evidence suggesting sustained "Arabization" and Islamization of the northernmost Nubian kingdom of Al-Maqurra (capital city at Dunqula) from the ninth to the twelfth century. Intermarriage between Nubians and Arabs from the tribe of Banu al-Kanzare well attested (Kropacek 1985: 437). In 1275, the northern part of Al-Maqurra kingdom was annexed by Mamluk Egypt

(1250–1517 AD), and ruled by a vassal dynasty of Banu al-Kanzdescent. The Banu al-Kanz were granted the territory situated between Aswan and the modern border of Sudan. From this territorial basis, they took total control of Al-Maqurra kingdom which was converted to Islam in 1317 (Garcin 1985: 416). The southward expansion of nomadic Arab tribes, which began during the Ayyubid period (1171–1250), was amplified after the rise to power of the Mamluk dynasty (1250–1517) and the collapse of the Nubian kingdoms. The Mamluks initiated a planned program to expel all the unruly Arab nomad tribes from the kingdom. They were then castigated as *"Bedouins," "urbans"* (i.e., rebels, uncivilized), and several military campaigns were launched against them. According to Kropacek (1985: 437), important Mamluk military expeditions are recorded as having occurred in 1302, 1351, 1353, 1375, and 1395. Mamluk military expansion left the Arab nomads one alternative: to trek southward to Sudan. Contrary to what is suggested by Hrbek (1977: 78), according to which nomadic Arab expansion to Sudan "was more akin to infiltration over centuries than a sudden invasion," it seems more likely that large-scale migration of relatively large groups of nomads was the outcome of at least some of the military campaigns launched by Mamluk rulers. The available historical sources summarized by Hrbek (ibid.) are, unfortunately, mostly silent with regard to the nature of the Arab expansion. However, the settlement process is not directly linked to commercial activities and religious proselytism. Nevertheless several tribal names are reported for nomadic Arab groups who settled in Nubia during the first half of the second millennium AD; the *Juhayna, Bali, Judham,* and *Tayy.* Of key importance to this study is the fact that these very tribal groups settled in Sudan and later expanded south and westward (Garcin 1985; Kropacek 1985; Hrbek 1977). As will be discussed later, the Judham tribe appears to have played an important role in the expansion of the Shuwa-Arab in the Chad basin in the fourteenth century.

As outlined by Hrbek (1977: 78), the disintegration of the northern Nubian kingdom facilitated the access of Arab nomads to rich pasture lands beyond the Nubian desert. Their expansion followed two main directions, with the Nile valley as the dividing axis—one easterly and the other westerly. It is the westerly one which will be considered in this discussion. According to Hrbek (1977), westward Arab expansion toward the Darfur in western Sudan followed two main routes, either directly from Upper Egypt along the Darb al Arba' in (the route of 40 days), or from Dunqula along the Wadi al Malik. In the Darfur, Islam "developed through three phases in which there was probably largely peaceful interaction between the new faith and established customs" (Mohammed 1986: 223). It was of little importance during the first phase (ca. 1100–1600), probably expanded by individuals, traders, and/or holymen who progressively acquainted with rulers and elite members of local communities. "The location of the mosques seems not to be of central importance to the settlements at this time. Bora's mosque was on the fringe of the settlement and not associated with other Islamic constructions. At Uri the mosque was small and rather isolated one, and at Ain Farah it seems to have been superimposed on an earlier stone structure. There is no evidence to suggest that there was a Muslim quarter in the settlement" (Mohammed 1986: 224). During phase two (ca. 1600–1800), with the rise to power of the Keira dynasty, Islam was adopted as the official religion of the court and was spread among the subjects of the kingdom. Mosques were built in different settlements, and the royal domains expanded to include Kordufan. "As a result Darfur was brought into more contact with its Muslim neighbours" (Mohammed 1986: 225). And finally, phase III, a later nineteenth and early twentieth century development, led to the consolidation and routinization of Muslim faith, laws, and practices (Hiskett 1994; Insoll 1996).

From the tenth to the fourteenth century, territories situated between the Nile and northern Darfur was settled by Arabs (MacMichael 1922). Their changing adaptation to their new ecological and cultural settings generated regional variations outlined by Hrbek (1977). Those settled along the northeastern part of the territorial range continued to rear camels and sheep. They consisted of different clans of various tribes but nonetheless formed large groups known as the *Kababish* (from *Kabsh*, i.e., "ram"). Those who migrated farther S, to southern Darfur and southern Kordufan, and westward to Wadai and the lake Chad region, adopted cattle husbandry and became known as *Baqqara* (from *Baqara*, i.e., "cow"). "Although they preserved their nomadic way of life and their tribal system intact, they intermarried with the local peoples, inaugurating thus another process, that of the gradual Africanization of the Sudanese Arabs" (Hrbek 1977: 79; Kropacek 1985; Cunnison 1966; Hassan 1973; McMichael 1922).

Arab Expansion in the Chad Basin (ca. 1300–1500)

The original aspects of the earliest phase of Shuwa-Arab expansion in the Chad basin is unknown. There may have been several routes toward the Ennedi, along the Darb al-Ar'bain in the Wadi Howar, the Wadi el Malik, as well as westward from the northern Darfur (fig. 1). The archaeology of the eastern part of modern Chad Republic is unknown. There are nonetheless a number of historical sources, both written and ethnohistorical records, which provide useful data (Zeltner 1979; Al-Qalqashandi in Levtzion and Hopkins 1981: 346–349). The presence of Arabs in the Chad basin is attested by a letter found by Al-Qalqashandi (1355–1418) in the Egyptian *Diwan* (State Archives) and published in his fourteen-volume compilation *Subh al-a'sha fi sina'at al-insha* (*The Dawn of the Night-Blind, on the Art of Letter-Writing*), completed in AD 1412: "This is the text of a letter which came to al-Malik al-Zahir Abu Sa'id Barquq. It arrived during 794/1391–2 in charge of the ruler of Barnu's cousin with a present. It was prompted by what is mentioned in it concerning the Arabs of Judham who are his neighbors. It is written on square paper with lines side by side, in a Maghribi hand, without margin at head or side. The conclusion of the letter is written on the verso, at the foot of the page" (Al-

Qalqashandi, quoted in Levtzion and Hopkins 1981: 347). The content of this letter, in which Abu 'Amr 'Uthman, king of Bornu, complained about the exactions of the Judham Arabs against his subjects, is particularly important for our discussion. Here is the quote of an important part of this document as it relates to the Chad basin and the history of the Shuwa:

> To the mighty King of Egypt, God's blessed land, Mother of the World:
> Upon you be peace more fragrant than pungent musk, sweeter than the water of cloud and ocean. . . .
> To proceed: We sent you our ambassador, my cousin, whose name is Idris b. Muhammad, because of the misfortune which we and our vassal kings have experienced. For the Arabs who are called Judham and others have snatched away some of our free people, women and children, infirm men, relations of ours, and other Muslims. Some of these Arabs are polytheists and deviate from true religion. They have raided the Muslims and done great slaughter among them because of a dispute which has occurred between us and our enemies. As a result of this dispute they have killed our king 'Amr the Martyr b. Idris, the son of our father al-Hajj Idris son of al-Hajj Ibrahim. . . . These Arabs have devastated all our country, the whole of al-Barnu, up to this day. They have seized our free men and our relatives, who are Muslims, and sold them to the slave dealers (jullàb) of Egypt and Syria and others; some they have kept for their own service.
> Now God has placed the control of Egypt from the sea to Uswan in your hands. These our people have been seized as merchandise, so pray send to all your territory, your emirs, ministers, judges, magistrates, jurists, markets overseers, that they may look and search and discover. If they find them, let them snatch them from their hands and put them to test. If they say: "We are free, we are Muslims" believe them. Do not take them for liars. When the truth is clear to you release them. Restore them to their freedom and Islam. For certain Arabs cause mischief in our land and do not act righteously. They are those who are ignorant of the Book of God and the Sunna of His Messenger (Al-Qalqashandi, quoted in Levtzion and Hopkins 1981: 247–8).

From the details contained in the letter quoted above, the Judham Arabs and other tribes were present in the Chad basin by the end of the fourteenth century (ca. AD 1380). The eastern boundary of the Bornu kingdom is not clearly known; however, according to Zeltner (1979: 19–20), Arab territories were situated between the Bahr el-Ghazzal and Lake Fittri. In addition, there seems to have been a permanent state of unrest between the Arabs and subjects of Bornu kingdom, suggesting a long-term interaction. King 'Amr b. Idris the brother of Uthman was killed in 1387. Arab raids resulted in the capture of slaves who were sold to dealers in Muslim market places situated in the Nile valley. Thus, at this point in time, the Shuwa-Arab were integrated de facto, in the long-distance trade network linking Egypt to the Central Sudan; they were in fact suppliers of slaves and not simply fleeing aggressive pastoralists as suggested by biased historical sources. In many respects the Shuwa-Arab worked to help link the Chadian plain/Sudanian

periphery with the growing Muslim/Mamluk core centered in Egypt. Finally, the
Shuwa-Arab do not appear to have been particularly good Muslims; they are presented as polytheists, deviant from true religion, and ignorant of the Book; and
their expansion was not linked to any kind of religious proselytism. The document
also provides some clues concerning the tribal identity of the fourteenth-century
Chad basin Arabs, indicating that they belonged to the Judham and other tribes.

Using written sources as well as ethnohistorical records and genealogies, Zeltner (1979: 20–22) provides an extremely useful general outline of the Judham
tribal history from its remote origin in the Arabian Peninsula. At the beginning of
the seventh century, Judham was a large and powerful tribe roaming to the N of
Medina with other tribes such as Lakhm, Sa'd Hudaym, and 'Udrah. "The first
mention of an agreement signed between Muhammad (The Prophet) and Judham
is dated to October 627, and Judham clans were part of the agreement which included the Wa'il" (Zeltner 1979: 20). The Judham were the first among the Arab
tribes to settle in Egypt. They were among General 'Amr ibn al As troops during
the Islamic conquest of Egypt and were granted territories and important privileges during the Fatimid period because of their participation in the *Jihad* (Holy
War). Their situation changed radically during the Ayyubid and the Mamluk periods;
when Judham clans or factions were reported to have been among the Kababish as
well as the Baqqara pastoral-nomads (Kropacek 1985: 449). Their presence in the
Chad basin in the fourteenth century is the direct consequence of the long process
of ethnogenesis initiated from their earliest settlement in Lower Egypt, but loosely
connected with explicit attempts to expand the new faith. According to Zeltner
(1979: 34), several Arab tribes and fractions distributed in the Chad basin today are
more or less directly linked to Judham ancestry. They used older Judham faction
names as self-appointed designations; this is the case for Wa'il, Bani Hasan, Uled
Ziyud, Uled Rachid, Uled Ghanim, Uled Malik, Uled Jabir, Halba and 'Uqbat.

Cultural Interaction in the Chad Basin (ca. AD 1500–1750)

Apart from the fourteenth century letter to the Mamluk Sultan of Egypt presented
above, there is no additional written record containing substantial information on
the Arab presence in the Chadian basin prior to the nineteenth century. At the beginning of the sixteenth century, Arab tribes were distributed over a relatively large
territory in the eastern part of the modern Chad Republic, extending from the
Ennedi-Darfur mountains in the E to Lake Fittri and Bahr el Ghazzal in the W
(fig. 1). According to Zeltner (1979: 23), the Bani Hasan started to expand in
Bagirmi, as well as along the northeastern and southern shores of Lake Chad during the first half of the sixteenth century.

The sketchy information available on the interaction between Arab nomads
and native local groups from the Chad basin is due to Imam Ahmad (or ibn) Furtu,
a sixteenth century Bornu scholar. Furtu was the author of two books on the mili-

tary expeditions of Sultan Idris Alaoma (1564–1596), the first one on Bornu and the second on Kanem (Lange 1977, 1987; Zeltner 1979, 1980). Without delving into the details concerning this poorly investigated history, Ahmad Furtu reported that Sultan Idris Alaoma, king of Bornu, launched several military campaigns in Kanem from 1574 to 1578 in order to support his ally Sultan Muhammad, king of Kanem, who was threatened by competitors backed by a coalition of Bulala and several Arab tribes. A peace treaty was signed on January 2–3, 1578, according to which Kanem recognized the overlordship of Bornu. It is in this "check and balance" policy between competing states and ethnic groups that the alliance with Arab nomadic tribes was sought after. At the end of his first military campaign in 1575, Sultan Idris Alaoma's diplomacy succeeded in shifting the balance of regional power by gaining the support of important Bulala chiefs and large fractions of Arab nomadic tribes. Bulala governors, emirs and office-holders, and even delegates of Arabs and Fittri tribes and others, and all those who joined him, were driven to support the cause of Sultan Muhammad" (Ahmad Furtu in Zeltner 1980: 150). Tribal names of Arab fractions involved in the alliance with the Bornu king are unfortunately unknown; it is nonetheless asserted that their support has been decisive for the victory of Bornu troops (Zeltner 1980: 176). Sultan Idris Alaoma is considered to have facilitated the westward expansion of Arabs in the Bornu kingdom. At the end of the first Kanem military campaign, some Arab fractions joined Bornu troops on their way back home. They left in Shitati and Manga and went back to their respective settlements (Zeltner 1979: 22).

It is thus possible to consider that by the middle of the second half of the sixteenth century, numerous Arab tribes and fractions were widely distributed all over the eastern half of the Chad basin, from N to S of the eastern shore of Lake Chad in the W to the modern Sudan boundary in the E. They were involved and caught in the shifting balance of power between competing polities, tribal groups, chiefdoms as well as states such as Wadday, Bagirmi, Kanem and Bornu (fig. 1). From that time, their west and southward expansion may have been characterized by "push and pull" according to the vagaries of shifting alliance and opportunities to escape from oppression and heavy state taxation. Prior to the nineteenth century, for which there is a richer body of historical record provided by European explorers (Denham et al. 1828; Barth 1965; Nachtigal 1980, 1987), two major episodes of Arab expansion are singled out by Zeltner (1979); the suggested reconstitution is based on comparative analyses of genealogies and ethnohistorical record.

The first episode, within the northern "stream," concerns the southward expansion of Arabs from their northern territories toward central Bornu, along the western shore of Lake Chad, up to the W of Maiduguri in modern Nigeria. This early seventeenth-century migration appears to have occurred during the reign of Sultan Ibrahim ibn Idris (1612–1619) and seems to have involved several tribes and fractions. These were the Jowama, Ulad Rashid, Hamediya, Sawarina, and Asale, according to Nachtigal (in Zeltner 1979: 24), or the Jowama, Juhayna, Hamadiya,

Habbaniya, Bani Hilal, Uled Rashid, and Bani Hassan, according to Palmer (in Zeltner 1979: 24). Their territorial range was extended westward to include the districts of Magumeri, Karagwaro, and Merkuban, and as far S as Uje (fig. 1).

The second episode of movement, within what may be considered the southern stream, concerns large-scale expansion of Arab tribes from Bagirmi westward during the first half of the eighteenth century (1730–1750). According to Barth (in Zeltner 1979: 60–61), Arab presence is attested as early as 1540 in the vicinity of Massenya, the capital city of the kingdom. From that area, several fractions of the Beni Hassan tribe expanded westward as far as the Mandara mountains; others including the Yesiye, expanded in the yaere, the floodplain situated on the W bank of the Chari-Logone river system, up to the Balge province, between Bodo and Ngala along the southwestern shore of Lake Chad. Ethnohistorical data referring to this migration and studied by Zeltner (1979) are supported by evidence provided by Nachtigal (in Zeltner 1979: 63; Reyna 1990) according to which Hajj Mohammad el Amin, king of Bagirmi (1751–1785), launched a military campaign against Logon and the Arabs living in that western region in southern Bornu. By the end of the eighteenth century, the western expansion of Arab nomads appears to have reached its modern limits in the southern part of the Chad basin. Nineteenth-century explorers provide interesting details concerning Shuwa-Arab changing relations with their sedentary and frequently oppressive neighbors. The patterns of relationships between the Arabs and their neighbors had framed their cultural behavior in their new homes. Understanding this part of their history may offer some clues for the explanation of their present-day situation and, thus, deserves a more detailed analysis.

Chadian Plain Shuwa-Arab and Their Neighbors in the Nineteenth Century

According to ethnohistorical records collected within the former limits of the Bornu kingdom, the nineteenth century is divided into two major periods: the first termed "the time of Kuka" (1811–1893) which is coeval with the Kanemiyyin dynasty founded by Mohammad el Amin el Kanemi with its capital city at Kuka; and the second much shorter period, termed the "time of Rabbeh" (1893–1900), starting from the collapse of Bornu initiated by Rabbeh's conquest, and ending with the latter's defeat and colonial takeover by European French troops.

From 1808 to 1811, backed by Kanembu and Shuwa-Arab followers and soldiers, Mohammad el Amin el Kanemi "took up arms on the *Mai's* behalf and in a series of campaigns scotched what had now became a thorough-going attempt by the Fulani to conquer Bornu" (Hiskett 1976: 142). He did not succeed in expelling the Fulani from the western province of the Bornu kingdom which became part of the Sokoto empire; nonetheless, as a result of his military campaigns, he gained increased prestige and fame, and finally initiated a new dynasty. The assistance given to the new dynasty by some Shuwa-Arab factions was reciprocated by the appointment of some of their members to high offices and governmental positions (Fisher 1975; Zeltner 1980). The position of *vizier*, the second in the state hierarchy, was held by the Shuwa-Arab family of Mohammad ben Tirab who was later succeeded by his son, Hajj Beshir. In the first half of the nineteenth century, Mohammad el Amin el Kanemi initiated a new policy favorable to Shuwa-Arabs, Some of their factions oppressed and harassed in the Bahr el-Ghazzal by Wadday rulers were welcomed in Bornu. The new dynasty refrained from interfering in Shuwa-Arab affairs; they kept their traditional ways of life, each settlement with its own sheikh, The vizier Mohammad ben Tirab played the role of intermediary by being in charge of Shuwa-Arab affairs (Zeltner 1980: 202). Shuwa-Arab women were married into the highest ranks of the social hierarchy, but "at the same time other Shuwa were regarded as dangerous rebels, and unruly frontier elements" (Fisher 1975: 111).

Major Denham, Captain Clapperton, and Dr. Oudney (1828) visited the area in 1822–1824, during the reign of Mohammad el Amin, and found the general political situation particularly chaotic. They visited several settlements along their W-E and N-S exploration routes. Their W-E route led them along the southern shore of Lake Chad, from Kukawa in the W to the Bahr el Ghazzal in the E, and along the course of the Shari river, from its delta in the N to Loggun in the SE. Their N-S route lead them from Kukawa to Mora. Unfortunately, they do not give information on tribal affiliations of the different Shuwa-Arab settlements but do provide important details on different facets of their interaction with their neighbors. "The Shouaas have brought with them the Arabic, which they speak nearly pure. They are divided into tribes, and bear still the names of some of the most formidable of the Bedouin hordes of Egypt. They are a deceitful, arrogant, and cunning race; great charm writers; and by pretending to a natural gift of prophecy, they find an easy entrance into the houses of the black inhabitants of the towns, where their pilfering propensities often show themselves" (Denham et al. 1828: 157).

On their way to Loggun on February 16, 1824, a few kilometers to the S of Kusseri, the Denham expedition faced some difficulties with Shuwa-Arabs. "What added to our distress was, that from this time until the evening of the 16th (February), the Shouaa Arabs, who occupy the frontier of the Loggun country, refused to allow us to pass until the Sultan had been consulted, and a number of his questions answered as to the purpose of our visit" (Denham et al. 1828: 15). In this case, some groups of Shuwa-Arabs were clearly employed as border guards of the Logone kingdom. At Loggun, the capital town of the kingdom, at the level of economic interaction, they noted that "the Shouaa are all around them, and to them they are indebted for the plentiful supply of bullocks, milk, and fat, with which the market abounds" (Denham et al. 1828: 18). There is a market every evening, but supplies are much more abundant at the weekly market every Wednesday.

Along the eastern shore of Lake Chad, in Kanem, where they are, above all, camel herders, there are some slight differences in dwellings and a relative political autonomy of Shuwa-Arabs. "The Shouaas live entirely in tents of leather, or rather of rudely dressed hides, and huts of rushes, changing but from necessity, on the approach of an enemy, or want of pasturage for their numerous flocks: they seldom fight except in their own defense. Their chiefs never leave their homes, but send bullocks to the market at Maffatai and Mekhari, and bring gussub (millet) in return: their principal food, however, is the milk of camels, in which they are rich, and also that of cows and sheep; this they will drink and take no other nourishment for months together. Their camps are circular, and are called *dowera,* or *frigue,* with two entrances for the cattle to enter at and be driven out" (Denham et al. 1828: 67).

Clearly, the Shuwa-Arab had diversified economic pursuits around Lake Chad and a range of relationships with their neighbors, ranging from high social positions in Bornu, border guards in Loggun, to relatively autonomous groups along the eastern shore of Lake Chad. In general, however, as social groups, Shuwa-Arabs were everywhere targets of heavy state taxation and tribute and, as such, were faced with a permanent dilemma: "they have the greatest contempt for, and hatred of, the negro nations, and yet are always tributary to either one black sultan or another: there is no example of their having peopled a town, or established themselves in a permanent home" (Denham et al. 1828: 67).

Heinrich Barth (1965) visited Bornu, Bagirmi, and Wadday in 1850–1855, and collected extensive historical material. In general, his observations support those published earlier by Denham et al. (1828) with Shuwa-Arabs treated with some indulgence and lenity in Bornu, "where they attained the highest degree of power and influence," while "being oppressed and very badly treated in Wadday." According to Barth (1965: 328), "their dialect is very peculiar, . . . its character is deteriorated, and becomes nearly ridiculous by the continued repetition and insertion of certain words . . . which at once bears testimony to the servile and degraded position which they occupy in Negroland." His data on tribal affiliations of some Shuwa-Arab settlements are more precise. A total of forty-one Shuwa-Arab settlements have been recorded from Ngala (in Bornu) in the NW to Logone in the SE. "With regard to the settlements of the Arabs in this district of Kotoko, I think that they are not more than two hundred years old. Most of these Arabs belong to the numerous tribe of the Salamat" (Barth 1965: 434). Rangana, in Bornu, is described as a "well inhabited district full of open hamlets. . . . All the inhabitants are Arabs, and belong to the tribe called Welad Megébel, whose chief is called I'sa A'she" (Barth 1965: 434). Farther E, a large proportion of the population of the province of Afadé consists of Shuwa principally, "of the tribe of E' Nejaime and Welad Abu Khodair" (Barth 1965: 436). Their relationship with the rulers was uneven: "The governor was absent just at the time on a small expedition to chastise some of these peoples who are very unsettled in their habits, and often refractory" (Ibid.). The border area along the eastern boundary of the Bornu kingdom was particularly unsafe. "The country is at present in such a state, principally owing to the turbulent spirit of the Shuwa-Arab, that even this road is regarded as unsafe; and we were

Table 1: General distribution of Shuwa-Arabs in the Chadian basin during the
nineteenth century

Wadday	Bagirmi	Kanem	Kotokoland and Mandara	Bornu
Salamat	—	Salamat	Salamat	—
Essala	Essala	Essala	Essala	Essala
Khozzam	Khozzam	—	—	Khozzam
Beni Hasan	—	—	Beni Hasan	—
Ouled Hamid	—	Ouled Hamed	Ouled Hamed	Ouled Hamed
Ouled Rachid				
Missiriya				
Djaadina				
Heimat				
Degena				
Dababa				
Mahamid				
Chourafa				
Chiggerat				
Tordjem				
Kolomat				
Zabalat				
Mahadi				
Zanatat				
Medjanin				
Korobat				
Issirre				
Beni Holba				
Zebeda				
Choukekat				
Kaoualima				

Source: Compiled from Gustav Nachtigal 1985 maps

therefore obliged to keep together, several inhabitants of Logon having attached
themselves to my little caravan" (Barth 1965: 437).

Gustav Nachtigal (1987a, b) provides additional data on Shuwa-Arab in the
whole area, in Bornu, Kotokoland, Bagirmi, as well as Wadday (table 1). There is
a particular emphasis on tribal affiliations with numerous details on social fractions. Wadday Arabs are divided into two major groups: cattle herders (el Bakkara
Arabs) divided into eighteen tribes, and camel herders (Abbala Arabs) divided into
5 tribes (Nachtigal 1987b: 70–72). In all the cases, Arab tribes were, in general,
involved in tributary relationships with their settled and dominant neighbors. These

tributary relationships will be studied here through one example from nineteenth century Bagirmi. The document, a report on tribute paid by different villages and ethnic groups to members of the Bagirmi kingdom elite, is written in Arabic; it was found among the archives of *Mbang* (King) Youssouf in the 1960s and published in 1987 (Lebeuf 1987). The document refers to the tribute paid for one year period, but it is not known exactly when. According to Lebeuf (1987: 193), the tribute distribution recorded in the document was possible after several military campaigns which resulted in the conquest of new territories with additional ethnic groups such as the Sokoro, Boa, Miltou, Toumak, and Sara; these campaigns were launched by Mbang Abd el Qader (1846–1858) and Mohammed Abu Sakin (1858–1885). Tribute was a fundamental aspect of the Bagirmi social system in endless cycles of predatory expansion and has been summarized by S. P. Reyna (1990: 132).

> Bagirmi had no formal budget. All the revenues became officials' private salaries, and as personal income they could be disposed of as the official saw it fit. Thus there was no institution that disbursed state funds, because these do not exist. There was only a multitude of officials with their private incomes. Officials, however, tended to expend their incomes on public enterprises because they were obliged to use their private incomes to implement policy once the *mbang* and the court had made a decision. In contrast to the contemporary state, where there are two discrete sectors, public and private, with public revenues expended for public purposes and private incomes for private ends, an important characteristic of Bagirmi fiscal system was that public revenues became private incomes that were expended upon public goals.

Some twenty-one ethnic groups are mentioned in the tribute report with the number of tributary villages varying from a maximum of thirty for the Shuwa-Arabs to one for the Boa, Miltou, Fulani, Kenga, Niellim, Gabre, Tounia, and Dam (table 2). As far as Shuwa Arabs are concerned, it appears that they constituted the largest ethnic group of the Bagirmi kingdom in the nineteenth century, a feature still true today (Lebeuf 1987: 173–177) with approximately 100, 000 Shuwa Arabs out of 200, 000 inhabitants. The tribute paid by Shuwa-Arab tribes consisted of domestic animals, horses, cattle and sheep/goats, butter from cow milk, iron tools and digging sticks, grain, salt, honey, and women. It was distributed among seventeen office holders organized into six categories (tables 2 and 3). The first, comprised of the members of the royal family, was represented by the *Magira* (Queen mother) with three villages, the *Shiroma* (first son of the king) with two villages, the *Ngar Mourba* (second son) and *Ngar Daba* (fourth son), with one village each. The second, with "chiefs of land," all members of the state council in charge of matters of peace and war, as well as the election of kings, consists of three officials: the Galadima with four villages, and the Milna (husband of the first king's daughter) and the Ngar *Mwaémanga with* one village each. The third with important district chiefs is comprised of a single official, the *Alifa* of Moito, owning a whole region as his tributary zone. The fourth consists of a single religious official, the

Table 2: Summary of a nineteenth century Bagirmi tribute report

Tribute payers		Recipients		Tribute components			
Ethnic group	Number of villages	Officials' titles	Number of tributary villages owned	Nature	Quantity	Arab contribution	Percent
1–Arabs	30	*The Royal family*		Horse	126	75	59.52
2–Barma	27	Magira	3	Cattle	108	87	80.55
3–Massa	13	Shiroma	2	Sheep/Goat	683	651	95.31
4–Sokoro	8	Ngar Mourba	1	Butter	246	246	100
5–Kanouri	6	Ngar Daba	1	Grain	213	152	71.36
6–Goulay	5	*Chiefs of land*		Tools	354	330	93
7–Babalya	4	Galadima	4	Salt	30	18	60.00
8–Kotoko	4	Milna	1	Honey	384	12	3.12
9–Kouang	3	Ngar Mwaemanga	1				
10–Kouka	3	*District chief*					
11–Toumak	3	Alifa Moito	Region				
12–Mopou	2	*Religious official*					
13–Saroua	2	Grand Imam	1				
14–Boa	1	*Army commanders*					
15–Dam	1	Mbarma	4				
16–Fulani	1	Patsha	3				
17–Gabre	1	Kirima	2				
18–Kenga	1	Ngaramane	2				
19–Miltou	1	*Court Officials*					
20–Niellim	1	Katakulay	1				
21–Tounia	1	Katakunji	1				
		Katakulangane	1				
		Naib	1				

Source: Compiled from Lebeuf 1987

Table 3: Tribute paid by the Shuwa Arabs in nineteenth-century Bagirmi

Tribe	Village	Horse	Cattle	Sheep/goats	Butter's calabash	Grain loads	Salt cones	Tools	Others	Women	Officials
Yesiye	Lapana	1	1	—	12	—	—	—	—	—	Ngaramane
	Djoba	12	12	200	—	—	—	—	—	4	Mbarma
	Abouguem	—	—	—	—	—	—	—	12	—	Kirima
	Meache	12	12	12	12	—	—	—	—	—	Galadima
	As	1	1	50	—	—	—	—	—	—	Galadima
Total	5	26	26	262	24	—	—	—	12	4	4
Khozam	Kaba	1	1	—	12	—	—	—	—	—	Ngaramane
	Balaniere	2	2	12	12	—	—	—	—	—	Shiroma
	Dagana	12	12	—	—	—	—	—	12	—	Patsha
	Ambidega	—	—	—	24	—	—	—	12	—	Katakunji
	Gama	2	2	12	12	—	—	—	—	—	Galadima
	Barie	1	1	50	12	—	—	—	—	—	Shiroma
Total	6	18	18	74	48	24	—	—	24	—	5
Assale	Djamatawak	1	1	—	12	—	—	—	—	—	Milna
	Abd el Salamat	—	1	50	12	—	—	—	—	1	Katakulangane
	Shawa	1	1	—	12	—	6	—	—	—	Katakulay
Total	3	2	3	50	36	—	6	—	—	1	3
Ouled	Bibil	1	1	1	12	—	—	—	—	—	Magira
Daoud	Kourswa	1	12	—	—	—	—	—	—	—	Naib
Total	2	2	13	1	12	—	—	—	—	—	2
Ouled eli	Arkwa	1	1	1	12	—	—	—	—	—	Ngar Mwaemanga
Ouled el Hadj	Mile	1	1	12	12	—	—	—	—	—	Ngar Daba
Dababa	Bodoro	1	1	1	12	—	—	—	—	—	Ngar Mourba

Table 3: Continued

Ital	Ital	—	1	1	12	12	—	—	—	—	—	Mbarma
Laday	Pourdia	—	1	1	12	12	—	—	—	—	—	Mbarma
Mayaguine	Idjili	—	2	2	12	12	—	—	—	—	—	Kirima
Maena	Korbol	—	1	1	—	6	—	—	—	—	—	Patsha
Toubo	Djoba	—	—	—	—	—	—	—	330	—	—	Patsha
Anga	Anga	—	1	1	—	12	—	—	—	—	—	Grand Inman
Idjis	Lobodo	—	2	2	12	12	—	—	—	—	—	Galadima
Tribal affiliation not specified												
	Odio	—	1	1	1	12	—	—	—	—	—	Magira
	Tchinga	—	1	1	1	12	—	—	—	—	—	Magira
	Moito Area	—	12	12	200	—	48	12	—	200	4	Alifa Moito
	Dekakire	—	2	2	—	—	80	—	—	—	—	Mbarma
TOTAL		30	75	87	651	246	152	18	330	260	9	17

Grand Imam, with one tributary village. The last two categories are composed of officials from servile origins. Army commanders are represented by four top-ranked officers, the *Mbarma* (Chief commander) with four villages, the *Patsha* (Chief commander) with three settlements, the *Ngar ngolo Kirima* and *Ngar ngolo ngaramane* (sub-commanders) with two settlements each. And finally, court officials granted with one village each, and represented by the *Naib* (speaker), *Kataku-lay* (chief of palace guards), *Katakunji* (chief of royal music band), and *Kataku-langane* (chief of palace servants).

At least fourteen tribal groups are listed in the tribute report, the affiliation being unspecified for four cases: Odio, Tchinga, Dekakire, and Moito region, (table 3). Tribute exactions appear to have been particularly heavy for the Yesiye, with five tributary villages shared by four officials, and the Khozam, with six villages belonging to five officeholders. In general, with minor exceptions as is the case for honey for which they provided only 3.12 percent of the recorded total with 12 *kulu* (a 12 liter jar) given to the Katakulangane by the Assale from Abd el Salamat (table 3), Shuwa-Arab contribution to the annual tribute flow was high to very high. The proportion varies from 100 percent for cow milk butter; 95.31 percent for sheep and goats; 93.22 percent for tools, with the set of 110 iron hoe-blades, 110 iron axe-blades, and 110 digging sticks given to the *Patsha* by the Toubo from Djoba, specialized in iron-working (table 3); 80.55 percent for cows and bulls; 71.36 percent for grain, mostly wild one with each share measuring 80 liters; 60 percent of locally made salt cones; 59.52 percent of horses; and finally, 28.12 percent of women (table 3).

Bagirmi was not an exception among the states of the Central Sudan. Shuwa Arabs were subject to comparable taxation elsewhere, in Wadday, Bornu, as well as Kotoko polities. During the nineteenth century, the whole area was plagued with endemic warfare (Reyna 1990; Lebeuf 1987; Zeltner 1980). Tribute flows helped to support armies, in order to increase the booty output intensify territorial conquests, which at their turn increased the return in term of booty and new tributary zones.

This particular type of social dynamics was particularly costly for dominated ethnic groups as has been the case for the Shuwa-Arab. It is, thus, not surprising that they welcomed Rabbeh as a liberator, a conqueror with remote Sudanese-Arab origins (Zeltner 1988: 143). Rabbeh's conquest of Bagirmi, Kotoko principalities, and Bornu was completed within five years, from 1889 to 1894. In Bagirmi, the Banu Salamat were among the first Arab tribes to join Rabbeh troops; some of their fractions, such as the Ulad Abu Daw, were defeated a few years before by Wadday troops. Other Arab sheikhs were at first reluctant but finally joined the side of the new conqueror after his victory over Bornu troops in May 1893. There were nonetheless few opponents among the Salamat and Ghawalme tribes (Hagenbucher-Sacripanti 1977: 231). The revolt of Sheikh Wobri, the headman of the Dar Begli fraction of the Banu Salamat, was crushed after few fights, while Jaggara, headman of the Abu Khader, a fraction of the Ghawalme, fled to Dagana with his followers and later joined French troops in their war against Rabbeh.

Rabbeh's Shuwa-Arab policy was radically different from the former ones and totally new. His main innovation was to organize Shuwa-Arab communities along tribal lines and not territorial ones. They were liberated from the oppression of their settled neighbors. Each settlement was led by a sheikh. A new position, lawan was created above the settlement level, concerning all the members of tribal fractions dispersed in different parts of the conquered territories. Thus, there was a lawan for each tribe, the Salamat, Hemmadiye, Bana Sayd, Ghawalme, etc., directly under the supervision of the *Nadir* (inspector) of Arabs, a new position in which Rabbeh appointed one of his lieutenants, Mendilga (Zeltner 1988: 145). Rabbeh's brutal domination and reign did not last for very long. After a series of battles, he was defeated by French troops in 1900–1901 (Abadie and Abadie 1989).

The Colonial Period (1900–1960)

The discussion of the Shuwa-Arab situation during the colonial period will be confined to the area situated in the northern part of modern Cameroon. The collapse of Rabbeh's regime and a hasty, untimely territorial reorganization initiated a period of serious unrest. Jaggara, the first Arab sheikh to have joined French troops, was appointed as sultan of a new and extensive *sultanate* created by Gentil (Zeltner 1988; Hagenbucher-Sacripanti 1977). The new political system included several competing Kotoko principalities: Gulfey, Makari, Wulki, Bodo, and Afade; warring Arab tribes, including the Hemmadiye, Banu Seit, Ghawalme, and Salamat, as well as Kanuri settlements. The capital city of the new Serbewel sultanate was Gulfey. An important change in the traditional politics of the region occurred with the appointment of a Shuwa-Arab to replace a Kotoko ruler within a Kotoko principality. This change generated serious difficulties in the region. Troubles went on unabated with the increased frequency of localized strife with Gulfey troops. From 1914 onward, there was a series of escalations followed by a cycle of punitive expeditions against the revolting Arab tribes; Hemmadiye and Salamat Lawans were executed. Formerly competing rulers of Makari and Afade joined their forces and launched an attack against Gulfey, and one high official of the Jaggara regime was killed. This expedition was followed by a strong reaction by the colonial administration; but paradoxically, the punitive military campaign was turned against the Shuwa Arabs (Hagenbucher-Sacripanti 1977: 233). Ghawalme, Hemmadiye, Salamat, and Banu Seit sheikhs and elders were arrested and put in jail at Maroua. Jaggara was destitute, and a new territorial organization initiated.

In 1953, the land was divided into five *cantons*—Gulfey, Wulki, Makari, Afade, and Bodo—corresponding to the traditional Kotoko political subdivisions. For the Shuwa-Arab, this meant a shift back to an ancient political organization characterized by the domination of Kotoko polities (Lebeuf 1969). The four major Shuwa-Arab tribal units (Ghawalme, Hemmadiye, Salamat and Banu Seit), with their factions dispersed all over the area, were split anew and divided among different and generally competing Kotoko principalities. The position of Lawan created by Rabbeh lost its content but remained a "prestige" tag. With minor changes, this situation remains more or less the same up to the present; with a very remote central government of the modern state, with marginal influence on daily Shuwa-Arab life. The situation is still characterized by largely traditional patterns of relationships between the seminomadic Shuwa-Arab and their neighbors (Holl 1993; Holl et al. 1991; Holl and Levy 1993).

Conclusion

With the introduction of new powers in the regional political scene (British, French, and German), the colonial period certainly added additional complexity to an already complex situation. It lasted for fifty to sixty years depending on the area around the Lake Chad basin, with the territories divided into three parts: (1) the Chad colony situated in the E and included in French Equatorial Africa (F. E. A.) encompassing former Bagirmi and Wadday territories; (2) the central part, comprising the largest part of the floodplain, which was initially a German colony, became a territory under Mandate, shared by the British and French following the first World War. They were later included in Nigeria for the western part, and Cameroon for the eastern one; and finally, (3) the western areas, formerly parts of the Bornu kingdom, were ruled by the British and later included in modern Nigeria. Thus, Shuwa-Arab communities were distributed under "three flags" following African independence in the 1960s: the Chad Republic, Cameroon, and Nigeria.

As far as northern Cameroon is concerned today, the area is divided into several administrative divisions organized into three levels. The canton at the lowest level, comprising varying amounts of villages settled by different ethnic groups and theoretically supervised by a chief, his main duty consisting of collecting taxes. Depending on areas, canton chiefs were appointed among members of the former traditional chiefs with their former palaces as headquarters, or among Shuwa-Arab elders. Cantons were distributed into two, three, and, finally, five intermediate levels, alternatively termed *Subdivision, District, Arrondisement* or *Sous-préfecture,* with their headquarters at Logone-Birni, Waza, Kusseri, Makari, and Gulfey. The officials in charge of administration are appointed by the Cameroonian government. The highest level of local territorial organization is subsumed under the term *Département* or *Préfecture.* The administrator is a high ranking official, generally appointed among specially trained students or political leaders.

As can be seen from the general summary of the Cameroonian state territorial administration presented above, social and political relationships at the canton level are primarily based on traditional rules and practices. This situation often generates serious social tension due to incompatibilities between the requirement of modern administrative standards and "deep time" traditional practices. Traditional political systems were financed by a combination of a tax per capita or households and annual tribute paid to a broad range of officials. Corvée labor was also used for productive activities in major officials' domains and the maintenance of important features, palaces, and earthen ramparts. A process of devolution started during the colonial period, and was amplified after the formation of independent modern states. Traditional authorities were deprived of their usual financial support and granted with unsatisfactory alternatives. Ancient buildings and palaces, part of an impressive architectural heritage, were doomed to collapse. In general, traditional authorities tried to revive former tributary relationships with Shuwa-Arab groups. The latter were summoned to pay in order to be allowed to use grazing lands for their flocks. Such a situation was not confined to the home range of Shuwa-Arab but appears to have been extended to nomadic Fulani groups in southwestern Cameroon. These difficulties were solved at the highest state levels, with stipulations emphasizing the "national character" of grazing lands.

> More important, perhaps, has been the establishment of a clear policy which asserted that Fulbe in Anglophone areas are no longer to be thought of as strangers and denied the civil rights available to all citizens. The 1974 ordinance, which declared all grazing lands to be 'national lands', probably marks a significant turnabout that may increase the economic, if not the political, status of pastoralists throughout the nation. Subsequent measures can be anticipated that will bring cadastral surveys, the registration of plots, and the issuance of deeds or titles (probably of usufruct, rather than *de jure* ownership). (Frantz 1981: 105)

It is not known if the measures anticipated by Frantz (1981) have been enacted and implemented in northern Cameroon. Field observations made during a ten-year period show important interaction between the Kotoko settled agriculturalists and Shuwa-Arab seminomadic groups. Shuwa-Arab cattle herds are allowed to graze on sorghum fields after the harvest at the beginning of the dry season. The details of the decision process leading to such an arrangement are not known. All the interviewed informants, among the Kotoko as well as Shuwa-Arab, simply replied that "it is an immemorial traditional arrangement." The intimate relationships between the Shuwa-Arab and the Kotoko have generated several patterns of behaviors concerning cooperation and competition, bilingualism, exchange of goods and services, unbalanced marriage patterns, as well as site-location strategies and settlement patterning. Thus, it is assumed that these relations reflect the "deep time" patterns of social interaction which are embedded in the long-term history of relationship between the Shuwa-Arab and other ethnic groups in the region. Seen from the perspective of the 1990s, this history of social relations between different ethnic groups, regional complex societies, and global super-powers have helped to shape the material culture of the Shuwa-Arab studied in this book. This historical trajectory has had widespread influence and permeates today's Shuwa-Arab spatial dynamics on a multitude of levels ranging from the household to regional settlement patterns.

Chapter 2

The Study Area:
Land, People, and Settlements

Introduction

The study area, termed the Houlouf region, is situated in the northernmost part of Cameroon along the southern margins of the Sahel (fig. 2). Its northern, western, and southern limits are arbitrary, with the eastern one coinciding with the course of the Logone river. It extends over 500 square kilometers, 20 kilometers N-S, from 12° 05' to 11° 55' latitude N, and 25 kilometers W-E, from 14° 50' to 15° 05' longitude W. It is the northern portion of the El Birke Canton, a lower-order, present-day, administrative division, ruled by a traditional Kotoko chief up to the first years of the 1980s (fig. 2).

The Land, Soils, Vegetation, and Climate

The Houlouf region is a flat Sudano-Sahelian landscape, usually flooded during the rainy-season and prone to cyclical droughts, with elevation varying from 296 m above sea level in the SE to 290 m in the N, W, and NW. The Logone river is the sole permanent river; but there are many fossil river channels as well as a dense network of seasonal streams, the Maligwa and the Abani being the most important.

Three major soils types have been recorded (Brabant and Gavaud 1985). These are (1) a dark gray to very dark gray and thick clay formation deposited at the bottom former lakes and marshes, containing a large amount of limestone nodules. This soil formation is extended over the western and southwestern half of the study area. Then (2) a dark to pale brown-gray sandy-silt and silty-sand soil distributed along the Logone river valley, in a SE-NW stretch of land, and in isolated patches; it provides good agricultural potential but is prone to fast soil exhaustion. And finally, (3) a brown, relatively shallow clay formation, with varying

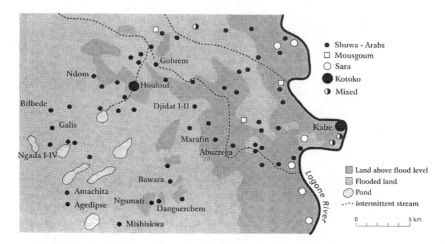

Figure 2: The Houlouf Region: settlement and ethnic groups

components of sand and silt extending over the northern part of the region. Geo-morphological processes and the accumulation of sediment by hydrologic agencies have generated the partition of the study area into two main components. The sea-sonally flooded lowlands cover approximately three-fifths of the region, with the remaining two-fifths consisting of land permanently above flood level (fig. 2). The location of permanent habitation sites is thus severely constrained.

The vegetation is typically a Sudano-Sahelian arbustive savanna with thorny trees; it is nonetheless divided into several plant associations which offer a mosaic of biomes. The seasonally flooded and marshy hinterland, locally called Yaere, is an extensive grassland dotted with numerous, more or less permanent, ponds, of-fering highly valued grazing opportunities. Three vegetation subtypes associated with different soils have been recorded (Letouzey 1985). The first, located in the northwestern portion of the study area, is predominantly a *Pennisetum ramosum* grassland with *Echinochloa obtusiflora, E. pyramidalis, Erichloa fatmensis, Oryza longistaminata, Vetiveria nigritana,* and *Hyparhenia rufa* (Letouzey 1985: 3). The second, extended in the W along the limit of the study area, is an *Echinochloa pyramidalis* grassland with *Brachiaria mutica, Echinochloa stagnina, Eliocaris dulcis, Oryza longistaminata, Panicum anabaptistum, Polygonum salicifolium, Hyparrhenia rufa,* and, here and there, a few groves of *Acacia seyal* and *Piliostygma reticulatum* (Letouzey 1985: 4). The third, located in the SW, is concentrated along major fossil or active channels; it is predominantly an *Echinochloa stagnina* and *Nymphea spp.* grassland with *Centrostchys aquatica, Polygonum senegalense* var. *albomentosum* (Letouzey 1985: 4).

The arbustive savanna with a more important tree component is the most extensive vegetation type found in the study area. It is divided into seven subunits according to the differential frequency of species, which are distributed into roughly parallel SE-NW bands; these are, from N to the S: (1) the *Ziziphus mauritiana* and *Acacia seyal* subtype; (2) the *Acacia nilotica* var. *adansonii* with *Mitragina inermis;* (3) the *Acacia nilotica* var. *adansonii* and *A. seyal;* (4) the *Acacia seyal;* (5) the *Mytragyna inermis* and *Crateva adansonii* with *Acacia polyacantha, A. sieberana;* (6) the *Anogeissus leiocarpus,* with *Balanites aegyptiaca, Guiera senegalensis;* and finally, (7) the *Sclerocarya birrea* and *Anogeissus leiocarpus.* The third vegetation type is represented by small, densely wooded patches located along the Logone river valley; it consists of *Acacia polyacantha, A. seyal, A. sieberana,* and *Combretum paniculatum.*

The climate is clearly a Sudano-Sahelian one with two clear-cut and contrasted seasons. Being located on the Sahel margins, the study area is prone to cyclical droughts, with erratic variations in the yearly amount of rainfall confined to a three- to five-month (June to October) rainy-season (table 4). It is followed by a five- to seven-month dry season (November to May). Depending on the amount of rainfall, the rainy-season is followed by a more or less long flood period (October/November to January/March), buffering and delaying the impact of the imperial sun of the dry season. The recorded annual temperatures range from 39 to 47° C for maxima to 8.2 to 18° C for the minima (table 5). On average, March is the warmest month of the year, with a diurnal amplitude of 34.4° C (12.6° to 47°) September, with daily temperatures ranging from 18° to 38°, is the coolest.

Table 4: Rainfall record from Ndjamena located 295 m above sea level

Month	Means on 28 years		Year 1960		Relative Humidity on 25 years	
	Amount (mm)	Number of days	Amount (mm)	Number of days	06 TU	12 TU
January	0.0	0.0	0.0	0	51	17
February	0.0	0.0	0.0	0	45	12
March	0.0	0.0	0.0	0	42	16
April	4.9	1.3	7.5	2	42	16
May	37.8	5.5	24.7	5	54	24
June	66.3	8	45.3	8	75	40
July	155.2	12.9	207.4	17	87	59
August	261.6	18.4	128.1	14	92	71
September	104.2	10.1	108.6	7	89	64
October	22.5	3.1	11.7	2	78	36
November	0.6	0.1	0.0	0	55	19
December	0.0	0.0	0.0	0	52	16

Source: La République du Tchad 1961–1962: Société des Editions Paul Bory, Monaco

Table 5: Temperature records from Ndjamena in degrees Celsius

Month	Extremes on 23 years		Means on 25 years		Year 1960	
	Max.	Min.	Max.	Min.	Max.	Min.
January	41.8	8.2	32.7	13.5	32.4	13.4
February	43.2	9.5	35.6	15.5	34.8	15.3
March	47.0	12.6	38.6	20.4	38.7	19.3
April	45.8	13.9	41.2	23.9	40.6	25.3
May	45.5	16.1	40.2	25.1	39.4	24.8
June	43.0	18.0	37.2	23.8	38.0	24.3
July	41.3	17.0	33.1	22.6	32.1	22.7
August	37.8	16.5	30.4	22.1	31.3	22.6
September	38.0	18.0	33.3	22.1	32.6	22.7
October	43.0	14.7	36.0	21.4	36.5	22.6
November	42.2	11.4	37.1	18.4	35.7	17.8
December	39.8	8.4	33.9	15.5	35.4	17.5

Source: La République du Tchad 1961–1962: Société des Editions Paul Bory, Monaco

Peoples: Ethnicity in Perspective

There are different definitions of ethnicity, emphasizing various kinds of characteristics (Abruzzi 1982; Barth 1956, 1969; Cohen 1969, 1974a, b; Duncan 1981; Dragadze 1980; Hjort 1981; Emberling 1997; Knutsson 1969; Nash 1989). It appears that ethnic groups are primarily characterized by more or less shared world views, language, and, depending on circumstances, a common territory. According to Dragadze (1980: 162), *ethnos* can be defined as a firm aggregate of people, historically established on a given territory, possessing in common relatively stable particularities of language and culture, also recognizing their unity and difference from other similar formations (self-awareness) and expressing this in a self-appointed name (ethnonym). Ethnicity is, at the same time, a sociological category and a sociohistorical construct. It is a complex phenomenon involving psychological, historical, economic and political factors, thus better considered as a variable interdependent with many others in any sociocultural milieu. According to Cohen (1974: iv), "an ethnic group can be operationally defined as a collectivity of people who share some patterns of normative behavior and form a part of a larger population interacting with people from other collectivities within the framework of a social system." Cohen's definition clearly aims to delineate the outlines of ethnicity in urban contexts. Contexts in which the overarching social system is, de jure, easily grasped.

In the Houlouf region, depending on the parameters used in the analysis of the data at hand, it is not easy to delineate one, two, or even more overarching social systems. The Kotoko is a general category of Chadic speakers, settled in walled settlements, and not a "self-appointed" ethnonym. This term was coined by the Arabs, and its use was later extended and generalized. They refer to themselves according to their towns: *Mia Lagwan* for those from Logone-Birni; *Mser* for those from Kusseri; *Mia Mpade* for those from Makari (Lebeuf 1969). Depending on the context, when asked about his/her identity, a Shuwa Arab will answer that he/she is Arab if situated in a multiethnic setting; will give the name of his/her tribe if addressed in the context of a large Shuwa-Arab audience; and will specify his/her faction or clan in smaller and nonambiguous contexts (Hagenbucher-Sacripanti 1977a). If considered from data arranged along varying criteria such as population size, number of settlements, site-location, regional distribution, or history, some ethnic groups may claim to have an autonomous social organization, while this claimed autonomy may be denied by others. Additional and untractable complexity appears as the rule if considered from the background of long-term history, with changing patterns of alliance, warfare, domination, and the rise and fall of competing peer-polities.

Data concerning the various populations inhabiting the study area have been collected from the administrative census of 1969 (Elingui 1978) and the report of the general census of population and habitation of 1976 (Bureau Central du Recensement 1985). Additional but more general population data reported at the scale of the whole Northern Cameroon have been published by Podlewski (1966) and A. Lebeuf (1959, 1969). The study area thus appears to be inhabited by six ethnic groups, the Kotoko, Shuwa-Arab, Mousgoum, Massa, Sara, and Kanuri, representing four linguistic families and distributed into thirty-four settlements (table 6).

The Massa and the Kanuri do not have any exclusive settlement of their own. The former are speakers of Central Eastern Chadic languages, the latter being speakers of a Saharan language (Dumas-Champion 1983; Caprile and Jungraythmayr 1973; Newmann 1977). They share settlements with other ethnic groups; with the Mousgoum at Kabe-Malo and Kabela, and the Shuwa-Arab at Ndou for the Massa, while the Kanuri are found at Kabe-Kilam with the Mousgoum and the Kotoko (table 7). The recorded ethnically mixed settlements are surprisingly confined to the bank of the Logone river (fig. 3). The Mousgoum, speakers of a Central southern Chadic language, are found in five villages: in an exclusive settlement of their own at Kawadji, and in association with other ethnic groups in four of them (with the Sara at Kabe-Bekoro, the Massa at Kabe-Malo and Kabela, and finally the Shuwa-Arab at Koumboula). The Sara, speakers of a Bongo-Bagirmi language, have two settlements of their own at Madana and Sabakalle I, and share one village with the Mousgoum at Kabe-Bekoro. The Kotoko, speakers of *Lagwan,* a Central Chadic language, are distributed into two large settlements: Kabe-Kilam on the bank of the Logone river in the E, and Houlouf in the NW (table 7). Both villages, sited at 15 kilometers from each other, are ancient fortified cities, attested by the remains of collapsed and eroded earthen ramparts still visible from place to place.

Table 6: Settlements, ethnic groups, and population distribution in the study area

Settlement	Ethnic group	Population (1969)	Population (1985)	Demographic trends
1–Abendourwa	Arab	29	35	+6
2–Abuzrega	Arab	21	—	—
3–Alaya	Arab	116	53	−63
4–Djidat I	Arab	37	63	+26
5–Djidat II	Arab	79	134	+55
6–El Birke I	Arab	77	138	+61
7–El Birke II	Arab	23	51	+23
8–Gaou Brahim	Arab	42	77	+35
9–Houlouf	Kotoko	286	1127	+841
10–Ibou	Arab	192	253	+61
11–Kabe-Bekoro	M/S	81	131	+50
12–Kabe-Malo	M/Ma	26	33	+7
13–Kabe-Kilam	*K/M/Ka	377	652	+275
14–Kabela	M/Ma	183	239	+56
15–Kawadji	M	102	80	−22
16–Koulkoule	Arab	—	19	—
17–Koumboula	Arab/M	55	98	+43
18–Madaf	Arab	62	130	+68
19–Madana	Sara	174	247	+73
20–Mahanna	Arab	26	40	+14
21–Magourde I	Arab	18	37	+19
22–Magourde II	Arab	20	27	+7
23–Magourde III	Arab	20	50	+30
24–Marafaine	Arab	56	98	+42
25–Mishiskwa	Arab	54	66	+12
26–Ndom	Arab	28	49	+21
27–Ndou	Arab/Ma	55	102	+47
28–Ngada	Arab	—	73	—
29–Ngumati	Arab	63	52	−11
30–Njagare	Arab	146	218	+72
31–Sabakalle I	Sara	49	121	+72
32–Sabakalle II	Arab	64	62	−2
33–Sabakalle III	Arab	66	98	+32
34–Wadjetouna	Arab	46	80	+34

Key: K = Kotoko; S = Sara; M = Mousgoum; Ma = Massa

Dwelling features organized into closed household compounds, settlement layouts, and spatial organization are clearly based on Kotoko cultural standards. In general, however, all the Houlouf and Kabe-Kilam inhabitants are not Kotoko stricto sensu; they include the Mousgoum, the Kanuri, and many other ethnic minorities

Table 7: Population distribution

Ethnic group	Number of settlements	Population	Min.	Max.	Mean	Range	Standard deviation
Arab	24	1903	19	253	82.73	234	57.22
Kotoko	2	1779	652	1127	889.5	475	237.50
Sara	2	368	121	247	184	126	63
Composite	5	603	33	239	120.60	206	67.31

as observed at Houlouf from 1982 to 1991. They are unfortunately not singled out in the 1985 census report. The Shuwa-Arab, speakers of a Semitic language, are distributed into twenty-six settlements, two of them being shared with the Mousgoum and the Massa, respectively at Koumboula and Ndou (table 7, fig. 2). The study area is thus a multiethnic setting with different groups arranged along an ethnic spectrum. The emerging patterns of co-residence and "avoidance" clearly show the Kotoko and the Shuwa-Arab to be situated at both ends of the observed ethnic spectrum; both represent the main ethnic groups of the study area, but they do not share any single settlement. The Kotoko are associated with the Mousgoum and the Kanuri; the Shuwa-Arab with the Mousgoum and the Massa; the Sara exclusively with the Mousgoum; the Massa with the Shuwa-Arab and Mousgoum; the Mousgoum with the Sara, Massa, Shuwa-Arab, Kotoko, and Kanuri. The pattern of settlement-sharing does not appear to be based on linguistic affinities.

The data summarized in the preceding paragraph can be used to investigate

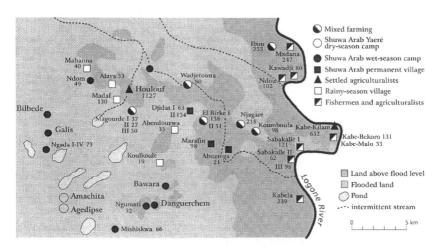

Figure 3: The Houlouf Study Area: Population distribution based on the 1976 census

Table 8: Trends in local demography

Ethnic group	Arab	Kotoko	Sara	Mousgoum	Composite	Total
Number of settlements	24	2	2	1	5	34
Population (1969)	1334	663	223	102	400	2722
Population (1985)	1903	1779	368	80	603	4733
Total increase	569	1116	145	−22	203	2011
Growth (percent)	42.65	168.32	65.02	−21.56	50.75	73.87
Annual growth (percent)	2.84	11.22	4.33	−1.43	3.38	4.9

several other aspects connected with the study area's sociocultural dynamics. Population distribution and major demographic trends, variation in socioeconomic systems and site-location strategies will be dealt with in more detail.

Data from the 1969 and 1976 censuses suggest some interesting demographic trends. In both cases, the Shuwa-Arab are the largest ethnic group in the study area, followed by the Kotoko. The regional population size shifted from 2,722 (1969) to 4,733 (1980) within a ten-year period, clearly beyond the optimal natural population growth potentials (table 8). The series of drought years which occurred in 1970–1974 all over the West African Sahel have certainly generated a new distribution of population. Permanent villages with deep wells and settlement located in areas with a relatively high water table attracted additional population. This may explain the growth of the Houlouf population from 286 (1969) to 1,127 (1976), as well as its later decrease to 450 inhabitants in 1982, during the first year of fieldwork in the area. In the 1980s, the population of Houlouf witnessed important changes almost from year to year, depending on the intensity of the political crisis that happened to take place in the nearby Chad Republic. With the exception of the Mousgoum, there is a general population growth of all the ethnic groups inhabiting the study area (table 8), with an inferred general annual growth of 10.55 percent. This inferred average annual growth rate varies from 6.09 percent for the Shuwa-Arab to 24.04 percent for the Kotoko, while being negative (−3.08 percent) for the Mousgoum.

Using the data from the 1976 census alone, the Shuwa-Arab appear to be the most scattered population, distributed into twenty-four villages with the number of inhabitants per site varying from 19 at Koulkoule in the SW in the Yaere to 253 at Ibou in the NE near the Logone river (table 8, fig. 3). Sites with less than 100 inhabitants are generally found clustered in the flooded Yaere in the W and SW, while those with population figures higher than 100 are located a few kilometers E-SE of Houlouf. The distribution patterns of the Kotoko and Sara populations, found in two settlements in each case, do not deserve any further discussion. Kotoko villages are clearly the most populated settlements; both villages are ancient important traditional political centers. Finally, in sites with an ethnically mixed population, the number of inhabitants varies from 33 at Kabe-Malo to 239 at Kabela, both on the bank of the Logone river and settled by the Massa and the Mousgoum.

Socioeconomic specialization partially generated by local environmental diversity appears to be the major driving force behind the observed pattern of regional distribution of ethnic groups (fig. 4). Agriculture, livestock husbandry, and fishing are practiced by almost all the study area ethnic groups, with subtle gradations and nuances but also sharp distinction. Four major socioeconomic systems are attested in the study area; pastoralism, mixed farming, farming, and farming-fishing.

Pastoralism involving the husbandry of cattle, sheep, and goats, based on seminomadism articulated on rainy-season villages on the one hand, and dry-season camps situated in the Yaere on the other, is exclusively a Shuwa-Arab socioeconomic system. They also grow *Sorghum* with a preference for *Sorghum durra* var. *Rubra* (red sorghum) which is not heavily attacked by birds, corn (*Zea mays*), and different kinds of calabashes used to process dairy products. Twelve seminomadic pastoralist villages have been recorded in the census reports used in this work; from field observation however, they are more numerous and widespread. It is highly doubtful that all seminomadic pastoralist settlements were visited by census officers. Whatever the case, all the seminomadic pastoralists villages are clustered within and on the edge of the Yaere (Fig. 4).

The mixed farming system involves agriculture and livestock husbandry with relatively equal shares in the subsistence in-put/out-put. It generally operates in the context of sedentary or almost-sedentary settlement strategy; in some cases, a more

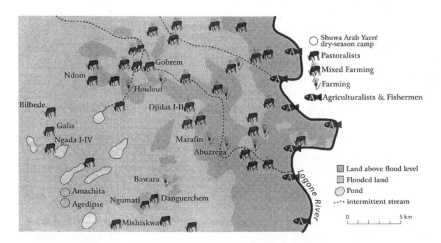

Figure 4: The Houlouf Study Area: Economic basis of Settlement

or less important portion of people may move from the village to stay in dry-season camps, but settlements are not totally emptied of their population. Fourteen mixed farming settlements are recorded; they are clustered in the northeastern half of the study area, sited in the part of land generally above the flood level. The largest proportion of mixed-farmers belongs to the Shuwa-Arab, associated with the Mousgoum at Koumboula and the Massa at Ndou. Village population size is, on average higher than in the seminomadic pastoralist case. It varies from a minimum of 27 at Magourde II to a maximum of 253 at Ibou (fig. 4), with the population of five settlements higher than 100 inhabitants in the case of Djidat II, El Birke I, Ibou, Ndou, and Njagare.

Farmers-fishermen settlements are confined to the banks of the Logone river. It is the socioeconomic system with the highest ethnic diversity, involving the Kotoko, the Mousgoum, the Massa, the Sara, and the Kanuri. Relatively intensive fishing activities, with specialized equipment comprising large flat-bottom boats, fishing nets, and large dug-outs, are carried out during the rainy-seasons and high-water periods. Agriculture involves the cultivation of sorghum and intensive gardening geared toward the production of onions, cucumbers, tomatoes, and green vegetables sold in the near-by cities of Kusseri and Ndjamena. Small plots of root crops, especially cassava, were seen at Kabe-Kilam. Settlement population size ranges from a minimum of 33 inhabitants at Kabe-Malo to a maximum of 652 at Kabe-Kilam (fig. 4). Five of the recorded farmers-fishermen settlements, Kabe-Bekoro, Kabe-Kilam, Kabela, Madana, and Sabakalle I, have population figures higher than 120 inhabitants.

Houlouf, with a population amounting to 1,127 inhabitants according to the 1976 census report, is a unique agriculturalist settlement. It is a genuine peasant community, with the ring of sorghum fields extending over a radius of 4.5 kilometers (Holl et al. 1991). But the situation is much more complex than suspected at first glance. In fact, as information spills over after several years of regular fieldwork, almost all the village elders in this Kotoko settlement own some livestock. It has been impossible to obtain more precise quantitative information. It was nonetheless specified that the Galadima (chief of land and second in the village hierarchy after the Sultan) and the *Marabout* (Muslim scholar) own large cattle herds dispersed among several Shuwa-Arab settlements in the Yaere. It thus appears that, through the development of the patron/client relationship, the ownership of livestock by Kotoko elders is practically invisible in the settlement record. As far as sheep and goats are concerned, Houlouf inhabitants have devised a system of herd management. During the dry season, animals are pooled in the morning for grazing and watering purposes; in a rotating system shifting from one family to the other, young boys 12 to 16 years old work as shepherds, at daytime and return the animals to each family in the evening. Thus, there is a small amount of animal husbandry practiced within the context of the Houlouf settled peasant socioeconomic system. Intensive gardening is also currently practiced at Houlouf.

Kotoko and Shuwa-Arab Interaction

As one moves from the Shuwa-Arab seminomadic pastoralists to the Kotoko sedentary peasants at the other end of the socioeconomic spectrum, there is clearly a population density gradient and an ethnic overlap in the middle of the spectrum. Socioeconomic interaction takes place in different contexts. The Shuwa-Arab buy their clay vessels from Kotoko potters. Exchanges take place at daily and weekly markets organized in each cluster of settlements. Market places are exclusively located in Kotoko settlements. The Shuwa-Arab sell dairy products, decorated calabashes, and gathered wild grain and fruits, and they perform services as blacksmiths. There is an unbalanced pattern of intermarriage, with generally Shuwa-Arab women married to Kotoko men rather than the opposite. And more important, Arab language is the lingua franca used among peoples of the entire region and even between the Kotoko from different settlement (Holl 1993; Holl and Levy 1993). The patron/client relationship alluded to above is but the tip of the complex web of long-term interaction between the Kotoko and the Shuwa-Arab which will be considered in more detail in the following section.

The Kotoko Side

The Kotoko are the aboriginal population. Their claim for prior settlement and possession of the land is expressed in genealogies linking the present-day inhabitants to their mythical ancestors, the "Sao" (Griaule and Lebeuf 1948; Lebeuf 1969). In fact, during the last millennium (ca. 1000–1900 AD), they had developed a highly centralized and ranked social system, at first organized into competing peer-polities and later into chiefdoms (Holl 2002). The political system is characterized by the existence of a paramount chief, prince of Logone-Birni (*Mra Lagwan*), and lower order local chiefs (Sultan). Before and even during the colonial period, Kotoko peer-polities were organized into a two- to three-tiered settlement hierarchy. The spatial layout of Kotoko political centers shares the same basic structure observed at a number of different places by nineteenth-century European explorers (Denham et al. 1828; Barth 1965; Nachtigal 1980) and ethnographers (Griaule and Lebeuf 1948, 1950, 1951; Lebeuf 1969) at Makari, Afade, Gulfey, Kusseri, Kala-Kafra, Houlouf, Logone-Birni, Logone-Gana, etc. All the settlements are surrounded by impressive earthen ramparts. Their spatial layout is focused on the ruler's palace and its adjoined plaza. Habitation units are organized into individual walled compounds (*Sare*) comprising courtyards and varying numbers of houses according to the size and wealth of the household. The compounds are generally quadrangular in shape. Main houses are also rectilinear with flat roofs, with some important officials' palaces being multistory buildings (fig. 5). Sun-dried bricks are the predominant building material. Aggregates of compounds are organized into distinct quarters or wards separated from each other by narrow streets and open

Figure 5: The Sultan's Palace from Logone Birni

places (fig. 6). Each ward is ruled by a chief (Bilama) elected or appointed among the elders. These elders are members of different councils in charge of community affairs under the leadership of the Sultan, his residence being located at the center of the settlement. The central location of the ruler's palace is thus a "spatial trans-lation" of the leading position of his office within the Kotoko social system.

The extended family comprising all the descendants of a *yarew* (founding ancestor) is the essential building block of Kotoko society. The unity of the *mi zili aduma* (member of the extended family) is primarily based on common residence in a more or less large compound. In terms of generations, the Kotoko extended family includes the elder household head and his wives, their sons with wives and children, their unmarried daughters, and usually children of some of their daugh-ters (Lebeuf 1969: 106–107). "Each adult has his own house; each married woman with a distinct kitchen, lives in her own house with her children" (Lebeuf 1969: 106). The proximity and aggregation of compounds into distinct wards, their loca-tion relative to the Sultan's palace which appears to be the central structuring fea-ture of Kotoko town planning, and their spatial relationship to each other are based on a subtle gradation of rank and occupation, ranging from the Sultan at top to slave at the bottom. The scaled rank/occupation groups encompass high ranking elite members with hereditary titles and privileges, officials appointed to specific positions from free-born citizens or from slave origins, free-born citizens, those from slave origins, and finally slaves.

Figure 6: Houlouf: View of a village street

The settlement patterning of Houlouf shares the same characteristics presented above: the former earthen rampart is almost completely eroded. The Sultan's palace is located at the center of the village, on the eastern side of a large plaza with a well and numerous trees. The village's elders like to meet each other formally and informally under a shelter built along the palace western wall, on the northern side of the entrance. The Friday Mosque and the residence of Agaga Salle, the elder in charge of important ritual ceremonies and the third in the village's political hierarchy aged approximately ninety years in 1991, are situated next to the Sultan's palace on the southern side of the plaza. Prior to the installation of a deep-bored pump in 1985, the well was the informal meeting place of the women of the whole village; different kinds of information were exchanged and dispatched. From 1982, the year of the first field season at Houlouf, some significant changes occurred. The first to be mentioned concerns the arrival of a Muslim scholar (Marabout) who built his compound, a mosque, and a Koranic school, on the northern edge of the village. With the exception of the elementary school, all the compounds located on the northern side of the main E-W street were built between 1984 and 1988 and are inhabited by recent settlers. There is a communal sheep-goat enclosure on the eastern edge of the site and a market place on the western one. The residence of the Galadima (Chief of land), the second in the village's political hierarchy, previously situated on the northern edge was later surrounded by recently built compounds. There is a third mosque in one of the western wards, as well as one engine-pulled mill. And finally, a deep-bored pump has been installed initially on the edge of the cluster of habitations.

From the colonial period onward, the political authority of the traditional system has been steadily eroded, a process amplified by modern Cameroonian administration. In present-day circumstances, the Sultan has been reduced to the function of a mere tax collector. In contrast, the Muslim local organization is relatively free from the burden of the administration. There seems to be a competition for followers between the Kotoko traditional organization, represented by the close proximity between the Sultan's palace and the Friday Mosque located at the center of the settlement, but with its vanished political influence, and the relative Muslim Revival, represented by the wealthy Marabout, his followers, and students. During the last five years of observation (1986–1991), the meeting place in front of the Marabout compound and the evening Koranic school have attracted a higher frequency of village elder gatherings at the expense of the Sultan's palace shelter and large plaza. This competition between Kotoko traditional system and different Muslim doctrinal obedience is not new in this region. It is deeply imbedded in Kotoko rulers' genealogies, characterized by two interesting features: first a systematic attempt to push backward in the remote past the period of conversion to Islam; and second, an eagerness to keep a right balance between pre-Muslim and Muslim periods, manifested in a certain proportionality between the number of converted and nonconverted rulers (Lebeuf 1969; Zeltner 1979). The discussion conducted on Houlouf settlement patterning clearly shows that the structuring of community space is far from being a neutral process. It shows that the spatial layout of sites is dependent upon the dominant ideological system.

Aspects of Houlouf Ethnohistory

The history of the city is organized along sultans' genealogies. The narrative style which cannot be translated here is rhythmic when concerned with the succession to sultanship. Additional information was obtained in January 1991, through "guided interviews" of the three oldest members of the Houlouf community: the *Galadima* and his friends, Agaga Salle, the sacrificator, and Awalou Abaka; all of them aged eighty to ninety years. The narrative runs as follows:

> This is the story of our village.
> We learned it from our fathers,
> Who also learned it from their fathers, and so on.
> This is the true history of our village.
> Houlouf was the first city in this part of the land,
> Everything started when the whole area was totally uninhabited.

1   Sao was the first Sultan.
    At the death of Sao,
2   His son, Maina Kirdi became Sultan.
    At the death of Maina Kirdi,
3   His son, May Abdou became Sultan.
    At the death of May Abdou,
4   His son, May Messala became Sultan.
    By May Messala time, there was no Logone, no Kusseri, no Kabe, no Kala,
    Houlouf was unique.
    May Messala brought Islam to this land.
    May Messala launched a Holy War against pagans,
    A Holy War to convert them to the true religion,
    A Holy War which lasted for seven years.
    At the death of May Messala,
5   His son, May Adam Gana became Sultan.
    At the death of May Adam Gana,
6   His son, May Messali became Sultan.
    At the death of May Messali,
7   His son, May Akki became Sultan.
    At the death of May Akki,
8   His son, May Ousmane became Sultan.
    At the death of May Ousmane,
9   His son, May Arouna became Sultan.
    At the death of May Arouna,
10 His son, May Ngouri became Sultan.
    At his time, Rabbeh destroyed Houlouf
    And its inhabitants were dispersed.
    At the death of May Ngouri,
11 His son, May Akki became Sultan.
    At the death of May Akki,
12 His son, May Deyne became Sultan.
    At the death of May Deyne,
13 His son, May Boukar became Sultan
    At the death of May Boukar,
14 His son, May Abdel Karim became Sultan.
    At the death of May Abdel Karim,
15 His son, May Moussa became Sultan.
    At the death of May Moussa,
16 His son, May Mahamat became Sultan.
    At the death of May Mahamat
17 His son, May Mahamat became Sultan.
    At the death of May Mahamat,
18 His son, May Idrissi became Sultan.
    At the death of May Idrissi,
19 His son, May Hassana became Sultan.

As is usually the case with ethnohistorical records, the narrative starts with the chain of transmission from remote ancestors to the present through successive father-son cohorts. Alternative narratives are discounted, the performed one being singled out as the "true history." There are also interesting paradoxes in this genealogy of Houlouf sultans. The most striking is the case of May Messala, the fourth sultan, who launched a seven-year long Holy War to expand Islam in an empty land. The feature, which nonetheless emerges from this ethnohistorical account of the history of the city, is probably the picture of a well-organized community, with a neat pattern of succession to sultanship, disturbed only once by an "uncivilized" outsider, Rabbeh. The heavy taxation and tribute exaction implemented on neighboring Shuwa-Arab villages is, in this regard, considered as a "normal" extension of their rights as "owners" of the land (Hagenbucher-Sacripanti 1977a,b; Zeltner 1979, 1980). According to A. Lebeuf (1969: 218), Kotoko financial contribution to their central government resources is minor in scale. It is partially based on volunteer contributions combined with a minor tax for those involved in productive activities. The bulk of government resources and support for elites' and officials' households are derived from tribute extraction and a broad spectrum of taxes paid by the members of dominated ethnic groups. "Neither European colonization, nor independent Cameroun state, have succeeded in abolishing the different taxes and tributes still collected by all traditional authorities, or their heirs" (Lebeuf 1969: 218). Ordinary folktales convey contrasted views on Kotoko/Shuwa-Arab interaction. On the Kotoko side, Shuwa-Arabs are considered untrustworthy, thieves, prone to violence, and bad Muslims. From Shuwa-Arab perspective, Kotoko are seen as witches, chauvinistic, and greedy for power and wealth (Holl 1993; Tijani 1986; Hagenbucher-Sacripanti 1977). It appears clear that there are several lines of tension between both ethnic groups; tension between natives and immigrants, between settled farmers and seminomadic pastoralists, between a centralized social system with its required financial imperatives and "dissipative" mobile flexible clan-tribal scale societies, and finally between contrasted historical and cultural experiences.

The interaction between the Kotoko and the Shuwa-Arab is not a one-sided phenomena, with the latter having to adapt to circumstances set by the former. There is a fair amount of syncretism on both sides. The Kotoko have integrated parts of Arab-Muslim practices in their cultural universe. The Shuwa-Arab, in their process of "Africanization," have adopted various aspects of local magic and witchcraft practices.

The Shuwa-Arab Side

Some Kotoko and Kanuri communities situated in areas with predominant Shuwa-Arab settlements went through economic and cultural adaptation leading to the assimilation of the latter's practices. This is the case at Abari II, a small village from the Serbewel Canton studied by Hagenbucher-Sacripanti (1977). He observed that the inhabitants of Abari II claim to be of Kotoko origin and use Kotoko-specific facial scarifications for their children. But they speak Arabic and have forgotten their original Chadic language, practice excision on their daughters, pay for the "blood-price" (*diye*) and ordinary administrative per-capita tax with the Salamat through the Lawan, have adopted mixed farming and a seminomadic way of life, sharing dry-season grazing lands with the Ulad Eli, and finally, more interesting, as is the case for the Shuwa-Arab, they despise the Kotoko and consider them as experts in witchcraft. Similar changes have been observed for other communities of the area, namely, the Kanuri of Abari I, the Hawsa of Bongor, the Fulani of Dilebil, Abu Dangala, and Atri I, all of them being under the "command" of the Lawan of the Salamat (Hagenbucher-Sacripanti 1977: 225–226).

Practices linked with the protection of one's life and goods and the cure for sickness are enmeshed in a general world view in which witchcraft appears efficient. For the Shuwa-Arab, almost any Kotoko is a witch; their visible social organization with the sultan at its top is a simple copy of the hidden hierarchy of the secret universe of sorcerers (Hagenbucher-Sacripanti 1977: 261). According to this conception, Kotoko Sultans are at the same time witch sultans, presiding over ceremonies during which bodies of victims are shared in secret festive circumstances. Kotoko fame for witchcraft is not a recent phenomenon; nineteenth century historical records point to well-entrenched belief and widespread stories, as reported by H. Barth on March 12, 1852, on his way from Kukawa to Logone-Birni:

> We then passed on our left the town U'lluf, Hulluf or Helib, surrounded by a high clay wall, and almost hidden behind wide-spreading fig-trees just as is the case with Kala. This town, the name of which is pronounced "Elf" by the Arabs, and of the origin of which they give very absurd accounts, is ill-famed for the presumed witchcraft and sorcery of its inhabitants; and this was the only reason which prevented my companions from staying here during the heat of the day. (Barth 1965: 440)

Oral history recorded at the Shuwa-Arab settlement of Alaya I in January 1991 provides some clues on their insertion in the social and political landscape of the study area. Information was obtained on different subjects through a "guided" interview of Bilama Harfi, the headman of the village, assisted by his younger brother. The story runs as follows:

> My father died when he was 98 years old. My brother is sitting next to me; we are from the same mother. This is what we were told by our father: our ancestors came from the East, from the village of Dababa in the region of Bokoro in Chad. It is Mahamat al Hajj who led the migration and was welcomed by the population of Houlouf. By the time of Mahamat al Hajj, 350 years ago, Logone-Birni was still nonexistent. He asked for land for himself and his people to settle, and was granted land. The inhabitants of Houlouf were very kind to them; their

hospitality was free, nothing had to be paid in exchange. When they arrived from the East, they did not possess any cattle but only a few sheep and goats.

At that time, there were no Arabs in the area, the Yaere was settled by mound-dwellers. They did not allow our ancestors to settle on their mounds; but after their death, Arabs started to move in the *Yaere,* attracted by the empty land and the abundance of fish. They were fishing and growing millet [sorghum].

After the death of Mahamat al Hajj, Sale was the successor; he was followed by Abdoulaye Dougourchi, then Ble, then Harfi, then myself, Harfi. Islam was introduced and imposed by May Messala. At his time, a single boy could take care of the herd in the dry-season camp. It was a peaceful period; thieves were sentenced to death.

The Salamat of the yaere arrived in this part of land before the Essala; they were allied with Houlouf to fight against the Essala who arrived later. There were also wars between the Salamat of the yaere and Logone-Birni; the Salamat were defeated. Since then they had to pay for taxes and an annual tribute in sheep and goats to Houlouf and Logone-Birni Sultans.

Our father was present at Alaya when Rabbeh passed by. Rabbeh troops humiliated all the men and murdered many of them.

There were many wars at that time. The Arabs possessed very few horses. Horses were particularly expensive. At least ten heads of cattle were needed to buy one horse; armed men were wearing wooden shoes and organized into rotating guarding squads in order to avoid surprise attacks and raids.

In former time, each settlement was autonomous; after Rabbeh, there were Lawans and Sheikhs (as is the case for Lawan Adum of Madaf). Weapons and tools in iron were made from ore collected on the surface in the yaere, at such places as Fangada, Ngada, and Choloba. With that ore, iron blooms were obtained after two to three hours of smelting in low furnaces. This way of producing iron tools was abandoned after the arrival of the Europeans. There were very few blacksmiths, each of them was working for several villages.

The narrative provided by Bilama Harfi and his brother does not integrate any kind of myth. It is coherent and aims to explain how their ancestors have managed to settle and survive in an alien context. The ancestor who led the migration, Mahamat al Hajj, was, according to standard Islamic practices, a pilgrim to the "Sacred House of God" at the Mekka. He was thus already a Muslim, and some of his tribesmen may have been converted. Both the Houlouf and Alaya narratives are in agreement on the point concerning the introduction of Islam in the area by May Messala, the fourth sultan of Houlouf. Unfortunately, the Alaya narrative does not tell if Mahamat al Hajj, who entered the Houlouf territory 350 years ago, arrived prior, during the reign, or after the rise of May Messala to sultanship. Both narratives share common features concerning the "emptiness" of the territories; Houlouf was unique and there were no Arabs. The Houlouf narrative is nonetheless exclusively "Kotoko-centric," while the Alaya one refers to different groups represented in the area—the Kotoko, the Essala, and the "yaere mound-dwellers"—and to warfare and changing alliances between them.

All the Shuwa-Arab from the study area belong to one large tribe, the Banu Salamat. The Salamat are divided into two major factions, those from the yaere, the Ulad Daoud and the Essala settled farther E and NE. These factions are divided into several clans, some of them confined to a single settlement while others are more widespread. The Essala are predominantly mixed-farmers, living in sedentary villages with their main settlements, Njagare, Djidat, El Birke, Abuzrega, and Marafaine, located in the N-NE of the study area. The Ulad Daoud are divided into eight clans: the U. Fokhara at Ngada I and IV; the U. Yesiye at Bawara; the U. Abdallah at Allaya I and II, Bilbede, Gallis, Madaf I and Mahanna; the U. Migebil at Mishiskwa; the U. Jubara at Sororo, Chouaram, Ngada II and III; the U. Bijime at Fangada; the U. Wanis at Madaf II; and finally, the U. Oukhoura at Ndom.

Shuwa-Arab sites are generally patterned in relation to herding activities, with varying numbers of livestock enclosures at the center surrounded by rings of houses. Households are based on the model of extended families (Tijani 1986; Conte and Hagenbucher 1977; Holl et al. 1991; Holl and Levy 1993; Holl 1993) and possess more or less clustered dwelling features. Settlements are in almost all the cases circular to elliptical in shape with inward oriented houses (fig. 7). Grown up and married sons achieved "social majority" after the birth and weaning of the first child; they can then leave from their fathers' domain to start their independent household.

Figure 7: View of Mishiskwa, a Shuwa-Arab semipermanent village in 1984

Research Expectations

With the formation of modern African states and, more important, their international boundaries, expanding populations have been confined to limited territories,
with few urban centers as outlets for out-migration. The Shuwa-Arab are a particularly interesting case; even during the colonial period, large clan groups and tribal
factions could move from one colony to another. After independence, African states
tried to exert a tighter control over movements of peoples and goods, and devised
administrative procedures impeding the movement of whole tribes factions. A comparative analysis of Kotoko and Shuwa-Arab demography carried out in the 1960s
by A.M. Podlewski (1966) suggests interesting patterns, some of them with important implications for the future of both populations, will be considered here.

Table 9: Comparative demographic patterns of Kotoko and Shuwa-Arabs from
          Northern Cameroon

Parameter	Kotoko	Shuwa-Arab
Population size	21,000	45,000
Sample size	1,406	2,368
Sampled localities	6	34
Age group (percent) 0–14 yrs	31	34
Age group (percent) 15–59 yrs	60	58.5
Age group (percent) >60 yrs	9	7.5
Male/Female Ratio	0.94	0.94
Av. Nb children/woman	3.28	4.26
Birth rate (0/1000)	29.9	40.5
Reproduction rate (percent)	1.59	2.12
Mortality rate (0/1000)	20.6	23
Growth rate (percent)	1.009	1.31
Survival table		
Age		
0	1,000	1,000
1	833	854
5	786	792
10	727	776
20	727	679
30	669	597
40	575	567
50	448	459
60	318	262
70	140	139

Source: Podlewsky 1966

As suggested by their age-pyramids and in birth, reproduction, and growth rates (table 9), the Kotoko are a stationary population; any additional growth can only be achieved through a farther decrease of the mortality rate, which is already relatively low. They are also particularly stable, with approximately 70 percent of them residing for all their life in their birthplace. The Shuwa Arab, in contrast, are a dynamic and growing population, characterized by a higher degree of mobility, with an important growth potential not yet fully enacted. A comparative study of Kotoko and Shuwa-Arab survival tables and curves (table 9) shows five dominant patterns. First, infant mortality up to fifteen years is systematically higher among the Kotoko. Second, in age groups ranging from fifteen to forty years, there is an important reversal with higher mortality among the Shuwa Arabs. Third, higher survival rate occurs for the Shuwa Arabs in the fifty years age set; followed by the fourth pattern characterized by a sharp increase in the Kotoko survival rate in the sixty years age groups. The last one shows an almost similar survival rate for both populations. In general, life expectancy is longer for the Kotoko while Shuwa-Arab growth rate is higher. Shuwa-Arab population size was already more than twice that of the Kotoko in the 1960s (table 9). A. M. Podlewski (1966) predicted that Shuwa-Arab population will continue to increase and after thirty years, by the end of the twentieth century, they will be three times more numerous, a situation which may generate increasing social tension.

Several scenarios can be outlined from the demographic evidence summarized above. Modern states' boundaries have created an unprecedented problem for expanding nomadic to seminomadic population. An assumption has to be specified at this point; it is considered that different Shuwa-Arab populations are confined within the boundaries of their respective states; individuals and small groups may

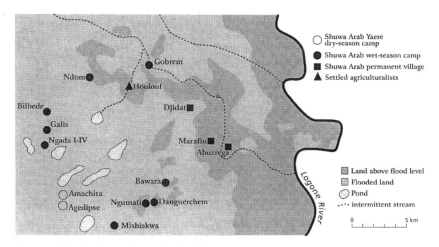

Figure 8: Distribution of the studied settlements

easily cross the boundaries, but, even if it is not impossible, the mass movement of whole factions or tribes is much more difficult. Three connected but distinct scenarios can be suggested. In the first, there may be a constant moving frontier of Shuwa-Arab expansion, particularly directed toward areas with low population densities; this is the case in the yaere and its southern extension in the Waza National Park, where human settlement is prohibited. Second, there may be a pull toward urban centers resulting in the withdrawal from the traditional Shuwa-Arab society but also alleviating pressure from the socioeconomic system. Third, there may be an increasing number of settlements, resulting in the reduction of pastoral-nomadic territorial range, increased population per settlement, decreased mobility, a shift toward mixed farming, and sustained trends toward a sedentary way of life. The third scenario may lead to important changes in the balance of power at the local level between the traditionally dominated Shuwa-Arab and the dominant Kotoko. The ethnoarchaeological research project conducted on the Houlouf region's Shuwa-Arab settlements aims to document the material correlates of the recent phase of the Kotoko/Shuwa-Arab interaction and test the hypotheses outlined above. In order to achieve this goal, twenty-seven Shuwa-Arab sites, permanent villages, semi-permanent settlements, and dry-season camps were investigated (fig. 8).

PART II

Semipermanent Villages

Semipermanent, or rainy-season, villages are found generally along the edge of the Yaere, in that part of the land subject to seasonal flood. They are permanent settlements, inhabited for the major part of the year. They are nonetheless abandoned for three to four months each year, their inhabitants then settling in the Yaere dry-season camps. The discussion is based on archaeologically relevant criteria, such as regional distribution of settlements, site size and shape, density and diversity of features, distribution and patterns of material culture items. Twelve semipermanent villages have been studied in detail; they will be presented according to their distribution in the regional landscape (fig. 8). Three village clusters are considered: these are the southern settlement group with four sites, Bawara, Danguerchem, Mishiskwa, and Ngumati; the western group with six sites—Bilbede, Gallis, and Ngada I, II, III, and IV; and finally, a looser, non-clustered group termed "northern settlement group" comprised of two villages, Gobrem and Ndom.

Chapter 3

The Southern Settlement Group

This chapter deals with four sites, Bawara, Danguerchem, Mishiskwa, and Ngumati, belonging to the southern settlement group. They are stretched on approximately 6 kilometers along a SW-NE axis. Mishiskwa, the southernmost site is found at 3 kilometers of its northern neighbor. Danguerchem and Ngumati are found almost at the middle of the settlement group; they are twin-settlements, located almost on the same spot but on different shores of a fossil river channel, with the former in the E and the latter in the W. Finally, Bawara is found at 2.5 kilometers NE (fig. 8).

Bawara

Bawara is the northernmost site of the southern settlement group. Subcircular in shape and measuring 130 m in length in its maximum NW-SE axis and 120 m in width in its minimum NE-SW one, the settlement is extended over 1.56 hectares of a fenced village space (fig. 9). The village layout, with houses situated on the perimeter, is organized around central livestock corrals. Four of these corrals, with their diameters varying from 4.9 m to 8.7 m, are used for sheep and goats. The larger, extended over 1,530 square meters (45 m W-E × 34 m N-S) with three entrances, is exclusively used for cattle. Two wells, with the water table reached at a depth of 13 to 15 m, are situated at ten to 15 m on the eastern side of the site. Houses and built features are organized into more or less clearly distinct clusters corresponding to households' installations (tables 10 and 11).

Proceeding clockwise from the S-SE of the site, cluster 1 consists of three features in a linear arrangement. At its center, there is a public shelter or discussion house (feature 1) measuring 5 m in diameter, built with one central pole, nineteen side posts, a thatched roof but without walls, a livestock house also used as barn (feature 19) measuring 8.8 m in diameter, built with wood and reeds and comprising six central poles, located a few meters to the E; while the habitation house (feature 2) measures 6 m in diameter, is built with mud-brick and two central poles,

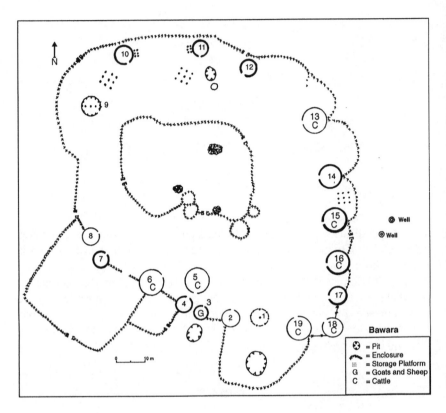

Figure 9: Map of Bawara

Table 10: Bawara household clusters

Cluster number	Number of units	Habitation houses	Livestock houses	Storage platforms	Others
1	1	1	1	—	2
2	1	1	2	—	1
3	1	2	1	—	1
4	1	1	—	2	1
5	1	2	—	2	—
6	1	1	2	1	—
7	1	1	2	—	—
Total	7	9	8	5	5

Table 11: Bawara general distribution of pottery

Cluster number	Features number	Service vessels	Cooking vessels	Storage vessels	Unknown	Total
1	4	—	5	2	—	7
2	4	—	—	—	—	—
3	4	—	1	1	—	2
4	4	—	1	1	—	2
5	4	1	2	4	—	7
6	4	—	—	—	—	—
7	3	—	—	2	—	2
Total	27	1	9	10	—	20

and is found 5 m to the W of the discussion shelter (fig. 9). The habitation house has two small windows, an unusual feature in semipermanent villages, a large bed, 3.50 m long and 1.80 m wide, extended over the southern half of the house opposite to the entrance, an elaborate hearth situated on the right-hand side of the entrance, and seven clay vessels and three enamelwares arranged in shelf along the wall between the door and the fireplace. There is an unstructured fireplace in the middle on the northern half of the house, next to a straw mat. A pair of slippers was found near the mat, with a clay vessel. A wooden rack used as a table is situated along the wall in the eastern part of the house. Ten flashlight batteries of "Hellessens" trademark were found scattered on the house floor.

The pottery material is divided into four morphological categories: (1) one necked pot decorated with a band of twisted roulette impression delimited by two parallel grooved lines on the shoulder, measuring 36 cm in total height (TH), 26 cm in maximum diameter (MaD), 11.5 cm in mouth diameter (MD), 17 cm in height of maximum diameter (HMD), and finally, a 0.9 cm thick wall (T); (2) two semiglobular pots, each with a slightly constrained neck and everted rim, both decorated with extensive twisted roulette impression on the body, overlined by one or two grooved lines, complemented by two to four symmetric buttons. They share comparable morphometric attributes, 22 and 23 cm in MD, 29 cm in MaD, 27 and 29 cm in TH, 14 and 17 cm in HMD, and 0.8 and 1.1 cm in T; (3) two straight-sided to holemouth pots, with their decoration motifs and syntax similar to that just described above, their morphometric attributes varying from 21 to 24.5 cm for MD, 21 to 28 cm for MaD, 21 to 25.5 cm for TH, 11 to 15 cm for HMD, and finally, 1.3 to 1.8 cm for T; and (4) two large-necked globular storage jars, measuring 28 cm in MD, 39 and 44 cm in MD, 46 and 50 cm in TH, 5 to 13 cm in NH, 23 to 24 cm in HMD, 1.3 to 1.4 cm in T, decorated with a band of twisted roulette impression delimited by two or three parallel grooved lines on the shoulder. One of the specimens is singled out by a series of six handles/lugs on the shoulder.

Cluster 2, with three houses arranged in a triangular pattern, is found only a few meters to the W of the previous one (fig. 9). It comprises a relatively large four-central-poles barn (feature 5), built with wood and reeds and measuring 10 m in diameter. The barn is situated in the inner part of the village, at the apex of the triangle, facing the other houses from the cluster. Feature 3 is a single-central-pole goat house, measuring 4.2 m in diameter and surprisingly built with mud-bricks. And finally, the habitation house (feature 4), built with mud-brick, two central poles, and measuring 6 m in diameter, comprises a large bed, a series of shelves, and an elaborate hearth.

Cluster 3 farther W also comprises three features in a linear arrangement. Feature 6, situated at the eastern end of the cluster, measures 7.6 m in diameter; it is a relatively large four-central-poles barn, built with wood and reeds. Features 7 and 8 are habitation houses with large beds, elaborate hearths, and diversified pieces of domestic equipment. House 7 measures 4.7 m in diameter being built in mud-brick with a single central pole; a single large clay vessel was found in the house. It is a round-base, hemispheric pot with a slightly restricted neck and everted rim, 23 cm in MD, 32 cm in MaD, 37 cm in TH, 18 cm in HMD, and 1 cm thick wall. The uncovered pottery has two handles and is decorated with a band of twisted roulette impression under- and overlined by two parallel grooved lines on the shoulder. House 8, slightly larger, measures 5.8 m in diameter; it is a two-central-poles feature, built with wood and reeds, comprising two raised grinding platforms, one clay vessel, and three enamel basins. Grinding platforms are built with four short poles, 50 to 70 cm in height, supporting an elliptically shaped and slightly concave grinding installation made with clay and straw, mixed with horse dung to enhance its resistance. The uncovered pottery is a large, ovoid storage pot. It is decorated with a band of twisted roulette impression under- and overlined by parallel grooved lines on the shoulder. Its morphometric attributes, 22 cm for MD, 31 cm for MaD, 36 cm for TH, 19 cm for the HMD, and 1 cm for T, are very close to those from the pottery from house 7. As suggested by similar decorative syntax and morphometric attributes, pottery from houses 7 and 8 were probably obtained from the same potter's workshop.

Cluster 4, with three main features in a linear arrangement, is situated at approximately 40 m N of cluster 3 (fig. 9). Feature 9, situated at the southern end is a public shelter or discussion house, measuring 6.5 m in diameter, built with three central poles, a thatched, dome-shaped roof and without walls. A large storage platform supported by twelve poles is found at the center, with the habitation house (feature 10) with an adjunct small shelter located at the opposite northern end of the linear arrangement. The habitation house is built with mud-brick and one central pole, measures 5.6 m in diameter, and comprises a large bed, an elaborate hearth, one enamel basin, and two clay vessels. One of the vessels is a necked storage jar with four lugs; it measures 30 cm in MD, 45 cm in MaD, 60 cm in TH, 14 cm in NH, 27 cm in HMD, and finally, 1.4 cm in T. It is decorated with a band of twisted roulette impression and three parallel grooved lines on the shoulder. The other one, measuring 22 cm in MD, 31 cm in MaD, 24 cm in TH, 14 cm in HMD, and finally, 1 cm in T, is a relatively large, rounded-base, hemispherical pot, with slightly constricted neck and everted rim. It is decorated with extensive twisted roulette impression on the body overlined by three parallel grooved lines and four pairs of appliqué buttons on the shoulder.

Cluster 5 is located 20 m W of the previous one. It consists of four features: one storage platform supported by a series of nine poles, a small circular chicken coop, and finally, two habitation houses at 15 m from each other. House 11, with an adjunct shelter on its western flank, is built in mud-brick with two central poles, and measures 5.5 m in diameter. It comprises a large bed, elaborate hearth, and a large amount of vessels: seven pottery and three enamelwares. House 12, also built in mud-brick with a single central pole, is smaller, measuring 4.8 m in diameter; a small bed as well as one enamel basin were found in the house which belongs to a young, unmarried man. The pottery material recorded in house 11 is distributed into five morphological categories: (1) food serving vessels are represented by one circular plate with slightly everted rim, decorated with extensive twisted roulette impression; the plate measures 27 cm in both maximum and mouth diameter, 8 cm in TH, and 1.1 cm in T. Cooking vessels are represented by two specimens; (2) one is a rounded-base, hemispherical pot, 20 cm in MD, 25 cm in MaD, 24 cm in TH, 14 cm in HMD, and 0.7 cm in T, decorated with extensive twisted roulette impression on the body overlined two parallel horizontal grooved lines on the shoulder; (3) and the other, a slightly elongated, necked pot with a globular body, measuring 21 cm in MD, 28 cm in MaD, 32 cm in TH, 5 cm in NH, and finally, 0.8 cm in T, with the motifs and pattern of decoration similar to those of the first specimen. Four of the recorded storage vessels are distributed into two morpho-logical categories; (4) a large ovoid, plain pot with everted rim, with its morpho-metric attributes varying from 28 cm for MD, 42 cm for MaD, 46 cm for TH, 25 cm in HMD, and finally, 1 cm in T; and (5) necked jars, which, despite minor varia-tions from one specimen to the other, appear to share fundamental characteristics. Two of them share similar decoration patterns, consisting of a band of twisted roulette impression associated to three horizontal and parallel grooved lines situ-ated on the jar's shoulder; while the other one is decorated with extensive twisted roulette impression on the body, overlined on the shoulder by two horizontal and parallel lines complemented by three pairs of appliqué buttons. Their morphometric attributes vary from 31 to 26 cm for MD, 41, 40 to 38 cm for MaD, 54 to 45 cm for TH, 13, 7 to 5 cm for NH, 26 to 25 cm for HMD, and finally, 1.8 to 1.1 cm for T.

Cluster 6, with its four features in a linear arrangement is located approxi-mately 25 m to the SE of cluster 5. Two of the recorded features, houses 13 and 15, are relatively large barns measuring respectively 10 and 7.2 m in diameter. They are built in wood and reeds, with seven central poles for the former and four for the latter. The habitation house (feature 14), measuring 5.8 m in diameter, built in mud-brick with two central poles, is located at the center of the cluster, with a storage platform supported by a series of nine poles on its southern side. It comprises a large bed, an elaborate hearth, and one enamel basin.

Cluster 7, located a few meters S, is also a linear arrangement of features, with two barns and one habitation house (fig. 9). House 16, the northern barn, is built in mud-brick with four central poles and measures 6.3 m in diameter. The southern barn, house 18, is slightly larger, built in wood and reeds with two central poles. A large, slightly necked storage jar probably used to water the livestock was found in house 18; it is decorated with a band of twisted roulette impression under- and overlined by parallel and horizontal grooved lines situated on the vessel's shoulder. Its morphometric attributes vary from 25 cm in MD, 45 cm in MaD, 50 cm in TH, 8 cm in NH, 27 cm in HMD, to 1.3 cm in T. The habitation house (feature 17) measures 5 m in diameter. It is built in mud-brick with a single central pole and comprises an elaborate hearth, a large bed, two enamel wares, and one clay vessel. The pottery recorded from house 17 is a large necked jug, with the upper part missing. It is decorated with four pairs of appliqué buttons, each pair associated to vertical grooved lines from the shoulder to neck bottom. The MD is unknown stricto sensu but the available measurement is 10 cm, with 32 cm in MaD, 30 (?) cm in recorded TH, 17 cm in HMD, and finally, 1.2 cm in T.

A detailed comparative analysis of settlement patterns will be carried out later, after a description of all the studied sites. At this point, there are two salient features which deserve to be singled out from the Bawara site. The first concerns building material selection; more than half of the houses (10 of 19) are built in mud-brick, a highly unusual proportion for a semipermanent village. It is clear from the Bawara architectural evidence that houses build in mud-brick are preferentially used for habitation; there is a single case of habitation in a wood and reeds house (house 8). Among the ten recorded cases, only two (houses 3 and 16) are devoted to sheep/goats and cattle. The second salient feature is slightly looser but nonetheless real. Habitation clusters with storage platforms are located in the northern half of the site, while those without such features but with livestock houses and even small enclosures, are situated in the southern half of the village. The concentration of pottery material in two houses (houses 2 and 11) belonging to the central house cluster of each "site-moitie" is striking.

Ngumati

Ngumati is located on the left bank of a fossil river channel at 11° 56' N and 14° 56' E, near a more or less permanent pond. The village extended over 1.18 hectare is elliptically shaped, measuring 125 m in length in its N-S axis and 95 m in width in its W-E one. It consists of twenty-one circular houses distributed into seven clusters, five livestock enclosures, and one garden plot (fig. 10, table 12).

Cluster 1, the habitation unit of the village headman (the Bilama) and the

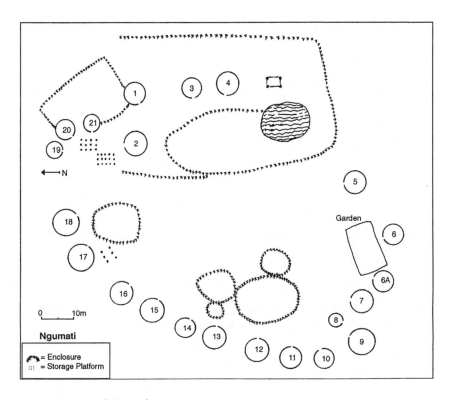

Figure 10: Map of Ngumati

Table12: Ngumati household clusters

Cluster number	Number of units	Habitation houses	Livestock houses	Storage platforms	Others
1	2	6	1	3	2
2	1	3	—	—	1
3	1	3	—	—	—
4	1	2	1	—	—
5	1	2	—	—	—
6	1	1	1	—	—
7	1	1	1	1	1
Total	8	18	4	4	4

most extensive of the settlement, is spread over the eastern half of the settlement. It comprises seven houses organized into two units and distributed over 3,600 square meters of fenced area set apart from the other features of the villages. Unit 1(A) comprises features 2, 19, 20, and 21, in a semicircular linear arrangement around two storage platforms with twelve and fifteen supporting poles. Unit 1(B) is slightly looser and consists of four features in a N-S linear arrangement, houses 1, 3, and 4, and a four-poles storage platform.

Feature 20, at the northern end of unit 1(A) is a public shelter measuring 5.5 m in diameter built with a single central pole. The Bilama habitation house of (feature 19) is located 1.5 m SW. It is a two-central-poles feature, measuring 6 m in diameter and built with wood and reeds. Still inhabited at the time of field-work it was not studied in detail; it nonetheless comprises a large bed, an elaborate hearth, and numerous clay vessels and enamel wares of varying size arranged in shelf distributed on both sides of the fireplace, situated on the right-hand side of the house's entrance, as is the case in all the studied Shuwa-Arab semipermanent villages. House 21, 5 m farther S, is also a habitation house with a large bed and an elaborate hearth, built in wood and reeds with a single central pole and measuring 5 m in diameter. House 2, located in the inner part of the village space, is situated approximately 10 m SSW of house 21; it is a relatively large two-central-poles barn, built with wood and reeds measuring 9.2 m in diameter.

In unit 1(B), house 1, situated at the northern end, is built in mud-brick and measures 5 m in diameter. It is a four-central-poles feature of unknown function. No traces of bed or fireplace have been recorded. One partially broken clay vessel was found in close proximity to house 1; it is a globular pot with a slightly constricted neck and everted rim, decorated with extensive twisted roulette impression on the body, overlined by a horizontal grooved line on the shoulder. Its morphometric attributes vary from 23 cm for MD, 28 cm for MaD, 20 (?) cm for the recorded TH, which is probably half of its original size, and, finally, 1 cm in T. House 3, at approximately 12 m S of the previous one, is a single-central-pole feature built in wood and reeds measuring 5 m in diameter. It is a poorly preserved habitation already abandoned and in an advanced stage of degradation; neither traces of bed nor fireplace have been found; its precise function is therefore unknown. The situation is similar for house 4, a two-central-poles feature built with wood and reeds, measuring 7 m in diameter and located some 5 m farther S (fig. 10). The unit installation is complemented by a four-poles storage platform situated near a dry, small-size watering basin. The fenced space in front of houses 3 and 4 was used as Bilama cattle corral.

Cluster 2 consists of four features: a rectangular garden plot, 15 m long and 10 m wide, and three houses disposed in a curvilinear arrangement on its southern side (fig. 10). House 5, a single-central-pole feature built with wood and reeds located at the northern end of the cluster measures 5 m in diameter. Houses 6 and 6A, found, respectively, at fifteen and 25 m farther SW were built with the same raw materials. They are slightly larger, measuring 6 m in diameter each with two central poles. All the cluster houses are very badly preserved, the complex having been abandoned for years.

Cluster 3 is situated in the SW of the settlement. It comprises three houses disposed in a triangular arrangement. The state of preservation is rather poor, no evidence of hearth or bed having been recorded. Houses 7 and 9, located 5 m from each other, are single-central-pole features measuring 6 m in diameter each. The former is built with wood and reeds, and the latter with mud-brick. House 8, situated in front of the larger dwelling, is smaller in size, measuring 3.6 m in diameter. It is a young man's house built in wood and reeds with a single central pole (fig. 10).

Cluster 4 comprises three houses arranged linearly, with each situated at 3 to 4 m from the other. House 10, at the southern end, measures 5 m in diameter; it is a single-central-pole habitation feature with an elaborate hearth. The bed was certainly dismantled. A necked storage jar was found on the house floor; it is decorated with extensive twisted roulette impression on the body, overlined by two horizontal and parallel grooved lines complemented by two symmetric pairs of appliqué buttons on the shoulder. Its morphometric attributes vary from 25 cm for MD, 33 cm for MaD, 36 cm for TH, 17 cm for HMD, 6 cm for NH, and finally, 0.9 cm for T. House 11, in a central position, is built in mud-brick with one central pole and measures 6.5 m in diameter. Nothing was left inside, not even traces of a fireplace; its use as a habitation feature is highly probable, but its precise function is unknown. Finally, House 12, at the northern end of the cluster, measures 8 m in diameter. It is a relatively large barn with four central poles, built with wood and reeds.

Cluster 5, with two houses, is situated in the central western part of the settlement. It consists of two features: A habitation house (feature 13) with an elaborate but poorly preserved hearth, with the bed missing, built in wood and reeds with a single central pole and measuring 6 m in diameter; and a slightly smaller single-central-pole wood and reeds house (feature 14) of unknown function, situated at 3 m to the N of the previous one and measuring 5 m in diameter.

Cluster 6 comprises two houses, features 15 and 16, at 4 m from each other. House 15 is a large barn in wood and reeds, built with six central poles and measuring 10 m in diameter. Habitation house 16 measures 6.3 m in diameter. As is the case for the barn, it is also built in wood and reeds but with a single central pole. A collapsed hearth was found in the house, but no traces of a bed have been recorded.

Cluster 7, situated NNW of the site, closes the perimeter of the settlement built features (fig. 10). It clearly consists of four features: a cattle enclosure (enclosure I), extended over 154 square meters, measuring 14 m in length N-S and 11 m in width W-E, a storage platform with six supporting poles, and two houses. House 17 is a relatively well-preserved habitation feature, with a large bed and an elaborate hearth. It is built in wood and reeds, with a single central pole and measures 6.5 m in diameter. One clay vessel used for cooking was found on the house floor. It is a slightly necked, rounded base, hemispheric pot with two handles, decorated with extensive twisted roulette impression on the body, with its morphometric attributes varying from 24.5 cm for MD, 27 cm for MaD, 30 cm for TH, 16 cm for HMD, 8 cm in NH, and, finally, 0.9 cm for T. House 18 is a two-central-poles barn, measuring 9 m in diameter, built with wood and reeds, and located 4 to 5 m NE of the habitation feature. A holemouth pot and an enamel basin, presumably used for watering the livestock, were found on the barn floor. The clay vessel measures 26 cm in MD, 31 cm in MaD, 31 cm in TH, 17 cm in HMD, and 0.9 cm in T. It is decorated with extensive twisted roulette impression on the body, overlined by two horizontal and parallel grooved lines on the shoulder.

The Ngumati site is an interesting case of scission. The fenced Bilama-houses complex is the material manifestation of a disrupted community life, partially supported by the tight clustering of livestock enclosures in the abandoned western half of the settlement. The four southwestern livestock enclosures, with their size ranging from 108 (enclosure II, 12 × 9 m) to 280 (enclosure IV, 20 × 14 m) meters square for cattle corrals, and from 19.62 (enclosure III, 5 m in diameter) to 28.26 (enclosure V, 9 m in diameter) meters square for goat enclosures, appear to have been used by the members of clusters 2 to 5 before deciding to leave. By the time of fieldwork in February 1988, the former village headman was the unique inhabitant of the settlement; he was abandoned not only by the other members of the village but also by his own family.

Danguerchem

Danguerchem is located opposite to Ngumati, on the right bank of a fossil river channel, at 11° 56′ latitude N and 14° 56′ longitude E. It is an elliptically shaped settlement extended over 1.08 hectare, measuring 135 m in length in its NW-SE axis and 80 m in width in the SW-NE one, already abandoned several years before fieldwork. It is, thus, a de facto archaeological site. The precise year of abandonment is not known; but judging from available maps and census records, Danguerchem was inhabited in the early 1960s but is not reported in the documents resulting from the 1969 and 1977 population censuses published in 1978 (Elingui 1978). The site features were in an advanced state of degradation, providing an interesting case of archaeological site formation. The village comprises twenty-six features, divided into twenty-three houses organized into five clusters and three livestock enclosures (fig. 11, table 13).

The site's communal installations are clearly located in the central part of the village. They consist of enclosures I, II, and III, fenced with thorny tree branches, and a public shelter or discussion house 9. Enclosure I, devoted to cattle and situated in the NE, is subcircular in shape and measures 32 m in MaD (c. 805 m square in surface). It comprises a large, high fodder storage platform, 7 m long and 6 m wide,

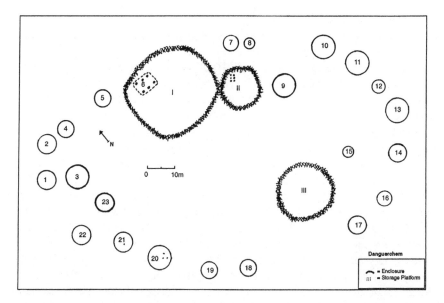

Figure 11: Map of Damguerchem

supported by six poles. Enclosure II, contiguous to the previous one, is the small-est among the recorded cases, measuring 14.2 m in diameter (c. 159 m square). It may have been devoted to goats; but due to several years of erosion, there is no positive material evidence to support this proposal. Enclosure III, measuring 20 m in diameter (c. 315 m square) is located in the southern part of the settlement, approximately 30 m from the others. It was clearly devoted to cattle as suggested by the recorded patchy, indurated dung deposits. Finally, House 9, the public shel-ter or discussion house, is located 5 m SE of enclosure II; it is a six-poles feature with a dome-shape thatched roof, built without walls and measuring 10.5 m in

Table 13: Danguerchem household clusters

Cluster number	Number of units	Habitation houses	Livestock houses	Storage platforms	Others
1	2	4	1	—	—
2	1	2	—	—	—
3	1	3	1	—	—
4	1	3	—	—	—
5	3	3	—	—	—
Total	8	15	2	—	—

diameter. An enamelware lid and two clay vessels were found on the public shelter floor. One of the clay vessels is a footed bowl, decorated with extensive twisted roulette impression on the body, 15 cm in mouth as well as MaD, 10 cm in base diameter, 18 cm in height as well as HMD, 4 cm in foot height, and 0.8 cm in T; the other is a large globular pot with constricted neck and slightly everted rim, found in an upside-down position. It is decorated with a horizontal band of twisted roulette impression overlined by two parallel grooved lines on the shoulder; its morphometric attributes vary from 25 cm for MD, 35 cm for MaD, 35 cm for height, 20 cm for HMD, and, finally, 1 cm for T. The main village entrance, measuring 33.5 m in width, is situated in the S between houses 17 and 18 (fig. 11).

Cluster 1, situated NNW, comprises five wood and reeds houses stretched over 45 m. Four of the recorded features are habitation houses arranged in a linear pattern, the remaining one being a barn. House 1, built with two supporting poles, measures 7.5 m in diameter. It comprises an elaborate five-niche hearth, a collapsed wooden rack, and a bed represented by a series of postholes and scattered supporting forks. House 2 is found 5.5 m NE of the previous one; it is also a two-poles feature, with an elaborate hearth and a disintegrated bed. Two piles of long straight twigs used as bed frames were found disposed along the house wall. Features 4 and 5, situated at 11 m from each other, are young men/women's houses. Both measure 5.5 m in diameter, the former built with a single central pole and the latter with two. The recorded material remains consist of an iron cutlass, two small flashlight batteries, and two rubber shoes for house 4, and an enamel teapot, a portion of flashlight, one female shoe, and a slipper for house 5. And finally, the barn (house 3), built with five supporting poles and measuring 9.5 m in diameter is situated in the inner part of the site at approximately 3 m SE of house 1. One enamel basin, a lid, and three clay vessels were found on the barn floor. One of the vessels is a two-lugged, necked, large globular pot, 21 cm in MD, 26 cm in MaD, 30 cm in height, 15 cm in HMD, and 1 cm in T, decorated with a horizontal band of roulette impression at the neck's base, overlapped and overlined by two horizontal and parallel grooved lines complemented by six equidistant appliqué buttons at the neck. The other two are comparable large necked pots, globular to slightly elongated, with more or less constricted necks and everted rims. The globular specimen measures 27 cm in MD, 41 cm in MaD, 47 cm in height, 23 cm in HMD, and 1 cm in T; it is decorated with two horizontal and parallel grooved lines overlapped by a band of twisted roulette impression on the upper part of the shoulder. The elongated specimen is decorated with a narrow horizontal band of twisted roulette impression delimited by two parallel grooved lines with an additional grooved wavy line in the middle, complemented by three pairs of equidistant appliqué buttons located on the upper part of the shoulder, its morphometric attributes varying from 28.5 cm for MD, 38 cm in MaD, 49 cm in height, 23 cm in HMD, and 1.2 cm in T.

Cluster 2, comprising two features, houses 7 and 8, is found in the northeastern part of the settlement, a few meters from enclosures I and II. Both features are single-central-pole habitation houses built in wood and reeds. House 7 measures 7 m in diameter, and comprises the remains of a bed, an elaborate hearth, two clay vessels, and one rubber shoe. Both recorded vessels are relatively large in size. One is a globular pot with constricted neck and slightly everted rim, 26.5 cm in MD, 38 cm in MaD, 45 cm in height, 24 cm in HMD, and 0.7 cm in T,decorated with a narrow horizontal band of twisted roulette impression delimited by two parallel grooved lines, with an additional wavy grooved line in the middle. The other is a slightly elongated, globular pot, with constricted neck and everted rim, 28 cm in MD, 48 cm in MaD, 52 cm in height, 23 cm in HMD, and 1 cm in T, decorated with a horizontal band of twisted roulette impression and superimposed parallel and horizontal grooved lines on the upper shoulder. House 8, at 3 m SE of the previous one, is a young man's habitation feature; the bed is small in size, being represented in this case by lines of postholes and a few scattered bed-supporting forks; a pair of worn-out slippers was found on the house floor.

Cluster 3, with four houses is located on the eastern side of the settlement. The features, built in wood and reeds, are stretched over 45 m and arranged in a N-S linear pattern; two of them (features 10 and 12) are habitation houses, one (feature 11) used for both habitation and livestock, and the remaining one (feature 13) being a barn. House 10, situated at the northern end of the cluster, approximately 10 m E of the discussion shelter (feature 9), is built with four supporting poles and measures 9 m in diameter. The bed, represented by a few postholes and scattered short forks, is situated at the center of the house, in the space delineated by the four supporting poles. The hearth is surprisingly small and crudely made for such a large house; it consists of three fire-hardened clay blocks used as "hearthstones." Two enamel basins were found on the house floor. House 11, located 5 m S of the previous one, has an ambiguous status as it comprises an elaborate hearth but no traces of a bed. Cases of barns with elaborate hearths, which may have been used for both human habitation and livestock, are well attested in many of the studied settlements, and this may be the case for feature 11. It is built with four roof-supporting poles and measures 9 m in diameter. The recorded material evidence consists of a small tin container, an enamel lid, and an enamel teapot. House 12, at 4 m farther S, measures 6 m in diameter; it is a young man's house built with a single central pole, comprising the remains of a bed represented by scattered short bed forks. And finally, house 13, located at the southern end of the cluster, measures 9.5 m in diameter. It is a barn built with four roof-supporting poles.

Cluster 4 is found in the south-southeastern part of the site; it comprises four wood and reeds features loosely organized into two units (fig. 11). Unit 1, in the E, consists of houses 14 and 15, both built with a single central pole. The former measures 7 m in diameter and comprises a built hearth but no visible evidence of a bed. One worn-out slipper was found on the house floor. The latter, situated in the inner part of the settlement, 12.5 m NW of the previous one, is a young man's house, much smaller in size and measuring 4 m in diameter; it comprises a simple hearth made with three fire-hardened clay blocks and scattered evidence of a bed. Unit 2, at some 10 m W, comprises houses 16 and 17, located approximately 7 m from each other. House 16, almost completely eroded and represented by shallow traces of the house circle, measures 5.5 m in diameter. Preservation is better for house 17, which is a single-central-pole feature, measuring 7 m in diameter, comprising scattered remains of a bed, no trace of hearth, two enamel basins, two enamel plates, and a worn-out 25-liter plastic jerry-cane.

Cluster 5 is stretched on 60 m on the western side of the site. It comprises six features arranged in a N-S linear pattern at distances varying from 4.4 to 8 m from each other (fig. 11). Two of the houses (features 21 and 22) are built with mud-brick with the others in wood and reeds. One of the features, house 23, is located on the inner side of the settlement. Houses 18 and 19, both measuring 6 m in diameter, are very poorly preserved. An iron spearhead was found on the house 18 floor. House 19 appears to have been built with a single central pole; an iron brasero fragmented into three pieces was retrieved on the floor. House 20 is located at the center of the cluster and measures 7.5 m in diameter. It is a three-supporting-poles feature, with two small postholes and scattered forked bed's supporting poles. The presence of a bed is nonetheless highly improbable; considered in relation to the absence of a hearth, house 20 appears to have been a barn. One pair of rubber shoes, one flashlight battery, and an empty powder milk can were found on the house floor. Houses 21 and 22, both built in mud-brick with a single central pole, measuring 6.5 m in diameter and located 4.4 m from each other, appear to have been the main habitation features from cluster 5. There is no clear evidence of beds, but elaborate hearths are found in each house. The domestic gear found in house 21 consists of two enamel plates and a storage jar, elongated and slightly globular in shape with a constricted neck and everted rim, decorated with vertical red bands on the body. The recorded vessel measures 16 cm in MD, 32 cm in MaD, 41 cm in height, 18 cm in HMD, and finally, 1.2 cm in T. Three enamel basins with their lids were found on the house 22 floor. Finally, house 23, approximately 7 m E of house 22, was badly preserved; its remains consist of a circle measuring 5.5 m in diameter, with a visible series of five postholes in the NE, presumably remains of wooden shelves.

The layout of Danguerchem is characterized by a relatively clear patterning, with features of communal interest located in the central part of the village, more or less surrounded by household, more "private" installations, with the number of houses varying from two (cluster 2) to six (cluster 5).

Mishiskwa

Mishiskwa is located approximately 4 kilometers SW of Ngumati, on the edge of the flooded hinterland depression, at 11° 49′ northern latitude and 14° 39′ eastern longitude. It is a subcircular settlement, extended over 2.1 hectares, measuring

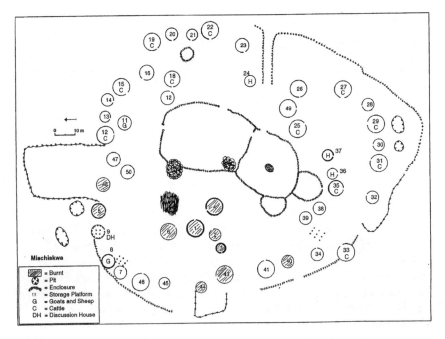

Figure 12: Map of Mischiskwa

150 m in length N-S and 140 m in width E-W. The southern and western limits of the site are marked by a fence made with branches of thorny trees, the layout being organized around a series of central livestock enclosures. Enclosures I and IV, measuring respectively 120 (ca. 12 m in diameter) and 28.26 (6 m in diameter) meters square, are devoted to sheep and goats. The larger specimens, enclosure II (26.5 × 21.5 m), extended over approximately 570 square meters, and enclosure III (34 × 28 m), measuring 952 square meters, are used for cattle. The central part of the settlement is also shaded by two large trees (fig. 12). Forty-eight houses distributed into six clusters have been recorded (tables 14 and 15). Almost all of the western half of the settlement was destroyed by a fire lit by a child playing with a matchbox a few days before the study of the village.

Cluster 1, the village headman's complex, is situated in the northwestern part of the site. It comprises eleven houses, among which eight are burned. Houses are distributed into distinct units. The first one includes five houses (1, 2, 3, 4, and 6), all of them burned and located in the inner side of settlement. House 1 was the Bilama main house, built in mud-brick and measuring 9 m in diameter. Two hurricane lamps, five enamelwares, and five clay vessels have been recorded among the burned house remains. Five morphological classes are represented: (1) a footed bowl, 13 cm in mouth and MaD, 12 cm in TH, 3 cm in foot height, and 0.9 cm in

Table 14: Mishiskwa household clusters

Cluster number	Number of units	Habitation houses	Livestock houses	Storage platforms	Others
1	4	6	5	1	1
2	2	2	2	—	—
3	3	5	3	—	—
4	3	3	3	—	1
5	4	4	8	—	—
6	3	3	3	1	—
Total	19	23	24	2	2

T, decorated with extensive twisted roulette impression on the body; (2) a rounded base, hemispheric pot with slightly constricted neck and everted rim, decorated with twisted roulette impression on the body, overlined by two horizontal and parallel grooved lines on the shoulder, complemented by two lugs and two handles. Its morphometric attributes vary from 21.5 cm for MD, 25.5 cm for MaD, 25 cm for TH, 14 cm for HMD, to 0.8 cm in T; (3) a necked, globular pot decorated with a horizontal band of twisted roulette impression under- and overlined by two parallel grooved lines on the shoulder, and measuring 12 cm in MD, 28 cm in MaD, 35 cm in TH, 5.5 cm in NH, 20 cm in HMD, and finally, 0.8 cm in T; (4) a globular jar with slightly constricted neck and everted rim, measuring 24 cm in MD, 35 cm in MaD, 40 cm in maximum height, 25 cm in HMD, and 1.2 cm in T, and decorated with a horizontal band of twisted roulette impression delimited by two parallel grooved lines and complemented by three pairs of appliqué buttons on the shoulder; and finally, (5) a large, plain, straight-side plate measuring 49 cm in diameter, 7 cm in height, and 1.9 cm in T. House 2 (Bilama's first wife) comprising an elaborate and decorated hearth and probably a large but burned bed, was built with wood and reeds and measured 6 m in diameter. It is located approximately

Table 15: Mishiskwa general distribution of pottery

Cluster number	Number of features	Service vessels	Cooking vessels	Storage vessels	Unknown	Total
1	13	2	10	6	—	18
2	4	—	—	—	—	—
3	8	2	4	2	—	8
4	7	—	1	1	—	2
5	12	—	3	5	—	8
6	7	—	—	1	—	1
Total	51	4	18	15	—	37

4 m SW of house 1. Two necked pots were found in house 2. The first specimen measures 11 cm in MD, 28 cm in MaD, 38 cm in maximum height, 7 cm in NH, 16 cm in HMD, and finally, 1 cm in T, and is decorated with four vertical, regularly space bands of twisted roulette impression, each delimited by parallel grooved lines. The second specimen, with its upper part broken, is decorated with a horizontal band of twisted roulette impression complemented by three parallel grooved lines, underlined by an appliqué cordon on the shoulder. House 3, almost contiguous to the previous one, is Bilama's second wife dwelling. It is built in mud-brick with four central poles and measures 4.5 m in diameter; it comprises an elaborate hearth and almost certainly a bed which has been reduced to ash. Houses 4 and 6, situated respectively, at 5 m SE and N of house 1, are barns; the former measuring 10.5 m in diameter, is built in mud-brick, with an unknown number of central poles, and the latter, built with wood and grass, measures 9 m in diameter. Nine enamelwares and four clay vessels were stored in house 4; the pottery assemblage is divided into three morphological categories. There are two necked storage jars with almost similar morphometric attributes, varying from 24 to 28 cm for MD, 40 cm for MaD, 50 cm for TH, 7 to 16 cm for NH, 18 to 27 cm for HMD, and finally, 1.2 cm for T. One jar is plain and filled with *kreb,* wild grain collected in the yaere at the beginning of the dry season. The other, decorated with extensive twisted roulette impression on the body overlined by two horizontal and parallel grooved lines on the shoulder, is filled with *Ziziphus* spp. fruits. The remaining vessels comprise a short-necked, globular pot with everted rim, measuring 11.5 cm in MD, 28 cm in MaD, 34 cm in height, 5 cm in NH, 17 cm in HMD, and 0.8 cm in T, decorated with a horizontal band of twisted roulette impression delimited by two parallel grooved lines on the shoulder; and a rounded base, hemispheric pot with a slightly constricted neck and everted rim with two handles and two lugs, decorated with extensive twisted roulette impression on the body overlined by two horizontal and parallel grooved lines on the shoulder. Newly collected reeds were piled in front of the burned houses' unit and reconstruction was already underway (fig. 12 and 13).

The second unit consists of burned features 43 and 44, situated a few meters to the W of unit 1 and adjunct to a fenced cultivated plot in the background. House 43 is a four-central-poles barn built with wood and grass and measuring 8.2 m in diameter. Feature 44, approximately 7 m NW of barn 43, also in wood and reeds, is the habitation house; it measures 8.25 m in diameter and comprises an elaborate and decorated hearth, three clay vessels, and certainly a (burned) bed. All the recorded vessels are cooking and liquid storage pots divided into two shapes: two rounded base, hemispheric pots with very slightly constricted necks and everted rims, with similar morphometric attributes. They vary from 20 cm in MD, 23 cm in MaD, 25 to 28 cm in height, 14 to 18 cm in HMD, to 0.8 cm in T. One of the specimens, with two handles, is decorated with extensive roulette impression on the body overlined by a horizontal grooved line on the shoulder. The other has an almost similar pattern of decoration, the difference being in the

Figure 13: Burned houses at Mischiskwa

presence of two horizontal and parallel lines, complemented by equally spaced appliqué buttons on the shoulder.The third vessel is a long-necked storage pot with everted rim, measuring 11.5 cm in MD, 30 cm in MaD, 40 cm in height, 7 cm in NH, 18 cm in HMD, and 1.1 cm in T, and decorated with a horizontal band of twisted roulette impression under- and overlined by two parallel grooved lines.

Unit 3, 10 to 13 m N, includes two houses set at 5 m from each other. The habitation house (feature 45), built in wood and reeds, comprises an elaborate hearth, probably a bed, too, and measures 5.85 m in diameter. The barn (feature 46), also built in wood and reeds, measures 10.5 m in diameter. Unit 4, 4 to 5 m N, consists of three features: (1) a storage platform with nine supporting poles; (2) a habitation house (feature 7), a single-central-pole dwelling, built with wood and reeds, and comprising a large bed and an elaborate hearth; and finally, (3) a goat house (feature 8) built in mud-brick with three central poles, and measuring 5.4 m in diameter. Two similarly globular storage jars with constricted necks and everted rims were found in house 7. The first one, measuring 29 cm in MD, 45 cm in MaD, 49 cm in height, 25 cm in HMD, and 0.9 cm in T, is decorated with extensive twisted roulette impression on the body overlined by two horizontal and parallel grooved lines on the shoulder. The second one is slightly smaller, its morphometric attributes varying from 28 cm for MD, 36 cm for MaD, 43 cm for height, 21 cm for HMD, to 1.1 cm for T. It is decorated with extensive twisted roulette impression overlined by three horizontal and parallel grooved lines on the upper body part.The unique public shelter or discussion house (feature 9) of the settlement, measuring 7 m in diameter and built with three central poles, is located slightly on the edge of the Bilama house cluster and can thus be set apart.

Cluster 2, situated on the northern edge of the settlement, is singled out by a large, rectangular, fenced plot and comprises four houses, all of them destroyed by fire. Houses 5, 10, and 11 are almost equidistant and set in a linear arrangement, while house 48 is located in the inner side of the village.The features are nonetheless organized into two distinct units, each with a habitation house and a barn. Houses 5 and 11, measuring respectively 6.2 and 5.25 m in diameter and used for habitation are built in mud-brick for the former and wood and reeds for the latter, each comprising an elaborate hearth. Three clay vessels have been recorded in house 5: there is one globular jar with slightly constricted neck and everted rim, measuring 30 cm in MD, 50 cm in MaD, 56 cm in height, 26 cm in HMD, and 1.3 cm in T, and decorated with extensive twisted roulette impression on the body overlined by two horizontal and parallel grooved lines, complemented by equally spaced appliqué buttons on the shoulder; and two similar, rounded base, hemispheric pots, with two handles, slightly constricted necks and everted rims. They measure 21 cm in MD, 26–28 cm in MaD, 28–30 cm in height, 14–16 cm in HMD, and 0.8–0.9 cm in T, and are decorated with extensive twisted roulette impression on the body, overlined by two horizontal and parallel grooved lines on the shoulder. Houses 10 and 48 are barns of almost equal size, their diameters varying respectively from 6.8 to 7 m. Both were built with wood and reeds.

Cluster 3, slightly in the E but still on the northern side of the settlement, comprises eight houses, all built with wood and reeds. They are spread on 55 m NW-SE and 25 m NE-SE (fig. 12) and organized into three units. Unit 1, situated in the W, consists of four houses. Feature 12 is a relatively large four-central-poles barn measuring 9 m in diameter. Feature 13, 1 m to the E, is a small single-central-pole house, 4.8 m in diameter. Feature 42 is approximately 5 m S; it is a single-central-pole young man's house with a bed but without hearth, measuring 4.4 m in diameter. And finally, house 14, built with two central poles, measures 6.4 m in diameter and comprises a large bed, an elaborate hearth, and one enamel basin and five clay vessels of varying shapes arranged on wooden shelves. Four morphological categories are represented in the recorded pottery assemblage. They consist of: (1) a flat base bowl decorated with twisted roulette impression on the body, measuring 14 cm in maximum and MD, 7 cm in base diameter, 8 cm in height, and 1 cm in T; (2) two rounded base, hemispheric pots with slightly constricted necks and everted rims, with one of the specimens possessing two handles; they measure 19–20 cm in MD, 22–24 cm in MaD, 22 cm in height, 11 cm in HMD, and 0.8–1 cm in T. Both are decorated with extensive twisted roulette impression on the body overlined by one or two horizontal grooved lines on the shoulder; (3) a slightly elongated and globular pot with constricted neck, decorated with twisted roulette impression on the body overlined by a horizontal grooved line on the shoulder; and finally, (4) two similar necked storage jars, decorated with a horizontal band of twisted roulette impression complemented by two or three parallel grooved lines on the shoulder. Their morphometric attributes vary from 26 to 27 cm for MD, 30 to 35 cm for MaD, 36 to 37 cm for height, 4 to 6 cm for NH, 15 to 22 cm for HMD, and finally, 1.1 to 1.2 cm for T.

Unit 2, situated a few meters E, comprises two houses, features 15 and 16. The former is a double-function house, a six-central-poles barn containing a hearth. Measuring 6.7 m in diameter, it was probably used as a kitchen from time to time. The latter, situated 6 m SW and measuring 6 m in diameter, is a single-central-pole house, with a large bed, an elaborate hearth, and three clay vessels. Three vessel shapes are represented; a plain plate 19 cm in diameter with a straight 9-cm-high and 1.2-cm-thick wall; a short, necked, large, globular pot with everted rim, 14 cm in MD, 30 cm in MaD, 40 cm in height, 5 cm in NH, 20 cm in HMD, and 1 cm in T, decorated with a horizontal band of twisted roulette impression under- and overlined by parallel grooved lines on the shoulder; and finally, a rounded base, slightly elongated pot with constricted neck, everted rim, and two handles, decorated with extensive twisted roulette on the body overlined by two horizontal and parallel grooved lines on the shoulder. Unit 3, also with two houses, features 17 and 18, is located in the inner side of the settlement, near the central cattle enclosure III (fig. 12). House 17 is a four-central-poles feature used for habitation; it measures 6.8 m in diameter and comprises a large bed and an elaborate hearth. House 18 is a double-function, barn-kitchen, seven-poles feature with a fireplace, 7.6 m in diameter.

Cluster 4 is located along the eastern side of the site. It is a linear arrangement of six wood and reeds houses stretched on 50 to 55 m N-S, associated with a small sheep-goat corral. The recorded features are distributed into three units with two houses each. The northern unit comprises a barn (feature 19) built with five roof-supporting poles measuring 7.7 m in diameter, and a habitation house (feature 20), slightly smaller in size, with a diameter of 6.2 m, built with four supporting poles and comprising a large bed and an elaborate hearth. One kerosene lamp, three enamelwares, and two clay vessels were found in house 20. One of the clay vessels is a rounded base, hemispheric pot with constricted neck, everted rim, and two handles, decorated with twisted roulette impression on the body overlined by two horizontal and parallel grooved lines on the shoulder, measuring 18.5 cm in MD, 27 cm in MaD, 26 cm in height, 14 cm in HMD, and 1 cm in T; and the other, a necked jar, 23 cm in MD, 29 cm in MaD, 44 cm in height, 6 cm in NH, 22 cm in HMD, 1.2 cm in T, decorated with a horizontal band of twisted roulette impression under- and overlined by two horizontal and parallel grooved lines on the shoulder.

Unit 2, with houses 21 and 22, is found 5 m S. Feature 21 is the habitation house; it is a single-central-pole dwelling, 6.2 m in diameter, comprising a large bed and an elaborate hearth. House 22 is a relatively large barn, 9.4 m in diameter, built with six roof-supporting poles. Both houses were devoid of any material remains, with the exception of an enamel basin found in house 21.

Unit 3 is located 10 m SW of house 22, and consists of two features, houses 23 and 24, 12 m from each other. The habitation house (feature 23) is built with three supporting poles and measures 6.2 m in diameter; it comprises a large bed, an elaborate hearth, five enamelwares, one pair of rubber shoes, and a raised grinding platform. Feature 24, a 5.3-m-diameter "horse house," built with two supporting poles, is located in the inner side of the settlement. A worn-out kerosene lamp was found on its floor.

Cluster 5, with twelve wood and reeds houses, is located on the southern side of the village. It is extended over 110 m NE-SW and 60 m NW-SE and delimited on its eastern, southern, and western sides by a fence made with branches of thorny *Acacia* spp. trees (fig. 12). The recorded features are distributed into four units, with two relatively isolated houses. Unit 1, situated in the NE, comprises two barns (features 25 and 47), both built with four supporting poles and measuring 9 m in diameter, and one habitation house (feature 26). The habitation house, 7.6 m in diameter is slightly smaller but nonetheless built with four supporting poles. It comprises a large bed, an elaborate hearth, two enamelwares, and four clay vessels. Three shapes are represented in the recorded pottery assemblage: (1) a rounded base hemispheric pot, with constricted neck, everted rim and two handles, 19 cm in MD, 27 cm in MaD, 30 cm in height, 17 cm in HMD, and 1 cm in T, decorated with twisted roulette impression on the body overlined by two horizontal and parallel grooved lines on the shoulder; (2) a slightly necked pot with decorative motifs and syntax similar to that described above, measuring 25 cm in MD, 36 cm in MaD, 41 cm in height, 4 cm in NH, 24 cm in HMD, and finally, 1.1 cm in T; and (3) two similar globular jars decorated with a horizontal band of twisted roulette impression under- and overlined by two parallel grooved lines on the shoulder, their morphometric attributes varying from 14.5 to 21 cm for MD, 30 to 31 cm for MaD, 37 to 39 cm for height, 16 to 18 cm for HMD, and finally, 0.8 to 0.9 cm for T.

Unit 2 consists of three features, houses 27, 28, and 29. It is situated in the S central part of the cluster near a series of large pits (fig. 12). The barn (feature 29) is built with six supporting poles and measures 10 m in diameter. The habitation house (feature 28) is comparatively smaller, built with two roof-supporting poles and measuring 6.1 m in diameter. It comprises a large bed, an elaborate hearth, one pair of rubber shoes, two enamelwares, and four clay vessels. The recorded pottery assemblage belongs to a single shape category, with nonetheless important variations in size. The smaller size group includes two rounded base, globular, short-necked pots with everted rim, with one handled specimen; their morphometric attributes vary from 21 cm for MD, 27 to 28 cm for MaD, 29.5 to 31 cm for height, 5 cm for NH, 15 to 18 cm for HMD, and 0.7 to 0.9 cm for T. Both specimens have broadly comparable decorative patterns; one is decorated with twisted roulette impression on the body overlined by two horizontal and parallel grooved lines on the shoulder, and the other with additional three pairs of appliqué buttons equally spaced on the shoulder. The larger size group with more constricted neck vessels comprises two similar specimens, in morphometric attributes as well as decorative patterns. The decoration is confined to the vessel shoulder and consists of a horizontal band delineated by two parallel grooved lines filled with three equally spaced panels of three triangles of grooved lines each. Their morphometric attributes vary from 15 cm in MD, 31 cm in MaD, 37 cm in height, 4 cm in NH, 18 cm in HMD, and 1 cm in T. House 27, a particularly large nine-supporting-poles barn, 10.5 m in diameter, is probably part of unit 2 despite the fact that it is located slightly aside.

Unit 3, a few meters W of the previous one, also consists of three features; a six-supporting-poles barn (feature 31), measuring 9.1 m in diameter; a habitation house (feature 30), 5.5 m in diameter built with two supporting poles. House 30 comprises a large bed and an elaborate hearth, as well as one enamel basin, a kerosene lamp, and five rubber shoes; and finally, a "horse house" (feature 37), partially built with mud-brick and a single-central-pole, measuring 5 m in diameter, and situated at some 20 m in the inner part of the settlement.

Unit 4, on the western side of the studied cluster, comprises three features, houses 32, 35, and 36, stretched on 20 to 25 m. Feature 36 is a "horse house" 5.1 m in diameter, built with a single central pole. Feature 35 is a dual-function house, built with six supporting poles and measuring 8 m in diameter, generally used as a barn, however, the presence of a fireplace suggests that it may have been utilized as kitchen from time to time. And finally, feature 32, a habitation house, 6.5 m in diameter, is built with two roof-supporting poles and comprises a large bed and an elaborate hearth.

Cluster 6, with a relatively central storage platform and six wood and reeds houses distributed into three neat units, is situated on the SW side of the settlement. Its outer side is delimited by a fence. Unit 1 comprises features 33 and 34, situated at 7 m from each other. The former is a four-supporting-poles barn, measuring 7.9 m in diameter, and the latter, a habitation house, 6.7 m in diameter, built with four-supporting-poles and comprising a large bed, an elaborate hearth, and one short-necked jar. The recorded jar measures 26 cm in MD, 32 cm in MaD, 47 cm in height, 3 cm in NH, 20 cm in HMD, and 1.2 cm in T. It is decorated with extensive roulette impression on the body overlined by two horizontal and parallel grooved lines on the shoulder. Unit 2, located 10 to 15 m NE of the previous one, comprises houses 38 and 39. The first is a habitation house built with a single-central-pole, measuring 5 m in diameter. The second is a burned barn measuring 6.5 m in diameter. And finally, unit 3, situated at the northern end of the cluster, consists of burned houses 40 and 41, located 4 to 5 m from each other. The habitation house (feature 40) measures 6.1 m in diameter; it was built with a single central pole and comprised an elaborate hearth and presumably a bed. Feature 41 was a relatively large 8.4-m-diameter goat house.

The Mishiskwa settlement layout appears clearly to be organized around collective cattle and goat enclosures. The recorded house clusters comprise two to four units. Only five houses out of a total of forty-eight are built with mud-brick, with four of them found in the Bilama cluster in the northwestern side of the site. The fact that almost half of the settlement burned a few days before fieldwork clearly points to fire as the major threat to Shuwa-Arab wood and reeds villages. This fact may explain the care with which hearths are built among the Shuwa Arabs.

Chapter 4

The Western Settlement Group

The Western settlement group is located approximately 10 kilometers NW of the southern one. Six sites have been investigated in that area; these are, from N to S, Bilbede, Gallis, and Ngada I, II, III, and IV. On average, the studied settlements are located 1 to 2 kilometers from each other, Ngada being constituted of four distinct villages, situated at distances varying from 300 to 800 m from one to its nearest neighbor.

Bilbede

Bilbede is the northernmost site of the western settlement group. It is an almost circular village, extended over 1.35 hectares, slightly elongated in its SW-NE axis which measures 135 m in length, while the SE-NW one is stretched over 100 m (fig. 14). The village layout consists of three main concentric rings; an outer ring of fenced maize fields measuring 50 to 100 m in width, the middle ring with habitation and settlement features, and finally, the inner one comprising dispersed chicken coops and livestock enclosures. Features of communal interest are located almost at the center of the village. They consist of five enclosures of varying size; the largest ones, enclosures I and II, measuring respectively 980 and 83 m square, are devoted to cattle. The three remaining enclosures, of almost standardized size of approximately 20 m square, being clearly for goats; each may have been used by related households. At first glance, judging from the density and diversity of features, with numerous chicken coops, fenced maize fields, storage platforms, as well as refuse scattered on the site surface which consists of a large amount of corn-cobs, Bilbede appears to be more involved in agriculture than livestock husbandry. The village was nonetheless totally deserted in March 1988, with all its inhabitants settled in dry-season camps, thus suggesting that they still adhere to a seminomadic way of life. Settlement installations are organized into nine clusters (tables 16 and 17, fig. 14).

Cluster 1 is located in the southern side of the site; it is clearly delineated by

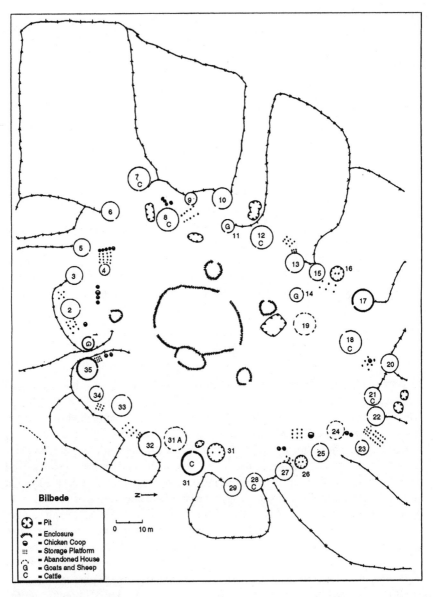

Figure 14: Map of Bilbede

Table 16: Bilbede household clusters

Cluster number	Number of units	Habitation houses	Livestock houses	Storage platforms	Others
1	1	2	1	2	6
2	1	3	—	1	5
3	1	2	—	1	4
4	1	1	2	2	—
5	1	2	2	1	2
6	1	3	1	3	4
7	1	2	—	2	4
8	1	1	2	—	2
9	1	3	1	4	2
Total	9	19	11	16	29

a fence and comprises three houses arranged in a linear pattern with distance from each other varying from 6 to 10 m (fig. 14). Other associated features include one goat enclosure 20 m square in extent, five chicken coops organized into a series of four with the fifth relatively isolated, and two storage platforms located on both sides of house 2. House 1, at the eastern end of the cluster, is built in mud-brick with a single central pole; it is a goat house measuring 4.2 m in diameter. House 2 is located 10 m W of the previous one; it is a four-poles wood and reeds feature measuring 7.2 m in diameter, comprising a large bed, an elaborate hearth, and two enamelwares. And finally, house 3, also built with wood and reeds, is a two-poles feature measuring 6.5 m in diameter with a large bed. A pair of rubber shoes, two enamel basins, and two clay vessels were recorded in house 3. Two vessel shapes

Table 17: Bilbede general distribution of pottery

Cluster number	Number of features	Service vessels	Cooking vessels	Storage vessels	Unknown	Total
1	11	—	2	—	—	2
2	9	—	1	—	—	1
3	9	—	2	1	—	3
4	5	—	6	4	—	10
5	7	—	4	2	—	6
6	11	—	7	1	—	8
7	8	—	3	9	—	12
8	4	—	3	4	—	7
9	10	—	6	5	—	11
Total	74	—	34	26	—	60

are represented: one is a rounded base hemispheric pot with slightly constricted neck and everted rim, 20 cm in MD, 24 cm in MaD, 24 cm TH, 14 cm in HMD, and 0.9 cm in T, decorated with extensive roulette impression on the body overlined by two horizontal and parallel grooved lines on the shoulder; and the other, a slightly elongated, globular pot with everted rim, with its decoration similar to the case just described above, its morphometric attributes varying from 21 cm for MD, 25 cm for MaD, 26 cm for height, 16 cm for HMD, and finally, 0.8 cm in T. Chicken coops are circular features, 0.3 to 0.5 m high built with a low mud wall, some with a flat roof, their diameter varying from 0.6 to 1.5 m. Poultry goes inside through a hole which is closed for the night, and is thus protected from predators. The recorded storage platforms are built with five and ten supporting poles.

Cluster 2, slightly W, comprises three wood and reeds houses situated at 6 to 10 m from each other (fig. 14). House 4 is a 4.2-m-diameter young-man feature. It is situated in the inner side of the settlement, built with a single central pole, and comprises a small bed. The furniture consists of two enamelwares. A large storage platform built with sixteen supporting poles as well as a series of five chicken coops arranged in a N-S line are adjunct to house 4. House 5, located 6 m SW and built with two supporting poles, measures 6.5 m in diameter. It includes an elaborate hearth and a large bed. Finally, house 6, the largest of the cluster measures 8.2 m in diameter. It is built with four supporting poles and comprises a hearth and a large bed. The house's furniture consists of one kerosene lamp, one pair of rubber shoes, four enamelwares, and one slightly necked pot with a rounded base and two handles. The recorded pottery measures 22 cm in MD, 27 cm in MaD, 31 cm in height, 6 cm in NH, 17 cm in HMD, and 0.9 cm in T, decorated with extensive roulette impression on the body overlined by two horizontal and parallel grooved lines on the shoulder.

Cluster 3 is situated on the western side of the village and comprises four wood and reeds houses stretched on 40 m N-S (fig. 14). Barns (houses 7 and 8) are found at the southern end of the cluster. House 7 is built with 6 supporting poles and measures 9.4 m in diameter. House 8, located 10 m NE, measures 8.4 m in diameter, being built with four supporting poles. A set of four chicken coops is situated on the western side of barn 8. A relatively large storage platform, built with two parallel lines of five supporting poles each, and measuring 5 m in length and 2 m in width, is sited between houses 8 and 9. It thus provides an open, sheltered area. Habitation houses are confined to the northern side of the cluster; House 9 is a 4.2-m-diameter young-man feature, built with a single central pole, and comprising a small bed and one enamelware. House 10, at the northern end of the cluster, measures 7.3 m in diameter. It is built with four supporting poles, comprises a large bed, an elaborate hearth, a grinding platform, and three pieces of pottery.

Three vessel shapes are represented: (1) a large jug with a rounded base and everted rim, 12 cm in MD, 30 cm in MaD, 34 cm in height, 6 cm in NH, 17 cm in HMD, and 0.7 cm in T, with the decoration restricted to the neck-shoulder area and consisting of four regularly spaced panels of twisted roulette impression each delimited by vertical grooved lines, under- and overlined by horizontal and parallel grooved lines; (2) a rounded base, globular pot, with slightly constricted neck, everted rim and two handles, decorated with twisted roulette impression on the body overlined by two horizontal and parallel grooved lines, and measuring 20 cm in MD, 24 cm in MaD, 28 cm in height, 13 cm in HMD, and 0.9 cm in T; and finally, (3) a slightly elongated pot, with constricted neck and everted rim, 19.5 cm in MD, 22 cm in MaD, 26 cm in height, 13 cm in HMD, and 0.7 cm in T, decorated with extensive twisted roulette impression on the body overlined by two horizontal and parallel grooved lines on the shoulder.

Cluster 4 is situated in the WNW of the village and comprises three almost equidistant wood and reeds houses, two storage platforms, and an adjoined fenced field measuring 45 by 35 m. The goat house (feature 11), built with a single central pole and measuring 4.5 m in diameter, is situated at the southern end of the cluster. The barn (feature 12) is found 7 m N; it is a four-supporting-poles house, measuring 8.7 m in diameter and containing an enamel basin. The habitation house (feature 13) is situated 8 m N, at the other end of the cluster. It is built with four roof-supporting poles and measures 7.5 m in diameter. It comprises a large bed, an elaborate hearth, two enamelwares, and ten clay vessels arranged in wooden shelves beside the fireplace. Two storage platforms, with six and nine supporting poles, are located on the western side of house 13.

The recorded sample of pottery is divided into three morphological categories: (1) four specimens of slightly elongated, globular pots with slightly constricted necks and everted rims, their morphometric attributes varying from 18 to 22.5 cm in MD, 21 to 25 cm in MaD, 22 to 33 cm in height, 14 to 19 cm in HMD, and, finally, 0.8 to 0.9 cm in T. Two patterns of decoration, each found on two vessels, have been recorded: one consists of twisted roulette impression on the body overlined by two horizontal and parallel grooved lines on the shoulder; and the other consists of twisted roulette impression on the body, overlined by two horizontal and parallel grooved lines complemented by 4 and 6 equidistant pairs of appliqué buttons on the shoulder; (2) three specimens of round based, globular, necked pots with everted rim, measuring 13 to 26 cm in MD, 30 to 35 cm in MaD, 38 to 39 cm in height, 4 to 5 cm in NH, 21 to 25 cm in HMD, and finally, 0.8 to 0.9 cm in T. Two of the potteries are decorated with a horizontal band of twisted roulette impression, under- and overlined by two to three parallel grooved lines on the shoulder, the remaining one being decorated with extensive twisted roulette impression on the body overlined by two horizontal and parallel grooved lines on the shoulder; and finally, (3) three specimens of necked, globular jars with everted rim, 25.5 to 28 cm in MD, 37 to 43 cm in MaD, 45 to 52 cm in height, 5 to 6 cm in NH, 23 to 30 cm in HMD, and finally, 0.9 to 1.1 cm in T. The decoration pattern consists of a horizontal band of twisted roulette impression on the shoulder, over- and underlined by parallel grooved lines for two specimens, and extensive twisted roulette impression on the body overlined by two horizontal and parallel grooved lines on the shoulder for the remaining one.

Cluster 5, situated in the NW of the settlement consists of seven features arranged in a circular pattern some 30 m in diameter. House 19 is an ancient abandoned feature reduced to a 8.5 m diameter circle on the ground. Feature 16, located in the middle of the cluster, next to the large storage platform built with six supporting poles, is a single-central-pole public shelter or discussion house, measuring 4.9 m in diameter. Feature 14, at the southern end of the cluster, is a goat house, measuring 4.9 m in diameter and built in wood and reeds with a single central pole. Feature 15, some 6 m NW is a wood and reeds habitation house with a bed but without hearth, built with a single central pole and measuring 5.3 m in diameter. House equipment consists of a single enamelware. Habitation house 17 is built in mud-brick with four roof-supporting poles; it measures 7.5 m in diameter and comprises a large bed, an elaborate hearth, three rubber shoes, one enamelware and six clay vessels disposed on wooden shelves.

The recorded pottery sample comprises four morphological categories: (1) two specimens of rounded base, globular, handled pot with constricted necks and everted rims, 22 to 22.5 cm in MD, 25 to 29 cm in MaD, 29 to 31 cm in height, 18 to 19 cm in HMD, and finally, 0.8 to 1 cm in T, decorated with twisted roulette impression on the body overlined by two horizontal and parallel grooved lines on the shoulder in one case, and complemented by additional appliqué buttons in the other; (2) two specimens of slightly elongated, globular pot, with slightly constricted necks and everted rims, both decorated with extensive twisted roulette impression on the body, overlined on the shoulder by one or two horizontal grooved lines, complemented by four or five appliqué buttons, their morphometric attributes varying from 15.5 to 23 cm for MD, 17.5 to 29 for MaD, 14.5 to 29 cm for height, 9.5 to 19 cm for HMD, and finally, 0.9 to 1.1 cm for T; (3) a necked, globular pot decorated with a horizontal band of twisted roulette impression under- and overlined by two parallel grooved lines, measuring 21 cm in MD, 33 cm in MaD, 38 cm in height, 6 cm in NH, 22 cm in HMD, and finally, 1.1 cm in T; and (4) a necked, globular jar with everted rim, 24 cm in MD, 38 cm in MaD, 44 cm in height, 4 cm in NH, 27 cm in HMD, and finally, 1.2 cm in T, with decoration confined to the neck-shoulder and consisting of a horizontal band of twisted roulette impression under- and overlined by two parallel grooved lines.

Cluster 6, located in the northern side of the site, comprises four or five wood and reeds houses stretched on 40 m in a W-E linear arrangement, three chicken coops, and three storage platforms (fig. 14). Feature 24, a remaining shallow 6.5 m diameter circle of an abandoned house, cannot be clearly attached to either of the neighboring clusters. Feature 20, located at the western end of the cluster, is a habitation house, built with four supporting poles, measuring 7.4 m in diameter, and comprising an elaborate hearth, a large bed, one pair of rubber shoes, and an enamelware. One chicken coop and a seven-supporting-poles storage platform are located in front of house 20. Barn 21 is found some 7 m SE; it is built with four supporting poles and measures 6.3 m in diameter. An enamel basin was found on the barn floor. Habitation house 22 is situated next to the barn, on its eastern side; it is a four-supporting-poles feature, measuring 7 m in diameter, with an elaborate hearth, a large bed, three enamelwares, and eight clay vessels. Two distinct but close storage platforms are located between houses 22 and 23; the smaller specimen is built with nine supporting poles arranged into three lines of three poles each, while the larger comprises fifteen poles in three lines of five each. House 23, at the eastern end of the cluster, measures 6.5 m in diameter, and is built with a single central pole. It comprises a bed and a grinding platform. A pair of rubber shoes was found on the house floor. Finally, two chicken coops are located a few meters S, in front of house 23.

Four morphological categories are represented in the recorded pottery assemblage: (1) four specimens of slightly elongated, globular pots with constricted necks and everted rims, 19 to 22.5 cm in MD, 23 to 28 cm in MaD, 20 to 28 cm in height, 14 to 17 cm in HMD, and finally, 0.7 to 1 cm in T; each of the pots has a specific decorative syntax based on differential arrangements of similar elements. The first case, found with minor variations on two vessels, consists of extensive twisted roulette impression on the body overlined by two horizontal and parallel grooved lines complemented by four or five pairs of equidistant appliqué buttons on the shoulder. In the second, the decoration is confined to the neck-shoulder and comprises two horizontal and parallel grooved lines with three equidistant pairs of appliqué buttons. And finally, in the third, there is extensive twisted roulette impression on the body with four equidistant appliqué buttons on the shoulder; (2) two specimens of handled rounded base globular pot with slightly constricted necks and everted rims, 19 to 23 cm in MD, 24 to 29 cm in MaD, 26 to 30 cm in height, 15 to 19 cm in HMD, and finally, 0.7 to 0.9 cm in T, decorated with twisted roulette impression on the body overlined on the shoulder by two horizontal and parallel grooved lines in one case, with the addition of two symmetric appliqué buttons in the other; (3) a necked, globular pot decorated with a horizontal band of twisted roulette impression over- and underlined by two parallel grooved lines on the shoulder, 15 cm in MD, 29 cm in MaD, 38 cm in height, 6 cm in NH, 20 cm in HMD, and 0.9 cm in T; and (4) a necked jar with everted rim, measuring 23.5 cm in MD, 40 cm in MaD, 45 cm in height, 5 cm in NH, 26 cm in HMD, and 1 cm in T, decorated with twisted roulette impression on the body overlined by two horizontal and parallel grooved lines on the shoulder.

Cluster 7 consists of three main wood and reeds features in a linear NW-SE arrangement stretched on 25 m and associated with two storage platforms and three chicken coops. It is located in the northeastern part of the settlement adjunct to a long, fenced maize field (fig. 14). The public shelter (feature 26), located at the centre of the cluster is built with a single central pole and measures 4.7 m in diameter. Habitation house 25 is found few meters N of the public shelter; it is a four-supporting poles feature, 6.6 m in diameter, comprising an elaborate hearth and a large bed. House equipment consists of four similar long-necked storage jars with everted rim. Their morphometric attributes vary from 25 to 29 cm for MD, 37 to 42 cm for MaD, 48 to 56 cm for height, 6 to 9 cm for NH, 26 to 34 cm for HMD, and finally, 1.1 to 1.3 cm in T. Three decoration patterns have been recorded; the first, found on two specimens, consists of extensive twisted roulette impression on the body overlined by two horizontal and parallel grooved lines on the shoulder. The second, confined to the neck and shoulder comprises a horizontal band of twisted roulette impression under- and overlined by two parallel grooved lines. And finally, the third, also confined to the neck-shoulder area, consists of a horizontal band of twisted roulette impression with superimposed three parallel grooved lines, complemented by four equidistant sets of three appliqué buttons.

House 27, the second habitation feature of the cluster with an adjunct, seven-supporting-poles storage platform, is located in the southern side of the public shelter. It is a two-supporting-pole house, 6.1 m in diameter, comprising a large bed and an elaborate hearth. House's furniture consists of four enamelwares and eight clay vessels carefully disposed in wooden shelves next to the fireplace. The recorded pottery is divided into three vessel shapes: (1) a globular, long-necked pot with everted rim, decorated with a horizontal band of twisted roulette impression under- and overlined by two parallel grooved lines on the shoulder, measuring 12 cm in MD, 28 cm in MaD, 37 cm in height, 6 cm in NH, 18 cm in HMD, and finally, 0.9 cm in T; (2) three specimens of slightly elongated, globular pots, with constricted necks and everted rims, their morphometric attributes varying from 20 to 23 cm in MD, 28 to 31 cm in MaD, 30 to 37 cm in height, 16 to 22 cm in HMD, and finally, 0.8 to 1 cm in T. Two decoration patterns have been recorded: the first, found on two vessels, consists of a horizontal band of twisted roulette impression delineated by two parallel grooved lines on the shoulder, and the second comprises extensive twisted roulette impression on the body overlined by two horizontal and parallel grooved lines on the shoulder. And (3) four specimens of necked to long-necked storage jars with everted rim, 25 to 28 cm in MD, 34 to 37 cm in MaD, 41 to 52 cm in height, 4 to 10 cm in NH, 22 to 24 cm in HMD, and finally, 0.8 to 1.3 cm in T. The decoration is confined to the neck-shoulder area in three out of four cases, but each of the recorded jars has a peculiar pattern. They are considered here in terms of increasing degrees of elaboration. The first case consists of a horizontal band of twisted roulette impression under- and overlined by two parallel grooved lines. The second comprises a horizontal band delimited by two parallel grooved lines, filled with four equidistant panels of twisted roulette impression each delimited by two short vertical and parallel grooved lines. In the third, a horizontal band delimited by two parallel grooved lines is filled with twisted roulette impression and superimposed, regular, zigzag, grooved and awl-stabbed lines. And finally, the fourth comprises extensive twisted roulette impression on the body overlined by two horizontal and parallel grooved lines, complemented by five equidistant pairs of appliqué buttons on the shoulder.

The remaining cluster 7 installations are situated in the inner side of the settlement, in front of houses; they include chicken coops, with a larger specimen near house 25 and two smaller ones in front of house 27, and a nine-supporting-pole storage platform in a relatively central location.

Cluster 8, with four main wood and reeds features, associated with a small fenced field, is situated in the eastern side of the village, arranged in a linear pattern stretched on approximately 30 m N-S (fig. 14). The public shelter (feature 30) is located in the inner side of the settlement; it is built with two roof-supporting poles and measures 5.7 m in diameter. Barns (features 28 and 31) are situated at both ends of the cluster. The northern one (house 28) is built with two supporting poles, measures 6.9 m in diameter, and comprises one enamel basin. The southern barn (house 31) is larger, measuring 9.8 m in diameter and built with six roof-supporting poles; four clay vessels were found on the barn floor. The habitation house (feature 29) is located at the center of the cluster; it is a two-supporting-poles feature, 6.4 m in diameter, comprising a large bed, an elaborate hearth, and three pieces of pottery as house domestic equipment. Feature 31A is a shallow 9-m-in-diameter circle, the remains of an abandoned house which cannot clearly be assigned to any cluster.

Cluster 9 is located in the southeastern part of the settlement. It is a clearly delineated household unit including four houses, one in mud-brick and the others in wood and reeds, four storage platforms, two chicken coops, and fenced maize and sorghum fields (fig. 14). Habitation houses 32 and 35 are located at both ends of the cluster. House 32 is built with four supporting poles and measures 7.9 m in diameter; it comprises a large bed, an elaborate hearth, and six potteries arranged on wooden shelves. House 35, some 38 m SW, is built in mud-brick with four supporting poles, an elaborate hearth, a large bed, and house equipment consisting of five enamelwares and five clay vessels.Three rubber shoes were abandoned on the floor. Two storage platforms of different size are found next to house 32; the smaller has six supporting poles, and the larger, nine, as is the case for the specimen located near house 34; the specimen attached to house 35, in line with two chicken coops, has twelve poles. Feature 34 is a young man's house, built with a single central pole, measuring 4.4 m in diameter, and comprising a small-size bed. Finally, the barn (feature 33) is located at the center of the house cluster. It is built with six supporting poles and measures 7.8 m in diameter.

Considering the frequency distribution of houses and the building material used, two general observations can be made at this juncture: with three houses out of thirty-five in mud-brick, wood and reeds are clearly the standard building materials; the range of variation, with three to five houses per cluster, is relatively narrow, suggesting an optimal size for household units in the settlement.

Gallis

Gallis is located approximately 2 kilometers S of Bilbede. The settlement is circular in shape, measuring 200 m in MaD and extending over 3.2 hectares. Its entrance, signalled by a 45-m-wide gap in the houses' circle, is situated in the southern side.With the notable exception of the well, which is 13 m deep and located to the S at the village entrance, there are virtually no communal features used by all the members of the settlement. The high frequency of storage platforms and the small number and size of livestock enclosures suggest that grain agriculture is superceding livestock husbandry, with nonetheless a seminomadic lifestyle still predominant. At the time of fieldwork, in March 1991, most of the village inhabitants were already in their dry-season camps, but an important number of individuals were still in the village. Fifty-three houses have been recorded, among them, seven (features 47, 48, 49, 50, 51, 52 and 53) are abandoned and worn-out features. The remaining forty-six, with some of them still inhabited, are distributed into nine clusters (tables 18 and 19). The still inhabited houses (1, 3, 4, 6, 7, 11, 43, 44, 45, and 46) were consequently not studied in detail; they are clustered in the SW of the site and appear to belong to kin groups, probably part of an extended family (fig. 15).

Cluster 1 is found in the southwestern side of the village; it comprises thirteen wood and reeds houses arranged around a cattle corral shaded by a large tree and measuring 15 m in diameter (fig. 15). It is spread over 85 m NE-SW and 40 to 50 m NW-SE and is divided into several units. Unit 1 is found in the SE. It consists of two houses set at 8 m from each other and three large storage platforms. Two of the recorded storage platforms are built with nine supporting poles, while the third, measuring 8 m in length and 6 m in width, comprises twenty-four poles. The habitation house (feature 1), measuring 6.2 m in diameter, was still inhabited;

Table 18: Gallis household clusters

Cluster number	Number of units	Habitation houses	Livestock houses	Storage platforms	Others
1	5	8	3	10	6
2	2	3	2	5	2
3	1	1	1	—	4
4	1	2	1	2	2
5	1	1	3	—	1
6	1	3	1	4	1
7	2	4	1	4	—
8	1	3	—	4	1
9	1	2	1	3	3
Total	15	27	13	32	20

Table 19: Gallis general distribution of pottery

Cluster number	Number of features	Service vessels	Cooking vessels	Storage vessels	Unknown	Total
1	27	?	?	?	?	?
2	12	—	3	1	—	4
3	6	—	7	2	—	9
4	5	—	4	5	—	9
5	5	—	—	1	—	1
6	9	—	3	6	—	9
7	9	1	2	5	—	8
8	7	—	1	8	—	9
9	9	—	—	2	—	2
Total	89	1	20	30	?	51

it comprises a bed, an elaborate hearth, and domestic equipment that was not studied. The barn (feature 2), at 8 m NW, is built with three supporting poles and measures 6.2 m in diameter. Unit 2, also with two houses (feature 3 and 4), is attached to a fenced field 50 m long and 45 m wide and is situated at some 15 m NW

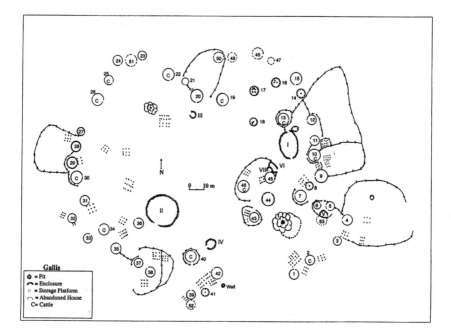

Figure 15: Map of Gallis

of the previous one. It also comprises three storage platforms, one with six supporting poles and the remaining two with nine. Both features still occupied are
habitation houses, with beds and hearths, and certainly some furniture, measuring
7.4 (house 3) and 6.9 (house 4) m in diameter. Unit 3 is found at some 8 m NE;
it is well-demarcated by a fence and consists of two houses (features 5 and 6)
and a goat enclosure 5 m on average diameter, overlapping partially with the remains of the abandoned house 53. The recorded unit 3 features are disposed in a
neat triangular pattern. The barn (house 5) is built with four roof-supporting poles
and measures 8.2 m in diameter, while the still occupied habitation at 4 m E, with
an elaborate hearth, a bed, and furniture, measures 5 m in diameter. Unit 4 is located at the northeastern end of the cluster, within a fenced area 35 m in length
and 15 m in width. It comprises two houses (features 45 and 46) set at 12 m from
each other, the former being a habitation house still occupied and measuring 6.2 m
in diameter, and the latter, a barn, built with four supporting poles and measuring
7.4 m in diameter; two storage platforms with 8 and 9 supporting poles; and finally, two goat enclosures, the larger measuring 7 by 4 m, and the smaller, 4.5 m
on average diameter. Unit 5 is a well-delineated and fenced context 15 m long and
13 m wide, with habitation house 43 measuring 7 m in diameter, and two storage
platforms with four and twelve supporting poles. Houses 7 and 44, each inhabited
by a single, elder person, are relatively isolated and situated at 15 m from each
other.

Cluster 2, located on the western side of the village, is a clearly defined and
fenced complex stretched on 55 m N-S, comprising one cattle corral 18 m long
and 13 m wide, six or seven wood and reeds houses, four storage platforms, and
two fenced fields. The recorded features are distributed into two units. Unit 1 is
found in the S with features 8, 9, and 10 and a 600 (30×20) meters square field.
The public shelter (feature 8), built with a single central pole and measuring 5.5 m
in diameter, is located at the southeastern end of the cluster with an adjunct twelve-
supporting-poles storage platform.The habitation house (feature 9), still occupied
and measuring 6.2 m in diameter, is found 4 m NW. And the barn (feature 10),
8.6 m in diameter and built with four roof-supporting poles, is 6 m N of the habitation house. Three storage platforms, two with nine poles and the remaining one
with twelve, are located between both houses and slightly W (fig. 15). Unit 2 farther N comprises three houses in a triangular arrangement, with distances varying
from 8 to 12 m from each other, a fenced field 45 m long and 23 m wide, and a
storage platform built with twelve-supporting-poles. House 12, 5.7 m in diameter,
with a single central pole, is a new feature that was being built during the period
of fieldwork. Feature 11, the habitation house 5.7 m in diameter, was still occupied but the pottery material consisting of four vessels distributed into three morphological categories was made available for measurement. And finally, the barn
(feature 13), located at the northeastern end of the cluster, is built with four supporting poles and measures 8.4 m in diameter.

The vessels' shapes recorded in house 11 assemblage are as follows: (1) a rounded base, hemispheric pot with slightly constricted neck, everted rim, and two handles, decorated with twisted roulette impression on the body overlined on the shoulder by two horizontal and parallel grooved lines with, in addition, two symmetric pairs of appliqué buttons; (2) two specimens of necked, globular pot with everted rim, both decorated with twisted roulette impression on the body overlined on the shoulder by two horizontal and parallel grooved lines, complemented by four equidistant appliqué single or pairs of buttons; and (3) a long-necked, globular jar decorated on the shoulder with a horizontal band of twisted roulette impression under-and overlined by two parallel grooved lines, with, in addition, four equidistant appliqué buttons.

Cluster 3, with six wood and reeds features, located in the northwestern part of the settlement, is particularly problematic for two main reasons. First, the arrangement of features appears to have been altered with the abandonment of houses 47, 48, 49, and 50. And second, the concentration of four public shelters in such a small area is unusual. The recorded discussion houses (features 14, 16, 17 and 18) almost spaced at regular intervals, set at 10 m (features 16 to 17), 13 m (features 14 to 16), and 14 m (features 17 to 18), are built with one to four supporting poles, their diameter varying from 5.2 to 6.4 m. The habitation house (feature 15) and the barn (feature 19) are situated at both E and W ends of the cluster, at 45 m from each other. The latter, measuring 8.2 m in diameter is built with six supporting poles, while the former, 8.7 m in diameter, has four supporting poles, one elaborate hearth, a large bed, a large set of thirty-one enamelwares, and finally, nine clay vessels arranged in wooden shelves near the fireplace.

The recorded vessel assemblage comprises three morphological categories: (1) a long-necked, globular pot with everted rim, 20 cm in MD, 32 cm in MaD, 34 cm in height, 6 cm in NH, 19 cm in HMD, and 1.1 cm in T, decorated with a band of twisted roulette impression over- and underlined by two parallel grooved lines on the shoulder; (2) six specimens of rounded base, globular pots with constricted necks and everted rims, their morphometric attributes varying from 19 to 24 cm in MD, 22 to 29 cm in MaD, 21 to 30 cm for height, 12 to 18 cm for HMD, and finally, 0.7 to 0.8 cm in T. Four of the specimens share a similar pattern of decoration, consisting of twisted roulette impression on the body overlined by two horizontal and parallel grooved lines on the shoulder. The remaining two cases, with minor variations have a slightly more elaborated decoration which is nonetheless articulated with the same syntax: in one, twisted roulette impression on the body overlined by three horizontal and parallel grooved lines with four equidistant appliqué buttons on the shoulder; and in the other, twisted roulette impression on the body overlined on the shoulder by two horizontal and parallel grooved lines complemented by three equidistant pairs of appliqué buttons. And finally, (3) two specimens of long-necked, globular jar with everted rim, 23 to 26 cm in MD, 35 to 40 cm in MaD, 45 cm in height, 7 cm in NH, 26 to 28 cm in HMD, and 1 to 1.1 cm in T; one being decorated with twisted roulette impression on the body overlined on the shoulder by two horizontal and parallel grooved lines, and the other, with a horizontal band of twisted roulette impression under- and overlined by two parallel grooved lines.

Cluster 4 is situated in the northern edge of the village and comprises seven features: a fenced field 35 m in length and 25 m in maximum width on the outer side, three wood and reeds houses and a small six-poles-storage platform set in SE-NE linear arrangement, and finally on the inner side, a small goat enclosure 5 m in diameter and a large twenty-poles storage platform. The large tree a few meters NE of the storage platform is probably a component of cluster 4; if this is the case, the features appear to delineate a circular pattern measuring slightly less than 40 m in diameter (fig. 15).The barn (feature 22) situated at the northeastern end of the cluster is built with six supporting poles and measures 7.9 m in diameter. A young man's house (feature 21) with a small bed and two clay vessels, built with a single central pole and measuring 5.3 m in diameter, is found at the middle of the houses' line. And finally, the main habitation house (feature 20) built with four supporting poles and measuring 8.5 m in diameter, is located at the southwestern end of the cluster. It comprises a large bed and an elaborate hearth, with furniture consisting of two enamelwares and nine clay vessels; one pair of rubber shoes was found on the house floor.

The recorded sample of vessels is comprised of four morphological classes: (1) two specimens of globular pots with slightly constricted necks and everted rims, measuring 17 to 22 cm in MD, 20 to 27 cm in MaD, 21 to 23 cm in height, 13 to 16 cm in HMD, and 0.8 to 1.1 cm in T, and decorated with extensive twisted roulette impression on the body overlined on the shoulder in one case, and by two horizontal and parallel grooved lines, with additional three equidistant appliqué buttons in the other; (2) a rounded base hemispheric pot, with slightly constricted neck, everted rim and two handles, decorated with twisted roulette impression on the body overlined on the shoulder by two horizontal and parallel grooved lines complemented by two symmetric appliqué buttons, and measuring 25 cm in MD, 30 cm in MaD, 29 cm in height, 18 cm in HMD, and 1.2 cm in T; (3) a short-necked, globular pot with everted rim, 14 cm in MD, 30 cm in MaD, 36 cm in height, 4 cm in NH, 17 cm in HMD, and 0.9 cm in T, decorated on the shoulder with a horizontal band of twisted roulette impression under- and overlined by two grooved lines; and finally, (4) four specimens of necked storage jars, measuring 24 to 27 cm in MD, 36 to 43 cm in MaD, 43 to 50 cm in height, 4 to 7 cm in NH, 26 to 32 cm in HMD, and 0.9 to 1.2 cm in T; three decoration patterns have been recorded: the first, found on two jars, consists of a horizontal band of twisted roulette impression under- and overlined by two parallel grooved lines on the shoulder; the second, seen on one vessel, is a farther elaboration of the first one, with, in addition, four equidistant appliqué buttons; and finally, the third, found on two jars, comprises extensive twisted roulette impression on the body overlined on the shoulder by two horizontal and parallel grooved lines.

Cluster 5 with four (or five) wood and reeds houses is found in the NNE of the village; it is a NW-SE linear arrangement of features set at a distance varying from 8 to 12 m from each other, and stretched on 50 m and comprising one habitation house (feature 24) and three barns (feature 23, 25, and 26). House 24 is built with two supporting poles, measures 7.2 m in diameter, and comprises an elaborate hearth, a large bed, as well as one enamelware and a necked storage jar. The uncovered jar measures 27 cm in MD, 40 cm in MaD, 49 cm in height, 6 cm in NH, 27 cm in HMD, and 1.2 cm in T. It is decorated with twisted roulette impression on the body overlined on the shoulder by a horizontal grooved line and small shallow depressions. The diameter of barns varies from 6.3 (features 23 and 25) to 7.3 m (feature 26), and the number of roof-supporting poles from two (feature 25) to four (features 23 and 26). Feature 51 is a shallow circle 8 m in diameter, and is the remaining evidence of an abandoned house.

Cluster 6 is a clearly demarcated set of features located in the eastern side of the settlement. It is stretched on 40 m N-S and comprises four houses, three (feature 27, 28, 29) in mud-brick and one (feature 30) in wood and reeds, a fenced field 30 m long and 25 m wide, and four (or five) storage platforms built with six to fourteen supporting poles (fig. 15). House 27, at the northern end of the cluster, measures 5.6 m in diameter; it is built with a single central pole and includes a bed and a hearth. House 28 is located some 5 m S of the previous one; built with two roof-supporting poles, it measures 6.5 m in diameter with a hearth, a bed, and a single enamelware. House 29, probably the main habitation, is found 3 to 4 m farther S. It is a four supporting poles feature, measuring 7.3 m in diameter and comprising an elaborate hearth, a large bed, as well as one enamelware and nine clay vessels. And finally, the barn (feature 30), located at the southern end of the cluster, is built with four-supporting-poles and measures 7.9 m in diameter.

Four morphological categories are represented in the pottery sample from house 29: (1) a globular pot with slightly constricted neck and everted rim, 23 cm in MD, 30 cm in MaD, 30 cm in height, 18 cm in HMD, and 1 cm in T, decorated with extensive twisted roulette impression on the body overlined on the shoulder by two horizontal and parallel grooved lines complemented by four equidistant pairs of appliqué buttons; (2) two specimens of rounded base hemispheric pot with slightly constricted neck, everted rim and two handles, 21 to 24 cm in MD, 30 to 33 cm in MaD, 32 to 33 cm in height, 19 to 22 cm in HMD, and 0.9 to 1 cm in T, both decorated with extensive twisted roulette impression on the body overlined by two horizontal and parallel grooved lines on the shoulder, with, in addition, three equidistant appliqué buttons in one case; (3) two specimens of short-necked, globular jar decorated on the shoulder with a horizontal band of twisted roulette impression under- and overlined by two parallel grooved lines, measuring 24 to 25 cm in MD, 36 to 42 cm in MaD, 38 to 45 cm in height, 6 to 8 cm in NH, 22 to 27 cm in HMD, and 1 to 1.1 cm in T; and finally, (4) four specimens of long-necked jar, with their morphometric attributes varying from 29 to 34 for MD, 34 to 55 cm for MaD, 50 to 67 cm for height, 10 to 15 cm for NH, 21 to 33 cm for HMD, and 1.4 to 1.7 cm in T. Three of the jars are decorated with twisted roulette impression on the body overlined on the shoulder by two horizontal and parallel grooved lines, and the remaining one with a horizontal band of twisted roulette impression under- and overlined by two parallel grooved lines, with, in addition, four equidistant lugs.

Cluster 7 is located in the SE of the village. It consists of five relatively dispersed houses (feature 31, 32, 33, 34, and 36) and four storage platforms (fig. 15). The orientation of houses doorways clearly indicates that they belong to the same social unit, presumably an extended family. The barn (feature 34), built with four supporting poles and measuring 7.6 m in diameter, is located at the center of the cluster, at 16 m from houses 31, 32, and 36. House 31, with its adjunct 6 by 6 m nine-pole storage platform found in the NE of the cluster, is built with two central poles, measures 6.3 m in diameter, and comprises a bed. House 32, 8 to 10 m SE, is surrounded by two storage platforms with four and nine supporting poles; built with two roof-supporting poles, and measuring 6.5 m in diameter, it has an elaborate hearth, a large bed, a petrol lamp, four enamelwares, and six clay vessels.

The recorded sample of pottery comprises two vessels shapes: one specimen of rounded base hemispheric pot, with slightly constricted neck, everted rim, and two handles, 25 cm in MD, 32 cm in MaD, 32 cm in height, 21 cm in HMD, and 0.9 cm in T, decorated with twisted roulette impression on the body overlined by two horizontal and parallel grooved lines on the shoulder; and five specimens of long-necked storage jar, their morphometric attributes varying from 26 to 31 cm in MD, 40 to 48 cm in MaD, 52 to 65 cm in height, 7 to 17 cm in NH, 25 to 32 cm in HMD, and 1.2 to 1.5 cm in T. Four of the jars present similar or almost similar patterns of decoration, consisting of a horizontal band of twisted roulette impression on the shoulder delineated by two or three parallel grooved lines, complemented in one case by three equidistant appliqué buttons. The remaining specimen is decorated on the shoulder with a horizontal band of twisted roulette impression underlined by an appliqué cordon with short vertical grooved lines and four equidistant lugs. House 33, at approximately 5 m SE of the barn (feature 34) is built with two supporting poles, measures 6.1 m in diameter, and comprises a bed and a hearth. Finally, feature 36, a 8.1 m diameter habitation house is found in the western end of the cluster; it is built with four roof-supporting poles, comprises a bed and an elaborate hearth, with one enamelware and two clay vessels. One of the pieces of pottery is a footed bowl, 13 cm in maximum as well as MD, 9 cm in foot diameter, 11 cm in height, 3 cm in foot height, and 0.9 cm in T, decorated with extensive twisted roulette impression on the body; and the other, a rounded base hemispheric pot with slightly constricted neck and two handles, decorated with twisted roulette impression on the body overlined on the shoulder by two horizontal and parallel grooved lines, complemented by six equidistant appliqué buttons.

Cluster 8 is located in the southern side of the settlement. It is a well-delineated, fenced complex with three wood and reeds houses and four storage platforms (fig. 15). House 35, at the northeastern end of the cluster, is built with two roof-supporting poles, measures 7 m in diameter, and comprises a hearth, a large bed, two enamelwares, and six clay vessels. A relatively large storage platform, 5 m long and 3.5 m wide, built with fifteen poles, is found 4 m in front of the house. Three vessel shapes are represented in the recorded pottery sample: (1) a globular pot with slightly constricted neck and everted rim, 22 cm in MD, 26 cm in MaD, 27 cm in height, 17 cm in HMD, and finally, 0.8 cm in T, decorated with extensive twisted roulette impression on the body overlined on the shoulder by two horizontal and parallel grooved lines, complemented by four equidistant appliqué buttons; (2) a short-necked, globular pot with everted rim decorated on the shoulder with a horizontal band of twisted roulette impression under- and overlined by two parallel grooved lines, measuring 13 cm in MD, 30 cm in MaD, 37 cm in height, 5 cm in NH, 18 cm in HMD, and finally, 1.2 cm in T; and (3) four specimens of long-necked jars, their morphometric attributes varying from 25 to 29 cm in MD, 39 to 43 cm in MaD, 45 to 60 cm in height, 8 to 16 cm in NH, 27 to 33 cm in HMD, and finally, 1.2 cm in T. One of the specimens is plain but comprises four equidistant lugs on the shoulder. The remaining three, with some variation from one case to another, share similar patterns of decoration; the decoration is confined to the shoulder-neck area and consists of a horizontal band of twisted roulette impression, under- and overlined by two parallel grooved lines in the first case, three parallel lines in the second, and three parallel lines and a chevron band in the third.

Feature 37, the second habitation house of the cluster, is located 12 m SW of the previous one. It measures 6.5 m in diameter, is built with three roof-supporting poles, and comprises a hearth, a large bed, one grinding platform, and a set of four necked storage jars. The recorded vessels measure 25 to 28 cm in MD, 36 to 42 cm in MaD, 45 to 52 cm in height, 6 to 7 cm in NH, 24 to 27 cm in HMD, and finally, 1 to 1.4 cm in T. The decoration is confined to the shoulder-neck area in all the cases, with a specific pattern for each specimen. One jar is plain but nonetheless decorated on the shoulder with four equidistant sets of three appliqué buttons; the second has a horizontal band of twisted roulette impression under- and overlined by two parallel grooved lines; a pattern similar to that of the third jar, with, in addition, two symmetric appliqué buttons; and finally, the fourth comprises a horizontal band of twisted roulette impression with three superimposed parallel grooved lines, with, in addition, four equidistant sets of three appliqué buttons.

Three storage platforms are located within the fenced area. They measure 4 by 4.5 m for the southern one, 5 by 5 m for the northern one, and 3.5 by 3.5 m for the western one, built respectively with nine, eleven, and nine supporting poles. Feature 38, located at the center of the fenced area, is a new house that was being built at the time of fieldwork, measuring 6.6 m in diameter. The absence of any livestock house within cluster 8 and the orientation of the entrance of the large 22-m-in-diameter cattle enclosure located 15 m N suggest that the installation is owned by/or shared with cluster 8 members.

Cluster 9 is located in the S-SW of the village on the eastern side of the entrance near the 14-m-deep well. It comprises nine features distributed into four (or five) wood and reeds houses, three storage platforms, a goat enclosure (fig. 15). Feature 52, located at the southern end of the cluster, is an abandoned house, reduced to a shallow circle 6.5 m in diameter. Feature 39, the habitation house, is found at the eastern end of the cluster. It is built with a single central pole, measures 5.6 m in diameter, and comprises a bed and a hearth, with domestic equipment consisting of a petrol lamp, an enamelware, and a long-necked storage jar. The recorded jar, 30 cm in MD, 42 cm in MaD, 55 cm in height, 18 cm in NH, 29 cm in HMD, and 1.7 cm in T, is decorated with three horizontal and parallel grooved lines on the shoulder with four equidistant lugs and pairs of appliqué buttons. A storage platform built with nine supporting poles is adjunct to house 39, on its southeastern side. The public shelter (feature 41) is located some 5 m W of the previous house not far from the well; it is a single-central-pole feature, measuring 4.8 m in diameter. A large 5 by 5 m storage platform built with twelve poles is located near the discussion house, on the inner side of the settlement, in continuity with another large 8 by 5 m nineteen-poles storage platform adjunct to house 42. Feature 42 is the second habitation house of the cluster, found at some 9 m NW of the discussion house. It is built with two roof-supporting poles, measures 7.4 m in diameter, and comprises a bed, a hearth, and four enamelwares. Livestock installations are located approximately 10 m N; the barn (feature 40), surrounded by a fence, is built with four roof-supporting poles and measures 7.9 m in diameter.

Gallis' spatial layout can be characterized by one striking feature—the partition of the village into two halves—western and eastern. The western half shows a frequent use of fences and larger, multiunit clusters, inhabited by members of extended families, most of them still present on the site during fieldwork; and the eastern half, exhibits almost equally sized groups (if judged by the frequency distribution of built features which varies from three to five) who were absent at the time of fieldwork, having already settled in their dry-season camping areas.

Ngada I

Ngada I is the easternmost of a series of four settlements sharing the same placename, arranged in an E-W linear pattern, with distance from one site to its nearest neighbor varying from 300 to 800 m. The Ngada settlement cluster is located 1.5 kilometers S of Gallis, not far from a series of more or less permanent ponds. Ngada I is sub-elliptical in shape and extended over 3.36 hectares comprising forty-five wood and reeds houses, four goat and six cattle enclosures, nine storage platforms, and a few chicken coops. The site measures 210 m in length SE-NE and 160 m in width SE-NW, with the inner side of the settlement devoted to communal features. Dwelling features and other settlement facilities are found in a circular linear pattern, organized into twelve clusters (tables 20 and 21, fig. 16).

Seven communal installations have been mapped; they are distributed into

Table 20: Ngada I household clusters

Cluster number	Number of units	Habitation houses	Livestock houses	Storage platforms	Others
1	1	2	2	—	—
2	1	2	2	2	—
3	2	3	1	2	2
4	1	2	1	1	—
5	2	3	2	—	1
6	1	3	1	—	—
7	1	1	1	1	1
8	2	4	2	1	3
9	3	3	2	2	1
10	3	4	2	1	2
Total	17	27	16	10	10

six large cattle enclosures and a unique public shelter (feature 39) located in the SSE near one of the village entrances (fig. 16).The discussion house is built with eight roof-supporting poles and measures 10.2 m in diameter. The recorded cattle enclosures are divided into two groups; the first one consisting of abandoned and worn-out enclosures from previous years, and the second comprising those in used at the time of fieldwork. Worn-out enclosures are arranged in a tighter cluster, with distance from one to another varying from 10 (enclosure III to IV, III to V and IV to V) to 15 m (enclosure V to VI). They are extended over 396 (enclosure IV: 22 × 18 m), 415 (enclosure III: 23 × 23 m), 448 (enclosure VI: 28 × 16 m)

Table 21: Ngada I general distribution of pottery

Cluster number	Number of features	Service vessels	Cooking vessels	Storage vessels	Unknown	Total
1	4	—	3	3	—	6
2	6	1	3	2	—	6
3	8	1	5	8	—	14
4	4	2	6	6	—	14
5	6	—	2	4	—	6
6	4	—	1	—	—	1
7	4	—	4	—	—	4
8	10	1	2	1	—	4
9	8	—	3	4	—	7
10	9	—	6	1	—	7
Total	63	5	35	29	—	69

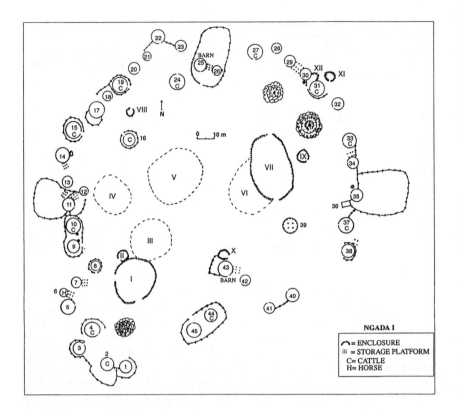

Figure 16: Map of Ngada I

and 806 (enclosure V: 31 × 26 m) square meters, with at least a total surface of
2,065 square meters devoted to cattle during the previous years. The corrals still
in use are set 75 m apart, one is extended over 575 square meters (enclosure I: 25 ×
23 m), and the other on 805 square meters (enclosure VII: 35 × 23 m), with at least
a total of 1380 square meters devoted to cattle at the time of fieldwork. Comparatively, the variation considered above suggests an important reduction in the size
of the Ngada I cattle herd, an issue which will be discussed in more detail later.

    Cluster 1 is located in the southern part of the village, on the western side
of the entrance (fig. 16). It is spread over 40 m NW-SE and 35 m SW-NE and
comprises four houses surrounded by a fence, with, in addition, a large tree situated in the inner side of the settlement. Houses are organized into two distinct units.
Unit 1 in the SE comprises an habitation house (feature 1), built with two roof-
supporting poles, measuring 6.9 m in diameter, with a large bed, an elaborate
hearth, a grinding platform, a petrol lamp, three enamelwares and six clay vessels;

and a barn (feature 2), 7.2 m in diameter, also built with two supporting poles, and located 3 to 4 m NW.

Unit 1 pottery assemblage includes three vessel shapes: (1) a rounded base hemispheric pot with slightly constricted neck and everted rim, 24 cm in MD, 31 cm in MaD, 31 cm in height, 17 cm in HMD, and finally, 1 cm in T, decorated with extensive twisted roulette impression on the body overlined on the shoulder by two horizontal and parallel grooved lines; (2) two specimens of globular pot with slightly constricted necks and everted rims, 21 to 22 cm in MD, 28 cm in MaD, 27 to 29 cm in height, 16 to 17 cm in HMD, and 0.8 to 1 cm in T, decorated with twisted roulette impression on the body, overlined on the shoulder by two horizontal and parallel grooved lines, complemented in one case by four pairs of equidistant appliqué buttons; and (3) three specimens of necked to long-necked storage jar, with morphometric attributes varying from, 20 to 30 cm in MD, 30 to 42 cm in MaD, 46 to 55 cm in height, 7 to 16 cm in NH, 26 to 37 cm in HMD, and 1.2 to 1.5 cm in T. Each jar has a specific decoration: one is plain but has an appliqué cordon on the shoulder with four equidistant lugs; another is decorated on the shoulder with a horizontal band of twisted roulette impression with three superimposed parallel grooved lines; and the third has extensive twisted roulette impression on the body, overlined on the shoulder by three horizontal and parallel grooved lines.

Unit 2, with two houses, is located approximately 10 m NW. The habitation house (feature 3) measures 6.9 m in diameter, is built with a single central pole, and comprises a large bed, an elaborate hearth, and a single enamel basin. The barn (feature 4) is found 5 m NE; it is built with five roof-supporting poles and measures 7.9 m in diameter. An enamel basin probably used for watering livestock was found on the house floor. The large tree 10 m E of the barn, is an integral part of the cluster, being a de facto discussion shelter.

Cluster 2 is located in the SSW of the settlement, 10 m NW of the previous one. It consists of four wood and reeds houses and two storage platforms stretched on 35 m NE-SW. Feature 5, one of the habitation houses built with four supporting poles and measuring 7.9 m in diameter, is situated at the southwestern edge of the cluster flanked on its northern side by a nine poles storage platform (fig. 16). It comprises an elaborate hearth, a large bed, and a grinding platform, domestic equipment being divided into one enamelware and four clay vessels. The recorded pottery assemblage comprises two vessels shapes: (1) Two specimens of globular pot with slightly constricted necks and everted rims, 19 to 22 cm in MD, 24 to 32 cm in MaD, 25 to 34 cm in height, 15 to 17 cm in HMD, and 0.7 to 1 cm in T, one decorated with a horizontal band of twisted roulette impression under- and overlined by two parallel grooved lines, and the other with extensive twisted roulette impression on the body overlined on the shoulder by two horizontal and parallel grooved lines. (2) Two specimens of necked to long-necked storage jars, morphometric attributes varying from 29 to 30 cm for MD, 43 to 55 for MaD, 50 to 65 cm for height, 7 to 13 cm for NH, 24 to 45 cm for HMD, to 1.1 to 1.5 cm in T. One jar is decorated with twisted roulette impression on the body overlined on the shoulder by two horizontal and parallel grooved lines, and the other with a horizontal band of twisted roulette impression on the shoulder, under- and over-lined by two parallel grooved lines complemented by four pairs of equidistant appliqué buttons.

A 'horse house' (feature 6), built with a single central pole and measuring 4.9 m in diameter is located 2 m NW of house 5, behind the storage platform. Feature 7, the second habitation house of the cluster with its adjunct nine-poles storage platform, is located at the center of the linear arrangement. It is built with a single central pole, measures 5.9 m in diameter, and comprises a large bed. House equipment consists of a wooden mortar, a plastic bucket, an iron hoe, six enamel-wares, and two clay vessels. One of the pieces of pottery is a footed bowl, 13 cm in mouth and MaD, 9 cm in foot base diameter, 11 cm in total as well as MaD height, 3 cm in foot height, and 1 cm in T, decorated with twisted roulette impression on the body. The other is a short-necked, globular pot with everted rim, decorated with a horizontal band of roulette impression on the shoulder, under- and overlined by two parallel grooved lines. The barn (feature 8), surrounded by a fence, is located at the northeastern end of the cluster at 7 m from the nearest habitation house. It is built with a single central pole and measures 5.2 m in diameter. One pair of rubber shoes was found on the floor. Goat enclosure II some 10 m NE of barn 8, probably belongs to cluster 2 as suggested by the southwestern orientation of its entrance (fig. 16). If the same criterium is applied to the large cattle enclosure I, it may belong to both cluster 1 and 2.

Cluster 3, on the western side of the village, comprises four wood and reeds houses, two chicken coops, and two storage platform set in a well-delineated and fenced context (fig. 16). The recorded features are organized in two distinct units. Unit 1 consists of a fenced space 22 m long N-S and 10 m wide E-W, with two houses set at slightly less than 5 m from each other, each associated with a chicken coop. The habitation house (feature 9), comprising a large bed and an elaborate hearth, is built with two roof-supporting poles and measures 6.7 m in diameter. House vessels consist of a single rounded base short-necked, globular pot with everted rim and two handles, decorated with extensive twisted roulette impression on the body, overlined by two horizontal and parallel lines on the shoulder, measuring 21 cm in MD, 28 cm in MaD, 31 cm in height, 5 cm in NH, 17 cm in HMD, and 0.9 cm in T. The barn (feature 10) is built with four supporting poles and measures 8.2 m in diameter.

Unit 2, 5 m farther N, attached to a fenced field 22 m long and 18 m wide, consists of two habitation houses and two nine-poles storage platforms. Feature 12 is a "young man" house, built with a single central pole, comprising a small bed and measuring 4.5 m in diameter. Feature 11, the main habitation house of the cluster, measures 7 m in diameter. It is built with two roof-supporting poles and comprises a large bed, an elaborate hearth, some supply of firewood, and a large sample of thirteen clay vessels. Three morphological categories are represented in the recorded pottery sample: (1) a plain footed bowl, 13 cm in mouth and MaD, 9 cm in foot base diameter, 11 cm in total and MaD height, 3 cm in foot height, and 1.2 cm in T; (2) four specimens of globular pot with slightly constricted necks and everted rims, all of them decorated with extensive twisted roulette impression on the body overlined on the shoulder by two horizontal and parallel grooved lines, with their morphometric attributes varying from 13 to 22 cm for MD, 19 to 27 cm for MaD, 22 to 29 cm for height, 14 to 16 for HMD, and finally, 0.7 to 0.9 cm in T; and (3) eight specimens of long-necked storage jar, measuring 24 to 26 cm in MD, 33 to 38 cm in MaD, 45 to 55 cm in height, 7 to 10 cm in NH, 25 to 37 cm in HMD. Three main patterns of decoration have been recorded among the studied sample of jars; proceeding from simple to complex, there are (1) three specimens decorated with a horizontal band of twisted roulette impression on the shoulder, under- and overlined by two parallel grooved lines; (2) two specimens decorated with a horizontal band of twisted roulette impression on the shoulder, combined in one case with three parallel grooved lines and four equidistant appliqué buttons, and the other with two parallel grooved and double chevron lines; and (3) two specimens with extensive twisted roulette impression on the body, overlined on the shoulder by two or three parallel grooved lines in two cases, with, in addition, a chevron line in the remaining one.

Cluster 4, with three wood and reeds houses arranged in a linear N-S pattern, is located in the western side of the settlement. It is stretched on 38 m, with features situated at 7 m from each other. Feature 13 is found at the southern end of the cluster; it is a habitation house, 6.5 m in diameter, built with a single central pole and comprising a bed and a hearth. Habitation house 14, with an adjunct nine-poles storage platform, is located 7 m farther N, at the center of the cluster; it is built with four roof-supporting poles, measures 8 m in diameter, and comprises a large bed, an elaborate hearth, a grinding platform, and a large sample of fourteen clay vessels carefully arranged on wooden shelves set above a curvilinear clay bench. One rubber shoe was also found on the house floor. The barn (feature 15) is located at the northern end of the cluster; it is surrounded by a fence, is built with six roof-supporting poles and measures 9.2 m in diameter.

Six morphological categories are represented in what is clearly the cluster's vessels assemblage: (1) a footed bowl decorated with extensive twisted roulette impression on the body, measuring 13 cm in maximum as well as MD, 8 cm in foot base diameter, 12 cm in height, 3 cm in foot height, and 1 cm in T; (2) a large, plain, shallow, hole-mouth bowl with rounded base, 23 cm in MD, 6 cm in height, and 0.8 cm in T; (3) a necked, globular pot with rounded base and everted rim, decorated with a horizontal band of twisted roulette impression on the shoulder, under- and overlined by two parallel grooved lines, and measuring 12 cm in MD, 30 cm in MaD, 39 cm in height, 6 cm in NH, 20 cm in HMD, and 1 cm in T; (4) a rounded base hemispheric pot, with slightly constricted neck, everted rim and two handles, 24 cm in MD, 28 cm in MaD, 29 cm in height, 18 cm in HMD, and 1.2 cm in T, decorated with extensive twisted roulette impression on the body overlined on the shoulder by two horizontal and parallel grooved lines with, in addition, two symmetric appliqué buttons; (5) four specimens of slightly elongated, globular pot, with constricted neck and more or less everted rim, their morphometric attributes varying from 21 to 24 cm in MD, 26 to 34 cm in MaD, 25 to 37 cm in height, 15 to 23 cm in HMD, and finally, 0.7 to 1 cm in T. One of the specimens is decorated with a horizontal band of twisted roulette impression on the shoulder under- and overlined by two parallel grooved lines; another has extensive twisted roulette impression on the body overlined on the shoulder by two horizontal and parallel grooved lines, with, in addition, four equidistant appliqué buttons for both remaining cases. And finally, (6) six specimens of necked to long-necked storage jar with thickened everted rim, measuring 24 to 29 cm in MD, 34 to 40 cm in MaD, 44 to 45 cm in height, 6 to 11 cm in NH, 27 to 34 cm HMD, and 1.2 to 1.8 cm in T. As far as decoration is concerned, three of the jars have a horizontal band of twisted roulette impression on the shoulder, delineated with two or three parallel grooved lines; two others are decorated with extensive twisted roulette impression on the body overlined on the shoulder by two horizontal and parallel lines; with the last specimen comprising extensive twisted roulette impression on the body overlined on the shoulder by a horizontal chevron band and a small, shallow depression line.

Cluster 5 in the W-NW consists of five wood and reeds houses and a small 4.5-m-in-diameter goat enclosure (enclosure VIII), located at a relatively central position. The recorded features are distributed into two units; the southern with features 16, 17, and 18, and the northern with features 19 and 20 (fig. 16). In the southern unit, the barn (feature 16) is located in the inner part of the village at 9 m S of the goat enclosure; it is a 7-m-in-diameter feature, built with two roof-supporting poles and surrounded by a fence. Habitation house 17 is located approximately 15 m W of barn 16; it is 8-m-diameter feature, built with four central poles, with an adjunct fenced area on its southern side. It comprises an elaborate hearth and a large bed, with the domestic gear consisting of two enamelwares and two clay vessels. One of the vessels is a globular pot with slightly constricted neck and everted rim, 21 cm in diameter, 23 cm in MaD, 23 cm in height, 15 cm in HMD, and 0.8 cm in T, decorated with twisted roulette impression on the body overlined on the shoulder by two horizontal and parallel grooved lines; and the other, a necked storage jar with everted, thickened rim, its decoration similar to that of the previous specimen, and measuring 27 cm in MD, 41 cm in MaD, 50 cm in height, 8 cm in NH, 26 cm in HMD, and 1.2 cm in T. House 18, a "young-man'" feature with a small bed, is built with a single central pole and measures 5 m in diameter.

The northern unit comprises two houses set at 5 m from each other. The barn (feature 19), built with four supporting poles and measuring 9 m in diameter, is surrounded by a fence. The habitation house (feature 20) with a large bed, an elaborate hearth, and a grinding platform located a few meters N, is built with three supporting poles and measures 7.2 m in diameter. House's furniture consists of two enamelwares, four clay vessels, as well as two rubber shoes. The recorded pottery assemblage comprises two vessel shapes: a globular pot with slightly constricted neck and everted rim, 24 cm in MD, 29 cm in MaD, 29 cm in height, 16 cm in HMD, and 0.9 cm in T, decorated with twisted roulette impression on the body, overlined on the shoulder by two horizontal and parallel grooved lines, with, in addition, four equidistant appliqué buttons; and three specimens of necked storage jar with everted rim, decorated with extensive twisted roulette impression on the body overlined on the shoulder by two horizontal and parallel grooved lines, their morphometric attributes varying from 26 to 30 cm in MD, 40 to 42 cm in MaD, 48 to 54 cm in height, 6 to 8 cm in NH, 29 to 35 cm in HMD, and finally, 1.2 to 1.8 cm in T.

Cluster 6, situated in the N, includes four houses. Three of them set in a triangular arrangement are connected by a fence, while the fourth one is located approximately 15 m in the inner side of the settlement (fig. 16). Feature 21, at the southwestern end of the cluster, is a "young-man" house built with a single central pole, comprising a small bed and measuring 4.6 m in diameter. Feature 22, the main habitation house measuring 8 m in diameter, is found 6 m further N. It is built with four roof-supporting poles and comprises a large bed, an elaborate hearth, and a grinding platform; the house containers consist of two enamelwares. In addition, one pair of rubber shoes was found on the house floor. Feature 23, the second habitation house, is located 7 m E of the previous one; it is built with a single central pole, measures 5.5 m in diameter, and comprises a bed and a hearth, with, in addition, one enamelware and one piece of pottery. The barn (feature 24) is found 12 m S of habitation house 23; it is built with four roof-supporting poles and measures 8.3 m in diameter.

Cluster 7, also located to the N of the settlement, is a well-demarcated and fenced complex with two wood and reeds houses and a nine-poles storage platform, 33 m in length and 20 m in maximum width (fig. 16). The barn (feature 25) in the W is built with two roof-supporting poles and measures 6.8 m in diameter. The habitation house (feature 26) measures 5.6 m in diameter. It is built with three poles, comprises an elaborate hearth and a large bed, with house equipment consisting of eleven enamelwares and four clay vessels. A storage bin made of sun-dried clay was found in the house, set above a curvilinear clay bench. Two vessels shapes are represented in the recorded pottery assemblage: (1) a rounded base hemispheric pot with slightly constricted neck, everted rim and two handles, 21 cm in MD, 26 cm in MaD, 29 cm in height, 20 cm in HMD, and finally, 1.1 cm in T, decorated with extensive twisted roulette impression on the body overlined on the shoulder by two horizontal and parallel grooved lines; (2) three specimens of globular pot with slightly constricted necks and everted rims, with their morphometric attributes varying from 18 to 24 cm in MD, 21 to 29 cm in MaD, 20 to 28 cm in height, 14 to 20 cm in HMD, and finally, 0.8 to 1 cm in T. They share similar decoration patterns although with some variations. Two of the potteries are decorated with extensive twisted roulette impression on the body overlined on the shoulder by two horizontal and parallel grooved lines, with, in addition, three equidistant pairs of appliqué buttons on the shoulder for the third specimen.

Cluster 8 is located in the NE of the settlement. It is stretched on 62 m NW-SE and comprises two units with three wood and reeds houses each (fig. 16), with, in addition, two large trees part of the cluster's space. Unit 1, at the western end of the cluster, consists of houses 27, 28, and 29, set at 5 m from one to next. Barn 27 at one end measures 8.3 m in diameter. It is built with four roof-supporting poles and comprises an enamel basin used for livestock watering. The main habitation house (feature 28) is located at the center of the unit; built with two supporting poles, it measures 7.2 m in diameter and comprises a large bed, an elaborate hearth, and a storage bin made in sun-dried clay, with house equipment consisting of three enamelwares and four clay vessels. The recorded pottery is divided into three vessels shapes: (1) a footed bowl decorated with extensive twisted roulette impression on the body, 14 cm in maximum and MD, 9 cm in foot base diameter, 11 cm in height, 3 cm in foot height, and finally, 0.9 cm in T; (2) two specimens of globular pot with slightly constricted necks and everted rims, measuring 21 to 22 cm in MD, 26 to 29 cm in MaD, 30 to 31 cm in height, 17 to 19 cm in HMD, and 0.9 cm in T, and both decorated with twisted roulette impression on the body, overlined on the shoulder by two horizontal and parallel grooved lines with four equidistant pairs of appliqué buttons; and finally, (3) a necked storage jar with everted thickened rim, 27 cm in MD, 42 cm in MaD, 50 cm in height, 7 cm in NH, 25 cm in HMD, and 1.2 cm in T, decorated with twisted roulette impression on the body, overlined on the shoulder by three horizontal and parallel grooved lines. The second habitation house (feature 29) comprises a hearth and a bed but no vessels; it is built with two roof-supporting poles and measures 6.6 m in diameter. A storage platform built with twelve supporting poles and measuring 4 by 5.5 m connects unit 1 to unit 2.

Unit 2 consists of three houses (feature 30, 31, and 32), two small goat enclosures (enclosure XI and XII) measuring 5 to 6 m in MaD, and a chicken coop (fig. 16). In this case, the barn (feature 31) is located in the center of the unit; it is built with five supporting poles and measures 7.9 m in diameter. Habitation house 30 with an adjunct chicken coop, located 4 m NW, is a single-central-pole feature, measuring 5.9 m in diameter, with a large bed and an elaborate hearth, a tin container, one enamelware, and two clay vessels. And finally, habitation house 32, 7 m SE of the barn, is built with two central poles and measures 6.5 m in diameter. It comprises a bed, a hearth, a storage bin, and a grinding platform, with house equipment consisting of a single piece of pottery.

Cluster 9 is a N-S linear arrangement of six wood and reeds features stretched on 70 m and situated on the eastern side of the village. It has an adjunct fenced field measuring 30 m in length and 25 m in width (fig. 16). The recorded features are organized into two units, the northern one (unit 1) with two houses (features 33 and 34) and a six-poles storage platform and the southern with four houses (feature 35, 36, 37, and 38), one chicken coop and one four-poles storage platform.

Barn 33, belonging to unit 1, is located at the northern end of the cluster; it is built with four roof-supporting poles, measures 7.6 m in diameter, and comprises an elaborate hearth. This house is thus used as a kitchen as well as a barn. Habitation house 34, with an adjunct storage platform, connected to the barn by a fence, is found 5 m S; it is built with a single central pole, comprises a large bed but no hearth, and measures 5.9 m in diameter. The goat enclosure IX, measuring 7 m in MaD and located some 25 m W in the inner side of the settlement, probably belongs to cluster 9 inhabitants.

Habitation house 35, with its adjunct chicken coop located at the center of the cluster, is the northernmost feature of unit 2. It is built with a single central pole, comprises an elaborate hearth and a large bed, with a single piece of pottery. The recorded clay vessel is a globular pot with slightly constricted neck and everted rim, decorated with extensive twisted roulette impression on the body overlined on the shoulder by two horizontal and parallel lines, measuring 21 cm in MD, 23 cm in MaD, 25 cm in height, 17 cm in HMD, and finally, 0.8 cm in T. Feature 36 is a rectangular discussion house built with wood and reeds, measuring 5 m in length and 2.5 m in width. It is almost attached to house 35 being located 1 to 1.5 m SW. The barn (feature 37) is found at 6 m S of the discussion house, built with four roof-supporting poles and measuring 8.6 m in diameter. And finally, feature 38, the second habitation house of unit 2, is set at 6 m S of the barn. It is built with two roof-supporting poles, measures 6.7 m in diameter, and is surrounded by a fence with an adjunct storage platform. It comprises a large bed, an elaborate hearth, and wooden shelves in which two enamelwares and seven clay vessels have been found.

Three morphological categories are represented in the recorded vessels assemblage: (1) three specimens of globular pot with slightly constricted necks and everted rims, measuring 21 to 24 cm in MD, 28 to 30 cm in MaD, 30 to 37 cm in height, 17 to 19 cm in HMD, and 0.8 to 1 cm in T. Each globular pot has a specific decoration pattern: one is decorated with a horizontal band of twisted roulette impression on the shoulder, under- and overlined by two parallel grooved lines; the second has an almost similar decoration with only one overlining horizontal grooved line. And finally, the third has extensive twisted roulette impression on the body overlined on the shoulder by two horizontal and parallel grooved lines, with, in addition, four equidistant appliqué buttons; (2) a globular storage jar, 29 cm in MD, 35 cm in MaD, 36 cm in height, 22 cm in HMD, and 1.5 cm in T, decorated with extensive twisted roulette impression on the body overlined on the shoulder by two horizontal and parallel grooved lines with four equidistant pairs of appliqué buttons; and finally, (3) three specimens of necked storage jar with everted thickened rim, their morphometric attributes varying from 25 to 27 cm in MD, 33 to 40 cm in MaD, 45 to 50 cm in height, 7 to 9 cm in NH, 26 to 30 cm in HMD, and

1.4 to 1.6 cm in T. Two specimens are decorated with a horizontal band of twisted roulette impression on the shoulder, under- and overlined by two parallel grooved lines; and the remaining one with extensive twisted roulette impression on the body overlined on the shoulder by three horizontal and parallel grooved lines.

Cluster 10, organized into three clearly distinct units with two wood and reeds houses each, is located in the S and SE of the settlement, arranged in a triangular pattern at 20 m from each other (fig. 16). Unit 1 in the SE consists of features 40 and 41, set at 8 m from each other and connected by a fence. Both are habitation houses, built with two roof-supporting poles, each comprising a large bed and an elaborate hearth, measure, respectively, 6.9 and 6.4 m in diameter. The equipment of house 40 consists of a single enamelware while that of house 41 is more diversified, with a grindstone on a raised platform, eight enamelwares and seven clay vessels. Three vessel shapes are represented in the recorded sample: (1) three specimens of globular pot with slightly constricted necks and everted rims, measuring 21 to 23 cm in MD, 27 to 30 cm in MaD, 29 to 30 cm in height, 17 to 19 cm in HMD, and 1 cm in T, decorated in one case with extensive twisted roulette impression on the body overlined on the shoulder by two horizontal and parallel grooved lines, with, in addition, four equidistant appliqué buttons for the remaining two specimens; (2) two specimens of short-necked, globular pots, both decorated with a horizontal band of twisted roulette impression on the shoulder under- and overlined by two parallel grooved lines, measuring 11 to 12 cm in MD, 25 to 29 cm in MaD, 32 to 35 cm in height, 5 to 6 cm in NH, 16 to 20 cm in HMD, and finally, 0.8 to 1.3 cm in T; and (3) two specimens of necked to long-necked storage jars with everted rims, one decorated with a horizontal band of twisted roulette on the shoulder under- and overlined by parallel grooved lines, and measuring 25 cm in MD, 37 cm in MaD, 45 cm in height, 6 cm in NH, 26 cm in HMD, and 1.5 cm in T; and the other, 29 cm in MD, 41 cm in MaD, 65 cm in height, 10 cm in NH, 37 cm in HMD, and 1.3 cm in T, decorated with extensive twisted roulette impression on the body overlined on the shoulder by two horizontal and parallel grooved lines.

Unit 2 is located in the inner side of the settlement and consists of two houses set at 5 m from each other, a 4 by 3 m storage platform with twelve supporting poles, a goat enclosure (enclosure X) measuring 6 m in MaD, and a fenced garden 10 m in length and 5 m in width. Feature 42, a young man habitation house, is built with a single central pole, measures 5.2 m in diameter, and comprises a small bed with a mosquito-net. The barn (feature 43) located a few meters NW, is built with four roof-supporting poles and measures 8.1 m in diameter.

Unit 3 is a well-delineated and fenced complex 30 m in length and 15 m in width. The houses are located 5 m from each other; the barn (feature 44), built with two roof-supporting poles, measures 6.5 m in diameter, and the habitation house (feature 45), also built with two roof-supporting poles, measures 7.4 m in diameter, and comprises an elaborate hearth, a large bed, and a grindstone set on a raised platform, with the house domestic gear consisting of four clay vessels.

Despite a relative decrease of the village herds as suggested by reduced cattle enclosures, livestock husbandry still appears to be predominant in the patterning of the Ngada I settlement. Communal features like discussion houses are located in the same part of the village, probably within the village headman's household complex.

Ngada II

Ngada II is located a few hundred meters W of the previous settlement. The village is subcircular in shape, extending over 1.2 hectares, stretched on 120 m in its E-W axis and 100 m in the N-S one. Ngada II comprises forty-three houses distributed into eight household clusters, three circular central cattle corrals, with two of them out of use, and finally, a single sheep/goat enclosure (tables 22 and 23, fig. 17). Cattle enclosures appear clearly as communal features; both worn-out specimens measure 20 and 25 m in diameter, while that still in use, and much larger in size, is extended over 1600 square meters (50 × 36 m).

Household cluster 1 is located in the S-SW, on the left side of the village entrance (fig. 17); it includes seven houses distributed into three units stretched over 50 m. Unit 1, located at the southeastern end of the cluster, consists of three houses, two devoted to habitation (features 1 and 2) and one barn/cattle house (feature 3). House 1 measures 6.4 m in diameter; it is built with wood and straw with two roof-supporting poles and includes an elaborate hearth and a bed. Domestic equipment consists of an enamelware, a petrol lamp, and a single clay vessel. The single recorded pottery is a relatively large necked jar used for storage, measuring 25 cm in MD, 29 cm in MaD, 45 cm in TH, 5 cm in NH, 22 cm in HMD, and finally 1 cm in T. It is decorated on the shoulder with a horizontal band of twisted roulette impression under- and overlined by grooved lines. House 2 is

Table 22: Ngada II household clusters

Cluster number	Number of units	Habitation houses	Livestock houses	Storage platforms	Others
1	3	4	2	2	—
2	1	3	1	2	1
3	1	3	1	2	1
4	2	3	2	1	1
5	1	4	1	2	—
6	2	3	2	1	—
7	2	3	1	1	1
8	3	6	2	2	1
Total	15	29	12	13	5

Table 23: Ngada II general distribution of pottery

Cluster number	Number of features	Service vessels	Cooking vessels	Storage vessels	Unknown	Total
1	8	—	4	7	—	11
2	7	2	8	7	—	17
3	7	—	2	—	—	2
4	7	—	3	6	—	9
5	7	—	6	12	—	18
6	6	—	1	5	—	6
7	6	—	3	8	—	11
8	11	—	7	18	—	25
Total	59	2	36	64	—	99

found approximately 12 m S of the previous one. It is built in mud-brick with four central poles, measures 7.5 m in diameter and comprises an elaborate hearth and a large bed. The recorded domestic equipment is similar to that of the previous house, with a petrol lamp, an enamel basin, and a large clay vessel. The pottery, a necked storage jar, measuring 28 cm in MD, 38 cm in MaD, 42 cm in TH, 10 cm in NH, 24 cm in HMD, and finally, 1 cm in T, is decorated with extensive twisted roulette impression on the body overlined on the shoulder by three parallel and horizontal grooved lines. House 3 is devoted to cattle. Located some 8 m NW of feature 2, it is a wood and straw house with four central poles, measuring 7.2 m in diameter.

Unit 2 comprises houses 4 and 5 both built with wood and straw with a six-poles storage platform 4 m long and 2 m wide (fig. 17). The former is a two-central-poles habitation feature with an elaborate hearth and a large bed measures 7.2 m in diameter, the latter is an 8-m-diameter barn and cattle house with four roof-supporting poles. The domestic gear found in house 4 consists of four enamel basins and eight clay vessels partitioned into four cooking and four storage wares. Two morphological classes are represented among the cooking vessels. The first-class consists of three specimens of slightly elongated, globular pot with more or less constricted neck, their morphometric attributes varying from 20 to 23 cm for MD, 27 to 31 cm for MaD, 29 to 35 cm in TH, 16 to 20 cm for the HMD, and finally, 0.8 to 1.1 cm in T. Each specimen has a specific pattern of decoration. Proceeding for the simplest to the more complex, there is one specimen decorated on the shoulder with a horizontal grooved line complemented by a band of twisted roulette impression; the second and third specimens share similar decorations, with extensive twisted roulette impression on the body, overlined on the shoulder by two parallel and horizontal grooved lines for both, with, in addition, four pairs of appliqué buttons for the third. The second morphological class comprises a single specimen, a rounded-base handled hemispherical pot with slightly constricted neck.

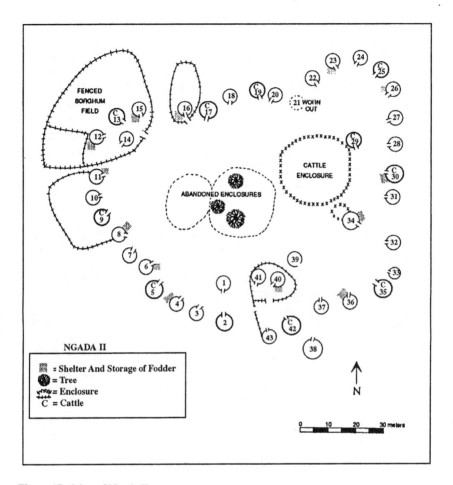

Figure 17: Map of Ngada II

It is decorated with extensive twisted roulette impression on the body overlined on the shoulder by two parallel and horizontal grooved lines, with, in addition, two appliqué buttons, and measures 20 cm in MD, 24 cm in MaD, 28 cm in TH, 10 cm in HMD, and finally, 0.8 cm in T. All the storage vessels belong to a single morphological class, that of necked jar. Their morphometric attributes range from 27 to 30 cm in MD, 37 to 43 cm in MaD, 45 to 65 cm in TH, 5 to 17 cm in NH, 28 to 42 cm in the HMD, and finally, 1.2 to 1.8 cm in T. Three of the specimens have similar decorations, with extensive twisted roulette impression on the body, overlined on the shoulder by two or three parallel and horizontal grooved lines, with, in addition, four pairs of equidistant appliqué buttons for the third jar. The remaining specimen is plain, with its decoration consisting of two symmetric appliqué buttons and four equidistant lugs on the shoulder.

Unit 3, at the northwestern edge of the cluster, also consists of two wood and straw features, houses 6 and 7, with an adjunct, four-poles 2 × 2 m storage platform (fig. 17). The habitation house (feature 6), with its standard elaborate hearth and extensive bed, is built with two roof-supporting poles and measures 6.9 m in diameter. The recorded domestic equipment comprises a single clay vessel, a globular, necked storage jar, decorated on the shoulder with a horizontal band of twisted roulette impression, with three superimposed parallel, grooved lines and three equidistant sets of four appliqué buttons. Its morphometric attributes vary from 27 cm for MD, 40 cm for MaD, 48 cm for TH, 8 cm for NH, 32 cm for the HMD, to 1.3 cm in T. Feature 7, the barn/cattle house, measures 7.2 m in diameter and is built with four roof-supporting poles.

Cluster 2 is situated on the western side of the settlement; it is spread on 30 m, comprises four wood and straw houses, two storage platforms, as well as a fenced maize field measuring 30 m in length and 15 m in width (fig. 17). Three of the recorded houses, 8, 10, and 11, are devoted to habitation, each of them comprising a more or less elaborate hearth and an extended bed. Feature 8, located at the southern edge of the household cluster with an adjunct 2 × 2 m, four-poles storage platform, is built with two roof-supporting poles and measures 6.3 m in diameter. Three rubber shoes were found on the house floor, and the recorded domestic equipment consists of one enamel basin and nine clay vessels. The pottery material is divided into two functional categories, with five cooking and four storage vessels. The cooking pots belong to two morphological classes. The first one has a single specimen of rounded base, globular, short-necked hemispheric pot with everted rim. It is decorated with extensive twisted roulette impression on the body overlined by two horizontal and parallel grooved lines on the shoulder, and measures 21 cm in MD, 26 cm in MaD, 29 cm in TH, 5 cm in NH, 18 cm in HMD, to 0.9 cm in T. The second morphological class comprises four specimens of slightly globular pot with constricted necks and everted rims, their size attributes ranging from 16 to 21 cm in MD, 22 to 25 cm in MaD, 24 to 28 cm in TH, 13 to 17 cm in the HMD, and finally, 0.9 to 1.1 cm in T. Their decoration shares most of the basic pattern consisting of extensive twisted roulette impression on the body, overlined on the shoulder by two horizontal and parallel grooved lines in three cases, complemented by three equidistant appliqué buttons on the shoulder for one specimen, with, in addition, a double chevron line made with carved roulette in the remaining case. The category of storage vessels is homogenous, with all four specimens being necked jars. Three of them are decorated with a horizontal band of twisted roulette impression, under- and overlined by two parallel grooved lines on the shoulder, the remaining one having extensive twisted roulette impression on the body overlined on the shoulder by two horizontal and parallel grooved lines. Their morphometric attributes range from 22 to 27 cm in MD, 32 to 38 cm in MaD, 40 to 47 cm in TH, 5 to 8 cm in NH, 25 to 29 cm in the HMD, to 1.1 to 1.2 cm in T.

House 10 is also built with two roof-supporting poles and measures 7.1 m in diameter. House 11, with almost similar technical characteristics even if slightly larger 7.3 m in diameter, is located approximately 4 m N of the previous one and has an adjunct eight-poles 3 × 2 m storage platform. The domestic gear consists of eight clay vessels, distributed into three slightly globular cooking pots with everted rims and slightly constricted necks, one hole-mouth pot, one plate, and three necked storage jars. The slightly globular cooking pots measure 16 to 21 cm in MD, 19 to 29 cm in MaD, 19 to 25 cm in TH, 13 to 17 cm in the HMD, and finally, 0.8 to 1 cm in T. They all share the same basic pattern of decoration, with extensive twisted roulette impression on the body, overlined on the shoulder, in one case, by two horizontal and parallel grooved lines, with, in addition, four equidistant appliqué buttons for both remaining specimens. The hole-mouth vessel is a small-size food-serving ware, measuring 15 cm in diameter and height, with an 0.8-cm-thick wall. Its decoration consists of extensive twisted roulette impression on the body, overlined a few centimeters below the rim by two parallel and horizontal grooved lines. The plate used for food-serving is decorated with twisted roulette impression on the rim. It measures 38 cm in diameter, 6 cm in TH, and finally, 1.6 cm in T. The recorded necked jars present quite similar morphometric attributes, with MD ranging from 23 to 28 cm, MaD from 32 to 41 cm, TH from 42 to 48 cm, NH from 3 to 7 cm, HMD from 26 to 28 cm, and finally, T from 1.1 to 1.2 cm. Each, however, has a specific decoration. The simplest case consists of a horizontal band of twisted roulette impression on the shoulder with three superimposed parallel, grooved lines; the next specimen in terms of decoration elaboration, comprises a horizontal band of twisted roulette impression, delimited at the bottom and top by two parallel grooved lines with, in addition, four equidistant pairs of appliqué buttons. The third specimen has extensive twisted roulette impression on the body overlined on the shoulder by two horizontal and parallel grooved lines. The fourth feature of the cluster, house 9, is a barn/cattle house, built with four roof-supporting poles and measuring 6.9 m in diameter.

Cluster 3 is a clearly delineated and fenced spatial unit located in the northwestern part of the settlement (fig. 17). The fenced space measures 55 m in length NE-SE and 35 m in width NW-SE and comprises four houses built with wood and straw, two storage platforms, and sorghum fields. There are three habitation houses, features 12, 14, and 15. The first one, with an adjunct 4 × 2 m, six-poles storage platform, is built with two central poles, measures 6.8 m in diameter and has an elaborate hearth and a large bed; the domestic equipment consists of two damaged and probably out of use enamel basins. The second (house 14) is located some 7.5 m E of the previous one; it is a small, 4.4 m in diameter young man's house, built with a single central pole and a small bed. The third (house 15) with a nine-poles, 3 × 3 m storage platform, is located some 8 m N of the young man's house; it is built with two roof-supporting poles, measures 5.4 m in diameter, and comprises a large bed and an elaborate hearth. The recorded domestic kit consists of three enamelwares and two clay vessels. Both clay vessels are cooking pots belonging to two distinct morphological classes. One is a short-necked rounded base globular pot with everted rim and two handles, 24 cm in MD, 28 cm in MaD, 31 cm in TH, 3 cm in NH, 22 cm in HMD, and finally 1.2 cm in T. It is decorated with extensive twisted roulette impression on the body overlined on the shoulder by two horizontal and parallel grooved lines complemented by two symmetric pairs of appliqué buttons. The other specimen is a slightly globular pot with constricted neck and everted rim, decorated with extensive twisted roulette impression on the body overlined on the shoulder by two horizontal and parallel grooved lines, measuring 22 cm in MD, 28 cm in MaD, 30 cm in TH, 19 cm in HMD, and finally, 1.1 cm in T. The barn/cattle house (feature 13) is at equal distance from houses 12 and 15; it is built with two roof-supporting poles and measures 6.2 m in diameter. Two relatively large enamel basin probably used for watering livestock were found on the house floor.

Household cluster 4 is located in the northern side of the village. It is stretched on 40 m W-E and comprises six houses, with one of them abandoned and worn-out (feature 21) having been reduced to a simple, shallow 4.5-m-in-diameter circle on the ground, one storage platform, and a fenced field 18 m long and 10 m wide (fig. 17). The recorded built facilities are divided into two units. Unit 1 is the western one with features 16 and 17; the former is a 6.4-m-in-diameter wood and straw house with an adjunct 2 × 2 m, nine-poles storage platform. It is built with two central poles and possesses an elaborate hearth and a large bed. One male rubber shoe was found on the house floor, with the recorded domestic equipment divided into five enamelwares and a single cooking clay vessel. The pottery, a slightly globular short-necked pot with everted rim, is decorated with extensive twisted roulette impression on the body, overlined on the shoulder by three horizontal and parallel grooved lines with, in addition, four equidistant appliqué buttons. It measures 23 cm in MD, 28 cm in MaD, 28 cm in TH, 3 cm in NH, 18 cm in height of the MaD, and finally, 1 cm in T. The latter feature, house 17, is a wood and straw barn/cattle house located some 3 to 4 m E of the previous one beyond the fence. It is also built with two central poles and measures 6.6 m in diameter.

Unit 2 comprises three wood and straw houses. Feature 18 is clearly a young man's house. It measures 6 m in diameter and is built with two roof-supporting poles. It comprises a small bed, with the house equipment reduced to a single enamelware. The barn/livestock house is situated at the middle of the subcluster; it is a relatively large feature built with four roof-supporting poles and measuring 8.9 m in diameter. Habitation house 20 is situated at the eastern end of the unit, built with four roof-supporting poles and measuring 7.7 m in diameter. House installations comprise an elaborate hearth and a large bed, while the domestic kit consists of a sample of eight clay vessels. The pottery material can be partitioned into two functional categories, with two cooking and six storage wares. There are two morphological classes represented among the cooking wares: one is a short-necked, rounded base, hemispherical handled pot, decorated with extensive twisted roulette impression on the body, overlined on the shoulder by two horizontal and parallel grooved lines, complemented by eight slightly elongated appliqué buttons. The specimen measures 21 cm in MD, 25 cm in MaD, 30 cm in TH, 3 cm in NH, 18 in HMD, and finally, 0.9 cm in T; the other is a slightly globular short-necked pot with everted rim, measuring 22 cm in MD, 26 cm in MaD, 28 cm in TH, 3 cm in NH, 21 cm in HMD, and finally, 1.1 cm in T. It is decorated with extensive twisted roulette impression on the body overlined on the shoulder by two horizontal and parallel grooved lines. All the recorded storage wares are necked jars; they share, with minor variations, a similar pattern of decoration which consists of a horizontal band of twisted roulette impression, delimited by two parallel grooved lines in four cases out of six, with, in addition, four equidistant pairs of appliqué buttons in one case and three superimposed parallel grooved lines in another one. Their morphometric attributes vary from 23 to 30 cm in MD, 31 to 44 cm in MaD, 37 to 49 cm for TH, 5 to 9 cm for NH, 24 to 34 cm for HMD, and finally, 1.1 to 1.3 cm in T.

Cluster 5 is located in the NE of the settlement (fig. 17). It is comprised of four wood and straw houses disposed in an in-curved arrangement, with distance from one feature to the next varying from a maximum of 6.7 m (house 22 to 23) to a minimum of 3.8 m (house 24 to 25). Four of the features are habitation houses; the fifth one is a barn/livestock construction. The livestock house (feature 25) is built with six central supporting poles and measures 10.5 m in diameter; it is the largest house of the whole site.

House 22, at the western end of the house cluster, measures 6 m in diameter, is built with a single central pole and comprises a small bed, with domestic equipment consisting of four clay vessels. The pottery material, divided into two functional categories, is distributed into three morphological classes. There is one necked storage jar, decorated on the shoulder with a horizontal band of twisted roulette impression, under- and overlined by parallel grooved lines, measuring 27 cm in MD, 39 cm in MaD, 52 cm in TH, 7 cm in NH, 30 cm in HMD, and finally, 1.1 cm in T. The sample of three cooking pots is divided into one rounded base slightly necked hemispheric pot with two handles, and two slightly globular pots, with constricted mouth or short neck. The rounded base specimen measures 21 cm in MD, 27 cm in MaD, 32 cm in TH, 5 cm in NH, 20 cm in HMD, and finally, 0.8 cm in T. Its decoration consists of extensive twisted roulette impression on the body overlined on the shoulder by two parallel and horizontal grooved lines with, in addition, two symmetric pairs of appliqué buttons. Even if they have similar general characteristics, both specimens of slightly globular pots present some important differences. One specimen measures 22 cm in MD, 31 cm in MaD, 34 cm in TH, 4 cm in NH, 20 cm in HMD, and finally 1 cm in T, and is decorated on the shoulder with a horizontal band of twisted roulette impression delimited at the bottom and top by two parallel grooved lines. The other is decorated with extensive twisted roulette impression on the body overlined on the shoulder by two horizontal and parallel grooved lines, its morphometric attributes varying from 20 cm for MD, 23 cm for MaD, 26 cm for TH, 15 cm for HMD, to 0.8 cm for T.

House 23, a few meters east of the previous one, measures 8.2 m in diameter. It is built with four roof-supporting poles and comprises an elaborate hearth and large bed. A worn-out metal container and a single man's rubber shoe were found on the house floor. Feature 23 is associated with a 2.5 × 3 m, nine-poles storage platform. House 24 is also built with four roof-supporting poles, and, similarly, is 8.2 m in diameter. As a habitation house, it comprises an elaborate hearth and a large bed, with domestic equipment consisting of five clay vessels, arranged on wooden shelves along the wall, and one plastic container. All the recorded vessels are necked storage jars; their morphometric attributes vary from 26 to 27 cm in MD, 34 to 39 cm in MaD, 43 to 45 cm in TH,6 to 9 cm in NH, 24 to 26 cm in HMD, and finally 1.1 to 1.4 cm in T. There is slightly more variation in decoration, which, nonetheless, shares some basic pattern. It is confined to the vessel shoulder and consists of a horizontal band of twisted roulette impression, delimited at the bottom and top by two parallel grooved lines in two cases, with, in addition, four or five elongated appliqué buttons in two cases, and four pairs of equidistant appliqué buttons in the remaining one.

Finally, feature 26, situated at the eastern end of the household cluster, appears to be the household head house. It is built with two roof-supporting poles, measures 7.4 m in diameter, contains an elaborate hearth, an extended bed, a large sample of nine clay vessels carefully arranged on wooden shelves, a raised grinding installation, and a saddle. It has an adjunct 2 × 1 m, six-poles storage platform. The recorded pottery assemblage comprises two sets of wares, four used for cooking and five for storage. The cooking vessels are divided into two morphological classes: one short-necked, globular pot decorated with a horizontal band of twisted roulette impression on the shoulder, under- and overlined by two parallel grooved lines, measuring 15 cm in MD, 28 cm in MaD, 38 cm in TH, 5 cm in NH, 20 cm in HMD, and finally, 1.1 cm in T. Three specimens are slightly globular pots with constricted neck, with morphometric attributes varying from 17 to 22 cm for MD, 19 to 26 cm for MaD, 20 to 27 cm for TH, 13 to 17 cm for HMD, and finally, 0.7 to 0.9 cm for T. They share similar patterns of decoration, with extensive twisted roulette impression on the body overlined on the shoulder by two horizontal and parallel grooved lines for the smaller specimen, with, in addition, four equidistant appliqué buttons for both remaining larger ones. All the five storage vessels are short to long-necked jars; they will be described here according to their decoration. One specimen, a water jar, is, strictly speaking, plain. It has nonetheless an appliqué cordon on the shoulder with four equidistant lugs, and measures 29 cm in MD, 38 cm in MaD, 50 cm in TH, 17 cm in NH, 26 cm in HMD, and finally, 1.4 cm in T. Two specimens share a similar decoration. It consists of a horizontal band of twisted roulette impression on the shoulder, under- and overlined by two parallel grooved lines. Their morphometric attributes vary from 25 to 26 cm in MD, 33 to 40 cm in MaD, 40 to 50 cm in TH, 5 to 7 cm in NH, 26 cm in HMD, and finally, 1 to 1.3 cm in T. There is one specimen with decoration comparable to that of both specimens just described above, but with, in addition, four equidistant appliqué buttons; it measures 26 cm in MD, 38 cm in MaD, 45 cm in TH, 7 cm in NH, 24 cm in HMD, and finally, 1.3 cm in T. And finally, there is one case with extensive twisted roulette impression on the body, overlined on the shoulder by two horizontal and parallel grooved lines complemented with four equidistant pairs of appliqué buttons; it measures 24 cm in MD, 36 cm in MaD, 40 cm in TH, 5 cm in NH, 24 cm in HMD, and finally, 1.1 cm in T.

Cluster 6, situated to the E of the site, consists of five features stretched on 40 m N-S, with one of the houses located in the inner space of the village (fig. 17). All the recorded features are built with wood and reeds. Feature 27, at the northernmost end of the house cluster, is a habitation house measuring 5.9 m in diameter, built with two roof-supporting poles, comprising an elaborate hearth and a large bed, with domestic equipment reduced to a single clay vessel. The recorded pottery is a storage jar decorated with a horizontal band of twisted roulette impression on the shoulder delimited at the bottom and top by two parallel grooved lines, measuring 24 cm in MD, 39 cm in MaD, 49 cm in TH, 5 cm in NH, 30 cm in HMD, and finally, 1.2 cm in T.

Feature 28, some 5 m S, is also a habitation house with an elaborate hearth, a large bed, five clay vessels, and one enamelware. It is built with two roof-supporting poles and measures 6.8 m in diameter. The pottery material is subdivided into two cooking and three storage vessels. One of the cooking vessels is a slightly globular pot with slightly constricted mouth, decorated with extensive twisted roulette impression on the body overlined on the shoulder with two horizontal and parallel grooved lines complemented by four equidistant appliqué buttons, and measuring 19 cm in MD, 22 cm in MaD, 22 cm in TH, 15 cm in HMD, and finally, 1 cm in T. The other is a necked rounded base hemispheric pot, decorated on the shoulder and neck base by three horizontal grooved lines supporting eight equidistant panels of four short vertical grooved lines each, and measuring 14 cm in MD, 31 cm in MaD, 39 cm in TH, 6 cm in NH, 18 cm in HMD, and finally, 0.8 cm in T. Storage vessels are divided into one necked and two long-necked jars. The necked specimen measures 25 cm in MD, 36 cm in MaD, 49 cm in TH, 7 cm in NH, 30 cm in HMD, and finally, 1.1 cm in T. It is decorated on the shoulder by a horizontal band of twisted roulette impression, under- and overlined by two grooved lines. Both long-necked jars are decorated with extensive twisted roulette impression on the body overlined on the shoulder by two or three horizontal and parallel grooved lines. They measure 29 to 30 cm in MD, 45 to 46 cm in MaD, 55 to 60 cm in TH, 10 cm in NH, 39 to 40 cm in HMD, and finally, 1.4 to 1.5 cm in T.

Features 29 and 30 are barn/livestock houses. Both are built with four roof-supporting poles, and measure, respectively, 8.9 and 8.3 m in diameter. Livestock house 30 is associated with a 3 × 3 m, nine-supporting-poles storage platform. Feature 31, the southernmost of the cluster is a habitation house, with an elaborate hearth and a large bed, but devoid of any domestic equipment. It is a 6.1-m-in-diameter house, built with two roof-supporting poles.

Cluster 7 is located in the E-SE of the settlement. It comprises four houses built with wood and reeds, one storage platform, and a sheep/goat enclosure. Three of the features are situated in the main circle of the site houses, the remaining one being in the inner side. Features 32, 33 and 34 are habitation houses. House 32 measures 8.4 m in diameter, comprises an elaborate hearth and a large bed, and is built with four roof-supporting poles. The domestic kit consists of eight clay vessels and two enamel basins. In addition, a petrol lamp and a single rubber shoe were found on the house floor. The recorded pottery assemblage comprises three cooking and five storage vessels. One cooking ware is a necked globular and rounded base pot decorated on the shoulder with a horizontal band of twisted roulette impression delimited at the bottom and top by a grooved line, measuring 15 cm in MD, 28 cm in MaD, 36 cm in TH, 6 cm in NH, 19 cm in HMD, and 1 cm in T. The second is a slightly globular pot with slightly constricted mouth, 24 cm in MD, 29 cm in MaD, 29 cm in TH, 20 cm in HMD, and finally, 0.9 cm in T, decorated with extensive twisted roulette impression on the body overlined on the shoulder by two horizontal and parallel grooved lines complemented by four equidistant appliqué buttons. And the third, 21 cm in MD, 26 cm in MaD, 27 cm in TH, 3 cm in NH, 20 cm in HMD, and finally 1 cm in T, is a short-necked rounded base hemispheric handled pot, with its decoration similar to that of the previous specimen, the minor difference being in the number of appliqué buttons, in this case two instead of four. All the storage wares are necked jars. Their morphometric attributes vary within a very narrow range, with 23 to 26 cm for MD, 35 to 39 cm for MaD, 40 to 48 cm for TH, 7 to 9 cm for NH, 23 to 31 cm for HMD, and finally 1.1 to 1.4 cm in T. Three of the jars are decorated on the shoulder with a horizontal band of twisted roulette impression delimited at the bottom and top by parallel grooved lines. Another specimen has its basic decoration pattern similar to that just described above, with, in addition, four equidistant pairs of appliqué buttons. And finally, the last one is decorated with extensive twisted roulette impression on the body overlined on the shoulder by two horizontal and parallel grooved lines.

House 34, located some 13 m NW of the previous one, is associated with a 5 × 3 m, nine-poles storage platform and a sheep/goat enclosure measuring 3.8 m in diameter. It is built with four roof-supporting poles, measures 8.5 m in diameter, and comprises an elaborate hearth and a large bed. The recorded domestic equipment consists of three necked storage jars, each with a specific decoration. The first specimen, measuring 25 cm in MD, 40 cm in MaD, 50 cm in TH, 7 cm in NH, 30 cm in HMD, and finally 1 cm in T, is decorated on the shoulder with a horizontal band of twisted roulette impression delimited by parallel grooved lines. The second one is decorated on the shoulder with a horizontal band of twisted roulette impression with three superimposed grooved lines, complemented by four equidistant appliqué buttons; it measures 26 cm in MD, 38 cm in MaD, 44 cm in TH, 10 cm in NH, 26 cm in HMD, and finally 1.3 cm in T. Finally, the third, 29 cm in MD, 41 cm in MaD, 50 cm in TH, 10 cm in NH, 30 cm in HMD, and 1.2 cm in

T, is decorated with extensive twisted roulette impression on the body overlined on the shoulder by two horizontal and parallel grooved lines.

Feature 33, located some 7 m S of house 32, is an adolescent's house; it is built with a single central pole, measures 4.2 m in diameter, and contains a small bed. Three rubber shoes were found on the house floor as well as an enamelware. The barn/livestock house 35 is located at the southwestern end of the house cluster, some 3.5 m from the adolescent's house. It is a relatively large feature measuring 9.1 m in diameter, built with four roof-supporting poles.

Cluster 8 is located in the southern part of the settlement; it is the Marabout [Muslim scholar] household and comprises eight wood and reeds houses distributed into three units spread over an area measuring some 60 m in diameter.

Unit 1, on the eastern part of the complex, comprises three habitation houses. House 36 is associated with a 4 × 4 m, eight-poles storage platform and measures 6.3 m in diameter. It is built with two central poles, contains an elaborate hearth as well as a large bed, with a large sample of eleven clay vessels carefully arranged on wooden shelves along the house wall. The pottery assemblage includes five cooking and six storage vessels. There are two morphological classes among the cooking wares. One consists of three slightly globular pots with constricted necks and everted rims; their morphometric attributes vary from 21 to 25 cm in MD, 27 to 31 cm in MaD, 27 to 31 cm in TH, 17 to 22 cm in HMD, to 0.8 to 1 cm in T. They are decorated with extensive twisted roulette impression on the body, overlined on the shoulder by two horizontal and parallel grooved lines for one of the specimens, with, in addition, four equidistant appliqué buttons for another specimen, and two single and two double symmetric appliqué buttons for the last one. The other morphological class comprises two specimens of rounded base, handled, hemispheric pots with constricted necks. They measure 19 to 22 cm in MD, 23 to 26 cm in MaD, 22 to 27 cm in TH, 16 to 19 cm in HMD, and finally, 1 to 1.2 cm in T. Their decoration consists of extensive twisted roulette impression on the body, overlined on the shoulder, in one case, by two horizontal and parallel grooved lines, and in the other, by three horizontal grooved lines complemented with two symmetric lugs. The storage jars are divided into one undetermined case (upper part broken) and one short- and four long-necked specimens. The undetermined specimen measures 21 cm in MD, 35 cm in MaD, 36 cm in TH, 27 cm in HMD, and finally, 2 cm in T; it is decorated with a horizontal band of twisted roulette impression on the shoulder delimited at the bottom and top by parallel grooved lines. The short-necked specimen, 24 cm in MD, 35 cm in MaD, 40 cm in TH, 4 cm in NH, 24 cm in HMD, and finally 0.9 cm in T, has a decoration pattern similar to that just described above. The four recorded long-necked jars have their morphometric attributes varying from 25 to 34 cm for MD, 40 to 55 cm for MaD, 48 to 65 cm for TH, 9 to 10.5 cm for NH, 23 to 30 cm for HMD, and 1 to 1.4 cm in T. Three specimens share the same decoration pattern, which consists of a horizontal band of twisted roulette impression on the shoulder delimited by two parallel grooved lines. The remaining one is almost plain; what can be considered as decoration comprises an appliqué cordon on the shoulder with short vertical incisions and four equidistant lugs.

House 37, 6 m W of the previous one, measures 6.9 m in diameter. It is built with two roof-supporting poles and comprises a hearth and a bed. House 39, 16 m NW, is smaller in size, measures 4.9 m in diameter, and is built with a single central pole. It nonetheless comprises a hearth and a bed as well as two clay vessels. Both vessels are necked storage jars. One, with an appliqué cordon on the shoulder complemented by four equidistant lugs and decorated with short vertical incised lines, measures 28 cm in MD, 39 cm in MaD, 47 cm in TH, 10 cm in NH, 27 cm in HMD, and finally 1.3 cm in T. The other, 26 cm in MD, 43 cm in MaD, 50 cm in TH, 6 cm in NH, 30 cm in HMD, and finally 1 cm in T, is decorated with a horizontal band of twisted roulette impression on the shoulder, delimited by parallel grooved lines and complemented by four equidistant pairs of appliqué buttons.

Unit 2 is located to the S of the cluster and comprises three features, one habitation and two barn/livestock houses. The habitation house is relatively small in size; it is built with a single central pole and measures 4.8 m in diameter. Both barn/livestock houses, features 38 and 42, have similar diameter of 8.8–8.9 m; both are built with four roof-supporting poles. Unit 3 is well-demarcated and fenced area extending over 20 by 15 m. Both habitation houses (features 40 and 41) comprise a hearth and a bed, and are the same size, measuring 7.9 m in diameter. They are built with four roof-supporting poles each. House 40 is associated with a 2 × 3 m, six-poles storage platform. Its domestic equipment consists of eight clay vessels, while a pair of rubber shoes has been found on the house floor.

The pottery assemblage from house 40 comprises two cooking pots and six storage jars. Both cooking pots have similar patterns of decoration, with extensive twisted roulette impression on the body overlined on the shoulder by two horizontal and parallel grooved lines, complemented, in one case, by two symmetric sets of three appliqué buttons, and in the other, by four equidistant appliqué buttons. One specimen is a rounded base, handled, hemispheric pot with slightly constricted neck and everted rim, 22 cm in MD, 27 cm in MaD, 31 cm in TH, 17 cm in HMD, and finally 0.9 cm in T. The other, a slightly globular, short-necked pot, measures 21 cm in MD, 28 cm in MaD, 30 cm in TH, 3 cm in NH, 16 cm in HMD, and finally, 0.8 cm in T. All the recorded storage vessels are necked jars; their morphometric attributes vary from 24 to 28 cm for MD, 40 to 44 cm for MaD, 42 to 56 cm for TH, 6 to 10.5 cm for NH, 20 to 30 cm for HMD, to 0.8 to 1.3 cm in T. Three patterns of decoration are attested among the six jars. One specimen is decorated with short, vertical, incised lines set on an appliqué cordon with four equidistant lugs at shoulder. Three jars are decorated with a horizontal band of twisted roulette impression on the shoulder delimited at the bottom and top by parallel grooved lines, complemented, for one of them, by three equidistant appliqué elongated vertical buttons. And finally, two specimens have extensive twisted roulette impression on the body overlined on the shoulder by two horizontal and parallel grooved lines.

Four clay vessels, all of them storage jars, and two enamelwares have been recorded from house 41. Two morphological classes are attested. One comprises a single specimen of a large necked jar, 32 cm in MD, 45 cm in MaD, 60 cm in TH, 7 cm on NH, 31 cm in height of MaD, and finally 1.4 cm in T, decorated with extensive twisted roulette impression on the body overlined on the shoulder by three horizontal and parallel grooved lines. The other consists of three specimens of necked, globular jars, with morphometric attributes varying from 28 to 29 cm in MD, 37 to 41 cm in MaD, 47 to 48 cm in TH, 4 to 7.5 cm in NH, 23 to 26 cm in HMD, to 1.2 to 1.6 cm in T. Two of the specimens are decorated with a horizontal band of twisted roulette impression on the shoulder delimited by two parallel grooved lines, and the remaining one with extensive twisted roulette impression on the body overlined on the shoulder by three horizontal and parallel grooved lines, complemented by four equidistant sets of three short, elongated, and vertical appliqué buttons.

In general, what can be called communal features, which in this case consists of a single cattle enclosure, is located in the eastern half of the settlement's inner space. It is as if there were an inverse relationship between "fencing" and communal features. The other remarkable aspect of this settlement is the total absence of any "public" or "discussion" shelter; it is true that the shade provided by the storage platforms is a genuine substitute. The observed situation is nonetheless special if compared to all the cases already described. The number of houses per household cluster vary from four to eight, with one to two barn/livestock features per cluster and three to six habitation houses.

Ngada III

Ngada III is laid out as an almost perfect circle, 160 m in diameter. The settlement thus measures two hectares in surface extent. The site's features are distributed into fourteen household clusters (tables 24 and 25), with the central part of the village devoted to large cattle enclosures (fig. 18). Three of the recorded cattle enclosures are worn-out features, presumably in use during the previous years. The abandoned enclosures located at the center of the settlement are circular in shape, two of them measuring 25 m in diameter with the last one slightly elongated and measuring 30 m in length and 20 m in width. At the time of fieldwork, there was a single, large cattle corral in use. Located in the eastern side of the site's inner space, it is oval-shaped with two opposite entrances, and measures 60 m in length in its N-S axis and 30 m in width in the E-W one. In terms of fenced cattle space, the large corral in use is larger than the cumulated surface of the three worn-out specimens. The interpretation of this transformation is far from easy. It can be argued that increased cattle space is the straightforward consequence of a larger herd's size. But

Table 24: Ngada III household clusters

Cluster number	Number of units	Habitation houses	Livestock houses	Storage platforms	Others
1	1	1	1	1	1
2	1	3	1	2	2
3	2	4	3	2	1
4	1	1	1	—	1
5	2	2	—	1	2
6	1	1	—	—	2
7	1	3	1	2	3
8	1	1	—	1	2
9	1	1	1	—	1
10	1	2	1	1	—
11	1	1	1	1	1
12	1	1	1	1	—
13	1	1	1	1	—
14	1	2	—	1	1
Total	16	24	12	14	17

Table 25: Ngada III general distribution of pottery

Cluster number	Number of features	Service vessels	Cooking vessels	Storage vessels	Unknown	Total
1	4	—	1	3	—	4
2	8	1	1	5	—	7
3	—	—	—	2	—	2
4	3	—	1	3	—	4
5	5	—	4	9	—	13
6	2	—	3	7	—	10
7	8	—	8	10	—	18
8	2	—	—	1	—	1
9	3	—	1	7	—	8
10	4	—	1	5	—	6
11	3	—	1	1	—	2
12	3	—	4	1	—	5
13	3	—	3	2	—	5
14	4	—	—	—	—	—
Total	55	1	28	56	—	85

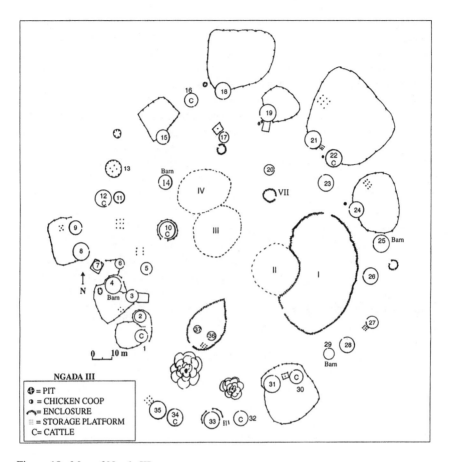

Figure 18: Map of Ngada III

this shift may also have resulted from a reduction in the size of the village's herd which previously divided into three management units and was then lumped into a single herding unit during the year of fieldwork. This last suggestion is at variance with what is suggested by the layout patterns of household clusters, which is discussed in the next paragraphs.

The main entrance to the village is located in the S-SW and consists of a 20-m-wide gap in the circle of houses. Proceeding from that entrance clockwise, there is cluster 1, a well-demarcated and fenced unit, extended over 23 m NE-SW and 20 m E-W, comprising two wood and reeds houses. Feature 1, in the S, is a barn/livestock house, built with two roof-supporting-poles and measuring 6.3 m in diameter. It is associated with an adjunct 2 × 2.5 m, five-poles storage platform. The habitation house, feature 2, is located some 4 m farther N; it is built with two central poles, measures 5.9 m in diameter, and comprises an elaborate hearth and a large bed. The recorded domestic equipment consists of four clay vessels and four enamel basins. The pottery is divided into two cooking and two storage wares. Two shapes are represented among the cooking wares. One specimen is a slightly globular short necked pot with everted rim, 18 cm in MD, 24 cm in MaD, 25 cm in TH, 3 cm in NH, 16 cm in HMD, and finally, 0.8 cm in T, decorated with extensive twisted roulette impression on the body overlined on the shoulder by two horizontal and parallel grooved lines complemented by two symmetric appliqué buttons. The other one is a globular rounded base necked pot decorated on the shoulder with a horizontal band of twisted roulette impression delimited at the bottom and top by parallel grooved lines, measuring 14 cm in MD, 30 cm in MaD, 33 cm in TH, 4 cm in NH, 19 cm in HMD, and finally, 0.9 cm in T. Both storage wares are necked jars, with nonetheless important differences in morphology. One specimen is a short-necked, slightly elongated jar, measuring 27 cm in MD, 36 cm in MaD, 42 cm in TH, 5 cm in NH, 27 cm in HMD, and finally, 1.1 cm in T, decorated on the shoulder with a horizontal band of twisted roulette impression under- and overlined by parallel grooved lines complemented by four equidistant pairs of appliqué buttons. The second specimen is a plain, long-necked water jar with four equidistant lugs appliqué cordon on the shoulder, with its morphometric attributes varying from 26 cm in MD, 40 cm in MaD, 52 cm in TH, 17 cm in NH, 29 cm in HMD, to 1.4 cm in T.

Household cluster 2 is stretched over approximately 40 m along the NE-SW axis (fig. 18). It consists of four features divided into three habitations (feature 3, 5, and 6) and one barn/livestock (feature 4) house. Houses 3 and 4, set at 4 m from each other, belong to a fenced almost square unit measuring 20 by 18 m, encompassing a four-poles, 2 × 2 m storage platform. House 3, the habitation feature of the unit, is built with three roof-supporting poles, measures 6 m in diameter, and comprises an elaborate hearth, a large bed, and a raised grinding platform. A single pottery, a necked storage jar, was found in the house. It is decorated with a horizontal band of twisted roulette impression on the shoulder under- and overlined by parallel grooved lines, and measures 24 cm in MD, 35 cm in MaD, 42 cm in TH, 6 cm in NH, 26 cm in HMD, and finally, 1.1 cm in T. The house is flanked on its eastern side by a rectilinear patio, a de facto discussion house, measuring 6 m in length and 4.5 m in width. The barn/livestock house is larger; it is built with four roof-supporting poles and measures 7.9 m in diameter. There is a large pit (3 × 2 m) behind the livestock house, probably used for the extraction of building material.

A looser unit 2, with two habitation houses (features 5 and 6) and a 3.5 × 3.5 m, six-poles storage platform is located in the inner part of the settlement. Feature 5 is an adolescent/young female adult's house built with a single central pole and measuring 4.9 m in diameter. It comprises a small bed and a raised grinding platform. Three clay vessels partitioned into three functional categories have been recorded. They consist of: (1) a footed service bowl, 13 cm in mouth as well as MaD,

9 cm in base diameter, 12 cm in TH as well as HMD, 4 cm in foot height, and finally, 1 cm in T, decorated with extensive twisted roulette impression on the body; (2) a cooking rounded base short-necked hemispheric pot with everted rim, decorated with extensive twisted roulette impression on the body overlined on the shoulder by two horizontal and parallel grooved lines with, in addition, two symmetric appliqué buttons, and measuring 23 cm in MD, 29 cm in MaD, 29 cm in TH, 3 cm in NH, 17 cm in HMD, and finally, 0.8 cm in T; and (3) a necked storage jar, 25 cm in MD, 40 cm in MaD, 45 cm in TH, 6 cm in NH, 25 cm in HMD, and finally, 1.3 cm in T, decorated on the shoulder with a horizontal band of twisted roulette impression delimited at the bottom and top by parallel grooved lines.

House 6 is located some 8 m W of the previous one; it is built with two central poles, measures 5.4 m in diameter, and possesses a relatively large bed. Domestic equipment consists of one 25-liters plastic container, an enamel basin, and three clay vessels. The pottery material is divided into two large rounded base necked storage pots and one necked jar. Both pots have missing or partially broken neck. They have the same pattern of decoration, consisting of a horizontal band of twisted roulette impression on the shoulder, under- and overlined by two parallel grooved lines. They also share similar morphometric attributes, 12 to 13 cm in MD, 30 cm in MaD, 30 to 33 cm in total observable height, 20 cm in HMD, and finally, 1 cm in T. The necked storage jar measures 28 cm in MD. 40 cm in MaD, 50 cm in TH, 7 cm in NH, 29 cm in HMD, and finally, 1.2 cm in T. It is decorated with a horizontal band of twisted roulette impression on the shoulder, delimited at the bottom and top by parallel grooved lines, with, in addition, four equidistant pairs of appliqué buttons.

Household cluster 3 is located in the western side of the settlement (fig. 18) and comprises seven houses, four used for habitation and three as barn/livestock features. The houses organized into three distinct units are disposed in a circular arrangement, with a 4 × 3 m, nine-poles storage platform in the central position. Unit 1, located in the W-SW of the cluster, consists of three features, houses 7, 8, and 9, with, in addition, a fenced field 22 m long and 15 m wide, and a 2 × 2 m, five-poles storage platform. House 7, at the southern end of the unit, is quadrangular in shape, with side measuring 4 m in length. It is a wood and reeds feature built with a single central pole. The function of this square house is partly ambiguous as neither hearth nor bed have been recorded inside. Domestic equipment consist of a globular, short-necked pot probably used for storage, measuring 12 cm in MD, 30 cm in MaD, 36 cm in TH, 5 cm in NH, 20 cm in HMD, and finally 0.9 cm in T, decorated on the shoulder with a horizontal band of twisted roulette impression under- and overlined by parallel grooved lines. House 8, some 4 m NW of the previous one, measures 7.7 m in diameter and is clearly a habitation feature with an elaborate hearth and a large bed. It is also a wood and reeds feature built with four roof-supporting poles. With the exception of a raised grinding installation, no domestic equipment was found in the house, all of them having probably been transported to the dry-season camp. House 9, a few meters N, is built with mud-brick;

it measures 6.6 m in diameter, has four roof-supporting poles and comprises an elaborate hearth and a large bed. A single clay vessel was left in the house; it is a globular, short-necked pot, similar to the specimen from house 7, and presumably used for storage. The recorded pottery, decorated with a horizontal band of twisted roulette impression on the shoulder delimited at the bottom and top by parallel grooved lines, measures 13 cm in MD, 30 cm in MaD, 34 cm in TH, 5 cm in NH, 18 cm in HMD, and finally, 0.9 cm in T.

Unit 2 is situated to the N of the cluster and comprises two features, one habitation and one barn/livestock house. The barn/livestock feature (feature 12) measures 8.2 m in diameter. It is a wood and reeds house comprising four roof-supporting poles. The habitation house 11 is located less than 2 m E of the previous one; it is built with mud-brick with two central poles, measures 5.6 m in diameter, and is surprisingly devoid of any significant domestic installations or equipment.

The third unit of the cluster is much looser; it consists of two relatively isolated wood and reeds barn/livestock houses, 10 and 14, set at 15 m from each other. The former is built with four roof-supporting poles and measures 8.3 m in diameter; it is entirely surrounded by a wooden fence. The latter, measuring 6.9 m in diameter, is surprisingly built with six roof-supporting poles. Some fodder was found in the house as well as two enamel basins, probably used to water the livestock.

Feature 13 is the unique public shelter of the settlement and is located due W. It is built with four roof-supporting poles without walls and measures 7 m in diameter. Its location seems to have been clearly designed to be relatively independent from all the household clusters.

Cluster 4 is located in the N-NW of the village. It comprises five wood and reeds houses stretched over 65 m W-E (fig. 18) with eight additional features including a fenced field, a sheep/goat enclosure, chicken coops, a patio, and a storage platform. Houses are fairly spaced, with distance from one to the next varying from 10 to 20 m. House 15, attached to a fenced field, quadrangular in shape, and measuring 18 by 15 m, is situated at the southwestern end of the cluster (fig. 18). The house is a wood and reeds feature, built with two central poles. House installations consist of an elaborate hearth, a large bed, and a raised grinding platform, while the domestic kit comprises four clay vessels and six enamelwares. The recorded pottery material is divided into one cooking and three storage wares. The cooking vessel is a slightly globular pot with constricted neck and everted rim, 29 cm in MD, 40 cm in MaD, 36 cm in TH, 20 cm in HMD, and finally, 1.4 cm in T, decorated with extensive twisted roulette impression on the body overlined on the shoulder by two horizontal and parallel grooved lines. All three storage wares are short-necked jars; their morphometric attributes vary from 23 to 24 cm in MD, 34 to 37 cm in MaD, 39 to 47 cm in TH, 5 to 6 cm in NH, 21 to 27 cm in HMD, and finally 1 to 1.5 cm in T. Each specimen has a specific pattern of decoration; two specimens are decorated with horizontal bands of twisted roulette impression on the shoulder delimited at the bottom and top by parallel grooved lines, with, in one case, four equidistant pairs of appliqué buttons, and in the other, a horizontal chevron line made with carved roulette impression. The last specimen has extensive twisted roulette impression on the body overlined on the shoulder by two horizontal and parallel grooved lines.

Feature 16, 16 m NE of the previous one, is a barn/livestock house, built with five roof-supporting poles and measuring 8.5 m in diameter. Habitation house 17 is located in the inner part of the site, approximately 20 m SE of the previous one. It is probably an adolescent/young adult feature, built with a single central pole, measuring 5.1 m in diameter, and comprising a small bed. It is flanked in the S and NW by a 5-m-diameter sheep/goat enclosure and a 4 × 5 m, ten-poles storage platform. Feature 18, the main habitation house, is attached to a relatively large fenced field, 35 m long and 30 m wide. It is a relatively large house, built with five roof-supporting poles, measuring 8.1 m in diameter, and comprising an elaborate hearth, a large bed, and a raised grinding installation. Domestic equipment consists of thirteen clay vessels and six enamelwares carefully arranged on wooden shelves. Among the thirteen recorded wares, there is one large, hole-mouth, flat base basin probably used for serving food, decorated with extensive twisted roulette impression on the body delimited on the shoulder by an appliqué cordon with four equidistant lugs; the basin measures 35 cm in MD, 37 cm in MaD, 16 cm in base diameter, 30 cm in TH, 24 cm in HMD, and finally, 1.6 cm in T. Three cooking vessels have also been found. Two are slightly globular pots with everted rim, measuring 21 to 35 cm in MD, 27 to 36 cm in MaD, 29 to 37 cm in TH, 18 to 22 cm in HMD, and finally, 0.9 to 1 cm in T, and decorated with extensive twisted roulette impression on the body overlined on the shoulder by two horizontal and parallel grooved lines, complemented in one case with four pairs of equidistant appliqué buttons. The last specimen of cooking ware is a rounded base short-necked handled hemispheric pot, 27 cm in MD, 34 cm in MaD. 34 cm in TH, 3 cm in NH, 20 cm in HMD, and finally, 1 cm in T, decorated with extensive twisted roulette impression on the body delimited on the shoulder by two horizontal and parallel grooved lines, complemented by two symmetric pairs of appliqué buttons. The sample of storage vessels is divided into four morphological classes, with two necked, globular pots, one hole-mouth, and four short-necked and two long-necked jars. Both necked, globular pots are used for the storage of dairy products; they measure 12 to 15 cm in MD, 30 cm in MaD, 37 to 38 cm in TH, 4 cm in NH, 18 to 20 cm in HMD, and finally, 0.8 to 1 cm in T. Each has a specific pattern of decoration; one specimen is decorated on the shoulder with a horizontal band of twisted roulette impression delimited at the bottom and top with two parallel grooved lines, and the other, also decorated with a horizontal band of twisted roulette impression on the shoulder combined with three parallel grooved lines, has, in addition, seven panels of four short, vertical, grooved lines on the upper part of the shoulder to the neck base. The specimen of hole-mouth jar measures 21 cm in MD, 37 cm in MaD, 41 cm in TH, 22 cm in HMD, and finally, 1.2 cm in T. It is decorated on the shoulder with a horizontal band of twisted roulette impression under- and overlined by two parallel grooved lines, complemented by four equidistant appliqué buttons.The sample of four short-necked jars has, with minor variations in the one case with additional four equidistant appliqué buttons, the same decoration pattern, which consists of a horizontal band of twisted roulette impression delimited at the bottom and top by two parallel grooved lines. The recorded specimens measure 22 to 26 cm in MD, 35 to 42 cm in MaD, 41 to 50 cm in TH, 5 to 7 cm in NH, 22 to 31 cm in height of the MaD, and finally, 1 to 1.2 cm in T. Finally, both long-necked jars are similar in morphometric attributes and decoration patterns. The former varies from 30 to 32 cm in MD, 50 cm in MaD, 70 cm in TH, 12 to 14 cm in NH, 40 to 41 cm in HMD, to 1.2 to 1.4 cm in T. And the latter consists of extensive twisted roulette impression on the body overlined on the shoulder by two parallel grooved lines.

Habitation house 19 is situated some 17 m SE. It is attached to a relatively small fenced field, 18 m in length and 12 m in width, a rectilinear patio 4.5 by 3 m, with two chicken coops. The house is built with two central poles and measures 6.3 cm in diameter. The recorded furniture consists of an elaborate hearth and a large bed, with the domestic equipment divided into two enamel basins and ten clay vessels. The pottery material is partitioned into three cooking and seven storage wares. Two vessels are represented among the cooking wares; there is one specimen of a slightly globular, short-necked pot with everted rim, 26 cm in MD, 33 cm in MaD, 33 cm in TH, 3 cm in NH, 20 cm in HMD, and 1.2 cm in T, decorated with extensive twisted roulette impression on the body overlined on the shoulder by two horizontal and parallel grooved lines complemented by four equidistant buttons. The remaining two are rounded base short-necked and handled hemispheric pots, with almost similar decoration consisting of extensive twisted roulette impression on the body overlined on the shoulder by two horizontal and parallel grooved lines, with, in one case, two symmetric appliqué buttons. Their morphometric attributes vary from 23 to 25 cm for MD, 29 cm for MaD, 28 to 34 cm for TH, 3 to 5 cm for NH, 18 to 19 cm for HMD, 1 to 1.2 cm for T. All the seven storage vessels are necked jars. They can be divided into two major groups according to their pattern of decoration. There are four specimens with decoration confined to the vessels' shoulder, consisting of a horizontal band of twisted roulette impression delimited at the bottom and top by two parallel grooved lines for three of them; the fourth being singled out by three horizontal grooved lines with, in addition, three equidistant sets of four appliqué buttons. Their size attributes vary from 25 to 27 cm in MD, 37 to 40 cm in MaD, 45 to 50 cm in TH, 5 to 7 cm in NH, 24 to 30 cm in HMD, and finally, 1.2 to 1.5 cm in T.The remaining three are decorated with extensive twisted roulette impression on the body overlined on the shoulder by two horizontal and parallel grooved lines, with, in two cases, an addition of three or four equidistant pairs of appliqué buttons. They measure 28 to 33 cm in MD, 38 to 42 cm in MaD, 40 to 45 cm in TH, 5 to 6 cm in NH, 23 to 29 cm in HMD, and finally, 1.3 to 1.7 cm in T.

Household cluster 5 is found in the northeastern edge of the settlement. It comprises four houses in a loose circular arrangement, a large fenced field measuring 45 by 40 m, a 7-m-in-diameter sheep/goat enclosure located in the inner part of the site, one chicken coop, and two storage platforms (fig. 18). The largest storage platform is located in the fenced field; it is built with nine poles and measures 5 by 4.5 m; the smaller specimen is adjunct to house 21, comprises twelve supporting poles, and measures 2.5 by 2 m. House 20 is located some 6 m N of sheep/goat enclosure VII; it is an adolescent feature built with a single central pole, comprising a small bed, an enamelware as domestic equipment, and measures 4.6 m in diameter.

House 21, 20 m NE of the adolescent feature 20, measures 8.1 m in diameter. It is built with four roof-supporting poles, contains an elaborate hearth and a large bed. Domestic equipment consists of three enamelwares and twelve clay vessels. A necklace of glass beads was found abandoned on the house floor. Five vessel shapes are represented among the recorded pottery. There is one specimen of handled, hole-mouth basin probably used for cooking; it measures 36 cm in mouth as well as MaD, 27 cm in TH as well as HMD, and finally, 1 cm in T. Its decoration, situated a few centimeters below the rim, is fairly elaborated and consists of a horizontal band of twisted roulette impression under- and overlined by two parallel grooved lines, with, in addition, ten equidistant pairs of appliqué buttons. Another specimen is a short-necked, slightly globular pot, 21 cm in MD, 30 cm in MaD, 35 cm in TH, 4 cm in NH, 19 cm in HMD, and finally 0.8 cm in T, decorated with a horizontal band of twisted roulette impression with three superimposed parallel and horizontal grooved lines on the shoulder. Three of the vessels are slightly globular pots with slightly constricted necks and everted rims; their morphometric attributes vary from 21 to 24 cm in MD, 27 to 28 cm in MaD, 26 to 31 cm in TH, 18 to 20 cm in HMD, and finally 1 to 1.2 cm in T. They share similar decorations with extensive twisted roulette impression on the body, overlined on the shoulder by two horizontal and parallel grooved lines, with, in all the cases, additional four to six equidistant appliqué buttons. There are two rounded base, globular, necked pots, one used for storage and the other for cooking. They measure 14 to 15 cm in MD, 30 to 31 cm in MaD, 36 to 40 cm in TH, 5 cm in NH, 19 to 20 cm in HMD, 1 to 1.1 cm in T. Both are decorated on the shoulder with a horizontal band of twisted roulette impression under- and overlined by two parallel grooved lines, with, in one case, seven small panels of four short, vertical, grooved lines at the neck base. Finally, there are five necked storage jars, 23 to 27 cm in MD, 35 to 40 cm in MaD, 36 to 48 cm in TH, 6 to 7 cm in NH, 21 to 27 cm in HMD, and finally, 1.1 to 1.3 cm in T. One of the jars is decorated with extensive twisted roulette impression on the body overlined on the shoulder by two horizontal and parallel grooved lines. The other four have a horizontal band of twisted roulette impression under- and overlined by parallel grooved lines on the shoulder, complemented, for two specimens, by four equidistant pairs of appliqué buttons in one case, and five panels of three short, vertical, grooved lines in the other.

Feature 22, approximately 5 m SE is a barn/livestock house. It is built with four roof-supporting poles and measures 8.7 m in diameter. Four freshly made wooden poles were found stored in the barn. Habitation house 23 is located 4 m S of the cluster's barn. It is built with five roof-supporting poles and measures 7.4 m in diameter. House's furniture consists of an elaborate hearth, a large bed, and a raised grinding installation, with domestic equipment divided into one enamel basin, an enamel teapot, and six clay vessels. The pottery material is partitioned into two cooking and four storage wares. One of the cooking wares is a slightly globular short-necked pot, 27 cm in MD, 30 cm in MaD, 32 cm in TH, 4 cm in NH, 20 cm in HMD, and finally, 1 cm in T, decorated with extensive twisted roulette impression on the body overlined on the shoulder by two horizontal and parallel grooved lines and three equidistant pairs of appliqué buttons. The other is a rounded base short-necked handled hemispheric pot, with its decoration quite similar to that of the previous specimen, but with two symmetric sets of three appliqué buttons instead. It measures 27 cm in MD, 30 cm in MaD, 28 cm in TH, 3 cm in NH, 19 cm in HMD, and finally, 1.2 cm in T. All the four storage wares are necked jars, their morphometric attributes varying from 24 to 27 cm for MD, 36 to 41 cm for MaD, 48 to 52 cm for TH, 7 to 8 cm for NH, 30 to 34 cm for HMD, and finally, 1.2 to 1.5 cm for T. In all four cases, decoration is confined to the vessel's shoulder and consists of a horizontal band of twisted roulette impression, delimited by two parallel grooved lines (one case) or three superimposed grooved lines (three cases) complemented by three equidistant sets of two to four appliqué buttons.

Household cluster 6 is located on the eastern side of the village. It comprises three wood and reeds houses, one chicken coop, a sheep/goat enclosure measuring 5 m in diameter, and a 30 by 22 m fenced field with a nine-poles, 3 by 4 m storage platform (fig. 18). The whole set of features is disposed in a linear almost N-S arrangement stretched on 55 m. Feature 24, located at the northern end of the cluster and attached to the fenced field, is a habitation house. It is built with four roof-supporting poles, measures 7.3 m in diameter, and contains an elaborate hearth, a large bed, and a raised grinding installation. Domestic equipment consists of one enamelware and a single clay vessel. The recorded storage ware is a necked jar, 30 cm in MD, 41 cm in MaD, 50 cm in TH, 8 cm in NH, 27 cm in HMD, and finally, 1.5 cm in T, decorated with extensive twisted roulette impression on the body overlined on the shoulder with two horizontal and parallel grooved lines. A worn-out rubber shoe was also found on the house floor. The barn/livestock house (feature 25) is located some 15 m SE of the previous one; it measures 8 m in diameter and is built with four roof-supporting poles.

House 26, the second habitation of the cluster, is found approximately 10 m S of the barn/livestock house. It is built with four roof-supporting poles and measures 8 m in diameter. House installations consist of an elaborate hearth and a large bed, and domestic equipment includes a set of eight clay vessels arranged along the wall in wooden shelves. A 25-liters plastic container was also found in the house. The recorded pottery material is partitioned into one cooking and seven storage wares. The cooking vessel is a rounded base short-necked handled hemi-spheric pot, 22 cm in MD, 31 cm in MaD, 32 cm in TH, 3 cm in NH, 15 cm in HMD, and finally 1 cm in T, decorated with extensive twisted roulette impression on the body overlined on the shoulder by two horizontal and parallel grooved lines. Storage vessels are distributed into two morphological classes. There are four specimens of short-necked jars, with their morphometric attributes varying from 22 to 28 cm for MD, 35 to 40 cm for MaD, 43 to 49 cm for TH, 3 to 6 cm for NH, 22 to 24 cm for HMD, and finally 1 to 1.3 cm for T. Their decoration, confined to the vessels' shoulder, belong to two patterns attested on two specimens each. One consists of a horizontal band of twisted or carved roulette (chevron) impression delimited at the bottom and top by two horizontal and parallel grooved lines, and the other is constituted of four equidistant pairs of appliqué buttons set in a hori-zontal panel delineated by two parallel and horizontal grooved lines. The three remaining specimens are long-necked and larger jars. They measure 27 to 35 cm in MD, 42 to 60 cm in MaD, 51 to 60 cm in TH, 8 to 10 cm in NH, 23 to 33 cm in HMD, and finally, 1.1 to 1.4 cm in T. Each specimen has a specific pattern of dec-oration. One is decorated on the shoulder by a horizontal band of twisted roulette impression delimited at the bottom and top by two horizontal grooved lines. The other has a horizontal band of twisted roulette impression with three superim-posed parallel grooved lines with, in addition, four equidistant sets of four short appliqué elongated buttons. And finally, the remaining specimen has extensive twisted roulette impression on the body delimited on the shoulder by two hori-zontal and parallel grooved lines.

Household cluster 7 is located in the southeastern side of the settlement. It comprises three wood and reeds houses stretched over 35 m, with an adjunct 2 by 2.5 m, nine-poles storage platform. Feature 27 at the northern end of the cluster is the main habitation house; it is built with two central poles, comprises an elabo-rate hearth, a large bed, and measures 6.4 m in diameter. Six vessels have been recorded; they were found arranged on wooden shelves along the wall on both sides of the hearth. There is a single, slightly globular, short-necked cooking pot, 23 cm in MD, 33 cm in MaD, 35 cm in TH, 3 cm in NH, 15 cm in HMD, and fi-nally 1.2 cm in T, decorated with extensive twisted roulette impression on the body overlined on the shoulder by two horizontal and parallel grooved lines. All five storage wares are short-necked jars. Following similarities in decoration patterns, the recorded jars can be partitioned into three groups. There are two specimens decorated on the shoulder by a horizontal band of twisted roulette delimited by two parallel grooved lines; they measure 25 to 26 cm in MD, 40 to 42 cm in MaD, 50 to 53 cm in total length, 7 cm in NH, 23 to 26 cm in HMD, and finally, 1 to 1.2 cm in T. There is another set of two specimens with broadly comparable decoration—a pattern of decoration which consists of two or three horizontal and parallel grooved lines on the shoulder, delineating a narrow band filled with four equidis-tant sets of three or four appliqué buttons. Their morphometric attributes vary from 24 to 27 cm in MD, 40 to 45 m cm in MaD, 46 to 50 cm in TH, 5 to 6 cm in NH,

22 to 25 cm in HMD, and finally, 0.9 to 1.4 cm in T. The last specimen, measuring 26 cm in MD, 42 cm in MaD, 46 cm in TH, 7 cm in NH, 23 cm in HMD, and finally, 1 cm in T, has the most elaborate decoration, also restricted to the vessel shoulder. It consists of a horizontal band delimited by two parallel grooved lines, filled with distinct panels of twisted roulette impression created by eight sets of three short vertical grooved lines each, with, in addition, six equidistant pairs of appliqué buttons. Feature 28, some 10 m S of the previous one and at the middle of the cluster, measures 7.2 m in diameter. It is built with four roof-supporting poles and comprises an elaborate hearth and a large bed. Several specimens of unfired clay figurines representing a cattle herd with two herders riding horses were found under the bed. They are probably children's toys. The southernmost feature of the cluster (house 29) is an average size barn/livestock house; it measures 6.1 m in diameter and is built with a single central pole. Two simple fireplaces have also been recorded in the livestock structure.

Cluster 8, located due S of the settlement, is spread over an area measuring 95 m E-W and 65 m N-S. It is the Marabout (Muslim scholar) household unit, which comprises four clearly distinct units of two wood and reeds houses each, set at distances varying from 10 to 30 m from each other. Unit 1 on the eastern side of the cluster is clearly demarcated by a fence with the enclosed area extended over 780 square meters (30 × 26 m). Feature 30 is a barn/livestock house, built with five roof-supporting poles, measuring 8 m in diameter. It is flanked on its western side by a 2.5 × 3 m, nine-poles storage platform. The habitation house, feature 31, is found some 5 m W of the barn. It is built with four roof-supporting poles, comprises an elaborate hearth, a large bed, and a raised grinding installation, and measures 7.9 m in diameter. The recorded domestic equipment consists of a metal bucket, three enamelwares, and two clay vessels. The pottery material is divided into one cooking and one storage ware. The former, a slightly globular short-necked pot, decorated on the shoulder by a horizontal band of twisted roulette impression under- and overlined by two parallel grooved lines, measures 23 cm in MD, 33 cm in MaD, 35 cm in TH, 3 cm in NH, 15 cm in HMD, and finally, 1.2 cm in T. The latter is a short-necked, globular jar, 27 cm in MD, 44 cm in MaD, 42 cm in TH, 5 cm in NH, 22 cm in HMD, and finally, 1.2 cm in T, with extensive twisted roulette impression on the body overlined on the shoulder by two horizontal and parallel grooved lines.

Unit 2 is found some 10 m farther W. It consists of two wood and reeds houses set at 8 m from each other, with a 2 × 3 m, six-poles storage platform in between. A large tree located in front of both houses is the fourth component of the unit (fig. 18), its shade used as "discussion shelter." Feature 32 is the barn/livestock house, built with two central poles and measuring 7.3 m in diameter. The habitation house (feature 33) measures 7.9 m in diameter and has a complementary wooden fence on its front half. It is built with four roof-supporting poles, comprises an elaborate hearth, a large bed, and a raised grinding platform, with domestic equipment consisting of five clay vessels. The recorded pottery material is divided into four cooking and one storage vessels. Two morphological classes are represented among the cooking wares. One consists of a single specimen of a rounded base, hemispheric, handled pot with constricted neck and everted rim, 20 cm in MD, 26 cm in MaD, 23 cm in TH, 13 cm in HMD, and 0.8 cm in T, decorated with extensive twisted roulette impression on the body overlined on the shoulder by two horizontal and parallel grooved lines. The other morphological class is represented by three specimens of slightly globular, constricted to short-necked pot, with their morphometric attributes varying from 19 to 21 cm in MD, 26 to 27 in MaD, 23 to 27 in TH, 13 to 15 cm in HMD, and finally, 0.6 to 1.1 cm in T. Two of the specimens share a similar pattern of decoration with extensive twisted roulette impression on the body overlined on the shoulder by two horizontal and parallel grooved lines in one case, complemented in the other by four equidistant pairs of appliqué buttons. The remaining one is decorated on the shoulder with a horizontal band of twisted roulette impression under- and overlined by two parallel grooved lines. The storage ware is a long-necked jar with an elaborate decoration confined to the shoulder-neck base area, which consists of a horizontal, appliqué cordon with six equidistant lugs, three appliqué zoomorphic figurines, and a band of twisted roulette impression. The jar measures 31 cm in MD, 45 cm in MaD, 61 cm in TH, 19 cm in NH, 28 cm in HMD, and finally, 1.6 cm in T.

Unit 3 with three features—two houses and a 3 × 3.5 m, nine-poles storage platform—is located some 10 m W of the previous one. There is less than 1 m between both houses; the barn/livestock feature (feature 34) is built with five roof-supporting poles and measures 8.9 m in diameter. The habitation house (feature 35) has almost the same size, measuring 8.2 m in diameter. It is built with four roof-supporting poles, contains an elaborate hearth, a large bed, and a raised grinding installation, with five clay vessels arranged on wooden shelves along the wall. The pottery material comprises three cooking and two storage wares. One of the cooking wares is a rounded base, short-necked and handled hemispheric pot; it is decorated with extensive twisted roulette impression on the body overlined on the shoulder by two horizontal and parallel grooved lines, with, in addition, two pairs of symmetric appliqué buttons, and measures 25 cm in MD, 34 cm in MaD, 34 cm in TH, 3 cm in NH, 20 cm in HMD, and finally, 1.3 cm in T. The other two are slightly globular, constricted to short-necked pots, 22 to 25 cm in MD, 32 to 33 cm in MaD, 28 to 31 cm in TH, 15 to 18 cm in HMD, and finally, 1.3 to 1.3 cm in T; they have important similarities in some parts of their decoration, which consists, in both cases, of extensive twisted roulette impression on the body overlined on the shoulder by two horizontal and parallel grooved lines; this basic pattern is complemented, for one specimen, by two symmetric single and double appliqué buttons, and three equidistant lugs and three pairs of vertical and elongated appliqué buttons for the other. Both recorded storage vessels are short-necked storage jars, with similar decorations confined to the shoulder and consisting of a horizontal band of twisted roulette impression under- and overlined by two parallel grooved lines, measuring 26 to 29 cm in MD, 42 to 45 cm in MaD, 49 to 50 cm in TH, 6 to

7 cm in NH, 26 cm in HMD, and finally, 1.2 to 1.3 cm in T. Unit 3 is located 30 m N in the inner part of the village. It is an oval-shaped fenced unit, measuring 30 m in length and 20 m in maximum width, comprising two houses and a 3 × 2 m, nine-poles storage platform. The large tree located a few meters S of the unit entrance is probably a component of the complex. Both houses, set at 4 m from each other, are relatively small in size. They measure 4.3 (feature 36) and 3.2 m (feature 37) in diameter, both built with a single central pole. House 36 comprises a single small bed, while the smaller house 37 has two beds. A small enamel basin was found in each of the houses which are devoid of any hearth or fireplace. Both houses are, in fact dormitories for three Marabout students, and the large tree is used as the Koranic school. According to informants, these students obtain their food by begging from one house to the next at a specific time of the day, while no one, with the exception of their teacher, is allowed to trespass the limit of the fenced unit. They devote all their time to the study of religion and the Koran and have to be fed by the whole community. At first glance, fencing appears to be frequently used at Ngada III. Each household cluster has at least one storage platform. There is a skewed spatial distribution of livestock enclosures and chicken coops, all of them located in the northeastern half of the settlement. The southwestern half has more storage platforms and barn/livestock houses; nine out of fourteen for the former, and eight out of twelve for the latter. Nucleation of different clusters seems well underway, as well as a limited use of rectilinear features.

Ngada IV

Ngada IV is the westernmost and last settlement from the village cluster under investigation. It is laid out in a broadly subcircular pattern extended over 2 hectares, measuring 220 m in length in its NW-SE axis and 185 m in width in the SE-NE one. It comprises fifty-three houses distributed into twelve household clusters (tables 26 and 27). The central part is filled with numerous livestock enclosures and an open-air Mosque. The open-air Mosque consists of a single course of two superimposed mud-brick 0.2 to 0.3 m in height delimiting a rectilinear perimeter of praying space. The religious feature located in the E-NE portion of the site measures 5 × 5 m with the *Mihrab* (the architectural feature indicating the direction of the Mecca) protruding 1 m farther E (fig. 19). The other communal features are all linked with livestock herding and management. There are two relatively large subcircular cattle enclosures, which were in use during the field study; the smaller measures 161.5 square meters (17 × 19 m), and the larger, 250 square meters (20 × 25 m). One of the predominant characteristics of Ngada IV is the high frequency of abandoned enclosures probably used during the year prior to fieldwork; eight such features have been recorded. They are arranged in a slightly incurved N-SE linear pattern, with one specimen located a few meters E. Two of the worn-out enclosures were devoted to sheep/goat. Both are perfectly circular

Table 26: Ngada IV household clusters

Cluster number	Number of units	Habitation houses	Livestock houses	Storage platforms	Others
1	1	2	—	1	2
2	1	2	2	—	2
3	1	3	—	3	4
4	2	3	1	1	8
5	4	6	3	5	12
6	1	2	1	2	5
7	1	4	1	—	—
8	2	3	2	1	1
9	1	1	1	2	2
10	1	2	2	1	—
11	3	4	3	3	7
12	1	2	1	1	3
Total	18	34	17	20	46

and measure 6 and 9 m in diameter. The remaining six were cattle corrals; they vary in size from 15 to 24 m in diameter, with five of them belonging to the larger size features. The implication of the shift in livestock feature size outlined above will be considered after the description of the settlement features. Finally, the remaining important communal feature is the well, located in the middle of what is clearly the village entrance in the SE, some 20 m behind the circle of dwelling

Table 27: Ngada IV general distribution of pottery

Cluster number	Number of features	Service vessels	Cooking vessels	Storage vessels	Unknown	Total
1	5	?	?	?	?	?
2	6	—	4	4	—	8
3	10	—	6	5	—	11
4	13	—	6	3	—	9
5	26	1	5	15	—	21
6	10	—	10	3	—	13
7	5	—	—	—	—	—
8	7	—	2	3	—	5
9	6	—	2	5	—	7
10	5	—	2	4	—	6
11	17	4	10	15	—	29
12	7	?	?	?	?	?
Total	117	5	47	57	?	109

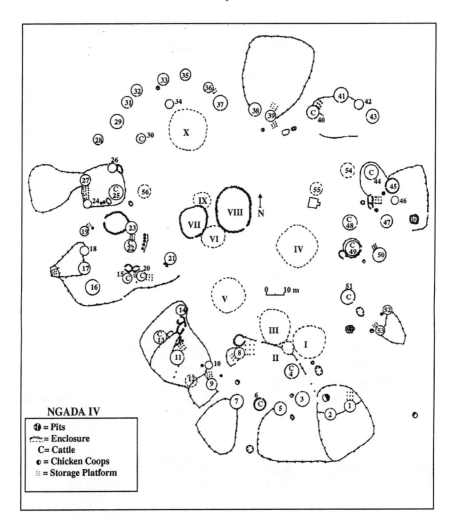

Figure 19: Map of Ngada IV

installations. The well is 13 m deep and surrounded by a raised, cemented, circular margin measuring 2 m in diameter.

Proceeding clockwise from the village entrance in the SE, there is household cluster 1 in the S-SE side of the settlement, a well-demarcated and fenced unit, measuring 40 m in its N-S axis and 32 m in the E-W one, and comprising two wood and reeds houses. The fenced space is divided into two parts by another fence connecting houses 1 and 2. The rear part is an already harvested sorghum field, while the front one is the courtyard with a relatively large chicken coop and a 3×4 m, nine-poles storage platform adjunct to house 1. Both houses were still inhabited during the fieldwork; the features' sizes were thus taken from outside. House 1 measures 4.8 m in diameter and has an elaborate hearth and a large bed; house 2 is larger, measuring 6.3 m in diameter with a large bed but without hearth. Enamelwares and clay vessels arranged on wooden shelves were observed but not studied in detail.

Cluster 2 is adjunct to the previous one with which it shares a fence (fig. 19). It comprises a fenced field 35 m in length and 30 m in width, one chicken coop, and four houses in a semicircular arrangement, with distance from one to the next varying from 6 to 8.2 m. There is another fence running along the NE and northern side of the cluster. Two of the features built with wood and reeds (features 3 and 5) are habitation houses. House 3 is built with four roof-supporting poles and comprises an elaborate hearth and a large bed. Domestic kit consists of two clay vessels for cooking and storage. The cooking ware is a short-necked, rounded base, globular pot, decorated on the shoulder with a horizontal band of twisted roulette impression under- and overlined by two parallel grooved lines, measuring 15 cm in MD, 26 cm in MaD, 36 cm in TH, 4 cm in NH, 18 cm in HMD, and finally, 0.8 cm in T. The storage vessel, with a decoration pattern similar to that of the previous specimen, is a necked jar, 26 cm in MD, 28 cm in MaD, 47 cm in TH, 6 cm in NH, 22 cm in HMD, and finally, 1.3 cm in T.

House 5 is 6 m W of the previous one; it is built with two central poles and measures 7.2 m in diameter. House's furniture consists of an elaborate hearth, a large bed, and a raised grinding installation. Domestic equipment comprises a tin container, two enamelwares, and six clay vessels. There are three cooking wares, all of them from a unique morphological class, that of a slightly globular, constricted to short-necked pot with everted rim. The recorded morphometric attributes vary from 19 to 24 cm in MD, 22 to 30 cm in MaD, 22 to 26 cm in TH, 13 to 15 cm in HMD, and finally 0.9 cm in T. One of the specimens is decorated with extensive twisted roulette impression on the body, the other two having a horizontal band of twisted roulette impression on the shoulder, delimited at the bottom and top by parallel grooved lines, complemented in one case by five equidistant pairs of appliqué buttons. All three storage vessels are necked jars, 27 to 30 cm in MD, 42 to 45 cm in MaD, 47 to 55 cm in TH, 6 to 10 cm in NH, 24 to 32 cm in HMD, and finally, 1 to 1.3 cm in T. Two specimens are decorated with a horizontal band of twisted roulette impression on the shoulder, under- and overlined by two parallel grooved lines complemented by two single symmetric or four equidistant pairs of appliqué buttons, and the last one has extensive twisted roulette impression on the body overlined on the shoulder by two horizontal and parallel grooved lines.

Features 4 and 6, approximately 20 m from each other, are barn/livestock houses. The former is located in the inner part of the village and measures 10 m in diameter. It is one of the largest houses of the settlement, built with six roof-supporting poles. An enamel basin and a metal bucket presumably used for livestock watering have been found on the house floor. Feature 6 is a mud-brick goat house; it is built with a single central pole and measures 5.8 m in diameter.

Cluster 3 is located a few meters W-NW of the previous one and comprises three houses disposed in a triangular arrangement at distances varying from 10 to 20 m, with, in addition, three storage platforms, two chicken coops, and a sheep/goat enclosure. The complex comprises two fenced fields, each attached to a habitation house. The largest of both fields, attached to house 7, measures 65 m in length and 50 m in width; the smaller, attached to house 9, is almost rectangular in shape, with 30 m in length and 26 m in width. Chicken coops are located in the courtyard.

Feature 7 is located at the southeastern end of the cluster. It is built with four roof-supporting poles and measures 7.7 m in diameter. Domestic furniture consists of a large bed, an elaborate hearth, and a raised grinding platform, and house wares are divided into ten clay vessels and five enamelwares. One man's rubber shoe was found on the house floor. The recorded pottery comprises six cooking and four storage vessels. Two morphological classes are represented among the cooking vessels. There is a single specimen of a globular, rounded base, and handled pot with slightly constricted neck and everted rim, measuring 23 cm in MD, 28 cm in MaD, 28 cm in TH, 3 cm in NH, 18 cm in HMD, and finally 1.1 cm in T, decorated with extensive twisted roulette impression on the body delimited on the shoulder by two parallel and horizontal grooved lines complemented by two symmetric appliqué buttons. The other five specimens are slightly globular pots, with constricted to short necks and everted rims. Three of the vessels present well-demarcated necks 2 to 4 cm in height; their morphometric attributes vary from 21 to 24 cm for MD, 28 to 33 cm for MaD, 29 to 36 cm for TH, 17 to 24 cm for HMD, and finally, 0.9 to 1 cm for T. Two patterns of decoration are attested; one, confined to the vessels' shoulder and recorded on two specimens, consists of a horizontal band of twisted roulette impression, delimited at the bottom and top by two parallel grooved lines. The other is constituted of extensive twisted roulette impression on the body, overlined on the shoulder by two horizontal and parallel grooved lines with, in addition, two symmetric appliqué buttons. The remaining two specimens, with slightly constricted necks, measure 23 to 27 cm in MD, 28 to 32 cm in MaD, 27 to 32 cm in TH, 16 to 20 cm in HMD, and finally 1 to 1.1 cm in T; both are decorated with extensive twisted roulette impression on the body, complemented on the shoulder by a horizontal band of chevron made with carved roulette delimited at the bottom and top by two parallel grooved lines with, in addition, four equidistant pairs of appliqué buttons in one case. In the other, the horizontal band on the shoulder is plain and comprises four equidistant appliqué *buttons.* All the storage vessels are necked jars; they measure 23 to 30 cm in MD, 34 to 47 cm in MaD, 37 to 65 cm in TH, 4 to 11 cm in NH, 20 to 45 cm in HMD, and finally 1 to 1.7 cm in T. Two specimens are decorated with extensive twisted roulette impression on the body overlined on the shoulder by two horizontal and parallel grooved lines. Both remaining vessels are decorated on the shoulder with a horizontal band of twisted roulette impression delimited at the bottom and top by two parallel grooved lines, complemented in one case by three equidistant sets of three elongated vertical appliqué buttons.

Feature 8 is located in the inner part of the village at 40 m from feature 7. The house was empty and devoid of any evidence of hearth, bed, or storage shelf. It is probably a habitation house. It measures 6.2 m in diameter and is built with mudbrick and two roof-supporting poles. It is surrounded by a circular sheep/goat enclosure measuring 10 m in diameter (fig. 19), an attached fence with a six-poles 6 × 2 m storage platform at its center, and finally a large 10 × 10 m, ten-poles storage platform.

Feature 9, at the northwestern end of the cluster, is a habitation house built in wood and reeds with a central roof supporting pole and measures 5.6 m in diameter. It has an adjunct 6 × 5 m, nine-poles storage platform, and comprises an elaborate hearth, a large bed, and a raised grinding platform. A single clay vessel and six enamelwares were recorded. The pottery is a large, necked storage pot, 14 cm in MD, 30 cm in MaD, 36 cm in TH, 5 cm NH, 18 cm in HMD, and finally, 0.7 cm in T; the decoration is confined to the pot's shoulder and consists of a horizontal band of twisted roulette impression under- and overlined by two parallel grooved lines.

Cluster 4 is a fenced complex measuring 85 m in length and 65 m in width, situated in the SW of the village. It is divided into two units. The southern one comprises features 10, 11, and 12, all of them wood and reeds houses, as well as six chicken coops, a 6 × 5 m, nine-poles storage platform, and an elliptically shaped sheep/goat enclosure 15 m in length and 8 m in width (fig. 19). Feature 10, associated with a chicken coop, is found at the eastern end of the unit; it is a teenager's habitation house, built with three roof-supporting poles and measuring 4.3 m in diameter. It comprises a small bed and an enamelware. Habitation house 11 measures 7.7 m in diameter. It is built with four roof-supporting poles and is located at the center of the unit with adjunct chicken coops and a storage platform. Domestic furniture consists of a large bed, an elaborate hearth, and a raised grinding platform. House wares are divided into four clays vessels and two enamel basins. The recorded pottery comprises four morphological classes distributed into two vessel categories, cooking and storage wares with two specimens each. Decoration patterns are also organized along the above mentioned functional variation. Cooking vessels are decorated with extensive twisted roulette impression on the body overlined on the shoulder by two horizontal and parallel grooved lines, complemented in one case by four equidistant appliqué buttons, and in the other, six equidistant elongated vertical appliqué buttons. One of the specimens is a rounded base, hemispheric short-necked, handled pot, 22 cm in MD, 29 cm in MaD, 33 cm in TH, 4 cm in NH, 18 cm in HMD, and finally 0.8 cm in T; the other is a slightly globular pot with constricted neck and everted rim, 21 cm in MD, 25 cm in MaD, 24 cm in TH, 15 cm in HMD, and finally 0.9 cm in T. Storage vessels are decorated on the shoulder with a horizontal band of twisted roulette impression under-

and overlined by parallel grooved lines, complemented in one case by four equidistant elongated vertical appliqué buttons, and the other by seven equidistant panels of four short, vertical, and parallel grooved lines each. One of the storage vessels is a large, necked pot, 14 cm in MD, 31 cm in MaD, 36 cm in TH, 5 cm in NH, 19 cm in HMD, and finally 0.8 cm in T, and the other a necked jar, 26 cm in MD, 43 cm in MaD, 48 cm in TH, 6 cm in NH, 29 cm in HMD, and finally, 1.2 cm in T.

Feature 12 is a worn-out habitation house with traces of the single roof-supporting pole, bed, and hearth still visible. It is reduced to a shallow 6.6-m-in-diameter circle.

The northern unit also comprises two wood and reeds features, with a subcircular sheep/goat enclosure measuring 10 m in diameter and a 7 × 5 m rectangular shelter. Habitation house 14 is located at the northern end of the unit; it is built with two roof-supporting poles and measures 6.6 m in diameter. It comprises an elaborate hearth and a large bed. Five clay vessels and a rubber shoe were recorded. The pottery material is divided into a single storage and four cooking wares. The storage specimen is a necked jar decorated with extensive twisted roulette impression on the body overlined on the shoulder by two horizontal and parallel grooved lines, measuring 23 cm in MD, 44 cm in MaD, 55 cm in TH, 8 cm in NH, 32 cm in HMD, and finally 1.4 cm in T. All four specimens of cooking vessels belong to a single morphological class, that of a slightly globular, constricted to short-necked pot with everted rim. Three of the specimens are decorated with extensive twisted roulette impression on the body overlined on the shoulder by two horizontal and parallel grooved lines; the remaining one having a horizontal band of twisted roulette impression under- and overlined by parallel grooved lines on the shoulder. Their morphometric attributes vary from 18 to 24 cm for MD, 24 to 28 cm for MaD, 24 to 33 cm for TH, 15 to 22 cm, and finally, 0.8 to 1.2 cm in T.

Feature 13, located approximately 25 m SW of the previous one, is a barn/livestock house. It is built with five roof-supporting poles and measures 7.5 m in diameter.

Cluster 5 is a partially fenced complex located in the western part of the settlement. It consists of nine wood and reeds houses, five storage platforms, eight chicken coops, and three livestock enclosures, distributed into four units.

Unit 1 is located to the W of the cluster and comprises features 16, 17, 18, and 19, set in a N-S linear arrangement with an adjunct fenced field 42 m in length and 35 m in maximum width. House 16 measures 5.7 m in diameter; it is built with a single central pole and comprises an average sized bed. House 17 a few meters N, is slightly larger and measures 6.6 m in diameter; it is built with three roof-supporting poles and comprises an elaborate hearth and a large bed. House wares consist of five clay vessels and an enamel basin. Three categories are represented in the recorded sample of pottery, namely, one service, two cooking, and two storage wares. The service ware is a footed bowl 13 cm in both MD and MaD, 9 cm in base diameter (BD), 11 cm in TH, 3 cm in foot height (FH), and finally 1 cm in T, decorated with extensive twisted roulette impression on the body. Both specimens of cooking vessels belong to the same morphological class, that of a slightly globular pot with constricted to short neck and everted rim, with morphometric attributes ranging from 25 to 30 cm for MaD, 27 to 35 cm for TH, 17 to 21 cm for HMD, and finally 0.8 cm in T. One specimen is decorated on the shoulder with a horizontal band of twisted roulette impression under- and overlined by parallel grooved lines, and the other with extensive twisted roulette impression on the body overlined on the shoulder by two horizontal and parallel grooved lines complemented with four equidistant appliqué buttons. Storage vessels comprise a large jug and a necked jar. The former measures 10 cm in MD, 31 cm in MaD, 38 cm in TH, 4 cm in NH, 18 cm in HMD, and finally 1.1 cm in T, decorated on its upper half with a large band of twisted roulette impression delimited at the bottom and top by parallel grooved lines, complemented by nine panels of two parallel and vertical grooved lines. The latter is plain with an appliqué cordon at the shoulder, and measures 30 cm on MD, 40 cm cm in MaD, 52 cm in TH, 16 cm in NH, 27 cm in HMD, and 1.5 cm in T.

Houses 17 and 18 are attached to a fenced field with a 5 × 5 m, nine-poles storage platform behind. House 18 is probably a young adult home. It is built with a single central pole, measures 4.8 m in diameter, and comprises a small bed. A sample of four potteries, divided into a single cooking and three storage vessels, have been recorded. The cooking ware is a slightly globular, short-necked pot with everted rim, 21 cm in MD, 28 cm in MaD, 30 cm in TH, 4 cm in NH, 18 cm in HMD, and finally, 0.9 cm in T, decorated with extensive twisted roulette impression on the body overlined on the shoulder by two horizontal and parallel grooved lines, complemented by four equidistant pairs of appliqué buttons. All the storage vessels are necked jars, with morphometric attributes varying from 25 to 30 cm for MD, 37 to 41 cm for MaD, 49 to 60 cm for TH, 6 to 11 cm for NH, 28 to 30 cm for HMD, and finally 1.2 to 1.8 cm for T. Two of the specimens share a similar decoration found on the shoulder and consisting of a horizontal band of twisted roulette impression delimited at the bottom and top by parallel grooved lines, with, in addition, three or four equidistant, round or elongated, and vertical appliqué buttons. The last specimen is plain but has an appliqué cordon with three equidistant lugs on the shoulder.

House 19 is located 10 m farther N and is associated with a 5 × 2 m, six-poles storage platform and a chicken coop. It is built with a single central pole, measures 5.1 m in diameter, and comprises an elaborate hearth and a large bed. Two storage vessels were recorded near the fireplace. One is a large, globular, short-necked pot, 25 cm in MD, 34 cm in MaD, 37 cm in TH, 4 cm in NH, 22 cm in HMD, and finally 1 cm in T, decorated on the shoulder with a horizontal band of twisted roulette impression under- and overlined by parallel grooved lines. And the other is a necked jar measuring 27 cm in MD, 40 cm in MaD, 50 cm in TH, 8 cm in NH, 30 cm in HMD, and finally 1.5 cm in T, decorated on the shoulder with a horizontal band of twisted roulette impression with three superimposed parallel, grooved lines and three equidistant sets of four vertical and elongated appliqué buttons.

Unit 2 is located to the S of the cluster. It consists almost exclusively of storage and livestock features. Feature 15 is a barn and cattle house built with five roof-supporting poles and measures 8.3 m in diameter. Feature 20, a few meters E, is smaller in size, built with a single central pole measuring 5 m in diameter, and used as sheep/goat house. It is attached in the W to a smaller 5 × 2 m, six-poles storage platform and to a larger 7 × 7 m, nine-poles one in the E. In addition, there are two sheep/goat enclosures; both are oval-shaped features measuring 8 × 6 m for the smaller and 10 × 8 m for the larger.

Unit 3, some 15 m N of the previous one, comprises two houses, one storage platform, five chicken coops, and a relatively large cattle enclosure. The recorded cattle enclosure is attached to a house, an uncommon situation which clearly departs from the collective use of the central part of the settlement. It is an oval-shaped feature measuring 27 × 25 m. The 5 × 5 m, nine-poles storage platform connects both houses, while the five chicken coops are set in a N-S line a few meters behind the houses and protected with a fence. Feature 22 is a barn/livestock house built with two roof-supporting poles and measuring 7.1 m in diameter. Feature 23, measuring 6.4 m in diameter and built with two roof-supporting poles, comprises an elaborate hearth, a large bed, and a raised grinding installation. Domestic equipment is reduced to a sample of eight clay vessels arranged on wooden shelves.

The pottery material comprises two major categories, with two cooking and six storage vessels. One of the cooking vessels is a short-necked, globular pot with everted rim, 13 cm in MD, 30 cm in MaD, 35 cm in TH, 3 cm in NH, 18 cm in HMD, and finally 1.8 cm in T, decorated on the shoulder with the classic horizontal band of twisted roulette impression delimited with parallel grooved lines. The other is a slightly globular, short-necked pot with everted rim, decorated with extensive twisted roulette on the body overlined on the shoulder by two horizontal and parallel grooved lines complemented with three equidistant pairs of appliqué buttons. Two morphological classes are represented among the storage vessels: one specimen of a long-necked, globular pot with everted rim, 12 cm in MD, 27 cm in MaD, 35 cm in TH, 9 cm in NH, 19 cm in HMD, and finally 1.2 cm in T, decorated on the shoulder with a horizontal band of twisted roulette delimited by parallel grooved lines. There are five specimens of long-necked jars; their morphometric attributes vary from 25 to 29 cm for MD, 36 to 44 cm for MaD, 44 to 70 cm for TH, 7 to 15 cm for NH, 23 to 43 for HMD, and finally 1.4 to 1.6 cm for T. One of the jars is plain but has an appliqué cordon with four equidistant lugs on the shoulder. There are two major decoration patterns for the remaining four specimens. Two of them are decorated with extensive twisted roulette impression on the body overlined on the shoulder by two or three horizontal and parallel grooved lines. The last two specimens have a horizontal band of twisted roulette impression with three superimposed parallel grooved lines on the shoulder, complemented in one case by three equidistant lugs and, for the other three, equidistant sets of three elongated, vertical, and parallel appliqué buttons.

Unit 4, located farther E in the inner space of the village, consists of feature 21 with its associated two chicken coops. House 21 measures 6.3 m in diameter, is built with two roof-supporting poles, and comprises an elaborate hearth and a large bed. The recorded domestic equipment consists of two clay vessels, four enamelwares, and one tin bucket. Both recorded potteries are storage vessels. They are similar with minor variations in some of their morphometric attributes, which vary from 28 to 31 cm for MD, 44 cm for MaD, 60 to 62 cm for TH, 9 to 10 cm for NH, 38 to 40 cm for HMD, and finally 1.3 to 1.4 cm for T. Both are decorated with extensive twisted roulette impression on the body overlined on the shoulder by three horizontal and parallel grooved lines.

Cluster 6, less than 10 m N of the previous one, is a clearly demarcated and fenced complex, with four wood and reeds houses, two chicken coops, a sheep/goat enclosure, and a storage platform. Houses are set in a square pattern, and the delimited space measures 50 × 45 m. A fenced field, 60 m in length and 50 m in maximum width, is attached to the complex. Feature 24, located at the southwestern corner of the complex, is probably a teenager's or young adult's house; it is built with a single central pole, measures 4.7 m in diameter, and comprises a small bed. House 24 is connected to neighboring house 27 by a 17 × 7 m, eighteen-poles storage platform. Habitation house 27, located at the northwestern corner of the cluster is built with two roof-supporting poles and measures 6 m in diameter. Furniture consists of an elaborate hearth, a large bed, and a raised grinding installation. Domestic equipment comprises six enamelwares and thirteen clay vessels.

The recorded pottery is divided into three storage and ten cooking vessels. All the storage vessels are necked jars. Their morphometric attributes vary from 25 to 26 cm for MD, 36 to 40 cm for MaD, 45 to 50 cm for TH, 7 to 9 cm for NH, 22 to 30 cm for HMD, and finally, 1.2 to 1.7 cm for T. All the jars are decorated on the shoulder with a horizontal band of twisted roulette impression with superimposed or delimited by three or two parallel grooved lines, complemented in two cases with three equidistant sets of four elongated, vertical, and parallel appliqué buttons. Three morphological classes are represented among the cooking vessels. There are two specimens of globular, necked pots with everted rims, both decorated on the shoulder with a horizontal band of twisted roulette impression combined with two or three parallel grooved lines, with, in one case, six equidistant panels of two short, vertical, and parallel grooved lines; they measure 13 and 16 cm in MD, 25 and 30 cm in MaD, 30 and 41 cm in TH, 4 and 5 cm in NH, 18 and 20 cm in HMD, and finally, 0.9 and 1.1 cm in T. There are also two specimens of a rounded base, hemispheric, handled, short-necked pot, 22 to 23 cm in MD, 28 to 32 in MaD, 30 to 36 cm in TH, 3 cm in NH, 17 to 20 cm in HMD, and finally, 0.7 to 0.8 cm in T, decorated with extensive twisted roulette impression on the body overlined on the shoulder by two or three horizontal and parallel grooved lines complemented, in one case, by two symmetric appliqué buttons, and in the other, eight equidistant, elongated, vertical appliqué buttons. Six of the recorded cooking vessels belong to the class of slightly globular, constricted to short-necked pot with more or less everted rim. Their mensurations vary from 13 to 23 cm for MD, 21 to 32 cm for MaD, 24 to 32 cm for TH, 3 to 5 cm for NH, 12 to 15 cm for HMD, and finally 0.7 to 1 cm for T. Two dominant patterns of decoration are attested in this ware class; one is recorded on a single specimen and consists of a horizontal band of twisted roulette impression with three superimposed, parallel, grooved lines. The other, found on five specimens, is constituted of extensive twisted roulette impression on the body overlined on the shoulder by two horizontal and parallel grooved lines, with, in one case, additional four equidistant appliqué buttons.

Feature 25, in the SE corner, is a barn/livestock house, associated with a pit and two chicken coops. The material used to build the coops was probably collected from the pit. The livestock house is built with four roof-supporting poles and measures 8.1 m in diameter. Feature 26, at the northeastern corner of the cluster, is built with a single central pole and measures 4.8 m in diameter. It is a straw-mat workshop adjunct to a sheep/goat enclosure; a supply of freshly collected and drying straw as well as a few completed mats were being stored there. The enclosure is oval-shaped and measures 11 m in length and 6 m in maximum width.

Cluster 7 is located in the NW of the settlement. It consists of five wood and reeds houses, with four arranged in a linear NE-SW pattern stretched on approximately 85 m. The fifth feature is found in the inner part of the village. Houses 31 and 32, located in the northeastern end of the cluster at 5 m from each other, were still inhabited at the time of the field investigation and, as such, were not studied in detail. They measure, respectively, 4.6 and 6.1 m in diameter, with each having a hearth and a bed. Feature 28, at the southwestern end of the cluster, is a young man's habitation house. It is built with a single central pole with furniture being reduced to a small bed. Feature 29, some 15 m NE of the previous one, measures 4.9 m in diameter, is built with a single central pole, and comprises an elaborate hearth and a relatively large bed. The barn/livestock house, feature 30, is found at 20 m in the inner side of the village; it has a single-central-pole and, surprisingly, a raised grinding installation.

Cluster 8 is located in the N-NW of the settlement. It comprises five wood and reeds houses, one storage platform, and a chicken coop, stretched on 90 m (fig. 19). Feature 33, at the western end of the cluster, is associated with a chicken coop; it measures 6.5 m in diameter and was still inhabited by the time of field study. House 34, at 15 m due S, is a new 4.7-m-in-diameter feature being built. House 35, at the center of the cluster, is built with two roof-supporting poles, measures 7 m in diameter, and comprises an elaborate hearth and a large bed. Domestic equipment consists of five clay vessels and a shoe polisher toolbox. The house's owner is clearly involved in part-time work in the nearby city of Kusseri.

The recorded pottery material consists of three storage and two cooking vessels. All the storage vessels are necked jars, with mensurations varying from 24 to 28 cm for MD, 38 to 41 cm for MaD, 42 to 55 cm for TH, 6 to 12 cm for NH, 23 to 35 cm for HMD, and finally 1.1 to 1.4 cm for T. Each specimen has a specific decoration; one is almost plain with an appliqué cordon and four equidistant lugs at shoulder. The other is decorated on the shoulder with a horizontal band of twisted roulette impression delimited by two parallel grooved lines complemented by four equidistant, elongated, vertical appliqué buttons. The last one has extensive twisted roulette impression on the body overlined on the shoulder by three horizontal and parallel grooved lines. Features 36 and 37, at the eastern end of the cluster, are barn/livestock houses. The former, attached to a 5 × 3 m, six-poles storage platform, is built with four roof-supporting poles and measures 9.6 m in diameter. The latter, at approximately 5 m per side, measures 8.9 m in diameter and is built with four roof-supporting poles.

Cluster 9 is found due N of the settlement. It is a well-demarcated and fenced unit comprising a 80 × 75 m field, two wood and reeds houses located approximately 5 m from each other, two storage platforms, and a chicken coop. Feature 38 is a 8-m-in-diameter barn/livestock house, built with four roof-supporting poles. Feature 39, the habitation house, is built with two roof-supporting poles and measures 6.2 m in diameter. House's furniture consists of an elaborate hearth, a large bed, and a raised grinding installation. Domestic gear comprises a set of seven clay vessels, one service-, one cooking-, and five storage wares. The flat the bottomed deep basin is used for food serving; the recorded specimen measures 31 cm in both MD and MaD, 12 cm in BD, 19 cm in both TH and HMD, and finally 1.5 cm in T; it is decorated with twisted roulette impression on the body overlined by two appliqué cordons and symmetric buttons. The cooking ware is a slightly globular pot with constricted neck, 20 cm in MD, 26 cm in MaD, 26 cm in TH, 17 cm in HMD, and finally 1.1 cm in T, decorated with extensive twisted roulette impression on the body overlined on the shoulder by two horizontal and parallel grooved lines complemented by four equidistant appliqué buttons. The storage vessels are divided into two morphological classes: a single specimen of necked, globular pot decorated on the shoulder with a horizontal band of twisted roulette impression delimited at the bottom and top by two parallel grooved lines; and four specimens of similar necked jars decorated with extensive twisted roulette impression on the body overlined on the shoulder by two or three horizontal and parallel grooved lines. Their morphometric attributes vary from 25 to 29 cm for MD, 37 to 44 cm for MaD, 47 to 55 cm for TH, 6 to 8 cm for NH, 25 to 34 cm for HMD, and finally 1.2 to 1.5 cm for T.

Cluster 10 is a partially fenced complex located in the NE of the settlement. It comprises four wood and reeds houses arranged in a slightly in-curved linear pattern stretched over 90 m E-W. The barn/livestock houses of the complex, features 40 and 43, are found at both ends of the cluster. The former is built with two roof-supporting poles and measures 6.7 m in diameter, while the latter measures 9.6 m in diameter and has four roof-supporting poles. Habitation houses are located at the center. House 42, the smaller, measuring 7 m in diameter and comprising a hearth and a bed of unknown size, was still inhabited by the time of fieldwork. The larger habitation house 41 is some 10 m NW of the previous one to which it is connected by a fence; it is built with four roof-supporting poles and measures 8.5 m in diameter. House's furniture consists of an elaborate hearth and a large bed, while domestic gear comprises six clay vessels and one plastic water canteen.

The recorded pottery material is constituted of two categories of wares: two cooking and four storage vessels. Both cooking wares are slightly globular, constricted to short-necked pots, 20 to 21 cm in MD, 25 cm in MaD, 23 to 25 cm in TH, 15 to 16 cm in HMD, and finally, 0.9 to 1 cm in T. One specimen is decorated with extensive twisted roulette impression on the body, overlined on the shoulder by two horizontal and parallel grooved lines complemented by four equidistant pairs of appliqué buttons. The other specimen seems to have a similar decoration but the pot frequently used for cooking is covered with a thick tar deposit. All the storage vessels are similar necked jars decorated on the shoulder with a horizontal band of twisted roulette impression under- and overlined by two horizontal and parallel grooved lines. Their morphometric attributes range from 25 to 26 cm for MD, 33 to 37 cm for MaD, 44 to 48 cm for TH, 6 cm for NH, 24 to 30 cm for HMD, and finally, 1.2 to 1.5 cm for T.

Cluster 11 is located due E of the settlement. It is a partially fenced complex comprising seven houses, with one in mud-brick, three storage platforms, three chicken coops, and three small sheep/goat enclosures, stretched over 115 m N-S and 110 m W-E. Even if the features are evenly distributed, there are clearly three distinct units. Unit 1 is found at the northern end of the cluster and comprises five features. Feature 44 is a wood and reeds barn/livestock house built with four roof-supporting poles and measures 8.2 m in diameter. Habitation house 45, approximately 10 m SE, measures 7.6 m in diameter. It is built in mud-brick with four roof-supporting poles and contains an elaborate hearth, a large bed, and a raised grinding installation. The chicken coop, the 10 × 7 m, fifteen-poles storage platform, and the 10 × 6 m, oval-shaped sheep/goat enclosure are located in the fenced courtyard (fig. 19).

The recorded pottery amounts to twelve specimens distributed into three service, five cooking, and four storage vessels. Two shape classes are represented among the service wares: one specimen of footed bowl, 16 cm in both MD and MaD, 9 cm in DB, 14 cm in both TH and HMD, 5 cm in FH, and finally 0.8 cm in T, decorated with extensive twisted roulette impression on the body; and two specimens of shallow, rounded base bowl, measuring 21 to 23 cm in MD and MaD, 6 to 8 cm in TH and HMD, and finally 1 cm in T, with decoration similar to that of the footed bowl. All the cooking vessels are slightly globular, constricted to short-necked pots with more or less everted rims. Their mensurations range from 17 to 25 cm for MD, 22 to 30 cm for MaD, 21 to 36 cm for TH, 14 to 20 cm for HMD, and finally 0.8 to 1 cm for T. One specimen is decorated on the shoulder with a horizontal band of twisted roulette impression delimited by two parallel grooved lines. The remaining four share a similar pattern of decoration consisting of extensive twisted roulette impression on the body overlined on the shoulder by horizontal and parallel grooved lines. This basic pattern is complemented by four equidistant appliqué buttons in two cases and, in one case, two symmetric single and double appliqué buttons.All the storage vessels are necked jars; their morphometric attributes range from 25 to 28 cm for MD, 36 to 40 cm for MaD, 31 to 47 cm for TH, 4 to 7 cm for NH, 21 to 27 cm for HMD, 1.2 to 1.4 cm for T. They are all decorated on the shoulder with a horizontal band of twisted roulette impression delimited by two or three parallel grooved lines, with, in addition, three sets of four elongated vertical, four single elongated vertical, and four double equidistant appliqué buttons.

House 46, a few meters S of the previous one, measures 4.5 m in diameter. It is a young man's dwelling unit, built with a single central pole and comprising a small bed, as well as an enamelware.

Unit 2 is set in linear E-W arrangement, with a fenced 7 × 5 m, twelve-poles storage platform in the background, the habitation house 47 in the middle at approximately 20 m W, and finally, the barn/livestock house 48 at 25 m farther W. The chicken coop and the small 7 × 5 m, oblong-shaped sheep/goat enclosure are located on the northern flank of the unit. House 47 is built with two roof-supporting poles, measures 6.4 m in diameter, and comprises an elaborate hearth and a large bed. Domestic equipment consists of three enamelwares and nine clay vessels. A pair of rubber shoes was found on the house floor.

The pottery sample comprises one service, two cooking, and six storage wares. There is one specimen of plain footed bowl measuring 14 cm in both MD and MaD, 9 cm in BD, 12 cm in both TH and HMD, 3 cm in FH, and finally 0.8 cm in T. Cooking vessels belong to two morphological classes: one is a globular, necked pot decorated on the shoulder with a horizontal band of twisted roulette impression delimited by parallel grooved lines, measuring 13 cm in MD, 27 cm in MaD, 35 cm in TH, 4 cm in NH, 18 cm in HMD, and finally 0.9 cm in T. The other is a slightly globular, necked pot, 22 cm in MD, 31 cm in MaD, 36 cm in TH, 4 cm in NH, 20 cm in HMD, and finally 0.9 cm in T, with its decoration similar to that of the previous specimen, but with four pairs of equidistant appliqué buttons. One of the storage ware is a necked pot, 11 cm in MD, 25 cm in MaD, 34 cm in TH, 6 cm in NH, 18 cm in HMD, and finally 0.9 cm in T. The remaining five are necked jars measuring 25 to 27 cm in MD, 36 to 40 cm in MaD, 42 to 55 cm in TH, 4 to 11 cm in NH, 22 to 30 cm in HMD, and finally, 1.2 to 1.6 cm in T. All the storage vessels share the same pattern of decoration: a horizontal band of twisted roulette impression delimited by parallel grooved lines on the shoulder, complemented in two cases by three or four lugs. Feature 48, the barn/livestock house is built with four roof-supporting poles and measures 8.9 m in diameter.

Unit 3, 10 to 20 m farther S, also consists of five features: two houses, a chicken coop, a storage platform, and a sheep/goat enclosure, with, in addition, a fence around the barn/livestock house 49.The sheep/goat enclosure is slightly elongated and measures 10 × 8 m; it is set in the fence surrounding the livestock house. The latter is built with four roof-supporting poles and measures 8.9 m in diameter. Habitation house 50, with its attached 4 × 5 m, twelve-poles storage platform, is located approximately 20 m E. It is built with five roof-supporting poles, measures 8.2 m in diameter, and contains an elaborate hearth and a large bed. A sample of eight clay vessels and one enamelware was recorded. There are three cooking vessels with similar decoration, but distributed into two morphological classes: two specimens of slightly globular, short-necked pots measuring 20 to 24 cm in MD, 23 to 29 cm in MaD, 22 to 32 cm in TH, 4 cm in NH, 15 to 17 cm in HMD, and finally, 0.9 to 1.1 cm in T; and one of globular, rounded based, short-necked, and handled pot, 23 cm in MD, 29 cm in MaD, 34 cm in TH, 4 cm in NH, 17 cm in HMD, and finally 0.9 cm in T. They are decorated with extensive twisted roulette impression on the body overlined by two horizontal and parallel grooved lines on the shoulder in one case. This basic pattern is complemented for the remaining two cases by four single and three double equidistant appliqué buttons. All five storage vessels are necked jars with morphometric attributes varying from 24 to 29 cm for MD, 34 to 42 cm for MaD, 37 to 50 cm for TH, 4 to 6 cm for NH, 21 to 36 cm for HMD, and finally, 1 to 1.3 cm for T. They are decorated on the shoulder with a horizontal band of twisted roulette impression delimited by two or three parallel grooved lines, with, in addition, four equidistant single appliqué buttons in one case, and four such sets of three vertical and elongated ones in the other.

Cluster 12 is located in the SE of the settlement; it includes three houses, two in wood and reeds, and one in mud-brick, two chicken coops, a storage platform, a fenced field, and a large tree. The barn/livestock house (feature 51) is located in the inner part of the settlement, approximately 40 m from the other houses. It is built with six roof-supporting poles and measures 10 m in diameter. Both habitation houses (features 52 and 53) were still inhabited at the time of fieldwork. They measure, respectively, 5.5 and 5.3 m in diameter, with the latter built in mud-brick. The adjunct nine-poles storage platform measures 4 × 5 m, and the fenced field 30 × 25 m.

Ngada IV has twelve houses clusters with the frequency of units varying from one to four (tables 26 and 27) The high number of worn-out features is a clear indication of the prior occupation of the same place a few years before. One of the striking characteristics of the Ngada IV layout is a certain degree of nucleation, indicated by frequent fencing, and the decreasing number and size of communal central corrals. Two competing hypotheses can be offered at this juncture: (1) the village may have witnessed a decrease in its livestock population; or (2) each household unit manages its own livestock which is kept in specially built features. At a higher level of spatial patterning, the settlement seems to be divided into four parts: the southern clusters complex with cluster 1 to 4; the western one with clusters 5 and 6, the northern with clusters 7 to 10, and finally the eastern complex with clusters 11 and 12.

Chapter 5

Two Northern Settlements

Ndom and Gobrem are the northernmost of the studied settlements. This group, with only two villages located 5 kilometers from each other, is particularly loose. The idea of a group itself is even weaker if one considers the fact that Gobrem is an abandoned village, a de facto archaeological site, while Ndom is still inhabited, and this as far back as the middle of the nineteenth century (Nachtigal 1980). Dealing with both settlements within the same rubric is thus a simple matter of convenience.

Ndom

Ndom is located 7–8 kilometers NNE of the Ngada village cluster. The village is almost circular in shape, measuring 120 m in its maximum SE-NW axis (fig. 20) and thus extended over 1.26 hectares. It comprises twenty-three houses distributed into six clusters (tables 28 and 29), located almost half a kilometer (450 m) S of the settlement. The central part of the site has three large *Tamarindus* sp. trees providing particularly thick shade. It is devoted to livestock, with a large 53 × 33 m, oblong shaped cattle enclosure, and four smaller circular sheep/goat corrals set in two groups. Those located on the northeastern flank of the cattle enclosure measure 10 and 8 m in diameter. The southwestern specimens are smaller and measure 8.5 m in diameter for the largest and 5 m for the smallest.

The village's main entrance is clearly in the S-SE. It is a 30.5-m-wide gap in the houses' ring, with two large trees set at 20 m from each other. There is a shallow 10-m-in-diameter circle of a worn-out feature (feature 24), suggesting that the house may have been relocated somewhere else to keep the entrance clear. A second gap, measuring 6 m in width, used as an exit, is to be found in the W (fig. 20).

Cluster 1 is located in the southern part of the settlement, W of the entrance. It is a completely fenced complex, as is the case for most of the household units of this village. It measures 65 m in its N-S axis and 55 m in the E-W one. It comprises

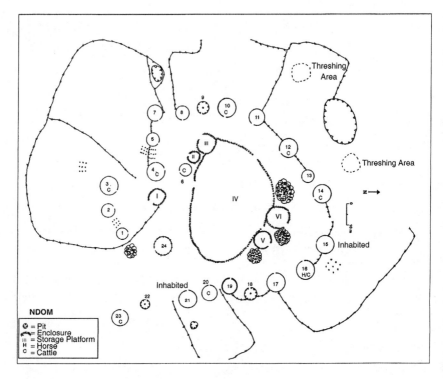

Figure 20: Map of Ndom

three wood and reeds houses, two storage platforms, a cultivated plot, and a sheep/goat corral.The corral, circular in shape and measuring 8 m in diameter, is situated in the inner part of the village at 15–20 m N of the houses. The houses are set in a linear E-W arrangement. Feature 1, at the eastern end of the cluster, is a bachelor's

Table 28: Ndom household clusters

Cluster number	Number of units	Habitation houses	Livestock houses	Storage platforms	Others
1	1	2	1	2	2
2	1	2	2	2	2
3	1	2	1	—	3
4	1	1	2	—	1
5	2	1	2	1	4
6	2	2	2	—	2
Total	8	10	10	5	14

Table 29: Ndom general distribution of pottery

Cluster number	Number of features	Service vessels	Cooking vessels	Storage vessels	Unknown	Total
1	7	—	4	5	—	9
2	8	—	7	10	—	17
3	6	1	10	9	3	23
4	4	—	—	4	1	5
5	8	—	—	—	—	—
6	6	—	—	—	—	—
Total	39	1	21	28	4	54

house built with a single central pole measuring 5 m in diameter. House furniture consists of a small bed. A 3 × 3 m, nine-poles storage platform is located a few meters W, set between features 1 and 2. Feature 2 is found 7 m W of the previous one; it is built with two roof-supporting poles, measures 7 m in diameter, and comprises an elaborate hearth, a large bed, and a raised grinding platform. The domestic equipment consists of nine clay vessels and a single enamelware. In addition, a pair of men's rubber shoes was found on the house floor.

The recorded pottery is divided into two categories, with five storage and four cooking vessels. Four of the storage wares belong to a single morphological class, that of short to long-necked jar. Their mensurations vary from 24 to 30.5 cm for MD, 36 to 43 cm for MaD, 38 to 61 for TH, 4 to 11.5 cm for NH, 29 to 40 cm for HMD, and finally, 1.1 to 1.4 cm for T. Each jar has a peculiar decoration; they can nonetheless be partitioned into two groups of two vessels each. One group comprises decoration restricted to the vessel's shoulder; in one case this consists of a horizontal band of twisted roulette impression under- and overlined by parallel grooved lines. In the other, there is a similar horizontal band of twisted roulette impression, but this time it is complemented with three parallel grooved lines and four equidistant sets of three appliqué buttons. The other group comprises vessels decorated with extensive twisted roulette impression on the body, overlined on the shoulder in one case by two horizontal and parallel grooved lines, a pattern to which three equidistant pairs of appliqué buttons are added in the last specimen.

There are three specimens of constricted to short-necked, slightly globular pots, one used for storage and the others for cooking. Their morphometric attributes vary from 18 to 26.5 cm for MD, 23 to 28 cm for MaD, 21 to 35 cm for TH, 4 cm for maximum NH, 13 to 22 cm for HMD, and finally, 0.7 to 1 cm for T. A single decoration pattern is represented and consists of extensive twisted roulette on the body overlined on the shoulder by one or two horizontal and parallel grooved lines.

The third morphological class comprises two vessel specimens used for cooking purposes. They are rounded base, globular, short-necked, handled pots, and are decorated with extensive twisted roulette impression on the body, overlined on the shoulder by two horizontal and parallel grooved lines. They measure 21 to 21.5 cm in MD, 23 to 28 cm in MaD, 27 to 29 cm in TH, 3 to 5 cm in NH, 17 to 18 cm in HMD, and finally, 1 cm in T.

The third feature of the complex (feature 3) is a barn/livestock house; it is located 4 m W of the main habitation, is built with eight roof-supporting poles, and measures 9.5 m in diameter. A 4.5 × 3 m, nine-poles storage platform is located in the cultivated plot, approximately 10 m behind the barn/livestock house. Finally, the part of the fenced complex devoted to the cultivated plot measures 55 m in length W-E and 34 m N-S.

Cluster 2, in the southwestern part of the village, is also completely fenced; it is spread over 75 m SW-NE and 45 m SE-NW, and comprises four wood and reeds houses, a sheep/goat corral, two storage platforms, and a fenced pit (fig. 20). Features 4, 5, and 7, set in a W-E linear arrangement, are tied to each other by a fence. Feature 4, the barn/livestock house, is located at the eastern end of the complex; it is built with seven roof-supporting poles and measures 10 m in diameter. Feature 6, located in the inner part of the village and next to the 6-m-in-diameter sheep/goat corral, is also a barn/livestock house. It is smaller in size, built with a single central pole, and measures 6.2 m in diameter. The 7-m-long space between features 4 and 5 is filled with storage platforms; the larger specimen, situated on the northern side of the fence, is built with nine supporting poles and measures 4 × 3.5 m. The smaller one, found in the southern side, has ten supporting poles and measures 3 × 2.5 m.

Feature 5 is built with a single central pole and measures 5.8 m in diameter. It has an elaborate hearth and no bed. It is one of the rare cases of a kitchen being used exclusively for cooking purposes. A single rubber shoe as well as an enamel, shallow basin were found in the house. The main habitation house, feature 7, is located at the western end of the complex. Built with a single central pole, it measures 6.9 m in diameter and comprises an elaborate hearth and a large bed. The domestic kit is particularly rich, with seventeen clay vessels arranged on wooden shelves on both sides of the hearth, as well as ten enamelwares. A pair of men's rubber shoes was recorded on the house floor.

The sample of recorded clay vessels is partitioned into two categories, with seven cooking, and ten storage wares. All the seven cooking wares belong to a single morphological class, that of slightly globular pot with constricted neck and everted rim. They are all decorated with extensive twisted roulette impression on the body, overlined on the shoulder by one (one case) or two horizontal and parallel grooved lines. Their mensurations vary from 15 to 24 cm for MD, 18 to 32 cm for MaD, 18 to 32 cm for TH, 11 to 19 cm for HMD, and finally, 7 to 1.2 cm for T. The storage vessels are divided into two morphological classes, with eight short to long-necked jars and two globular jars with slightly constricted neck. The latter measures 29 to 30 cm in MD, 37 to 41 cm in MaD, 40 cm in TH, 20 to 25 cm in HMD, and finally, 1.1 to 1.2 cm in T; both are decorated with extensive twisted roulette impression on the body, overlined on the shoulder in one case by two horizontal and parallel grooved lines and, in the other, by a single horizontal grooved line, complemented by a horizontal band of chevron impression made with carved roulette and five equidistant pairs of appliqué buttons. The former, the set of eight short- to long-necked jars, measure 21 to 30 cm in MD, 32 to 45 cm in MaD, 39 to 60 cm in TH, 3 to 9 cm in NH, 22 to 34 cm in HMD, and finally, 0.9 to 1.3 cm in T. Two patterns of decoration are represented: one, confined to the vessel's shoulder and found on five specimens, consists of a horizontal band of twisted roulette impression under- and overlined by horizontal and parallel grooved lines. The other, with extensive twisted roulette impression on the body overlined on the shoulder by two horizontal and parallel grooved lines, is found on three specimens, with, in one case, additional five equidistant appliqué buttons.

Cluster 3 is located in the western part of the village on the northern side of a 6-m-wide gap, which is the village exit (fig. 20). It is a well-delineated complex comprising four wood and reeds features set in a N-S linear arrangement, a 49 × 28 m fenced cultivated plot, a small 1 × 1 m, four-poles storage platform, and what is probably an 8-m-in-diameter sheep/goat corral located in the inner part of the site and attached to the large cattle enclosure.

Habitation house 8, attached to the cultivated plot fence with the adjunct small storage platform, is situated at the southern end of the cluster. It is built with two roof-supporting poles and measures 6.5 m in diameter. House's furniture consists of an elaborate hearth and a large bed. Domestic equipment comprises sixteen clay vessels and three enamelwares arranged on wooden shelves; a single rubber shoe was found of the house floor. The sample of clay vessels is divided into two use categories, with nine cooking and seven storage wares. Seven out of nine cooking vessels are slightly globular pots with constricted necks and everted rims. Their morphometric attributes vary from 18 to 26 cm for MD, 23 to 37 cm for MaD, 22 to 35 cm for TH, 13 to 20 cm for HMD, and finally, 0.7 to 1.2 cm for T. Three patterns of decoration are attested; one is found on a single specimen and consists of a horizontal band of twisted roulette impression on the shoulder, under- and overlined by parallel grooved lines. The second, with extensive twisted roulette impression on the body overlined on the shoulder by one or two horizontal and parallel grooved lines, is recorded on two specimens. And finally, the third, found on four vessels, is the most elaborate and consists of extensive twisted impression on the body, overlined on the shoulder by one to two horizontal and parallel grooved lines with, in addition, 3, 4, or 5 equidistant appliqué buttons. The remaining two specimens of cooking vessels as well one storage ware are globular short-necked pots, measuring 12 to 14 cm in MD, 29 to 33 cm in MaD, 35 to 36 cm in TH, 4 to 6 cm in NH, 16 to 21 cm in HMD, and finally, 0.9 to 1.1 cm in T. Two of the globular, short-necked pots are decorated on the shoulder by a horizontal band of twisted roulette impression delimited at the bottom and top by two parallel grooved lines. In addition to the pattern described above, the remaining specimen has, from the shoulder to neck base, five vertical panels filled with zigzag grooved lines.

With the exception of the globular, short-necked pot presented above, storage vessels are divided into two morphological classes. Four of the specimens are necked jars, with mensurations varying from 25 to 27 cm for MD, 35 to 47 cm for MaD, 41 to 50 cm for TH, 4 to 9 cm for NH, 24 to 31 cm for HMD, and finally, 1 to 1.2 cm for T. Three of the necked jars are decorated on the shoulder by a horizontal band of twisted roulette impression delimited by two parallel grooved lines, while the last one has extensive twisted roulette impression on the body overlined on the shoulder by two horizontal and parallel grooved lines. The remaining two wares are jars with slightly constricted neck; one is decorated on the shoulder by a horizontal band of twisted roulette impression delimited by two parallel grooved lines, and the other has extensive twisted roulette impression on the body, overlined on the shoulder by two horizontal and parallel grooved lines. They measure 19 and 30 cm in MD, 41 and 42 cm in MaD, 37.5 and 43 cm in TH, 23 and 24 cm in HMD, and finally, 1.1 and 1.4 cm in T.

Feature 9, located 3.5 m N of house 8, is an open, 5.3-m-in-diameter public shelter,built with a single central pole. The barn/livestock house (feature 10) is built with four roof-supporting poles and measures 9.5 m in diameter. It is located 3.5 m N of the discussion house. An enamel basin presumably used for watering the livestock was found on the house floor. Feature 11, the second habitation house, is located at the northern end of the complex, 6.5 m from the barn/livestock feature. It is built with two roof-supporting poles, measures 7.2 m in diameter, and comprises an elaborate hearth, a large bed, and a raised grinding table. Domestic kit consists essentially of seven clay vessels and three enamelwares. A man's rubber shoe was found abandoned on the house floor.

The pottery material is partitioned into three use categories, with one service, two storage, and four cooking vessels. The service vessel is a large bowl, measuring 20 cm in both MD and MaD, 8 cm in base diameter (BD), 13 cm in both TH and HMD, and finally, 1.2 cm in T. The vessel is decorated on the rim with four equidistant sets of three short incised lines, with, in addition, a horizontal band of twisted roulette impression on an appliqué cordon 2 cm below the rim. Four equidistant lugs are attached to the cordon. There is a clear correspondence between the lugs and the sets of incised lines.

Three shapes are represented among the cooking vessels. There are two specimens of slightly globular pots with constricted necks, measuring 20 and 26 cm in MD, 24 and 39 cm in MaD, 27 and 38 cm in TH, 14 and 22 cm in HMD, and finally, 1 and 1.1 cm in T. Both are decorated with extensive twisted roulette impression on the body, overlined on the shoulder by two horizontal and parallel grooved lines, complemented in one case by four equidistant appliqué buttons. There is one specimen of a globular, necked pot, 14 cm in MD, 30 cm in MaD, 36 cm in TH, 5.5 cm in NH, 17 cm in HMD, and finally, 1 cm in T, decorated on the shoulder by a horizontal band of twisted roulette impression delimited by two parallel grooved lines. The third morphological class is represented by a single vessel, a rounded base, hemispheric, two-handled, and short-necked pot, decorated with extensive twisted roulette impression on the body, overlined on the shoulder by two horizontal and parallel grooved lines, complemented by two symmetric appliqué buttons, measuring 21.5 cm in MD, 29 cm in MaD, 32 cm in TH, 2 cm in NH, 16 cm in HMD, and finally, 1.1 cm in T.

Both storage vessels are decorated on the shoulder with a horizontal band of twisted roulette impression delimited by two parallel grooved lines. One is a necked jar, 25 cm in MD, 34 cm in MaD, 39 cm in TH, 3 cm in NH, 22 cm in HMD, and finally, 1 cm in T, and the other, a globular jar with a broken and missing upper part, measuring approximately 22 cm in MD, 42 cm in MaD, 41 cm in TH, 28 cm in HMD, and finally, 1.3 cm in T.

Cluster 4 is located in the northwestern part of the settlement and comprises three wood and reeds features set in a linear SW-NE arrangement (fig. 20). Two of the features are attached to a fence enclosing part of the cultivated plot located in the outer side of the village. Two grain-threshing areas measuring 8 to 10 m in diameter have been recorded within the cultivated plot set on both sides of a large, oblong-shaped pit. The pit measures 21 m in length, 13 m in width, and 1.5 m in depth. It is clear that the clay used to build the circular threshing areas was collected from this pit.The fenced portion of the cultivated plot measures 44 m in length and 28 m in width.

Feature 12, the southwestern-most of the cluster is found 11.5 m NE of the last house of the previous complex; it a relatively large barn/livestock house built with seven roof-supporting poles and measures 9.6 m in diameter. Habitation house 13 is set at the center of the complex, at 8.35 and 3.75 m from its nearest neighbors. It is built with a single central pole, measures 5.7 m in diameter, and comprises an elaborate hearth and a large bed as furniture. The domestic kit consists of five clay vessels and two enamelwares. The pottery material is divided into four morphological classes. There are two necked jars used for storage. One, measuring 26 cm in MD, 46 cm in MaD, 48 cm in TH, 5 cm in NH, 31 cm in HMD, and finally, 1 cm in T, is decorated with a horizontal band of twisted roulette impression on the shoulder, under- and overlined by two parallel grooved lines. The other is similarly decorated with a horizontal band of twisted roulette impression on the shoulder, but complemented with three overlapping horizontal and parallel grooved lines as well as four equidistant lugs and an appliqué button; it measures 28 cm in MD, 41 cm in MaD, 56 cm in TH, 13 cm in NH, 29 cm in HMD, and finally, 1.3 cm in T. Each of the remaining three specimens belongs to a different morphological class. One is a slightly globular, short-necked pot used for cooking, decorated with extensive twisted roulette impression on the body overlined on the shoulder by two horizontal and parallel grooved lines, with its mensurations varying from 24 cm in MD, 36 cm in MaD, 37 cm in TH, 3 cm in NH, 27 cm in HMD, to 1 cm in T. The other, used for storage, is a rounded base, necked pot with everted rim, 20 cm in MD, 29 cm in MaD, 34 cm in TH, 5 cm in NH, 22 cm in HMD, and finally, 1 cm in T, decorated on the shoulder by a horizontal band of twisted roulette impression delimited at the bottom and top by two parallel grooved lines, complemented by four equidistant, short, elongated, vertical appliqué buttons. And the last specimen, a necked, globular jar, measures 27 cm in MD, 48 cm in MaD, 49 cm in TH, 8 cm in NH, 30 cm in HMD, and finally 1 cm in T. It is also decorated with a horizontal band of twisted roulette impression delimited by two parallel grooved lines on the shoulder complemented by four equidistant sets of two parallel and vertical grooved lines from shoulder to neck base.

Feature 14, at the northeastern end of the complex, is another barn/livestock house. It is built with four roof-supporting poles and measures 8.5 m in diameter.

Cluster 5, with three wood and reeds houses set in a slightly in-curved S line, a 4.5 × 4 m, twelve-poles storage platform, and a partially fenced cultivated plot, is situated in the northeastern part of the settlement. There is a fence connecting feature 14 of the previous cluster to house 15 at 15.5 m E. The partially fenced cultivated field measures 65 m in length and 25 m in width. Two sheep/goat corrals, 10 and 8 m in diameter, as well as two large trees located in the inner portion of the site, are part of the cluster

Feature 15 was still inhabited at the time of fieldwork; it is built with two roof-supporting poles, measures 6.8 m in diameter, and comprises an elaborate hearth and a large bed. Clay vessels and enamelwares were observed carefully arranged on wooden shelves, but they were not studied in detail. Feature 16, at 16.2 m SE, is a barn/livestock house built with five roof-supporting poles and measuring 7.5 m in diameter. Feature 17, at the southern end of the cluster, is also a barn/livestock house; it is the largest built feature of the whole settlement measuring 11.1 m in diameter, with twelve roof-supporting poles.

Feature 18 is an open public shelter; it is set at the middle of a previous village entrance, at equal distance (3.8 m) from houses 17 and 19 to which it is attached by a fence. It is built with a single central pole and measures 6.2 m in diameter. Clearly, the discussion house and its fence have been used to close the eastern gap and earlier village entrance/exit. Remarkably, it is sited almost symmetrically relative to feature 9, the other discussion house located in the western side of the settlement (fig. 20).

Cluster 6, at the southern end of the settlement, comprises three houses stretched on 60 m N-S, and a rectangular fenced field 26 × 24 m. A subcircular pit, measuring 3.5 m in maximum diameter and 1 m in depth, has been recorded in the fenced plot. The sediment used to make mud-bricks for house 19 was certainly collected from that pit. House 19 was inhabited during the fieldwork; the number of roof-supporting poles is unknown, but judging from its size, 5.3 m in diameter, there is probably a single one. There is an elaborate hearth and a large bed. Feature 20, at 3 m S, is a wood and reeds barn/livestock house built with four roof-supporting poles, measuring 7.9 m in diameter. House 21, 2.5 m S, was still inhabited; it measures 6.4 m in diameter and comprises a hearth and a bed. The remaining features 22 and 23 are set aside, at slightly more than 14 m from the nearest house. Feature 22 is an open discussion house, 4.8 m in diameter, and is built with a single central pole. The barn/livestock house 23, approximately 6.5 m S of the discussion house measures 8 m in diameter. It is built with four roof-supporting poles and is set at the southern end of the house complex.

The larger portion of the inner settlement space is devoted to the large cattle enclosure. Household units are clearly demarcated by a series of fences. Four of the recorded clusters are single unit complexes, the remaining two having two units. The number of habitation as well as barn/livestock houses varies from one to two, with three of the clusters having one to two storage platforms. The domestic kits from clusters 5 and 6 were not accessible, distorting any serious comparison; the recorded number of clay vessels per household nonetheless varies from four in cluster 4 to twenty-three in cluster 3. There are three discussion shelters for six house clusters; but as far as the settlement layout is concerned, the symmetric location of shelters 9 and 18 is particularly remarkable. If considered in relation to their nearest features, specifically sheep/goats corrals, it can be suggested that both discussion shelters signal a pooling of units in the matter of livestock herding.

Gobrem

Gobrem is located 3 kilometers NE of Houlouf, on the shore of the Abani, a seasonal river. As shown in aerial photographs from the late fifties, the studied site located on the left bank of the seasonal river was part of a twin settlement, with its complementary site on the right bank. Dense scatters of animal bones were recorded from the location of the former right bank site which has disappeared from the record. What is left generally consists of weathered and dispersed tiny fragments of former hearths and fireplaces. Evidence collected from aerial photographs, topographic maps, and census records suggests Gobrem to have been abandoned in the seventies, probably during the 1973–1974 Sahelian drought which plagued large parts of intertropical Africa. Data in support for this suggestion come from the site's well, which is, contrary to all the observed cases, located in the inner part of the settlement (fig. 21). The depth of the well, 8.5 m in total, has been increased three times. If the recorded step-like well's levels were dug according to the height of the water table, one can argue that at its first stage, when the well was originally dug, the water table was higher than 4.55 m, the depth of the upper step. This upper step was followed by an important drop of the water table. The well's depth was then increased to the middle step at 5.45 m. The second drop of the water table was the most important as suggested by the well's bottom at 8.5 m, a difference of slightly more than 3 m. By the time of fieldwork in 1987, the well was completely dry; in this part of the study area, the water table is reached at depths varying from 12 to 15 m.

Being an abandoned settlement, and this for at least thirteen years prior to the ethnoarchaeological project reported here, Gobrem is a de facto archaeological site (fig. 22). The site was colonized by vines, plants, and grasses and some of the features were in advanced stage of collapse. The settlement was thus investigated after

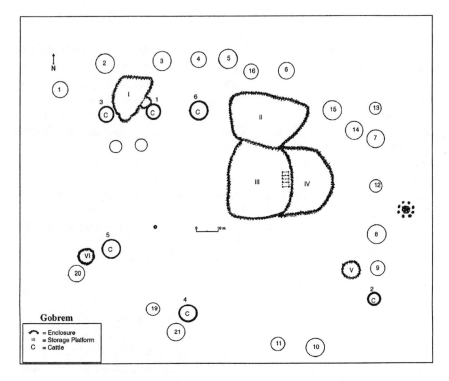

Figure 21: Map of Gobrem

a strict archaeological methodology: it was cleaned with machetes and shovels; the collapsed roofing material was removed from some features; and finally, the furniture, dispersed items, and artifacts found on houses' floors were mapped and photographed. Six refuse dumps were sampled with 3×1 m trenches. The accumulated material consists mostly of cattle dung and sheep/goat droppings mixed with ash. What may be termed cultural remains is composed of pieces of rubber shoes, broken glass bottles, potsherds, and a few corroded pieces of iron wires.

Gobrem is almost circular in shape, measuring 175 m in its maximum SE-NW axis, and 135 m in the minimum SW-NE one (fig. 21). It is extended over 2.40 hectares, with the village's main entrance, a gap 43 m in width, being located in the W. Settlement facilities are distributed into thirty-four features, twenty-seven circular wood and reeds as well as mud-brick houses, six livestock enclosures, and one well. The ring of houses is quite loose, with dwelling features set in distinct and distant clusters. Communal features are located in the inner part of the settlement; they comprise the well, which is oval shaped, measuring 1.45×1.10 m and 8.5 m deep, and three large clustered cattle enclosures. They measure 32 by 28 m for the largest specimen (corral III), which has a 7×3 m, ten-poles fodder storage

Figure 22: Abandoned house at Gobrem

rack; 35 × 22 m for corral II, the second in size; and finally, 28 × 18.50 m for the smallest corral IV. Feature 12 is the "discussion" house situated in the eastern part of the site. It is built with a single central pole and measures 7.1 m in diameter. A large tree surrounded by ash dumps signals a place for gatherings and probably tea parties; it was presumably an extension of the discussion house.

Settlement features are distributed into seven clusters (tables 30 and 31).

Table 30: Gobrem household clusters

Cluster number	Number of units	Habitation houses	Livestock houses	Storage platforms	Others
1	2	4	2	—	1
2	1	2	3	—	—
3	1	3	1	—	—
4	1	2	1	—	1
5	1	1	1	—	—
6	1	2	1	—	—
7	1	1	1	—	1
Total	8	15	10	—	3

Table 31: Gobrem general distribution of pottery

Cluster number	Number of features	Service vessels	Cooking vessels	Storage vessels	Unknown	Total
1	8	—	4	2	—	6
2	5	—	2	2	—	4
3	4	—	5	1	3	9
4	4	—	—	—	—	—
5	2	—	—	—	—	—
6	3	—	1	1	—	2
7	3	—	—	—	—	—
Total	29	—	12	6	3	21

Cluster 1 is located at the northwestern end of the houses' ring, on the northern side of the village's main entrance. It comprises seven wood and reeds houses and one cattle and one sheep/goat enclosures, and is spread over 45 m N-S and 50 m W-NW-E-SE. Houses are distributed around the cattle/ sheep/goat enclosures; the former measures 20 × 14.5 m, and the latter 4.5 m in diameter.

House 1, at the western end of the cluster, measures 7.4 m in diameter; it is built with four roof-supporting poles and comprises a bench, a hearth, and a bed reduced to a scatter of forked poles (fig. 23). The bench, generally used for the storage of pottery, is located on the right-hand side of the house; it measures 3 m in length, 0.55 m in width, and 0.15 m in height. As is usually the case in Shuwa-Arab houses, the hearth is located on the right-hand part of the dwelling. The specimen recorded in this case is semi-elliptical in shape, measuring 1.15 m in length, 0.35 m in height, and 0.50 m in maximum width. Two "clay balls" used as hearthstones complement the cooking installation. Artifacts recorded on the house floor include an almost complete clay vessel, a plastic bag, an empty can, and a goat's metapodial bone. The recorded clay vessel is a slightly globular and elongated cooking pot with constricted neck and everted rim, its base missing. It measures 21 cm in MD, 26.5 in MaD, ?26 cm in TH, ?15 cm in HMD, and finally 1 cm in T, decorated with extensive twisted roulette impression on the body overlined on the shoulder by two horizontal and parallel grooved lines, complemented by four equidistant appliqué buttons. House 2 is located 14.20 m E of the previous one. It is quite large in size measuring 9.30 m in diameter, having been built with six roof-supporting poles. The bed, reduced to a scatter of seven short, forked poles, was located between the rows of roof-supporting poles. The fireplace consists of three "clay balls" found near the scatter of bed poles in the left-hand side of the house. It is clearly not a standard cooking hearth but more probably a heating installation and smoke-making device to keep mosquitoes away. A wooden rack is found next to the wall at approximately 1 m SW of the fireplace. Dispersed remains found on

Figure 23: Floor of a collapsed house exposed at Gobrem

the house floor include a bundle of feathers, an enamel basin, and one flashlight battery.

House 3 is located 17 m farther E; it is built with four roof-supporting poles and measures 7.6 m in diameter. The house roof had collapsed and part of the wall was lying on the ground. The hearth consists of a three clay balls set in a triangular pattern on a circular, fired clay installation. It is located on the right-hand side of the house, 1 m S of the bed's corner. The bed is set at the house's center; five of its forked poles still set in situ. The material remains dispersed all over the house floor include an empty box of powder soap (Omo trade mark), an iron hoe blade, a worn-out flashlight, an empty sardine can, a flashlight battery, a small glass pot, an enamel plate, a plastic lid, a teapot lid, and finally, a large enamel basin lid.

Feature stable 1, measuring 6 m in diameter, is a goat house located some 15 m S of house 3. It is built with two roof-supporting poles, with the wall made of intertwined tree branches. Stable 3, the additional barn/livestock house of the cluster, is situated at 15 m W, on the other side of the cattle enclosure. It is built with a single central pole and measures 8.8 m in diameter.

The remaining two houses, located in the inner part of the settlement, are devoted to habitation. Both are similar and are found 10 m S of the livestock features. Each is built with a single central pole and measures 5.2 m in diameter. Habitation 17 was a practically empty collapsed feature, its central pole having been taken away recently; a crescent-shaped hearth, measuring 1.10 m in length, 0.65 m in maximum width, and 0.10 in height, is located in the standard right-hand side of the house. Habitation 18, 5.40 m E of the previous one, was also a collapsed feature, with two of its roof poles laid on the floor. The house's furniture, however was well-preserved and consists of a 2.70 × 1.80 m bed materialized by three lines of short forked poles, a simple heating fireplace located behind the bed, and a more elaborate five-niche hearth, 1.35 m in length and 0.45 m in width, complemented by two hearthstones, situated in the standard right-hand side of the house. The material items dispersed on the house floor include four complete clay vessels and the upper part of a fifth one, one plate and two large enamel basins, a petrol lamp, a goat skin, empty cans of insecticide spray, tomato sauce, soft drink cans, a calf-weaning lace, as well as an empty box of powder soap (Omo).

The recorded pottery material is divided into three cooking and two storage vessels. Two of the cooking wares are slightly globular pots with constricted necks and everted rims; both are decorated with extensive twisted roulette impression on the body overlined on the shoulder in one case by two horizontal and parallel grooved lines, and in the other, by a line of stabbed, shallow, triangular depressions and a zigzag grooved line. They measure 20 and 23 cm in MD, 26 and 28.5 cm in MaD, 25.5 and 32 cm in TH, 14 and 15.5 cm in HMD, and 0.8 to 1.1 cm in T. The third specimen is a rounded base, hemispheric pot with constricted neck, everted rim, and three equidistant lugs, measuring 28 cm in MD, 35 cm in MaD, 37 cm in TH, 21 cm in HMD, and finally, 0.9 cm in T, decorated with extensive twisted roulette impression on the body, overlined on the shoulder by two horizontal and parallel grooved lines complemented by three equidistant pairs of appliqué buttons. The storage vessels comprise the upper part of a necked pot, 10 cm in MD and 20 cm in MaD, and one specimen of elongated and globular jar with constricted neck and everted rim. Its mensurations range from 26 cm in MD, 40 cm in MaD, 46 cm in TH, 24.5 cm in HMD, to 1.2 cm in T. Both are decorated on the shoulder with a horizontal band of twisted roulette impression delimited at the bottom and top by two parallel grooved lines.

A text excavation, 3 × 1 m, was carried out in an oval-shaped rubbish dump located in front of house 3. The deposit, measuring 0.6 m in maximum thickness, consists essentially of accumulated cattle dung and sheep/goat droppings mixed with ash and charcoal. The collected material remains comprise three pieces of textile, a fragment of an undetermined fired clay item, 3 fragments of glass bottles, two fragments of flashlight batteries, one metal lid, one fruit of *Borassus* palm, seven animal bone fragments, and finally, twelve potsherds. The sample of sherds includes two rim-sherds, one decorated, and ten body-sherds, eight decorated. Twisted roulette impression is represented on all the decorated sherds, with one sherd comprising a band of twisted roulette impression delimited by parallel grooved lines. The modal sherds' thickness is in the 0.8–1 cm class with six sherds, followed by the 0.65–0.75 cm with three sherds, and finally, classes 0.4–0.6, 1.0–1.2, and 1.25–1.5 cm with one sherd each.

Cluster 2 is located in the northern part of the settlement, 9 to 12.40 m from the previous house complex. It comprises five houses, with four set in a linear W-E pattern, at distances varying from 3.80 (house 5 to 16) to 9.20 m (house 16 to 6). The last house is located in the inner part of the settlement, 12.80 m S of house 4 (fig. 21). Four of the features are built in wood and reeds, the remaining one being in mud-bricks.

Feature 4, at the western end of the complex, is a 7-m-in-diameter barn/livestock house, built in mud-bricks with four roof-supporting poles. A small triangular "window," $28 \times 28 \times 35$ cm, is built in the northern side of the house. Habitation 5, built in mud-brick, is found 5.50 m E of the previous one; its heavy straw roof had collapsed. The house measures 8.40 m in diameter and was built with four roof-supporting poles, two of them found lying on the floor. The house floor, hard, compact, and well maintained, was "plastered" with a mixture of clay and horse dung. The bed, originally set in the central part of the house between the roof-supporting poles, was reduced to a series of ten scattered, short, forked poles. The fireplace found in the left-hand side of the house, consists of two series of three hearthstones decorated with finger impressions. The rest of the recorded material remains includes two broken clay vessels, a 20-liters tin container, half of a "Tornado" trademark bicycle air pump, a plate and a lid, both in enamel metal, a large bowl made with horse dung, and finally, a sub-spherical, clay spindle whorl.

The recorded pottery material belongs to the category of cooking wares; one is a slightly globular and elongated pot with constricted neck and everted rim, 26.5 cm in MD, 36 cm in MaD, 38.5 cm in TH, 23 cm in HMD, and 0.9 cm in T, decorated with extensive twisted roulette impression on the body, overlined on the shoulder by a horizontal band of chevrons complemented by three equidistant sets of three appliqué buttons each. And the other is a two-handled, rounded base, hemispheric pot, decorated with extensive twisted roulette impression on the body overlined on the shoulder by two horizontal and parallel grooved lines, with mensurations ranging from 25.5 cm in MD, 31.5 cm in MaD, 34 cm in TH, 15 cm in HMD, to 0.9 cm in T.

House 16, 3.80 m E of the previous feature, is reduced to a shallow, 6 m in diameter circle on the ground. Structural features, such as a three-niche hearth and the posthole of the central pole, are nonetheless still visible. There is one short, forked bed pole and an oval-shaped ash dump in the northern half of the house. It is far from certain that all the material remains found on the house floor belong to the actual house owner. Clearly, evidence like a calf's vertebras, humerus, proximal femur, scapula, and metapodial were brought in by unknown scavengers, like wandering dogs, or jackals, or both. Conversely, the four recorded flashlight batteries, the enamel basin, and the large potsherds may have been part of the house owner's belongings.

House 6, 9.20 m E is a collapsed feature, measuring 7.2 m in diameter, originally built with two roof-supporting poles. Both poles were found lying on the house floor. Feature 6 is a barn/livestock house, almost empty with the exception of a pair of rubber shoes and the remaining part of a plastic bag. Feature stable 6, 12.80 m S of house 4, was built with four roof-supporting poles and measures 8.7 m in diameter. All the four roof-supporting poles were found lying on the house floor, in a similar S-N orientation. In addition, an enamel basin lid, a knotted rope, and an iron knife with a wooden handle were recorded.

Two test-excavations measuring 3 × 1 m each were carried out on subcircular refuse dumps one located between houses 4 and 5, and the other between houses 16 and 6. As in the case for the cluster 1 trench, the accumulated material consists of cattle dung and sheep/goat droppings mixed with ash and pieces of charcoal. The material record collected from the first trial trench comprises one fragment of plastic bag, two glass sherds, and thirty potsherds. Twenty-four, all body-sherds, are decorated. There are three rim-sherds among the six undecorated pieces. Incised lines are recorded on three sherds, twenty being decorated with twisted roulette impression, with the remaining piece combining twisted roulette impression with two parallel grooved lines. The sherds material is distributed into four thickness classes: three in the 0.65–0.75 cm class, fourteen in the 0.8–1.0 cm, ten in the 1.05–1.2 cm, and finally four in the 1.25–1.50 cm one. The sample from the second trench includes one fragment of a plastic box, one piece of fabric, one piece of bicycle tire, one metal bottle lid, one dorsal spine of catfish, one vertebra of sheep/goat, one proximal femur of cattle, one clay pot-leg, and finally, twenty-one potsherds. Thirteen of the sherds, two rim-sherds and eleven body-sherds, are decorated; the undecorated pieces are divided into two rims and six bodies. Twisted roulette impression recorded on eleven sherds is largely predominant; there is one instance of combined twisted roulette impression and parallel grooved lines, and two of single or double grooved lines. Three thickness classes are represented; the 0.8–1.0 cm class with fourteen sherds, the 1.05–1.15 cm with three, and finally, the 1.2–1.35 cm one with four sherds.

Cluster 3, in the NE of the village at 18.50 m SE of the previous house complex, comprises four wood and reeds houses. They are set in a triangular pattern, with features 7, 14, and 15 in line along the 32-m-long basis, and house 13 at the apex (fig. 21). House 7, located at the southern end of the complex, is built with four roof-supporting poles and measures 7.40 m in diameter. The lozenge-shaped hearth measures 0.70 m in length and 0.30 m in width. It is found in the standard right-hand side of the house and consists of four elements: one clay ball and three pots filled with clay set at 0.30 to 0.40 m from each other. Evidence for a bed is reduced to a set of five dispersed short, forked poles. Two clay vessels were found smashed on the house floor, and the rest of the material record consists of a stone-thrower, a small glass pot, a piece of blue fabric, and a worn-out enamel basin.

The pottery material collected from house 7 amounts to five vessels, even if three of them were actually used as "hearthstones" and not as containers. Each of the represented ware, is unique. There is one specimen of a globular storage jar with constricted neck and everted rim, 27.5 cm in MD, 39 cm in MaD, 45.5 cm in TH, 26 cm in HMD, and finally, 0.8 cm in T, decorated by extensive twisted roulette impression, overlined on the shoulder by two horizontal and parallel grooved lines. Cooking vessels are represented by a single specimen of a rounded base, hemispheric, two-handled pot, decorated with extensive twisted roulette impression on the body, overlined on the shoulder by a horizontal line of stabbed, shallow circles and a grooved line, measuring 18 cm in MD, 23 cm in MaD, 26 cm in TH, 16 cm in HMD, and finally, 1.1 cm in T. The recycled wares are divided into: one globular and slightly elongated pot with constricted neck and everted rim, 21 cm in MD, 25.5 cm in MaD, 25.5 cm in TH, 13.5 cm in HMD, and finally, 0.7 cm in T, decorated with extensive twisted roulette impression on the body, overlined on the shoulder by two horizontal and parallel grooved lines, with, in addition, four equidistant appliqué buttons; one globular pot with constricted neck and everted rim, decorated with extensive twisted roulette impression on the body overlined on the shoulder by two horizontal and parallel grooved lines, and measuring 19 cm in MD, 23 cm in MaD, 21.5 cm in TH, 17 cm in HMD, and finally, 0.9 cm in T; and a rounded base, hole-mouth pot, 26 cm in MD, 29.5 cm in MaD, 29 cm in TH, 16 cm in HMD, and finally 0.8 cm in T, decorated with extensive twisted roulette impression on the body, overlined on the shoulder by two horizontal and parallel grooved lines.

House 13, approximately 7 m N of the previous one, is a smaller, presumably adolescent's feature. It is built with a single central pole and measures 5 m in diameter. The bed was situated in the eastern half of the house, as suggested by the scatter of short-forked poles. A simple fireplace materialized by a shallow ash deposit was probably used for light, heating, and/or tea-making. A relatively large enamel lid as well as an enamel plate were found of the house floor. House 14, in the center of the cluster, was found in an advanced state of collapse. It is a barn/livestock feature built with two roof-supporting poles, found lying on the floor, and measures 7.90 m in diameter. Two large-forked poles were found still in position, and an iron chain 4.50 m in length was found hung at one of the wall posts. An enamel plate was also recorded.

House 15, the last feature of the cluster, is located at the northwestern end of the complex at 5.5 m from house 14. It is a relatively large house, built with four roof-supporting poles, measuring 8.5 m in diameter. The heavy thatch roof had collapsed and was lying on the house floor with two of the roof-supporting poles. The bed seems to have been located in the central part of the house, in the area delimited by the four roof-supporting pillars, as suggested by the scatter of seven short-forked poles, with two of them still in situ. The hearth comprises six fire-hardened clay balls, partially disturbed and stretched over 2 m in the northern half of the house. The recorded material remains consist of four clay vessels, a glass bottle, a can of orange soft drink made in Nigeria, a lid of a plastic teapot, two rubber shoes, a worn-out kerosene lamp, and finally a hammer-stone in syenite probably collected from an archaeological site. The sample of clay vessels comprises two broken and two complete wares. The complete specimens are both slightly elongated, globular, rounded base pots with constricted necks and everted rims, measuring 23 and 26 cm in MD, 28 and 29 cm in MaD, 29 to 30 cm in TH, 15 cm in HMD, and finally, 0.8 cm in T, decorated with extensive twisted roulette impression on the body, overlined on the shoulder by two horizontal and parallel grooved lines, complemented in one case by two symmetric sets of three appliqué buttons each. The remaining two broken specimens are upper parts of storage jars. One is a slightly elongated jar with constricted neck and everted rim, decorated on the shoulder with a narrow band of twisted roulette impression, combined with two horizontal and parallel grooved lines, and measuring 23 cm in MD, 34 cm in recorded MaD, 1 cm in T, with unknown TH and HMD. The other is a two-handled, short-necked jar, with measurable morphometric attributes varying from 22.5 cm in MD, 5 cm in NH, to 0.7 cm in T; it is decorated on the body by extensive twisted roulette impression overlined at the neck base by two horizontal and parallel grooved lines.

A trial trench, 2 × 1 m, was sunk in a circular rubbish heap located on the southern side of house 15. The accumulated refuse consists essentially of cattle dung and sheep/goat droppings mixed with ash and tiny pieces of charcoal. The collected material remains are distributed into five potsherds, one fragment of land-snail shell, one rubber piece, one plastic fragment, two fragments of undetermined clay figurines, and the rear part of a terra cotta figurine. The terra cotta figurines were clearly collected from archaeological sites as is the case for the syenite hammer-stone found in house 15. The recorded rear-part of the zoomorphic figurine has a transversal hole bored at its middle, as is the case for most of the figurines collected in archaeological sites in the area (Holl 1988, 2002); it is decorated on the legs, tail, and vertebral axis with convergent, short, incised lines defining chevron-like motifs. The sample of sherds comprises five body-sherds, three decorated with twisted roulette impression and two plain. Two thickness classes are attested, with four sherds in the 0.8–1 cm class and one in the 1.05–1.2 cm one.

Cluster 4 is found 14.80 m S of the discussion house (fig. 21) and consists of three houses set in a linear N-S arrangement, stretched on 35 m, with a 7.20-m-diameter sheep/goat enclosure located in the inner part of the village. House 8, at the northern end of the complex, is built with four roof-supporting poles, measures 7.90 m in diameter, and comprises a composite hearth with six "hearthstones" in an oval-shaped arrangement located in the standard right-hand side of the house. The bed area, set between the four roof-supporting poles, is clearly delimited by in situ poles and postholes. A circular shallow pit, 1 m in diameter, was found in the northern part of the house at less than a meter from the wall; its function is unknown. A piece of a man's garment was found on the house floor, as well as a "shepherd stick" hung at a wall post, and a knotted rope.

House 9 is located 8.80 m farther S. It is also a habitation feature, built with two roof-supporting poles, measuring 7.20 m in diameter, with poorly preserved evidence of a bed with two short-forked poles and a bench-like hearth, 1.15 m in length, 0.55 in maximum width, and 0.20 m in height, located in the right-hand side of the house. As is the case for the previous dwelling feature, this one also has a shallow, subcircular pit, 0.60 × 0.40 m. Finally, a sheep/goat scapula, probably intrusive, was found in the SE of the house, not far from the fireplace. Feature 22 is located 8.85 m S of house 9; it is a very poorly preserved sheep/goat house, built with a single central pole and measuring 5 m in diameter. The recorded architectural remains consist of a few thorny branches set in a discontinuous circle, the central pole lying on the floor, the central posthole, and finally a set of twin wall poles.

Two trial trenches were tested within the confines of the cluster 4 complex. One, measuring 3 × 1 m, was carried out in a rubbish heap located on the northern side of house 8; ten potsherds, one kernel of *Borassus* sp. palm, and one cattle thoracic vertebra were collected. The potsherds sample comprises four plain (one rim and three body), and five decorated body-sherds. Twisted roulette impression is the exclusive decoration technique attested in this sample. As far as sherds' thickness is concerned, the sample is spread over three classes, with seven sherds in the 0.8–1.0 cm class, and one each in the 1.15–1.3 cm and 1.35–1.5 cm ones. The other trial trench, also measuring 3 × 1 m, was sunk in a subcircular refuse heap located in the southern side of the sheep/goat corral. Four pieces of textiles were collected, as well as one portion of a plastic bag, one piece of rubber, a metal lid, a kernel fragment of *Borassus* sp. palm, three potsherds, and an undetermined fired clay fragment. one body-sherd is decorated with twisted roulette impression, the remaining two, also body-sherds being plain.

Cluster 5 comprises two features set at 9.30 m from each other and located in the southeastern part of the settlement, approximately 30 m SW of the previous house complex. House 10, the eastern feature, measures 8.20 m in diameter, and is built with three roof-supporting poles. The feature was used as a barn/livestock house. A fireplace was found in the western part of the house, and the material remains consist of a single large enamel vessel lid. The house's central poles were removed shortly before fieldwork. They were found piled along the road. Feature 11, the habitation house, is found 9.30 m W of the barn/livestock facility; it is built with a single central pole, measures 6.60 m in diameter, and comprises evidence for a bed and a three-niche hearth. The hearth, partly broken and located in the standard right-hand side of the house, measures 0.90 m in length and 0.45 m in width. The niches' width varies from 0.30 to 0.24 m. The house's central pole has also been removed, probably by firewood dealers, and was found piled along the road with those from house 10.

Cluster 6, farther W, at almost 40 m from the previous one, comprises three features set in a triangular pattern. Feature 19, in the northwestern end of the complex, is a relatively small habitation house built with twin central poles and measuring 5.20 m in diameter. Evidence for a bed is attested by a line of postholes along the central SW-NE axis of the house, suggesting the northwestern half of the feature to be the sleeping area. The hearth, which consists of a built, low, clay bench-like feature measuring 0.50 m in length, associated with two large clay "hearthstones," is found in the right-hand part of the house. The scattered material remains are divided into two clay vessels, an enamel basin, two bed-supporting forks, one glass bottle, one plastic oil bottle, a glass bottle of "eau de cologne," and finally, a single leather shoe.

One of the recorded clay vessels is a complete, slightly elongated, rounded base, globular pot with constricted neck and everted rim, 24 cm in MD, 32 cm MaD, 34.5 cm in TH, 18 cm in HMD, and finally, 1.0 cm in T, decorated with extensive twisted roulette impression on the body, overlined on the shoulder by two horizontal and parallel grooved lines. The damaged one consists of the upper part of a necked pot, with its observable morphometric attributes varying from 27 cm in MD, 38 cm in MaD, (?)25.5 cm in TH, 8 cm in NH, and finally, 1.2 cm in T. It is decorated on the shoulder by a narrow twisted roulette impression band underlined by a horizontal grooved line, with, in addition, an appliqué cordon.

Feature 21, at the southeastern end of the cluster, measures 7.60 m in diameter. It is built with two roof-supporting poles, one of them found lying on the house floor. The thatched roof collapsed within the house and was found in an advanced state of degradation. A circular fireplace was recorded in the northwestern side of the house, and the scattered material remains are distributed into a long iron cutlass, a glass flask, two pieces of an enamel plate, and finally, a sheep horn-core. The absence of a bed and built hearth suggests the feature to have been probably used as a barn/livestock house.

The third feature of the complex, stable 4, was devoted to sheep/goats. It is located some 4 m NE of feature 21, in the inner side of the settlement. Due to its poor state of preservation, it has been impossible to determine the number of roof-supporting poles. It measures 7.20 m in diameter, with several wall postholes still visible, associated to thorny branches. The scattered material remains include two soft drink aluminum cans, a large potsherd, and several goat's bones: one metacarpal, one distal metapodial, one frontal with horns, one humerus, and one tibia, belonging to the same animal. A trial trench 3 × 1 m was sunk in an elongated rubbish heap located between features 19 and stable 4. The collected material remains comprise two rope fragments, three pieces of fabric, two rubber fragments, two pieces of plastic, a broken iron blade, one plastic lid, four snail shell fragments, one steel piece of bicycle wheel, two fragments of undetermined fired clay pieces, and finally, twenty potsherds. The sherds sample consists of one rim-sherd, seventeen body-sherds, and two base-sherds. Six of the sherds, four from the body and two from the base, are decorated. The recorded decoration pattern consists of twisted roulette impression combined with one, two, or three parallel grooved lines. Four thickness classes are represented, with two sherds in the 0.65–0.75 cm class, fourteen in the 0.8–1.0 cm, one in the 1.05–1.15 cm, and finally, three in the 1.2–1.35 cm one.

Cluster 7, the last of the studied settlement, is located on the southern side of the village entrance, 25.30 m NW of the previous complex. The village's well is found less than 20 m NE of one of cluster 7's features. The complex comprises three features: house 20, stable 5, with in between a 6-m-in-diameter sheep/goat

enclosure built with thorny tree branches. House 20 was found as a heap of collapsed material, including the roof, wall, and all the poles. It is a two roof-supporting poles house, measuring 7.60 m in diameter. These two poles were found lying
on the house floor. The recorded material remains consists of a metal container
of engine oil with "Shell" trademark, two enamel plates and one enamel bucket.
Feature stable 5, at 10.20 m NE of the habitation house, is a sheep/goat house; it
is built with five roof-supporting poles and measures 8.90 m in diameter. A set of
five enamelwares, including three relatively large plates and two shallow, superimposed basins, were found along the western side of the house. One preserve can
and one man's rubber shoe were also recorded.

The layout of Gobrem presents some striking patterns. If an E-W line running from the discussion house 12 to the middle of the village entrance (fig. 21) is
drawn, the northern half of the settlement appears to have been inhabited by three
households with four (cluster 3) to seven (cluster 1) built features; and the southern one by four households with two (clusters 5 and 7) to three (clusters 4 and 6)
built features. The location of the communal cattle enclosures is skewed and clearly
within the northern half of the site. Cluster 1 has its own relatively large cattle enclosure. Those from the southern half seem to have owned sheep and goats. However, the location of large cattle enclosures in the northern half of the settlement
does not necessarily mean that southern half households were denied access to
such communal facilities. Finally, in the northern part of the village, house clusters are relatively close to each other, with distances varying from 9 (house 3 to 4)
to 18.50 m (house 6 to 15). A nucleation process with relatively distant house clusters is the major characteristic of the southern half's layout. The distance between
dwelling complexes then varies from 22.80 m (house 22 to 10), 25.30 m (stable 5
to house 19), to 39.20 m (house 20 to 21).

The number of built features, excluding livestock enclosures, varies from seven
(cluster 1) to two (clusters 5 and 7), with one to four habitation and one to three
livestock houses (table 30). The largest part of the recorded pottery material has
been collected from the three northern house clusters (table 31). The material from
the tested trial trenches clearly matches that recorded on house floors; the same
range of evidence is attested in both contexts. Refuse heaps probably resulted from
the cleaning of both habitation and livestock houses.

PART III

Dry-Season Camps

Dry-season camps are located in the southwestern part of the study area, in the Yaere, the hinterland depression flooded during the rainy-season and a few months after. This component of the Chadian plain landscape is extended more than 150 kilometers farther S and comprises well-known, first-class grazing lands. Despite modern African states' boundaries, several pastoralist groups from nearby Nigeria spend a significant part of the dry season in the Yaere. The dry-season camps presented in this chapter were settled in 1990 for three to four months, between February/March and May. Due to a catastrophic, 1990 rainy season with insignificant rainfall, the annual flood has been nonexistent, thus enhancing an excellent preservation of the architectural record. Two dry-season camps' clusters have been investigated. They are named in local Arabic language after the predominant tree species. One is called Amachita and the other Agedipse; they are located 1.5 kilometers from each other, the former comprising seven camps and the latter four. In contrast to those from semipermanent rainy-season villages, dry-season houses, or one may say huts, are generally built in lighter material, with long, arched twigs, and are lower and dome-shaped.

Chapter 6

The Amachita Camps Cluster

Introduction

The Amachita cluster comprises seven individual camps set in a trapezoidal spatial arrangement (fig. 24), with distances from one camp to the next varying from 100 (between Amachita II and III) to 800 m (between Amachita V and VI). A straightforward nearest-neighbor approach shows the settlements to be arranged into subgroups of two to three camps stretched on 250 m maximum. The northern subgroup thus comprises Amachita I, II, and III, located 110 and 100 m respectively. The southeastern subgroup consists of Amachita IV and V, set at 250 m from each other, and located at 450 and 800 m from the other subgroups. And finally, the western subgroup consists of Amachita VI and VII, also set at 250 m from each other and located 400 and 800 m from the others. Is the recorded distribution pattern random, or does it result from deeper and stronger sets of social relationships? This issue will be investigated in detail in the chapters devoted to inter-site spatial analyses.

Amachita I

Amachita I is an elongated, fenced camp extended over 0.77 hectare, measuring 110 m NW-SE and 70 m SW-NE. It is located in the N-NE of the camp cluster and comprises fourteen houses and four sheep/goat enclosures distributed around a large central cattle corral (fig. 25). The central corral measures 44 m in diameter and has four entry/exits connecting it to all the dwelling units of the camp. At first glance, the settlement layout is organized into four house clusters with three to five features each. In the dry-season camps, house clusters are not coeval with household units; with minor exceptions (widows, bachelors), each hut is inhabited by a nuclear family.

House cluster 1 is located in the eastern side of the camp (fig. 25). It comprises three huts set in an in-curved linear arrangement at distances varying from 5 to 9 m, within a distinct portion of the camp's fence. The unit is extended over

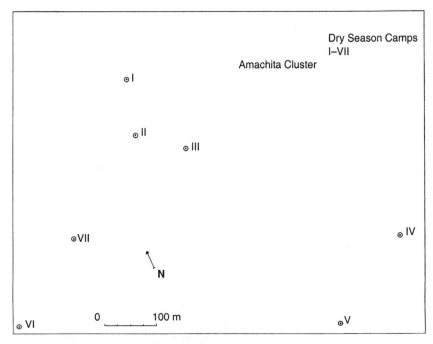

Figure 24: The Amachita camps' cluster

40 m NW-SE and 28 m W-SW-E-NE. House 1, located at the middle of the cluster, measures 3.9 m in diameter, is built with a single central pole, and comprises
a bed and an elaborate hearth. There is clearly a functional imperative for the
recorded hearths' shapes; an imperative to protect the wood and reeds house
structures from direct contact with sparks or incandescent wood. House 1's hearth,
located in the right-hand side of the house, measures 0.90 m in length and 0.60 m
in height; it is complemented by a set of three relatively large, clay "hearthstones."
Its panel has rounded edges in the upper side. The upper third of the hearth panel
is decorated with six equidistant upward arrows. The bed has been dismantled but
is nonetheless represented by a series of postholes.

House 2 is found at 5 m W of the previous one (fig. 25). It measures 3.8 m in
diameter, with a single central pole. It comprises a set of shelf 1.5 m long, 1.05 m
high, and 0.30 m wide, a bed, and an elaborate hearth found in the standard right-
hand part of the hut. The recorded hearth is rectilinear with three built sides and
measures 1.10 m in length and 0.50 m in width and height; the hearth's installation is complemented by a series of three "hearthstones." The upper part of the
hearth's rear panel is decorated with six equidistant upward arrows. A relatively
large two-handled storage jar was found crushed on the hut floor.

House 17, the third of the cluster, is found at 9.5 m SE of feature 2. It measures

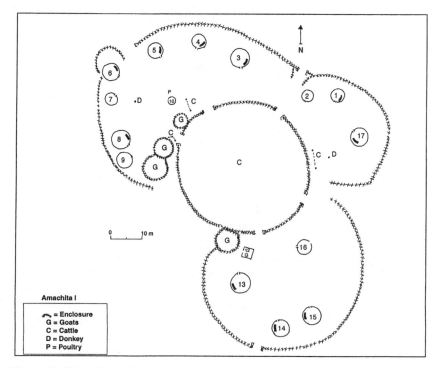

Figure 25: Map of Amachita I

5.60 m in diameter, is built with one central pole, and comprises a large bed, a set of shelf, and an elaborate but undecorated hearth that has the upper third of the rear panel underlined by a horizontal, appliqué cordon. A mud pot-stand was found next to the hearth, on its eastern side. Additional cultural remains include a smaller fireplace, located at the center of the western half of the house, and a large spoon handle found near the hearth and shelf. Finally, there is a series of calf and donkey-tethering poles in the inner part of the site, at 5 to 12 m SW of house 17.

House cluster 2 is located in the northern side of the camp and comprises features 3, 4, and 5, which are set in a linear E-W arrangement, associated with a long fence portion, and stretched over 52 m (fig. 25). House 3, at the eastern end of the complex, is built with one central pole, measures 5.7 m in diameter, and comprises a 3 × 1.5 m bed in the NW, a set of wooden shelves in the E, and an elaborate hearth in the SE, at the expected standard location. The recorded hearth is semi-circular in shape, with rounded upper edges, and includes two "hearthstones."

House 4, at approximately 8 m NW is slightly smaller than the previous one but was poorly preserved; it is built with one central pole and measures 4.4 m in diameter. The bed is located in the northern half of the house and measures 2 × 1.55 m. A set of shelf 1.55 m long and 0.35 m wide is found along the eastern side, next to the bed. The hearth, located due S, is rectangular in shape with an additional three "hearthstones" on its open northern side. The recorded installation, 1.10 m in length, 0.50 in width, and 0.65 m in height, is undecorated; the upper part of its rear panel is partly damaged. Finally, the upper part of a handled pot was found in the S, outside but next to the house wall.

House 5 is located 10 m W-SW of the previous one; it is built with one central pole and measures 4.60 m in diameter, with its entrance in the S-SE. The built hearth is located in the standard right-hand side of the house, along the eastern wall. It is rectangular in shape with three walls, complemented on the fourth side by a series of three "hearthstones." The installation measures 0.95 m in length, 0.45 m in width, and 0.55 m in height, with parts of the upper rear panel missing. The preserved decoration consists of a horizontal, appliqué cordon at two-thirds of the hearth panel height, underlining, presumably, six short, vertical appliqué cordons, of which portions of two have been preserved. It is not known if these vertical cordons were parts of arrow designs or simple vertical lines. The set of wooden shelves, stretched along the northern side of the house and measuring 2.10 m in length and 0.45 m in width, is almost adjunct to the built hearth. The bed, 2.50 m long and 1.80 m wide, is found in the northwestern part of the house. Finally, there is a short pole in the SW, next to the wall; in general, such poles are used as tethering devices. In this case, the pole was set indoors instead of outside, as is the case in house cluster 1.

House cluster 3 is located in the western part of the camp; it comprises five houses and three sheep/goat enclosures, combined with a distinct portion of the camp's fence, spread over 45 m NW and 30 m E-W (fig. 25).The house cluster seems to be divided into two units, here termed northern and southern.

The northern unit comprises houses 6, 7, and 10 and sheep/goat corral 9. House 6 is built with one central pole and measures 5.30 m in diameter, with its doorway in the S. The 3.20 × 1.70 m bed is located in the western half of the house. The shelf, measuring 2 m in length and 0.45 m in width, is located along the northern edge, between the bed and the hearth. The hearth, rectangular in shape, with three adjunct hearthstones, is found in the E, in the expected standard location. It measures 1.10 m in length, 0.50 m in width, and 0.60 m in height, with its rear panel built with right angles. House 7 is found 3 to 4 m S of the previous one. It is a young man's house, built with a single central pole and measuring 3.80 m in diameter. All the house's furniture has been dismantled; a tethering pole was left in situ near the central pole, while the house's door is located in the E. There is a donkey pole at 5.50 m E of house 7, in what can be called a courtyard. Feature 10 is not precisely a house; it is a 2.10-m-in-diameter chicken coop located 20 m SE of house 6. A large and shallow enamel plate, probably used for watering the poultry, was found on the feature's floor. Feature 9 is attached to the central cattle corral and located 3 m S of the chicken coop. It is an almost rectangular goat house with rounded corners, built with one central pole, and measuring 4 m in length and 3 m in width. Its entrance is situated on the northern wall, facing houses 6 and 7. Finally, there is a calf-tethering device at few meters E of the chicken coop and goats house (fig. 25). The installation measures 4.50 m in length and is oriented N-S.

The southern unit comprises two houses and two sheep/goat corrals. The latter, located in the proximity of the central cattle corral, are circular in shape and made with intertwined, thorny tree branches; the smaller measures 6 m in diameter, and the larger, 8 m. House 8 entrance is oriented SE it is built with one central pole and measures 5.3 m in diameter. The large 3.4 × 2.2 m bed is found in the western half of the house; the ten-poles, 1.50 × 0.40 m wooden shelves are located along the wall, NE of the bed. The rectangular hearth, including three hearthstones on its open side, measures 1.10 m in length, 0.75 m in height, and 0.50 m in width. It is located at the expected place in the house's inner space, and its rear panel is decorated with seven equidistant appliqué upward arrows underlined by a horizontal, appliqué cordon. House 11, set next to house 8, is a young man's habitation feature with its entrance oriented E. It is built with a single central pole and measures 5 m in diameter. A portion of the mud floor, 2.7 m in diameter on average, was preserved around the central pole. The bed was dismantled but its postholes were still visible.

The third and last house cluster is located on the southern part of the camp. It includes five houses and one sheep/goat enclosure set in a circular, fenced space measuring 50 m in diameter (fig. 25). Features are distributed into two units, with one case of an isolated house. Feature 16, slightly set aside, is a young man's house located 15 and 20 m E and N of northern and southern units. It is built with a single central pole and measures 4.50 m in diameter. Its doorway is oriented W, and the bed has been dismantled.

The northern unit comprises a 7-m-in-diameter sheep/goat enclosure attached to the central cattle corral, and a quadrangular goat house with sides measuring 3.60 to 3.70 m and door oriented W-NW. House 13 is the largest feature of the camp with its entrance oriented NW. It is built with one central pole and measures 5.80 m in diameter. The bed, certainly located in the southern half of the house, has been dismantled, but there were still four in situ supporting poles. The set of shelf located next to the entrance and on the right-hand side measures 2 m in length and 0.50 m in width. The hearth, adjusted to the house wall, is found due W; it is rectangular in shape, measuring 1.10 m in length, 0.40 m in width, and 0.70 m in height. It is complemented with two "hearthstones," and its rear panel is decorated in its upper part by five equidistant appliqué upward arrows underlined by a horizontal, appliqué cordon. Finally, there is a gourd-hanging forked pole at 1.50 m of the entrance in the left-hand side of the house.

The southern unit consists of houses 14 and 15, both with entrances oriented N. Feature 14 is built with one central pole and measures 5.10 m in diameter. House's furniture comprises a 2 × 1.10 m bed in the SE, a rectangular, four-niches hearth, 1.10 m in length, 0.52 m in height, and 0.40 m in width, complemented by two large clay "hearthstones" in the S-SW, and a set of shelf, 1.75 m in length and

0.45 m in width, disposed along the wall in the W. The hearth's rear panel is decorated with finger impressions arranged in a rectangular arch-like design. Two mud pot-stands, generally used as support for water jars, have been recorded; one is located near the house's entrance, on the right-hand side, and the other next to the hearth a few centimeters E. Finally, a few sherd scatters and a pile of ash, signalling an occasional fireplace, were recorded in the northwestern half of the house. House 15, found at 5 m E of the previous one, measures 5.6 m in diameter. It is built with a single central pole with house's furniture consisting of a bed, a hearth, and two sets of shelf. The bed is located in the southern half of the house and measures 2.60×1.70 m. A four-poles shelf set, 0.70×0.40 m, is found next to the bed, on its eastern side. The other shelf set is located in the NE along the wall, on the right-hand half of the house; it measures 1.20 in length and 0.4 m in width, and is adjunct to the hearth. The recorded hearth was poorly preserved, broken into four conjoinable pieces. It is a rectangular-shaped feature with rounded upper corners, measuring 1.10 m in length, 0.60 m in height, and approximately 0.40 m in width, complemented with two "hearthstones." The hearth's rear panel is plain, although its upper half is singled out by an appliqué cordon outlining its perimeter. Two mud pot-stands have been recorded, one located next to the hearth, in the western part of the house, and the other in the E, at slightly more than 1 m from the entrance. Finally, a piece of reed mat was found abandoned between the mud pot-stand and the smaller shelf set.

As shown by the above description, the pattern of furniture distribution within the house space is recurrent and consistent. The alluded pattern comprises three basic elements: the bed, the hearth, and the shelf, arranged in two main configurations. Proceeding counterclockwise from the houses' entrances, one configuration found in six cases (houses 2, 3, 4, 5, 6, 8) involves the placement of the hearth next to the door, then the shelf, with the bed on the opposite half. The other, recorded in four cases (houses 13, 14, 15, 16), clearly within the same cluster, involves the placement of the shelf next to the door, then the hearth, with the bed on the same opposite half of the house.

Amachita II

Amachita II is located 110 m S-SW of Amachita I; it is a slightly elongated, subcircular camp set next to a relatively long-lasting pond, with nineteen houses, a large central cattle corral, five sheep/goat enclosures, two wells, and livestock drinking troughs (fig. 26).The site measures 85 m in its maximum NE-SW axis and 60 m in width in the NW-SE one, and is thus extended over 0.51 hectare. The central cattle corral is circular in shape with six entry/exits and measures 35 m in diameter. Both wells and livestock drinking troughs are located 30 m from the ring of built features, one in the NE and the other in the SE. At the time of fieldwork, the water table was at 3 to 4 m below ground; water is fetched with plastic buckets

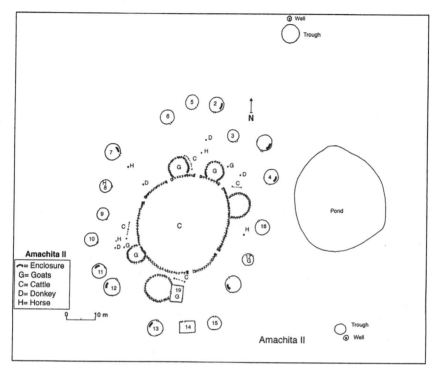

Figure 26: Map of Amachita II

and poured into the drinking troughs by adolescent males. These drinking troughs are circular features with diameters varying from 4 to 6 m; livestock is prevented from stepping in by a fence made of thorny branches set at less than a meter from the edge. Four of the five sheep/goat enclosures abut the central cattle corral; they range in size from 6 m in diameter for the smaller specimens to 8 to 9 m for the larger. The recorded built features are distributed into six house clusters.

House cluster 1 is located in the northeastern side of the camp and consists of features 1, 3, and 4 (fig. 26).These features are probably associated with the 6-m-in-diameter goat enclosure attached to the central cattle corral, and with goat-milking, donkey, and calf poles dispersed in the "courtyard." House 1 is found at the center of the cluster; it is built with two roof-supporting poles at 2 m from each other, and it measures 5.3 m in diameter, with its doorway oriented W. The bed is set parallel to both roof-supporting poles in the northeastern half of the house and measures 2.50 × 1.50 m. The hearth, located next to the bed in the standard right-hand side of the house, measures 1.10 m in length, 0.55 m in height, and 0.60 m in width. It is rectangular in shape and is built with two distinct niches; its rear panel has straight angles even if one is partly broken; the decoration, set on the upper half consists of a horizontal, appliqué cordon with finger impressions underlining five equidistant appliqué upward arrows. The shelf set is found between the hearth and the house door and measures 2 m in length and 0.40 m in width. A mud pot-stand is located next to the hearth, on its northeastern side. Two clay vessels have been recorded: a footed bowl, 14 cm in MD and MaD, 7 cm TH, 11 cm in BD, and finally 1.0 cm in T, decorated with extensive twisted roulette impression on the body; and a slightly elongated and globular pot, with constricted neck and everted rim, 20 cm in MD, 24 cm in MaD, 24 cm in TH, 12 cm in HMD, and finally, 1.0 cm in T, decorated with extensive twisted roulette impression on the body overlined on the shoulder by two horizontal and parallel grooved lines. Finally, a can of preserved fish and a glass bottle were found on the house floor. House 3, at 7 m W, is a relatively small habitation feature. It is a young man's house built with one central pole, measuring 3.80 m in diameter. The bed has been dismantled and no artifact has been recorded on the house floor. Finally, house 4, the third of the cluster, located 6 m S of house 1, measures 5.1 m in diameter. It is built with two roof-supporting poles set at 1.50 m from each other, and comprises a 3.2 × 2.0 m bed located in the eastern half of the feature, a two-niches hearth, and a set of wooden shelves. The doorway is located due W and the hearth is found in the S along the house central axis. It measures 1.0 m in length, 0.45 m in width, and 0.50 m in height, and the rear panel is decorated at mid-height by two horizontal and parallel lines of pinched finger impressions. The shelf is found in the SE, between the doorway and the hearth. The set measures 1.60 m in length and 0.60 m in width. Finally, there is a small ash dump and a scatter of potsherds in the western half of the feature.

House cluster 2 is found in the northern side of the camp; it consists of features 2, 5, and 6, and is associated to a 7-m-in-diameter goat enclosure attached to the central cattle corral, as well as a set of calf, donkey, and horse-tethering poles. The complex is thus extended over 26 m N-S and 22 m E-W. House 2, located at the eastern end of the cluster, measures 5.10 m in diameter. It is built with a single roof-supporting pole, with the doorway situated in the SW. House furniture consists of a 3.20 × 1.60 m bed located in the northeastern half of the feature; a four-niche hearth, 0.83 m in length, 0.40 m in width, and 0.54 m in height, with a triangular rear panel decorated with a horizontal, appliqué cordon, located in the E-SE; and finally, a set of wooden shelves, 1.70 m in length and 0.40 m in width, found in the S. A fireplace with a shallow pile of ash was also recorded in the southwestern half of the house. Feature 5, located at the center of the complex at 3 to 4 m W of the previous one, measures 4.30 m in diameter. It is a young man's house built with a single central pole, with its doorway located almost due S. The house floor was devoid of any furniture or artifacts, the bed having been dismantled. House 6, 5 m farther W, measures 4.7 m in diameter, with the doorway oriented S. It is built with a single central pole. The canopied bed, measuring 2.80 m in length and 1.50 m in width, is located in the northern half of the house. A circular, clay pot-stand has been recorded at approximately 1 m from the door, on the left-hand side. The remaining part of the recorded material evidence consists of a wooden pole of unknown function located in the southern half of the house and a large piece of reed mat.

House cluster 3 consists of features 7, 8, 9, and 10, and is associated with calf, donkey, and horse-tethering poles. House 7, at the northern end of the complex, measures 5.6 m in diameter. It is built with two roof-supporting poles set at 2.9 to 3.0 m from each other, with the entrance found in the E. The bed is located in the northwestern half of the house and measures 3.30 × 1.45 m. The hearth, carefully designed and built with three niches, is located next to the bed, on its eastern side. It measures 1.0 m in length, 0.50 m in width, and 0.53 m in height for the rear panel. It is lavishly decorated with extensive pinched finger impressions organized into two main registers: one is found on the pot-supporting part which is divided into four distinct niches; the other is found in the upper half of the hearth's rear panel and consists of five upward-oriented arrows set in a rectilinear frame of pinched finger impressions lines. The 1.70 m long and 0.50 m wide set of wooden shelves abuts the hearth and is stretched S to the door. Feature 8, at approximately 8 m S, is a single-central-pole, 4.6-m-in-diameter horse house. A rectangular feature, 4.4 m in length and 2.7 m in width, consisting of regularly spaced wooden poles was recorded within the horse house. Feature 9 is a young man's house with the entrance oriented SE, measuring 4.2 m in diameter and built with a single roof supporting pole. The bed is relatively small in size if compared to the specimens described already; it measures 1.60 m in length and 1.0 m in width. A small fireplace has been recorded in the southern half of the feature. Feature 10 located at the southern end of the complex, measures 4.7 m in diameter. It is built with one central pole with its entrance located in the E. It is a grandmother's house and, as such, is devoid of a built hearth. There are, nonetheless, clustered remains of clay "hearthstones" in the middle of the house, next to the central pole. A canopied bed, 2.50 m in length and 1.45 m in width, was found in the western half of the house. Finally, the house's furniture is complemented by a set of wooden shelves 1.50 m in length and 0.50 m in width located in the northern side.

House cluster 4 is found in the southwestern part of the camp. It consists of two features, houses 11 and 12, associated with a goat enclosure attached to the central cattle corral. The recorded goat enclosure measures 7 m in diameter and is situated at some 8 to 9 m E-NE of the houses within the camp's inner space. House 11 measures 5.1 m in diameter. It is built with two roof-supporting poles set at 2 m from each other along the house's central axis. The house's entrance is located in the E, and furniture consists of four elements: a bed, two hearths, and a set of wooden shelves. The bed is found in the western half; it measures 2.7 m in length and 1.7 m in width. One of the hearths, located along the door's axis in the eastern half of the house, is relatively small in size and consists of remains of fire-hardened clay and ash. The other one, located next to the bed but on its northern side, is much more elaborate, comprises three niches, and is lavishly decorated with pinched finger impressions. It measures 1.0 m in length, 0.50 m in width, and 0.60 m in height. Decorated registers are partitioned into two parts; one is found on four protruding pot-supports at the house floor level, and the other on the upper part of the rear panel where it defines a rectangular design. Finally, the set of shelves, located between the hearth in the W and the entrance in the E, is stretched on 2.0 m and measures 0.65 m in maximum width. There is a gap of less than 2 m between houses 11 and 12. The latter is slightly larger than the former, measuring 5.7 m in diameter. Its entrance is oriented N, and it is built with two roof-supporting poles set at 2.60 m apart. The bed is located in the southern half and measures 3.2 m in length and 1.65 m in width. The hearth is located next to the bed along the western side of the house. It is a three-niche installation, 1.0 m long, 0.55 m wide, and 0.60 m in height. The decoration consists of a horizontal, appliqué cordon at mid-height of the rear panel. A clay jar-stand was recorded next to the hearth on its southern side. The set of wooden shelves abuts the hearth's northern edge, is stretched on 1.50 m, and measures 0.45 m in width.

House cluster 5 is found due S of the camp. It comprises features 13, 14, 15, and 19, as well as a 9-m-in-diameter goat enclosure and a set of calf poles. Cluster 5 features are spread over 28 m E-W and 20 m N-S. House 13, located at the western end of the complex, measures 5.5 m in diameter; it is built with a single central pole with its entrance oriented N-NE. The bed is found in the southern half of the house and measures 3 m in length and 1.4 m in width. The hearth, located in the W, is semi-elliptical in shape, measures 1.1 m in length, 0.50 m in width, and 0.50 m in height, and comprises two niches. It is decorated with parallel lines of pinched finger impressions, with one set of parallel lines at the middle of each of the three pot-supporting features, and three equidistant and vertical sets attached to an arched line-set on the rear panel. Two wooden poles and a broken calabash were also recorded. Feature 14 is located at the center of complex, at 5 m E of the previous one. It is a rectangular horse house measuring 5.1 m in length and 4 m in width. Its entrance is oriented N and is found near the western edge. Surprisingly, the horse house is built without roof-supporting poles; a heavy log used to tether the horse and a small scatter of potsherds were found on the house floor. House 15, 4 m farther E, is relatively small in size and measures 4.7 m in diameter; it is a widow's house, built with one central pole, with its entrance oriented N. Furniture consists only of a 3 × 1.5 m bed found in the southeastern half of the house. A clay jar-stand is found at approximately 1 m W of the bed corner. And finally, a posthole was recorded next to the bed. The remaining feature (feature 19) of the complex is located in the camp's inner space. It is a 5.2-m-long and 4.2-m-wide rectangular goat house attached to an enclosure, built without roof-supporting poles but with two doors in the eastern and western walls.

House cluster 6 is found in the SE of the camp. It comprises three features set in a linear NE-SE arrangement, with a horse pole and presumably 8-m-in-diameter goat enclosure abutting the central cattle corral (fig. 26). The complex is thus stretched on 30 to 35 m along its N-S axis. Feature 16, located at the southern end of the complex, measures 5 m in diameter. It is built with a single central pole with its entrance oriented NW. The hearth is poorly preserved with only three recorded clay "hearthstones" located on the standard right-hand side of the house. A collapsed set of wooden shelves, measuring 3 m in length, was found in the southern part of the house. And finally, a canopied bed, measuring 2.5 m in length and 2 m in width, has been recorded in the eastern half of the feature. Feature 17, at 5 m N, measures 4.3 m in diameter. It is a small goat house built without a central pole with its entrance oriented N-E. Feature 18, at the northern end of the cluster, measures 4.8 m in diameter with its doorway oriented NW. It is used as habitation by a grandmother but also as shelter for a horse. The house is built with a single central pole, and comprises a relatively small 2 × 1.5 m canopied bed located in the northeastern quadrant. The central pole is integrated in the bed structure and constitutes its southwestern corner. Finally, the horse pole is found in the S and next to the wall, at 2 m of the bed.

The Amachita II camp has a relatively high frequency of donkey and horse poles. Elder females, grandmothers, or widows are present in three house clusters out of six. Beyond architectural evidence, significant cultural remains, confined to two clay vessels and one calabash, are rare. The arrangement of house furniture is highly patterned and consistent. If the houses of widows, grandmothers, and young-men are not considered, six habitations out of eight are characterized by the same pattern; starting from the house's entrance and moving counterclockwise, this pattern consists of the set of shelters, then the hearth, and finally the bed in the half of the house opposite the door. The decoration of the hearths is also predominantly made with pinched finger impressions arranged in diverse motifs.

Amachita III

Amachita III is located 100 m SE of Amachita II. The camp is circular in shape and measures 60 m in diameter. Houses are distributed around a large 35-m-in-diameter central cattle corral, to which six smaller goat enclosures are attached. The camp thus consists of three concentric rings of features spread over 0.28 hectare. A well, built with two adjunct livestock drinking troughs, is located 25 to 30 m SE of the camp's outer perimeter (fig. 27). A 25-m gap in the circle of houses located in the S is probably the main entry/exit to the camp.

House cluster 1 is located in the NW of the camp. It comprises features 1, 2, and 14, as well as donkey, goat, and calf poles dispersed in the courtyard, and finally, a 7-m-in-diameter goat enclosure. Feature 1 is a 5-m-in-diameter grandmother's house built with a single central pole with its entrance oriented SE. The house comprises a single furniture, a bed measuring 3.2 m in length and 1.5 m in width, located in the north/northwestern half of the feature. Feature 2, at 4 m NE of the previous one, is a relatively small goat house. Its entrance is oriented S, and it is built with a single central pole. Finally, feature 14, located at the southern end of the complex, measures 5.8 m in diameter. It is the second largest house of the

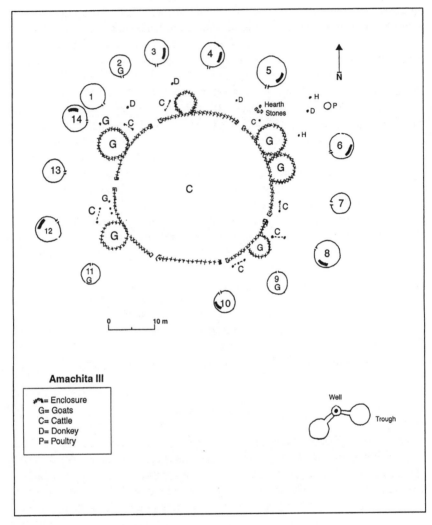

Figure 27: Map of Amachita III

camp, built with a single central pole, with its entrance oriented E. The bed, located in the western half of the feature, is poorly preserved with only seven in situ
forked bed-poles. The hearth is found due N on the house's central axis. It is a plain
five-niches features, 1.2 m in length. 0.50 m in width, and 1.0 m in height. Its rear
panel has rounded upper corners. A broken portable hearth with three clay "hearthstones" was found midway between the entrance and the central poles. A supply
of straw confined by two logs was abandoned in the southeastern part of the
house.

House cluster 2 is located in the northern part of the camp. It comprises features 3 and 4, as well as a 5-m-in-diameter goat enclosure and donkey and calf poles (fig. 27). House 3 measures 5.1 m in diameter. It is built with a single central pole, with its entrance oriented S. The house's furniture consists of two sets of shelf, two hearths, and one bed. The bed is located in the northern half of the feature and measures 3.0 in length and 1.6 m in width. A three hearthstones fireplace is found midway between the entrance and the central pole. The more elaborate one, associated with a clay pot-stand, is located due E along the wall. It is a five-niche feature, measuring 1.1 m in length, 0.45 m in width, and 0.50 m in height. The rear panel is decorated with a horizontal, appliqué cordon with pinched finger impressions, underlining six more or less equidistant vertical *appliqué* upward arrows with the same motif. The larger set of shelf is stretched on 1.7 m from the main hearth westward, and measures 0.50 m in width. The smaller one, 1.0 m in length and 0.50 in width, is found along the wall in the W, next to the bed. House 4 is located 7 m E. It measures 5.2 m in diameter, is built with one central pole, with its entrance oriented SW. As is the case for house 3, this one, too, has two hearths; the less elaborate specimen is located between the entrance and the central pole; it comprises two large, fire-hardened clay blocks associated with ash. The elaborate hearth is found along the wall in the SE. It measures 1.0 m in length, 0.40 m in width, and 0.55 m in height, and has, in addition, one large clay block. Its rear panel is decorated in its upper part by a horizontal, appliqué cordon with pinched finger impressions. A canopied bed, measuring 2.9 m in length and 1.7 m in width, is found in the northern half of the house. Finally, a small gourd-shaped calabash was recorded on the house floor near the entrance.

Cluster 5 in the N-NE of the camp consists of a single house (feature 5), an out-door fireplace, one horse, one calf, and two donkey poles, a chicken coop, and finally, a 7-m-in-diameter goat enclosure. Cluster 5 installations are thus distributed over 20 m E-W and N-S. House 5 is the largest of the camp. It is built with two roof-supporting poles set at 2.2 m from each other, with its entrance oriented SW. House furniture consists of a clay jar-stand next to a set of wooden shelves, 2.2 m in length and 0.50 m in width, located between the entrance and the hearth in the right-hand side of the feature. The hearth, with crenellated top, measures 1.1 m in length, 0.45 m in width, and 0.50 m in height, and is decorated with pinched finger impressions in two registers; one consists of a horizontal, appliqué cordon almost at mid-height of the rear panel, and the other is found on the crenellated part of the hearth made of short, vertical, impressed lines. A canopied bed measuring 4.1 m in length and 1.9 m in width is found in the northeastern half of the house. An installation consisting of a horizontal wooden pole supported by two forked ones was also recorded in the W; and finally, clustered charcoal remains, presumably evidence of an unstructured fireplace, were found midway between the house's entrance and the central poles.

Cluster 4 comprises features 6 and 7, a set of calf poles, as well as a 6-m-in-diameter goat enclosure. It is located in the eastern part of the camp. House 6, to the N of the cluster, measures 5.3 m in diameter and is built with a single central pole with its entrance oriented W. The bed is located in the eastern half of the house and measures 2.8 m in length and 1.4 m in width. The main hearth, located due E and along the wall next to the bed, is plain. It is a four-niche feature measuring 1.1 m in length, 0.45 m in width, and 0.55 m in height. The wooden shelves are poorly preserved; they are nonetheless stretched on 2 m E-W between the main hearth and the house's entrance, and measure 0.40 m in width. There are remains of a destroyed fireplace as well as a pile of ash and charcoal in the western half of the house. Feature 7 is a young man's house located 7 m S of the previous one. It measures 4.7 m in diameter and is built with a single central pole, with its entrance oriented W. All the furniture, and in this case probably only the bed, has been dismantled. What was left consists of a shallow ash dump.

House cluster 5 is located in the southeastern portion of the camp. It comprises three features stretched on 30 m NE-SW, with, in addition, two sets of calf-tethering poles and a small 5-m-in-diameter goat enclosure. House 8 measures 5.5 m in diameter. Its entrance is oriented W, and it is built with a single central pole. A canopied bed, measuring 3 m in length and 1.7 m in width, is found in the eastern half of the house. The main hearth is located due S; it is a 1.2-m-long, 0.50-m-wide, and 0.52-m-high five-niche feature, decorated on its upper part by a horizontal, appliqué cordon with pinched finger impressions. A set of wooden shelves, 2.1 m in length and 0.45 m in width, is stretched between the main hearth and the entrance. There are scattered remains of burned clay blocks and ash in the central part of the western half of the house. A calabash and a clay vessel were also recorded on the house floor. The recorded clay ware is a slightly globular pot with constricted neck and everted rim, 22 cm in MD, 25 cm in MaD, 27 cm in TH, 15 cm in HMD, and finally, 1.1 cm in T. It is decorated with extensive twisted roulette impression on the body overlined at the neck base by two horizontal and parallel grooved lines, complemented by four equidistant appliqué buttons. Feature 9, located at the center of the house cluster, measures 4.8 m in diameter. It is a goat house built with one central pole with its entrance oriented N. House 10, at the southwestern end of the cluster, is built with a single central pole and measures 4.8 m in diameter, with its entrance oriented N. The house's furniture includes a set of wooden shelves, 2 m long and 0.50 m wide, located between the door and the main hearth. The latter is a highly elaborate five-niches feature incorporating a clay pot-stand at its northern end. It measures 1.5 m in length, 0.70 m in width, and 0.45 m in height for its arched rear panel. The decoration consists of pinched finger impressions organized into a horizontal line connected to an arched one, thus delimiting a decorated register in the upper half of the hearth's rear panel. A canopied bed, 2.5 m long and 1.5 m wide, is found in the southern half of the house's inner space. Finally, two large, fired clay blocks associated with scattered ash and charcoal were found midway between the door and the house's central pole.

House cluster 6 is located in the W-SW of the camp, on the edge of the major entry/exit. It comprises three almost equidistant features: three goat-milking poles, a set of calf-tethering poles, and finally, a 6-m-in-diameter goat enclosure. Feature 11, at the southern end of the house complex, is a relatively small goat house. It measures 4.3 m in diameter built with one central pole, with its entrance oriented NE. Feature 12, at 8 m farther NW is larger and measures 5.2 m in diameter. It is built with a single central pole with its entrance oriented NE. A 3.3 × 1.5 m canopied bed is located in the southwestern half of the house. The hearth is found in the same half of the house at less than 1 m W of the bed. It is an almost plain hearth, with a horizontal, appliqué cordon, consisting of a simple trapezoidal panel 1.2 m long and 0.45 m high. A set of wooden shelves, 1.7 m in length and 0.4 m in width, is found between the main hearth and the door. Finally, three large, fired clay blocks and pieces of charcoal and ash remains of a fireplace have been found next to the house's central pole. Feature 13, at the northern end of the house cluster, measures 4.5 m in diameter; it built with a single central pole, with its entrance oriented E. It is a grandmother's house and, as such devoid of a hearth. The bed measures 2 × 2 m and is located in the western half of the house. The house floor was clear of any significant piece of cultural remains, with the exception of a fired clay ball, part of a disturbed hearth.

Amachita IV

Amachita IV is located approximately half a kilometer SE of Amachita III. The camp is subcircular in shape, measuring 100 m N-S and 80 m E-W. The camp is completely fenced with intertwined thorny tree branches and comprises two large cattle corrals, twelve houses, and a well. The well, with its adjunct 4-m-in-diameter drinking trough, is found in the southwestern margin of the camp (fig. 28).The camp's fence is interrupted by four entrances/exits; there is, however, a neat N-S partition materialized by wooden posts without thorny tree branches. There are five houses in the northern part divided into three clusters, two with two features (feature 1 and 2, 11 and 12) and the last with only one (feature 3). Seven houses are found in the southern half; they are almost equidistant, with distance between neighbors varying from 9 to 12 m. However, even within this even distribution of features, there seems to be four units, one with a single house (feature 4) and three with two houses (features 5 and 6, 7 and 8, 9 and 10). The central cattle corral measures 50 m in maximum diameter; it has seven entrances/exits leading to almost all the house clusters. The second cattle enclosure is located in the SE of the camp; it is an elongated feature measuring 45 m in its NE-SW axis and 23 m in its NW-SE one. The camp is remarkable for the absence of any goat feature.

Cluster 1 comprises features 1 and 2 located in the northern part of the camp on both sides of an entrance/exit (fig. 28). House 1 measures 5.6 m in diameter and is built with a single central pole with its entrance oriented SE. The furniture

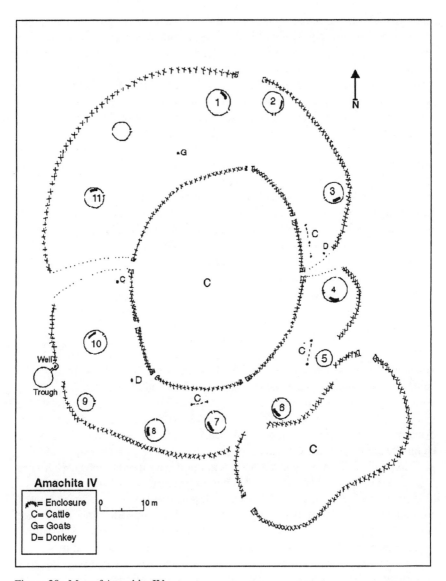

Figure 28: Map of Amachita IV

consists of a canopied bed, 2.8 m in length and 1.7 m in width, located on the northwestern side of the feature; a hearth with an in-curved panel and two hearthstones situated next to the wall in the NE but along the house's central axis. It is a plain four-niches hearth, 1.0 m long, 0.45 m wide, and 0.45 m high and a set of wooden shelves, measuring 1.8 m in length and 0.45 m in width, stretched between the hearth and the house's entrance. A shallow deposit of ash and charcoal, associated with a log, found in the southeastern half of the house, between the entrance and the central pole, suggests that the area may have been used for discussions and tea parties. House 2 is located 8 m E of the previous one. Its entrance is oriented S, and it measures 4.8 m in diameter. The feature is built without any roof supporting pole and comprises the three standard pieces of house's furniture: a canopied bed, measuring 3.0 m in length and 1.5 m in width, located in the northern half of the house; a plain, four-niches hearth with two additional hearthstones, 1.30 m in length, 0.50 m in width, and 0.40 m in height, located due E along the wall and along the house's central axis; and finally, a set of wooden shelves located between the hearth and the house's entrance, measuring 1.3 m in length and 0.50 m in width.

House 3 is found at 19 m SE of feature 2. As a single element unit, it is nonetheless associated with donkey and calf-tethering poles found at 10 to 12 m SW. It measures 4.6 m in diameter and is built with a single central pole with its entrance oriented SW. The house comprises a canopied bed, located in its northern half, measuring 2.5 m in length and 1.4 m in width. The hearth is found next to the wall in the E; it has three niches, two hearthstones, and measures 1.1 m in length, 0.50 m in width, and 0.45 m in height. It is surrounded on both the northern and southern sides by clay jar-stands. The set of wooden shelves is stretched between the hearth and the house's entrance on 1.4 m, and measures 0.50 m in width. Finally, there is a shallow ash and charcoal heap in the southern half of the feature, located between the door and the central pole.

House 4, 15 m farther S, appears at first glance to be a single feature unit associated with a distinct portion of the camp's fence. But features 4, 5, and 6 are equidistant and set at 10 m from one to the next; they may well have been part of the same house cluster with a young man's feature located at the center. House 4 measures 5.4 m in diameter. It is built with a single central pole with its entrance oriented W. The bed, found in the eastern half of the feature, measures 3.0 m in length and 1.5 m in width. The hearth is located due S; it is an in-curved, plain feature with six hearthstones, measuring 0.98 m in length, 0.45 m in width, and 0.60 m in height. A clay jar-stand was recorded next to the hearth, at its eastern end. The set of wooden shelves is found between the hearth and the house's entrance. It is a 1.8-m-long and 0.50-m-wide feature. Finally, there is a shallow ash pile in the western part of the house, between the door and the central pole.

Feature 5, associated with a set of calf-tethering poles, is a young man's house. It is relatively small in size, measuring 3.7 m in diameter. Built with a single central pole, it has its entrance oriented W. All the furniture, which in this case generally consists of a bed only, was dismantled. Depending on the situation, a larger cluster with three features or a smaller one with only two, the position of the described feature may shift from the center or middle to the northeastern end. House 6, at 10 m SW, is built with a single central pole and measures 4.3 m in diameter, with its entrance oriented NW. Proceeding counterclockwise from the door, there is the set of wooden shelves, measuring 1.8 m in length and 0.45 m in width; then, an in-curved, plain hearth with two hearthstones, 1.2 m long, 0.50 m wide, and 0.40 m in high; and finally, a canopied bed, measuring 2.3 m in length and 1.3 m in width, located in the southeastern half of the house. A small amount of ash and charcoal as well as a footed bowl were found between the door and the central pole. The recorded footed bowl is decorated on the body with extensive twisted roulette impression; the specimen measures 6 cm in TH, 10 cm in both MD and MaD, 7 cm in BD, and finally, 1 cm in T.

House cluster 5 is located due S of the camp. It consists of features 7 and 8, set at 10 m from each other, with, in addition, a set of calf-tethering poles (fig. 28). House 7's entrance is oriented N. It is built with a single central pole and measures 4.4 m in diameter. The canopied bed is located in the southern half of the feature; it measures 2.5 m in length and 1.5 m in width. The hearth is slightly crescent-shaped and located next to the wall in the W, along the bed's longitudinal axis. The recorded hearth is a three-niches feature, 0.90 m in length, 0.40 m in height, and 0.45 m in width, with two additional hearthstones. Finally, there is a set of wooden shelves along the northwestern part of the house wall, stretched on 1.8 m and measuring 0.50 m in width. House 8 measures 4.2 m in diameter. Its entrance is oriented N, and it is built with one roof-supporting pole. The canopied bed is found in the southern portion of the house's inner space and measures 2.5 m in length and 1.3 m in width. The hearth, located due W next to the wall, is crescent-shaped, has four niches and two additional hearthstones, and measures 1.1 m in length, 0.40 m in height, and 0.55 m in width. The set of wooden shelves is located between the hearth and the house's entrance; it is stretched on 1.8 m and measures 0.45 m in width. Finally, an enamel lid was found next to a shallow ash pile in the middle of the northern half of the house, between the entrance and the central pole.

Cluster 6 is found at approximately 14 m W and is comprised of features 9 and 10 and one donkey- and one calf-tethering pole (fig. 28). House 9 is located at the southern end of the cluster, its entrance oriented E. It is the smallest feature of the camp, measuring 4.3 m in diameter, built with one central pole, and used as a young man's house. All furniture was dismantled. There is, nonetheless, a shallow concentration of ash and charcoal near the central pole. House 10 is found at 9 m N. Its entrance is oriented NE. It is built with a single central pole and measures 5.2 m in diameter. There are relatively large portions of fire-hardened floor in the northeastern quadrant of the house. In addition, there is a scatter of ash and pieces of charcoal between the entrance and the central pole. The canopied bed is located in the southern half of the house's inner space; it measures 3.1 m in length and 1.6 m in width. The hearth, found slightly farther and along the wall, is a plain, three-niches feature, 1.2 m long, 0.40 m high, and 0.40 m wide, complemented by two hearthstones. The set of wooden shelves is located along the wall between the hearth and the door, in the northwestern quadrant. It is stretched on 2.0 m and measures 0.50 m in width.

The seventh and last house cluster of Amachita IV is located in the northwestern part of the camp (fig. 28). It consists of two features set at 12 to 13 m from each other, with, in addition, one goat-milking pole. House 11 measures 4.7 m in diameter. It is built with a single central pole with its entrance oriented E. It is associated with an outdoor wooden rack found next to the door. The canopied bed and the hearth are located in the western half of the house's inner space. The bed measures 2.5 m in length and 1.5 m in width. The hearth, found along the wall in the N, is a plain, four-niches feature, 1.2 m in length, 0.50 m in width, and 0.30 m in height. It has two additional hearthstones and is associated with a clay jar-stand found a few centimeters from its western flank. The wooden shelves measure 1.6 m in length and 0.4 m in width. They are stretched between the hearth and the house's entrance. A thin scatter of ash associated with a fire-hardened clay block, possibly a hearthstone, was recorded in the house's southeastern quadrant. Finally, a worn-out metal cup was found abandoned on the floor next to the wall, due S. House 12 is a young man's habitation feature, also used to shelter a donkey. It measures 4.1 m in diameter and is built with one central pole, with its entrance oriented E. The house floor was clear of any material evidence, with the exception of a relatively heavy log used to tether a donkey.

The spatial distribution of furniture within the houses' inner space is surprisingly uniform and monotonous at Amachita IV. Proceeding from the houses' entrance counterclockwise, the recorded spatial arrangement consists of: (1) a set of wooden shelves; then (2) the hearth; and finally, (3) the bed. If young men's houses are not considered, a secondary fireplace represented by a more or less extensive scatter of ash and charcoal, is found in seven houses out of nine. The general homogeneity of the Amachita IV camp is farther supported by a similarly shaped, plain hearth. From the accessible material evidence, it is clear that the camp was settled by a tightly knit social group.

Amachita V

Amachita V is located 250 m SW of Amachita IV. The camp, partially fenced with intertwined, thorny tree branches, comprises eighteen houses, one large central cattle corral, two smaller sheep/goat enclosures, and an elaborate livestock watering installation with three drinking troughs connected to a well (fig. 29). The site is circular in shape with a diameter of 70 m and thus measures 0.38 ha. The central cattle corral is slightly elongated in its N-S axis and measures 40 × 30 m with five entries/exits leading to each of the recorded houses' clusters. There are four smaller enclosures. Two of them, measuring 6 and 7 m in diameter, are sheep/goat enclosures attached to the central corral on its northeastern side. One of the features found within the cattle corral was used for the storage of reeds, and the remaining part was used for calves, as suggested by the presence of a set of calf-tethering poles at its center. The well, with its elaborate livestock watering installation, is found in the NW of the camp. Each of the drinking troughs measures 5 m in

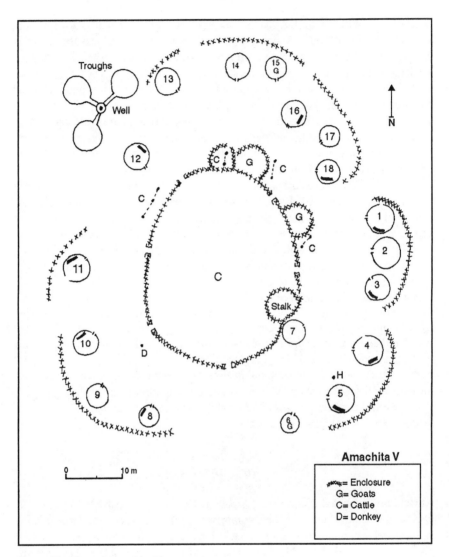

Figure 29: Map of Amachita V

diameter and is linked to the well by a 2- to 3-m-long channel. The camp's layout
is clearly organized into well-delineated house clusters. Five such clusters have
been identified, while two of the houses (features 11 and 12) are single component
units.

House cluster 1 is located along the eastern side of the camp (fig. 29). It is
surrounded by a distinct fence portion and consists of features 1, 2, and 3, set in a
N-S linear arrangement. In addition, a calf-tethering installation and a sheep/goat

enclosure are part of the complex. Feature 1 measures 5 m in diameter. It is built with a single central pole, with its entrance oriented W. The canopied bed is located in the eastern half of the house's inner space and measures 2.5 m in length and 1.5 m in width. The hearth is plain, with four protruding elongated vertical humps defining four niches, and measures 1.0 m in length, 0.40 m in width, and 0.40 in height. It is found along the wall in the S-SE of the house. The recorded wooden shelves are located between the hearth and the house's entrance; they measure 1.50 m in length and 0.50 m in width. Finally, there is a shallow scatter of ash and charcoal in the middle of the house's western half, between the door and the central pole. Feature 2, located at the center of the complex, measures 3.7 m in diameter. It is built with a single central pole with its doorway oriented W. All the house's furniture has been dismantled and no piece of material culture has been found on the floor. Feature 3, at the southern end of the complex, also has its entrance oriented NW; it is built with one central pole and measures 4.3 m in diameter. The canopied bed, 3 m in length and 1.5 m in width, is located in the eastern half of the house. The hearth is found due S next to the wall. It is a plain, four-niches feature with two additional hearthstones, associated with two clay jar-stands, one at each end. The hearth's rear panel is trapezoid in shape with rounded upper corners and measures 0.90 m in length and 0.45 m in height. The set of wooden shelves abuts the hearth on its southeastern side and measures 1.50 m in length and 0.45 m in width. Finally, a shallow scatter of ash and charcoal was found in the middle of the northwestern quadrant of the house.

House cluster 2 is comprised of four features spread over 20 m N-S W-E (fig. 29). Three are arranged in a linear pattern in association with a fence portion. House 4 measures 5.3 m in diameter; it is built with two roof-supporting poles set at 1.4 m from each other with its doorway oriented W. The canopied bed, found in the eastern half of the house, measures 2.5 m in length and 1.8 m in width. The hearth is located in the SE and along the wall. It is a two-niches, plain feature, with a relatively large hearthstone at its center measuring 0.90 m in length, 0.50 m in width, and 0.35 m in height. A 2.5-m-long and 0.50-m-wide set of shelves, located between the hearth and the doorway, complements the recorded house furniture. A casual fireplace represented by a shallow ash dump was found between the entrance and the central line of poles. House 5, with its associated horse-tethering pole located 5 m farther S measures 5 m in diameter. Its doorway is also oriented W, and it is built with a single central pole. The canopied bed and the hearth are located in the eastern half of the house's inner space. The bed measures 3 m in length and 1.8 m in width. The hearth is a four-niches, plain feature complemented by a large hearthstone. It measures 1.4 m in length, 0.6 m in maximum width if the position of the hearthstone is taken into consideration, and 0.44 m in height. There is a shallow scatter of ash and charcoal in the middle of the house's SW quadrant, while the set of 0.50-m-wide wooden shelves is stretched on 2 m along the southern wall portion, between the hearth and the doorway. Feature 6 is a relatively small goat house found at 6 to 7 m W. Its entrance is oriented NE, is built with one central pole, and measures 3.1 m in diameter. Feature 7, the last of the house cluster, is located approximately 10 m in the camp's inner space, abutting the central cattle corral. It is a young man's house with its doorway oriented E-NE, built with a single central pole and measuring 4.4 m in diameter. As is generally the case in young men' houses, the unique piece of furniture is found in the house's western half, and consists of a bed measuring 2.2 m in length and 1.4 m in width.

House cluster 3 is located in the southwestern part of the camp (fig. 29). The relatively large 20-m-gap between clusters 2 and 3 served as the camp's main entrance/exit. The cluster is comprised of three features associated with a distinct fence portion and a donkey-tethering pole. Feature 8 is located at the southeastern end of the complex. It is built with a single central pole and measures 4.3 m in diameter with its doorway oriented N. The canopied bed is found in the southern half of the house's inner space. It measures 2.5 m in length and 1.5 m in width. The hearth, located 0.20 to 0.30 m W of the bed, is poorly preserved. It was a three-niches feature measuring 0.90 m in length, 0.40 m in width, and 0.40 m in recorded height. The decoration consists of pinched finger impressions distributed into two registers. One is found on both recorded pot-supports, and the other, a horizontal line, is recorded at mid-height of the hearth's rear panel. The set of wooden shelves is located next to hearth, on its northern side. It measures 1.5 m in length and 0.50 m in width. Finally, there is a shallow 0.30-m-diameter fire pit in the middle of the house's northwestern quadrant. Feature 9 is a young man's house at the center of the complex, at 6 to 7 m NW of the previous one. It is devoid of any furniture and is built with one central pole. Its entrance is oriented N, and it measures 4.2 m in diameter. Feature 10, built with a single central pole and measuring 4.4 m in diameter, is found at the northwestern end of the cluster. Its entrance is oriented NE, with the house's furniture consisting of a 2.80-m-long and 1.40-m-wide bed located in the western half of the feature's inner space, and a 1.40-m-long and 0.50-m-wide set of wooden shelves found in the NE along the wall. The fireplace is represented by a scatter of ash and charcoal pieces located due N between the bed and the shelf.

Cluster 4, located due W in the Amachita V camp, is a single house complex, with feature 11 and a distinct portion of the fence (fig. 29). The recorded feature is built with one central pole and measures 4.9 m in diameter, with its entrance oriented E. The canopied bed, located in the western half of the house's inner space, measures 2.70 m in length and 1.80 m in width. The hearth is found NW; it is a two-niches feature, 0.90 m long, 0.50 m wide, and 0.50 m high, flanked on both the SW and NE sides by clay pot-stands. The decoration is confined to the hearth's rear panel. It consists of parallel lines of pinched finger impressions outlining three of the sides, with, in addition, a horizontal line slightly above mid-height. Finally, the set of wooden shelves is stretched between the hearth and the doorway and measures 2.30 m in length and 0.60 m in width.

Cluster 5 is also a single feature complex. It is located in the N-NW of the camp houses' ring, at 18 to 20 m of cluster 4. It is associated with a series of calf-tethering poles (fig. 29). House 12 has its doorway oriented S. It is built with one central pole and measures 5.00 m in diameter. The canopied bed, situated in the northern half of the house, measures 3.10 m in length and 1.45 m in width. The hearth was destroyed; it is nonetheless represented by a fire-hardened clay surface, ash, and pieces of charcoal found E of the bed at the wall base. Another casual fire-place was recorded between the doorway and the central pole, in the southern half of the house. The wooden shelves are stretched on 1.80 m between the destroyed hearth and the house's entrance.

House cluster 6 is found due N of the camp and is comprised of three features set in a linear W-E arrangement associated with two distinct portions of the outer fence (fig. 29). Feature 13, located at the western end of the complex, is a grand-mother's house with the doorway oriented SE. It is built with two roof-supporting poles set at 1.90 m from each other and measures 4.40 m in diameter. The bed, measuring 2.40 m in length and 1.40 m in width, is found in the northwestern half of the house's inner space. Finally, a shallow scatter of ash, evidence of a casual fireplace, was recorded in the northeastern quadrant of the house. Feature 14, at approximately 10 m E, is an empty, young man's house. It is built with a single central pole and measures 4.40 m in diameter with its entrance oriented S. Feature 15, a few meters E of the previous one, is a relatively small 3.60-m-in-diameter goat house built with a single central pole, with its doorway oriented S.

The seventh and last house cluster of the Amachita V camp is situated in the NE. It is comprised of three features associated with a distinct fence portion, as well as goat enclosures and calf-tethering poles (fig. 29). House 16, at the north-ern end of the complex, measures 4.7 m in diameter. It is built with one central pole, and its doorway is oriented S. A shallow scatter of ash and charcoal has been recorded between the entrance and the central pole, in the center of the south-southwestern half of the feature. The bed and the hearth are found in the north-northeastern half. The former is a canopied specimen measuring 2.50 m in length and 1.50 m in width. The latter is a U-shaped, three-niches, plain feature, 0.90 m in length, 0.50 m in width, and 0.45 m in height, complemented with two hearth-stones located due E, next to the bed. The set of wooden shelves abuts the hearth and is stretched 2 m W toward the doorway; it measures 2.00 m in length and 0.50 m in width. Feature 17, located at the center of the cluster, measures 3.70 m in diameter. It is a relatively small grandmother's house built with a single central pole, with its entrance oriented SW. House equipment consists of a single piece of furniture; the recorded bed is located in the eastern half of the house and meas-ures 1.80 m in length and 1.40 m in width. Feature 18, found at the southern end of the complex, is built with one central pole and measures 4.20 m in diameter, with its doorway oriented W. The set of wooden shelves is found on the right-hand side of the house and is stretched 2 m S, where its abuts the hearth; it measures 2.00 m in length and 0.45 m in width. The hearth is a plain three-niches feature with two additional hearthstones measuring 0.95 m in length, 0.40 m in width, and 0.50 m in height, situated in the southern part of the house. The bed is spread all over the eastern half of the house. It measures 2.70 m in length and 1.80 m in width. Finally, there is a shallow scatter of ash and charcoal in the middle of the house's western half, between the central pole and the doorway.

As far as intra-house spatial patterning is concerned, Amachita V appears as a highly homogeneous site with a unique mode. Proceeding clockwise, this mode consists of the bed, then the hearth, the set of wooden shelves, and the house doorway. Eight out of the ten recorded hearths are plain with elongated, vertical, protruding, clay lumps, while two are decorated with pinched finger impressions. The decorated hearths are found in houses 8 and 11, located in the same southwestern part of the camp. As can be seen on the camp map (fig. 29), on both eastern and northern sides, the distance between southwestern house clusters and the nearest units is significant, varying from 15 to 23 m.

Amachita VI

Amachita VI is a relatively small camp of nine houses spread over 0.38 hectare. It is located approximately 800 m NW of Amachita V. The central cattle corral with three entries/exits is subcircular in shape and measures 33 and 25 m in maximum and minimum diameters. It is surrounded by three donkey- and two sets of calf-tethering poles, as well as three attached, circular goat enclosures, with diameters varying from 6 to 7 m. The ring of houses is loose and features are situated at 10 to 17 m from the cattle corral. Two wells, an older abandoned one and a newly dug one connected through a clay channel to a 5-m-in-diameter livestock drinking trough, have been recorded at 30 to 35 m SE of the camp (fig. 30).

There is a single, neat cluster of features that consists of houses 4 and 5 in the W-NW of the camp. The recorded camp facilities will be described starting from the S clockwise. House 1 is built with a single central pole and measures 4.8 m in diameter, with its entrance oriented N. The bed, located in the southern half of the feature, measures 2.40 m in length and 1.50 m in width. The hearth is an elaborate three-niches feature, 0.90 m long, 0.50 m wide, and 0.50 m high, with an additional hearthstone. It is located next to the bed on its southwestern side, and its rear panel is decorated at mid-height with a horizontal, appliqué cordon. The last piece of house's furniture is found along the wall in the W; it consists of a 2.00-m-long and 0.45-m-wide set of wooden shelves.

House 2 is located 10 to12 m NW of the previous one; it is built without any roof-supporting pole and measures 5.2 m in diameter, with its doorway oriented N (fig. 30). A wooden rack, 1.00 m long and 0.50 m wide, is found due W next to the wall, abutting the hearth. The latter is a two-niche feature measuring 1.20 m in length, 0.50 m in width, and 0.45 m in height, located to the W of the house. It is decorated with pinched finger impressions organized into two registers. One includes

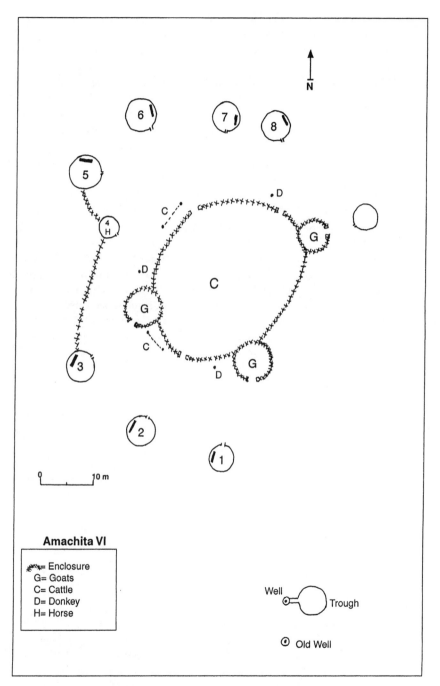

Figure 30: Map of Amachita VI

the three pot-supporting devices at the hearth's bottom, and the other at the upper half of the hearth's rear panel as two parallel lines on a horizontal, appliqué cordon. Finally, the bed, located in the south-southeastern half of the feature's inner space, measures 2.60 m in length and 1.60 m in width.

House 3 is located in the SW, at 10 m NW of house 2. It is built with one central pole measures 5.20 m in diameter, with its entrance oriented E. Two elements of house's furniture, both located in the western half of the feature's inner space, have been recorded. One is a canopied bed, measuring 2.55 m in length and 1.40 m in width, and the other is the hearth. It is a two-niches feature with a crescent-shaped rear panel, 1.20 m long, 0.50 m wide, and 0.45 m high. It is decorated with pinched finger impressions confined to the pot-supporting devices at the bottom, with, in addition, a horizontal, appliqué cordon in the upper half of the rear panel. The eastern half is clear of any feature, not even a scatter of ash.

House 4 is connected to the previous feature (3) and the next house (5) by a fence of thorny tree branches, interrupted by an entry/exit (fig. 30). It is the smallest house of the whole camp, measuring 3.70 m in diameter, built with a single central pole, with its entrance oriented SE. The feature serves as a horse house for the owner of house 5 and is found 5 to 6 m NW. The latter feature is built with one central pole and measures 6.00 m in diameter, with its entrance oriented E. The bed is found in the western half and measures 3.20 m in length and 1.80 m in width. The hearth is located along the wall, at 1 m N of the bed; it is a plain, four-niches feature, 1.20 m long, 0.50 m wide, and 0.50 m high, with two additional clay hearthstones. The set of wooden shelves is found along the wall in the house's northeastern quadrant, where it is stretched on 2.30 m, for a width of 0.60 m.

House 6, on the camp northern side, measures 6.00 m in diameter (fig. 30). It is built with one central pole, and its doorway is oriented SE. The bed is located in the N-NW half of the house and measures 3.40 m in length and 1.70 m in width; most of the bed's supporting poles were removed but postholes were still clearly visible. A large piece of reed mat was found on the floor. The hearth, found along the wall due N, measures 1.50 in length, 0.50 m in width, and 0.40 m in height. It is an elaborate feature with a rectilinear rear panel with rounded upper edges, two in-curved pot-supporting devices delineating a central niche at its middle, and low walls on both W and E sides. The rear panel is decorated with a line of pinched finger impressions defining a rectilinear pattern. The set of wooden shelves abuts the hearth and measures 1.70 m in length and 0.40 m in width.

House 7 is found 10 m E of the previous one (fig. 30). It is built with two roof-supporting poles set at 1.65 m from each other measures 5.10 m in diameter, with an entrance oriented S. The bed was completely dismantled and the hearth, reduced to the fire-hardened surface and superstructure fragments, destroyed. The recorded evidence does not seem to result from poor preservation but appears to have resulted from purposeful action of the house's owner.

House 8 is located in the N-NE of the camp (fig. 30), its entrance oriented SE. There is a donkey-tethering pole located next to the central cattle corral at 10 m

S of feature 8. It is built with one central pole and measures 5.40 m in diameter. The wooden shelves are located along the wall in the E, between the doorway and the hearth. The set measures 2.00 m in length and 0.50 m in width. The hearth, found in the NE, is a 1.10 m long, 0.50 m wide, and 0.45 m high two-niches feature with one additional clay hearthstone. The rear panel is decorated at mid-height with parallel lines of pinched finger impressions on a horizontal, appliqué cordon. And finally, the bed, situated in the northern half, measures 2.40 m in length and 1.60 m in width.

House 9 is relatively isolated from the others, located in the E at 19 to 20 m from its nearest neighbor, house 8. It is a young man's house, built without roof-supporting pole, measuring 4.6 m in diameter, with its entrance oriented SW toward the entry/exit of a goat enclosure (fig. 30). The house floor was devoid of any material evidence, the bed having been dismantled.

The absence of any casual fireplace in all the studied features is the most striking aspect of the Amachita VI camp. The spatial arrangement of furniture within the houses' inner space is also highly homogeneous, with, nonetheless, two undecidable cases in houses 3 and 7. A horizontal, appliqué cordon on the upper half of hearths' rear panels, with or without pinched finger impressions appears to be a common decorative element in the site's material culture repertoire. Finally, the size of habitation houses varies from 4.6 (house 9) to 6.00 m (houses 5 and 6) in diameter.

Amachita VII

Amachita VII is located 250 m NE of Amachita VI and 400 m SW of Amachita II. It consists of fourteen houses spread over 0.38 hectare. The camp is subcircular in shape, measuring 90 m in its SW-NE axis, and 70 m in the SE-NW one (fig. 31). The central cattle corral is elliptically shaped, measures 40 m N-S and 20 m E-W, and has four entries/exits. Three goat enclosures are attached to the central corral. All are circular in shape and measure 5 in diameter for the smallest specimen situated in the SE, 7 m in diameter for the northwestern enclosure, and finally, 10 m in diameter for the largest, southwestern one. The central livestock features are surrounded by one donkey-, two goat-milking, and four calf-tethering poles. The ring of houses is situated at 12 to 20 m away from the central cattle corral, with a 50-m-wide gap in the S, probably used as the camp's main entry/exit.

Dwelling facilities are organized into six house clusters with feature frequency varying from one to three. Cluster 1 is located in the W-SW of the camp (fig. 31). It is comprised of three houses arranged in a N-S linear pattern stretched on 35 m. The recorded houses are associated with one horse- and two donkey-tethering poles, and a goat enclosure measuring 10 m in diameter. Feature 1, found at the northern end of the complex, is a young man's house built with a single central pole, measuring 5 m in diameter, with its doorway oriented E. All the house's

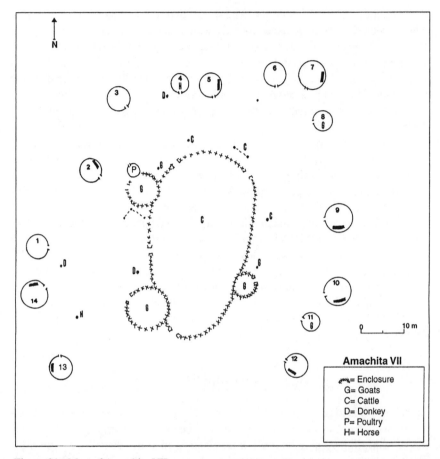

Figure 31: Map of Amachita VII

furniture was dismantled. The recorded remains consist of a shallow charcoal pile found in the southeastern quadrant of the house floor. House 14 is located at the center of complex, at 4 to 5 m S of the previous one. It is built with two roof-supporting poles set at 2.20 m from each other, measures 6.40 m in diameter, with the doorway oriented NE. The bed is located in the west-southwestern half of the house; it is a particularly long feature, measuring 4.00 in length and 1.70 m in width. The hearth is located due W next to the bed. It is a plain, 0.44-m-high and 1.00-m-long five-niche feature, consisting essentially of a rectangular panel with rounded upper corners. There is a second casual fireplace next to the house door. As far as furniture is concerned, the third element consists of a set of wooden shelves stretched between the main hearth in the W and the doorway in the NE, measuring 2.10 m in length and 0.50 m in width. Three different artifacts were recorded on the house floor: a fragment of iron chain used for horse-tethering, found between the main hearth and the shelf; an iron knife with a wooden handle, found under the bed, and finally, a metal pipe presumably used for metalworking. House 13, at the southern end of the cluster, has its doorway oriented N. It is built with a single central pole and measures 5.00 m in diameter. The bed measures 2.80 m in length and 1.30 m in width, and is located in the southern half of the house's inner space. The hearth is found due W; it is a six-niches feature, 1.30 m long, 0.55 m high, and 0.60 m wide, comprising a convex rear panel and three hearthstones. The panel is decorated with pinched finger impressions organized into two distinct registers. One, mid-height of the panel, consists of two parallel lines on a horizontal, appliqué cordon. The other is a narrow band at the top of the panel. The shelf are found along the house's northwestern wall portion; they measure 2.10 m in length and 0.50 m in width.

Cluster 2 is located in the northwestern part of the camp; it consists of three features spread over 400 m square, associated with one goat-milking post, a set of calf-tethering poles, and a goat enclosure measuring 7 m in diameter (fig. 31). Feature 15 is located in the inner part of the camp and is attached to the goat enclosure fence. It is a chicken coop with a doorway oriented NW, built with one central pole and measuring 2.50 m in diameter. House 2 is built with two roof-supporting poles set at 2.00 m from each other; it measures 4.8 m in diameter with its entrance oriented SE. The bed and the hearth are located in the northern half of the house. The former measures 3.00 m in length and 1.70 m in width, and the latter, located due E along the wall, is a 0.95-m-long, 0.38-m-high, and 0.50-m-wide installation. The hearth is a three-niche, plain, convex feature with an appliqué horizontal cordon connecting the four vertical and elongated clay bumps. It is complemented by two additional hearthstones. The wooden shelves are stretched between the hearth and the house's entrance and measures 1.80 m in length and 0.50 m in width. Feature 3 is a young man's house located 11 m N-NE of the previous one. It is built with two roof-supporting poles set at 2.00 m from each other measures 4.80 m in diameter, with its doorway opening in the SE. The house's floor was clear of any material remains, the furniture having been dismantled. There was, nonetheless, a shallow concentration of ash and charcoal between the door and one of the roof-supporting poles.

Cluster 3, found due N of the camp, consists of two houses, one donkey- and one calf-tethering pole (fig. 31). Both houses are close to each other, separated by 2 m only. Feature 4 is a horse house, built with one central pole. It measures 3.30 m in diameter, with its entrance oriented S. House 5 measures 5.70 m in diameter. It is built with two roof-supporting poles located 2.00 m from each other, its doorway oriented S-SW. The bed is found in the north-northeastern half and measures 3.20 m in length and 1.60 m in width. The main hearth is located next to the bed, on its eastern side. It is a plain, three-niche installation, 1.00 m long, 0.40 m wide, and 0.40 m high, its rear panel having rounded upper corners. There is, however, a horizontal, appliqué cordon mid-height the panel which may be considered as a decoration. The hearth is surrounded by a clay pot-stand on its northern side and a set of wooden shelves on the southern one. The latter measures 1.50 m in length and 0.45 m in width. Finally, there is a second fireplace located at the center of the house's southern half which appears to have been used frequently. The recorded concentration of ash and pieces of charcoal is associated with two relatively large hearthstones and a 1-m-in-diameter fire-hardened surface.

Cluster 4 is located in the northeastern part of the camp (fig. 31). It is comprised of three features set in a triangular pattern, associated with a set of calf-tethering poles located 12 to 15 m SW, near the central cattle corral. Feature 6, at the western end of the complex, is a young man's house built with a single central pole. It measures 4.30 m in diameter, with its doorway oriented S. The house floor was totally clear of any material evidence, even traces of ash. House 7 is located 3 m E of the previous one. It is slightly larger, measuring 5.40 m in diameter, but is nonetheless built with a single central pole with its entrance also oriented S. There are traces of two distinct hearths, both having been destroyed. One, the casual one, is represented by two hearthstones, and the other, the main one, is attested by fire-hardened clay. The bed is located in the northeastern half of the house's inner space. It measures 2.80 m in length and 1.40 m in width. The set of wooden shelves is 1.90 m long and 0.50 m wide and is stretched between the main hearth and the house doorway. Finally, a broken calabash was found next to the house, on its southern side. Finally, feature 8, at 5 m S of the previous one, is a relatively small goat house. It is built with one central pole and measures 3.80 m in diameter, with its door oriented W.

Cluster 5 is a single feature complex located in the eastern side of the camp (fig. 31). House 9 is found 15 m from its nearest northern neighbor and 10 m from the southern one. It is a relatively large, 6.00-m-in-diameter feature, built with a single central pole, its entrance being oriented W, and associated with a calf-tethering pole. The wooden shelves in the house's southwestern quadrant have been dismantled, but recorded postholes suggest that the set may have measured 2.00 m in length and 0.50 m in width. The hearth is found due S, along the wall. It is a plain convex feature, 0.95 m long, 0.70 m wide, and 0.40 m high, complemented with two clay "hearthstones." Finally, the bed, located in the eastern half of the house's inner space, measures 3.00 m in length and 2.00 m in width.

Cluster 6, at the southeastern end of the camp, consists of three houses set in a NE-SW linear arrangement, a goat-milking pole, and a 5-m-in-diameter goat enclosure attached to the central cattle corral (fig. 31). Feature 10, at the northern end of the complex, is built with two roof-supporting poles set at 2 m apart. It measures 5.60 m in diameter, with its doorway oriented W. Evidence for a casual fireplace has been recorded at the center of the house's western half, between the door and the central poles; the evidence consists of a shallow concentration of ash, a fire-hardened surface, and a clay "hearthstone." The main hearth, the set of wooden shelves, and a clay pot-stand are located along the southern wall portion. The hearth has a convex rear panel with a horizontal, appliqué cordon at mid-height; it is essentially a plain, three-niches feature measuring 1.00 in length, 0.50 m in width, and 0.60 m in height. The wooden shelves are poorly preserved; but as suggested by the still visible postholes, they were stretched on 2.00 m for a width of 0.50 m. The bed, measuring 3.40 m in length and 1.50 m in width, is found in the eastern half of the house. A worn-out flashlight, an empty glass bottle, and a metal teapot handle were found in the house's northeastern quadrant. Feature 6 is located at the center of the complex, at 4 to 5 m from the neighboring houses. It is a relatively small, 4.30-m-in-diameter goat house, built with one central pole, with its doorway oriented W. The house floor, covered with a loose scatter of goat droppings, was clear of any material evidence. House 12 is found at the southern end of the cluster, with its doorway oriented NW. It is built with a single central pole and measures 5.00 m in diameter. The bed is located in the house's eastern half and measures 2.90 m in length and 1.30 m in width. The hearth is situated next to the bed, on its southern side. It is a convex, plain, three-niches feature, measuring 0.80 m in length, 0.50 m in width, and 0.30 m in height, complemented by two hearthstones. Evidence for shelf has been found between the hearth and the entrance, but it is very poorly preserved. As suggested by the still visible postholes, the shelves may have measured 0.60 m in width and at least 1.30 m in length.

The Amachita VII intra-house spatial structure follows the same strict patterns. Proceeding counterclockwise and from the right-hand side of the house, the recorded pattern consists of: (1) a set of wooden shelves, (2) the main hearth, and (3) the bed. With one exception in house 13, all the recorded main hearths (six out of seven) are made with four elongated, vertical, protruding clay bumps, with a horizontal, appliqué cordon in three cases.

Chapter 7

The Agedipse Camps Cluster

The Agedipse cluster is located 1.5 kilometers SW of Amachita VI. It is comprised of four sites arranged in a trapezoidal pattern, at distances varying from 120 to 300 m from one camp to its neighbor (fig. 32).

Agedipse I

Agedipse I contains the northernmost camps of the studied cluster. It is a fenced, circular settlement measuring 105 m in diameter (fig. 33). The camp, extended over 0.86 hectare, is divided into six main livestock features located at the center, surrounded by a neat ring of thirty houses, and finally, an outer fence located 30 to 40 m from the central cattle corral. The central cattle corral measures 50 m in diameter with five entries/exits and five attached goat enclosures. The recorded goat enclosures range in size from 9 to 5 m in diameter and are located 10 to 25 m from one to the next. The well and its associated livestock watering complex is found at 15 to 20 m due W of the camp. The watering complex consists of four elements: a well connected through 1.50-m-long clay channels to two symmetric, 5.00-m-in-diameter troughs, with a third one located 4 to 5 m W.

The camp's dwelling features are distributed into nine house clusters and six isolated habitations. Cluster 1 is found in the north-northeastern side of the camp and consists of features 2 and 3 (fig. 33). Feature 2 is a 4.30-m-in-diameter horse's house, built with one central pole with its entrance oriented S. House 3 is located 4 m E; it is a single-central-pole feature, measuring 5.20 m in diameter, with its doorway oriented S. A canopied bed, measuring 3.00 m in length and 1.50 m in width, has been recorded in the northern half of the house's inner space. The hearth was destroyed; it was located at the wall base due W, combined with a straw upper shelf. A set of wooden shelves, stretched on 1.50 m and measuring 0.45 m in width, is found between the hearth and the house doorway. Finally, a clay pot-stand was recorded abutting the shelf on the left-hand side of the entrance.

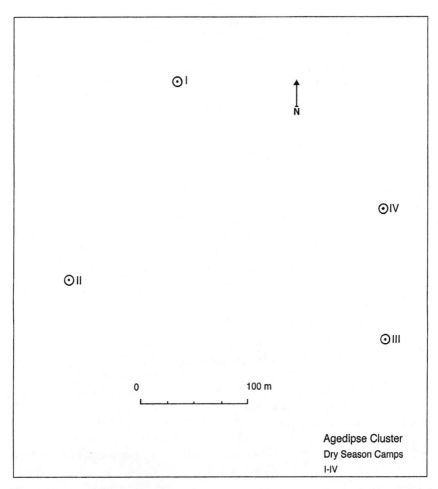

Figure 32: Agedipse camps' cluster

Cluster 2 comprises features 4, 5, and 6, set in linear arrangement along the camp's northeastern part, with a donkey-tethering pole a few meters within the site (fig. 33). Feature 4, at the northern end of the complex, is built with one central pole and measures 5.50 m in diameter, its doorway oriented SW. It is a grand-mother's house and, as such, devoid of any hearth. The bed, found in the house's northern half, measures 3.20 m in length and 1.70 m in width. A 1.50 × 0.50 m set of wooden shelves was found next to the bed but on its eastern side. The southern half of the feature is almost clear of any furniture, with the exception of a straw upper shelf. Finally, a clay pot-stand was recorded next to the door, on the right-hand side. Miscellaneous pieces of cultural remains were found scattered on the

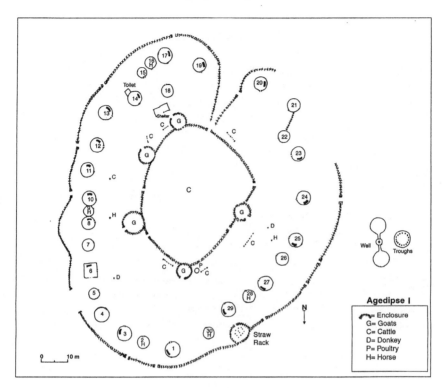

Figure 33: Map of Agedipse I

house floor or very close; they include a calabash, uncovered behind the bed, a pair of rubber slippers next to the door on the left-hand side, and finally, a child's colorful ball. Feature 5 is located 3 to 4 m S of the previous one. It is a small 3.70-m-in-diameter house, built with one central pole with the entrance oriented SW. The bed, situated in the northeastern half of the feature, measures 2.10 m in length and 1.20 m in width. A relatively large clay pot-stand, as well as one calabash and a truncated plastic container were recorded on the floor. Finally, what was probably used as a door reed blind was found outside next to the house doorway. Feature 6 is rectangular house measuring 5.30 m in length and 5.00 m in width. It is found at the southern end of the complex, at 4 m from the previous centrally situated feature. House 6 is built with two roof-supporting poles set at 2.00 m from each other, its entrance oriented W. The bed is located in the eastern half of the feature and measures 3.00 m in length and 2.00 m in width. Two sets of wooden shelves have been recorded; one, found along the northern wall measures 2.80 m in length and 0.40 m in width, and the other, located along the southern wall, is 2.70 m long and 0.45 m wide. A smaller wooden rack is situated next to the northwestern corner, with the hearth found in the opposite southeastern corner.

The later installation is an elaborate five-niches feature measuring 1.30 m in length, 0.60 m in width, and 0.75 m in height, with, in addition, three large hearthstones. A straw upper shelf was built above the hearth. The rear panel has five equidistant upward pointing tips; the upper half is decorated with two parallel bands of two pinched finger impressions lines. A straw upper shelf was built above the hearth. Finally, there is shallow scatter of ash and charcoal next to the house door, while a mirror fragment, one flashlight battery and a worn-out piece of cloth were found on the house floor.

Cluster 3, with four features, is stretched on slightly more than 20 m N-S along the eastern part of the camp (fig. 33).A horse-tethering pole is found a few meters within the camp's inner space, and the nearby 8-m-in-diameter goat enclosure may have belonged to the cluster's members. Feature 7, located at the northern end of the complex, is a 4.50-m-in-diameter young man's house, built with one central pole, with its entrance oriented SW. As is generally the case for young men's houses, this one, too, is devoid of any furniture. House 8 is located 3 to 4 m S. It is built with one central pole and measures 5.10 m in diameter, its doorway oriented W. The bed is found in the house's eastern half, and measures 2.80 m in length and 1.50 m in width. The hearth is located along the wall, due S of the bed. It is a four-niches feature, 1.25 m long, 0.50 m wide, and 0.50 m high, with the upper part of the rear panel decorated by parallel lines of pinched finger impressions. There are two sets of wooden shelves, one in the N and the other in the S, both measuring 1.70 m in length and 0.40 m in width. Finally, a calabash spoon was found on the house floor, next to the hearth. In addition to feature 8, houses 9 and 10 are adjunct to each other and form a continuum. Feature 9 is a small 3.90-m-in-diameter horse house, built with one pole with the entrance oriented SW. A horse-tethering pole and a relatively large wooden log were found on the house floor. Finally, a shallow clay depression, the horse water jar stand, was recorded in the southeastern quadrant of the feature. House 10 is the largest of the complex. It is built with a single central pole, with an entrance oriented W, and measures 5.30 m in diameter. The bed measures 3.00 m in length and 1.70 m in width. It is located in the eastern half of the house, as is the case for the hearth. The latter is a four-niches feature with two additional hearthstones, 1.25 m long, 0.45 m wide, and 0.63 m high, with a straw upper shelf above. Its rear panel is rectangular in shape with two pointed upper corners, decorated in its upper half with a rectangular grid of pinched finger impressions. Two sets of wooden shelves were recorded in the house; the southern measures 2.20 m long and 0.40 m wide, and the northern 1.30 m in length and 0.35 m in width. A clay jar-stand was found at the western end of the southern shelf, next to the door. A piece of worn-out cloth, a plastic bowl, an empty box of powder soap, and one flashlight battery were also found scattered on the house floor. Finally, the remaining part of the door reed blind, was abandoned outside, next to the doorway.

Houses 11 to 14 are almost equidistant, located 5 to 6 m from each other (fig. 33). Each is a distinct nuclear family dwelling unit. It is not known if the

7.00-m-in-diameter goat enclosure found at 10 to 15 m within the camp's inner space belonged to one, two, or all four houses. House 11 is built with one central pole, its entrance oriented W, and measures 5.10 m in diameter. The bed, the hearth, and the smaller set of wooden shelves are located in the eastern half of the house. The bed measures 2.70 m in length and 1.70 m in width. The smaller shelf with an overlying reed mat are found along the northern wall and measure 1.70 m long and 0.40 m wide. The hearth, rectangular in shape with three additional hearthstones, is located in the SE, on the bed's southern flank. It is a 1.20-m-long, 0.45-m-wide, and 0.55-m-high feature, with the upper half of its rear panel decorated with two horizontal and parallel series of pinched finger impressions. The larger set of wooden shelves is stretched on 2.50 m along the southern wall between the hearth in the E and the doorway in the W. It is a 0.45-m-wide feature divided into four vertical parts. A wicker plate with a small amount of sorghum flour and a piece of plastic mat were found on the shelf. Finally, the remaining part of the door blinds was lying outside, and one flashlight battery, a piece of used reed mat, and a worn-out cloth were found scattered over the house floor.

House 12, at 4 to 5 m S, has its doorway also oriented W. It is built with one central pole and measures 5.00 m in diameter. As is the case for house 11, this one, too, has most of its furniture concentrated in the eastern half; this is the case for the smaller 0.70-m-long and 0.35-m-wide northeastern shelf, the 2.70-m-long and 1.70-m-wide bed, and finally, the 1.25-m-long, 0.50-m-wide and 0.62-m-high hearth. The latter feature, located in the southeastern part of the house and overlain by a straw upper shelf, is rectangular with three complementary hearthstones. Its rear panel is trapezoidal in shape, decorated with six elongated, vertical, slightly protruding clay bumps overlined at mid-height by a horizontal, appliqué cordon. The remaining element of the house's furniture consists of a relatively large set of wooden shelves located along the southwestern wall portion, measuring 1.80 m in length and 0.45 m in width.

House 13 measures 5.30 m in diameter. It is located 7 m S of the previous feature, with its entrance oriented NW. It is built with a single central pole, with the bed and a small shelf located in its eastern half. The bed measures 2.90 m in length and 1.50 m in width. The hearth is situated along the house's N-S axis, at the southern end. It is a rectangular feature, 1.10 m long, 0.50 m wide, and 0.55 m high, comprising two additional hearthstones and overlain by a straw upper shelf. The hearth's rear panel is rectangular with two pointed upper ends, decorated at mid-height with pinched finger impressions set on a horizontal, appliqué cordon. Another set of wooden shelves is located along the southwestern portion of the house wall; it measures 1.30 m in length and 0.55 m in width. A raised grinding platform was recorded between the house door and the wooden shelves. Finally, a few plastic bags, a sole of a rubber shoe, and a piece of worn-out cloth were found dispersed on the house floor.

House 14 is the last of the set under consideration here; it is found at 7 to 8 m SW of house 13 and has a smaller rectangular extension behind it, which is, in fact, a "toilet" booth. The habitation measures 5.00 m in diameter and is built with one central pole, with its doorway oriented NW. A canopied bed, measuring 2.80 m in length and 1.70 m in width, is found in the house's eastern half; it is flanked by a 0.70-m-long and 0.40-m-wide wooden rack in the N and an elaborate hearth overlain by a straw upper shelf in the S. The recorded hearth is rectangular in shape, measures 0.90 m in length, 0.40 m in width, and 0.66 m in height, with three hearthstones, two of which were removed from their original position. The hearth's rear panel is rectangular with three equidistant, pointed tips at its middle, decorated at mid-height with pinched finger impressions on a horizontal, appliqué cordon. A larger set of wooden shelves, measuring 1.70 in length and 0.50 m in width, is found along the western wall portion. On average, house 14 has a relatively high density of abandoned material remains; they consist of one flour sieve, a man's shoe sole, two milk calabash rims, a large piece of reed mat, a woven vegetal fan, a fish trap, and finally, an extended but shallow scatter of ash and charcoal situated at the center of the house's western half, between the doorway and the central pole.

Cluster 4 is located in the southeastern portion of the settlement (fig. 33). It consists of six features: four houses, a 6-m-in-diameter goat enclosure attached to the central cattle corral with an adjunct set of calf poles, and finally, a 5 × 2 m rectangular shelter. Houses 15 to 17 are arranged in a NE-SW line. The first is a relatively small, 3.6-m-in-diameter grandmother's house built with a single central pole with its entrance oriented NW. A canopied bed, measuring 2.0 m in length and 1.20 m in width, is found in the southeastern half of the house. A worn-out piece of reed mat was abandoned next to the bed, on its northern side. Feature 16, at less than 1 m SW, is a horse house. It is also built with a single central pole measures 3.80 m in diameter, its doorway being oriented N-NW. The house floor was clear of any debris; there was, nonetheless, a set of straw upper shelves along the wall in the S and a relatively large enamel plate next to the door. Habitation 17 is the main house of the cluster. It is built with a single central pole and measures 5.30 m in diameter, with its entrance oriented N. The bed is found in the southern half and measures 2.70 m in length and 1.70 m in width. Large logs, a piece of reed mat, and an empty bag of powder soap were found clustered next to the bed, on its eastern side. The hearth overlain by a straw upper shelf is located in the W; it is a rectangular feature, 1.30 m in length, 0.45 m in width, and 0.70 m in height, with two complementary clay "hearthstones." The hearth's rear panel is not decorated; it is nonetheless divided into two equal parts by a horizontal, appliqué cordon. The upper part is crenellated and the lower one has four equidistant, vertical, and elongated clay bumps. A set of wooden shelves, 2.40 m in length and 0.45 m in width, is found between the hearth and the house's entrance. Finally, feature 18, located in the inner part of the settlement at 6 to 8 m from the others, is a young man's house clear of any material remains. It is built with a single central pole and measures 4.30 m in diameter, with its doorway oriented S.

House 19 measures 4.60 m in diameter and is located some 10 m W of the previous house cluster. It is built with a single central pole, with its entrance oriented N. A well-preserved, canopied bed, 2.60 m in length and 1.50 m in width, was found spread all over the southern half of the house. It is surrounded on the eastern side by a carefully made 0.80 × 0.40 m wooden shelves with reed mats; on the S side by another small set of wooden shelves; and finally, on the W side by the main hearth. The recorded hearth is a plain feature, 1.10 m in length, 0.45 m in width, and 0.60 m in height, with, in addition, three complementary clay "hearthstones." Its rear panel has four equidistant, vertical, and elongated clay bumps. Finally, there is a relatively large set of wooden shelves located between the hearth and the house door, measuring 1.50 m in length and 0.50 m width. A secondary fireplace represented by a shallow ash scatter, was recorded at the center of the house's northern half, between the central pole and the door.

Cluster 5 consists of features 20 and 21 and is found in the southern part of the settlement (fig. 33). They are located 10 m from each other; the former being the main dwelling unit and the latter a young man's house. House 20 measures 5 m in diameter. It is built with a single central pole, with its entrance oriented N. The bed is a well-preserved, canopied specimen located in the southern half of the house. It measures 2.70 m in length and 1.80 m in width. The hearth is located along the wall W of the bed, adjunct to a raised upper shelf and a clay pot-stand. It is a rectangular feature, 1.00 m in length, 0.45 m in width, and 0.57 m in height, with a plain rear panel comprising four equidistant, vertical, elongated clay bumps. A set of wooden shelves, 2.00 m long and 0.60 m wide, is stretched between the hearth and the doorway. Finally, there is a second fireplace located between the door and the central pole and comprising three "hearthstones" and probably the burned log found nearby. Two corncobs, a small piece of reed mat, an enamel bowl, a child's small ball, and finally, the remains of a broken calabash were found scattered over the house floor. As is generally the case with young men's houses, feature 21 is devoid of any furniture. It is a 4.60-m-in-diameter house, built with a single central pole with its doorway oriented NE.

Cluster 6, with houses 22 and 23 located 3 to 4 m from each other, is found to the S of the settlement, slightly NW of cluster 5 to which it is attached by fence (fig. 33). Feature 22 is a grandmother's house, measuring 4.30 m in diameter built with a single central pole, with its doorway oriented NE. The material remains recorded on the house floor consist of a 0.60-m-long metal pipe, two small gourd-like calabashes, and three burned logs near the central pole. House 23 is also built with a single central pole but is larger, measuring 5.20 m in diameter, with its entrance oriented E. The recorded canopied bed is located in the western half of the house and measures 2.30 m in length and 1.50 m in width. The hearth, overlain by an upper shelf, is situated along the wall in the N; it is a collapsed plain feature, comprising a 1.40-m-long and 0.50-m-high rear panel with five almost equidistant, vertical, and elongated clay bumps, and three clay "hearthstones." A 2.00 by 0.45 m set of wooden shelves is stretched along the northeastern quadrant of the house, between the doorway and the main hearth. And finally, an elongated piece of fire-hardened clay was recorded along the wall in the southeastern part of the house; it is not known if it was an additional fireplace.

House 24 is located to the W of the site, at 10 m N of the previous cluster camp (fig. 33). It is a 4.90-m-in-diameter habitation unit, built with a single central pole, with its doorway oriented NE. House furniture consists of a relatively large cano-pied bed measuring 2.70 m in length and 1.80 m in width situated in the western half of the feature, and a poorly preserved hearth found along the wall in the NW. The recorded hearth is a rectangular feature, 0.90 m long, 0.40 m wide, and ap-proximately 0.50 m in height, with two additional hearthstones and an adjunct clay pot-stand. Its rear panel is decorated on the upper half with pinched finger im-pressions on two horizontal and parallel appliqué cordons, three equidistant, ver-tical, and elongated clay bumps on the lower part, and finally, three pointed ends on the top side. An upper shelf, 2.00 m long and 0.40 m wide, was found above the hearth. Finally, one flashlight battery, a tong's sole, and a powder soap plastic bag were found scattered on the house floor.

Cluster 7 consists of features 25 and 26 located along the western edge of the site, at 3 to 4 m from each other (fig. 33).They are associated with a 6.00-m-in-diameter goat enclosure attached to the central cattle corral, as well as one horse-, one donkey-, and a set of calf-tethering poles. House 25 is built with a single cen-tral pole and measures 5.60 m in diameter with the doorway oriented E. The large 3.00 × 2.00 m bed is found in the house's western half. The collapsed hearth, found along the wall due N, was rectangular in shape and comprised three additional hearthstones. The preserved rear panel measures 1.25 m in length and 0.50 m in width. It is decorated on the upper half with six equidistant upward appliqué ar-rows delimited at the bottom and top by two horizontal and parallel appliqué cordons, the lower half having four equidistant, protruding, vertical, and elongated clay bumps. A set of wooden shelves, measuring 2.00 m in length and 0.50 m in width, is stretched along the northeastern part the house, between the hearth and the doorway. A shallow pile of ash remains of an additional fireplace was recorded at the center of the eastern half of the house, between the doorway and the central pole. Finally, a flashlight battery, a piece of reed mat, an empty matches box, and an enamel bowl were found scattered on the house floor.

Feature 26 is a young man's house. It is also built with a single central pole and measures 4.60 m in diameter, its doorway oriented SE. The furniture, particularly the bed in this case, was dismantled. The material remains found on the house floor consist of a large log, pieces of reed mat, and finally, a large clay jar-stand.

Cluster 8 is situated along the northwestern edge of the settlement (fig. 33). It has three houses set in a linear arrangement, with distances from one to the next varying from 3 to 4 m. They are associated with a 8.00-m-in-diameter enclosure attached to the outer fence and used for the storage of straw. House 27, at the south-western end of the cluster, measures 5.60 m in diameter. It is built with a single central pole, with its entrance oriented SE. The bed is found in the northwestern half of the house and measures 2.00 m in length and 1.80 m in width. The hearth and the wooden shelves, stretched along the northeastern quadrant, are particularly elaborate in this case. The hearth, a rectangular, five-niches feature, measures 1.60 m in length, 0.70 m in width, and 1.10 m in height, and has two additional clay hearth-stones. The rear panel is decorated on the upper half by three equidistant appliqué upward arrows underlined by a horizontal, appliqué cordon with parallel lines of pinched finger impressions. The lower half has four equidistant, protruding, vertical, and elongated clay bumps. The wooden shelves, 2.00 m long and 0.50 m wide, are attached to the hearth with sticks embedded in clay. Finally, a straw basket and two logs were found on the house floor. Feature 28, at the middle of the cluster, is a 4.70-m-in-diameter horse house. It is built with a single central pole with the entrance oriented SE. The floor is clear of material remains with the exception of a log, a tethering pole, and a stick. House 29, at the northeastern end of the cluster, measures 5.50 m in diameter. Its doorway is oriented SE, and it is built with a single roof-supporting pole. The bed was dismantled. An upper shelf was recorded in the western side of the house, and the hearth, found in the standard right-hand side of the feature, is surprisingly located as far as 0.80 m from the wall. It is an elongated, 1.20-m-long, three-niches feature with rounded edges, associated with five fire-hardened clay balls in disturbed secondary positions.

Cluster 9 is located due N of the site and consists of features 30 and 1, set at 9 to 10 m from each other (fig. 33). Feature 30 is a 4.10-m-in-diameter horse house and is built with a single central pole with its doorway oriented S. The house floor is clear of any material evidence, and the whole feature is, on average, poorly preserved. Habitation house 1 measures 5.00 m in diameter, is built with one roof-supporting pole, and has its doorway oriented S. House furniture consists of a canopied bed, 2.80 m in length and 1.40 m in width, located in the northern half of the feature; a rectangular hearth overlain by an upper shelf along the wall in the NE and a 2.00-m-long and 0.50-m-wide set of wooden shelves stretched between the hearth and the doorway. The recorded hearth is a five-niches feature, measuring 1.00 m in length, 0.40 m in width, and 0.60 m in height, with, in addition, two large hearthstones. The rear panel is decorated with five appliqué upward arrows on its upper half, the lower one having four equidistant, protruding, vertical, and elongated clay bumps. A clay pot-stand, pieces of a broken calabash, and an empty plastic oil bottle were found on the house floor.

The Agedipse I camp is clearly a well-designed and tightly organized settlement. As far as the intra-house spatial patterning is concerned, two predominant modes have been recorded. Proceeding clockwise, one mode consists of (1) a bed located in the opposite side of the entrance, then (2) the hearth with or without an overlying upper shelf, and finally, (3) a set of wooden shelves. This mode is found in houses 1, 3, 12, 13, 17, 20, 23, 25, and 27. It is thus recorded in three houses in the eastern half of the settlement (features 12, 13, and 17) and exclusive in the western one. The other mode, found exclusively in the eastern half of the site, in houses 6, 8, 10, 11, 14, and 19, consists of (1) a set of wooden shelves in the left-hand side, (2) the bed all over the feature's half opposite to the door, (3) the hearth with or without an upper shelf in the right-hand side, and finally, (4) a larger set of wooden shelves between the hearth and the doorway. The patterning outlined above is partially supported by the distribution of hearth decoration. Five (houses 6, 8, 10, 11, and 14) out of six hearths found in houses with the mode 2 layout are decorated with pinched finger impressions on appliqué cordons. Appliqué upward arrows in the upper half of the hearth's rear panel (houses 1, 3, 25 and 27) and plain registers (houses 12, 17, 20, and 23) are found in the mode 1 layout.

Agedipse II

Agedipse II is a relatively small dry-season camp 0.38 hectare in surface extent located 225 m SE of Agedipse I. It is a fenced settlement roughly circular in shape and measuring 70 m in diameter. It is comprised of ten houses, three goat enclosures, a well, and a central cattle corral (fig. 34).The central cattle enclosure is elliptical in shape and measures 35 m in its NW-SE axis and 30 m in the NE-SW one. It has four entrances/exits, with roughly one at each cardinal point. The goat enclosures attached to the central cattle corral measure 9.00 m in diameter for the largest southeastern specimen, 7.00 m for the northern, and finally, 6.00 m for the smallest western one. These central livestock features are surrounded by tethering poles, then the houses, the well located in the site's northeastern part, and finally the outer fence, which has six entrances/exits and is opened on the northwestern side. Houses are roughly distributed into four clusters, with one isolated case.

Proceeding clockwise from the N, cluster 1 consists of features 7 and 8, set at 10 to 11 m from each other, with, in addition, a goat enclosure (fig. 34). The former is a habitation house, measuring 5.50 m in diameter, built with a double central pole, and a doorway oriented SE. A canopied bed, 3.00 m in length and 1.70 m in width, is found in the western half of the feature, with a three-niches, rectangular hearth next to it, on its northern side. The recorded hearth has pointed upper corners and measures 1.25 m in length, 0.50 m in width, and 0.50 m in height, with two additional hearthstones. Its rear panel can be considered plain; there are, nonetheless, a horizontal, appliqué cordon at mid-height, with four equidistant, protruding, vertical, and elongated clay bumps in the lower half. A 2.00-m-long and 0.50-m-wide set of wooden shelves is stretched between the hearth and the house door. There is a shallow ash concentration between the entrance and the central pole. Finally, the remains of a broken large pot were found behind the hearth, as well as red-slipped sherds, small cosmetic bottles, and fragments of a calabash. Feature 8 is a 4.00-m-in-diameter horse house, built with a single central pole, with its entrance oriented W. The house floor is clear of any material remains with the exception of two log pieces found on its eastern side.

Cluster 2 is located along the eastern edge of the settlement. It comprises fea-

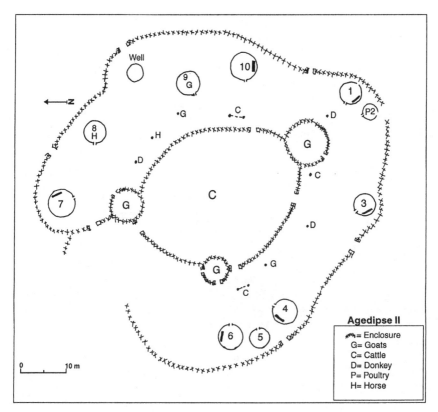

Figure 34: Map of Agedipse II

tures 9 and 10 found at 6 to 7 m from each other, due S of the well (fig. 34). The complex has, in addition, one set of calf-tethering poles as well as one goat-milking post. Feature 9 is an empty, 4.90-m-in-diameter young man's house, built with a single roof-supporting pole, with the entrance oriented SW. House 10 is slightly larger, measuring 5.50 m in diameter, built with two roof-supporting poles, with the doorway oriented W. The bed, located in the eastern half of the feature, measures 3.10 m in length and 1.60 m in width. A small wooden shelf, 0.70 m long and 0.30 m wide, is found along the wall on the northern edge of the bed. The hearth is situated on the opposite southern edge; it is a plain, rectangular, three-niches feature, measuring 0.95 m in length, 0.50 m in width, and 0.60 m in height for the rear panel. It is complemented by two relatively large hearthstones. A 2.40-m-long and 0.30-m-wide set of wooden shelves abuts the hearth in the E and is stretched westward toward the doorway. A three-hearthstones fireplace with a thick ash deposit and charcoal is located in the center of the house's southwestern quadrant. Finally, fragments of a broken mirror and an empty bottle of perfume were found dispersed on the house floor.

Cluster 3, located in the southeastern part of the settlement, at 18 to 20 m S of the previous one, consists of features 1 and 2, with, in addition, a donkey-tethering pole (fig. 34). Feature 2 is a small, 2.80-m-in-diameter chicken house, built without roof-supporting pole with a door oriented NW. The habitation house (feature 1) measures 4.00 m in diameter. It is built with a single central pole, its doorway oriented W. The bed, found in the eastern half of the feature, measures 2.00 m in length and 1.60 m in width. The rest of the recorded furniture is concentrated in the southern side, with, from N to S, a 1.50-m-long and 0.40-m-wide set of wooden shelves, a clay pot-stand, and finally, a semicircular, three-niches, plain hearth, 0.90 m in length, 0.40 m in maximum width, and 0.50 m in height. The relationship between both houses and the nearby goat enclosure is far from clear. Judging from the orientation of the enclosure's entrance/exit, house 3 is a better candidate for its ownership; but both units may have pooled their small livestock in order to build just one enclosure. This may be the reason why this goat enclosure is the largest of all the specimens recorded in the settlement.

House 3 is located due S of the settlement (fig. 34); it is associated with donkey- and calf-tethering poles found at 9 to 10 m N. The feature is built with two roof-supporting poles set at 0.30 m from each other and measures 4.20 m in diameter, with the doorway oriented N. The bed, with its overlying round canopy, measures 2.00 m in length and 1.55 m in width and is located in the southern half of the feature. The hearth is found along the wall, at 1.50 m E of the bed; it is an elongated, sub-rectangular, three-niches feature with rounded edges and two additional hearthstones, 0.90 m long, 0.50 m wide, and 0.50 m in height. The hearth decoration can be partitioned into three components. The hearthstones are decorated all over their surface with finger impressions. The lower part of the rear panel has four equidistant, vertical, and elongated clay bumps. And the upper part has a rectangular register delimited by appliqué cordon, and filled with designs organized on both sides of an upward appliqué arrow. The motifs consist of (1) an appliqué circle located in the middle, (2) a panel of two parallel and vertical lines of finger impressions, and (3) another panel similar to the previous one but with three lines. A 2.00-m-long and 0.50-m-wide set of wooden shelves abuts the hearth in the S and is stretched northward. There is a relatively large jar-stand next to the door, on the right-hand side, and finally, a shallow scatter of ash in the center of the house's northern half. One flashlight battery and an empty can of preserved milk were found dispersed on the floor.

Cluster 4 is located along the western part of the settlement and consists of features 4, 5, and 6, with, in addition, a goat-milking post, a set of calf-tethering poles, and a goat enclosure (fig. 34). Feature 4, at the southeastern end of the cluster, measures 5.10 m in diameter. It is a habitation house built with a single central pole and a doorway oriented NE. The bed is stretched over the southwestern half of the feature, and measures 3.20 m in length and 1.80 m in width. The hearth, found along the wall on the northwestern side of the bed, is a rectangular, three-niches feature, 0.90 m long, 0.50 m wide, and 0.50 m high, complemented by two clay hearthstones. The decoration consists of four equidistant, vertical, and elongated clay bumps in the lower half of the rear panel, and a rectangular register in the upper half delimited by appliqué cordons and filled with roughly alternating two upward appliqué arrows and two appliqué circles. The last element of furniture consists of a set of wooden shelves measuring 1.70 m in length and 0.50 in width, stretched between the hearth and the doorway. A shallow scatter of ash was recorded between the door and the central pole. Finally, a worn-out enamel basin with its lid were found to the N of the house, next to the door. Feature 5, at the middle of the cluster, is a small 3.40-m-in-diameter young man's house. It is built without roof-supporting pole, with the entrance oriented E. The house floor is clear of cultural remains. A relatively large, shallow, and circular depression, a presumable water-jar stand, was found next to the door, on the right-hand side. Feature 6, at the northern end of the set, measures 5.20 m in diameter. It is built with one roof-supporting pole, its entrance oriented E. The bed is found in the western half and measures 3.50 m in length and 2.00 m in width. The hearth is located 0.50 m from the bed, on its northern side. It is a rectangular, three-niches feature with rounded corners and two complementary hearthstones, measuring 1.20 m in length, 0.50 m in width, and 0.55 m in height. Both hearthstones are decorated with parallel lines of pinched finger impressions. The rear panel has four equidistant tips on the top, the lower half being decorated with four equidistant, vertical, and elongated bumps, and the upper one with a rectangular register delimited by appliqué cordons, divided into two equal parts by a vertical appliqué cordon, each filled with two symmetric panels of vertical and parallel lines of finger impressions, set on both sides of a central appliqué circle.

There is no significant variation in the intra-house arrangement of furniture. There is a single case (house 10) with an additional set of wooden shelves located on the bed's side opposite to the hearth. All the others have their furniture arranged following the pattern described clockwise and consisting of (1) the bed, (2) the hearth, and (3) the wooden shelves, and (4), in five cases out of six, an additional fireplace found between the doorway and the central pole. Hearth decoration provides another clue on the spatial layout of the camp. Hearths found in houses 1, 7, and 10, found in the northeastern half of the camp, are essentially plain features; those from houses 3, 4, and 6, located in the southwestern half, have elaborate decoration with motifs including similar elements, upward arrows, circles, pinched finger impressions, and a "framed" upper register.

Agedipse III

Agedipse III is the largest of all the studied dry-season camps. It is a circular settlement located 120 m S of Agedipse II, measuring 150 m in diameter and

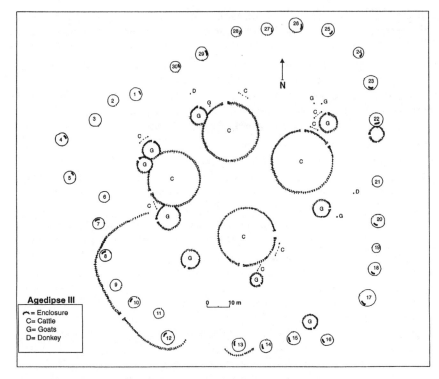

Figure 35: Map of Agedipse III

extended over 1.76 hectares. Settlement facilities are organized into three roughly concentric circles, with cattle corrals at the center, surrounded by goat enclosures and tethering poles, and finally, the ring of houses at 20 to 30 m outward (fig. 35).

There are four central cattle corrals of almost similar size, 25 to 26 m in diameter, located 8 to 15 m from each other. The specimens situated in the north-western half of the site have one entrance/exit each, those from the southeastern one have two. There are ten goat enclosures, with eight of them attached to or in the immediate proximity of the central cattle corrals. They vary in size from 6 m in diameter, for three of them, to 10 m for the largest specimen. The thirty houses are set at almost regular intervals; they are nonetheless organized into five large units of five to seven features each.

Unit 1 is found in the settlement's northwestern quadrant (fig. 34). It consists of seven houses stretched on 65 m N-S, a central cattle corral (CI) with its two attached goat enclosures (G1 and G2), and finally, a set of calf-tethering poles. Houses 1 to 3, located at the northern end of the unit at 20 m from the livestock features, and arranged in a roughly W-E line, are almost equidistant, located 5 to 6 m from each other. House 1 is built with two roof-supporting poles set at 2.00 m from each other and measures 5.50 m in diameter, with a doorway oriented south-eastern. The bed, measuring 3.00 in length and 1.60 in width, is spread all over the northwestern half of the house. The hearth is found along the wall, NE of the bed. It is a three-niches feature, 1.10 m long, 0.45 m wide, and 0.55 m in height; its rear panel is rectangular with rounded upper corners. It is decorated with a rectangular grid of appliqué, perpendicular cordons. The last element of the house's furniture is a set of wooden shelves, measuring 2.00 m in length and 0.55 m in width, stretched between the hearth and the doorway. House 2, at the center, is a 4.80-m-in-diameter young man's habitation, built with a single central pole with the door-way also oriented SE. The house floor has been cleared of everything. Feature 3, at the western end of the complex, is built with two roof-supporting poles set at 1.75 m from each other. It measures 5.30 m in diameter with its entrance oriented SE. The bed, found in the northwestern half of the house has been partially dis-mantled, but its original size, 3.00 m in length and 2.00 m in width, was still easily recordable.

Houses 4 and 5, at the center of the unit, are located some 10 m W at 10 to 11 m from each other (fig. 35). House 4 measures 5.60 m in diameter with its door-way oriented E. All the furniture, roof-supporting poles, and wall posts were dis-mantled. The presence of a bed in the western half of the house and wooden shelves in the NE, between the hearth and the doorway, is clearly indicated by the recorded series of postholes. The hearth, surprisingly well-preserved, was still present. It is located due N at 0.50 m from the wall. It is three-niches, slightly in-curved feature measuring 1.10 m in length, 0.50 m in width, and 0.55 m in height. The rear panel is rectangular and decorated at mid-height with two horizontal and parallel lines of pinched finger impressions on an appliqué cordon. House 5, with its doorway oriented E, measures 5.20 m in diameter. It is built with two roof-supporting poles set at 2.50 m from each other. The bed, measuring 3.00 m in length and 1.50 m in width, is found in the northwestern half of the house. The hearth is located NE, in the axis of the roof-supporting poles, along the wall. It is a three-niches feature, 1.20 m long, 0.50 m wide, and 0.45 m high, with, in addition, two hearthstones. The rear panel is plain stricto sensu with nonetheless a horizontal, appliqué cor-don overlining a set of four equidistant, vertical, and elongated clay bumps. A set of wooden shelves, 1.50 m long and 0.50 m wide, is stretched between the doorway and the hearth.

Houses 6 and 7, at the southern end of the unit, are located 6 to 7 m from each other (fig. 35). House 6's entrance is oriented E; it is a young man's habitation, built with a single central pole, and measuring 4.60 m in diameter. The bed, found in the feature's western half, measuring 2.60 m in length and 1.20 m in width, is the only piece of furniture recorded in the house. House 7, a few meters S, also measures 4.60 m in diameter. It is also built with a single roof-supporting pole, with its doorway oriented E. The bed, located in the house's western half, meas-ures 2.70 m in width and 1.50 m in width. The hearth is found along the wall on the northern side of the bed. It is a three-niches, slightly in-curved feature, 1.50 m long, 0.45 m wide, and 0.40 m high, with its rear panel decorated at mid-height with two horizontal and parallel lines of pinched finger impressions set on an appliqué cordon. Finally, a 2.00-m-long and 0.50-m-wide set of wooden shelves, stretched from the hearth to the doorway, complements the recorded house's furniture.

Unit 2 is situated in the settlement's northern quadrant. It is comprised of a central cattle corral (CII) with an attached goat enclosure (G3), one goat-milking post, one donkey- and a set of calf-tethering poles, and six houses (house 25 to 30) stretched on 75 m. They are arranged in a linear W-E pattern at distance varying from 8 to 14 m between neighbors and located 20 to 45 m from the livestock features.

House 25 is found at the eastern end of the unit. It is built with two roof-supporting poles set at 3.00 m from each other and measures 5.70 m in diameter, with the entrance oriented SW. A shallow depression, used as a jar-stand was found next to the door, on the right-hand side. Proceeding counterclockwise, there is a 1.50-m-long and 0.40-m-wide set of wooden shelves stretched between the jar-stand and the hearth. The latter is a three-niches, 1.25-m-long, 0.50-wide, and 0.50-m-high sub-rectangular feature with rounded corners. In this case, in fact, each of the hearth niches is a Kotoko portable hearth inserted in a larger clay masonry. The hearth's rear panel is decorated along its three sides by parallel lines of pinched finger impression and a horizontal, appliqué cordon in its lower part. A clay pot-stand was found at the hearth's eastern end. Finally, the bed is spread over the house's eastern half; it measures 3.20 m in length and 1.40 m in width. A piece of cloth and a blue girl's dress was found abandoned on the house floor.

House 26, at 8 m W of the previous one, measures 6.10 m in diameter. It is built with two roof-supporting poles located 2.20 m from each other, with the doorway oriented S. Three among the recorded four elements of furniture are found in the house's northern half. This is the case for the 1.00×0.50 m wood stand found along the wall in the W; the well-preserved canopied bed, measuring 2.50 in length and 1.60 m, located in the central part; and finally, the four-niches, rectangular hearth with its complementary two hearthstones. The recorded hearth measures 1.25 m in length, 0.50 m in width, and 0.65 m in height. Its rear panel, rectangular with rounded upper angles, is decorated all along its sides with parallel lines of pinched finger impressions, defining an upper plain register; this is complemented in the lower part by five equidistant, vertical, elongated clay bumps, two of them, smaller in size, are connected by a short, horizontal, appliqué cordon decorated with pinched finger impressions. The set of wooden shelves is located in the southern half of the house. It is stretched between the hearth and the doorway and measures 2.60 m in length and 0.50 m in width. Finally, an additional fireplace, represented by a shallow scatter of ash and charcoal, was found between the door and the roof-supporting poles. A piece of cloth and an empty plastic bottle were recorded on the house floor.

House 27, at 8 m farther W, measures 5.00 m in diameter. It is built with a single central pole with its entrance oriented S. The bed, situated in the northern half of the feature, has a canopy and measures 3.00 m in length and 1.60 m in width. A 0.70 m × 0.30 m wood stand is found along the wall next to the bed's western corner. The hearth is located due E. It is a 1.00-m-long, 0.45-m-wide, and 0.50-m-high three-niches, rectangular feature with rounded corners. The rear panel is decorated in the upper half by a rectangular frame made of pinched finger impressions set on appliqué cordon; on the lower half, there are four equidistant, vertical, and elongated clay bumps. A set wooden shelves, 1.10 m in length and 0.50 m in width, is located next to the hearth, on its southern side. Finally, an additional fireplace abutting the shelf comprises three large clay balls decorated with finger impressions. A piece of reed mat was found on the house floor next to the eastern corner of the bed.

House 28 is located at the center of the unit, at 8 m W of the previous one. It is a 4.50-m-in-diameter feature built with two roof-supporting poles situated at 2.30 m apart, with the doorway oriented S. The hearth, partly destroyed, is located close to the door, on the right-hand side. It is a 1.20-m-long, 0.45-m-wide, and 0.45-m-high, three-niches, rectangular feature with rounded corners. The lower part is decorated with scattered finger impression, and a horizontal, appliqué cordon is found in the upper third of the round cornered rear panel. The 1.70-m-long and 0.40-m-wide wooden shelves are stretched from the hearth eastward. The bed is spread on almost all the available space of the house's northern half and measures 3.00 in length and 1.60 m in width. Finally, a piece of reed mat was found under the bed's frame.

Houses 29 and 30 are set slightly aside, at 13 m W from the other unit's features. Feature 29, with its entrance oriented S, measures 5.80 m in diameter. It is built with a single central pole. The bed and hearth are located in the northern half; the former measures 3.20 m in length and 2.00 m in width, and the latter, a slightly in-curved, three-niches feature, is 1.10 m long, 0.45 m wide, and 0.45 m high. The hearth's rear panel has rounded corners, the upper part being decorated with a framed register made of parallel lines of pinched finger impression on appliqué cordons. The pot-supporting parts are also decorated with finger impression. The third element of the house furniture consists of wooden shelves stretched between the hearth and the door, measuring 2.20 m in length and 0.40 m in width. Finally, a loose ash scatter was found between the door and the central pole. House 30, at the western end of the unit, also built with a single central pole, measures 4.60 m in diameter, its doorway being oriented SE. The bed, 2.70 m in length and 1.40 m in width, is found in the northeastern half. The hearth, poorly preserved, is located due E along the wall. It is a three-niches, rectangular feature, 1.25 m long, 0.40 m wide, and 0.45 m high; the rear panel is decorated at mid-height with finger impressions on a horizontal, appliqué cordon. Finally, the wooden shelves, stretched between the hearth and the door, measure 1.70 m in length and 0.40 m in width. A shallow ash pile was found between the door and the central pole.

Unit 3 is located in the eastern part of the settlement (fig. 35). It consists of central cattle corral CIII with its two entrances/exits oriented NE, goat enclosures G4, G5, and G6, two sets of calf-tethering poles, three goat-milking and one donkey posts, and finally, houses 20 to 24 stretched on 76 m N-S. House 20, situated at the southern end of the unit, measures 6.00 m in diameter. It is built with two roof-supporting poles set at 2.50 m from each other, with its entrance oriented NW. The wooden shelves, situated along the wall in the southwestern quadrant, measure 2.20 m in length and 0.50 m in width and abut the hearth in the S. The latter is a 1.40-m-long, 0.50-m-wide, and 0.55-m-high three-niches, rectangular feature with rounded corners. The rear panel is decorated at mid-height with parallel lines of finger pinched impression on a horizontal, appliqué cordon. Finally, the bed, situated in the southeastern half of the house, measures 2.70 m in length and 1.50 m in width. There are two wooden posts of unknown function on the western side of the bed.

House 21, found 12 m farther N, is a 4.30-m-in-diameter young man's house. It is built with a single central pole with the doorway oriented SW. The house's floor is clear of any piece of material remains. House 22, roughly at the center of the unit is attached to goat enclosure G5. It is built with two roof-supporting poles set at 1.80 m from each other, the doorway oriented W, and measures 5.80 m in diameter. A relatively large but informal fireplace, with partially burned wooden logs, was recorded in the central part of the house's western half, between the door and the central poles. The bed and the hearth are found in the eastern half. The former measures 3.00 in length and 1.70 m in width. The latter is a two-niches, trapezoid-shaped feature with two complementary hearthstones. It measures 1.00 m in length, 0.55 m in width, and 0.50 m in height. The rear panel, with three pointed tips, is decorated at mid-height with two horizontal and parallel appliqué cordons, complemented in the lower half by three equidistant, vertical, and elongated clay bumps. An empty matchbox and a flashlight battery were dispersed on the house floor.

House 23, located 10 m N of the previous one, measures 5.90 m in diameter. Its entrance is oriented due W, and it is built with two roof-supporting poles set at 2 m from each other. The canopied bed, found in the eastern half, is 3.30 m long and 1.80 m wide. The hearth is located along the wall in the S. It is a 1.10-m-long, 0.56-m-high, and 0.50-m-wide three-niches, rectangular feature with rounded corners. The rear panel, rectangular in shape with rounded upper corners, is decorated with horizontal and parallel lines of finger impressions on an appliqué cordon. Finally, the wooden shelves, measuring 1.80 m in length and 0.50 m in width, are found between the hearth and the house doorway. A few additional material remains were found dispersed on the house floor; they consist of an empty paper box, a child's shoe sole, and a clay bowl.

House 24, at the northern end of the unit, is a 4.70-m-in-diameter feature, built with a single central pole, with the entrance oriented SW. The hearth and the wooden shelves are found in the southwestern half of the house. The former is a 1.25-m-long, 0.40-m-wide, and 0.55-m-high three-niches, rectangular feature with rounded corners, obtained through the insertion of three Kotoko portable hearths in a larger clay masonry. The wooden shelves abut the hearth's southeastern side and measure 1.80 m in length and 0.45 m in width. The bed, 2.40 m in length and 1.00 m in width, is found in the house's eastern half.

Unit 4 is located in the S-SE of the site. It comprises a central cattle corral (CIV) with two entrances/exits, one oriented S-SW and the other oriented E, two goat enclosures (G7 and G8), two sets of calf-tethering poles, and seven houses distributed into two clusters (fig. 35). The eastern cluster consists of houses 17 to 19, arranged in a linear N-S pattern, at distances varying from 4 to 6 m from each other. The western cluster is composed of five features, a goat enclosure (G7) and houses 13 to 16, laid out in a W-E line, at distances ranging from 6 to 9 m.

House 19, situated at the northern end of the cluster, is a relatively small 4.10-m-in-diameter feature. It is a young man's habitation built with a single central pole and an entrance oriented W. A bed found in the eastern half of the feature is the sole piece of furniture. It is a canopied bed measuring 2.10 m in length and 1.30 m in width. Feature 18, at the middle of the cluster, is larger, measuring 5.60 m in diameter. It is built with a single roof supporting pole and a doorway oriented W. The bed, found in the eastern half of the house, measures 3.30 m in length and 1.70 m in width. A storage bin, 0.70 m in maximum diameter and made with sun-dried clay, was found next to the wall, on the southern side of the bed. The hearth and the wooden shelves are found in the southwestern quadrant. The latter measures 1.00 m in length and 0.50 m in width. The former is a 1.30-m-long, 0.50-m-wide, and 0.45-m-high, three-niches feature with rounded corners. The rear panel with rounded corners is decorated at mid-height with horizontal and parallel lines of pinched finger impression set on an appliqué cordon. House 17 is found at the southern end of the cluster. It is the largest of the settlement, measuring 7.40 m in diameter, and is built with four roof-supporting poles and an entrance oriented W-NW. The four roof-supporting poles define a 3.00-m-long and 2.00-m-wide rectangle in the central part of the house, where the bed is located. The latter measures 4.00 m in length and 1.80 m in width. The hearth is found along the wall in the SW. It is a 1.10-m-long, 0.55-m-wide, and 0.50-m-high, three-niches, rectangular feature, with its round-cornered rear panel decorated with two horizontal and parallel appliqué cordons. A shallow ash scatter was found next to the door, and a footed bowl between the bed and the hearth.

The western cluster is stretched on approximately 50 m E-W. House 13, the westernmost feature, measures 5.65 m in diameter, with a doorway oriented N. It is complemented on the outer side by a fence portion.The habitation is built with two roof-supporting poles set at 2.20 m from each other, and is located in the northern half of the house instead of defining the symmetry axis, as is generally the case.The bed measures 3.10 m in length and 1.70 m in width; it is located in the center and southern half of the feature. It is surrounded in the S and E by two pairs of wooden posts used to hang light, daily, life items. The hearth is found due W, along the wall. It is a 1.30-m-long, 0.50-m-wide, and 0.45-m-high, three-niches feature with rounded corners. The rear panel, rectangular in shape with rounded upper corners, is decorated in the lower half with more or less equidistant, vertical, and elongated clay bumps, and a horizontal, appliqué cordon at mid-height. A set of wooden shelves, 2.00 m long and 0.50 m wide, is stretched between the house doorway and the hearth in the northwestern quadrant. Finally, a clay pot-stand was found between the shelf and the hearth, as well as a crushed, two-handled pot decorated with extensive twisted roulette impression on the body, overlined on the shoulder by two horizontal and parallel grooved lines. House 14, at 6 m E of the previous one, has its entrance oriented N; it is built with a single central pole and measures 5.30 m in diameter. The bed and the hearth are located in the house's southern half; the former, 2.60 m long and 1.60 m wide, has been partially dismantled; the latter, found along the wall in the southwestern quadrant, is a jumble of collapsed material 0.50 m wide and 1.30 m long. House 15, at 7 m E, has its doorway oriented NW-NW. It is a 5.60-m-in-diameter habitation house built with two roof-supporting poles set at 2.00 m from each other. A footed bowl, decorated on the body with twisted roulette impression, was found on the floor in the house's northern half. The bed is spread over almost all the southern half and measures 3.00 m in length and 2.00 m in width. The hearth is found along the wall, due W. It is a slightly in-curved, rectangular, three-niches feature 1.20 m long, 0.50 m wide, and 0.50 m high. The rear panel, decorated at mid-height with horizontal and parallel lines of pinched finger impression on an appliqué cordon, is rectangular in shape with rounded corners. House 16, the easternmost of the cluster's features, is a relatively small, 4.50-m-in-diameter habitation. Its doorway is oriented N and, despite its small size, is built with two roof-supporting poles set at 2.00 m from each other. The bed, measuring 2.50 m in length and 1.60 m in width, is found in the house's southern half, with the hearth along the wall, on its western side. The latter is a plain, 1.00-m-long, 0.45-m-wide, and 0.50-m-high four-niches installation, with a semicircular rear panel. The set of wooden shelves abuts the hearth on its southern side and is stretched northward; it measures 1.50 m in length and 0.40 m in width.

Unit 5, located in the southwestern part of the settlement, is well-delineated by a surrounding fence with an entrance at the middle of the complex (fig. 35). It consists of two large, sized 12 to 15-m-in-diameter goat enclosures (G9 and G10), five houses set in a NW-SE linear arrangement with features at 6 to 9 m from one to the next.

Feature 8, at the northwestern end of the complex, measures 5.00 in diameter. It is built with a single central pole, with the doorway oriented NE. The bed, located in the southwestern half, measures 2.50 m in length and 1.70 m in width. The hearth, found along the wall due N, is a three pseudo-niches convex feature, 1.30 m long, 0.50 m wide, and 0.50 m high with two additional hearthstones. The rear panel is trapezoid-shaped with rounded corners; it is decorated in the lower part with four equidistant, vertical, and elongated clay bumps, overlined at mid-height by two horizontal and parallel lines of finger impressions. Finally, the set of wooden shelves, measuring 1.60 m in length and 0.45 m in width, is stretched between the hearth in the W and the doorway in the E.

House 9 is found at 8 m SE of the previous one. It is a habitation feature with the doorway oriented E, measuring 4.80 m in diameter and built with two central poles located 2.00 m from each other. The bed, found in the house's western half, measures 3.00 m in length and 1.50 m in width. The hearth is located due north, along the wall; it is a crescent-shaped, 1.20-m-long and approximately 0.60-m-wide, collapsed, three-niches installation.

House 10 is located at the center of the complex, next to the entrance. It is a 5.00-m-in-diameter habitation feature with the entrance oriented NE and is built with two roof-supporting poles set at 1.80 m from each other. There is a raised grinding platform next to the door, on its left-hand side. The bed is found in the southwestern half and measures 2.80 m in length and 1.70 m in width. The hearth is located along the wall in the house's northwestern quadrant; it is a slightly incurved 1.00-m-long, 0.45-m-wide, and 0.50-m-high, three-niches installation. The rear panel, rectangular with rounded upper corners, is decorated at mid-height with two horizontal and parallel appliqué cordons underlying four almost equidistant sets of two short and vertical lines of finger impressions. Finally, there is a set of wooden shelves stretched along the house's northern quadrant measuring 2.00 m in length and 0.50 m in width.

Feature 11, 7 m SE, is a relatively small, 4.20-m-in-diameter young man's habitation. It is built with a single central pole, with the doorway oriented N. The bed measures 2.80 m in length and 1.40 m in width, and is located in the southern half of the house. A series of wooden shelves, 1.40 m long and 0.35 m wide, is found along the wall in the northwestern quadrant.

House 12, located at the southeastern end of the complex, measures 5.75 m in diameter. It is built with two roof-supporting poles set at 2.00 m from each other, with the entrance oriented NE. There is a casual fireplace, represented by a shallow ash pile, found between the door and the central poles. The bed, 4.00 m long and 2.00 m wide, is located in the southwestern half of the house, as is the case for the set of wooden shelves and the hearth. The shelves, stretched on 2.00 m and 0.50 m wide, are found along the wall and behind the bed in the SW. The hearth is also located along the wall, but in the house's northwestern quadrant. It is a 1.10-m-long, 0.45-m-wide, and 0.50-m-high, four-niches, rectangular installation. The rear panel is rectangular with rounded upper angles, decorated with parallel and horizontal lines of pinched finger impressions on an appliqué cordon, underlying four equidistant sets of two parallel and vertical lines of finger impressions.

The settlement appears to have been inhabited by five "herding" units. As can be expected in a dry-season camp as large as Agedipse III, there is more diversity in the intra-house arrangement of features as well as hearth shapes and decoration. As far as hearth decoration is concerned, half (12) of the recorded sample of twenty-four have motifs made of finger impressions. In terms of intra-house's furniture arrangement, the standard clockwise pattern with the bed in the feature's half opposite to the door, then the hearth, and finally, the wooden shelves, has been recorded in fourteen cases out of twenty-seven, with an additional element in houses 10 (a raised grinding platform) and 26 (a wood stand). Nine of the houses (houses 1, 5, 7, 8, 25, 26, 27, 29, and 30) (fig. 35) are located in the northwestern half of the settlement and belong to units 1, 2, and 5. The rest is distributed between units 3 (one occurrence) and 4 (four cases).

Agedipse IV

Compared to the previous camp, Agedipse IV is a rather small settlement located 200 m S of Agedipse I, and 300 m W of Agedipse III. The camp is roughly circular in shape, measuring 75 m in diameter and delimited by a fence. Livestock and human dwelling facilities are spread over 0.44 hectares and comprise a central cattle corral with four entrances/exit, one in each cardinal direction, and measuring 31 m in diameter; three goat enclosures attached to the cattle corral, two on the northern side and one on the southern one, with their diameters varying from 5.80 to 6.80 m; a small, 2.00-m-in-diameter chicken house; four sets of calf-tethering poles; a ring of thirteen almost equidistant houses; and finally, the camp fence with twelve entrances/exits (fig. 36). The well and a 6.00-m-in-diameter livestock watering trough are located 45 to 50 m SW of the camp. A large pile of straw shaded by three relatively large trees was recorded a few meters W of the well. Finally, an unused shallow water cistern, 14 m in diameter, was found at some 10 m W of the camp.

Camp facilities seem to be organized into three major units, each with four or five houses. Unit 1 is found in the N-NW of the settlement and consists of houses 1 to 4 and 13, two goat enclosures, one chicken house, and one donkey- and a set of calf-tethering poles (fig. 36). House 13, at the eastern end of the complex, is a small, 4.00-m-in-diameter goat feature devoid of any material culture item. It is built with a single central pole, with the doorway oriented S.

Feature 1, located 6.00 m W, measures 4.60 m in diameter. It is a habitation house with a doorway oriented S built with a single roof supporting pole. The bed, 2.10 m long and 1.40 m wide, is located in the northwestern half of the feature. It is flanked on the W by a 0.70-m-long and 0.35-m-wide wood stand, and a poorly preserved hearth in the E. The latter, comprising two additional hearthstones, measures 1.10 m in length, unknown width, and 0.50 m in height for the collapsed rear panel. The panel is rectangular in shape with rounded corners. It has on its upper half two parallel and vertical upward appliqué arrows underlined by a horizontal, appliqué cordon, all decorated with two parallel lines of pinched finger impressions. On the lower half, there are four equidistant, vertical, and elongated clay bumps. Finally, there is a set of wooden shelves located along the wall in the house's southeastern quadrant. Two large pieces of reed mat were found in the

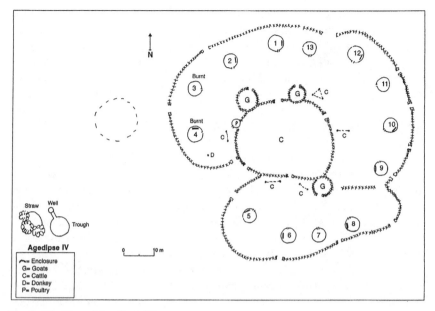

Figure 36: Map of Agedipse IV

central part of the house's southeastern half as well as a plastic teapot next to the wall in the SW, but outside.

House 2 is located at the center of the unit, at 10 m W of house 1. It is built with a single central pole, with the entrance oriented S, and measures 4.80 m in diameter. The distribution of features within the house space is similar to that of the previous house, with the 2.80-m-long and 1.40-m-wide bed in the northwestern half; a small 0.80 m × 0.30 m shelf next to the bed's southwestern corner; a collapsed hearth along the wall NE of the bed; and finally, a larger 1.80 m × 0.45 m set of wooden shelves in the southeastern quadrant. The hearth's 1.00-m-long and 0.40-m-high rear panel was found collapsed on the rest of the installation which comprises two additional hearthstones. It is decorated in the lower half with three equidistant, vertical, and elongated clay bumps, overlined at mid-height by a horizontal, appliqué cordon.

House 3, at 10 m W of feature 4, measures 4.40 m in diameter. It is a partially burned young man's feature clear of any material evidence, built with a single central pole with the doorway oriented E. Feature 4, 10 m S, is also partially burned. It is a habitation house with the entrance oriented E, built with one roof-supporting pole and measuring 4.90 m in diameter. The bed, located in the house's western half, measures 2.80 m in length and 1.60 m in width. A wood stand, 1.00 m long and 0.25 m wide, was found along the wall next to the bed's southwestern corner.

The hearth is on the opposite northeastern side. It is a 0.90-m-long, 0.60-m-wide, and 0.6-m-high, three-niches, rectangular installation with rounded edges, complemented by three hearthstones. The recorded rear panel is rectangular with rounded corners. It is decorated in the lower part by four equidistant, vertical, and elongated clay bumps overlined by a horizontal, appliqué cordon. The set of wooden shelves, measuring 1.70 m in length and 0.40 m in width, is found stretched between the hearth and the house door. A shallow scatter of ash was recorded between the door and the central pole. And finally, there was a large tin container found outside next to the wall in the NW.

Unit 2 is located in the southern side of the camp (fig. 36). It is a well-delineated and fenced complex with six entrances/exits, comprising a 6.10 m in diameter goat enclosure, two sets of calf-tethering poles, and four houses stretched on 40 m W-E. House 5, at the western end, measures 4.60 m in diameter. It is built with one central pole with the doorway oriented NE. The hearth is found along the wall in the NW; it is a rectangular, three-niches feature with two hearthstones, measuring 0.90 m in length, 0.50 m in width, and 0.70 m in height. The hearthstones are decorated at their middle with four parallel lines of pinched finger impressions. The rear panel is rectangular in shape with a crenellated top. It has two decorated registers; the lower one has three equidistant, vertical, and elongated clay bumps, and the upper one has two upward, parallel, appliqué arrows set within a frame of two horizontal and parallel *appliqué* cordons. The bed is found in the house's southwestern half and measures 2.20 m in length and 1.30 m in width. Finally, the set of wooden shelves, stretched on 1.70 m W-E and measuring 0.40 m in width, is situated in the northern quadrant between the hearth and the doorway.

Feature 6 is found 9 to 10 m SE of the previous one. It is a 4.50-m-in-diameter habitation house with the entrance oriented N. The bed , 2.20 m long and 1.30 m wide, is located in the southern half. The hearth is found along the wall due W; it is a rectangular, three-niches installation with rounded edges, complemented by three hearthstones and measuring 0.90 m in length, 0.50 m width, and 0.50 m in height. The rear panel is rectangular and decorated with five more or less equidistant, vertical, and elongated clay bumps, each attached to an upward, appliqué arrow with pinched finger impressions. The wooden shelves, 1.60 m long and 0.40 m wide, are the third element stretched along the wall in the northwestern quadrant. House 7, 5 m farther E, is a small, 4.00-m-in-diameter feature with the entrance oriented N, built with a single central pole. It is a young man's habitation with the floor cleared of any piece of cultural remains.

Finally, house 8, at the eastern end of the complex, is built with one central pole, with a doorway oriented NW, and measures 4.70 m in diameter. The bed, found in the house's southeastern half, is 2.80 m long and 1.50 m wide. The hearth is found due S along the wall; it is a largely destroyed feature with two complementary hearthstones. The collapsed rear panel is trapezoid-shaped. It is decorated with four equidistant, vertical, and elongated clay bumps in its lower half and a horizontal, appliqué cordon in the upper one. The set of wooden shelves, 0.40 m in width, abuts the hearth in the S and is stretched on 2.30 m northward. Finally, there is a large 1.00 m × 0.40 m piece of burned clay in the E, next to the bed's corner.

Unit 3 is found along the eastern side of the settlement, stretched on 45 m N-S. The outer fence has four entrances/exits, and houses are almost equidistant, with distances from one to the next varying from 8 to 9 m. Two sets of calf-tethering poles, located next to the central cattle corral, seem to belong to this unit (fig. 36).

House 9, at the southern end of the complex, measures 4.10 m in diameter. It is built with a single central pole, with the entrance oriented NW. The bed, located in the southeastern half, measures 2.30 m in length and 1.30 m in width. The hearth, found due S along the wall, was badly damaged, restricted to two hearthstones and a 1.10 m × 0.50 m burned surface. The wooden shelves are 0.50 m wide and are stretched on 1.80 m N-S along the western wall portion. Finally, a few potsherds were found clustered between the door and the central pole in the northwestern part of the feature.

House 10, at 9 m N, has its doorway oriented SW. It is built with a single central pole and measures 4.20 m in diameter. The bed is found in the northeastern half and measures 2.20 m in length and 1.50 m in width. The hearth is a rectangular, 0.90-m-long, 0.50-m-wide, and 0.5-m-high three-niches feature with two complementary hearthstones. The rear panel is semicircular in shape, decorated in the lower half with four equidistant, vertical, and elongated clay bumps, overlined at mid-height with horizontal and parallel lines of pinched finger impressions. The wooden shelves are set between the hearth in the E and the door in the W and measure 1.60 m in length and 0.40 m in width. A small, empty glass bottle, a piece of reed mat, and a wooden log were found scattered between the bed, the hearth, and the shelves.

House 11, at 8 m N of the previous one, is a young man's feature. It is built with a single central pole, with the entrance oriented W, and measures 3.85 m in diameter. The recorded floor is clear of any material remains. Feature 12 is found at the northern end of the unit, its doorway oriented SW. It is a habitation house built with one central pole and measuring 4.80 m in diameter. The wooden shelves measure 1.40 m in length and 0.40 m in width; they are located in the house southeastern quadrant. The hearth is found due E. It is a collapsed installation, 0.90 m long and 0.60 m wide, with a portion of plain rear panel. The bed, 2.60 m long and 1.30 m wide, is located in the house's northeastern half.

The size of dwelling features from Agedipse IV varies within a narrow range of 1.05 m (4.90 m [house 4]–3.85 m [house 11]), and all are built with a single central pole. As far as intra-house spatial organization is concerned, two patterns have been recorded. One is found in houses 1, 2, and 4, from unit 1 in the N-NW of the settlement, and consists of four elements: proceeding clockwise, the pattern comprises (1) a small set of shelves or wood stands, then (2) the bed in the half of the house opposite to the entrance, (3) the hearth along the wall, and finally, (4) the larger or main wooden shelves. The second pattern, with (1) the bed, (2) the hearth, and (3) the wooden shelves, is documented in units 2 and 3, with houses 5, 6, and 8 in the former, and houses 9, 10, and 12 in the latter.

PART IV

Permanent Villages

Chapter 8

Abuzrega

Introduction

Abuzrega is situated at 12° 02′ latitude N and 15° 01′ longitude E, in the bend and on the right bank of the Abani river channel. Census data from 1975 show the village to have a population of twenty-one inhabitants (Elingui 1978: 4). The village is not recorded in the 1976 census published in 1985 (Recensement General, 1985), suggesting the site to have been abandoned or, more probably, that census officers carried out their survey during the dry season when the inhabitants were elsewhere. The settlement is subcircular in shape, with an average diameter of 230 m. The village is thus extended over 4.15 hectares (fig. 37). It is surrounded by a ring of fenced sorghum fields, with some stretched along the bottom of the fossil river channel. The settlement's main entrance is located in the S, with the site's layout organized into nine habitation complexes, each inhabited by an extended family (table 32). They are distributed around a central space, 80 to 90 m in diameter, in which communal features are located. They include a well, 13 m deep with a 4.90-m-in-diameter curb and a 1.60 × 1.00 m trough in the S, found E of the roadway; two barns, the southern one (feature 12), at approximately 40 m N of the well, being a 8.50-m-in-diameter wood and reeds house filled with straw and surrounded by a fence, with the doorway oriented S, and the larger northern specimen, empty during the period of observation, 10.90 m in diameter with the entrance oriented SE; and finally, two central cattle corrals, the eastern specimen (CII) measuring 18 m in diameter, and the western one (CI), 25 m.

Habitation Complex 1

Habitation complex 1 is found in the southeastern part of the settlement. It is comprised of seven houses, two storage platforms, and two goat enclosures, stretched on 68 m SW-NE, with, in addition, a partially fenced rear space 100 m long and 38 m wide (fig. 37). House 1, at the southwestern end of the complex, is built with

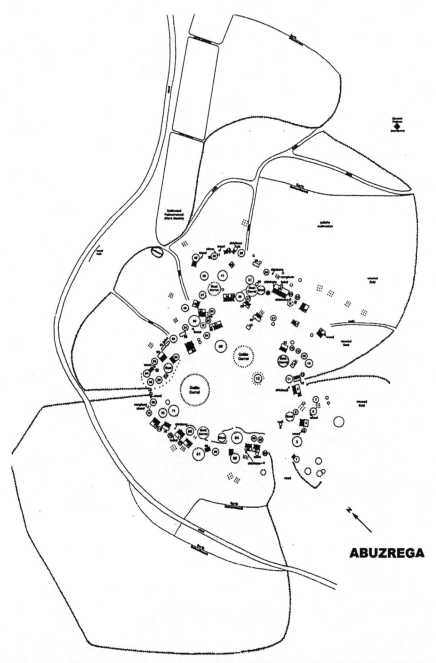

ABUZREGA

Figure 37: Map of Abuzrega

Table 32: Abuzrega houses and features distribution

Cluster number	Number of features	Number of units	Habitation houses		Livestock houses	
			C	R	C	R
1	11	3	5	1	1	—
2	13	5	5	6	1	—
3	27	7	6	7	3	—
4	13	5	6	3	1	—
5	17	5	4	7	2	—
6	13	4	5	5	1	—
7	7	3	4	2	1	—
8	8	3	4	2	1	—
9	12	2	3	2	2	—
Total	121	37	42	35	13	—

mud-brick and measures 4.00 m in diameter. It is a grandmother's habitation with the doorway oriented N, opening under a 2.00 m × 2.00 m raised storage platform/verandah. Feature 2, at 8.00 m NE, is a 8.50-m-in-diameter cattle house built in mud-brick, with its entrance oriented N.

House 4, at the center of the complex, belongs to the household head. It is a rectangular, mud-brick feature, 6.70 m long and 3.50 m wide, facing NW and complemented by a 5.50-m-long and 3.00-m-wide sheltered patio. The kitchen is located a few meters SW; it is a relatively small, 3.60-m-in-diameter house, built in mud-brick with its door oriented NE. A wood stand was found attached to the feature, and the hearth is a plain, two-niches, 1.00-m-long, 0.60-m-wide, and 0.5-m-high installation. Feature 5 is found at 5.00 m N of the household head's habitation; it is the grandmother's dry-season house, built in wood and reeds with the doorway oriented S, measuring 3.90 m in diameter. It is attached to a 9.00-m-in-diameter goat enclosure (GIII) situated on its western side. There is another smaller goat pen, adjunct to a 4.00 m × 4.00-m-nine-poles storage platform, both situated at 9 to 10 m NE of the central house 4 (fig. 37). Houses 6 and 7, located in the southeastern end of the complex at 5.00 m from each other, belong to the married son. The former, built in mud-brick with the doorway oriented N-NW and measuring 5.40 m in diameter is the son's first wife's house. The latter, belonging to the second wife, also built with mud-brick and a doorway oriented W, is slightly smaller, measuring 4.80 m in diameter. The hearth is a three-niches installation decorated on top with a line of shallow, finger-made depressions, three equidistant, upward, appliqué arrows on the upper half, and finally, three equidistant, vertical, and elongated clay bumps on the lower half. The sorghum storage platform, located between both houses, measures 4.00 m in length and 3.50 m in width. Behind the line of houses, there are a number of pits from which the material used for mud-brick was collected. They are distributed into two clusters, with four in the SW and three in the NE (fig. 37).

Habitation Complex 2

Habitation complex 2 is located in the E-SE of the settlement. It comprises twelve features distributed over 50 m NE-SW and 45 m E-W, and incorporates on the outer side a sorghum field 67 m long and 27 m in maximum width, delimited by a fence and a footpath (fig. 37). Five of the recorded features are rectangular, the remaining seven being circular. Two features, the 10.60-m-in-diameter goat corral, located in the northwestern side of the complex, and the "entertainment" wood and straw, square, 4.30-m-long and 3.40-m-wide house, in a relatively central position, are installations of general interest. The latter is flanked on its eastern side by a sorghum storage rack.

House 8 is found at the southwestern end ⸱f the complex. It is a rectangular feature built with mud-brick, measuring 6.60 m long and 3.30 m wide, with the doorway oriented NW. The adjunct verandah, built with six supporting poles, provides an additional sheltered space of 6.00 m × 3.00 m. The rectangular, mud-brick building with its attached wood and straw kitchen are inhabited by a young married couple. Feature 9, the kitchen, is attached to house 8's southwestern wall and measures 3.80 m in length and 3.20 m in width. The hearth is a two-niches, rectangular feature, 1.40 m in length, 0.70 m in width, and 0.80 m in height, decorated in its upper part with appliqué raised clay lines defining a horizontal, E-shaped motif. Finally, a small sized chicken coop was found a few meters in front of houses 8 and 9.

House 10, owned by the elder brother and found at 4 to 5 m N of the previous one, is also inhabited by a married couple. It is a rectangular, mud-brick building, 6.30 m in length and 3.40 m in width, with the entrance oriented NE. The adjunct shelter, also used as a storage platform, measures 5.30 m long and 2.80 m wide. Feature 13, located 1 to 2 m E, is a 3.20-m-in-diameter kitchen built in mud-brick; its doorway is oriented NW. The hearth is a two-niches, plain feature, 1.00 m long, 0.50 m wide, and 0.60 m high. House 11 is built in mud-brick and measures 6.10 m in diameter with its entrance oriented N. It is found a few meters NW of house 10 and is inhabited by boys who share it with a few goats.

House 14, approximately 10 m E of feature 10, is built in mud-brick and measures 6.60 m in diameter, with its doorway oriented NW. It is inhabited by the extended family head and his wife. The hearth is a rectangular, three-niches installation with crenellated top, decorated in its upper half by a plain rectangular register delimited by appliqué cordons. There is a small circular chicken coop next to the feature (fig. 37). House 15, 3 to 4 m N of the previous one, is a small, 4.80-m-in-diameter feature, built in mud-brick, with the doorway oriented W. It is the family headman's horse house, with a few meters N of it, a 4.00-m-in-diameter chicken mud-brick house, with an entrance oriented E-SE.

Features 18 and 22, located at the northern end of the complex, are inhabited by a married couple for which no information was available. The former, built with mud-brick, with its entrance oriented SW, measures 4.10 m in diameter. The latter, also built in mud-brick, is a rectangular house, 5.90 m long and 2.90 m wide, facing W. It has an additional sheltered space built with four supporting poles and measuring 5.30 m in length and 2.80 m in width.

House 19 is withdrawn from the main concentration of the extended family features, located 20 m aside in the E (fig. 37). It is the second house of the elder son for his other wife. He has two wives, and seven children, four girls and three boys. The house, built with mud-brick, measures 6.20 m long and 3.20 m wide, and faces W. The additional sheltered area measures 5.50 m in length and 2.90 m in width. It is built with eight supporting poles and is used as a storage platform for fodder. Finally, a wood stand was recorded along the house's southern side.

With the exception of houses 8, 9, and 19, habitation complex 2 features are laid out around the discussion house (feature 17) and the extended family goat enclosure in an arch-like arrangement, 20 to 23 m in maximum diameter.

Habitation Complex 3

Habitation complex 3 is located due E of the settlement, where it is spread on 60 m N-S and 55 m E-W. It is the village headman's (Bilama) complex comprising seventeen houses, three goat enclosures, and five storage platforms (fig. 37). Five pits, from which construction material has been collected, are found dispersed behind the houses. There are two relatively large sorghum fields adjunct to the complex. The largest, with NW-SE earth embankment and delimited by a footpath, measures 156 m in length and 110 m in width. The smallest, located farther E, is 105 m long and 20 m wide. Details on houses ownership was not available; it was nonetheless clearly asserted that the village headman has two wives.

House 20 is located in the southeastern end of the complex. It is a rectangular feature facing N and built with mud-brick. It measures 7.30 m in length and 3.30 m in width, with an adjunct shelter 6.40 m long and 2.80 m wide and is built with six supporting poles. Four straw storage racks stretched on 50 m N-S are found at 20 m E of the Bilama's house. They are nine-poles installations measuring 5 to 4 m in length and 4 to 3 m in width (fig. 37). Four features are located in the space before the house; they include a nine-pole straw storage rack (feature 95), a chicken coop, a 5.00-m-in-diameter goat enclosure, and finally, kitchen 23, circular in shape, built in mud-brick with the doorway oriented N, and measuring 4.50 m in diameter. The hearth, found in house 23, is a two-niches, plain installation with a rectangular rear panel.

House 21, located 10 m W, is also built in mud-brick. It faces N and measures 4.40 m long and 3.50 m wide; its attached verandah is built with seven supporting poles and is 4.60 in length and 3.00 m in width. House 25, located at the center of the complex and measuring 13 m in length and 3.40 m in width, consists of two attached rectangular houses, mapped as features 25 and 25a, built in mud-brick and facing W. The verandah is clearly divided into two parts; the northern one, built with four supporting poles, measures 6 m in length and 2.90 m in width, and the southern part is 7.00 m long, with a similar width built with a similar number of supporting poles. A toilet booth and a chicken coop were found attached to house 25. Feature 24, next to house 25's southern wall, is a circular kitchen measuring 4.00 m in diameter, with the entrance oriented SW. A decorated hearth and a raised grinding platform were recorded in the kitchen. The decoration of the hearth consists of an upper register with five parallel and equidistant appliqué upward arrows; while equidistant, vertical, and elongated clay bumps are found in the lower part. Feature 26, a few meters NW of house 25, is the latter's kitchen. It is circular in shape, with its doorway oriented SE, and measures 3.60 m in diameter. The recorded hearth is decorated in its upper half with three distinct grids of appliqué lines overlined by a horizontal cordon.

House 30 is located in the inner part of the settlement, 25 m W of houses 25/25a. It is a rectangular building, 7.20 m long and 3.00 wide, facing E. The additional sheltered space, built with six supporting poles, measures 6.70 m in length and 3.00 m in width. A nine-poles-straw storage rack, 2.50 m wide and 3.50 m long, is located in the courtyard, next to the verandah. Feature 31, at approximately 10 m SE, is house 30's kitchen. It is a 4.90-m-in-diameter mud-brick house with the doorway oriented SW. A raised grinding platform and a decorated hearth were found in the kitchen. The latter installation is decorated in its upper part with five parallel and equidistant appliqué upward arrows underlined by a horizontal, similarly appliqué, cordon. House 32, at some 2 m from house 31's door, measures 3.60 m in diameter. It is used as house 30's donkey house.

Feature 33, located farther within the settlement's inner space, at 10 m from the nearest house, is the extended family's discussion house. It is built with wood and straw and measures 3.90 m in length and 2.90 m in width. Houses 34 and 35, located 6 to 7 m from each other, are found in the NE of the habitation complex. Feature 34 is the grandmother's house. It measures 5.70 m in diameter and is built in mud-brick with a doorway oriented W. The recorded hearth is a plain, two-niches installation. A chicken coop and a 3.50 m × 2.50 m, nine-poles sorghum storage platform (feature 101) were found a few meters S of the grandmother's house. House 35, farther N, is a rectangular, mud-brick building, 6.00 m long and 2.90 m wide, facing W. Two pits, presumably from which the construction material was collected, were found behind the house (fig. 37).

Seven features are clustered in the N-NW of the complex. They include two relatively large goat enclosures, two barns, and three habitations. The smallest of the goat enclosures is circular in shape, and measures 8.00 m in diameter; the largest is slightly elongated with 13.50 m in its maximum NW-SE axis and 10 m in the minimum SW-NE one. Barns 29 and 37, both built with mud-brick are oriented in almost opposite directions. The former, measuring 7.00 m in diameter, is attached to the rest of livestock features by a fence and is oriented SW. The latter, oriented E, measures 8.40 m in diameter and is attached to the largest goat enclosure. Houses 27 and 28, facing each other, are part of a functional complex, with the first used as a kitchen and the last as a living and sleeping facility. The kitchen is a circular mud-brick house, 4.10 m in diameter, with the doorway oriented W leading immediately to the main house's verandah, which is built with six supporting poles and measures 6.00 m in length and 2.90 m in width. The recorded hearth is plain with a crenellated upper side. The main house, facing E, measures 7.00 m in length and 3.00 m width. And finally, house 36 is a relatively small habitation feature, 4.30 m in diameter, built with wood and reeds with an adjunct 4.00 m × 2.80 m verandah. It is the grandmother dry-season house, the rainy-season one being located 10 m farther E.

Habitation Complex 4

Habitation complex 4 is located in the northeastern part of the settlement (fig. 37). It consists of fourteen features spread over an area measuring approximately 50 m in diameter. Two of the features are rectilinear mud-brick buildings, eight are round, mud-brick houses, three are storage platforms or racks, and finally, one is a circular goat enclosure. The complex is equally associated with field 5, located behind the line of habitation facilities in the NE. The recorded field, limited along its outer side by a fence, measures 110 m in length and 62 m on average width.

Five of the round houses, all used for habitation, are arranged in a NW-SE line along the northeastern edge of the complex. House 38 is located at the southern end of the line. It measures 5.60 m in diameter with its doorway oriented W. The recorded hearth is a two-niches feature with an appliqué horizontal cordon at mid-height of the rear panel. House 40, at 2 m N, is much smaller, with an entrance also oriented W. It measures 3.70 m in diameter has a bed but no hearth. It is complemented on its western side by a 2 m × 2 m sheltered area built with four supporting poles, and a chicken coop in mud-brick in the E. House 42 is found at 5 m NW of the previous one. Its verandah also used for storage and measuring 3.70 m in length and 2.80 m in width, is located on the left-hand side. The habitation measures 4.40 m in diameter, with the doorway oriented SW, and comprises a bed and a hearth. The latter is a two-niches feature with its rear panel decorated in the upper half by two horizontal and parallel appliqué cordons. House 43, at some 7 to 8 m farther NW, is surrounded by a four-poles, square (1.50 m × 1.50 m) storage platform and a pile of firewood in the SE, an attached chicken pen made of straw in the NE, and a 2.60 m × 2.60 m verandah with four supporting poles in the NW. The house, belonging to an elder woman, has a doorway oriented W and measures 4.70 m in diameter. The recorded hearth is a simple fireplace with three hearthstones. Finally, house 45, at the northwestern end of the line, has its doorway oriented S. It is the largest feature of the whole line, measuring 7.20 m in diameter. A pile of firewood was found next to the house door, on the right-hand side. The verandah, 4.30 m in length and 3.70 m in width, is built with four supporting poles on the house's western flank. The hearth, divided into three niches, measures 1.40 m in length, the rear panel being decorated in its upper half with three equidistant, short, vertical, and parallel appliqué cordons underlined by a horizontal, equally appliqué, cordon.

Livestock features and the discussion house are found in what may be called the central part of the habitation complex (fig. 37). Feature 39, the extended family's discussion house, located in the S with its doorway facing houses 38 and 40, is rectangular in shape, built in wood and straw, and measures 4.00 m long and 3.50 m wide.The goat enclosure measures 11.00 m in diameter; it is surrounded in the NE by a 6.60-m-in-diameter mud-brick goat house, and in the E by a cattle barn 8.10 m in diameter.

Two habitation houses are found on the westernmost side of the complex; feature 44 and 93 in the S and 47 in the N. The former is a relatively long, rectangular, mud-brick building facing SW, 10.30 m in length and 3.50 m in width, with an adjunct 7.30-m-long and 3.10-m-wide verandah built with eight supporting poles, divided in two parts, mapped as features 44 and 93. House 44 is the living and sleeping component, 6.80 m long and 3.50 m wide. House 93 is the kitchen, square in shape with each side measuring 3.50 m. The recorded hearth is decorated on the upper part of its rear panel with a horizontal register delimited by two parallel appliqué cordons filled with six equidistant, upward, appliqué arrows; the lower half has three equidistant, vertical, and elongated clay bumps. The latter, house 47, found at 15 to 17 m N of the previous one, measures 7.20 m in diameter. Its doorway is oriented S, and it contains a bed and a hearth. The recorded hearth is decorated in the upper part of its panel by five equidistant appliqué upward arrows underlined by a horizontal, appliqué cordon.

Finally, two straw storage racks were found in the field behind the dwelling installations; they are nine-poles features, set at 50 m from each other, and measuring 5.00 m in length and 4.00 m width.

Habitation Complex 5

Habitation complex 5 is found due N of the settlement. Built structures are spread over an area measuring 40 m in diameter (fig. 37). The complex is attached to a partially fenced field (field 8), 61 m long and 55 m wide, delimited in the W and E by footpaths. Two features were recorded in the harvested field: one is an oval enclosure, 12 m in length and 9 m in width, attached to the field's fence and located in the NE; the other (feature 104), at some 30 m SW of the previous one, is a 3 m × 3 m rectilinear, nine-poles storage rack. Habitation houses are distributed around central livestock features, which include a small goat enclosure, measuring 5.00 m in diameter; a relatively large, 10.90-m-in-diameter cattle barn built in mud-brick with its entrance oriented S; and finally, a small, 4.90-m-in-diameter mud-brick goat house with a doorway oriented W.

Four habitation houses, all built with mud-brick, are found in the eastern half of the complex. Three are rectangular and one circular. House 48, the northernmost, is 6.10 m long and 3.30 m wide and faces SE. The adjunct verandah is built with eight supporting poles and measures 6.10 m in length and 2.80 m in width. Houses 57 and its kitchen, house 56, located at the center, define a more elaborate layout with what may be termed a sheltered courtyard. House 57 is oriented along the NW-SE axis measures 6.10 m long and 2.90 m wide, with its door situated at the middle of the southwestern wall. House 56, the kitchen, is set perpendicular to and attached to the southwestern corner of feature 57. Oriented along the SW-NE axis and facing NW, feature 56 measures 4.00 m in length and 2.60 m in width, with the entrance located at the middle of the northwestern wall. The hearth is situated along the northeastern wall, on the left-hand side of the room. It is a rectangular, two-niches installation, 1.20 m long and 0.75 m high. The panel is decorated in its upper part by five equidistant, grooved, upward arrows in combination with small circles, delimited at the bottom by a horizontal grooved line and at top by an appliqué cordon. The additional sheltered space, built with five supporting poles, measures 6.10 m in length and 2.60 m in width. Feature 58 is located a few meters E of kitchen 56. It is a round, mud-brick house, measuring 5.80 m in diameter, with a doorway oriented S. It was an abandoned feature at the time of fieldwork; some of the furniture was still present. This was the case for the hearth, located in the standard right-hand side and decorated in its upper half by two horizontal and parallel appliqué cordons with pinched finger impressions; the bed, represented by two parallel lines of postholes found in the northern half opposite the entrance; and finally, a raised grinding platform, found next to the door on the right-hand side. Features 91 and 92 are found in the SE; the former is the living and sleeping room facing SW and measuring 9.20 m in length and 3.40 m in width; it is complemented by a walled sheltered area, 9.60 m long and 3.30 m wide. The shelter's roof is equally used as sorghum storage platform. House 92, the kitchen, which is much smaller and is attached to house 91's northwestern wall measures 3.40 m in length and 3.30 m in width.

There are three features along the central N-S axis of the complex. Because the large cattle barn in the central position has already been described (fig. 37), there are two left. One is house 49, located in the N at 5 m behind the barn; it is a round, mud-brick feature measuring 4.90 m in diameter with a small undecorated hearth, its doorway oriented S. The other, feature 54, is a small 4.60-m-in-diameter, round, mud-brick kitchen, with the entrance oriented E. The recorded hearth is plain and located to the W of the feature, opposite the door. A clay bench was also found along the southern side of the house.

Four features arranged along a N-S axis are found in the western part of the habitation complex. A nine-poles, straw storage rack (feature 105), 3.80 m in length and 3.50 m in width, is located in the northernmost position. Features 51 and 52, complementary parts of the same unit, are situated at the center. House 51 is a round, mud-brick kitchen with a doorway oriented SW, measuring 5.00 m in diameter. It contains a small undecorated hearth. House 51 has its door set at the middle of the southwestern wall. It is a rectangular, mud-brick building oriented NW-SE, measuring 6.10 m in length and 3.00 m in width. Finally, house 53, located at the southwestern end of the complex, measures 6.50 m in length and 3.10 m in width. The house doorway is oriented N and its adjunct verandah is probably among the largest of the village; it is 6.50 m long and 5.70 m wide, built with ten supporting poles.

Habitation Complex 6

Habitation complex 6 is found in the north-northwestern part of the settlement (fig. 37). It is comprised of a fenced field (field 9), measuring 90 m in maximum length and 50 m in width, and thirteen features delimited in the W and S by a series of posts. With the exception of the nine-poles, straw storage rack 106, located approximately 10 m behind the main concentration of built installations and measuring 3.50 m × 3.00 m, the habitation complex facilities are arranged in two roughly parallel W-E lines with a relatively large tree at the center of the western part.

The southern lines comprise five features. House 65 is located at the western end with its doorway oriented E. It is a grandmother's habitation unit without hearth, built with mud-brick and measuring 4.60 m in diameter. Feature 66, at approximately 2 m SE of the previous one, is a mud-brick goat house; it measures 5.80 m in diameter and is built with the entrance oriented E. The wood and reeds rectilinear house 67, 3.70 m long and 3.50 m wide, located at the center of the features, is the grandmother's dry-season habitation. The extended family's goat enclosure is found a few meters E of the grandmother's house. It is a circular feature measuring 8.00 m in diameter. Finally, house 68, built with wood and straw, is located at the eastern end of the line. It is a young man's habitation, measuring 7.50 m in diameter, with the doorway oriented W. It comprises an adjunct rectangular verandah, 4.70 m long and 2.90 m wide, built with eight supporting poles.

The northern line of features also consists of five individual elements, set very close to each other, with distances from one to the next varying from 1 to 2 m. House 60, at the eastern end, approximately 10 m NE of feature 68, is another grandmother's habitation built in wood and straw. It is a 5.90-m-in-diameter house without hearth, with its doorway oriented SW. House 61, 1.5 m W, is a two-room, rectangular, mud-brick building with a single door oriented S. It measures 9.10 m in length and 3.20 m width and has an adjunct toilet room behind it but no additional sheltered area, as is generally the case for such buildings in the village. House 62 is the household head's habitation unit. It is a mud-brick, rectangular building, 5.80 m in length and 3.10 m in width with the doorway oriented S. It has an attached verandah, also 5.80 m long but only 2.70 m wide, which is also used as a sorghum storage platform. House 63, a few meters farther W, is the complex main kitchen; it is a mud-brick, round feature, 5.20 m in diameter, with an undecorated hearth and the entrance oriented S. A pile of firewood located a few meters N of a relatively large tree was recorded next to the kitchen (fig. 37). Features mapped as 64 and 94 are located at the western end of the line; they are attached to each other but are used for different activities. House 64 is built in wood and straw and measures 6.80 m in diameter with the entrance oriented SE. It is the mother's house, and as an already senior woman, she was entitled to a simple, three-hearthstone fireplace. Finally, feature 94 is a rectangular wood and straw discussion house, 3.50 m in length and 2.90 m in width, with a door on its southern wall.

As far as the general layout of habitation complex 6 is concerned, there is a clear process of nucleation at work, as suggested by the series of posts geared to delineate the extended family's spatial unit. Such kinds of evidence are absent from the eastern half of the settlement already described. Also noteworthy is the position of livestock features, the goat house (66) and corral, virtually at the center of the habitation complex, before most of the habitation houses (fig. 37).

Habitation Complex 7

Habitation complex 7 is located in the northwestern part of the settlement. It is stretched on 35 m N-S, measures 30 m in maximum width, and consists of seven houses arranged into two roughly parallel lines. Features 69, 70, and 71 are found in the front line, while 72 to 75 belong to the rear line (fig. 37). An extensive fenced field, measuring 289 m in length and 180 m in width, is owned in common by inhabitants of complexes 7, 8, and 9, without any clearly visible limits for individual family plots.

Feature 69, at the northern end of the front line is a round, mud-brick house, measuring 5.90 m in diameter, built with the doorway oriented SE. It is a grandmother's habitation unit and, as such, is devoid of any hearth. A pile of firewood was found behind the house, on its northeastern side. House 70 is located 5 m S, roughly at the center of the front line. It is a 6.80-m-in-diameter, mud-brick round house with an undecorated hearth and an entrance oriented E. House 71, at 2 m SE, has its doorway oriented S. It is a relatively large, round, mud-brick barn/cattle feature, measuring 9.80 m in diameter.

House 72 is a round kitchen, 4.50 m in diameter, built with mud-brick, and located at the northern end of the rear line. Its doorway is oriented E, and it comprises a decorated hearth, 1.10 m long and 0.88 m high. The hearth's rear panel is decorated with three parallel and equidistant, appliqué, upward arrows with pinched finger impressions, set in a register delimited at the bottom and top by two parallel and horizontal, appliqué cordons. A four-poles sorghum stand measuring 2 m × 2 m was found next to the kitchen, on its northern side. House 73 is situated at 4 to 5 m S, in the central part of the habitation complex. It is a rectangular building, 6.90 m long and 3.30 m wide, oriented N-S with the door set in the eastern wall. It has an adjunct mud-brick patio which doubles the size of the habitation with an additional area of 6.90 m × 3.00 m. Feature 74 measures 5.50 m in diameter. It is attached to feature 75's northwestern corner with its entrance oriented E. The recorded hearth has two decorated registers. The upper one comprises a horizontal register delimited at the bottom and top by two parallel grooved lines, filled with eight short, equidistant, and parallel appliqué cordons. The lower one, underlain by a horizontal grooved line, is constituted of a set of three equidistant vertical motifs made with grooved lines and consisting of a vertical line attached to a circle with a central dot. Finally, house 75, found at the southern end of the rear line, is a rectangular, mud-brick feature, 6.10 m long and 3.20 m wide, facing W and oriented N-S. It has an adjunct verandah built with six supporting poles, measuring 6.10 m in length and 3.20 m in width, with a small pile of firewood on its northern side. A pit, which provided building material, was found behind the barn (feature 71) and before house 70.

Habitation Complex 8

Habitation complex 8 consists of thirteen features: five round, mud-brick houses, two rectangular buildings, three storage platforms, one shelter, and one goat corral. The complex is located due W of the settlement, stretched along 50 m N-S, with a maximum width of 30 m (fig. 37). The eastern limit of the complex is delineated by a distinct fence portion, including the goat corral, which is the easternmost feature, measuring 10 m in diameter.

Houses 76 and 77, as well as storage platform 108, are parts of the same "functional" aggregate, as is the case for houses 78 and 79 and storage platform 109. The first aggregate is located at the northern end of the complex with the features arranged in a triangular pattern at distances varying from 2 to 8 m. The kitchen (feature 76) is located at the apex of the triangle. It has a pile of firewood on its southern side, and its doorway is oriented E. The recorded hearth is decorated with three equidistant and parallel appliqué upward arrows delimited at the bottom and top by two horizontal and parallel appliqué cordons. The upper side of the hearth's rear panel is built with three equidistant, protruding tips. A small size chicken coop was recorded a few meters before the kitchen door. Storage platform 108, located 7 to 8 m SW of the kitchen, is a nine poles feature measuring 5 m in length and 4 m in width. House 77, the third element of the aggregate, is a rectangular building 6.60 m long and 3.10 m wide facing E and oriented N-S. It is complemented by a verandah 6.60 m in length and 2.90 m in width built with six supporting poles, which is also used for storage of sorghum stalks.

The second aggregate, also organized in a triangular arrangement, is much more compact, with distances between features varying from 1 to 2 m. House 78, the kitchen, is located at the apex. It is a relatively small, 3.70-m-in-diameter, round, mud-brick feature, with the doorway oriented E. The hearth's rear panel is rectangular with rounded corners, and measures 1.10 m in length and 0.70 m in height. The recorded decoration consists of five parallel and equidistant appliqué upward arrows. Feature 109, the storage platform, is built with nine supporting poles and measures 4 m long and 3.50 m wide. House 79 is the third element of the aggregate. It is a rectangular, mud-brick building, 6.50 m long and 3.20 m wide, oriented N-S and facing E. The adjunct verandah, 6 m in length and 3.30 m in width, is built with six supporting poles.

The remaining four features are spread over the southern half of the complex. House 80 is found slightly NE. It is a round construction, 5.60 m in diameter, with a doorway oriented W and no fireplace. A small 2 m × 1.5 m storage platform built with four poles is found a few meters S. Feature 81, a relatively large barn/cattle house, 10.50 m in diameter, is found 4 m S of house 79. It is built in mud-brick with the entrance oriented NE. A sheltered reception area (feature 82), 3.90 m long and 3.20 m wide, is located next to the barn, at less than 2 m SE. The construction is made with seventeen poles, with two of them used for roof support. Finally, house 83, the southernmost feature from the habitation complex, is a grandmother's wood and reeds dry-season habitation. It measures 4.90 m in diameter with its entrance oriented NE.

As is the case for almost all of the habitation complexes already described, this one also has its livestock features located more or less in the central part of the extended family space. The barn/cattle house 81 and the goat corral are precisely located on the median W axis of the complex. In this case, however, the distribution of habitation is more skewed, as all of them are found in the northern half, while the grandmother's dry-season house and the reception shelter are located in the S.

Habitation Complex 9

Habitation complex 9 is located in the southwestern part of the settlement. The features are spread over an area measuring 45 m × 40 m, fenced on its northeastern and southern sides. The recorded built installations are distributed into seven houses, three storage platforms, two chicken coops, and a 7-m-in-diameter goat enclosure found at the northern end of the complex (fig. 37).

With the exception of straw storage racks 110 and 111, each built with nine poles and both measuring 4 m in length and 3.50 m in width, located some 10 m behind the nearest habitation complex installation, built features are arranged in three roughly parallel NW-SE lines. The rear line comprises two features, house 85 and storage platform 113. The former is a round, mud-brick construction, 8.40 m in diameter, the doorway oriented E, with, on its northeastern flank, an attached 4.90 m × 4.30 m verandah built with five supporting poles. The hearth is decorated with two horizontal and parallel appliqué cordons delimiting a register filled with four vertical and parallel short appliqué lines. Storage platform 113 is found at 3 to 4 m SE; it is a 5-m-long and 3-m-wide installation built with four rows of three supporting poles.

The middle line is confined to the southern half of the complex and comprises three houses. House 88, at the southern end, measures 5.10 m in diameter. It is a round, mud-brick construction with a decorated hearth and a doorway oriented N. The recorded hearth decoration consists of a line of five equidistant appliqué squares in the upper half of the rear panel. A large pit and a chicken coop are found behind the kitchen, at 12 and 5 m W respectively. House 87, at the middle of the line, is a rectangular, mud-brick building oriented roughly N-S with an attached toilet behind and a verandah before. It measures 5.90 m in length and 3.30 m in width, and the adjunct verandah built with six supporting poles, is 5.20 m long and 2.90 m wide; both face E. House 86, located 1 m N of the previous one, shares almost all of its architectural characteristics and orientation. There are minor variations in size, with the latter measuring 6.50 m in length and 3.10 m in width. A chicken coop was recorded next to house 86, on its western side.

The front line comprises four features, the northernmost (the goat corral) has already been described. Feature 84 is a 9.60-m-in-diameter barn/cattle house, claimed by an informant (in 1991) to have been built fourteen years ago. It is built in wood and straw with the entrance oriented NE. House 90 is found at some 9 m S. It is a round, mud-brick goat feature, 5.40 m in diameter, with the doorway oriented W. Finally, house 89, located at the southern end of the line, is a young man's wood and straw, round house, measuring 5.10 m in diameter with the entrance oriented NW.

In the case of habitation complex 9, livestock features are clearly surrounded by habitation houses. The series of earth embankments, located approximately 50 m behind habitation complexes 8 and 9, in fact materialize the banks of the *Abani,* the intermittent stream bed, with one of the cultivated plots, as shown by field 6, in the northeastern part of the village catchment.

Located in the bend of the Abani, Abuzrega is surrounded by prime agricultural land. At first glance, and judging from the size of communal cattle corrals, the village cattle herd does not seem to be particularly important. But the presence of large barns/cattle houses in most of the habitation complexes suggests that this may in fact not be the case; some families may have pooled their cattle while others may have decided to keep theirs within the habitation complex. The issue—how many cattle heads do you own?—is such a sensitive one that it is generally better not to ask for precise answers. As far as the settlement layout is considered, there is a striking division of the village into two parts. The limit is set on the fields' fences defining two narrow alleyways on both sides of the settlement in a NW-SE axis (fig. 37). Four habitation complexes, 1, 7, 8, and 9, are found in the southwestern part. They are, on average, smaller, with seven to eight houses, among which one or two are rectangular. There are five habitation complexes—2, 3, 4, 5, and 6 in the northeastern part of the village. They are larger, in general, with the number of houses varying from ten to seventeen (in the village headman's complex), among which three to seven are rectangular, mud-brick buildings. Each habitation complex belongs to an extended family, with three generations frequently represented. Finally, the recorded patterns of hearth decoration do not seem to provide any significant information on the relationships between the villagers. But it is worth noting that the standard hearth position—in the right-hand side—as recorded in the semipermanent villages and dry-season camps is more at variance at Abuzrega, and probably in other permanent villages.

Chapter 9

Djidat I

Introduction

Djidat I is part of a twin settlement; the other one, Djidat II, is founded at some 200 m N. The settlement is located 12° 01′ latitude N and 14° 57′ longitude E, 4.5 kilometers NW of Marafaine. The village was inhabited by thirty-seven individuals in 1969 (Elingui 1978: 32). The number of inhabitants was increased to sixty-three, divided into thirty-three females and thirty males, in the 1977 census (Recensement General 1985: 320). Djidat I is circular in shape and measures 150 m in diameter. It is surrounded by a ring of fenced fields which increases the site diameter to 300 m (fig. 38). The settlement and its ring of fields are thus extended over 7.07 hectares, with the village stricto sensu measuring 1.77 hectares. Eighty-two houses, forty-five rectangular and thirty-seven circular, have been recorded. They are divided into eleven habitation complexes of varying size distributed around the central cattle corral and the mosque (table 33). The village is accessed through two roads, a larger, 12-m-wide road situated in the N, and a narrower road, 5-m-wide in the SE, and a footpath 1 to 2 m wide, in the W.

Three sets of features are for communal use. One is the central cattle corral, 27 m in diameter, with three entrances/exit opening in the NW, the S, and the E. Because the village herds were in the dry-season camping area at the time of fieldwork, the enclosure was used as a protected space to dry the freshly harvested sorghum. Another is the mosque complex, with three features located along the northern flank of the central cattle corral, including the mosque, the guesthouse and the guest's horse house. The mosque (feature 14) is a rectangular, mud-brick building with corrugated tin roof, oriented N-S and facing W. It is 6.90 m long and 4.10 m wide without the mihrab, which is found at the middle of the eastern wall and measures 1.10 m × 1.10 m. Feature 15, the guesthouse, located 8 m behind the mosque, is a round 4.40-m-in-diameter, mud-brick construction with the doorway oriented N. The guest's horse house (feature 16), at 3 m NE is also a round, mud-brick construction of a similar size with the entrance oriented W (fig. 38). Finally,

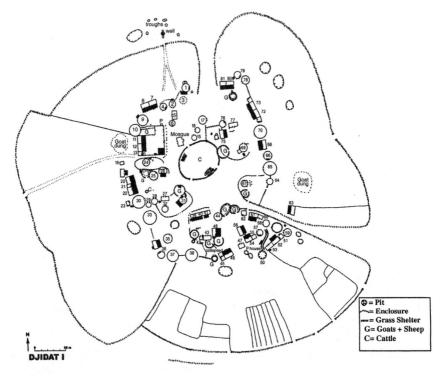

Figure 38: Map of Djidat I

Table 33: Djidat I houses and features distribution

Cluster number	Number of features	Number of units	Habitation houses		Livestock houses	
			C	R	C	R
1	2	1	2	—	—	—
2	7	3	2	3	2	—
3	6	2	—	3	—	1
4	16	7	4	8	4	—
5	6	1	1	1	3	—
6	7	2	—	5	—	—
7	8	2	—	4	1	—
8	16	4	—	9	4	—
9	5	2	2	1	1	—
10	14	5	3	8	2	—
11	5	2	2	2	—	—
Total	92	31	16	44	17	1

the third set of communal features is the well and its associated watering troughs, found to the N of the settlement, beyond the fenced fields. The well, with a 4-m-in-diameter curb, is 12 m deep and comprises two adjunct symmetric rectangular troughs. Six additional watering troughs are found at 5 to 10 m around.

Habitation Complex 1

Habitation complex 1 is found due N of the settlement, located on the W road's side. It is a partially fenced, single house complex, attached to the neighboring construction by a fence portion. Feature 1 is a round, mud-brick house measuring 6.40 m in diameter with the entrance oriented SW (fig. 38). There is a toilet booth built with straw in the rear side and a verandah in the front part. The latter, built with six supporting poles, measures 3.70 m in length and 3 m in width. The house's hearth is located along the wall in the E, in the standard right-hand side position. It is a rectangular installation with two niches and a decorated rear panel. The recorded decoration is confined to the upper part of the panel and consists of four equidistant and parallel appliqué upward arrows underlined by an equally appliqué, but horizontal cordon. A pile of firewood and a chicken coop are found in the courtyard on both the W and E sides of the house. Finally, there is a shallow, 5.40-m-in-diameter circle 3 m in the inner part of the site, the remaining foundation of an older, worn-out house. Habitation complex 1 shares with its western neighbor a large field (field 1), 130 m long W-E and 42 m wide N-S, limited in the SW by an earth embankment. Habitation complex 1's field is probably limited by the fence in the N and E, and the footpath in the W, and, as such, measures 30 m in length and 27 m in width.

Habitation Complex 2

Habitation complex 2 is located SW of the previous one, in the northwestern part of the settlement. It is comprised of seven houses—four circular and three rectangular—and a relatively large tree in the courtyard. The features are disposed in a crescent-shaped pattern measuring 35 m in diameter and open in the S. Two of the round, mud-brick features, houses 6 and 9, are used to shelter livestock. The former, located at the southern end of the complex, is a 4.60-m-in-diameter goat house with a doorway oriented W and an old abandoned hearth, and the latter, a 8.40-m-in-diameter barn with the door opening E, is found at the southwestern end.

Houses 2 and 4, both circular and built in mud-brick, are located next to each other in the northeastern part of the complex and are linked with a fence. House 2 measures 5.60 m in diameter with the doorway oriented S. It has an undecorated hearth made of three hearthstones, and a toilet booth built in straw attached on the rear side. The entrance of house 4 is oriented SW; the feature measures 5.40 m in diameter and comprises a small hearth located in the SE, in the standard right-hand side position. The recorded hearth measures 0.90 m in length, 0.70 m in width, and 0.50 m in height, and the decoration, confined to the upper part of the rear panel, consists of an elongated, rectangular frame made of appliqué cordons filled with four equidistant, short, vertical appliqué lines.

Features 5, 7, and 8 are rectangular, mud-brick buildings. House 5, found in the eastern part of the complex, is oriented N-S, faces W, and measures 6.70 m in length and 4.10 m in width. It was an unfinished, roofless construction used, in the meantime, for goats. Houses 7 and 8 can be considered as distinct parts of the same building measuring 13 m in length and 5.90 m in width, including in both cases, living and sleeping rooms, cooking areas, and enclosed courtyards delimited by mud-brick walls. House 7, at the eastern end, measures 6.90 m long and 3.10 m wide. The sheltered courtyard is also 6.90 m long but only 2.80 m wide. The hearth is found in the courtyard, along the southern wall on the left-hand side; it is a plain 1.25-m-long feature with four equidistant, pointed tips on the upper side, and a horizontal, appliqué cordon at mid-height of the rear panel. House 8, the western component of the building, is slightly smaller, measuring 6.10 m in length and 3.10 m in width for the room, and 6.10 m long and 2.80 m wide for the sheltered courtyard. The hearth, 1.25 m long and 0.55 m high, is found in a similar left-hand side position in the courtyard, also along the southern wall. The hearth's rear panel is decorated in its upper part by five equidistant, appliqué, upward arrows under-lined by an equally appliqué, horizontal cordon. A chicken coop, built against the next complex's wall is found a few meters W of goat house 6. The habitation complex portion of field 2 is delimited in the E by the footpath and in the W by an earth embankment; it thus measures 105 m in maximum length and 42 m in width.

Habitation Complex 3

Habitation complex 3, located in the western part of the settlement, departs radi-cally from the standard Shuwa-Arab architecture (fig. 38). It is a large, rectangular complex measuring 22 m in length W-E and 21.50 m in width N-S, with the main entrance set in the eastern wall. There is a line of small wooden posts running par-allel to the eastern wall. The main components of the habitation complex distrib-uted around a large courtyard are located along the western wall; they include features 10 and 10a, used for goats, houses 11 and 12, used as living and sleeping rooms, house 13, as the kitchen, a toilet room, a shelter, and finally a pile of fire-wood. The complex estate is complemented by the northern part of field 2, delim-ited by an earth embankment in the N and a footpath in the S, measuring 100 m in length and 65 m in maximum width. A large heap of accumulated goat droppings, subcircular in shape and measuring 12 to 15 m in diameter, has been recorded in the field, a few meters behind the complex.

Features 10 and 10a are located along the northern wall and the northwestern corner of the complex. The former, used to shelter goats, is a round, mud-brick house measuring 8.80 m in diameter with the doorway oriented E. It opens in an unroofed milking area, 15 m long and 6.50 m wide, with a door oriented S and located at the eastern end of the southern wall. The area is equipped with a line of ten equidistant, short wooden milking poles set along the northern wall.

The living and sleeping rooms as well as the kitchen are oriented N-S facing E. They are rectangular, mud-brick buildings attached to each other. House 11 measures 6.40 m in length and 3.30 m in width. The adjunct verandah, 6.40 m long and 3.50 m wide, is built with three supporting poles. House 12 has an almost similar size, 6.10 m in length and 3.30 m in width, with an adjunct sheltered area, 6.10 m long and 3.20 m wide, built with three supporting poles. The kitchen shares the complex's southwestern corner with the toilet room. The former measures 3.30 m long and 3.10 m wide, with a decorated hearth found along the eastern wall, in the non standard left-hand side position. The recorded hearth is a two-niches, rectangular feature, 1.25 m long, 0.50 m wide, and 0.80 m high, with a pseudo-crenellated upper side consisting of five equidistant, pointed tips. The decoration is confined to the upper half of the rear panel; it is a rectangular frame filled with five short more or less equidistant, appliqué, upward arrows. The toilet room is smaller, 2.50 m × 2 m, attached to the kitchen eastern wall. Finally, a relatively large square shelter, 5 m × 5 m, built with seven supporting poles, is found at the complex's southeastern corner.

Habitation Complex 4

Habitation complex 4 is located in the W-SW of the settlement. It is comprised of nineteen features: sixteen houses and three enclosures spread over an area measuring 55 m in length N-S and 45 m in width E-W (fig. 38). The recorded features are organized into three more or less consistent clusters, a northern cluster with features 24–26 and two enclosures, a southern fenced one with features 26–27, 31–32, and one goat corral, with, in addition, the nearby house 33, and finally, a western linear one with houses 18–23, 29, and 30.

The northern cluster measures 30 m in length and 20 m in width. House 24 is located at the center of an elliptically shaped enclosure 24 m long and 10 m wide. It is a grandmother's round, mud-brick habitation unit, 5.70 m in diameter with the doorway oriented E. A small storage rack and a pile of firewood were recorded next to the house, on its northeastern side. A goat corral (CII) is attached to the southern flank of the grandmother's enclosure and the neighboring house 25. It is roughly circular in shape, measuring 7 m in diameter, with the entrance/exit opening S. It is a "specialized" goat-milking area with more than twenty poles distributed all over the corral. House 25 is a 7-m-in-diameter, round, mud-brick kitchen with the doorway oriented SE. The hearth is located in the NE, in the standard right-hand side position. It was rebuilt recently with the upper part of the previous feature still visible, thus providing an interesting "stratigraphy." The previous hearth was decorated with three equidistant, appliqué, upward arrows. The recent one is a two-niches, rectangular feature, 1.50 m long, 0.50 m wide, and 0.80 m high, with the decoration confined to the upper part of the rear panel and consisting of a rectangular frame made with appliqué cordons, filled with ten short and equidistant appliqué, upward arrows. House 26, the remaining feature of the northern cluster, is found at less than 1 m E of the kitchen. It is a rectangular, mud-brick living and sleeping room, 6.80 m long and 3.30 m wide, oriented W-E and facing S. It has an adjunct 4.80 m in length and 2.80 m in width verandah supported by eight poles. Finally, the rectangular house is surrounded on its northeastern side by a short fence (fig. 38).

The southern cluster is rectangular with rounded edges. It measures 30 m in length SW-NE and 20 m in maximum width NW-SE. The cluster's inhabitants were in the dry-season camping area at the time of fieldwork. Goat corral III is found at the northeastern end of the cluster. It measures 9 m in diameter with the entrance/exit oriented S. At the time of fieldwork, the enclosure was used as a sorghum drying area. House 31 is less than 1 m S of the enclosure. It is a round, mud-brick habitation unit, 6.30 m in diameter, with the doorway oriented SW opening on a 5.70-m-long and 3.90-m-wide verandah built with eight supporting poles. A two-niches, rectangular hearth, 1.25 m long, 0.50 m wide, and 0.80 m high, was recorded in the northern part of the house. It is decorated on the rear panel upper half with a rectangular frame made of appliqué cordons filled with four equidistant, short, appliqué, upward arrows. A pile of firewood was recorded behind feature 31, on its northeastern flank. The rest of the cluster's features are found on the western side where they are arranged in a triangular pattern. House 27, located more or less at the center, is a rectangular, mud-brick living and sleeping feature, 6.30 m long and 3.20 m wide, oriented W-E, and facing N. There is a pile of firewood between houses 27 and 28, the latter being the kitchen, found at 2 to 3 m W. The kitchen is a round, 5.20-m-in-diameter, mud-brick construction, with a doorway oriented N. The hearth is found next to the door on the left-hand side. It is a rectangular, two-niches feature, 1.25 m long, 0.50 m wide, and 0.80 m high, decorated on the upper third of the rear panel with a rectangular register delineated by appliqué cordons and filled with eight more or less short, equidistant, appliqué, upward arrows. Feature 32, found at 5 m S of 27, is a 5.10-m-in-diameter mud-brick goat house with the entrance oriented NE. The break in the fence and the northeastern orientation of the doorway show that feature 33, a relatively large, 11-m-in-diameter round, mud-brick barn, located 6 m behind goat house 27, is part of the southern cluster despite its positioning in the western features' line.

House 19, at the northern end of the western features' line, was a rectangular, mud-brick kitchen, 3.60 m long and 2.40 m wide, built by a newly married young man for his wife. The woman left and went back to her family and the angry husband systematically destroyed the kitchen. One may guess that, with the feature being oriented W-E, its doorway may have been on the southern wall opening S. House 18, the living and sleeping room of the recently wed, is a 6.40-m-long and 3-m-wide rectangular, mud-brick building, oriented N-S and facing E. It has an adjunct verandah built with four supporting poles and measuring 2.10 m × 2.10 m. Houses 20 to 22 form a long succession of three rectangular, mud-brick rooms built sequentially. The set is oriented roughly N-S and faces E. Feature 20, the northern room, used as, living and sleeping facility, measures 5.90 m in length and 2.60 m in width. It has an attached 6.70-m-long and 3.10-m-wide verandah built with four supporting poles. Room 21, located at the middle of the series, is the kitchen. It is 3.10 m long and 2.80 m wide with a 3.60 m × 2.80 m verandah. The hearth is located along the southern wall, in the left-hand side of the feature. It is a two-niches, rectangular installation, 1.25 m long, 0.50 m wide, and 0.80 m high. The panel is decorated with two parallel, appliqué, upward arrows in a rectangular frame. In addition, two water jars were recorded on a narrow mud bench located along the eastern wall on the left-hand side of the doorway. House 22, the southern living and sleeping room, is 6.70 m long and 2.60 m wide and its adjunct verandah 2.90 m in width and 6.70 m in length. In fact, the combined verandahs of all three rooms form an uninterrupted sheltered area 17 m long and 2.80 m wide. House 23 is found at 4 to 5 m SW of the previous one; it is a rectangular kitchen, 4 m long and 2.40 m wide, oriented N-S and facing E. The doorway is set at the northern end of the eastern wall, with the hearth found along the southern one. The latter is a two-niches, 1.25-m-long installation, with the rear panel decorated in its upper half with five more or less equidistant, *appliqué,* upward arrows connected to each other by a horizontal, *appliqué* cordon. Finally, a water jar was found next to the hearth, on its eastern side. A pile of firewood has been recorded next to the kitchen's southeastern corner and behind feature 30, a relatively large, 10.40-m-in-diameter round, mud-brick barn with an entrance oriented E. House 29, the remaining feature of the western set, is located less than 1 m SE of barn 30. It is a 4.50-m-in-diameter round, mud-brick goat house with the doorway oriented N. Finally, a horse-tethering pole, a mud chicken coop, and a small pit have been recorded in the central part of the complex.

Habitation complexes 4 and 5 share the fenced field 3, limited in the N by a footpath. There is no visible physical evidence for each unit's part, and the whole parcel measures 133 m in length and 80 m in width.

Habitation Complex 5

Habitation complex 5 is located in the southwestern part of the settlement; it is stretched on 45 m SE-NW and consists of five features: four houses and a goat corral (fig. 38). Goat enclosure IV is located in the inner part of the site; it measures 6.30 m in diameter with an entrance oriented SW. Feature 35, at the center of the complex, is an abandoned, round, mud-brick house, 6.30 m in diameter with a doorway oriented NE. The remaining houses are arranged in a crescent-shaped pattern with some linked by fences.

House 34, a living and sleeping room, is found at the northern end of the line. It is a rectangular, mud-brick building, 7 m long and 3.10 m wide, oriented N-S and facing E. It is complemented by a sheltered 6.80 m × 2.60 m area built with six supporting poles. A pile of firewood has been recorded behind the house, along its western wall. The round, mud-brick kitchen is located 2 to 3 m S. It is a 6-m-in-diameter feature with the entrance oriented NE. The recorded hearth is plain and found in the northern part of the house, in the standard right-hand side position. Finally, feature 37, the complex's barn, is found a few meters E of the kitchen. It is a round, mud-brick construction measuring 9.40 m in diameter with the doorway oriented NE. Habitation complex 5 is clearly a single nuclear family unit of two elder persons with grown-up children.

Habitation Complex 6

Habitation complex 6 is located due S of the settlement. It is comprised of eight features spread over an area measuring 40 m in length N-S and 20 m in maximum width W-E (fig. 38). The complex is delineated in the S, W, and N by distinct fence portions aligned posts with tied rope, with features arranged into two well-demarcated sets and an additional isolated house farther S.

The northern set consists of a long, rectangular, mud-brick building oriented W-E, facing S, and divided into three rooms. House 39 is a living and sleeping room situated at the western end of the building. It is 6.20 m long and 3 m wide, with an adjunct, 5.30-m-in-length and 2.80-m-in-width verandah built with five supporting poles. The latter installation is also used for the storage of sorghum stalks. Room 40, the kitchen, is found at the middle of the construction. It measures 3.80 m in length and 3 m in width, with a verandah in continuity with that of the previous room. This part of the verandah, measuring 4.30 m in length and 3 m in width is also used as a sorghum storage platform. A hearth was recorded along the kitchen's eastern wall, in the standard right-hand side position; it is a rectangular two-niches installation, 1.30 m long, 0.50 m wide, 0.80 m high, decorated in the upper part of the rear panel by a horizontal band filled with short, vertical, and parallel appliqué lines. The hearth mud installation is extended northward with a low bench supporting two water jars. House 41, at the eastern end, is the second living and sleeping room; it is 6.60 m long and 3 m wide, with an attached and distinct 4.10 m × 3.20 m verandah built with five supporting poles. Finally, a pile of firewood has been recorded on the western edge of the building, next to room 39's verandah.

The middle set consists of two goat corrals and two rectangular, mud-brick houses. Goat corral V is located to the W of the set; it is a circular, 7-m-in-diameter feature inserted in the complex's fence with its entrance oriented NW. Enclosure VI, the second goat corral, was a worn-out, collapsed feature at the time of field-work. It is attached to the neighboring house 43 on its northern side and measures 8 m in MaD. Rooms 42 and 43 are parts of a long, rectangular, mud-brick building oriented W-E and facing N. House 42, 3.10 m in length and 2.90 m in width, used as the kitchen, is situated at the western end. The hearth, a plain, rectangular, two-niches installation, 1.25 m long, 0.60 m wide, and 0.75 m high, is located along the eastern wall, in a non standard left-hand side position. Two water pots were found next to the hearth, on the southern side. Finally, there is a small, circular chicken coop attached to the kitchen's northern wall. House 43, the living and sleeping room located at the eastern end, is larger. It measures 6.20 m in length and 2.90 m in width, with the doorway at the middle of the northern wall. The remaining feature of the complex is relatively isolated from the others, situated at 8 to 9 m S of goat corral V. It is a large, 9.80-m-in-diameter, round, mud-brick barn with the entrance oriented N.

A larger rectangular chicken coop with rounded angles was recorded in the central part of the complex, and a second pile of firewood was found a few meters behind kitchen 42. The habitation estate is complemented by a share of the large fenced field 4. The whole field measures 120 m in maximum length W-E and 76 m in width N-S. Habitation complex 6's share is located in the western part of field 4, with a series of earth embankments in its southern half (fig. 38).

Habitation Complex 7

Habitation complex 7 is also located due S of the village (fig. 38), and consists of three distinct sets of features stretched along 50 m N-S. The northern set is comprised of two features, a round, mud-brick goat's house and an oval-shaped goat corral. Feature 49, the goat house, measures 5.60 m in diameter with a doorway oriented SE. Corral VIII, attached to house 49 on its northeastern side, measures 11 m long and 8 m in maximum width, with the entrance oriented SE. The enclosure also serves as a goat-milking area equipped with twenty-two more or less equidistant wooden posts arranged in an oval-shaped pattern.

The middle set, also with two features, is located 7 m S of the northern one. House 48 is a rectangular, mud-brick construction oriented N-S, facing E, with an adjunct verandah. The room measures 6.30 m in length and 3 m in width, with a series of wooden shelves along the southern wall, the bed along the northern one, and finally, the hearth along the eastern wall, in the non standard left-hand side position. The recorded inside hearth is a rectangular, two-niches installation, 1.10 m long, 0.50 m wide, and 0.85 m high. The rear panel is pseudo-crenellated with four more or less equidistant, protruding tips along the upper side. The decoration, confined to the upper third of the panel, consists of four appliqué, upward arrows underlined with a horizontal, appliqué cordon. The verandah is built with six supporting poles and measures 6.30 in length and 3.60 m in width. The outside hearth, adjacent to the inside one, is a plain, rectangular, two-niches feature, 0.90 m long, 0.50 m wide, and 0.40 m high. Goat corral VII, in the S, is partially attached to house 48. It is an 8-m-in-diameter, circular enclosure with the entrance oriented NE. Finally, a pile of firewood has been recorded at the southwestern corner of house 48.

The southern set, at approximately 5 m S of the previous one, is constituted of one round and one rectangular, mud-brick building. The round specimen, feature 44, is a 5.10-m-in-diameter goat-milking house with a doorway oriented N. The house is equipped with twelve milking posts arranged in a series of concentric circles. Houses 45 and 46, a few meters E of the goat-milking installation to which it is linked by a fence, belong to the same rectangular building, oriented SW-NE, and facing N-NW. The rectangular building is divided into four parts, with two rooms, a reception patio, and a courtyard. The kitchen, room 45, is 3.60-m-long and 3.10-m-wide, and is located at the southwestern end of the building complex, with its doorway opening in the reception patio 45a. The hearth, a two-niches, rectangular installation, 0.80 m long, 0.55 m wide, and 0.75 m high, is located along the western wall, in the standard right-hand side position. It is decorated on the panel's upper half by three equidistant, appliqué, upward arrows underlined by a similarly appliqué horizontal cordon. The reception patio, on the northern side of the kitchen, measures 3.60 m in length and 3.40 m in width, with a door set at the middle of the eastern wall leading to the enclosed courtyard. Room 46 measures 7.10 m long and 3.60 m wide. Two large four-poster beds with canopies were found along the eastern and western walls; two large rectangular mats were laid in the central part of the house, with a glass cabinet along the southern wall. Finally, the enclosed courtyard measures 7.10 m in length and 3.40 m in width.

House 47 is found at 7.60 m E of the previous one. It is a rectangular discussion house built in mud-brick, oriented roughly W-E and facing N. It is also used for entertainment, tea-drinking parties, as well as a guesthouse. Habitation complex 7's part of field 4 has a large oval-shaped pit along its northern limit, and a series of parallel earth embankments delimiting tomato and onion parcels (fig. 38).

Habitation Complex 8

Habitation complex 8 is located in the southeastern part of the settlement, delineated along its northeastern side by a fence with a single entrance (fig. 38). The complex's fifteen features are arranged in a roughly triangular pattern, 35 m in maximum width at the basis and 50 m in height. They are distributed into three units with an almost similar range of structures.

The northern unit consists of five features arranged in a NW-SE line facing S-SW. Goat corral IX is located at the northwestern end. It is a 8-m-in-diameter, circular enclosure used as a milking area with the entrance oriented S. It is equipped with a series of fifteen short wooden poles arranged in a concentric inner circle. House 62, at 2 to 3 m SE, is a rectangular, mud-brick kitchen, 4 m in length and 3.80 m in width. The recorded hearth, consisting of three clay "hearth-stones" is located along the southern wall in the left-hand side. Houses 61 and 60 are distinct rooms of a long, rectilinear mud-brick building found at 2 to 3 m SE of the previous one. The former, house 61, measures 7.40 m in length and 2.90 m in width. It has an adjunct courtyard, 6.30 m long and 2.70 m wide, surrounded by a mud-brick wall with the reed roof nonetheless supported with five poles. House 60, attached to the previous feature's eastern wall, measures 4.10 m long and 2.90 m wide. It is inhabited by an elderly woman, one of the grandmothers. House 58, the remaining feature of the NW unit, is found next to the southeastern corner of the previous room 60. It is a round, 5.30-m-in-diameter goat house with a doorway oriented W.

The southwestern unit is comprised of four features organized in an L-shaped arrangement. House 56 is oriented roughly N-S and faces E. It is a 7.10-m-long and 3.30-m-wide rectangular building with an adjunct 7.10-m-long and 2.90-m-wide verandah built with four supporting poles. A small rectangular chicken coop with rounded angles was recorded in the southern part of house 56's verandah. House 54 and 55 are part of the same rectangular building oriented roughly W-E and facing N. Room 54, at the western end, measures 5.90 m in length and 3 m in width. It has a relatively large verandah of exactly the same size built with six supporting poles. Room 55, the kitchen, is 3.60 m long and 3 m wide and comprises a decorated hearth located along the eastern wall, in the left-hand side position. The recorded hearth is a 1.40-m-long, 0.50-m-wide, and 0.70-m-high rectangular installation with three niches. The rear panel is pseudo-crenellated with six equidistant, protruding tips along its upper side, while the decoration, confined to the upper third, consists of five more or less equidistant, appliqué, upward arrows. House 57, at approximately 1 m E, is a round, 5.80-m-in-diameter, mud-brick construction, with the doorway oriented N. Originally used as a kitchen, as shown by the presence of a hearth, it was turned into a goat house equipped with a series of four milking posts found W, in the right-hand side of the feature. The recorded hearth is located along the wall in the southern part of the house, almost opposite the entrance. It is a rectangular, three-niches installation, 0.90 m long, 0.20 m in observable width, and 0.50 m in height, with a pseudo-crenellated rear panel consisting of six more or less equidistant pointed tips along the upper side. The decoration is limited to the panel's upper half delineated by a horizontal, appliqué cordon, with some extension in the lower half along the hearth's northern side. Parallel lines of pinched finger impressions are used to create four rectangular frames, and three are filled with grooved upward arrows. Pinched finger impressions are found all along the N vertical side of the installation.

The southeastern unit consist of six features arranged in a SW-NE line. A mud-brick drain was built in the central part of the complex to shift rainwater away from the main houses (fig. 38). Goat corral X is located at the northwestern end of the unit. It is an 8-m-in-diameter enclosure, with the entrance oriented W. A pile of firewood was recorded in the E, behind the corral. Feature 59, at 1 to 2 m SE, is a 6.70-m-in-diameter, round goat house with a doorway oriented W-NW. Rooms 51 to 53 belong to the same long, rectangular building. The kitchen, house 51, is located at the northeastern end and measures 3.80 m in length and 3 m in width. It has two hearths, one inside at the western end, thus, in the standard right-hand side position, and the other outside at the eastern end along the northern wall. The inside hearth measures 1.40 m in length, 0.60 m in width, and 0.70 m in height, and comprises three niches. Four equidistant, pointed tips are found along the rear panel's upper side, with a horizontal, appliqué cordon at mid-height. The decoration is confined to vertical parallel lines of pinched finger impressions along the hearth's N side. The outside hearth is a smaller, 0.90-m-long, 0.50-m-wide, and 0.70-m-high feature with two niches. The rear panel is crenellated with the decoration organized into a frame delineated by two horizontal and parallel appliqué cordons with finger impressions filled with four equidistant, grooved, upward arrows; and vertical and parallel lines of pinched finger impressions along the feature's eastern side. House 52, the main living and sleeping room, is found in the middle part of the building. It measures 7.30 m long and 3.30 m wide, with an adjunct sheltered area, 7.50 m in length and 3.50 m in width built with eight supporting poles. Room 53, the second living and sleeping area located at the western end, is 7 m long and 3.30 m wide. A pile of firewood was found behind room 53, along the southeastern wall. House 50, the remaining feature of the southeastern unit, is found at 2 to 3 m W of the long , rectilinear building. It is a round, 6.80-m-in-diameter, mud-brick goat house, with the doorway oriented N. It was also used as a milking area and, as such, was equipped with ten equidistant wooden posts arranged in a series of concentric circles. A relatively large pile of firewood has been recorded at 5 m N of feature 50, next to the water drain.

Finally, habitation complex 8's share of field 4 is located in the eastern part, as shown by the network of earth embankments abutting the habitations in the N (fig. 38).

Habitation Complex 9

Habitation complex 9 is found in the E-SE of the settlement. It is a well-delineated unit sharing the large fenced field 5 with the neighboring complexes 10 and 11 (fig. 38).The fenced field 5 measures 185 m in length in its N-S axis and 50 m in width. Habitation complex 9's structures are stretched along 50 m NW-SE, and are organized into a tight group, with three house and one enclosure and an isolated, rectilinear, mud-brick building.

House 63 is the isolated, rectangular, 7.10-m-long and 3.10-m-wide building. It is oriented roughly N-S and faces W-NW. Its adjunct verandah is built with 6 supporting poles and adds 7.10 m × 2.70 m to the structure size. A large oval-shaped goat droppings dump, 18 m long and 16 m wide, is found at some 15 m NE of house 63. The rest of the complex, with four features, is fenced and situated at 25 to 30 m W of the previous house. Goat corral XI, partially inserted in the enclosing fence and located in the western part of the complex, measures 6 m in diameter with an entrance oriented NE. House 67, a few meters N, measures 5.30 m in diameter. It is a round kitchen built in mud-brick with an attached, 4.40-m-long and 3-m-wide verandah supported with six poles. The kitchen hearth is located along the wall in the northern part of the feature, in the standard right-hand side position. It is a rectangular installation, 1 m long and 0.80 m high, decorated on the panel's upper half with appliqué motifs: two parallel, wavy lines delimiting a register filled with eight more or less equidistant, upward arrows. Feature 64, a round, 5.30-m-in-diameter young man's house, is located some 15 m E of the kitchen, with its doorway oriented W. It is inserted in the complex's fence and linked to the neighboring barn 65. The latter, built in mud-brick, measures 10.60 m in diameter, with the doorway oriented W.

Habitation Complex 10

Habitation complex 10, the Bilama (village headman) houses cluster is located in the eastern part of the settlement (fig. 38). It is spread over 50 m W-E and N-S and comprised of fourteen features organized into three units. The northern one, that of Bilama's son Hamat, consists of a series of four rooms, part of a long rectangular building oriented N-S and facing W. Rooms 71 and 74, at both ends of the construction, are kitchens; the former, belonging to Hamat's first wife, is a rectangular kitchen, 3.70 m long and 3.10 m wide, with the hearth located along the southern wall in the standard right-hand side position. The recorded hearth is a rectangular, two-niches, 1.40-m-long, 0.60-m-wide, and 0.80-m-high pseudo-crenellated installation. The decoration, confined to the upper half of the rear panel, consists of an elongated, rectangular frame delineated by appliqué cordons filled with six short, appliqué, upward arrows. The latter feature 74, Hamat's second wife's kitchen is slightly smaller, measuring 3.50 m in length and 3.10 m in width, with the hearth located along the northern wall, in the left-hand side. The hearth installation comprises two niches, and its plain rear panel has four equidistant, pointed tips along its upper side. Houses 72 and 73, for the first and the second wife, respectively, are similar in shape and size. Both measure 7 m long and 3.10 m wide with an additional walled courtyard 7 m in length and 3 m in width.

The southern unit is stretched E-W across the complex and includes five features. House 68, the Bilama's living and sleeping room, is found along the eastern edge of the unit, between an unused kitchen (feature 66) in the S and a barn (feature 70) in the N. It measures 7.10 m in length and 2.10 m in width and has an enclosed courtyard 7.10 m long and 3.10 m wide. House 66 is a round, 6.40-m-in-diameter, mud-brick construction with a decorated hearth located along the wall in the S. Its doorway is oriented NW, and the cooking feature, 1 m long, 0.20 m wide, and 0.60 m high, has a convex rear panel decorated along its edge with two parallel lines of pinched finger impressions. An appliqué, horizontal cordon underlines a series of four equidistant, vertical, grooved motifs. The barn is a relatively large, 10.90-m-in-diameter, round, mud-brick house built with its entrance oriented SW. The remaining features, delineated by a fence, are found in the inner part of the settlement at approximately 10 m W of the Bilama's house. Goat corral XII, at the western end, is attached to the central cattle corral. It is a circular, 10-m-in-diameter enclosure with the entrance oriented NE, and is also used for goat-milking, as shown by the in-curved line of eleven short wooden poles set across the feature. House 69, the Bilama's kitchen, with an attached toilet booth, is found 8 to 9 m E of the corral. It is a round, 6.70-m-in-diameter, mud-brick construction with the doorway oriented N and a hearth located in the right-hand side. The recorded hearth is a rectangular, three-niches feature, 1.20 m in length, 0.80 m in width, and 0.70 m in height, decorated in the upper half of the rear panel with eight equidistant, appliqué, upward arrows underlined by an appliqué, horizontal cordon. Finally, a pile of firewood was found behind the village headman's kitchen.

The third unit is also located in the inner part of the settlement but slightly farther N. It is constituted of five features delineated and connected by a fence with two perpendicular parts. House 17, at the northwestern end, is a round, 6.50-m-in-diameter, mud-brick barn with a doorway oriented E. House 75 is a rectangular, mud-brick building, 6.40 m long and 3 m wide, oriented N-S and facing E. It has an additional sheltered area built with six supporting poles and measuring 6.40 m in length and 2.10 m in width. A low storage rack is found next to the house, along its northern wall. Behind, there is a distinct, square, 3 m × 3 m toilet room, a chicken coop, and a pile of firewood. Kitchen 76, found at 2 m N, is a 5.10-m-in-diameter mud-brick house, with a doorway oriented SE. The hearth is a two-niches, rectangular feature, 1.25 m long, 0.50 m wide, and 0.72 m high, decorated in the upper half of the rear panel with a rectangular register filled with four equidistant, short, appliqué, upward arrows. There are also four equidistant, pointed tips along the hearth upper side. Finally, house 77 at 3 m E of the kitchen, is oriented W-E, faces S, and measures 6.30 m in length and 3 m in width. The verandah was still being built and consisted then of a series of wooden poles defining a 2.60 m × 2.40 m area.

Habitation Complex 11

Habitation complex 11 is located in the northeastern part of the settlement on the E of the main road. It consists of five features arranged in an almost perfect circle, measuring 25 m in diameter, and attached to the neighboring southern complex by a fence linking kitchen 74 and house 78. Goat corral XIII is found at the southern end of the complex and has its entrance oriented N-NW. It is a 6-m-in-diameter, circular enclosure, used exclusively for goat-milking purposes and is equipped with twenty-five densely packed wooden posts. There is, in addition, a small, circular chicken coop attached to the milking corral and found on its northern side.

Rooms 80 and 81 are parts of the same rectangular, mud-brick building oriented W-E and facing S, with an adjunct verandah 6.30 m long and 2.60 m wide, built with eight supporting poles. The former, measuring 6.30 m in length and 3 m in width, was surprisingly used as shelter for goats, and the latter, 4.50 m long and 3 m wide, as a storage room. Feature 79, located at the northern end, is a round, mud-brick kitchen, 5.80 m in diameter, with the doorway oriented SW. The hearth is located in the southeastern side of the house, in the standard right-hand side position. It is a rectangular installation with four equidistant, pointed tips along the upper side, measuring 1.20 m long, 0.60 m wide, and 0.80 m high. The decorated register, found in the upper half of the rear panel, consists of a rectangular frame made with appliqué cordons filled with six equidistant, equally appliqué, upward arrows. A pile of firewood was recorded between the kitchen (house 79) and the rectangular building (houses 80 and 81). House 78, the remaining feature of the complex, is a round, mud-brick house inhabited by a young man; it measures 6.40 m in diameter with the doorway oriented W.

There is a series of three large pits found in the northern part of field 5, behind the houses of habitation complexes 10 and 11. One of the striking aspects of Djidat 1's spatial layout is the increased variation in feature frequency between habitation complexes, with a range of 1 to 16, respectively, in complexes 1 and 4. The rectangular buildings, amounting to forty-five, are slightly predominant over the circular ones with thirty-seven. In all the cases, mud-brick is the "universal" building material used at Djidat I, and goat-milking is particularly well attested in the studied material record.

Chapter 10

Djidat II

Introduction

Djidat II, the second of the Djidat twin settlements resulted from the growth of Djidat I's population and the later split between different families and factions. According to informants, these sets of events happened thirty-six years ago. The site is located 12°02′ northern latitude and 14°57′ eastern longitude, 200 m N of Djidat I. The settlement population amounted to seventy-nine inhabitants in the 1969 census (Elingui 1978: 32). It increased to one hundred and twenty-three individuals, divided into sixty-four males and seventy females in the 1976 census (Recensement General 1985: 320). The population of the settlement was probably larger than that of 1976 at the time of fieldwork in January 1991, but precise figures are not available. It is difficult to escape from the straightforward impression of a high density settlement at a simple glance at the village map (fig. 39). The settlement is subcircular in shape and measures 240 m in maximum diameter. The 4.52 hectares of densely built area is comprised of 172 round and rectangular houses. The densely built area is surrounded by a ring of fields increasing the village diameter to 390 m. The village and its nearest ring of fields extended over 11.94 hectares, are part of a large, intensively exploited, 2.3-km-in-radius site-catchment area.

The recorded settlement facilities are divided into twenty-five habitation complexes distributed around a central area with communal features like the mosque, the well, and central cattle corrals (table 34). The village's well is located virtually at the center of the settlement (fig. 39) surrounded in its immediate periphery by the mosque in the S, cattle corrals 1 and 2 in the W, and 3 and 4 in the NW. It is a 3-m-in-diameter and 19 to 20-m-deep feature, with a 4.60-m-in-diameter and 1-m-high curb comprising two small, symmetric livestock watering troughs.

The mosque (feature 147) is located 15 m S of the well. It is surrounded by a fence with two entrances on the northern and western sides delimiting a subcircular space measuring approximately 13 m in diameter. The religious building, situated on the northern edge of the Marabout (Muslim scholar) habitation cluster, is

261

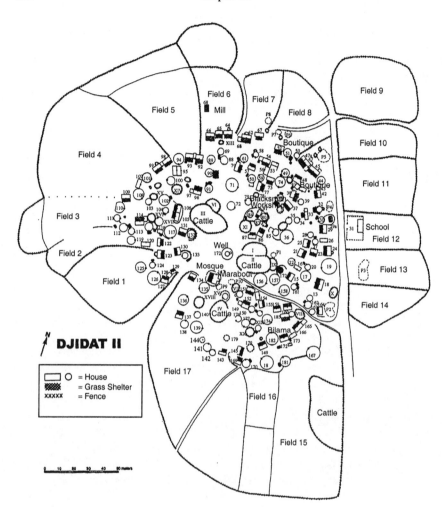

Figure 39: Map of Djidat II

a rectangular feature oriented N-S. It measures 7.90 m in length and 4.40 m in width with an adjunct verandah 7.90 m long and 3.60 m wide built with seven supporting poles. The building has two doors set in the northern and western wall, with the Mihrab measuring 1.5 m × 1.5 m protruding in the middle of the eastern wall.

Cattle corrals 1 and 2 are located 5 to 10 m W of the village's well. Both are elongated, more or less oblong-shaped features, measuring, respectively, 23.50 and 38 m in length W-E, and 14.50 m and 14.30 m in width N-S. Corral 1 has its main entrance on its western side, with that of corral 2 situated in the SW. Cattle corral 3 and goat enclosure 4 are found at some 15 m NW of the well. Both are

Table 34: Djidat II houses and features distribution

Cluster number	Number of features	Number of units	Habitation houses		Livestock houses	
			C	R	C	R
1	8	3	1	3	2	—
2	14	3	3	6	4	—
3	1	1	1	—	—	—
4	5	1	—	2	2	—
5	9	3	3	4	1	—
6	4	2	—	3	1	—
7	2	1	—	2	—	—
8	5	2	1	2	2	—
9	12	4	2	6	2	—
10	6	2	1	4	1	—
11	2	1	1	1	—	—
12	4	1	1	—	3	—
13	3	2	—	3	—	—
14	5	2	1	3	—	—
15	5	3	—	3	1	—
16	5	3	—	3	1	—
17	3	1	1	2	—	—
18	6	3	1	4	1	—
19	9	3	3	3	2	—
20	6	2	2	2	1	—
21	5	1	2	1	1	—
22	5	2	1	2	1	—
23	9	3	2	5	2	—
24	31	7	11	9	7	—
Total	156	56	37	70	35	—

attached to each other, with the larger elliptically shaped feature measuring 33 m in length and 18 m in width, and the smaller semicircular one being 13 m long and 8 m wide (fig. 39).

Three additional features of communal interest are not located in the central part of the settlement. They consist of a deep-bored mechanical water pump found in the S, at 45 m of the field's outer fence; a "students" house complex comprising a rectangular, mud-brick house and a fenced courtyard located in the E along the eastern road side; and finally, a diesel-engine powered mill found N-W-N of the site. Two students attending the Mosque Koranic school operated by the Marabout were residents of the complex at the time of fieldwork. The students' complex is rectangular in shape, oriented N-S, and measures 20 m in length and 13.20 m in width, with a single doorway at the middle of the eastern wall. The enclosing wall is built with wooden logs (fig. 39).The students' house (feature 31), attached to the eastern wall, measures 9.90 m in length and 4.20 m in width, with a doorway in the central part of the western wall. Finally, the students' complex is situated in a land plot, field 12, almost rectangular in shape, 60 m long and 30 m wide, cultivated by the residents in order to grow part of their food. In general, young students of Koranic schools are living from alms and food collected daily in the village. The engine-pulled mill is found in feature 68, located in field 6, in the northern part of the village. It is a rectangular, mud-brick building oriented N-S with the doorway at the southern end of the eastern wall. It measures 5.40 m in length and 3.40 m in width (Fig. 39). The feature's roof is made of coarse reed mats. The mill belongs to a Kotoko entrepreneur from Houlouf and is operated by a young man commuting daily from Houlouf to Djidat II.

Due to the particularly high density of features, the identification of individual household complexes is slightly more complicated than in all the previous cases. Information obtained from the village inhabitants was crucial in the clarification of the observed spatial patterns (table 34).

Habitation Complex 1

Habitation complex 1 is located a few meters E of cattle corrals 1 and 2 and con-sists of eight features stretched on 60 m NW-SE, from goat enclosures IX to X (fig. 39). Enclosure IX, located in the central part of the settlement and attached to one of the central cattle corrals, is semi-elliptical in shape and measures 11 m in length and 6 m in maximum width. Enclosure X, on the other hand, is located in the outer periphery of the village along the western road's side; it is an oval-shaped feature 9 m in length and 7.50 m in width. Feature 172, the goat house, is constituted of a 5.00-m-in-diameter thatched enclosure surrounded by a semi circular, mud-brick wall open on its southeastern side and measuring 8.00 m in diameter. House 15 is found 4 to 5 m SE of goat house 172; it is a rectangular, mud-brick building oriented NE-SW, measuring 6.60 m in length and 3.60 m in width, with the doorway in the middle of the northwestern wall. The house has an adjunct verandah, 6.40 m long and 2.10 m wide built with four supporting poles. It is inhabited by Gida, a widowed father of two deaf daughters. House 16, the third feature of the complex, is found at 5 m NE; it is a rectangular, mud-brick building oriented NW-SE, measuring 4.80 m in length and 2.40 m in width, with the door in the middle of the southwestern wall. At the time of fieldwork it was used as a provisional goat shelter. House 161 is located in the central part of the complex along its southwestern side. It is a round, mud-brick house inhabited by the mother of Gida and Idrisa. The construction measures 6.30 m in diameter, with its door-way oriented NE, shaded by a 3.80 × 2.60 m rectangular verandah. The recorded hearth measures 0.90 m in length and 0.60 m in height; its rear panel is decorated on three sides by two parallel lines of finger impressions divided into two plain frames by an additional vertical set of parallel lines. Finally, a pile of firewood was recorded next to the house's wall, on its eastern side. House 17, located 5 m NE of the mother's dwelling unit, is a former habitation used as a goat shelter. It is a round, mud-brick house, measuring 7.50 m in diameter, with its door oriented SE. Finally, house 18, the remaining feature, is located at the southeastern end of the complex. It is inhabited by Idrisa, the other son and Gida's brother, with his wife and three children. The construction is a rectangular, mud-brick building, oriented N-S, and divided into two parts. The house measures 8.40 m in length and 3.40 m in width, with the door at the middle of the western wall. The enclosed courtyard is also rectangular, 8.40 m long and 3.10 m wide

The spatial layout of the habitation complex features is clearly structured around house 161, the dwelling unit of the most senior person of the extended family unit, with each son's architectural facilities and goat enclosure stretched on 30 m on both the NW and the E.

Habitation Complex 2

Habitation complex 2 is found due E of the settlement. It is comprised of thirteen features spread over an area measuring 50 m × 40 m, and, partitioned into three subclusters (fig. 39). The southern subcluster, stretched on 40 m W-E constituted of six features, belong to Udai and his family, while the remaining central and northern ones, with, respectively, four and three houses, belong to Udai's deceased brother's sons, Omar and Abubakar.

In Udai's subcluster, rectangular and circular houses are arranged in distinct and parallel W-E lines (fig. 39). Features 19 and 22, at both ends of the line, are livestock houses. The former, used as a barn, measures 11.60 m in diameter with a doorway oriented W. The latter, much smaller, is a 5.70-m-in-diameter goat shelter with the door oriented NE. The kitchen (feature 20), located at the center of the line and measuring 4.90 m in diameter, has its entrance oriented NW. The recorded hearth is a two-niches, rectangular installation, 1.10 m long, 0.48 m wide, and 0.70 m high, the rear panel being decorated with six equidistant and short upward arrows set in a rectangular frame delimited by appliqué cordons. Finally, a relatively large pile of firewood was recorded next to the kitchen door, slightly on its northwestern side.

Each of the rectangular buildings has a specific orientation. House 21, located at the western end of the line, is oriented N-S facing E. It measures 6.30 m in length and 3.40 m in width with an attached 6.30-m-long and 2.65-m-wide verandah built with four supporting poles. It is inhabited by Udai, his wife Mariam, and their seven children. Feature 23, at some 3 m E of the previous building, is Udai's reception and discussion house. It is oriented W-E, facing S, and measures 5.30 m in length and 3 m in width. The complementary verandah, 5.30 m long and 2.50 m wide, is built with four supporting poles. Finally, house 24, at the eastern end of the complex, is inhabited by the most senior members of the extended family, Mohammed and Dia, who had two sons, Udai and his deceased brother. The construction, measuring 7.30 m in length and 3.40 m in width, is oriented roughly N-S, faces W, and, connected to the neighboring barn by a fence. The verandah is built with eight supporting poles and adds an additional area of 7.30 m × 2.90 m. Finally, a small toilet room has been recorded and is attached to the house's eastern wall.

Omar's and Ngasi's subcluster consists of four features (25, 26, 27, and 28), two rectangular buildings, and two round ones located at the center of the extended family's habitation complex, a few meters N of Udai's one (fig. 39). Feature 27, Ngasi's kitchen, is found at the center of the subcluster; it is a circular, mud-brick construction measuring 5.60 m in diameter, with the doorway oriented SW. The recorded hearth is located S along the wall in the standard right-hand side of the house. It is a plain rectangular feature. Finally, a relatively large pile of firewood was found next to the kitchen's wall, on its northern side. House 25, located 2 to 3 m W of the kitchen, is inhabited by the nuclear family and their five children. It is a rectangular, mud-brick building measuring 5.90 m in length and 2.70 m in width, oriented N-S, and facing E. The attached verandah, built with four supporting poles, measures 5.90 m long and 1.80 m wide. Feature 28, the second round house of the subcluster, is found at 2 to 3 m NW of the kitchen. It is a 5.10-m-in-diameter goat house with an entrance oriented W. House 26, in the eastern side of the subcluster, is an unfinished, rectangular, mud-brick building. It measures 6.90 m in length and 3.00 m in width; the new house is being built for Omar's first born son, who was expected to be married soon.

The third subcluster, that of Omar's brother Abubakar, his wife Fani, and their two children, is found to the N of the complex. It is constituted of three main features: a rectangular building, a round house, and a fenced, circular straw storage area. House 29, the rectangular building, is found in the southern side of the subcluster. It is oriented N-S, facing W, and measures 7.30 m in length and 3.00 m in width. The adjunct verandah, built with four supporting poles, is 7.00 m long and 2.70 m wide. The kitchen, feature 30, is located N of the main house and measures 5.80 m in diameter with its entrance oriented W. The hearth is a plain, rectangular installation, and a pile of firewood has been recorded along the kitchen's wall, on its northwestern side (fig. 39). The fenced straw storage area is subcircular in shape and measures 8.00 m in maximum diameter. A chicken coop in mud-brick was recorded at 5 m W of the kitchen; it is square in shape with rounded corners. Finally, the nuclear family's barn, feature 36, is found at some 25 m W in the inner part of the settlement (fig. 39). It is a relatively large, round, mud-brick house measuring 10.60 m in diameter with its doorway oriented E.

Habitation Complex 3

Habitation complex 3 is a nuclear family's dwelling unit. It is found along the eastern edge of the settlement as part of the outer ring of features, a few meters N of complex 2 (fig. 39). House 32 is inhabited by Jaber, his wife Zara, and their six children. At the time of fieldwork, they had been settled in the village for two years, coming from Ngada in the western part of the study area. Feature 32 is a round, mud-brick house measuring 5.90 m in diameter with the doorway oriented NW. There is an adjunct room attached to the western part of the main mud-brick feature, built with wooden posts and reed mats; it is rectangular in shape, 4.80 m in length and 3.70 m in width, with the entrance set in the northern wall. The family hearth, located in the main house, is a plain, rectangular installation. In addition, a toilet room is attached to the main house, on its eastern side, and a pile of firewood was recorded in the S. Finally, a large pit (pit 4), 8.00 m long, 5.00 m wide, and 1.50 m deep, was found behind the complex.

Habitation Complex 4

Habitation complex 4 is also located in the eastern part of the settlement but in the inner side of the village. It is comprised of four main features—houses 33, 34, and 35 as well as goat enclosure XXI—stretched on 30 m W-E (fig. 39). The complex belongs to Hassana. His first wife left with their two children, and the second one was at Kusseri, the nearby town, at the time of fieldwork. House 33 is a rectangular, mud-brick building, measuring 8.70 m in length, 2.40 m in width, oriented roughly N-S, facing W, and divided into three parts. What may be termed the living room, in the southern part of the building, measures 6.90 m in length, with a doorway opening on an enclosed patio, almost square in shape, measuring 2.60 m by 2.20 m. It is built with woven reed mats and a few wooden posts, with the entrance set in the northern wall. Finally, the third component of the building (feature 33a), is the hand-operated mill room, measuring 2.80 m in length and 2.40 m in width. Feature 34, located 4 to 5 m W of the previous one, is a round, 4.60-m-in-diameter, mud-brick goat house, with the doorway oriented E. Feature 35, the round, 5.50-m-in-diameter bull house, with an entrance oriented N, is found at 1 to 2 m NW. Finally, the goat enclosure, located at the western end of the complex, is an oval-shaped feature measuring 8.00 in length and 6.00 m in maximum width (fig. 39). Clearly, as the owner of a hand-operated mill, Hassana can be considered an entrepreneur providing a much needed service to the women of his community and beyond.

Habitation Complex 5

Habitation complex 5 consists of nine main features arranged in an almost circular pattern located next to the eastern set of central cattle enclosures, on the northern side (fig. 39). The recorded features are divided into two subclusters and one relatively isolated dwelling unit. Feature 85, the isolated dwelling unit inhabited by the eldest male and his wife, is located at the eastern end of the complex. It is a 6.00-m-in-diameter, round, mud-brick house with the doorway oriented W, opening on a roofless, mud-brick wall patio, 4.80 m in length and 3.60 m in width. The recorded hearth is a rectangular installation with a horizontal, appliqué, cordon at mid-height of the rear panel and a series of four equidistant, vertical, and elongated bumps on the lower half. The southern side of the dwelling space is delimited by a fence attached to the nearby barn 36. Goat corral XI is located at the western edge of the complex. It is a perfectly circular feature measuring 10 m in diameter.

The northern subcluster is surrounded by a fence and comprises three features (fig. 39). House 81, the rectangular building inhabited by a young adult male, is located at the center of the unit. It is oriented N-S, faces W, and measures 3.95 m in length and 3.20 m in width. The added verandah, 3.10 m long and 2.80 m wide, is found along the house's southern side. Features 80 and 84 are both round, mud-brick houses. The former, found immediately E of the rectilinear building measures 5.80 m in diameter with its doorway oriented N. The latter, at 2 m W with the entrance also oriented N, measures 6.90 m in diameter. It is inhabited by a grandmother. Surprisingly, the hearth recorded in house 84 is decorated, an unusual fact for grandparents' habitations. The decoration consists of parallel lines of pinched finger impressions on both vertical sides of the rear panel, complemented on the upper half by seven short, vertical, and equidistant appliqué cordons resting on a longer transversal appliqué cordon. Finally, a pile of firewood was recorded behind the grandmother's house in the SW.

The southern subcluster has four features arranged in a semicircular pattern (fig. 39). House 87 is a rectangular, mud-brick building oriented W-E, facing N, and measuring 6.40 m in length and 3.10 m in width. It has an adjunct 5.10 m × 2.20 m verandah built with six supporting poles. House 86, located next to the northeastern corner of the previous one, faces NE. It has a roofed, mud-brick patio, 5.80 m long and 3.35 m wide, added to a living room of approximately the same size, 5.80 m in length and 3.20 m in width. In fact, the building measures 6.55 m in total length and 5.80 m in width. Feature 82, the kitchen, is parallel to the main house and found at 4 to 5 m N. It is a relatively small, 2.60 m × 1.80 m rectangular, mud-brick construction with the door set in the southern wall. The recorded hearth is a plain, rectangular installation, and a pile a firewood was found along the eastern wall. Finally, feature 83, the goat house, inserted in the fence and located on the N of the subcluster, measures 5.80 m in diameter with its entrance oriented S.

The demographic structure of habitation complex 5's members is poorly documented in comparison to all the previous cases.The data available nonetheless show that there are at least three generations represented with the grandmother, the eldest male and his wife, and presumably, their sons' houses. The location of the complex within the central part of the settlement is, so far, unique.

There are two features next to a large tree located approximately 10 m N of habitation complex 5 (fig. 39). They consist of house 37 and shelter 76; the former inhabited by Abisuya, a single mother and her son, the latter being a blacksmith's

Figure 40: The Blacksmith workshop from Djidat II

shelter. Abisuya's house is a rectangular, mud-brick building oriented roughly W-E and facing S. It measures 7.20 m in length and 2.40 m in width, with an attached 7.20 m × 2.90 m verandah built with seven supporting poles. The blacksmith's workshop is located 2 to 3 m W of Abusiya's house (fig. 39). It consists of a shelter, measuring 3.80 m in length and 3.60 m in width built with twelve supporting side-poles and a central one, and a forge installation (fig. 40). The forge is structure around a 0.50-m-in-diameter, shallow open hearth where the metal pieces being processed are heated. There is a 0.50-m-long and 0.20-m-wide tunnel built in clay on the northern side of the hearth. Two blow pipes or tuyeres, attached to leather bellows are set in the tunnel with an additional flat metal piece to minimize the inflow of colder air. A relatively large metal sheet set along the western side of the installation serves as a windbreak, and a large tin can is used as a charcoal container and/or, trash bin depending on the smithing work schedule. An anvil, consisting of a quartzite cobble set on top of a wooden piece, is located in the eastern part of the forge, next to a pile of charcoal, a wooden log, a steel hammer, the blacksmith's mat, and a hoe being manufactured.

Habitation Complex 6

Habitation complex 6 is found in the northern part of the settlement (fig. 39). It is comprised of four features set in a 15 m × 15 m quadrangular arrangement.

Feature 38, a rectangular, mud-brick house oriented N-S and facing E, is inhabited by Abdulai, his second wife, Ejela, and their six children. The building measures 6.30 m in length and 3.00 m in width. The patio added to the house is longer (8.30 m), narrower (2.70 m), and open ended on its northern side. The family's goat house, feature 39, is found a few meters E of the main house; it is a 5.40-m-in-diameter, round, mud-brick construction with its entrance oriented W. Features 40 and 41 are located along the northern side of the complex. The former is a thatched, 3.80-m-long and 3.50-m-wide kitchen facing S; the recorded hearth is a two-niches, rectangular installation with decoration confined to the upper half of the rear panel. The decoration consists of six equidistant, short, upward, appliqué arrows resting on a horizontal, appliqué cordon. The latter, inhabited by Gambu, Abdulai's eldest son, measures 5.50 m in length and 3.10 m in width. It still has a straw roof. A pile of 1,170 mud-bricks has been recorded along the eastern end of the southern wall. They are to be used in the construction of the house's flat mud roof. Finally, a chicken coop was recorded a few meters E of house 40 eastern wall, and a pile of firewood was found at the northwestern corner of feature 38.

Habitation Complex 7

Habitation complex 7 is located in the N-NE part of the settlement, in the outer features' ring (fig. 39). It consists of a single, relatively long, mud-brick building divided into two rooms, oriented N-NW-SE, facing SW, and inhabited by Adam, his wife, and their five children. Feature 42, the living/sleeping room, located at the southern end of the building, measures 6.20 m in length and 2.90 m in width. It has an adjunct verandah, 6.20 m long and 2.40 m wide, built with eight supporting poles and two lateral mud-brick walls. The kitchen or room 43, at the northern end measures 3.10 in length and 2.90 m in width. The recorded hearth is a rectangular installation, 1.10 m long and 0.60 m high, with the upper part of the rear panel decorated with two short, vertical, and parallel appliqué cordon, underlined by a longer transversal one. Finally, a pile of firewood was recorded at the northwestern corner of the kitchen, along the northern wall.

Habitation Complex 8

Habitation complex 8, belonging to Ahmed and his family, consists of five features (feature 73, 74, 75, 77, and 78) arranged in a circle, open in the S, and measuring 25 m in diameter on average. The complex is located in the northern part of the settlement, a few meters N of habitation complex 5 (fig. 39). Two of the features are rectangular, mud-brick buildings, and the remaining three are round houses equally built with mud-bricks. The kitchen (feature 75) is located at the southeastern end of the complex with its doorway oriented NW, surrounded by a chicken coop in the SW and a pile of firewood in the NE. It measures 6.00 m in diameter and has a decorated hearth. The hearth's rear panel is framed on three sides with an appliqué cordon. The upper half, delineated by an additional transversal cordon, is filled with seven more or less equidistant, parallel series of pinched finger impressions. The same motif is also found on all the appliqué cordons. House 74, the barn, is located at the complex's northeastern corner, at 5 m N of the kitchen. It measures 7.00 m in diameter with an entrance oriented S. House 73, at 2 m W, measures 6.30 m in length and 2.80 m in width. It is oriented W-E, faces S, and has an attached 4.60 m by 2.90 m verandah. House 77 is located along the western flank of the complex. It is oriented N-S, faces E, and measures 7.00 m in length and 3.00 m in width. The adjunct verandah, extended over 6.10 m × 2.80 m, is built with eight supporting poles. Finally, feature 78, found at the southwestern end of the complex, is a round, 4.40-m-in-diameter goat house, with the door oriented NE. A horse pole was found in the central part of the complex courtyard.

Habitation Complex 9

Habitation complex 9 belongs to an extended family of blacksmiths. It is located in the northern part of the settlement in the outer houses' ring, comprised of ten features arranged into two roughly parallel W-E lines (fig. 39). The complex features, stretched on 55 m W-E and 25 m N-S, are owned by three nuclear families of brothers, all of them active blacksmiths.

Feature 44 is located at the eastern end of the complex. It is a round, 6.50-m-in-diameter, mud-brick goat house belonging to Ramat's family. Their main house, feature 45, inhabited by the husband, wife, and their six children, is found 2 to 3 m W. It is a relatively long, rectangular, mud-brick building oriented NW-SE, facing SW, and measuring 9.60 m in length and 3.10 in width. It has an added enclosed and sheltered courtyard, 9.90 m long and 2.40 m wide, and an attached 2.10 m × 2.00 m toilet room at the eastern end of the northern wall.

Features 46, 47, 47a, 48, and goat enclosure XII belong to the eldest son's family. Gidah has married a new wife after the death of the first one, and has four children. Features 46, 47, and 47a are distinct rooms of the same long, rectangular, mud-brick, attached to Ramat's house, oriented NW-SE, facing SW, and measuring 11.70 m in length and 3.10 m in width. The kitchen, found in room 46 at the eastern end of the building, is a narrow, 3.10 m × 1.70 m, confined area extended southward by mud-brick walls. The remaining part of the feature is divided into two rooms, both sharing the adjunct verandah. The larger room measures 6.00 × 3.10 m, and the smaller, 3.60 × 3.10 m. The adjunct verandah is built with five supporting poles and two parallel mud-brick walls, thus creating two distinct patios, one for each room. Finally, there is a 2.30 m × 1.40 m toilet room attached to the eastern end of the building's northern wall. Feature 48, Gidah's wife's house, is found at 7 to 8 m S. It is a rectangular, mud-brick building oriented W-E, facing

N, and measuring 6.10 m in length and 3.70 m in width. The attached verandah measuring 6.10 long and 1.70 m wide, built with four supporting poles, is used as a retail shop where daily-life items like matches, sugar, oil, cigarettes, etc., are sold. Goat enclosure XII is located next to Amina's house southwestern corner. It is a circular feature measuring 5.00 m in diameter. Finally, a pile of firewood was recorded next to house 48 and the goat corral (fig. 39).

Feature 50 is located a few meters W of Gidah house 47; it is a 4.80-m-in-diameter, round, mud-brick house, with the doorway oriented S, inhabited by an elderly woman, the mother of three brothers: Gidah, Ramat, and Ahmat. A relatively small chicken coop has been recorded next to the house's entrance, on the eastern side.

Features 49, 51, 52, and 53, located at the western end of the complex, belong to Ahmat's family. House 49, with its abutting pile of firewood and its entrance oriented W, is a 5.40-m-in-diameter, round, mud-brick kitchen. The recorded hearth is a rectangular, three-niche installation. The decoration, confined to the hearth's rear panel, is divided into two parts. There are six equidistant clay tips set along the upper side of the panel. The lateral and upper sides are overlined with appliqué cordons defining a two-frames register; the lower is plain and the upper is filled with five more or less equidistant, short, appliqué double-arrows. The appliqué cordons and double-arrows are decorated with parallel pinched finger impressions. House 51, located 10 to 11 m N, with its doorway oriented S, is used as a goat shelter. It is a 5.30-m-in-diameter, round, mud-brick construction, with a relatively large pile of firewood and a small chicken coop found next to its entrance on the southeastern side. House 52, at the western end of the outer features' line, is inhabited by Ahmat, his wife, and their four children. It is a rectangular, mud-brick construction oriented W-E, facing S, and measuring 7.40 m in length and 3.30 m in width. The adjunct verandah is slightly shorter than the house. It is built with four supporting poles and measures 5.70 m long and 3.00 m wide. Finally, feature 53, the remaining dwelling unit of the complex, is inhabited by Mahamat, Ahmat's twelve-year-old firstborn son. It is located 7 to 8 m S of the parents house, oriented W-E, facing N, and measuring 6.00 m in length and 3.00 in width. The house has two parallel mud-brick walls, the western one abutting the corner of the nearby house 56.

The grandmother's house and the goat corral are located along what can be considered as the central N-S axis of the habitation complex. This suggests that the corral may have been used by all the members of the extended family, and not exclusively Gidah's family.

Habitation Complex 10

Habitation complex 10, spread over 20 m E-W and 22 m N-S, is found in the N-NW part of the settlement and consists of six features arranged in a loose rectilinear pattern (fig. 39). There are two round, mud-brick houses located opposite corners of the complex. House 58, in the NW, used as a kitchen, measures 5.10 m in diameter with a doorway oriented S. The recorded hearth has a decorated register on the upper part of its rear panel. The decoration, made with appliqué cordons, consists of a horizontal band filled with short, vertical, and equidistant lines. A toilet booth is attached to the feature, and a pile of firewood was recorded next to the wall on the western side. Feature 59, in the SE and at 15 m from the previous one, is used as a goat house; its entrance is oriented NW, and it measures 6.00 m in diameter.

Each of the three rectangular buildings has a specific orientation (fig. 39). The largest, situated along the northern side of the complex, is a 9.00-m-long-two-rooms construction oriented W-E and facing S; room 54, at the eastern end, measures 6.40 m in length and 2.90 m in width. It has an attached, 6.40 m × 2.90 m verandah, built with four supporting poles. The kitchen, found in room 55 at the western end, is 3.50 m long and 2.90 m wide. The recorded hearth is a rectangular, three-niches installation. The decoration consists of a single, horizontal, appliqué cordon on the upper half of the rear panel. Finally, a pile of firewood was recorded at the western end of the kitchen's southern wall. House 56, in the E, is oriented N-S facing W. It measures 6.20 m in length and 3.20 m in width. House 57, the remaining feature, is oriented W-E facing N. It is a 6.20-m-long and 2.80-m-wide construction with an adjunct. 4.60 m × 2.10 m verandah, built with four supporting poles.

The complex is inhabited by two families of presumably close kin; but detailed information was not obtained from the features' owners.

Habitation Complex 11

Habitation complex 11 is comprised of two features, one circular (feature 61) and the other rectangular (feature 70), found in the northwestern part of the settlement at few meters W of the previous complex (fig. 39). House 61, used for habitation, measures 7.00 m in diameter with the doorway oriented SE. A pile of firewood was found next to the wall on the western side. House 70, located a few meters S, is oriented N-S, facing E. It is a 7.30-m-long and 3.00-m-wide rectangular, mudbrick building with an attached 6.20 m × 2.30 m mud-brick patio. In fact, the patio consists of a 1.00-m-high, lower course mud-brick wall, with its upper part built of straw.

Habitation Complex 12

Habitation complex 12 is also found in the northwestern part of the settlement, along the southern flank of habitation complexes 10 and 11, in the inner side of the village (fig. 39). It consists of four almost equidistant, round, mud-brick and wood and straw houses, stretched on 35 m N-S and 28 m W-E, and arranged in a lozenge pattern. House 60, in the N, measures 7.20 m in diameter with a doorway oriented W. A plain, multi-niches hearth was recorded as well as a relatively elaborate, 3.60 m × 3.30 m toilet room and a pile of firewood. House 71, located in the W, is a relatively large, 10.10-m-in-diameter barn with its entrance oriented. The goat house (feature 72) is found in the S. It measures 5.50 m in diameter with an entrance oriented E. Finally, feature 79, a grandmother's 5.00-m-in-diameter, round, wood and straw house, is located in the E with its doorway oriented W.

Habitation Complex 13

Habitation complex 13, found in the outer features' ring in the northwestern part of the settlement, is comprised of two rectangular houses arranged in an E-W line (fig. 39). Both buildings are oriented W-E and face S. House 67, located at the eastern end of the complex, measures 7.40 m in length and 3.40 m in width. It has an adjunct, slightly smaller, 5.00 m × 2.70 m verandah, built with four supporting poles. Houses 62 and 63 are part of a building complex located 4 m W of the previous one. The former measures 6.90 m in length and 3.00 m in width, and the latter, oriented N-S and facing E, is 3.30 m long and 2.90 m wide. Both rooms share the enclosed, 6.90 m × 3.30 m courtyard space. Finally, a toilet room, built with mud-brick walls, is attached to room 62's northern wall.

Habitation Complex 14

Habitation complex 14 is located in the outer features' ring in the northwestern part of the settlement. It is constituted of five features distributed over 25 m × 20 m three rectangular, mud-brick buildings, one round straw house, and a small, oval-shaped, 3.00 m × 5.00 m goat corral (corral XIII) at the center (fig. 39). The recorded rectangular houses are arranged along an E-W line facing S. Building 64, at the eastern end, measures 7.00 m in length and 3.10 m in width, with an additional enclosed 6.50 m × 3.10 m courtyard. House 65, at 1 m W, is located in the center; it is a 6.20-m-long and 3.10-m-wide construction with an adjunct, 6.20 m × 3.20 m verandah built with four supporting poles. House 66, at the western end of the features' line, consists of an enclosed courtyard and a room. The former measures 7.30 m in length and 3.30 m in width, and the latter is 7.30 m long and 3.00 m wide. House 69, the remaining feature, is located in the southern part of the complex. It is a 5.00-m-in-diameter straw construction used as a "discussion house" by young men.

Habitation Complex 15

Habitation complex 15, stretched on 20 m W-E and 18 m N-S, is located to the S of the previous one and consists of three round, mud-brick houses set at 4 to 5 m from each other (fig. 39). House 88, in the NE, measures 6.80 m in diameter with a doorway oriented S. A pile of firewood was recorded on its western flank. House 89, in the NW, is of almost the same size as the previous one, 6.90-m-in-diameter, with a doorway also oriented S. The recorded hearth is a rectangular, three-niches installation, with an appliqué, horizontal cordon at mid-height of the rear panel, and four protruding, equidistant clay tips along the upper side. House 90, the third feature of the complex, located in the SW at 5 m S of the previous house 89, is a 5.30-m-in-diameter horse house with the entrance oriented E. It is attached to a 4.90-m-long and 4.10-m-wide shelter built with eight supporting poles.

Habitation Complex 16

Habitation complex 16 is found in the west-northwestern part of the settlement and is part of the outer features' ring. It is spread over 25 m W-E and 20 m N-S and comprised of four features; three rectangular, mud-brick buildings and one round house (fig. 39). Two of the rectangular, houses, features 92 and 93, are attached to each other and constitute a single 14-m-long construction oriented roughly W-E and facing S. House 92, at the eastern end, measures 6.50 m in length and 3.00 m in width. It has an enclosed and sheltered courtyard, 5.90 m long and 3.10 m wide, with a plain hearth found along the western wall; a pile of firewood was recorded at the western end of the house's southern wall. Room 92a, a small and narrow feature measuring 3.00 in length and 2.20 m in width, used as goat shelter, is attached to both houses. House 93, at the western end, is 6.30 m long and 3.00 m wide. It has an attached, enclosed, and sheltered space extended over 5.90 m × 3.70 m. As is the case for the previous house 92, this one, too, has a plain hearth built in the courtyard but along the eastern wall, and a pile of firewood at exactly the same western end of the southern wall. Feature 94 is a round, mud-brick barn located at the western end of the complex. It is a relatively large house measuring 8.50 m in diameter, with its entrance oriented S. House 95, the remaining feature of the complex, found 2 m S of the barn, is oriented N-S, facing E. It measures 7.40 m in length and 3.20 m in width with an additional 7.50 m × 3.30 m patio.

Habitation Complex 17

Habitation complex 17 is constituted of two or three features located in the inner part of the settlement at 15 to 20 m S and SE of the previous one (fig. 39). House 91, located at the eastern end of the complex, measures 6.20 m in diameter with a doorway oriented NW. It is a round, mud-brick feature used for habitation, with a decorated hearth. The recorded decoration confined to the rear panel consists of an appliqué cordon with finger impressions at mid-height supporting a series of five equidistant, grooved, upward arrows. A small, elliptically shaped chicken coop and a pile of firewood were recorded in the northern side, along the house wall. The complex' second feature is comprised of two rooms (features 96 and 97), part of a 9.10 m, rectangular, mud-brick building oriented W-E and facing N. House 96, the living and sleeping component, at the eastern end, measures 6.10 m in length and 3.20 m in width and includes an adjunct, 6.10-m-long and 3.50-m-wide patio. Room 97, the kitchen, located at the western end, is almost square in shape and measures 3.20 m by 3.00 m. The recorded hearth is a two-niches, rectangular installation with a decorated rear panel. The decoration at mid-height of the rear panel consists of a horizontal band filled with five equidistant, grooved, upward arrows delimited by parallel appliqué cordons. Finally, there is a pile of firewood a few meters of the house's northwestern corner.

Habitation Complex 18

Habitation complex 18 is located due W of the settlement. Five of its six houses are found aligned NE-SW within the outer features' ring where they are stretched on approximately 40 m (fig. 39). The remaining feature is found at 10 m in the inner part of the village, with a relatively large tree located in the southern portion of the complex.

Houses 98 and 99 are distinct parts of a long tripartite, rectangular, mud-brick building oriented NNE-SSW, facing SE. The former, found at the northeastern end, measures 6.90 m in length and 3.10 m in width. It has an attached verandah, also 6.90 m long and 3.10 m wide, with two lateral mud-brick walls and two supporting poles. Room 98a, on the southwestern flank, is a toilet room, 2.60 m wide and 3.10 m long. The latter, at the opposite end, is a slightly larger room, 7.20 m in length and 3.10 m in width, with an enclosed patio 7 m long and 2.60 m wide. It has a small, semicircular toilet booth attached to the rear wall. Feature 101, the round goat house, is located 4 to 5 m SW. It measures 7 m in diameter with the entrance oriented E. House 107 is a new building not yet completed located at the southwestern end of the complex. It is oriented N-S faces E, and measures 7 m in length and 3.30 m in width. The kitchen, (feature 100) found in the eastern side of the complex, measures 5.80 m in diameter with a doorway oriented W. The recorded hearth is an almost plain, three-niches, rectangular installation. The rear panel is decorated in the upper part by two horizontal and parallel grooved lines in addition to six equidistant pointed tips along the upper side. Finally, there is a chicken coop, built in clay and located in the southern side of the complex, a few meters W of the large tree.

There is an 8.00-m-in-diameter goat corral at the junction of habitation complexes 16, 17, and 18. It is not known if this feature was used collectively by the three units or if it belongs to only one of them.

Habitation Complex 19

Habitation complex 19 is found due W of the settlement and includes two outer features' lines. It is constituted of nine features, inward oriented, and arranged in an oval-shaped pattern measuring 40 m in length NE-SE, and 30 m in width NW-SE (fig. 39). The complex's goat corral is located at the northeastern end; it is a sub-circular feature with a diameter varying from 5 to 6 m.

There are two rectangular, mud-brick buildings in the central part of the complex, dividing the extended family space into two equal parts. House 109, in the NW, is oriented roughly W-E, facing S. It is a 6.70-m-long by 3.00-m-wide feature, with an adjunct verandah built with four supporting poles and straw stores, 6.70 m in length and 2.70 m in width. Houses 114 and 115, located on the opposite side, are complementary parts of an L-shaped building, with the longest room (feature 114) oriented W-E and facing N. The living/sleeping room measures 6.90 m in length and 3.00 in width. It has an attached, 6.90 m × 2.70 m verandah abutting a recently added kitchen (feature 115), in fact, a small, 3.00-m-long and 2.8-m-wide perpendicular extension.

Goat house 103 and barn 108 are found in the northeastern half of the complex. They are located at 3 to 4 m from each other, with their doorways oriented S to SE. The former is a relatively small, 4.20-m-in-diameter, round, mud-brick feature, and the latter, a much larger 8.20-m-in-diameter one. Three round houses are found in the southwestern half. Barn 110, with a rectilinear rear-side measuring 8.60 m in length, has its entrance oriented E. The feature in fact measures 9.30 m in diameter. The grandmother's house, feature 111, is found at less than 2 m S of the previous one. It is a small, 4.60-m-in-diameter, round building with the doorway oriented E. A small chicken coop built in clay was found at 4 m E in the doorway axis. House 112, the remaining feature of the complex, is located a few meters SE; it measures 6.60 m in diameter, has a doorway oriented NE, and a small 3.00 m × 3.00 m verandah built with four supporting poles. Finally, there is a pile of firewood a few meters in the outer side between houses 111 and 112.

Habitation Complex 20

Habitation complex 20 is found in the western part of the settlement but, this time, in the inner part of the village. It is comprised of six features spread over a sub-circular area measuring some 25 m in average diameter (fig. 39). The houses are arranged into two roughly parallel N-S lines. Houses 105 and 106 are distinct parts of a long, rectangular, mud-brick building facing W, located along the complex's eastern edge, and partially surrounded by a wooden fence.The former, house 105, is found at the southern end of the building. It measures 6.50 m in length and 2.60 m in width and has an attached, small, 3.90-m-long and 2.50-m-wide verandah built with five supporting poles. The latter, house 106, at the northern end, is slightly smaller, measuring 6.30 m in length and 2.80 m in width. Its verandah, 4.40 m long and 2.10 m wide, is delimited on both southern and northern sides by mud-brick walls.

Round houses are found along the central axis of the complex. Feature 102, at the northern end, is a 6.20-m-in-diameter kitchen with a doorway oriented E. The recorded hearth is a three-niches, rectangular installation with the upper part of the rear panel decorated with two horizontal and parallel grooved lines and four equidistant, protruding tips. Finally, a pile of firewood was found next to the kitchen door, on the northern side. House 104, a few meters S and in a central position, is also a kitchen, measuring 4.20 m in diameter, with the entrance oriented SE. The hearth is a three-niches, rectangular installation with a decorated rear panel. The decoration consists of four registers delimited by two vertical and parallel grooved lines, each with an appliqué, upward arrow. A pile of firewood was recorded next to the wall, on the southern side. Feature 116, the goat house, is found at the southern end of the line. It has a doorway oriented NW and measures 5.30 m in diameter. The remaining feature of the complex consists of a circular, 7.00-m-in-diameter goat corral found in the W.

Habitation Complex 21

Habitation complex 21 is also located in the western part of the settlement, along the southern side of complexes 19 and 20 (fig. 39). It is comprised of four houses and one goat corral spread over a subcircular space measuring 25 m in average diameter. The recorded features are distributed into two sets, one consisting of two elements found in the NE and the other with three along the southwestern outer line. The goat corral, in the northeastern set at the edge of the complex, is elliptically shaped and surrounded by three other features. It measures 8.00 m in length in its SE-NW long axis and 4.00 m in the short NE-SW one. A small, circular, mud chicken coop has been recorded on the SE side. House 121 is a round, mud-brick construction found on the corral's western flank. It is a kitchen also used for sleeping, measuring 5.70 m in diameter with a doorway oriented SE. A small, 2.00 m × 2.00 m verandah built with four supporting poles shelters the feature's entrance. House 120, located 10 m S of the previous one, is a newly built, rectangular, mud-brick structure. It is oriented W-E, faces N, and measures 7.20 m in length and 3.10 m in width. House 119, at 5 m W, is a collapsed young man's house, measuring 5.90 m in diameter with its entrance oriented E. In fact, the house had been destroyed purposefully to be replaced by the new rectangular building. Finally, feature 113, the remaining house of the complex, is found less than 1 m N of the broken, down, young man's house. It is a horse house, measuring 5.10 m in diameter, with a doorway oriented E.

Habitation Complex 22

Habitation complex 22 is located in the western part of the settlement, within the village's inner space (fig. 39). It is constituted of five features arranged in an L-shaped pattern stretched on 34 m E-W and organized into two distinct subunits—one with houses 122 and 118 in the W, the other with features 131 and 132 in the E, with a relatively large barn in the middle.

The western subunit has two rectangular, mud-brick houses with different orientations. Feature 118, the kitchen, oriented W-E and facing S, measures 4.40 m in length and 2.90 m in width. It has a two-niches, rectangular hearth with two horizontal and parallel appliqué cordons on the rear panel. A pile of firewood was recorded along the kitchen's southern wall, on the eastern side. House 122, the living and sleeping room, is located 4 to 5 m S. It is oriented N-S, faces E, and measures 6.70 m in length and 3.00 m in width, with an adjunct 5.60-m-long and 2.50-m-wide verandah built with four supporting poles. Feature 117, the barn at the center of the complex, is a large, 10.40-m-in-diameter, round, mud-brick house with the doorway oriented SE.

The eastern subunit is comprised of one round and one rectangular building in a W-E linear arrangement. Feature 132, at the eastern end, is the kitchen surrounded by a 10-m-in-diameter fence. The construction measures 6.00 m in diameter with a doorway oriented S. The recorded hearth is a three-niches, rectangular installation with a decorated rear panel. The decoration is organized into two parts; the lower half has four equidistant, grooved, upward arrows and the upper half has two horizontal and parallel appliqué cordons with finger impressions. Kitchen 132 is attached to the living and sleeping room 131 with a mud-brick wall delimiting a toilet room. House 131 is, thus, a rectangular building, 6.70 m long and 3.10 m wide, with an adjunct verandah measuring 6.70 m in length and 2.60 m in width, built with four supporting poles.

Habitation Complex 23

Habitation complex 23 is found in the southwestern part of the settlement and consists of nine houses: four round and five rectangular spread over an elliptically shaped area 50 m long and 30 m wide. The complex features are distributed into three distinct subunits, one with houses 130 and 133 in the NE, the second in the

SE with features 126–129, and the third with houses 123, 124, and 125 in the NW (fig. 39).

Both features from the northeastern subunit have their doorways oriented W. The living and sleeping room 130 measures 6.10 m in length and 2.85 m in width. The added verandah, 6.00 long and 2.10 m wide, is built with four supporting poles. Feature 133, the 4.80-m-in-diameter kitchen located a few meters E, is surrounded on the rear side by a crescent-shaped fence abutting a pile of firewood. The kitchen hearth, a 1.60-m-long and 0.60-m-high, three-niches clay installation has a pseudo-crenellated rear panel decorated with a horizontal, appliqué cordon.

The southeastern subunit has four tightly knit features. House 129, located at the northeastern end, is a relatively small, rectangular building oriented NE-SW, facing NW, measuring 4.30 m in length and 2.90 m in width, with an attached 4.30-m-long and 1.80-m-wide verandah built with four supporting poles. Feature 128, the kitchen, is attached to the neighboring southern building by a mud-brick wall. It measures 3.60 m long and 2.90 m wide, with the doorway set in the southwestern wall. The recorded hearth is a four-niches, rectangular installation. The rear panel is decorated with three horizontal and parallel lines of pinched finger impressions, two of them on two appliqué cordons. The base has random finger impressions. House 127, the living and sleeping room of the subunit, is oriented W-E, faces N, measures 5.90 m in length and 3.00 m in width, and has an attached 5.90-m-long and 2.00-m-wide verandah shared with the kitchen and built with three supporting poles. Finally, house 126, the large 11.20-m-in-diameter barn with a doorway oriented N, is found at less than 1 m W (fig. 39).

The northwestern subunit is slightly looser, with two round houses and one rectangular building. Feature 124, the 5.80-m-in-diameter kitchen with an entrance oriented E and a pile of firewood, is located at the center of the subunit at equal distance from both the living/sleeping room and the barn. The recorded hearth is a plain, rectangular clay installation. House 123, at 4 m N, is oriented N-S, faces E, and measures 6.60 m in length and 3.20 m in width. It has a toilet room attached to its western wall and a 6.60-m-long and 2.90-m-wide verandah built with two lateral mud-brick walls and two supporting poles. Finally, the barn (feature 125) is found at the western end of the complex. It is a 8.50-m-in-diameter, round, mud-brick house with the doorway oriented E.

Habitation Complex 24

Habitation complex 24, owned by the Marabout (the Muslim scholar) is found due S of the settlement. It is the largest of the whole village with thirty-three features spread over 100 m E-W and 70 m N-S, with, in addition, fields 16 and 17. The latter field is fenced and measures 150 m in its longer SE-NW axis and 75 m in the shorter SW-NE one. The former, rectangular in shape, is delimited on the E

by an earth embankment and measures 100 m in length and 30 m in width. There
are nine rectangular buildings, nineteen round houses, and five livestock corrals
distributed into more or less patterned groups. Cattle corral 4 is clearly located at
the center of the complex (fig. 39). It is an elliptically shaped feature measuring
18.50 in length and 15.00 m in width. Feature 148, located in the N, is a 5.00-m-
in-diameter goat house with an entrance oriented SW surrounded by a 8.00-m-in-
diameter fence open on its southwestern flank.

The features found in the western part of the complex are arranged in two
roughly parallel N-S lines, with the westernmost one slightly looser. House 134 is
located at the northern end of the westernmost line; it is a relatively small, rectangular, mud-brick building oriented E-W, facing S, and measuring 5.90 m in length
and 3.10 m in width. It has an adjunct, 5.90-m-long and 2.50-m-wide verandah
built with six supporting poles. Feature 136, at 13 to14 m S, is a round, 8.80-m-
in-diameter barn with its doorway oriented NE. At the time of fieldwork, with livestock in the yaere dry-season camps, it was used as a habitation. Finally, house 37,
at the southern end of the line, is oriented E-W, facing N. It measures 6.90 m in
length and 3.00 m in width with an attached verandah of almost the same size,
6.90 m long and 3.10 m wide, built with four supporting poles. A two-niches hearth
with a decorated rear panel was found along the northern wall in the verandah. The
recorded decoration consists of a frame made with an appliqué cordon with the
delineated register filled with five parallel, short, vertical, appliqué cordons, all
decorated with single finger impressions. Houses 138, 139, and 140 caught fire and
burned out completely a few weeks before fieldwork. The first was the mother's
house, measuring 6.50 m in diameter. With the doorway oriented N; the second, a
8.90-m-in-diameter barn with the entrance oriented E and the third, a relatively
small, 4.90-m-in-diameter goat house. House 135, at the northern end of the second line, measures 8.40 m in diameter with the doorway oriented SW. The feature
is a temporary house built in wood and reeds after the destruction of part of the
compound. The recorded hearth is a three-niches, rectangular installation with a
decorated rear panel. Five equidistant, protruding tips are found along the upper
side, and the decoration consists of two parallel and horizontal, appliqué cordons
with single finger impressions with the intermediate space filled with six equidistant, grooved, upward arrows. Finally, goat corral XVIII, located at the center of
the line, is a subcircular feature with a diameter varying from 8.50 to 9.00 m.

A group of five features is found in the southern part of the complex (fig. 39).
It is comprised of two worn-out, round houses, one rectangular, mud-brick building, and two round dwellings still in use. Feature 144, one of the worn-out houses,
is found at the northwestern end of the subunit; it was a 4.20-m-in-diameter
grandmother's straw hut, which collapsed with the roof-supporting and five wall
poles left. The other, feature 146, is located 15 m E and consists of a simple
5.20-m-in-diameter shallow mud ring. Houses 141 and 142 are found at the center of the features' group. The former measures 4.90 m in diameter, with the doorway oriented N and a decorated hearth. The rear panel, on which the decoration is

found, is built with four equidistant, protruding clay tips. The motifs are organized
into two registers, an upper and a lower one. Two horizontal and parallel appliqué
cordons with single finger impressions are found in the upper register. The lower
one has five more or less equidistant, parallel, and vertical grooved upward arrows
underlined by a horizontal, appliqué cordon with single finger impressions. The
latter, located 1 m SE and inhabited by a great-grandmother, is of the same size, measuring 4.90 m in diameter, with the doorway also oriented N. Finally, house 143,
the remaining feature of the subunit is found at the eastern end. It is oriented
W-E, facing N, and measures 6.60 m in length and 2.90 m in width. The adjunct
verandah, 4.30 m long and 2.50 m wide, sheltering slightly more than the eastern
half of the house's front, is built with three supporting poles.

The southeastern subunit is comprised of seven features—three rectangular,
mud-brick buildings, three round houses, and the remains of a worn-out feature
delimited on the outer side by a fence (fig. 39). House 145, located at the western
end of the subunit, is a round, mud-brick feature used as a kitchen and sleeping
room. It measures 5.20 m in diameter, with a doorway oriented N and a decorated
hearth. The hearth's rear panel has two pointed upper corners with the decoration
consisting of pinched finger impressions on appliqué cordons along the lateral and
upper sides as well as the mid-panel. Building 169, in the SE, is a rectangular feature oriented W-E, facing N, and measuring 7.30 m in length and 3.00 m in width.
It has an adjunct patio slightly larger than the house itself, being 7.30 m long and
3.30 m wide. House 168, at 1 to 2 m N, is also rectangular and oriented N-S. It
faces E, measures 7.00 m in length and 3.00 m in width, with an attached 7.00-m-
long and 2.50-m-wide verandah built with four supporting poles. Feature 171, a
few meters E of the previous one, was a round, mud-brick house measuring
6.80 m in diameter, with a shallow, old foundation circle left. House 170, located
6 to 7 m S, is also a round, mud-brick house used as a kitchen and sleeping room.
It measures 6.30 m in diameter and has a doorway oriented N. The recorded hearth
is an almost plain, three-niches, rectangular installation with a horizontal, appliqué
cordon at mid-height of the rear panel. Finally, a pile of firewood was found next
to the house's wall, on its northeastern side. Feature 180, found at the complex's
southeastern corner, is a relatively large, 11.00-m-in-diameter barn with the entrance oriented NW. House 179, the remaining feature of the subunit is located 6
to 7 m N of the barn. It is a rectangular, mud-brick building oriented NE-SW and
facing NW. It measures 6.80 m in length and 3.00 m in width, with an attached
6.80-m-long and 2.80-m-wide verandah built with four supporting poles.

The central-eastern subunit is constituted of five features: two goat corrals and
three round, mud-brick houses arranged along a W-E line and stretched on 25 m
(fig. 39). Feature 176, at the western end, is a 5.60 m in diameter grandmother's
house with a doorway oriented SW. House 177, at 1 m E, is used as a donkey shelter; it also measures 5.60 m in diameter with the entrance oriented S. House 178,
at the eastern end of the line, used as a kitchen and sleeping room, is a 5.30-m-in-

diameter feature with the doorway oriented SE. The recorded hearth is a plain, two-niches, rectangular installation with a pseudo-crenellated rear panel. A pile of fire-wood was recorded next to the house's entrance in the SW. Finally, both circular goat corrals, XIX and XX, are found between houses 177 and 178. The former, in the N, is smaller, measuring 5.00 m in diameter, while the latter, in the S, is much larger, with a diameter of 8.00 m.

The northeastern subunit is comprised of six features—three rectangular con-structions, two round houses, and one goat corral. The latter, feature VII, found in the northwestern edge of the subunit, is oval-shaped and measures 8.00 in its long axis and 6.00 m in the short one. The houses are arranged in a U-shaped pattern with the rectangular buildings facing each other (fig. 39). House 150, the Mara-bout's main living and sleeping room, is found along the southern flank of the sub-unit. It is oriented W-E, facing N, and measures 6.60 m in length and 3.30 m in width. It has an adjunct, 6.60-m-long and 2.60-m-wide verandah built with four supporting poles. A smaller, almost square room, used as a kitchen and measuring 3.20 m × 3.00 m, was added on the western edge of the Marabout's house. Its door-way is oriented N and is set in the eastern part of the northern wall. The hearth is a three-niches, rectangular installation with a decorated rear panel. The recorded decoration consists of a frame delineated by appliqué cordons on all four sides filled with four parallel and equidistant, grooved, upward arrows. House 152 is lo-cated some 10 m N of the previous one. It is also oriented W-E, but faces S with a fence portion along its rear side. It measures 6.80 m in length and 3.00 m in width. The verandah is built with two short, mud-brick walls at its western end, in com-bination with three supporting poles, and provides an additional 6.80 m × 2.80 m space. Feature 151, abutting the goat corral and measuring 5.60-m-in-diameter with the entrance oriented NE, is used as a goat shelter. A small, rectangular chicken coop and a toilet room were found along the rear side of the goat house. Fea-ture 153, at the eastern end of the subunit, is also a round goat house. It is smaller than the previous one, measuring 4.60 m in diameter, with the entrance oriented S and two piles of firewood along its eastern flank.

Clearly, the Marabout's complex is inhabited by at least four generations, starting with the great-grandmother from house 142. Judging from the number and diversity of structural features, the Muslim scholar also appears to be the wealth-iest member of the Djidat II community.

Habitation Complex 25

Habitation complex 25, the village-headman (Bilama) extended family unit, is located in the southeastern part of the settlement. It is comprised of twenty-five features spread over an area measuring 86 m in its SE-NW axis and 58 m in the SW-NE one. The complex has an attached field (field 15) measuring 115 m in length and 58 m in width, delineated on its western side by an earth embankment. Part of the fenced field is devoted to a relatively large bull corral (corral V), 52 m long and 32 m wide. Depending on their location and orientation of doorways, habitation complex 25's features seem to be organized into two main subunits, with a few isolated cases (fig. 39).

The central subunit consists of twelve features arranged into two converging SW-NE lines. Five of the recorded features are round, mud-brick houses, six are rectangular buildings, and the remaining one, goat corral VIII, is an elliptically shaped pen, 10 m long and 7 m wide. House 174 is found at the western end of the northern features' line. It is a round, 6.30-m-in-diameter construction without hearth with the doorway oriented SE and is owned by Maimona, the village headman's first wife. House 183, found 7 to 8 m E, is a rectangular, mud-brick building oriented roughly W-E and facing S. The construction measures 7.10 m in length and 2.90 m in width, with an attached 6.80-m-long and 2.50-m-wide verandah built with four supporting poles. Feature 168, the kitchen, at less than 1 m E, measures 4.90 m in diameter with the doorway oriented SW. The hearth is a rectangular, three-niches installation, 1.30 m in length and 0.50 m in width, with a 0.90-m-high rear panel. The latter, decorated with two horizontal and parallel appliqué cordons delineating a register filled with five more or less equidistant, appliqué, upward arrows, has four equidistant, pointed tips along its upper side. House 162, located at the eastern end of the line, is the previous kitchen of Maimona with a collapsed hearth. It measures 6.90 m in diameter with a doorway oriented W. A pile of firewood was recorded next to the kitchen wall, on its northwestern side. Feature 13, N of the previous one, is a worn-out, round house reduced to a shallow circle measuring 5.30 m in diameter.

House 163 is located at the eastern end of the southern line. It is also an abandoned kitchen with an undecorated hearth, measuring 6.10 m in diameter, with the doorway oriented W. Rooms 165 and 166 are complementary parts of the same long, mud-brick building oriented roughly N-S and facing W, inhabited by Korsa, Maimona's and Bilama's firstborn son, his wife Ramata, and their three children. Room 165, the kitchen, found at the northeastern end of the building, measures 5.00 m in length and 3.10 m in width. Feature 166, the living and sleeping component, is slightly larger, 6.90 m long and 3.10 wide, with an adjunct, 6.90 m × 2.60 m verandah built with four supporting poles. House 173 is located at the center of the line. It is a rectangular kitchen oriented SW-NE, facing NW, and measuring 5.80 m in length and 3.20 m in width. The recorded hearth is decorated with a series of three equidistant, grooved, upward arrows underlined by a horizontal, appliqué cordon. Feature 172, the living and sleeping room is found 1 m W. It is also a rectangular, mud-brick building facing NW, oriented SW-NE, measuring 7.20 m in length and 3.10 m in width, with an attached 7.20-m-long and 2.40-m-wide verandah built with four supporting poles. An independent mud-brick toilet, 2.80 m long and 2.00 m wide, was built a few meters behind the main house, and two piles of firewood were recorded at both ends. Finally, house 182, with its entrance oriented NW, is a relatively large, 11.20-m-in-diameter barn located at the western end of the line.

The northern subunit consists of eight houses—four round and four rectangular arranged into a subcircular pattern measuring 30 m in average diameter (fig. 39). Houses 156 to 158 are large barns located along the northwestern side of the subunit. Barn 156, at the western end, belongs to Amina, the Bilama's third wife. It measures 10.50 m in diameter with a doorway oriented SE. Barn 157, owned by Maimona and located a few meters E, measures 9.00 m in diameter, with the entrance oriented S. And the third of the series, barn 158, located at the eastern end, belongs to Hepseta, the Bilama's second wife; it has an entrance oriented W and measures 8.50 m in diameter. The fourth round house is found at the southwestern corner of the subunit; it is a relatively small, 3.90-m-in-diameter feature, with the doorway oriented NE and an undecorated hearth. Rectangular constructions are organized along two perpendicular axes, with features 155 and 156 on the NW-SE axis facing NE, and buildings 159 and 160 along the WSW-ENE one, roughly facing N. House 155 belongs to Amina, the Bilama's third wife; it measures 7.10 m in length and 3.30 m in width, and has an adjunct, 7.10-m-long and 2.90-m-wide verandah built with four supporting poles. House 154, located a few meters N, is being built. It is 6.50 m long and 3.00 m wide. Houses 159 and 160 are located 2.40 m from each other along the southeastern side of the subunit. The former measures 6.10 m in length and 3.00 in width, with an attached verandah extended over 6.10 m by 2.00 m and built with four supporting poles. The latter is slightly longer, with 7.10 m in length, but narrower, with 2.70 m in width, with a larger verandah built with four supporting poles and measuring 7.10 m long and 2.30 m wide.

Three features are relatively isolated. House 181, an out of use round kitchen located in the southwestern part of the complex, measuring 7.80 m in diameter, with a doorway oriented NW and a three-niches hearth decorated with five more or less equidistant, grooved, upward arrows underlined by a horizontal, appliqué cordon. It is connected to barn 167, the second isolated structure, found at some 15 m NE with a fence. The latter is a relatively large feature measuring 11.20 m in diameter, with its entrance oriented NW. Finally, house 164, the third isolated feature, found in the eastern side of the complex, is a rectangular, mud-brick house oriented NNW-SSE, facing W, with a short fence along its southern side. It is inhabited by a refugee from the nearby Chad Republic; and as is generally the case, it is up to the village headman to implement the hospitality requirement for any person in need. The house measures 6.90 m in length and 3.30 m in width, with an adjunct, 6.90-m-long and 3.90-m-wide verandah built with four supporting poles. All the round kitchens located around house 164 were left to collapse, supporting the view that part of the complex was granted to the refugee's family and the features that belonged to the Bilama's wife were relocated elsewhere in the complex.

Djidat II is the most densely inhabited settlement of all the localities considered in this study. As can be seen from the average density of features and their distribution into different habitation complexes, larger extended families are found clustered in the southeastern half of the village (table 34). The habitation complexes of the Marabout (the Muslim scholar) in charge of the Friday Mosque and the Bilama (the village headman) are found next to each other in the southeastern quadrant of the settlement. The rest of the site is inhabited by smaller family units, with what can be termed craft specialists clustered in the north-northeastern quadrant. The ring of fields, with seventeen fenced and well-demarcated plots ranging in length from 45 m (field 7) to 110 m (field 17), and width from 20 m (field 2) to 90 m (field 4), is but a minute part of the settlement's cultivated field systems. In this case, with the exception of fields 15, 16, and 17 belonging to the Marabout and the Bilama, the ownership of fenced fields was not tracked systematically. Finally, with the Friday Mosque, the engine-pulled and the hand-operated mills, the "retail shops," and the metalworkers servicing the whole area at approximately 8 to 10 kilometers around, Djidat I and II are clearly components of an important emerging center.

Chapter 11

Marafaine

Introduction

Marafaine is located 12° latitude N and 14°58′ longitude E, along the Houlouf-Logone-Birni road track and at 1.5 kilometers NW of Abuzrega. As is the case for the latter settlement, this one too is found in that part of the landscape permanently above flood level. According to census data published in 1978, the population of Marafaine amounted to fifty-four inhabitants in 1969 and sixty-six in 1976–1977 (Elingui 1978). The latter 1976–1977 census provides more precise information on the sex ratio, with thirty-six males and thirty females.

Marafaine has a perfectly circular shape and comprises a ring of houses surrounded by an outer ring of fenced fields (fig. 41). The inner ring of built facilities measures 160 m in diameter; the settlement is thus extended over a surface of 2.01 hectares. The width of the outer ring, with the fenced fields, varies from 45 m in the E to 100 m in the W. If combined, the village and its intensively cultivated area are spread over 8.04 hectares.

The village is accessed through three roads and one footpath set according to the cardinal directions. The principal and larger road, 12 m in width, is found in the W and connects the village directly to the main Houlouf-Logone-Birni traffic (fig. 41). The village well is found at some 30 m behind the ring of houses, on the northern side of the main access road. It is 13 m deep with a 4-m-in-diameter curb with two symmetric 1 m × 1 m drinking troughs. The southern and eastern roads are 6 to 4 m wide on average, with the former closed with a heavy log. Finally, the footpath is found in the N. It is 2.5 m wide, closed at the southern end by a fence. The central part of the village is almost empty with two features of communal interest, the mosque and a large cattle corral. The mosque, still being built, is found in the eastern part of the central area. It is a rectangular, mud-brick building oriented N-S with the doorway at the middle of the western wall. The construction measures 6.70 m in length and 4.70 m in width. The Mihrab indicating the direction of the Mekka, protruding at the middle of the eastern wall, measures 1.60 m in length and 1.0 m in width. A large 5-m-in-diameter pit (pit 1), from which the

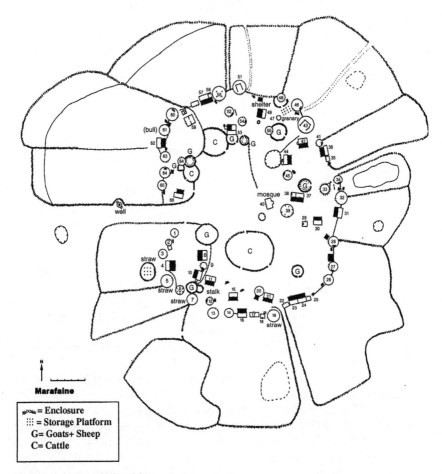

Figure 41: Map of Marafaine

construction material used for the mosque was probably collected, is found at 3 to 4 m SW. The large cattle corral is found in the southern part of the village's central area. It is an oblong feature, 35 m long in its W-E axis and 28 m wide in the N-S one, with three entrances/exits. Finally, Marafaine is comprised of sixty-seven round and quadrangular houses, distributed into ten habitation complexes with frequency of features varying from three to twelve (table 35).

Habitation Complex 1

Habitation complex 1 is located in the southwestern part of the village, along the southern road's side. It consists of nine houses: three rectilinear and six round; two

Table 35: Marafaine houses and features distribution

Cluster number	Number of features	Number of units	Habitation houses		Livestock houses	
			C	R	C	R
1	12	3	2	3	4	—
2	13	3	2	6	4	—
3	9	3	2	4	1	—
4	10	3	1	5	3	—
5	6	3	2	4	—	—
6	7	1	1	—	3	—
7	5	1	1	1	1	—
8	8	2	1	5	1	—
9	6	2	1	2	2	—
10	6	2	1	1	2	—
Total	82	23	14	31	21	—

goat corrals, one straw rack, and two fenced fields. The complex's features are arranged in a horseshoe shape open in the N (fig. 41).

Features 1 to 5 are arranged in what can be termed the western line. Feature 1, located at the northwestern end, measures 5.80 m in diameter. It is a circular, mud-brick horse house, built with its entrance oriented S. House 2, a 4.40-m-in-diameter, round, mud-brick kitchen is found at 2.5 m S. It is also built with the doorway oriented S, opening into a square, 2.3 m × 2.3 m verandah supported by four poles. The hearth, a plain, two-niches feature with a rectangular rear panel, is found to the N of the house, opposite the entrance, and a pile of firewood has been recorded next to the kitchen wall, on its eastern side. Feature 3, at 3.5 m SW of the kitchen, has its entrance oriented SE. It is a round, mud-brick construction used as a bull house, measuring 6.60 m in diameter. House 4, in a relative central position, is surrounded by the bull house (feature 3) in the N, the straw enclosure (feature 68) at 8 m W, and barn/cattle house 5 at some 3 m S. It is a rectangular, mud-brick building with a patio built with mud-brick and, as such, delineating an enclosed courtyard. The house, oriented N-S and facing E, measures 6.80 m in length and 3.10 m in width. The patio adds a sheltered courtyard 6.80 m long and 3.95 m wide. The straw storage enclosure, located behind house 4, measures 12 m in diameter; it comprises a 5 m × 4.5 m nine-poles rack. The barn/cattle house 5, at 3 m S of feature 4, is a 9-m-in-diameter wood and straw construction, with the entrance oriented NE. It is attached to the field fence in the rear part and, surrounded on its front side by another fence.

Feature 6, at the southern end of the complex, at 3.6 m SE of the barn, measures 6.5 m in diameter; it is a goat house built in mud-brick, with the entrance oriented NE, and seven milking poles arranged in a circular pattern. The eastern line is comprised of two goat enclosures at both ends, with, in between, features 8 to 10. The smaller goat corral is found at the southern end of the line. It measures 8 m in diameter with an entrance oriented NW. The northern, and larger, goat enclosure is 15 m in diameter, with, surprisingly, an entrance opening E in the central part of the village.

There is virtually no significant space left between eastern line dwelling structures, with gaps varying from 1.20 m (feature 8 to 9) to 2.20 m (feature 9 to 10). House 10, separated from the southern goat corral by the end part of the complex's eastern fence, faces W and is oriented roughly N-S. It is a rectangular, mud-brick building with a complementary sheltered area and an attached chicken coop. The house measures 6.20 m in length and 3.20 m in width, and the verandah is supported by eight poles and measures 6.30 m long and 2.80 m wide. The gap between houses 10 and 9 is filled with a four-pole wooden rack. The latter feature is a 4.80-m-in-diameter, round, mud-brick kitchen with a doorway oriented W. The hearth is found in the standard position, in the right-hand side of the house. It is a two-niches, 1.25-m-long, 0.70-m-wide and 0.75-m-high feature with a decorated, rounded corners rear panel. The recorded decoration, found in the upper part of the panel, consists of five equidistant, vertical, and parallel appliqué upward arrows underlined by a horizontal, appliqué cordon. House 8, 6.20 m long and 3.20 m wide, is the third rectangular, mud-brick building in the complex. It is oriented N-S, faces W, and has a corrugated tin roof. The verandah, 6.30 m long and 2.80 m wide, is also built with mud-brick, providing an enclosed courtyard.

Finally, fields 12 and 13 complement the complex estate. The former measures 62 m in length and 25 m in width, and the latter, 48 m long and 40 m wide. With the exception of the northern goat corral, the layout of habitation complex 1's features, delineated by an enclosing fence, is clearly inward-oriented with an open space in the middle.

Habitation Complex 2

Habitation complex 2, the Bilama's extended family unit, is found due S of the settlement. It is stretched on 70 m W-E and measures 30 m in maximum width (fig. 41). The complex, with two large trees, is constituted of twelve houses: six quadrangular and six circular; one sorghum-stalk storage enclosure, and two fenced fields. With the exception of the subcircular, 5.00-m-in-diameter storage enclosure and the straw barn (feature 7) located in the western end and attached to habitation complex 1's southern goat corral, the features are arranged into two roughly parallel lines. Houses 11, 15, 20, and 21, in the northern line, are facing S; and features 12 to 14 and 16 to 19 have their doorways generally oriented N. House 7 measures 8 m in diameter. It is a barn/cattle construction built with wood and straw with its entrance oriented NE.

House 13 is located at the western end of the southern line (fig. 41). It is a grandmother's habitation unit with the lower wall part built in mud-brick and the

upper one with straw. The construction measures 8.10 m in diameter with a doorway oriented NE. Goat house 14 is located 4 m E of the grandmother's dwelling.
It is a round, mud-brick feature, 6.20 m in diameter, with the entrance oriented NE,
attached to neighboring house 16 by a short, 3-m-long fence. The latter is a rectangular, mud-brick building with an adjunct shelter oriented W-E and facing N.
It measures 6.80 m in length and 3.40 m in width, while the verandah built with
six supporting poles, is also 6.80 m long but only 3 m wide. House 17, at 2.60 m E,
is, similarly, a rectangular, mud-brick building facing N, oriented W-E, and measuring 6.80 m long and 3.50 m wide. Feature 18, the almost square kitchen, 3.5 m
in length and 3.3 m in width, is found at 1 m E of house 17. The hearth is found
along the southern wall opposite to the door. It is a four-niches, 1.25-m-long, 0.90-m-
wide, and 0.75-m-high rectangular feature, with a lavishly decorated panel. The
recorded decoration consists of a general frame made with parallel lines of pinched
finger impressions on an appliqué cordon divided into two equal parts by a horizontal cordon also with pinched finger impressions. The upper and the lower register are filled with four more or less equidistant, parallel, appliqué, upward arrows.
A low, square, 1.1 m × 1.1 m, four-pole firewood rack was found next to the
kitchen's N wall, on the eastern side. House 19, at the eastern end of the line, at
1.5 m from the square kitchen, is a round barn 9.4-m-in-diameter, built with wood
and straw with the entrance oriented N-NW; it is surrounded on the E by the end
portion of field 10's fence.

   The northern line, with four houses, is slightly looser. House 11, at the western end, is a rectangular, mud-brick building with an adjunct shelter built with six
supporting poles. It is oriented W-E and measures 7.5 m in length and 3.7 m in
width for the house proper and 7.5 m in length and 3 m in width for the verandah.
A large tree and a large pile of firewood are found at 7 to 8 m E of the previous
house. Feature 15, a rectangular, young man's house, not strictly in the axis of the
northern line, is located, nonetheless, in the central part of the habitation complex.
It is a 6.2-m-long and 3-m-wide mud-brick building with an adjunct, 6.2-m-long
and 2.2-m-wide verandah built with six supporting poles. Another pile of firewood
was recorded a few meters from the young man's house's northeastern corner. Finally, there are two features at the eastern end of the northern line. One, house 20,
is a round, mud-brick construction used to shelter goats. It measures 6.4 m in diameter, with a doorway oriented SW, and an attached, square shelter measuring
2.90 × 2.90 m built with four supporting poles. The other, house 21, is a rectangular, mud-brick house 7 m long and 3.4 m wide, with a complementary 7 m ×
2.4 m verandah built with six supporting poles. House 12, the last built feature of
the complex, is found in the western half, between houses 11 and 13. It is a round,
mud-brick construction, 5.9-m-in-diameter, with the entrance oriented NE, used
as a kitchen. The hearth, situated in the western part of the house, in the standard
right-hand side position, measures 1.25 m in length, 0.90 m in width, and 0.60 m
in height. It is a plain, rectangular feature with four niches. A storage rack, 1.6 m
long and 1 m wide, was recorded next to the kitchen, on its eastern side.

Fields 10 and 11 (fig. 41) are extended southward. The former, measuring 85 m in length and 65 m in width, has a large heap of goat droppings used as fertilizer. The latter is smaller with 75 m in maximum length and 55 m in width. Even if the habitation complex is not an entirely fenced unit, the inward disposition of dwelling features is clearly attested, as was the case for habitation complex 1.

Habitation Complex 3

Habitation complex 3 is found in the southeastern portion of the settlement. It is comprised of seven houses arranged in a crescent-shaped, linear pattern, with features generally connected by a fence, a circular 8-m-in-diameter goat corral situated in the inner part of the village, with the entrance/exit oriented S, and finally, a fenced sorghum field (field 9) measuring 100 m in length and 60 m in width (fig. 41). The dwelling facilities are organized into three distinct units, with four houses in the southern, two in the central, and one in the northern.

House 22, at the western end of the southern unit, was built to be a kitchen but was used in the interim as a goat shelter. It is a small, rectangular, mud-brick building facing NW and oriented roughly W-E, measuring 4.5 m in length and 3 m in width. Houses 23 to 25 form a coherent long, rectangular, mud-brick building divided into three parts. Feature 23, measuring 6.60 m in length and 3.10 m in width faces N and has an adjunct, enclosed courtyard delimited by mud-brick walls. The enclosed additional space is 6.60 m long and 3 m wide. House 24, attached to the previous one, is 6.10 m long and 3.10 m wide with a doorway oriented N. Its verandah, built with seven supporting poles, measures 6.10 m in length and 2.5 m in width. Feature 25, the kitchen, is a square 3.10 m × 3.10 m room with the entrance set in the W end on the northern wall. The hearth, a rectangular, 1.25-m-long, 0.60-m-wide, and 0.67-m-high two-niche feature, is located at the southeastern corner. The decoration is confined to the upper half of the rear panel. It consists of a rectangular frame of appliqué cordons with parallel lines of pinched finger impressions filled with five equidistant, vertical, appliqué, upward arrows also with pinched finger impressions. Finally, a pile of firewood was recorded at 1 to 2 m NE of the kitchen corner.

A 10-m-long fence connects the firewood pile to house 26 of the central unit. It is a 7-m-in-diameter mud-brick construction, with the doorway oriented NW, and is used as a goat shelter. Another pile of firewood was found next to the feature's wall, on the southwestern side. House 27, at 2 to 3 m N, is also a round, mud-brick construction, with the entrance oriented due W. It is used for habitation, measures 6.80 m in diameter, and comprises a decorated hearth found in the standard right-hand side position. The recorded hearth is a three-niches, rectangular feature, 1 m in length, 0.75 m in width, and 0.70 m in height. The decoration in the upper half of the rear panel is similar in all aspects but one (the number of upward arrows) to that found in kitchen 25, in other words, four equidistant appliqué upward arrows with pinched finger impressions in a frame of appliqué cordons also with parallel lines of pinched finger impressions. The shelter, built on the northern side of house 27, is used as a retail-shop, selling matches, cigarettes, sugar, et cetera. It is built with six supporting poles and measures 5 m in length and 4 m in width. A chicken coop was recorded at the southwestern corner of the shelter.

House 28, at 8.80 m N, is located at the northern end of the complex. It is surrounded by a pile of firewood in the S and a square 3 m × 3 m shelter built with nine supporting poles in the NW. The feature is a round, 7.20-m-in-diameter, mud-brick house, with a doorway oriented W. The hearth is found in the S, in the standard position; it is a four-niches, rectangular installation, 1 m long, 0.60 m wide, and 0.60 high, decorated in the upper third of the rear panel by a rectangular frame filled with short, vertical, and parallel appliqué cordons, all with corncob impression.

Habitation Complex 4

Habitation complex 4 is located due E (fig. 41). It is constituted of eight houses and one goat corral arranged into an elliptically shaped pattern, 50 m long W-E and 35 m wide N-S. The goat corral measures 8.60 m in diameter; fifteen regularly spaced goat-milking posts were found arranged in a circle along the enclosure's inner perimeter. Two fenced fields (field 7 and 8), measuring 50 m in length and 35 m in width for the larger field 8,and 53 m × 23 m for the smaller field 7, complement the habitation complex's estate. A large circular pit, 8-m-in-diameter and 1.5 m deep, was found in field 8; it is the source of the construction material used for the complex houses. A relatively large dump of goat droppings, 35 m long and 15 m in maximum width, was recorded in field 7; the device aims to produce animal manure to be used as fertilizer later.

Habitation complex 4 houses, all built with mud-brick, are distributed into five quadrangular and four round features. Most of the round houses are located in the N-NE, with one case in the W. Three of them are livestock houses, the last one being a habitation. The round habitation, house 34, is found in the NE of the complex. It is a 6-m-in-diameter mud-brick construction with the doorway oriented SW. The hearth, located in the standard right-hand side position, is a rectangular, three-niches feature, 1.10 m long, 0.50 m wide, and 0.70 m high, with three equidistant, pointed tips on the upper side of the rear panel. The hearth decoration consists of a horizontal band of six equidistant, short, vertical, appliqué, upward arrows. Both goat house 33 and barn/cattle house 32 are located 5 m S of the round habitation, SW for the former and S for the latter. House 33 measures 6.20 m in diameter with its entrance oriented SW. It has an attached chicken coop in the rear side and is entirely surrounded with regularly spaced goat-milking posts. House 32, the barn/cattle feature, is attached to its neighbor by a fence. It has its doorway oriented SW and measures 9 m in diameter. Two piles of firewood disposed on both sides of the fence were recorded on the northern flank of the barn. The remaining round house 39, is also a barn located among rectilinear constructions. It measures 9.10 m in diameter with the entrance oriented SE. Two symmetric sets of three equidistant tethering poles were found in the barn.

Rectilinear features are found in the southern half of the complex, with one located in the NW. The latter comprises a living/sleeping room, termed house 37, and an attached kitchen in house 38. The building is oriented W-E and faces S. The living/sleeping room is 6 m long and 3 m wide, the kitchen measuring 3.4 m in length and 3 m in width, both sharing the 9.4 m × 2.7 m verandah built with eight supporting poles. The hearth, recorded in kitchen 38, is located along the western wall; it is a rectangular, five-niches, 1.50-m-long, 0.70-m-wide, and 0.60-m-high with a decorated rear panel. The rear panel has four equidistant, pointed tips on its upper side and the uncovered decoration consists of parallel lines of pinched finger impressions on appliqué cordons defining a rectangular frame. The remaining three rectilinear features are set in a W-E line. Feature 30, at the western end, is a newly built wood and straw kitchen, 3.80 m long and 3.40 m wide, with the entrance oriented N and situated at the eastern end of the northern wall. Located 4 m E, House 29 has a doorway in the middle of the northern wall. The building is 6.30 m long and 3.30 m wide, with an adjunct 6.30 m × 2.30 m verandah built with four supporting poles. House 31, found at 15 m E, is oriented N-S facing W. It is linked to its neighbors by the complex's fence, measures 7 m in length and 3.10 m in width, and has an additional sheltered space, 7.00 m long and 2.90 m wide, built with six supporting poles.

The layout of habitation complex 4 and the disposition of houses' doorways show a clear trend toward an inward orientation, already seen in habitation complexes 1 and 2. The complex also has the advantage of the presence of two relatively large trees.

Habitation Complex 5

Habitation complex 5 is located in the northeastern side of the village (fig. 41). It is constituted of six houses: two round and four rectangular, arranged in a semi-circular pattern open in the S. It is delimited in the NW by a fence abutting a very large pit, 12-m-in-diameter and 1 m deep, and is attached to field 6 stretched eastward and measuring 75 m in length and 28 m in width. The complex's features are organized into three "functional" units, each inhabited by a nuclear family.

Unit 1 is located in the eastern side of the complex and consists of a long, rectangular, mud-brick building oriented N-S and facing W (fig. 41). The building is divided into two rooms, the southern (house 35) being the kitchen, and the northern (house 36), the living and sleeping area. The kitchen measures 4.40 m in length and 2.90 m in width. The doorway is set in the middle of the western wall and the hearth is located along the northern wall, on the left-hand side. The latter is a rectangular, two-niches, 1.10-m-long, 0.60-m-wide and 0.70-m-high installation with decoration confined to the upper part of the rear panel. The recorded decoration consists of four equidistant and parallel appliqué upward arrows underlined by an appliqué, horizontal cordon. House 36, the living/sleeping room, is 6.80 m long and 2.90 m wide. It has an adjunct verandah 6.80 m in length and 2.70 m in width, built with six supporting poles. The nuclear family's supply of firewood was found piled next the kitchen southern wall.

Unit 2, to the N of the complex, is comprised of houses 41 and 42 located 5.50 m apart. Feature 41, the kitchen, is a round, mud-brick construction measuring 4.80 m in diameter with the doorway oriented W. The hearth is located in the eastern part opposite to the entrance. It is a two-niches feature, rectangular in shape, with a round cornered rear panel, measuring 1.25 m long, 0.70 m wide, and 0.80 m high. The hearth decoration consists of a double frame made with appliqué cordons, with, in both upper and lower registers, three equidistant and parallel appliqué upward arrows. House 42, oriented W-E and facing S, is a rectangular, mud-brick building, 6.60 m in length and 3.20 m in width. It has a complementary 6.60 m × 2.70 m shelter built with six supporting poles. Finally, a small, mud chicken coop is attached to the house's western wall.

Unit 3 is situated in the western side of the complex and comprises two houses. House 44, the living and sleeping room, is a rectangular, mud-brick construction, oriented N-S and facing E, and measuring 6.80 m long and 3 m wide. The attached verandah built with six supporting poles, is 6.80 m in length and 2.60 m in width. In addition, there is a toilet room, 2.70 m long and 1.90 m wide, built in mud-brick and attached to the house's western wall. House 45, the kitchen, is found at 4 m S. It is a round, mud-brick feature. 6 m in diameter, with the entrance oriented NE. The hearth is found in the northwestern part and, as such, in the standard right-hand side position. It is a four-niches installation, 1.25 m long, 0.70 m wide, and 0.75 m high. The rear panel is decorated with six equidistant and parallel appliqué upward arrows underlined by an appliqué, horizontal cordon. Finally, a pile of firewood was recorded next to the kitchen wall, on the eastern side.

Habitation complex 5 features are facing each other with what can be termed the extended family courtyard in the middle. The use of the same decorative motif on all the extended families hearths, that of equidistant and parallel appliqué upward arrows, is particularly striking in this case.

Habitation Complex 6

Habitation complex 6 is comprised of eight features; four round houses, two corrals, a wood rack, and a granary; all located in the north-northeastern part of the village. The complex's estate is complemented by field 5, measuring 77 m in length and 65 m in width and divided into two almost equal parts by a footpath (fig. 41). A relatively large heap of goat droppings, future fertilizer, was recorded. The complex is clearly a single family unit with features arranged into two groups. One group with three houses is organized into a NW-SE line with the habitation in central position. House 46 is inhabited by an elderly couple. The feature is built in mud-brick and measures 8 m in diameter with its doorway oriented SW. The hearth is found in the southeastern part of the house, in the standard right-hand side position. It is a two-niches, rectangular feature, 0.80 m long, 0.60 m wide, and 0.65 m high, and, as is generally the case for elderly people's fireplaces, is undecorated. A small shelter, 2.20 m × 2.10 m, also used for storage and built with six supporting poles, is found next to the house on its southern side. A large low storage platform, 5.40 m in length and 3.20 m in width, built with four rows of three poles each, is located before the main house. Barn 43, at 5 m S, is attached to the previous one by a fence. It is a large, 11.80-m-in-diameter mud-brick construction with the entrance oriented SW. An installation with seven tethering poles connected to each other with wooden sticks and defining a square with three sides was found in the barn. House 48, with its attached enclosure located at the northwestern end of the line, is a horse feature. The house built in mud-brick with its door oriented S measures 5.80 m in diameter. The attached enclosure, elliptical in shape, is 10 m long and 4 m wide. A pile of firewood was recorded at the eastern end of the horse corral.

The second group of features is located in the inner side of the site. Feature 47 is a relatively large Mousgoum-style granary made with sun-dried clay. It is a tronconically shaped installation measuring 2.40 in base diameter and more than 2 m in height. It is set at 0.50 m above ground resting on four thick logs. House 50 measures 5.90 m in diameter. It is a mud-brick goat feature with the doorway oriented E, opening on a relatively large, 11-m-in-diameter enclosure.

Habitation Complex 7

Habitation complex 7, a single nuclear family unit, is found due N of the village. It is comprised of five features; three houses, a shelter and a goat corral; stretched on 45 m N-S. It is complemented by a rectangular, fenced field (field 4), 50 m long and 45 m wide, divided into two parts by a footpath (fig. 41). The goat corral, 6 m in diameter, is located in the inner part of the site, with an entrance/exit oriented N; it comprises nine milking posts arranged in a circular pattern. House 54, at 7 m N of the enclosure, is a round, mud-brick kitchen measuring 6 m in diameter, with the doorway oriented NE. The hearth is located in the eastern part of the feature, on the left-hand side. It is a rectangular, two-niches installation, 1.10 m long, 0.60 m wide, and 0.80 m high. The rear panel is decorated on both vertical sides by two parallel lines of pinched finger impressions on appliqué cordons, with, on the upper third, a horizontal register filled with four appliqué rectangles. House 49, at 10 m E, is the living and sleeping room. It is a rectangular, mud-brick building,

6.50 m in length and 2.80 m in width, oriented N-S and facing W. It has an attached verandah built with six supporting poles and measuring 6.50 m long and 3.60 m wide. A pit, 2 m in diameter, is found a few meters S of the house's southern wall. The barn, feature 51, is located 15 m NW of the main house, at the northern end of the complex, and inserted in the field's fence. It is a relatively large, 10.20-m-in-diameter, round, mud-brick construction with the door oriented S. A set of five tethering poles arranged in a U-shaped pattern has been recorded in the central part of the barn. Finally, there are a set of three tethering poles along the western side of the complex, a pile of firewood, and a sorghum storage rack along the field's fence in the N. The latter, built with six supporting poles, measures 3.20 m in length and 2.50 m in width.

The layout of the habitation complex's features is an unusual one; livestock installations are found at both southern and northern ends, with the living/sleeping room and kitchen in between.

Habitation Complex 8

Habitation complex 8 is also located in the north-northwestern part of the village. It consists of seven features; a goat corral and six houses arranged in L-shaped pattern, 42 m long N-S and 30 m wide W-E, with a fan-shaped field 3, 95 m in maximum length and 55 m in width (fig. 41). An earth embankment oriented W-E runs parallel to the field's northern fence, at some 40 m behind the line of houses. The relatively large, 20-m-in-diameter cattle corral, attached to one of the complex's feature, is probably a communal installation, as suggested by the SE orientation of its entrance.

The S-N line is comprised of three features. The goat corral, measuring 8 m in diameter, is found at the southern end attached to the rear wall of the neighboring house, with an entrance oriented SE. House 53 is the most complex building of the village; it is an almost square, mud-brick construction, 6.70 m long W-E and 6.40 m wide N-S, with an attached chicken coop. The house is divided into three parts: a sheltered courtyard in the NW, 4 m long and 3.10 m wide, with a doorway oriented N; a storage room, 4 m in length and 3.60 m in width, in the NE with the door oriented W and opening in the courtyard; and finally, the living/sleeping room, 6.70 m long and 2.40 m wide, with the entrance oriented N and opening in the courtyard. House 52 is located 5 m N of the previous one and has its entrance oriented S. It is the habitation complex's kitchen, built in mud-brick, and measuring 5.40 m in diameter. The recorded hearth is found in the standard right-hand side position in the SE. It is an undecorated, two-niches, rectilinear feature, 1.70 m long, 0.60 m wide and 0.64 m high.

Feature 55 is located at the eastern end of the W-E line. It is a 10.10-m-in-diameter, mud-brick barn, attached to the neighboring complex barn 51 by a fence, with the doorway oriented S. Four tethering poles were recorded in the central part of the feature, and a pile of firewood was found next to the wall, on the south-western side. House 56 and 57 are complementary parts of the same 9.10-m-long and 3.10-m-wide rectangular, mud-brick building, oriented W-E and facing S. The former at the eastern end is a 3.10-m-long and 2.30-m-wide kitchen, with the hearth located along the northern wall opposite the entrance. The recorded hearth has two niches, rectangular in shape; it measures 1.10 m in length, 0.65 m in width, and 0.66 m in height. The decoration consists of a register framed with appliqué cordons filled with four appliqué upward arrows with, in addition, an anchor-like motif. The latter is a 6.80-m-long and 3.10-m-wide living and sleeping room. Both rooms share the 9.10-m-long and 2.90-m-wide verandah built with seven support-ing poles. Finally, feature 58, located at the western end, is attached to the neigh-boring complex by a short fence. It is a rectangular "discussion house" facing S, built with wood and straw, and measuring 5.80 m in length and 3.10 m in width.

Habitation Complex 9

Habitation complex 9 is found along the northwestern part of the settlement. It is a fenced unit with five houses, three round and two rectangular, a goat corral, and a storage rack, with, in addition, an elongated fenced field 2, which measures 95 m in length and 52 m in width. An earth embankment, in fact, the continuation of that already reported for the neighboring complex 8, runs parallel to the outer fence at 40 to 84 m behind the houses (fig. 41). Two relatively large trees are found in the central part of the complex with its features organized into three subunits.

The northwestern subunit consists of houses 60 to 62 connected to each other by short fences and arranged in a roughly N-S line. House 60, at the northern end, is a round, mud-brick kitchen measuring 9 m in diameter, with the doorway ori-ented E. The hearth, found in the northern part of the feature, measures 1.25 m in length, 0.60 m in width, and 0.65 m in height. It is a rectangular feature with two hearthstones and a rear panel decorated in the upper part by three equidistant, ver-tical, appliqué cordons underlined by an additional horizontal one. A pile of firewood and a storage platform are found in the space between house 60 and 61, the for-mer in the outer side, and the latter, built with four supporting poles and measuring 2 m × 2 m, in the inner one. Located 4 m SW of the previous feature, house 61 is also a round, mud-brick construction used as a bull shelter. It measures 7.70 m in diameter and has a doorway oriented E. House 62, at the southern end, is found at 2 m from the central bull house. It is a rectangular building with an enclosed court-yard oriented N-S and facing E. The room measures 6.80 m in length and 3.30 m in width, and the mud-brick verandah 5.80 m by 3 m. There is a short fence link-ing house 62 to its southern neighbor, and a pile of firewood, recorded next to the southeastern corner.

The southern subunit comprises two features, one house and a goat corral. The former, house 64, is a round, mud-brick construction, 5 m in diameter, with the entrance oriented N; it is used to shelter goats. The latter, is an 8-m-in-diameter goat enclosure with an entrance/exit oriented NE. Two concentric series of milking posts have been recorded in the corral, the inner ring with seven poles and the outer one with thirteen.

The northern subunit consists of a house and a storage rack. The storage rack is built with seven supporting poles and measures 3 m in length and 2.5 m in width. House 59 is a rectangular, mud-brick building oriented NW-SE facing SW. The room measures 6.40 long and 3.20 m wide. The adjunct patio, built with a mud-brick wall, is unfinished, no roofing material having been laid yet. The enclosed courtyard thus obtained is 6.40 m long and 3.50 m wide.

Habitation Complex 10

Habitation complex 10 is located in the western side of the village. It is a fenced unit with the main entrance oriented eastward and an elongated, almost rectangular, field 1, measuring 65 m long and 40 m wide. There is an earth embankment running parallel to the field's western fence (fig. 41). The complex's built facilities amount to six, with four houses: one rectangular and three circular and two corrals. Both enclosures, with their entrances/exits oriented S, are attached to each other and are located in the inner side of the village; the smaller specimen, used for goats, is circular in shape and measures 5 m in diameter, and the larger, elliptically shaped enclosure, 10.20 m long and 8.10 m wide, is used for cattle.

House 67, the rectangular, mud-brick building, is oriented W-E, faces N, and measures 6.70 m in length and 3.10 m in width. Its adjunct verandah, 5.20 m long and 2.90 m wide, is built with six supporting poles. The remaining three features are round, mud-brick houses arranged in a N-S line. House 63, at the northern end, is a 7.30-m-in-diameter barn with the doorway oriented S. House 65 is found in a central position at 3 to 4 m S of the previous one. It is the kitchen of the complex, with the entrance oriented E-SE and a hearth found on the northern side, in the standard right-hand side position. The recorded hearth is a plain, rectangular installation with three niches, measuring 1 m in length, 0.55 m in width, and 0.70 m in height. A storage platform, 3 m × 2 m, built with four supporting poles, is located next to the kitchen's wall, on the eastern side. Finally, feature 66, at the southern end of the line, has its doorway oriented E and measures 6 m in diameter. It is a goat house which is attached to field 1 by a short fence portion. A pile of firewood was recorded next to the goat house, on its southern flank.

As is the case for Abuzrega, Marafaine is also divided into two halves. Four of the larger habitation complexes, 1 to 4, with seven to twelve houses, are located in the southern half, as is also the case for the larger cattle corral and the Mosque. Smaller habitation complexes with three to six houses are found in the northern half. The accumulation of goat droppings in some of the fields indicates a move toward agricultural intensification.

PART V

Patterns and Trends

Chapter 12

Location Tactics, Space Allocation, and Site Structures

Introduction

The patterns of regional distribution of settlements have been outlined in chapter 2. Permanent villages are found on that part of the land situated above the annual average flood level. Semipermanent villages are more widespread, found on the edge of the land above flood level. And finally, dry-season camps are confined to the Yaere, the hinterland depressions where the water table is found at 2.00 to 4.00 m below the surface. The availability of water and the high-quality grazing attract pastoralists from an extensive area. The studied dry-season camps' clusters were settled by people from different villages. The Amachita camps' cluster preferentially included peoples from the NW, N and NE; from Djidat at 15 kilometers NE for Amachita I; Magourde at 14 kilometers NNE for Amachita II; Chouaram at 15 kilometers N for Amachita III; Bam Kala at 17 kilometers NW for Amachita IV; Krene near Tilde in the Afade Canton at 20 kilometers NW for Amachita V; Alaya I at 11 kilometers N for Amachita VI; and finally, Mahanna next to Alaya I at 11 kilometers N for Amachita VII. The groups from the Agedipse cluster came from Kulkule at 12 kilometers ENE for Agedipse I; Magourde at 15 kilometers NNE for Agedipse II; Hinduk for Agedipse III; and finally, Tumam for Agedipse IV.

The minimum distance between the semipermanent settlement and the selected dry-season camping area revolves around 11 kilometers, approximately three to four hours walk with a small size cattle herd. The maximum documented distance fluctuates between 20 and 25 kilometers. Each dry-season camp is inhabited by families from the same village, with camps' clusters based on preferential association between groups from different settlement and clan affiliations.

It is tempting to lump all the settlements described so far within the same temporal frame of reference and consider them more or less contemporaneous. There are sound reasons for such a decision, as all the studied sites have been

303

settled during the last century, or more precisely, during the last fifty years. However, if the implemented research aims to document change in the use of space as well as shifting patterns in the organization of material culture, it is probably more appropriate to devise a more detailed and precise chronology of the material under investigation. Depending on issues being tackled, both tactics will be used in the remaining part of this work.

The Chronological Framework

The chronology of the tested Shuwa-Arab settlements to be worked out is based on a combination of different sources: the description of the Kotoko country published by Denham et al. (1828), Barth (1965), and Nachtigal (1987); low altitude aerial photographs of the *Institut Geographique National* from the late 1950s, and topographic maps also published by the *Institut Geographique National;* Cameroon national census data (Elingui 1978 and Recensement General 1985); informant interviews; and finally direct field observations.

The Early Group includes four villages: Danguerchem, Gobrem, Ndom, and Ngumati. Of all the tested settlements, Ndom is the only one mentioned by H. Barth during his travel from the Bornu Kingdom to Logone that lasted from March 5 to August 21, 1850 (Barth 1965: 425). The site is located next to the fortified town of Kala-Kafra; and in the published maps, the nineteenth century Ndom [Ndum] is found precisely where it is today. The remaining three, Gobrem, Danguerchem, and Ngumati, are totally or almost totally abandoned settlements. Gobrem was abandoned in the mid-seventies, as seems to be the case for Ngumati. The latter village, however, still had one inhabitant who, in fact, does not reside anymore on site. Danguerchem is represented on topographic maps based on aerial photographs from the 1950s but is not mentioned in the 1969 census; and, as such, can be considered to have been abandoned in the late 1960s. The headman from Mishiskwa at the time of fieldwork was born at Gobrem, where he spent his childhood and adolescence. He moved to the former village late in his adult life when he was married with children. These semipermanent settlements thus appear to have been founded between the late nineteenth and early twentieth century.

The Middle Group is particularly ambiguous. It includes five villages, one semipermanent, Mishiskwa, and four permanent, represented in the studied sample by Abuzrega, Djidat I and II, and Marafaine. They were probably already settled in the nineteenth century but are not clearly mentioned in the available historical sources. As far as their location is concerned, they may have been part of the series of Shuwa-Arab sites observed and described by G. Nachtigal in the 1870s. First, he specified that "from Alph [Houlouf] our road ran to the SE through a region densely populated by Kanuri and Shuwa" (Nachtigal 1987: 241). He then adds that "the inhabitants, exclusively Shuwa, for the most part protect the villages of this low lying country. Exposed every year to inundation, against the penetration of the water by low earthen walls, customarily made more resistant by the insertion of reeds" (ibid). And finally, he outlines the major characteristics of Shuwa houses and how they were usually used: " the villages are distinguished by their spacious, clumsy and very solid huts of reeds and straw, which apart from people shelter all the domestic animals. Generally, in addition to some low clay benches in the peripheral part of the hut, where the inhabitants stay during the day, there is also in the middle an apparatus of poles about 3 m high covered with mats, in which the family spend the night, while hens, cows, horses and goats crowd together on the flat earth" (Nachtigal 1987: 242).

Djidat II is clearly a more recent settlement resulting from a split between the inhabitants of Djidat I. Informants' estimates of the foundation date of the new village vary from thirty-five to fifty years. Whatever the case, however, Djidat II is clearly a mid-twentieth, century village.

And finally, the Late Group includes recent villages. Bawara, Bilbede, Gallis, and Ngada I–IV are absent from topographic maps based on low altitude aerial photographs from the late 1950s. With the exception of Ngada I, they are not found in the 1969 and 1977 census record. They were presumably nonexistent at that time and, as such, appear to have been founded during the latter part of the twentieth century. Finally, dry-season camps were all settled precisely between February and May 1990.

The Spatial Structures of Shuwa-Arab Sites

A settlement can be partitioned into four more or less imbedded components: (1) the size of the site delineated by the outer periphery of the settlement's features is the most encompassing level. (2) The settlement's built space revolves around the proportion of the site devoted to human construction or installations. The non-built space is as important as the built one, and is generally used for the movement of people and livestock in and out of the settlement. (3) The built space is, at its turn, geared toward livestock and human uses. (4) Livestock space stricto-sensu is partitioned into cattle and sheep/goat corrals and houses, as well as barns. And finally, (5) human space stricto-sensu includes houses, workshops, Mosques, as well as public "discussion" shelters. Some of the variables just outlined above are taken into account in the discussion of the spatial organization of the investigated Shuwa-Arab sites. They include settlement size, the number and diversity of built features, the proportion of built versus non-built space, as well as patterns of space allocation to activities like human habitation and livestock sheltering (table 36).

Settlement Size

Settlement size varies from a minimum of 0.25 hectares at Amachita II to a maximum of 4.52 hectares at Djidat II. There is a discernible trend toward increasing size from the Early to the Late Groups (table 36) with mean site size shifting

Table 36: Structures of the tested sites

Settlement group	Site size (ha)	Features		Density (ha)	Built space (m. sq.)	Livestock (m. sq.)	Human (m. sq.)
		Number	Diversity				
Early Group							
Danguerchem	0.54	21	3	38.88	2,136.59	1,276.75	862.84
Gobrem	1.20	35	4	29.16	3,704.13	2,826.13	878.00
Ndom	0.63	36	3	57.14	3,022.27	2,640.28	381.99
Ngumati	0.59	30	4	50.84	1,536.02	892.38	634.64
Middle Group							
Abuzrega	4.15	105	7	25.30	3,826.58	1,415.11	2,411.47
Djidat I	1.76	92	8	52.27	3,129.50	1,010.90	2,118.61
Djidat II	4.52	190	9	42.03	8,646.66	4,051.11	4,595.56
Marafaine	2.01	74	6	36.81	3,467.34	1,375.46	2,091.88
Mishiskwa	1.05	55	3	52.38	3,791.67	2,885.94	905.73
Late Group							
Bawara	0.78	27	3	34.61	2,337.17	2,071.68	265.49
Bilbede	0.67	74	4	110.44	2,348.50	1,626.91	706.40
Gallis	3.20	92	3	28.75	2,250.23	1,099.60	1,150.63
Ngada I	3.36	63	3	18.75	3,207.82	2,202.86	964.03
Ngada II	0.60	59	3	98.33	3,464.99	1,611.33	1,167.40
Ngada III	2.00	67	4	33.50	3,759.37	2,438.56	1,300.40
Ngada IV	2.03	107	5	52.70	2,603.03	1,433.58	1,077.61
Dry-Season Camps							
Amachita I	0.38	23	2	60.52	1,883.89	1,615.39	268.50
Amachita II	0.25	29	3	116.00	1,509.90	1,183.80	326.00
Amachita III	0.28	27	3	96.42	1,382.50	1,155.36	227.00

Table 36: Continued

Amachita IV	0.40	19	3	47.50	2,198.04	2,000.00	198.04
Amachita V	0.38	25	3	65.78	949.67	684.67	265.00
Amachita VI	0.38	15	3	39.47	1,118.00	930.23	187.77
Amachita VII	0.38	21	3	55.26	1,204.02	952.29	251.73
Agedipse I	0.86	38	2	44.18	2,688.82	2,132.63	556.29
Agedipse II	0.38	15	3	39.47	1,096.79	934.60	162.19
Agedipse III	1.76	44	2	25.00	3,001.05	2,344.35	656.70
Agedipse IV	0.44	23	3	52.27	1,047.21	859.27	187.94

from 0.74, then 2, and finally 3 hectares, with, however, increasing standard deviations (0.30 to 2.15). The extent of sites from the Early Group varies from 0.54 hectares at Danguerchem to 1.2 hectares at Gobrem. The situation is dramatically different in the Middle Group that consists predominantly of permanent villages. Sites size ranges from a minimum of 1.05 hectares at Mishiskwa to 4.52 hectares at Djidat II, and three out of the five investigated sites are larger than two hectares. In the Late Group, four out of the seven studied settlements are larger than 2 hectares, and site size ranges from a minimum of 0.60 hectares at Ngada II to a maximum of 3.36 hectares at Ngada I. Dry-seasons camps are clearly a special case. Two sites, Agedipse I and III, measuring respectively 0.86 and 1.76 hectares are exceptionally large and depart significantly from the general trend documented from the rest of the sample. The "standard" size of the dry-season camp seems to fluctuate between 0.25 and 0.44 hectares.

The Built Space

In general, less than half of the recorded settlement surface is built. There are, however, significant variations between the documented sites' groups. In the Early Group, the extent of the built space ranges from a maximum of 3,704.13 m square at Gobrem to a minimum of 1,536.02 m square at Ngumati (table 36). The built space/site size ratio varies from 0.47 at Ndom to 0.26 at Ngumati. The non-built space, geared to facilitate movements of people as well as livestock, appears to be a more critical element in the organization of more compact, permanent villages (tables 36 and 37). The extent of the built space documented among the Middle Group settlements varies from a minimum of 3,129.50 m square at Djidat I to a maximum of 8,646.66 m square at Djidat II, for a mean of 4,572.35 m square. The ratio of built space to settlement size is significantly smaller among the permanently settled villages, ranging from a minimum of 0.09 at Abuzrega to a maximum of 0.19 at Djidat II (table 37). The one documented at Mishiskwa, 0.36, is within the range recorded for the Early Group villages and congruent with semi-permanent villages. The Late Group presents a series of interesting situations. In general, the extent of the built space fluctuates between a minimum of 2,250.23 m square at Gallis to a maximum of 3,759.37 m square at Ngada III. The range, amounting to 1,509.14, is significantly narrower when compared to the Early and Middle groups' settlements, but the situations are more diverse if ratios are taken into account. In fact, the documented ratios of built space to settlement size vary from a minimum of 0.07 at Gallis to a maximum of 0.57 at Ngada II, and can be partitioned into three situations. The first situation includes Gallis and Ngada I, with ratios varying from 0.07 to 0.09. The second, with ratios ranging from 0.12 to 0.18, is documented at two sites, Ngada III and Ngada IV. And finally, the third, recorded at Bawara, Bilbede, and Ngada II, is characterized by higher ratios, varying from 0.29 to 0.57. The recorded variations are difficult to interpret. The

Table 37: Patterns of space allocation

Settlement Group	Site size (Ha)	Built space	Livestock space	Human space	Livestock/ Human
Early Group					
Danguerchem	0.54	0.39	0.23	0.15	1.47
Gobrem	1.20	0.30	0.23	0.073	3.21
Ndom	0.63	0.47	0.41	0.060	6.91
Ngumati	0.59	0.26	0.15	0.10	1.38
Middle Group					
Abuzrega	4.15	0.09	0.03	0.058	0.58
Djidat I	1.76	0.17	0.05	0.12	0.47
Djidat II	4.52	0.19	0.08	0.10	0.88
Marafaine	2.01	0.17	0.06	0.10	0.65
Mishiskwa	1.05	0.36	0.27	0.08	3.18
Late Group					
Bawara	0.78	0.29	0.26	0.03	7.80
Bilbede	0.67	0.35	0.24	0.10	2.30
Gallis	3.20	0.07	0.03	0.03	0.95
Ngada I	3.36	0.09	0.06	0.02	2.28
Ngada II	0.60	0.57	0.26	0.19	1.38
Ngada III	2.00	0.18	0.12	0.06	1.87
Ngada IV	2.03	0.12	0.07	0.05	1.33
Dry-Season Camps					
Amachita I	0.38	0.49	0.42	0.07	6.01
Amachita II	0.25	0.60	o.47	0.13	3.63
Amachita III	0.28	0.49	0.41	0.08	5.08
Amachita IV	0.40	0.54	0.50	0.04	10.09
Amachita V	0.38	0.24	0.18	0.06	2.58
Amachita VI	0.38	0.29	0.24	0.04	4.95
Amachita VII	0.38	0.31	0.25	0.06	3.78
Agedipse I	0.86	0.31	0.24	0.06	3.83
Agedipse II	0.38	0.28	0.24	0.04	5.76
Agedipse III	1.76	0.17	0.13	0.03	3.56
Agedipse IV	0.44	0.23	0.19	0.04	4.57

lower ratios documented at Gallis and Ngada I appear to result from a significant decrease in the importance of livestock, or more precisely, cattle, in the villages' economies.

As far as the tested eleven dry-season camps are concerned, the extent of built space ranges from a maximum of 3,001.05 m square at Agedipse III to a minimum of 949.67 m square at Amachita V. There are significant variations between both camps' clusters. In the Amachita cluster, the built space fluctuates between 949.67

and 2,198.04 m square, with an average of 1,463.71 m square. In terms of proportion, four out of the seven Amachita camps present high built space to settlement size ratios, varying from 0.49 to 0.60 (table 37). The ratios of the three remaining ones are significantly lower, ranging from 0.24 to 0.31. Camps from the Agedipse cluster are significantly large with, however, lower built space to settlement size ratios. The lowest ratio, amounting to 0.17, is documented at the largest Agedipse III camp, with 3,001.05 m square of built space. The highest, 0.31, is recorded at Agedipse I, for a built space measuring 2,688.82 m square (table 37).

Significantly, there is a general overlap in the distribution of built space to settlement size ratios in all the groups. Even if all the tested permanent villages are clustered at the lower end of the spectrum with ratios ranging from 0.09 to 0.19, sites' built space appears as a poor predictor of settlement categories. It is, however, not totally unreliable but has to be probed farther regarding the nature and diversity of the built features under consideration.

Livestock Space

The amount of space devoted to livestock and connected activities is a critical element in the settlement's layout and an accurate indicator of the socioeconomic status of the community under investigation. In the Early Group, livestock space ranges in size from a minimum of 892.38 m square at Ngumati to a maximum of 2,826.13 m square at Gobrem (table 37), with the ratio of livestock area to settlement size fluctuating between 0.15 documented at Ngumati, and 0.41, recorded at Ndom. In general, the amount of livestock space is considerably larger in Middle Group settlements. It varies from a minimum of 1,010.90 m square at Djidat I to a maximum of 4,051.11 m square at Djidat II, but its share of the settlements' area is smaller, with ratios varying from a maximum of 0.27, recorded at Mishiskwa, to 0.03, documented at Abuzrega. In fact, in all the tested permanent villages, the proportion of settlement space devoted to livestock ranges from 3 to 8 percent. The situation is much more diversified among Late Group settlements. The space allocated to livestock ranges from a minimum of 1,099.60 m square at Gallis to a maximum of 2,438.56 m square at Ngada III. In terms of livestock space to settlement size ratios, the tested Late Group sites can be divided into three classes. Class 1 includes three sites, Gallis, Ngada I, and Ngada IV, with ratios ranging from 0.03 to 0.07 (table 37). Class 2 consists of a single settlement, Ngada III, with a recorded ratio of 0.12. And finally, class 3, with three sites, Bilbede, Bawara, and Ngada II, is comprised of settlements with ratios varying from 0.24 to 0.26. Class 1 sites appear to have, on average, a higher amount of storage platforms, suggesting the emergence of a socioeconomic system tilting toward a heavier reliance on grain production.

Dry-season camps are clearly livestock settlements. The extent of the camp's space devoted to livestock varies from a maximum of 2,344.35 m square at

Agedipse III to a minimum of 684.67 m square at Amachita V (table 37). The variation in the size of livestock space is narrower in the Amachita camps' cluster, where it ranges from a maximum of 2,000 to a minimum of 684.67 m square, with the documented ratios of livestock space to settlement size fluctuating between 0.18, at Amachita V, and 0.50, at Amachita IV. The range of variation is broader in the Agedipse camps' cluster, with livestock space extended over a maximum of 2.344.35 m square at Agedipse III and a minimum of 859.27 m square at Agedipse IV. The recorded ratios fluctuate within a narrower range, from 0.13 at Agedipse III to 0.24 at Agedipse I and II.

The built livestock space under scrutiny includes different kinds of facilities. They range from specially built houses to sheep/goat pens, cattle corrals, and milking installations. Specially built watering troughs found around some wells in the dry-season camping area have not been included in the computation of livestock space in the Amachita and Agedipse camps' clusters.

In the Early Group settlements, the number of livestock facilities varies from a minimum of 5 to a maximum of 17, respectively, at Danguerchem and Gobrem (table 37). They are partitioned into 3 to 7 pens/corrals and 2 to 10 houses. Danguerchem and Ngumati have, respectively, 2 and 4 livestock houses; both, with 3 and 5 pens/corrals, are part of the southern settlement cluster and appear to rely more on communal enclosures. Two Danguerchem households out of five have one livestock house each. That is also the case for four households out of the seven documented at Ngumati. Gobrem and Ndom on the other hand have more livestock houses than communal enclosures. The former has 7 pens/corrals and 10 livestock houses, and the latter, respectively, 6 and 10. The distribution between households is also skewed with frequencies varying from 1 to 2 livestock houses at Ndom, to 1 to 3 at Gobrem.

Among the Middle Group settlements, there is no convincing case of a central cattle enclosure used by all the community members. The nucleation process underway results in each extended family building most of its needed livestock facilities. The number of livestock features varies from a minimum of 26 at Abuzrega to a maximum of 55 at Djidat II. The frequency of pens/enclosures ranges from a minimum of 5 at Mishiskwa to a maximum of 20 at Djidat II, and that of houses from a minimum of 13 at Abuzrega to a maximum of 35 at Djidat II (table 38). With the exception of Mishiskwa, the frequency of livestock pens/corrals is high on average fluctuating between 10 and 20 respectively, at Djidat I and Djidat II.

The tested Middle Group settlements can be divided into two classes according the patterns of distribution of livestock houses. Class I includes three sites, Abuzrega, Djidat I, and Marafaine, with 1 to 4 livestock houses per household unit. There are 13 livestock houses for 9 households at Abuzrega, with frequencies varying from 1 to 3; 18 for 11 households at Djidat I, ranging from 1 to 4; and finally, 21 for 10 households at Marafaine, varying from 1 to 4. Class II is comprised of two sites, Djidat II and Mishiskwa, with 1 to 8 livestock houses per household unit. The former site has 35 livestock houses for 25 households, with frequencies ranging

Table 38: The distribution of built features

Settlement Groups	Number of units	Number of features	Human houses			Livestock houses		
			n	Min.	Max.	n	Min.	Max.
Early Group								
Danguerchem	5	22	15	2	4	2	1	1
Gobrem	7	34	15	1	4	10	1	3
Ndom	6	34	10	1	2	10	1	2
Ngumati	7	31	18	1	6	4	1	1
Middle Group								
Abuzrega	9	159	77	5	13	13	1	3
Djidat I	11	155	60	2	12	18	1	4
Djidat II	25	283	107	1	20	35	1	7
Marafaine	10	141	45	1	8	21	1	4
Mishiskwa	6	54	23	3	6	23	2	8
Late Group								
Bawara	7	28	9	1	2	8	1	2
Bilbede	9	77	19	1	3	11	1	2
Gallis	9	78	27	1	8	13	1	3
Ngada I	10	63	27	1	4	16	1	2
Ngada II	8	58	29	3	6	12	1	2
Ngada III	14	61	24	1	4	12	1	3
Ngada IV	12	121	34	2	6	17	1	3

from 1 to 7. The latter includes 24 such houses for 6 households, with frequencies varying from 2 to 8.

In general, however, the space devoted to sheep/goats appears to be consistently on the rise among the Middle Group settlements, with the notable exception of Mishiskwa. Goat-milking is practiced at a relatively high intensity at Djidat I, a phenomenon materialized by the large number of specialized milking stations. At a lower intensity scale, few milking stations have been recorded at Abuzrega and Marafaine. Part of the production is diverted to the large markets of the nearby towns of Logone-Birni and Kusseri.

In the Late Group settlements, the frequency of livestock features varies from 20 to no pens/corrals and 8 to 17 houses. Gallis stands out as a special case with no livestock enclosure at all, and 13 houses distributed among 9 households with frequency ranging from 1 to 3. Ngada IV is also a special case with 20 enclosures and 17 houses. The total amount of enclosures is inflated by the high number of abandoned and worn-out pens/corrals still visible in the village. The recorded 17 livestock houses are distributed among 12 households, with frequencies varying from 1 to 3. With the exception of these two special cases, the total number of livestock features per site varies from a minimum of 13 at Bawara, with 5 pens/

corrals and 8 houses, to a maximum of 21 at Ngada I with in this case 16 houses and 5 pens/corrals. In general, the number of pens/corrals per site fluctuates between 7 and 4 respectively, at Ngada III and Ngada II. The range is broader for houses with frequencies varying from a minimum of 8 at Bawara to a maximum of 16 at Ngada I. However, their distribution within sites is almost even. In four cases documented at Bawara, Bilbede, Ngada I, and Ngada II, the number of livestock houses per household varies from 1 to 2 with 8 to 16 available for 7 to 10 households. Among the three remaining cases, Gallis, Ngada III, and Ngada IV, the frequency of livestock houses ranges from 1 to 3 with 13 to 17 documented features for 9 to 14 households.

In dry-season camps, livestock houses are a minor component of the settlement's facilities. They are absent from four out of eleven tested sites. The documented frequency varies from a minimum of 1 at Amachita I and Amachita II to a maximum of 5 at Agedipse I. In the Amachita camps' cluster, there are two sites, Amachita IV and Amachita VI, without livestock houses, two, already alluded to above with one each, two, Amachita V and Amachita VII, with two, and finally, one, Amachita III, with three. In the Agedipse camps' cluster, on the other hand, two of the sites, Agedipse III and Agedipse IV, are devoid of livestock houses. The remaining two, Agedipse I and Agedipse II, have, respectively, 5 and 2. Livestock enclosures are found in all the tested camps and are systematically more numerous. Their frequency varies from a minimum of 2 at Amachita IV to a maximum of 14 at Agedipse III. Both extremes are clearly unusual when nine out of the eleven tested sites have 4 to 7 pens/corrals. There is no straightforward correlation between the number of enclosures and that of livestock houses. This is partly due to the fact that more than half of the livestock houses documented in the dry-season camps were used as horse or donkey shelters.

As far as space allocated to livestock is concerned, the studied settlements can be divided into two neat categories. The dry-season camps are livestock driven sites in which most of the corralling is communal. In more elaborate settlements, the dominant trend is that of an increasing reliance on livestock houses at the expense of communal corralling, as can be seen with changing livestock house/pens/corrals ratios. They vary from a minimum of 0.66 (2/3) to a maximum of 1.66 (10/6) among the Early Group sites, at Danguerchem and Ndom respectively. In the Middle Group, they range from a minimum of 1 (13/13) at Abuzrega to a maximum of 4.8 (24/5) at Mishiskwa. And finally, in the Later Group, with the exception of Gallis and Ngada IV, both special cases, the lowest ratio, 1.6 (8/5), is documented at Bawara, and the higher one, 3.2 (16/5), is recorded at Ngada I.

Human Space

The component of the settlement devoted exclusively to human use is divided into public and private spaces. Public space includes such features as open-air or built mosques, discussion shelters, blacksmith workshops, retail shops, as well as mills. Private space is comprised of habitation features more or less divided into function-specific installations such as cooking, living, sleeping rooms, bathrooms and toilets, et cetera. depending on sites and circumstances. The extent of the human space varies considerably from one settlement group to another. In the Early Group, human space ranges from a minimum of 381.99 m square at Ndom to a maximum of 878.00 m square at Gobrem (table 38). The ratio of the recorded human space to settlement size varies from a minimum of 0.060 to a maximum of 0.15, at Ndom and Danguerchem, respectively.

Among the Middle Group settlements, human space is consistently more important than the livestock space and varies in extent from a minimum of 905.73 m square at Mishiskwa to a maximum of 4.595.56 m square at Djidat II. In fact, if Mishiskwa is not taken into account, the human space from permanent villages is, in general, larger than 2,000 m square. In terms of human space to settlement size ratios, the documented cases range from a minimum of 0.058 at Abuzrega to a maximum of 0.12 at Djidat I.

In Late Group sites, the extent of human space ranges from a minimum of 265.49 m square at Bawara to a maximum of 1,300.40 m square at Ngada III. Four out of the seven tested settlements have their human space component larger than 1,000 m square. The recorded human space/settlement size ratios fluctuate between 0.02, documented at Ngada I, and 0.19, at Ngada II (table 38). In fact, ratios higher than 0.10 have been recorded at two sites only, Bilbede and Ngada II. The remaining five sites present ratios varying within a narrow 0.04 range, from 0.02 (Ngada I) to 0.06 (Ngada III).

In the dry-season camps, the share of human space is understandably a small one. The recorded extents vary from a minimum of 162.19 m square at Agedipse II to a maximum of 656.70 m square at Agedipse III. In the Amachita camps' cluster, the range of variation is relatively narrow, from 187.77 m square at Amachita VI to 326 m square at Amachita II, for an average human space extent of 246.29 m square. The situation is different in the Agedipse camps' cluster, not only because of the larger range of variation but also because of an emerging dual pattern. The cluster appears to include two sets of one large and one small site. In set one, the extent of human space varies from a minimum of 162.19 m square at Agedipse II to a maximum of 556.29 m square at Agedipse I. In set two, Agedipse III has a human space extended over 656.70 m square compared to 187.94 m square at Agedipse IV. As far as human space/settlement size ratios are concerned, the situation is more diversified in the Amachita camps' cluster where they vary from a minimum of 0.04 at Amachita IV and VI to a maximum of 0.13 at Amachita II. In the Agedipse cluster, on the other hand, the range is much narrower, from a minimum of 0.03 at Agedipse III to a maximum of 0.06 at Agedipse I.

The nature and frequency distribution of features built for human use suggest a more subtle understanding of patterns of change that can be documented through well-tailored ethnoarchaeological research. In the Early Group, public discussion shelters are found at two sites, Danguerchem and Ndom, with frequencies varying from 1 to 3 (table 39). All the recorded houses are circular in shape, their total amount per site varying from 10 (Ndom) to 18 (Ngumati) for five to seven households. In fact the number of houses per household unit ranges from 1 to 6. Minima vary from 1 (in three cases) to 2 at Danguerchem, and maxima from 2 (Ndom) to 6 (Ngumati).

The situation is radically different in the Middle Group. With the exception of Mishiskwa, without public features but 23 circular houses for 6 household units, (3 to 6 houses per unit), all the permanent villages have more diverse uses for architectural features. Houses are circular and rectilinear. The use of mud-brick as building material is predominant. The allocation of space tends to be more and more function-specific. Cooking areas tend to be separated from the living and sleeping ones. They are located in rectangular houses' patios or in specially built kitchens. Bathrooms and toilet booths are attached to most of the houses. Three out of the four permanent villages have mosques. The number of public features varies from 2 to 3. That of rectangular houses ranges from a minimum of 27 at Abuzrega to a maximum of 67 at Djidat II (table 39), and finally, that of circular ones, from a minimum of 36 at Marafaine to a maximum of 85 at Djidat II. Nine to twenty-five households are documented to be living in the tested sites. The minimum number of houses per household varies from 1 at Djidat II and Marafaine to 5 at Abuzrega, and the maximum, from 8 at Marafaine to 20 at Djidat II. Clearly, large extended families appear to be an accurate indicator of social success.

All the houses documented from the Late Group settlements are circular in shape. There are nonetheless two rectilinear features, an open-air mosque and a wood and straw discussion house, recorded at Ngada III and Ngada IV. One of the sites, Ngada II, is devoid of public features. Their frequency among the remaining six villages varies from 1 to 6. Gallis is unusual with six discussion houses for nine household units; in this case, the shelters seem to have been preferentially used by the members of each of the extended families. For the remaining five villages, there are 1 to 3 shelters for 7 to 14 household units.

The number of habitation houses ranges from a minimum of 9 for seven households at Bawara to a maximum of 34 for twelve households at Ngada IV (table 39). Four out the seven tested sites have 24 to 29 houses for nine to fourteen households. At Bawara and Bilbede, each household unit has one to three houses. Habitation clusters thus seem to house small, single family units with their children. At Ngada I and Ngada III, the number of houses per household unit ranges from 1 to 4. In these cases, family groups are larger, on average, and generally consist of polygamous households. In the remaining three sites, Gallis, Ngada II, and Ngada IV, the frequency of houses per household varies from 1–3 to 6–8. At Gallis, with a range of 1 to 8, some of the largest houses' clusters were still inhabited by members of extended families at the time of fieldwork. With 2 to 3 houses minimum per household unit, Ngada II and Ngada IV appear to be inhabited by family groups larger than average, comprised of polygamous units and two-generations extended families.

Table 39: Frequency distribution of features built in the tested settlements

Settlement group	Number of households	Habitations		Public shelter	Livestock installations	Corrals	Storage platforms	Chicken coops	Milking stations	Others
		Circle	Rectilinear							
Early Group										
Danguerchem	5	15	—	1	3	2	1	—	—	—
Gobrem	7	15	—	—	7	10	1	—	—	1
Ndom	6	10	—	3	6	10	5	—	—	—
Ngumati	7	18	—	—	5	4	4	—	—	1
Middle Group										
Abuzrega	9	42	27	2	13	13	55	8	—	1
Djidat I	11	37	45	2	10	19	25	7	10	—
Djidat II	25	85	67	3	20	35	59	9	—	5
Marafaine	10	36	31	3	13	20	28	5	5	—
Mishiskwa	6	23	—	—	5	24	2	—	—	—
Late Group										
Bawara	7	9	—	1	5	8	5	—	—	—
Bilbede	9	19	—	3	6	11	16	22	—	—
Gallis	9	27	—	6	—	13	32	—	—	—
Ngada I	10	27	—	1	5	16	10	4	—	—
Ngada II	8	29	—	—	4	12	13	—	—	—
Ngada III	14	24	1	2	7	12	14	1	—	—
Ngada IV	12	34	1	1	20	17	20	27	—	1
Dry-Season Camps										
Amachita I	4	14	—	—	5	1	—	—	—	3
Amachita II	6	17	1	—	6	1	—	—	—	4
Amachita III	8	11	—	—	7	3	—	—	—	6

Table 39: Continued

Amachita IV	9	12	—	—	2	—	—	—	3
Amachita V	7	15	—	—	5	2	—	—	4
Amachita VI	8	9	—	—	4	—	—	2	—
Amachita VII	7	11	1	1	4	2	—	—	1
Agedipse I	8	24	—	—	7	5	1	1	6
Agedipse II	5	7	—	—	4	2	1	1	2
Agedipse III	16	30	—	—	14	—	—	—	7
Agedipse IV	5	13	—	—	4	—	1	1	5

Among the dry-season camps, there is a single case of public shelter recorded at Agedipse I. Two rectilinear features, both them attached to specific houses and used as discussion and goat shelters, were found at Amachita II and Agedipse I. In general, the nuclear family is the main social unit to settle in the dry-season camps, with younger children and adolescents as well as elder persons, widows and/or grand mothers. The frequency of habitation houses varies from a minimum of 7 at Agedipse II to a maximum of 30 at Agedipse III, with significant differences between both camps' clusters. In the Amachita camps' cluster, the number of houses varies from a minimum of 9 at Amachita VI to a maximum of 17 at Amachita II; but five out of seven sites have a house total ranging from 11 to 15. The Agedipse camps' cluster presents another pattern associating a larger to a smaller site. In one case, with Agedipse I and Agedipse II, there are 24 houses distributed into eight clusters in the former, and 7 divided into 5 in the latter. In the other case, 30 houses arranged into 16 clusters are found at Agedipse III, the larger camp, and 13 organized into 5 are documented at Agedipse IV, the smaller one.

The ratio of livestock to human space provides an elegant summary of the major forces driving the space allocation systems implemented among the tested sites. There are three main situations: (1) a situation of equilibrium when the space devoted to livestock is equal to that devoted to humans, a case in which the ratio is equal to 1 (L/H = 1); (2) a situation in which the space devoted to humans is more important than that allocated to livestock. L/H is, in this case lower than 1, tending to 0 (zero) if the site is exclusively for human use (L/H = 0 < (1); and finally, (3) a situation of predominance of livestock space, with L/H > 1, tending to + infinite if the allocated human space is not nil.

Livestock space requirements and needs are predominant in shaping the spatial organization of three of the four categories of settlements studied in this work. In the Early Group settlements, the L/H ratios vary from 1.38 and 1.47 at Ngumati and Danguerchem, respectively, to 6.91 at Ndom. The range is comparatively narrow. In the Late Group sites, the range is much broader, stretched from a minimum of 0.95 at Gallis to a maximum of 7.80 at Bawara. In fact, four out of seven sites, Gallis, Ngada II, Ngada III, and Ngada IV, have ratio values fluctuating between 0.95 and 1.87, not very far from a balanced distribution. Two, Bilbede and Ngada I present a similar ratio, 2.30 and 2.28, respectively. Bawara, then, has the structural consistency of a dry-season camp that recently became a rainy-season village. Finally, the range is at its broadest among the dry-season camps and varies from a minimum of 2.58 at Amachita V to a maximum of 10.09 at Amachita IV. Surprisingly, the range among ratios is narrower within the Agedipse camps' cluster, 3.56–5.76, and both larger camps have close ratio values, 3.83 and 3.56.

Distributional Patterns of Built Features

The number and diversity of built features recorded in the sample of tested settlements vary enormously. The category of built features includes houses, pens, enclosures, shelters, wells, storage racks and platforms, chicken coops, as well as workshops. The range of variation is relatively narrow in the Early Group and dry-season camps. In both cases, the frequency of built features fluctuates between 21 and 36, and the diversity between 3 and 4 in the Early Group (table 39). Within the dry-season camps, the range in the frequency of features is larger, varying from 15 to 44 with, however, less diversity, which fluctuates between 2 and 3. There are more variations within the Middle and Late Groups. In the former, there are 55 to 190 built features among the five tested settlements, with diversity ranging from 3 at Mishiskwa, a semipermanent village, to 9 at Djidat II where blacksmith workshops, "retail shops," an engine-powered and a hand-operated mill, a boarding school, a relatively large Friday Mosque, et cetera, have been recorded. In the latter, features diversity ranges from 3 to 5 for frequency varying from a minimum of 27 at Bawara to a maximum of 107 at Ngada IV. Bawara is clearly an exception, with a low frequency of built features that departs significantly from the rest of the Late Group sites. The general trend is that of a frequency of built features amounting to 59 and higher, well above the maximum recorded for the Early Group sites. The trend toward an increasing number of built features can be singled out as another aspect of the structural changes through time that can be deciphered from the evidence at hand.

The density of features provides another access to the structuration of Shuwa-Arab settlements. The recorded densities tend to increase through time, shifting from an average of 44 per hectare in the Early Group, 41.75/hectare in the Middle Group, 53/hectare in the Late Group, to 58.35/hectare in dry-season camps. More precisely, the density of features varies from a minimum of 29.16/hectare at Gobrem to a maximum of 57.14/hectare at Ndom in the Early Group. The range, 27.98, is comparatively narrow and surprisingly similar to that from the Middle Group sites (i.e., 27.08). In the latter category, the density varies from a minimum of 25.30/hectare at Abuzrega to a maximum of 52.38/hectare at Mishiskwa. The situation is much more diverse for the Late Group and dry-season sites. In the former, features density varies from a minimum of 18.75/hectare at Ngada I to a maximum of 110.44/hectare at Bilbede. The range, amounting to 91.69, is significantly broader and each settlement appears to have dealt with very specific patterns of space allocation to sociocultural activities. In the latter, densities vary from a minimum of 25/hectare at Agedipse III to a maximum of 116/hectare at Amachita II, for a range of 91, similar to that of the previous settlement category.

Other Built Features

There are four categories of built features distinct from houses and bulky enough to be part of the spatial organization of the settlements. These are, in order of decreasing frequency, storage platforms, chicken coops, milking installations, and tethering devices.

Storage platforms are used for a range of purposes including sun-drying of grain, fodder, as well as straw and reeds for roofing and/or door blinds and mat making. Depending on their size and height, they are also used as convenient shelters during the hot hours of the day. Among the Early Group sites, the frequency of storage platforms varies from 1 to 5. Danguerchem and Gobrem are de facto archaeological sites; the documented presence of a single storage platform in each for five and seven household units is probably an artifact of features dismantling that may have occurred at the time of abandonment. The distribution is slightly more balanced at Ndom and Ngumati, with, respectively, five storage platforms for six households and four for seven. At Ngumati, however, three out the four recorded storage platforms were located within the confine of the Bilama's (village headman) cluster. In general, architectural features devoted to the processing of plant materials appear to be underrepresented among Early Group sites. This may suggest a stronger emphasis on livestock husbandry at the expense of agricultural activities.

The Middle Group settlements present a totally different situation, with the exception of Mishiskwa, which replicates the trend outlined for the Early Group sites. The number of storage platforms varies from a minimum of 25 for 11 household at Djidat I to a maximum of 59 for 25 at Djidat II. In all the documented cases, there are at least two storage platforms per household, rising up to 6 per household at Abuzrega. In these permanent settlements, agriculture is as important as livestock husbandry with each village surrounded by a ring of cultivated fields.

Storage platforms are constant and recurrent features of the Late Group settlements. Their frequency varies from a minimum of 5 for 7 household units at Bawara to a maximum of 32 for 9 at Gallis. The latter site has no communal livestock enclosures and appears to rely much more on agriculture. There is no correlation between the number of household units and that of storage platforms, even if there are 10 and 14 such units for 10 and 14 storage platforms at Ngada I and Ngada III. There are more households than storage platforms at Bawara, with 7 for 5. In general, however, the number of storage platforms is higher than that of households in four out of seven cases, fluctuating between 13 and 32 for 9 to 12 house clusters.

Dry-season camps are devoid of storage platforms. There is a single case documented at Agedipse I, and it consists of a feature used for drying roofing reeds. Despite the relatively broad range of specific use, the largest number of storage platforms is geared to the processing of agricultural products. Their frequency distribution among the tested settlements can thus be used as a proxy measure of the importance of agriculture in the villages' economies.

The general distribution of chicken coops is more restricted. They are found predominantly among Middle and Late Groups settlements, with four specimens in dry-season camps. Three out of four sites from the Agedipse camps' cluster, Agedipse I, II, and IV, have one chicken coop each, as is the case for Amachita VII in the Amachita camps' cluster (table 39). Among Middle Group settlements, all four permanent villages have chicken coops. The recorded frequency varies from a minimum of 5 at Marafaine to a maximum of 9 at Djidat II. In the Late Group sites, three villages out of seven, Bawara, Gallis, and Ngada II, are devoid of chicken coops. The remaining four have 1 to 27 such features. Bilbede and Ngada IV with 22 and 27 chicken coops, respectively, are clearly special cases of a slight shift toward "economic specialization." Chickens are given as presents to visiting guests; they are, nonetheless, an increasing economic asset, sold in the nearby town markets of Logone Birni, Kusseri, as well as Ndjamena, the capital city of Chad Republic on the right bank of the Chari river.

Milking installations are confined to permanent villages from the Middle Group settlements. They consist of a high number of small tethering poles equidistant from each other and generally spread over the whole surface of a goat pen. They suggest a well organized and tightly scheduled goat-milking program. Sour goat-milk is a crucial and omnipresent ingredient of a broad range of sauces. Goat milk is sold locally, as well as in the nearby town markets, where it is transported in calabashes. Intensive goat-milking has been documented at two villages, Djidat I and Marafaine. In the former village, the production of goat's milk appears to be a widely shared activity. Milking installations are found in seven household clusters out of eleven. In the latter, goat's milk production appears to be similarly intensive even if the number of installations amounts to only five. In fact, this means that five households out of ten are involved in goat-milk production.

There are a number of miscellaneous, more or less elaborate built features that are found in many different sites. These include wells, simple, with or without cemented margins in Middle and Late Groups settlements, or associated with elaborate livestock watering troughs in the dry-season camps; a blacksmith workshop; three tiny retail shops; an engine-pulled mill; a hand-operated mill; and finally, numerous horse-, donkey-, calf-, and sheep/goat-tethering installations found mostly in the dry-season camps.

The Djidat I and II complex is the largest of all the tested settlements. It has the greatest diversity of features, evidence for craft specialization, and services attracting the population from the surrounding villages. Its geographic location at the center of the study area seems to have enhanced its recently achieved regional primacy, an issue that will be dealt with in more detail later.

Conclusion

Shuwa-Arab settlements share some distinctive characteristics, some being more extensive than others. All settlements share a similar circular to elliptical shape. The archetype is probably that of a large central cattle byre surrounded by houses located along the site's perimeter. Such an archetype is clearly visible in dry-season camps, slightly blurred in some semipermanent villages, and despite significant alteration and intensive nucleation, can still be recovered from the spatial structures from permanent villages.

The Shuwa-Arab house is round in shape and is generally built in wood and straw with a thatched roof. There are few examples of mud-brick, round houses in semipermanent villages. In permanent villages, however, there is an important shift toward the preferential construction of rectangular, mud-brick houses with flat earthen roofs. The intra-house spatial organization is radically altered with different house shapes. In the circular house module inhabited by a married woman, the hearth is always located on the right-hand side when moving in; the bed is always located opposite to the doorway; and finally, shelf sets are built on one or both sides of the hearth. In the rectangular house module, there is an increasing functional differentiation between rooms. Cooking is separated from the living and sleeping areas. In some cases, the hearth is built along the house wall in the sheltered patio; and in others, there are kitchens in round as well as rectilinear houses. The recorded extended families' habitation complexes are, for the vast majority, still open on all sides, or surrounded by low wooden fences. There is a single case of a Kotoko-like habitation unit found at Djidat I, (feature 10–13), a walled compound with high, mud-brick walls delineating a large courtyard with round and rectangular houses.

The pottery material recorded from all the tested settlements was obtained from Houlouf female potters. In fact, beside, architectural evidence, Shuwa-Arab self-signaling cultural material statements are found on hearths. These features are represented in diverse shapes and decorated with an array of motifs that will be dealt with in more detail in the next chapter.

Chapter 13

Patterns in the Material Record

Introduction

There are several significant material blueprints differentiating Shuwa-Arab settlements from those of other local ethnic groups. Their settlements are systematically inward-oriented with a central, more or less open space surrounded by one to several rings of houses on the perimeter. Houses are still predominantly round in shape with, however, a significant departure from the standard in permanent villages, where rectilinear buildings tend to become the norm. Wood and straw are preferentially used as building materials. Mud-brick is increasingly favored in permanent settlements, slightly less in semipermanent villages. In general, each married couple with children tends to use a large family bed, and the building of an elaborate hearth is the exclusive privilege of married women. The spatial organization of the standard Shuwa-Arab house has been shown to be tightly patterned. Using the house's entrance as the reference point, and facing inside, the hearth is always located on the right-hand side, surrounded in most of the cases by storage, cooking, and service gear. The family bed, on the other hand, is always located in the left-hand half the house.

Variations in the use of space have been discussed extensively in the description of the material record from each studied site. The allocation of space to such activities as cooking, food consumption, bathing, entertainment, living, and sleeping is, on average, much more elaborate in permanent villages. Each of the activities mentioned above thus tend to be confined to a specific room or area of the house complex. In all the semipermanent villages and dry-season camps, there is more embeddedness in the patterning of activity areas. Cooking, storage, food consumption, and sleeping tend to take place in the same house. All the material products associated with these activities thus tend to be clustered within the space of a single house. These cultural products can be more or less ethnic-specific, allowing the researcher to probe the "self-centered" expression of cultural preference. In the cases under investigation here, pottery material is obtained from producers' workshops located Houlouf and, as such, refers more to the owner's taste and supply

Figure 42: Building a hearth at Djidat II

network. Depending on circumstances, few Shuwa-Arab women are involved in
the production and decoration of calabashes. The hearth, however, appears to be a
critical household feature among the Shuwa Arab. It is an explicit social statement
asserting a change of status. An elaborate hearth is built by a married woman exclusively (fig. 42). Hearths are built in clay, progressively hardened through their
continual use for cooking. They are comprised of two main parts, horizontal and
vertical. The horizontal part includes a number of connected pot-supporting devices termed *niche*. The vertical part consists of a panel, with or without vertical and
elongated clay bumps, instrumental in the stabilization of the cooking pots. Most
of the recorded decoration is found on the hearths' rear panel. In some cases, however, hearthstones, in fact clay balls, are also decorated.

    One would thus expect the hearths to highlight the married women's cultural
preferences. Such preferences may express links with the women's families, families that may live in the same or a different village.This chapter is devoted to the
discussion of hearth shapes and decoration. These features are located inside, in the
intimate part of the married couple's house, accessible only to the closest relatives
and friends of the household. Their decoration is thus not targeted to outsiders, but
self-signaling. It certainly involves aesthetic, stylistic, and functional preferences.
Are hearths' shapes and decorations patterned according to house, household, village, or clan affiliations? What is the range and diversity of decorative themes?
How are they distributed among the investigated settlements? Are there meaning-

ful variations between settlement categories? These are some of the issues that will be addressed in the rest of this chapter.

Hearths from the Early Group Settlements

Hearth preservation was particularly poor in most of the investigated Early Group sites (table 40). At Gobrem, no hearth was well-preserved enough to allow for an acceptable and reliable recording of the decoration.A single badly damaged hearth was recorded at Ngumati (fig. 43) from house 18. The decoration consists of pinched finger impression on a horizontal, appliqué cordon at mid-height of the rear panel.

Four hearths were more or less well-preserved at Danguerchem (fig. 43). Each is a unique blend of characteristics. Two shape categories are represented, rectangular and trapezoidal. The former is attested by a single case from house 22. The latter includes three specimens from houses 1, 14, and 21. All the recorded Danguerchem hearths share an important decorative feature, a horizontal, appliqué cordon dividing the rear panel into two registers. In the upper register, there are three to six appliqué upward arrows (houses 1 and 14), four short, vertical appliqué cordons (house 21), and a plain, rectangular framed space (house 22). The lower register is plain for the specimen from house 14, and includes four equidistant, vertical, and elongated clay bumps for features from houses 1, 21, and 22. The studied sample is too small for subtle patterns to emerge; what is striking, however, is the uniqueness of each of the documented feature, even when they are found within the same household unit, as is the case for specimens 21 and 22. The Danguerchem material tends to support the suggestion of the uniqueness of each married woman's aesthetic preferences.

Five hearths have been recorded from Ndom. Two of the village's house clusters still inhabited at the time of fieldwork were inaccessible. The documented hearths can be partitioned into three shape categories: (1) rectangular with rounded angles; (2) rectangular with crenellated top; and (3) trapezoidal with rounded angles (fig. 44).The first category includes three specimens found in houses 2, 11, and 19. Hearth 19 is the simplest. It has four vertical and elongated clay bumps in the lower third, a horizontal, appliqué cordon delineating the upper third part of the panel, with the middle horizontal portion left plain. Hearth 11 has an asymmetric, horizontal, downward, L-shaped decoration arrangement (fig. 44). The decorative motif consists of pinched finger impressions arranged in parallel lines on appliqué vertical and horizontal cordons and the panel. And hearth 2, the last one of the category, has an elaborate decoration. The panel is divided into two almost equal registers. The upper one consists of a rectangular frame delineated by appliqué cordons filled with six more or less equidistant upward-oriented arrows (fig. 44). The lower register has an intriguing combination of signs, arranged into three distinct syntactic units: a left bracket, an upside down triangle, and an upward

Table 40: Frequency distribution of hearths' taxa

Settlement	Number of Hearths	Plain	Decorated	Categories / classes				Diversity
				I/cl.	II/cl.	III/cl.	IV/cl.	
Early Group								
Danguerchem	4	—	4	1	3	—	—	4
Gobrem	?	—	—	—	—	1	—	—
Ndom	5	2	3	3	1	—	—	5
Ngumati	1	—	1	—	—	—	—	1
Total	10	2	8	4	4	1	—	9
Middle Group								
Abuzrega	33	16	15	29/11	2/2	2/2	—	15
Djidat I	23	4	19	4/2	5/2	14/4	—	8
Djidat II	31	10	21	12/10	3/3	15/8	—	21
Marafaine	18	5	13	12/6	4/4	2/2	—	12
Mishiskwa	7	1	6	7/6	—	2/2	—	6
Total	112	36	74	64/11	14/4	33/8	—	23
Late Group								
Bawara	3	—	3	—	1/1	2/2	—	3
Bilbede	7	2	5	5/5	1/1	1/1	—	7
Gallis	7	2	5	6/5	—	—	1/1	6
Ngada I	13	4	9	7/5	3/3	2/2	1/1	11
Ngada II	19	3	16	11/8	3/2	—	4/3	13
Ngada III	11	4	7	6/6	—	5/5	—	11
Ngada IV	17	1	16	11/4	1/1	3/2	2/2	9
Total	77	16	61	46/8	9/3	13/5	8/3	19

Table 40: Continued

Dry-season Camps

Amachita I	6	3	3	4/2	—	—	2/1	3
Amachita II	5	1	4	3/3	—	1/1	1/1	5
Amachita III	8	2	6	4/3	—	1/1	3/3	7
Amachita IV	6	6	—	—	—	—	6/1	1
Amachita V	8	6	2	1/1	—	—	7/2	3
Amachita VI	6	3	3	1/1	—	—	5/3	4
Amachita VII	8	5	3	6/4	1/1	1/1	—	6
Agedipse I	17	7	10	6/4	2/1	9/6	—	11
Agedipse II	6	3	3	2/2	3/3	1/1	—	6
*Agedipse III	21	7	14	11/5	2/2	5/3	2/1	12
Agedipse IV	7	4	3	5/3	1/1	1/1	—	5

* An additional fifth category of bi-concave hearth was found in this site.

NGUMATI

22

21

01

Figure 43: Hearth designs from Ngumati and Damguerchem

arrow in the left; a left bracket, a double arrow, and a right bracket in the middle; and finally, a double arrow, a phi symbol, and a right bracket in the left.

The specimen from the second category with the crenellated top was recorded in house 13. Besides the crenellation, the decoration consists of a set of two superimposed, upward-oriented arrows at the vertical symmetry axis of the panel (fig. 44), overlined on the upper third by a horizontal, appliqué cordon with pinched finger impressions and complemented by series of pinched finger impressions of "hearthstones." The specimen from the third category, recorded in house 8, is probably the simplest of the Ndom sample. It has thickened sides and a series of four equidistant, vertical, and elongated clay bumps in the lower third (fig. 44).

Each of the recorded hearths is unique. There is, nonetheless, some overlap in terms of shape and/or motif elements: arrows are found on hearths 2 and 13 located in opposite parts of the village; pinched finger impressions are found on hearths 11 and 13 in neighboring house clusters; equidistant, vertical, and elongated clay bumps are found on hearths 8 and 19 from house clusters situated on opposite sides on the settlement; and a horizontal, appliqué cordon is found on hearths 2,

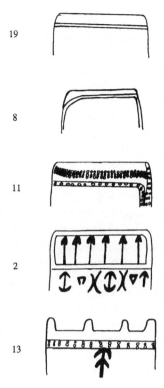

Figure 44: Hearth designs from Ndom

11, 13, and 19. Clearly, Ndom hearths do not appear to have any peculiarity of their own.

As far as Early Group settlements are concerned, the documented hearths share a certain number of characteristics, namely, horizontal, appliqué cordons at Danguerchem, Ngumati, and Ndom, upward-oriented arrows at Danguerchem and Ndom. In general, however, the recorded samples are still too small to allow for the emergence of significant patterns.

Hearths from the Middle Group Settlements

The Middle Group settlements include all four investigated permanently inhabited villages and one semi permanent one. The number of recorded hearths varies from a minimum of 7 at Mishiskwa to a maximum of 31 at Abuzrega and Djidat II (table 40). The sample recorded from the permanent villages is far below the effective number of hearths present in the settlements. This discrepancy results from the fact that fieldwork was carried out with the minimum possible disruption of villagers daily lives. Accordingly, most of the recorded hearths were accessible from the outside.

Thirty-three hearths have been recorded from Abuzrega, in the eastern part of the study area. They can be partitioned into three categories: (1) rectangularly shaped with rounded upper angles; (2) rectangularly shaped with two to three protruding tips; and (3) pseudo-crenellated shape.

Category 1 includes 29 specimens distributed into 11 classes. Class 1 includes features with plain panels (fig. 45). Thirteen such hearths have been found all over the site with, however, some significant clustering for houses belonging to the same habitation complex. It is the case for houses 3 and 9; houses 13, 18, and 19; houses 23 and 34; and houses 51 and 54. The remaining specimens from houses 43, 48, 63, and 70, are unique in their respective habitation complexes. Class 2 includes two occurrences found within the same habitation complex to the N of the site, in houses 38 and 42. The hearth's panel is divided into two plain registers by a horizontal, appliqué cordon (fig. 45). The upper register is a narrow band. The lower one is much broader and rectangular in shape. Class 3 has a single specimen found in house 7, in the S. The panel is divided into three registers. The upper one is decorated with a horizontal line of seven more or less equidistant appliqué buttons (fig. 45). The middle one has three equidistant upward-pointing arrows. And the lower one has three similarly equidistant, vertical, and elongated clay bumps adjusted to the arrows above. Class 4 is documented by the feature from house 58, an out-of-use kitchen. The hearth's decoration consists of two horizontal and

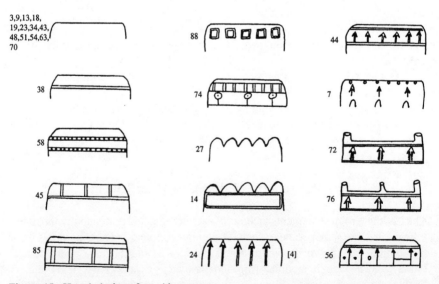

Figure 45: Hearth designs from Abuzrega

parallel appliqué cordons decorated with pinched finger impressions dividing the panel into three more or less equally sized registers (fig. 45). Class 5 hearths are found in house 9 in the S and house 45 in the N. The southern specimen is decorated with a horizontal upward capital *E* made of appliqué cordons (fig. 45). The northern one is divided into two registers by a horizontal, appliqué cordon, complemented in the upper half by three equidistant, short, vertical appliqué cordons (fig. 45). Class 6 includes four specimens. Two, from houses 24 and 31, within the same habitation complex,and those found in houses 47 and 78. The hearth's decoration consists of a series of five more or less equidistant, upward pointing arrows. Class 7 consists of two variants of a horizontal ladder motif made of appliqué cordons. The variant from house 26 (fig. 45) has a horizontal, appliqué cordon overlying three distinct more or less equidistant squares with one and two vertical partition lines. The specimen from house 85 has two horizontal and parallel appliqué cordons connected by four equidistant perpendicular short cordons (fig. 45). Class 8, with a single occurrence found in house 44, is a farther elaboration of house 85's variant, with, this time, six equidistant upward pointing arrows (fig. 45). Class 9, with a single case from house 88, has a horizontal line of five appliqué squares in the upper register. Class 10, recorded in house 74, has a horizontal ladder motif in the upper register, above three equidistant encircled dots supported by short, vertical, incised lines. Finally, class 11, recorded in house 56, has two protruding tips in addition to a horizontal, appliqué cordon, appliqué buttons, grooved horizontal lines, as well as five more or less equidistant, upward pointing grooved arrows (fig. 45).

Category 2 hearths have been documented in houses 72 and 76, and, as such, belong to the same habitation complex. The specimen from house 72 has two protruding tips at both right and left ends. The decoration consists of two horizontal and parallel appliqué cordons delimiting a framed space filled with three equidistant upward pointing arrows with pinched finger impressions (fig. 45). The specimen from house 76 lacks pinched finger impressions but has a third central protruding tip (fig. 45). Category 3, with pseudo-crenellated features, is comprised of two occurrences. The simplest, found in house 27, is plain. And the remaining one, from house 14, has a rectangular frame made of appliqué cordons, but left plain.

Besides the relatively high number of simple plain hearths, the upward pointing arrow motifs recorded on nine features appear to be a frequent decorative element, incised, grooved, or applied to the features panels. The horizontal, appliqué cordon documented on twelve hearths is even more frequent.

Twenty-three hearths have been recorded at Djidat I (Fig 45). They can be partitioned into three major shape categories: (1) rectangular with rounded upper angles, (2) rectangular with more or less right angles, and finally, (3) rectangular with protruding pointing tips. Category 1 is comprised of four hearths belonging to two classes. Class 1 includes three specimens from houses 1 and 8 in the N, and house 69 in the central E. In all three cases, a horizontal grooved line or an appliqué cordon divides the panel into two registers.The upper register is filled with four (house (1), five (house 8), and eight (house 69) more or less equidistant, upward-pointing arrows (fig. 46). Class 2 has a single specimen found in house 66 in the eastern part of the village. The panel is divided into two by a horizontal, appliqué cordon delineating a smaller upper register. The delineated upper register is filled with equidistant incised "tridents," and the panel's perimeter is decorated with a double line of finger impressions (fig. 46). Interestingly enough, category 1 hearths are distributed in pairs as far as the location is concerned. Houses 1 and 8 are situated in the northern part of the village but belong to distinct habitation complexes. Houses 66 and 69 in the E belong to the village headman's (Bilama) complex, each being the kitchen of a distinct wife.

Category 2, of rectangularly shaped features with more or less right upper angles, is comprised of five hearths divided into two classes. Class 1 has two specimens, found in house 4 in the N, and 41 in the S. Both are decorated on their upper register with a horizontal ladder motif. In house 4's hearth, the motif is made with four equidistant, vertical appliqué cordons (fig. 46); in house 41, the motif is narrower with twelve short, vertical lines. Class 2 consists of three specimens clustered in the western part of the village, in houses 21, 25, and 28. All three are two-pot-supporting hearths decorated with upward-pointing arrows (fig. 46). They differ in the structure and arrangement of their decoration. Hearth 21 has thickened sides delineating a rectangular, framed area filled with two parallel arrows. Hearth 25 has ten equidistant arrows resting on a horizontal cordon filling the upper register. And finally, hearth 28 has a narrow framed band in its upper third filled with eight more or less equidistant arrows.

Category 3, rectangular in shape with protruding, pointing tips, includes fourteen hearths out of twenty-three. They are divided into four classes with two to eight specimens each. Class 1, with a plain panel and four equidistant, pointing tips on the upper side, has two specimens, found in house 43 in the S and 74 in the N (fig. 46).

Class 2 has two specimens. One from house 7 in the N and the other from house 51a in the S. The latter specimen has a horizontal, appliqué cordon at mid-height with a vertical double line of finger impressions on the right side (fig. 46). The former has five equidistant, pointing tips instead of four, with a horizontal, appliqué cordon at mid-height. Class 3 is the largest with eight specimens. Despite some variations they all share three characteristics: (1) they are decorated with upward-pointing arrows; (2) they have three to six protruding, pointing tips; and (3) the decoration is set on the upper register. The specimens from house 13 in the NW, 31 in the central-W, and 79 in the N have four to five equidistant, pointing tips. The three to six upward, pointing arrows are set in a horizontal, more or less narrow, framed space of the upper register (fig. 46). The hearths from houses 45 and 48 in the S share a similar decoration, consisting of three to five upward-pointing arrows resting on a horizontal, appliqué cordon. Each of the remaining features has specific characteristics. The specimen from house 22 has two pointing tips at both left and right sides with the five floating arrows set on a horizontal, appliqué

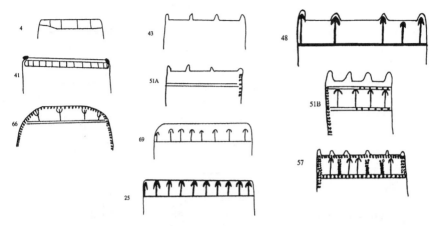

Figure 46: Hearth designs from Djidat I

cordon (fig. 46). That from house 55 has six pointing tips and five floating, upward-oriented arrows. And finally, house 67's hearth has its upper register decorated with two parallel meandering lines, the delineated space filled with eight upward-oriented arrows (fig. 46). Finally, class 4 is comprised of two occurrences from the same habitation complex located to the S of the village, in houses 51b and 57. They combine protruding, pointing tips with upward-oriented arrows, horizontal, appliqué cordons, and double-finger-impressions lines (fig. 46).

There is a handful of cases of preferential clustering of hearths with more or less similar motifs, decoration patterns and shapes. The reason for the widespread distribution of a motif such as the upward-pointing arrow will be discussed in the final part of this chapter.

Djidat II is the most packed and complex settlement studied during the research project. The sample of recorded hearths amounts to thirty-one specimens distributed into three categories with 3 to 10 classes (fig. 47). Category 1, rectangularly shaped with more or less right upper angles, is comprised of three classes each with a single specimen. Class 1, the simplest, is documented in house 43 in habitation complex 7 in the outer NE perimeter of the village. The upper third of the hearth's panel, delimited by a horizontal line, is decorated with two short, vertical, and parallel appliqué cordons (fig. 47). Class 2 is represented by the feature from house 118 in the W in habitation complex 22. It is a two-niches hearth with the rear panel decorated by two horizontal and parallel appliqué cordons (fig. 47). And finally, the class 3 installation is found in house 149 from the Marabout [Imam] habitation complex 24 in the S. The lower register has four more or less equidistant, vertical, and elongated clay bumps, and the upper one has four thickened sides delineating a framed space filled with four unevenly spaced, upward-pointing arrows (fig. 47).

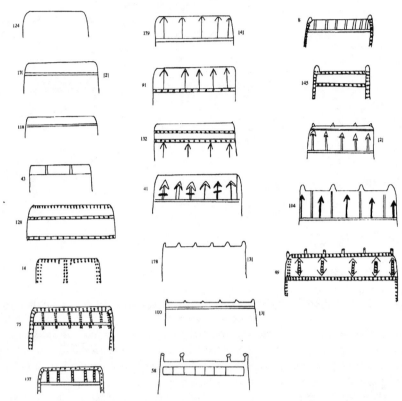

Figure 47: Hearth designs from Djidat II

Category 2, rectangularly shaped with more or less rounded upper angles, has
13 specimens divided into 10 classes. Class 1, an undecorated hearth, is found in
house 124 from habitation complex 23 in the SW of the site. Class 2 includes two
hearths, one from house 85 in habitation complex 5 in the centre-N and the other
from house 170 in the Marabout's habitation complex 24. The panel is divided into
two registers by a horizontal, appliqué cordon. The upper is left plain, and the
lower has four equidistant, vertical, and elongated clay bumps (fig. 47). Class 3
has one specimen recorded in house 15 from habitation complex 1 in the E. It is
decorated with double-finger impressions lines all along the sides with an additional vertical set at the panel's middle (fig. 47). Class 4 consists of three hearths with
minor variations in decorative elements. They all include a horizontal, appliqué
cordon at mid-height underlying five to eight more or less equidistant, upward-
pointing arrows (fig. 47). The specimen from house 91, in habitation complex 17
in the NW, has finger impressions on the horizontal cordon. That from house 112
in habitation complex 19 in the W has eight arrows in the upper register and four

vertical and elongated clay bumps in the lower. And finally, the house 179 specimen from the Marabout's habitation complex has the standard characteristics. Class 5 has one specimen found in house 128 in habitation complex 23 in the SW of the settlement. The panel is divided into three registers by two horizontal and parallel appliqué cordons. Both cordons and the upper side are decorated with finger impressions lines. Class 6 is attested by the hearth from house 41 in habitation 6 in the NE. A horizontal, appliqué cordon divides the panel into two registers. The lower one is narrow and plain. The upper one is filled with six upward-pointing arrows arranged in alternating dashed-non-dashed elements, a longer vertical line setting the right side limit of the decorated frame (fig. 47). Class 7, with a single specimen, is documented in house 132 from habitation 22 in the central-W of the site. The hearth's panel is divided into three registers by two horizontal, appliqué cordons decorated with finger impressions. The upper and the middle registers are plain (fig. 47). The lower one has four more or less equidistant upward-pointing arrows. Class 8's feature is found in house 75 in habitation 8 in the northern part of the village. It has a two-register panel with thickened sides (fig. 47). The thickened sides and the horizontal, appliqué cordon are decorated with pinched finger impressions. The upper register is filled with seven more or less evenly spaced, vertical double lines of finger impressions that "spilled" over the top side of the lower register. Class 9's hearth has been documented in house 137 in the Marabout's habitation complex in the S. The panel, divided into two registers by a horizontal, appliqué cordon, has a thickened edge. The lower register is narrow and plain. The upper one is filled with five more or less equidistant, vertical cordons. The thickened outlines as well as the vertical cordons are decorated with pinched finger impressions (fig. 47). Finally, class 10, also with a single occurrence, has been recorded from house 20 in habitation complex 2 in the E. The panel has a frame made of appliqué cordons delineating two registers. The lower one is broader and plain. The narrower upper one is filled with six evenly spaced, short, upward-oriented arrows (fig. 47).

Category 3, rectangularly shaped with protruding, pointed tips, is comprised of 14 hearths divided into eight classes. Class 1 has a single specimen found in house 178 of the Marabout's habitation complex 24 in the S. The hearth's panel is plain with, however, six more or less equidistant, pointing tips along the upper side (fig. 47). Class 2 includes five occurrences from house 55 in habitation complex 10 in the N, house 89 in complex 15 in the NW, house 100 in complex 18 in the W, house 102 in complex 20 in the central-W, and finally, house 133 in complex 23 in the SW. The number of pointing tips along the upper side of the hearth's panel varies from 3 (house 55) to 6 (house 100) with one pseudo-crenellated case (house 133). In all the cases, a horizontal, appliqué cordon divides the panel into two registers of varying size depending on specimens. The lower register has four more or less equidistant, vertical, and elongated clay bumps (fig. 47). Class 3, with one case, is represented by the hearth from house 58 in habitation complex 10 in the N. The four pointing tips are arranged into symmetric pairs at both left and right

ends of the panel. The decoration, representing a horizontal ladder with two horizontal lines and seven short, vertical ones, is a narrow band in the upper third portion of the panel (fig. 47). Class 4 is represented by the hearth from house 145 in
the Marabout's habitation complex 24. It has two pointing tips, one at each corner,
thickened edges, and a horizontal, appliqué cordon at mid-height. Both upper and
lower registers are plain, the pinched finger impressions being confined to the
thickened sides and the cordon (fig. 47). Class 5's feature from house 84 in habitation complex 5 in the central-N, is a farther elaboration of the class 4 one. The
right and left sides of the panel are thickened and decorated with finger impressions.
The upper register is filled with seven more or less evenly spaced, short, vertical
lines (fig. 47). Class 6's hearth has been recorded in house 104 in habitation
complex 20 in the W. The rear panel has four evenly spaced, pointing tips. It is divided into lower and upper registers by a horizontal, appliqué cordon.The lower
register has four vertical and elongated clay bumps arranged into two symmetric
pairs (fig. 47). The upper one is divided into five smaller rectangular frames, each
one filled with an upward-oriented arrow. Class 7 has two specimens from houses 7
and 97. The former has four pointing tips and four vertical and elongated clay bumps,
and the latter, five tips and two "burners." Both have a space delimited at the bottom and top by parallel horizontal, appliqué cordons filled with five more or less
equidistant, upward-oriented arrows (fig. 47). Finally, class 8 has three occurrences.
One is documented in house 49 in habitation complex 9 in the N, and the remaining two from houses 135 and 141 in the S in the Marabout's habitation complex.
They have 4 (house 141) to 6 (house 49) pointing tips along their upper side and
a certain amount of variation in their decoration. Specimen 46 has four vertical and
elongated clay bumps in the lower register and a framed upper register filled with
five unevenly spaced, double headed arrows (fig. 47). The arrows, the horizontal
cordon, as well as the panel's sides are decorated with pinched finger impressions.
Specimen 135 also has vertical and elongated clay bumps in the lower register; but
they are smaller in size. The middle register, delineated by two horizontal, appliqué
cordons, is filled with six equidistant, upward-oriented arrows. And the upper register is reduced to a very narrow horizontal band between two cordons. The bottom and top cordons are decorated with pinched finger impressions. House 141's
specimen is a farther elaboration of the preceding variant, with three horizontal
and parallel appliqué cordons decorated with finger impressions delineating three
registers. The lower one, the broader, is filled with five unevenly spaced, upward-
oriented arrows. The remaining upper two are plain, narrow, horizontal bands
(fig. 47).

   The distribution patterns of the Djidat II hearths provide two striking features.
Nine hearths are undecorated, and thirteen out of twenty-two decorated panels include arrows as a principal design element. The Marabout's habitation complex
emerges as the one with the highest diversity of hearth shape and design.

   Eighteen hearths have been documented at Marafaine.They are divided into
three categories, each with 2 to 6 classes of specimens (fig. 48). Category 1 consists

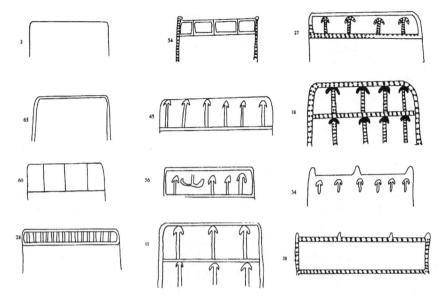

Figure 48: Hearth designs from Marafaine

of hearths with rectangularly shaped panels and more or less right angles. They are divided into four classes, each with a single specimen. Class 1 has been recorded in house 2 in the southwestern portion of the site. It is a "two-burners" hearth with a plain panel (fig. 48). Class 2 is found in house 60 in the NW. The feature has two complementary hearthstones. Its panel is divided into two registers by a horizontal, appliqué cordon. The lower is narrower and plain, and the upper filled with three equidistant, vertical, and parallel lines (fig. 48). Class 3, from house 56 in the N, is a "two-burners" hearth. Its panel has thickened sides. The framed space is filled with uneven, poorly designed, thick, upward-oriented arrows, with an additional anchor-like motif (fig. 48). Finally, class 4, documented in house 54 in the same northern habitation complex is also a "two-burners" hearth. The rear panel has thickened left and right sides, both decorated with pinched finger impressions. The lower register is slightly broader and plain. The upper one is filled with a horizontal succession of smaller rectangles made of appliqué cordons (fig. 48).

Category 2, rectangular with more or less rounded upper angles, includes twelve hearths divided into six classes. Class 1 consists of plain panel hearths with two to four "burners" (fig. 48). Three such specimens have been recorded in house 12 in the S, house 46 in the NE, and house 52 in the N. Class 2 has a single specimen documented in house 65 in the W. It has four "burners" and an undecorated panel with thickened sides (fig. 48). Class 3 includes three occurrences recorded in house 9 in the SW, and houses 35 and 45 in the NE. There are minor variations from one specimen to the other, specifically in the number of burners and arrows.

In all the cases, a horizontal, appliqué cordon divides the panel into two registers. The lower one is narrower and left plain. The upper is filled with four to six more or less equidistant, upward-oriented arrows (fig. 48). Class 4, with two specimens, from houses 25 and 27 in the SE, is a farther elaboration of class 3 features. In this case, the four and five upward-oriented arrows are within a framed space in the upper (house 27) and middle (house 25) registers. The frame's sides and arrows are decorated with pinched finger impressions (fig. 48). Class 5 has one specimen, found in house 28 to the E of the site. The upper third of the panel has a framed, narrow, horizontal band filled with evenly spaced, short, vertical lines, creating a horizontal ladder design (fig. 48). Finally, class 6 includes two occurrences, found in houses 18 in the S and 41 in the NE. In both cases, the panel is framed by thickened sides and divided into two symmetric registers by a horizontal, appliqué cordon. The lower and the upper registers have the same number of superimposed, upward-oriented arrows (fig. 48), three on three in house 41 and four on four in house 18. The latter is farther decorated with pinched finger impressions.

Category 3, rectangular with pointing tips, consists of two classes of hearths, each with a single specimen. Class 1's feature, documented in house 34 in the E, has three equidistant, pointing tips along its upper side (fig. 48). The decoration consists of a line of upward-oriented arrows set in the upper third of the hearth's panel. Class 2's hearth is found in house 38 in the central-E. It has four equidistant, pointing tips as well as four thickened sides delineating a perfectly framed space, left plain. The lower register has six small, vertical, and elongated clay bumps. And the frame is decorated with pinched finger impressions.

With the notable exception of houses 25 and 27, located in the same part of the village and sharing strong similarities in hearth shape and design, there is no other case of preferential clustering documented in the Marafaine case.

Seven out twenty-two hearths have been recorded from Mishiskwa. They all belong to the same category of rectangular features with more or less rounded upper angles (fig. 49) and can be divided into six classes. Class 1's hearth is found in house 5 in the N. The panel is divided into two symmetric registers by a horizontal and appliqué cordon (fig. 49). The lower register has four equidistant, vertical, and elongated clay bumps, and the upper one is left plain. Class 2 is documented in house 20 in the E. The panel has thickened sides and a horizontal, appliqué cordon decorated with pinched finger impressions. The upper register is plain, and the lower one has four equidistant, vertical, and elongated clay bumps (fig. 49). Class 3 has been recorded in house 23, also in the E. The hearth's panel has a thickened outline and two horizontal and parallel appliqué cordons, with the upper one decorated with pinched finger impressions. The middle and upper registers are plain, and the lower has four equidistant, vertical, and elongated clay bumps (fig. 49). Class 4 includes two specimens, both from the western part of the site, in houses 40 and 44. They have a framed upper register filled, respectively, with four and six more or less equidistant, upward-oriented arrows. The framed sides and the arrows are decorated with pinched finger impressions. The lower

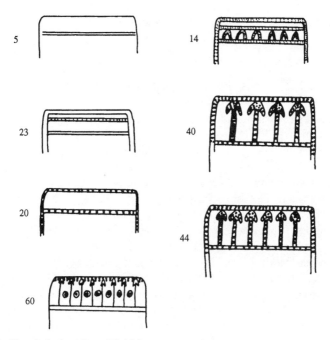

Figure 49: Hearth designs from Mishiskwa

registers have four to five more or less evenly spaced, vertical, and elongated clay bumps (fig. 49). Class 5 has one specimen, found in house 3 in the central-W. The panel is divided into two registers by a horizontal, appliqué cordon. The lower register has four vertical and elongated clay bumps. The upper one is decorated with a combination of three design elements: a double horizontal line of finger impressions along the upper side, a series of eight evenly spaced, upward-oriented arrows, and at mid-height, a line of small appliqué circles filling the inter-arrows space (fig. 49). And finally, class 6, which includes the most elaborate specimen documented from the site, is recorded in house 14 in the N (fig. 49). The hearth's panel is framed by a thickened rim decorated with finger impressions. Two horizontal and parallel appliqué cordons, also decorated with finger impressions generate a tripartite space. The lower, and broadest one, has five more or less evenly spaced, vertical, and elongated clay bumps. The upper, and narrowest, register is left plain. And finally, the middle one, of intermediate size, is filled with unevenly spaced, horseshoe shaped appliqué motifs decorated with finger impressions (fig. 49).

The sample documented from Mishiskwa represents approximately one third of the represented features. Finger impressions appear to be the predominant decoration technique. Appliqué horizontal cordons are found on all the documented cases, and five out of seven hearths have a framed upper half. All the recorded cases belong to the northern half of the settlement, the specimens from houses 40 and 44 being the closest in terms of stylistic similarity.

Hearths from the Late Group Settlements

The frequency of hearths documented among the Late Group settlements ranges from a minimum of 3 at Bawara to a maximum of 17 at Ngada IV (table 40). Each of the three hearths recorded at Bawara is unique. The specimen found in house 4 in the S is rectangular in shape with more or less right upper angles (fig. 50). The panel is divided into two registers by a horizontal, appliqué cordon decorated with finger impressions. The lower register is plain and has four more or less equidistant, vertical, and elongated clay bumps. The upper one is filled with a series of six unevenly spaced vertical double lines. The feature from house 10 in the N was poorly preserved but broken parts were still accessible. The hearth belongs to the rectangularly shaped with pointing tips category. In this case there are four such tips arranged along the upper side of the panel. The latter is divided into three registers by two horizontal and parallel appliqué cordons (fig. 50). The upper register is a narrow, plain band. The lower one, much broader, has three evenly spaced, vertical, and elongated clay bumps. And finally, the middle one, of intermediate size, is filled with five equidistant, appliqué, vertical lugs. The specimen from house 8 in the SW is also rectangular in shape with six pointing tips and low lateral walls (fig. 50) The rear panel is divided into three registers. The lower has four equidistant, vertical, and elongated clay bumps. The upper one is left plain while the middle

Figure 50: Hearth designs from Bawara

register is "lavishly" decorated. The design includes two horizontal and parallel appliqué cordons, a superimposed set of five perpendicular, upward-oriented arrows, with the delimited square frames filled with short horizontal lines of finger impressions (fig. 50).

Seven hearths were recorded at Bilbede. They can be divided into three categories—rectangularly shaped with rounded upper angles, rectangular with right upper angles, and rectangular with pointing tips (fig. 51). The first category includes five specimens, each unique. Class 1, the simplest feature, is documented in house 29 in the E. The panel is divided into two registers by a horizontal, appliqué cordon. The lower part has five evenly spaced, vertical, and elongated clay bumps, and the upper is a narrow, plain band (fig. 51). Class 2's hearth is found in house 35 in the S. Its panel has thickened sides and a horizontal, appliqué cordon delineating two registers. The lower register is much broader and has seven

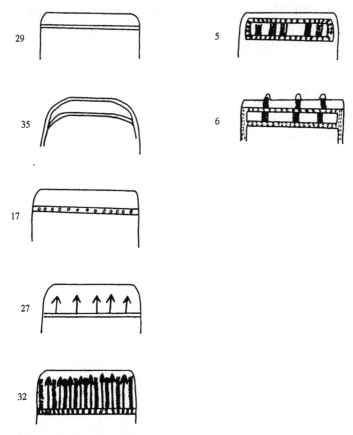

Figure 51: Hearth designs from Bilbede

equidistant, small, vertical, and elongated clay bumps (fig. 51). The upper is a narrower framed but plain space. Class 3, with a single specimen, is recorded in house 27 in the NE. The rear panel is divided into two symmetric parts by a horizontal, appliqué cordon. The lower register is plain. The upper one is decorated with five more or less equidistant, short, upward-oriented arrows (fig. 51). Class 4 is represented by the hearth from house 5 in the S. The lower register has five equidistant, vertical, and elongated clay bumps, and the upper one is a framed, rectangular space. The frame is decorated with pinched finger impressions and the delimited space is filled with five sets of vertical finger impressions lines (fig. 51). Finally, class 5 is found in house 32 in the SE. The whole rear panel is decorated. It is divided into two by a horizontal, appliqué cordon decorated with finger impressions. The lower register is narrow and plain.The upper one is filled with alternating vertical, double-finger impression lines and upward-oriented arrows (fig. 51).

The second and third categories include one specimen each. The second category occurrence, rectangular in shape with right upper angles, is found in house 17 in the N. The rear panel is divided into two by a horizontal, appliqué cordon decorated with finger impressions. The lower register is broader and includes two vertical and elongated clay bumps. The upper one is narrower and plain (fig. 51). The remaining category 3 case, rectangular with pointing tips, is recorded in house 6 in the SW. The hearth's rear panel is divided into three horizontal registers by two parallel appliqué cordons. These cordons, complemented by vertical, perpendicular appliqué lines, are all decorated with finger impressions. Three in the center are adjusted to the pointing tips (fig. 51), and two are found on the sides.The overall design thus consists of a lower register with six more or less evenly spaced, vertical, and elongated clay bumps, a middle register with four plain, rectangular frames, and the upper one with a horizontal succession of plain surfaces.

With each specimen unique, there is clearly no pattern to be discerned in the spatial layout of the documented hearths. finger impressions are, however, found on four features, with houses 5 and 6 as neighbors in the SW. Arrows are found in two occurrences, in houses 27 and 32, both located in the eastern part of the village.

More than half of the Gallis house clusters were still inhabited at the time of fieldwork. Despite the relative large size of the settlement, the number of recorded hearths amounts to seven only. They belong to two categories: rectangularly with more or less rounded upper angles; and a hybrid, rectangular with rounded and right upper angles (fig. 52). The first category includes five variants. Class 1, the simplest, has been recorded in house 4 in the southeastern part of the settlement. The hearth's panel is divided into two equal registers by a horizontal, appliqué cordon. The upper half is plain and the lower one has six evenly spaced, vertical, and elongated clay bumps (fig. 52). Class 2 is found in house 28 in the W. The hearth's panel has thickened sides with a horizontal, appliqué cordon at mid-height, all decorated with finger impressions. The lower register has five equidistant, vertical,

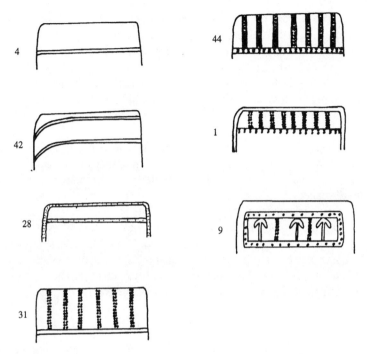

Figure 52: Hearth designs from Gallis

and elongated clay bumps, and the upper one is left plain (fig. 52). Class 3 includes two specimens with minor differences. Both have a horizontal, appliqué cordon dividing the panel into two registers with the lower one left plain and the upper decorated with six/seven sets of vertical, double lines of finger impressions. House 31, located in the western part of the site, has a specimen with an undecorated cordon, while that from house 44 in the central-E has pinched finger impressions. Class 4 has one occurrence, found in house 1 in the SE. The upper half of the hearth's panel has thickened sides on the right, left, and top, with the bottom delineated by a horizontal line of pinched finger impressions. The framed space is filled with eight more or less equidistant sets of vertical, double lines of finger impressions. The lower register, on the other hand, has three evenly spaced, vertical, and elongated clay bumps (fig. 52). Finally, class 5, with one specimen, has been documented in house 9 to the E of the site.The hearth's panel has a framed space in the upper half. The frame's perimeter, made of appliqué cordons, is decorated with a single finger impressions. The inside is divided into three smaller, square frames by vertical, double lines of finger impressions. Each of the smaller frames has an upward-oriented arrows at its center (fig. 51).

Category 2 includes a single specimen found in house 42 to the S of the settlement. The hearth's panel is divided into three registers by parallel, rectilinear-convex appliqué cordons. The lower register has six more or less evenly spaced, vertical, and elongated clay bumps. The middle as well as the upper ones are plain (fig. 52).

As far as the Gallis hearths' sample is concerned, double-finger impression lines are found on five specimens and horizontal, appliqué cordons on all but one. There is, however, no perceptible preferential clustering, either of shapes or motifs.

Thirteen hearths have been documented at Ngada I (fig. 53). They can be partitioned into four categories: (1) rectangularly with rounded upper angles; (2) rectangularly with lateral, low walls; (3) rectangularly with pointing tips; and finally, (4) trapeze shaped.

Category 1 is comprised of five variants. The simplest hearth class is found in house 30 to the N of the settlement. The rear panel is plain with two vertical and elongated clay bumps in the lower half (fig. 53). Class 2 is recorded in house 11 in the W. The panel is divided into two equal registers by two parallel and horizontal, appliqué cordons, both decorated with finger impressions. The upper register is left plain. The lower one has seven small, unevenly spaced, vertical, and

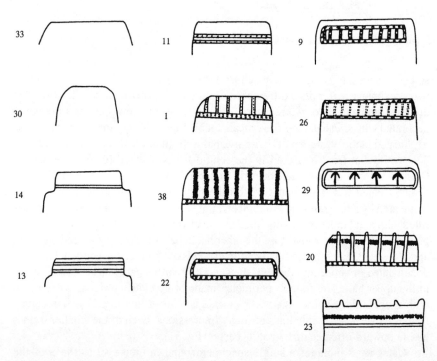

Figure 53: Hearth designs from Ngada I

elongated clay bumps (fig. 53). Class 3 is represented by a single specimen from house 38 to the E of the settlement. The hearth's panel is divided into two by a horizontal cordon decorated with pinched finger impressions (fig. 53). The lower register is plain. The upper one is filled with eight unevenly spaced sets of vertical, double lines of finger impressions (fig. 53). Class 4 hearth is found in house 29 in the N. The panel is divided in two parts. The lower part has five more or less equidistant, vertical, and elongated clay bumps. The upper one has a rectangular, framed space filled with four evenly spaced, short, upward-oriented arrows. Class 5 is a farther elaboration of the preceding one. It includes two specimens, one from house 9 in the W and the other from house 26 in the N (fig. 53). In both cases, the upper register has a rectangular frame decorated with finger impressions, the delineated space filled with nine sets of short, vertical, single or double lines of finger impressions. The lower register has five (house 9) and seven vertical and elongated clay bumps.

Category 2, rectangular in shape with low lateral walls, is comprised of three occurrences, all documented in the same northwestern part of the settlement, in houses 13, 14, and 22. Class 1 is represented by the hearth from house 14, the simplest in terms of decoration. The panel is divided into two registers by a horizontal, appliqué cordon. The upper half is plain, and the lower half has two pairs of vertical and elongated clay bumps. Class 2 is recorded in house 13. Two horizontal and parallel appliqué cordons decorate the upper half of the panel, the lower one having five more or less equidistant, vertical, and elongated clay bumps (fig. 53). Finally class 3, documented in house 22, has five equidistant, vertical, and elongated clay bumps in the lower register. The upper register, on the other hand, has a rectangular framed, but plain, space. The frame is however decorated with pinched finger impressions (fig. 53).

Category 3, rectangular in shape with pointing tips, consists of two specimens recorded from the same household to the N of the site, in houses 20 and 23. Class 1 is the pseudo-crenellated hearth from house 23. Six more or less evenly spaced, pointed tips are found along the top side of the rear panel. It is divided into two registers by a horizontal and appliqué cordon. The upper register is decorated with a horizontal, double line of finger impressions. The lower one has four vertical and elongated clay bumps arranged into pairs (fig. 53). Class 2, from house 20, has its panel also divided into two symmetric registers by a horizontal, appliqué cordon decorated with pinched finger impressions. The lower has five unevenly spaced, vertical, and particularly elongated clay bumps. The upper part has six vertical appliqué cordons tipping above the panel's upper side and supported by the mid-height horizontal cordon. Finally, there is a horizontal, double line of finger impressions along the panel's upper edge.

Category 4, trapezoidal in shape, is represented by one occurrence, the plain hearth from house 33 in the eastern part of the settlement (fig. 53). As far as design elements are concerned, Ngada I hearths appear to be predominantly decorated with finger impressions and appliqué cordons.

Nineteen hearths have been recorded at Ngada II. They are divided into three main categories with frequencies varying from three to ten (fig. 54). Category 1, rectangular in shape with rounded upper angles, includes eight variants. Class 1 is comprised of two specimens with minor differences. House 40's hearth, found in the southern part of the settlement, has a panel divided into two registers by a horizontal, appliqué cordon.The lower register has seven narrow, vertical, and elongated clay bumps more or less evenly spaced. The upper one has the perimeter decorated with finger impressions delineating a framed plain space (fig. 54). The second specimen, from house 26 in the NE, has a rectangular, framed, plain space

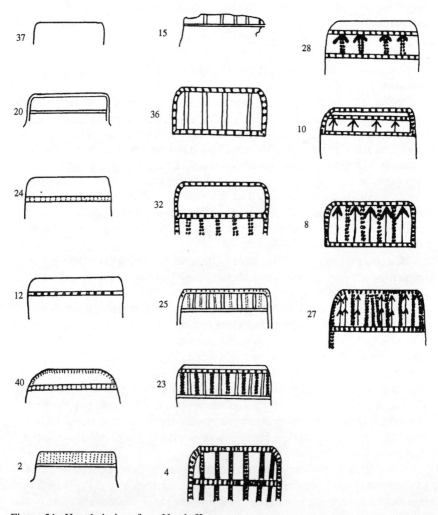

Figure 54: Hearth designs from Ngada II

made of cordons decorated with finger impressions in the upper register. The lower register, on the other hand, has five equidistant, vertical, and elongated clay bumps. Class 2 is represented by one specimen from house 36 in the SE of the village. The perimeter of the panel is framed with appliqué cordons decorated with pinched finger impressions. The delineated space is then filled with four unevenly spaced appliqué, vertical cordons (fig. 54). Class 3 is documented in house 32 in the eastern part of the settlement. The panel has a thickened perimeter decorated with pinched finger impressions. It is divided into two registers by a horizontal, appliqué cordon also decorated with finger impressions (fig. 54). The lower register has five equidistant, vertical, and elongated clay bumps alternating with five vertical, double lines of finger impressions (fig. 54). Class 4 hearths are represented by two specimens found in houses 23 and 25 in the NE. There are slight variations between the recorded installations. House 25's case has a thickened panel perimeter and two registers. The lower one is plain. The upper one is framed and divided into six smaller square surfaces by short, vertical, appliqué cordons. Each of the smaller square frame has a vertical, double line of finger impressions in its central bottom-top axis, with the upper side decorated with a line of finger impressions (fig. 54). House 23's hearth has no thickened sides but, instead, a framed upper register with a decoration pattern similar to that from the house 25 feature (fig. 54). Class 5 is represented by one specimen, found in house 28 in the E. The hearth's panel is divided into three registers by two horizontal and parallel appliqué cordons decorated with pinched finger impressions. The upper register is a narrow plain band (fig. 54). The lower one has five unevenly spaced, vertical, and elongated clay bumps. And finally, the middle one, and the broadest, is filled with four more or less equidistant, upward-oriented arrows partly made of pinched finger impressions (fig. 54). Class 6, documented by the hearth from house 10 in the western part of the village, is a farther elaboration of the preceding occurrence. In this case, the framed space from the upper register, filled with four equidistant, upward-oriented arrows, is set within another frame, with all the appliqué cordons decorated with pinched finger impressions (fig. 54). The lower register, on the other hand, has six evenly spaced, vertical, and elongated clay bumps. Class 7 includes one hearth found in house 4 to the S of the village. The panel has a thickened perimeter and two registers delimited by a horizontal, appliqué cordon. Both upper and lower registers are filled with six unevenly spaced, vertical cordons. The perimeter, the horizontal, as well as the vertical cordons are decorated with pinched finger impressions (fig. 54). Finally, class 8 includes two specimens, one from house 8 in the W and the other from 27 in the NE. The former has two registers; the lower with five unevenly spaced, vertical, and elongated clay bumps, and the upper with a framed and decorated space. The design pattern consists of a framed perimeter decorated with pinched finger impressions, five smaller rectangular frames delimited by vertical, double lines of finger impressions, and an upward-oriented arrow at the vertical axis of each of the rectangles (fig. 54). The latter specimen has its perimeter decorated with finger impressions as is the case for the horizontal, appliqué cordon (fig. 54). The framed space is then filled with superimposed upward-oriented arrows alternating with vertical double lines of finger impressions.

Category 2, rectangular in shape with more or less upper right angles, is comprised of two classes with one to two specimens each. Class 1 includes two occurrences, found in house 12 in the NW and 24 in the NE. The panel is divided into two registers by a horizontal, appliqué cordon decorated with finger impressions. In both cases, the upper register is left plain. The lower one has five (house 12) or nine (house 24) unevenly spaced, vertical, and elongated clay bumps (fig. 54). Class 2 has a single specimen, from house 15 located in the northwestern part of the site. A horizontal, appliqué cordon delineates an upper register on the upper third of the hearth's panel (fig. 54). The lower two-thirds incorporates five more or less evenly spaced, vertical, and elongated clay bumps. The decoration of the upper register consists of five unevenly spaced short, vertical cordons (fig. 54).

Category 3, rectangularly shaped with low lateral walls, consists of three hearth classes, each with a single specimen. Class 1 hearth, the simplest, was recorded in house 37 in the SE of the village. It is an undecorated feature with six more or less equidistant, vertical, and elongated clay bumps (fig. 54). Class 2 is documented in house 20 in the N. The hearth's panel has a thickened perimeter and a horizontal, appliqué cordon at mid-height, both undecorated. The lower register has six evenly spaced, vertical, and elongated clay bumps (fig. 54). Finally, class 3, found in house 2 in the S has the upper register delineated by a horizontal, appliqué cordon decorated with lines of fingers' impression. The lower register has four vertical and elongated clay bumps arranged into two pairs (fig. 4).

There is no significant pattern emerging from the detailed examination of the spatial distribution of shape and design of Ngada II hearths. In terms of frequency, however, finger impressions, single or pinched, as well as horizontal, appliqué cordons are clearly the most recurrent decorative and design elements.

Eleven hearths have been recorded at Ngada III. They are divided into two categories: rectangular with rounded upper angles, and rectangular in shape with upward-pointing tips (fig. 55). Category 1 includes six specimens, each unique in its combination of characteristics. Class 1, a plain feature and the simplest hearth of the category, is found in house 35 to the S of the settlement (fig. 55). Class 2 is documented in house 18 in the N. The hearth's panel, with a thickened perimeter, is divided into three registers by two horizontal and parallel appliqué cordons (fig. 55). The lower register has four unevenly spaced vertical and elongated clay bumps. The middle and upper ones are plain horizontal bands. Class 3 is found in house 2 in the SW. The hearth's panel is divided into symmetric registers by a horizontal, appliqué cordon set at mid-height. The lower register is left plain, and the upper is decorated with nine sets of unevenly spaced, vertical, double lines of finger impressions (fig. 55). Class 4 has been recorded in house 8 to the W of the site. The panel has a thickened perimeter and a horizontal cordon delineating a framed upper register. The delimited space is then filled with six sets of more or less equi-

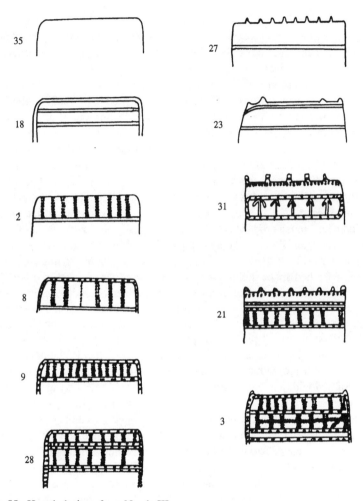

Figure 55: Hearth designs from Ngada III

distant, vertical, double finger impressions lines (fig. 55). Class 5, from house 9, also W of the site, is a farther elaboration of the preceding case. The hearth's panel has a thickened perimeter decorated with pinched finger impressions. It is divided into two registers by a horizontal, appliqué cordon also decorated with pinched finger impressions. The lower register has five equidistant, vertical, and elongated clay bumps. The upper one is filled with twelve parallel sets of vertical, double finger impressions lines (fig. 55). Class 6 is recorded in house 28 in the SE of the settlement. The hearth's panel, with a thickened perimeter, is lavishly decorated with simple or pinched finger impressions (fig. 55). It is divided into three registers by two sets of horizontal and parallel, appliqué cordons. The lower register has six equidistant, vertical, and elongated clay bumps. The middle one is a rectangular framed space filled with six sets of more or less equidistant, vertical, double finger impressions lines. And finally, the upper register, also a framed space, is decorated with eight sets of unevenly spaced, vertical double lines of finger impressions.

Category 2 is comprised of five specimens, each of them equally unique, as is the case for the preceding group. Class 1 is documented in house 27 in the eastern side of the site. The hearth's panel has eight equidistant, pointing tips along its upper side and a horizontal, appliqué cordon at mid-height (fig. 55). The upper register is left plain, and the lower one has six evenly spaced, vertical, and elongated clay bumps. Class 2, found in house 23, slightly N but still in the eastern part of the site, has four pointing tips arranged into pairs at both left and right ends of the panel (fig. 55). The latter has two horizontal and parallel appliqué cordons delineating three registers. The upper one is reduced to a very narrow horizontal band. The middle one, much broader, is left plain. And finally, the lower one has five equidistant, vertical, and elongated clay bumps. Class 3's hearth, recorded in house 31 in the southern side of the village, has five equidistant, pointing tips along its upper side. A framed space delimited by appliqué cordons is set at mid-height and decorated with pinched finger impressions. The delineated middle register is filled with five equidistant, upward-oriented arrows. The lower register has six evenly spaced, vertical, and elongated clay bumps. And finally, the upper one is decorated with a horizontal line of pinched finger impressions (fig. 55). Class 4 is documented in house 21 in the northeastern side of the settlement. The hearth's panel is pseudo-crenellated with eight evenly spaced, pointing tips along its upper side, each decorated with pinched finger impressions (fig. 55). The design is organized into three registers generated by three horizontal and parallel appliqué cordons decorated with single finger impressions and arranged into units of two and one. The lower register has six equidistant, vertical, and elongated clay bumps. The upper one is a relatively narrow band decorated with a horizontal double finger impressions line. And finally, the middle register is filled with nine sets of unevenly spaced, vertical, double lines of finger impressions (fig. 55). Class 5, the remaining specimen, is found in house 3 in the SW. The hearth's panel has two pointing tips, one at each upper corner. It has a thickened perimeter and three horizontal and parallel appliqué cordons, all decorated with finger impressions (fig. 55). The lower register is a narrow, horizontal, plain band. The upper one is broader and filled with nine sets of unevenly spaced vertical double lines of finger impressions. The finally, the middle one is decorated with intersecting finger impressions lines delineating fourteen small rectilinear frames (fig. 55).

The use of a horizontal, appliqué cordon as a key design element appears to be the dominant characteristic of Ngada III hearths. It is absent from a single house 35. Finger impression lines, and more precisely short, vertical, double lines are particularly noteworthy in the sample from this settlement. Despite the specificity of each of the recorded hearths, the features documented from houses 2, 3,

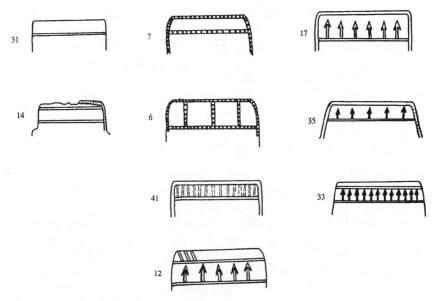

Figure 56: Hearth designs from Ngada IV

8, and 9, in neighboring household units located in the SW of the settlement, share common design elements: horizontal cordons, thickened perimeters, and sets of vertical double-finger-impression lines (fig. 55).

Seventeen hearths have been recorded at Ngada IV (fig. 56). They can be partitioned into four categories: (1) rectangular with rounded upper angles; (2) rectangular with right upper angles; (3) trapezoidal in shape with more or less rounded upper angles; and (4) rectangularly with rounded upper angles with low lateral walls. Category 1 is comprised of ten specimens divided into four classes. Class 1 has four occurrences, documented in houses 3 and 7 in the S, 45 in the E, and 39 in the N. The hearth's panel has a thickened perimeter decorated with pinched finger impressions. It is divided into two registers by a horizontal, appliqué cordon also decorated with pinched finger impressions. The lower register has five to seven vertical and elongated clay bumps, and the upper one is a framed, plain space (fig. 56). Class 2 consists of three specimens, found in neighboring houses 5 and 6 in the S and house 53 in the SE. The hearth's panel is divided into two registers. The lower one has four to six vertical and elongated clay bumps. The upper register corresponds to a framed space subdivided into four to seven smaller units by vertical cordons and/or double finger impressions lines (fig. 56). Class 3 has a single specimen, recorded in house 12 in the SW of the settlement. The hearth's panel is divided into three registers by two horizontal and parallel appliqué cordons. The lower register is plain. The middle one is filled with five equidistant, upward-oriented arrows. And finally, the upper one, a relatively narrow horizontal band, has a set of three slightly oblique appliqué cordons on the left (fig. 56). Class 4 includes two hearths; from house 17 in the W and 27 in the NW. In both cases, the panel has a thickened perimeter and a horizontal, appliqué cordon generating two almost symmetric registers. The lower register has four (house 17) to six (house 27) vertical and elongated clay bumps. The upper is filled with six (house 17) to five (house 27) equidistant, upward-oriented arrows (fig. 56).

Category 2, rectangular with right upper angles, is comprised of a single specimen, documented in house 31 in the NW of the village. A horizontal, appliqué cordon divides the hearth's panel into two equal parts. The lower register has three equidistant, vertical, and elongated clay bumps and the upper one was left plain (fig. 56).

Category 3, rectangular in shape with rounded upper angles and low lateral walls, includes two classes of hearth with one specimen each.The specimen found in house 14 in the SW of the village is partly damaged on its upper side. The panel has a thickened right side decorated with pinched finger impressions and divided into three registers by two horizontal and parallel appliqué cordons. The upper and middle registers are plain. The lower one has six evenly spaced, vertical, and elongated clay bumps (fig. 56). The specimen from house 41 in the NE has its panel divided into symmetric registers. The upper is perfectly framed with a thickened perimeter. The delineated rectangular space is then filled with a series of eleven vertical double-finger-impression lines (fig. 56). The lower one has five more or less evenly spaced, vertical, and elongated bumps.

Category 4, the remaining one, trapezoidal in shape with more or less rounded upper angles, includes two variants. Class 1 is found in house 35 in the NW of the settlement. The hearth's panel has a thickened perimeter decorated with finger impressions on the right side, with, in addition, a horizontal, appliqué cordon delimiting two registers. The lower and broader one has five equidistant, vertical, and elongated clay bumps. The upper, and narrower, is filled with five unevenly spaced, upward-oriented arrows (fig. 56). Class 2 has been recorded in the neighboring house 33 in the same northwestern part of the village. The hearth's panel is divided into three horizontal registers by two parallel appliqué cordons. The upper register is a narrow, plain band. The lower one is broader but equally plain. The middle one, intermediate in size, is filled with twelve short, upward-oriented arrows (fig. 56).

As far as the spatial distribution of Ngada IV hearths is concerned, features with arrow motifs found in houses 12, 17, 27, 33, and 35, are confined to the western half of the village. Those with finger impressions on appliqué cordons, documented in houses 3, 5, 6, 7, 41, 45, and 53, are preferentially located in the eastern half, with the notable exception of house 14. The design similarities and motif selection documented in Ngada IV seem to derive from clear elective affinity between household members from distinct extended family groups.

Hearths from the Dry-Season Camps

The state of preservation of dry-season camps' hearths varies enormously. In some settlements, almost all the fireplaces were destroyed by livestock trampling. In others, virtually all the built hearths appear to have been preserved (table 40).

Six hearths out of a total of ten were well-preserved enough to be recorded at Amachita I [Djidat] in the Amachita camps' cluster. Two shape categories, convex and rectangular, are represented (fig. 57). There are two cases of convex hearths found in houses 3 and 6. Both are undecorated with three equidistant, vertical, and elongated clay bumps in the lower half (fig. 57). The rectangular hearths are divided into two classes. Class 1 includes a single specimen, found in house 5. It has three equidistant, vertical, and elongated clay bumps in the lower half and a horizontal, appliqué cordon in the upper one (fig. 57). Class 2 is comprised of three specimens, found in houses 2, 8, and 13. The hearth's panel is divided into two symmetric registers by a horizontal, appliqué cordon. The lower register has two vertical and elongated clay bumps at its center (fig. 57). The upper one is filled with more or less equidistant, parallel, upward-oriented arrows. As far as the spatial distribution of the documented hearths is concerned, there is no preferential clustering in either shape or design to be singled out.

Five hearths out of eight are documented from Amachita II [Magourde]. Three shape categories are attested with one to three specimens in each. Class 1, convex in shape, is represented by house 13's hearth. The panel's perimeter is made of an appliqué cordon decorated with pinched finger impressions; the lower half has three more or less equidistant, vertical, and elongated clay bumps, and the upper

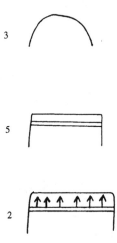

Figure 57: Hearth designs from Amachita I

one is decorated with three sets of parallel, double, vertical lines of finger impressions (fig. 58). Class 2, of rectangular features with rounded upper angles, includes three variants (fig. 58). The simplest variant is found in house 11. The panel is divided into two registers by a horizontal, appliqué cordon decorated with pinched finger impressions. The upper register is plain, and the lower has four more or less equidistant, vertical, and elongated clay bumps (fig. 58). Variant two is found in house 1. A horizontal, appliqué cordon divides the rear panel into two registers; the lower is plain and the upper decorated with four equidistant, upward-oriented arrows (fig. 58). And finally, variant three has an elaborate decoration (fig. 58); the rear panel is divided into three registers by two horizontal and parallel appliqué cordons, both decorated with pinched fingers' impression. The lower register has four equidistant, vertical, and elongated clay bumps. The middle register at mid-

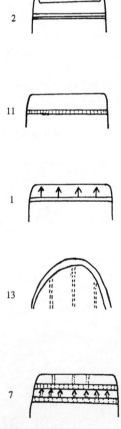

Figure 58: Hearth designs from Amachita II

height is filled with seven more or less equidistant, upward-oriented arrows partly made of finger impressions. And finally, the upper register is decorated with three sets of vertical and parallel lines of finger impressions found on the left half of the feature. Class 3, rectangular with upward pointing upper corners, has a concave upper side, and includes a single specimen found in house 2 (fig. 58). The recorded hearth's rear panel is divided into three registers. The middle one is plain. The lower has four equidistant, vertical, and elongated clay bumps, and the upper is delimited by a set of three horizontal and parallel grooved lines. Each of the hearths documented at Amachita II is unique.

All of the eight attested hearths have been recorded from Amachita III, a camp settled by family groups from Chouaram. They are divided into three shape categories with one to three variants each (fig. 59). The first convex category includes three classes with one specimen each. Class 1, the less elaborate, is found in house 14. The feature has four more or less equidistant, vertical, and elongated clay bumps in the lower third of the panel, with the rest left plain (fig. 59). Class 2's feature, found in house 6, shares all the characteristics of the previous class 1 but has, in addition, a series of horizontal and parallel finger impression lines on the upper register (fig. 59). Finally, class 3 is found in house 10. The panel is divided into two by a horizontal, appliqué cordon, an element also delineating the perimeter (fig. 59), and, decorated with finger impression lines. The upper and lower registers are left plain.

The second category, rectangular with rounded angles, also includes three classes. Class 1, the less elaborate, is found in house 12. The panel is divided into two symmetric registers by a horizontal, appliqué cordon. The lower has three vertical and elongated clay bumps, and the upper is a framed, plain space (fig. 59). Class 2 features are found in two specimens, in houses 13 and 8. The panel is divided into two registers by a thick, horizontal, appliqué cordon decorated with finger impressions (fig. 59). The lower register is wider and has four equidistant, vertical, and elongated clay bumps. The upper one is narrower and decorated with series of vertical and parallel fingers' impression lines. Finally, class 3 is found in house 3. The hearth panel is divided into two symmetric registers by an undecorated horizontal, appliqué cordon. The lower register has four equidistant, vertical, and elongated clay bumps. The upper one is filled with six upward-oriented arrows made partly of parallel finger impression double lines (fig. 59).

Finally, the third category is found in a single occurrence in house 5. It is a rectangular feature with right angles and pseudo-crenellation (fig. 59). There are two sets of three protruding tips along the upper side of the panel in the central and right parts. A double horizontal, appliqué cordon generates two symmetric registers. The lower has four vertical and elongated clay bumps arranged in two distinct pairs, and the upper has four more or less equidistant, short, vertical appliqué cordons decorated with finger impressions (fig. 59). As far as the spatial distribution of hearths is concerned, there is no apparent preferential clustering discernible in the material record from Amachita III.

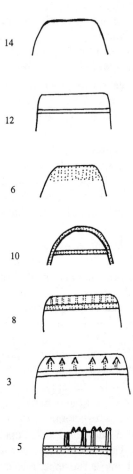

Figure 59: Hearth designs from Amachita III

Nine hearths have been documented at Amachita IV, a camp settled by family groups from the village of Bam Kala. Three of them were destroyed beyond recognition, and six were preserved well enough to be recorded. All the recorded specimens belong to a single variant from the same category, a convex-shaped hearth with four equidistant, vertical, and elongated clay bumps in the lower register, with the upper one left plain. The spatial distribution suggests some preferential clustering in pairs of neighboring houses, with occurrences from houses 1 and 2 in the N, houses 6 and 7 in the S, and finally, houses 10 and 11 in the W. The homogeneity of Amachita IV hearths stands in striking contrast to the diversity observed so far in the other sites. It is, however, the simplest hearth variant with the

1,3,
5,16

8

11

Figure 60: Hearth designs from Amachita V

required basic characteristics. The group of settlers from that year may have emphasized technical parameters and down played the aesthetic/symbolic one.

Eight out of ten hearths have been recorded from Amachita V, a camp inhabited by household groups from Krene. The documented hearths can be divided into two categories (fig. 60). The rectangularly shaped with rounded angles is represented by a single specimen found in house 11 to the W of the camp. The hearth's rear panel is partitioned into two symmetric registers by a horizontal, appliqué cordon decorated with pinched finger impressions. Both lower and upper registers are plain, but the left, right, and upper sides are decorated with parallel lines of pinched finger impression. The convex-shaped category includes two variants. The class 1 variant is represented by six specimens found in houses 1, 3, 4, 5, 16, and 18, all of them located in the eastern half of the camp. The hearth is undecorated with four more or less equidistant, vertical, and elongated clay bumps in the lower register (fig. 60). The class 2 variant includes a single specimen found in house 8 in the SW of the camp. The upper register is underlined by a horizontal, appliqué cordon decorated with pinched finger impressions. The middle register is plain, and the lower one has three equidistant, vertical, and elongated clay bumps (fig. 60).

Six out of a total of seven hearths have been recorded from Amachita VI, a camp settled by groups from the village of Alaya I. The documented features can be partitioned into two categories (fig. 61). One, with a single occurrence found in house 6, belongs to the category of rectangular shape with rounded angles, with, however, low lateral walls and two "burners." The rear panel sides are decorated with a line of finger impressions (fig. 61). The other, the convex shape category, includes three variants. Class 1's variant, the simplest, is represented by a single specimen found in house 5 located in the NW of the camp. It is undecorated with three equidistant, vertical, and elongated clay bumps in the lower half (fig. 61). Class 2's variant is attested in two cases, in houses 2 and 8. The rear panel has in the upper third register a broad sub-horizontal, appliqué cordon decorated with

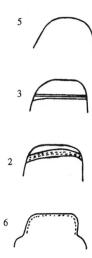

Figure 61: Hearth designs from Amachita VI

horizontal and parallel lines of pinched finger impressions. Finally, class 3, also represented by two specimens from houses 1 and 3, combines the characteristics of class 1 and 2 hearths. The panel is divided into symmetric registers by a set of three parallel and horizontal grooved lines. The lower register has three equidistant, vertical, and elongated clay bumps, and the upper one was left plain. In spatial distribution terms, there is no emerging significant pattern to be outlined.

All eight hearths documented at Amachita VII were well-preserved enough to be recorded. They can be divided into three categories. The convex shape category includes six specimens belonging to four classes. Class 1's variant, found in two occurrences in house 10 and 12, consists of a plain hearth with four equidistant, vertical, and elongated clay bumps in the lower register (fig. 62). Class 2 is also documented in two cases, in houses 2 and 5. The hearth's panel is divided into symmetric registers by a plain horizontal, appliqué cordon. The lower register has four more or less equidistant, vertical, and elongated clay bumps, and the upper is plain (fig. 62). Class 3 includes a single specimen from house 7. A horizontal, appliqué cordon decorated with parallel lines of pinched finger impressions divides the hearth's panel into two registers. The upper is left plain, and the lower has three equidistant, elongated, vertical clay bumps (fig. 62). And finally, class 4 variant is also attested by a single occurrence from house 13. The hearth's panel is decorated along its sides by a double line of pinched finger impressions. The identical motif is used at mid-height to create two symmetric registers, the upper one plain and the lower one with six more or less equidistant, elongated, vertical clay bumps (fig. 62).

The category of rectangular shape with rounded angles is represented by the hearth from house 10. In addition to the higher rear panel, decorated along its sides

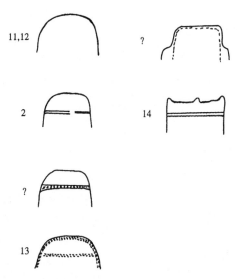

Figure 62: Hearth designs from Amachita VII

with a finger impressions line (fig. 62), it has low lateral walls and two "burners."
Finally, the third category, rectangular with pseudo-crenellation (fig. 62) is represented by a single occurrence from house 14.The hearth's rear panel has three
equidistant, pointed tips along its upper side, a plain horizontal, appliqué cordon
at mid-height creating two registers. The upper register is narrower and plain. The
lower one is broader and has four equidistant, elongated, vertical clay bumps. In
this case too, there is no apparent preferential spatial clustering.

All seventeen hearths from Agedipse I have been recorded. The camp was
settled by family groups from the semipermanent village of Kulkule and the documented features can be arranged into three categories: rectangular with right to
rounded angles, convex, and rectangular with crenellations (fig. 63).

The first category includes eight specimens belonging to five distinct classes.
Class I hearths, the simplest of the documented sample, are represented by three
specimens found in houses 18, 19, and 20, all located in the southern part of the
camp. The hearth's rear panel, built with right upper angles, is plain with four equidistant, vertical, elongated clay bumps in the lower register (fig. 63). Class 2 is
comprised of two specimens from houses 8 and 11 to the W of the camp. The panel
is divided into two registers. The lower has five equidistant, elongated, vertical clay
bumps. The upper one consists of a plain space delineated at the bottom and top
by horizontal and parallel appliqué cordons with double lines of finger impressions
(fig. 63). Classes 3 to 5 are represented by one specimen each. The class 3 hearth,
found in house 1 has right angles with the left, right, and upper sides overlined with
an appliqué cordon. The upper register is filled with five more or less equidistant,

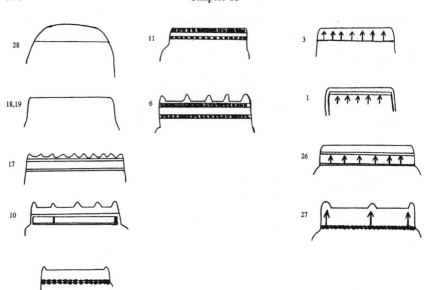

Figure 63: Hearth designs from Agedipse I

grooved, short, upward oriented arrows. The lower has four small elongated, vertical clay bumps (fig. 63). The documented class 4 hearth, from house 3, is a farther elaboration of the class 3 specimen (fig. 63), with, however, rounded angles.
A horizontal, appliqué cordon divides the rear panel into symmetric registers. The
lower has five equidistant, elongated, vertical clay bumps and the upper has seven
equidistant, short, grooved, upward-oriented arrows. Finally, class 5's feature is
found in house 25 in the western part of the camp. It has low lateral walls and a
rear panel divided into three registers by two horizontal and parallel appliqué cordons (fig. 63). The upper register is a narrow, plain band. The middle one is filled
with six equidistant, short, upward-oriented arrows. And finally, the lower one has
four equidistant, vertical, and elongated clay bumps.

The convex-shape category includes two hearths, found in houses 12 and 28,
in the E and N of the camp, respectively. The panel is divided into symmetric
registers by a horizontal, appliqué cordon (fig. 63). The upper register is left plain,
and the lower one has four equidistant, elongated, vertical clay bumps. The third
category of rectangular, more or less crenellated features includes seven occurrences, belonging to five classes. Class 1 is comprised of two specimens, found in
houses 13 and 14 in the SE of the camp. The panel is built with two pointing tips,
one at each end. A horizontal, appliqué cordon, decorated with pinched finger impressions is set at mid-height creating two symmetric registers. The upper one is
plain, and the lower one has four equidistant, elongated, vertical clay bumps (fig. 63).
Class 2's hearth, found in house 27, is a farther elaboration of the previous one,

with, this time, three equidistant, pointing tips with superimposed, upward-oriented arrows and low, curved lateral walls (fig. 63). Class 3 includes two hearths recorded in house 6 and 24.The panel is built with five equidistant, pointing tips (fig. 63). The lower register has four equidistant, vertical, and elongated clay bumps. The upper one consists of a plain space delineated at the bottom and top by a horizontal double line of pinched finger impressions. Class 4 is represented by a single occurrence, that from house 17 to the S of the camp. The rear panel crenellation consists of ten evenly spaced, pointing tips. The lower register has four vertical and elongated clay bumps, and the upper one is a plain space under- and over-lined by horizontal and parallel appliqué cordons (fig. 63). Finally, class 5, also represented by a single specimen found in house 10, consists of a hearth built with evenly spaced, pointing tips along its upper side, and low lateral walls with a rear panel divided into three registers. The upper one is plain. The middle one is unevenly filled with short, vertical lines generating two rectangles of appreciably different size. And finally, the lower register has four centrally located and equidistant, elongated, vertical clay bumps (fig. 63).

As far as spatial distribution is concerned, two striking and dissimilar cases can be singled out. In the first, three and two similar hearths, respectively, are found in neighboring houses 18, 19, and 20 located in the S and 13 and 14 in the SE of the camp. In the second, identical hearths are found in houses located some distance apart, houses 8 and 11 in the E, as well as 6 and 24, the former in the E and the latter in the W.

Agedipse II was settled by household groups from the permanent village of Magourde. Six hearths have been documented, all of them well-preserved and recorded. In fact, each of the features is unique in one way or another. They can, nonetheless, be partitioned into three categories with one to three variants (fig. 64). The convex category is represented by the hearth from house 1 in the SE of the camp. It is a plain feature with thickened perimeter and four vertical and elongated clay bumps in the lower half (fig. 64).

The category of rectangular with pointing tips includes three variants. Class 1 is found in house 7 in the N. It has two pointing tips at each upper corner and low lateral walls. A horizontal, appliqué cordon divides the rear panel into two registers. The upper one is a narrow, plain band, and the lower one, much broader, has four protruding vertical and elongated clay bumps (fig. 64). Class 2 has been recorded in house 10 to the E of the camp. It has four equidistant, pointing tips along the upper side, low lateral walls, and four evenly spaced, elongated, vertical clay bumps (fig. 64). And finally, class 3 is represented by an elaborate specimen found in house 6 in the W. It has four evenly spaced pointing tips along its upper side, low lateral walls, with the rear panel divided into two almost-equal-sized registers. The lower one has four equidistant, vertical, and elongated clay bumps. The upper one consists of a bilateral frame with a symmetric pattern of decoration. The decoration is organized around an appliqué central circle with, on the left and right, a series of two and four vertical finger impression lines (fig. 64).

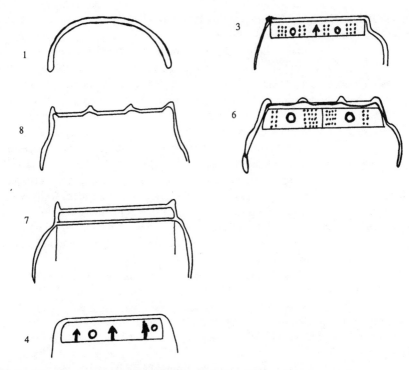

Figure 64: Hearth designs from Agedipse II

The category of rectangular with rounded angles includes two specimens. They differ in two parameters: the shape of the lateral walls and decoration richness. Class 1 has been recorded from house 4 to the W of the camp. It has a thickened perimeter, triangle-shaped lateral low walls, with the rear panel divided into two equal-sized registers. The lower part has four vertical and elongated clay bumps. The upper one, designed as a framed space, is decorated with three evenly spaced, upward-oriented arrows intertwined with two small circles. The composition's syntax suggests one small circle to have been forgotten or explicitly omitted (fig. 64). Class 2 is found in house 3 to the S of the camp. The hearth's perimeter is also thickened and the low lateral walls are rectangular in shape. The lower register is twice as broad as the upper one and includes four equidistant, vertical, and elongated clay bumps. The upper register has an elaborate framed decoration organized in a bilateral symmetry around a central upward-oriented arrow (fig. 64). Each half panel is structured around an appliqué central circle with, on the right and left, sets of two and three vertical finger impression lines.

If the spatial distribution of the hearth is taken into consideration, undecorated features found in houses 1, 7, and 10 are all located in the eastern half of the camp.

The decorated ones from houses 3, 4, and 6, all including small appliqué circles in their design, are found in the western half.

All twenty-one hearths from Agedipse III were preserved well enough to be recorded. The camp, the largest of all the tested cases, was settled by household groups from the semipermanent village of Hinduk. With a single exception from house 5, all the documented hearths integrate two to four Kotoko-made portable fireplaces and can be partitioned into five categories (fig. 65). Category 1, that of convex-shaped features, includes five specimens divided into three variants. Class 1 is found in house 16 in the SE of the camp. It is a four-niches feature with a plain, thickened perimeter panel (fig. 65). Class 2 is represented by three specimens from houses 13, 28, and 29 in the S and N. The panel has thickened sides and is decorated at mid-height by a horizontal, appliqué cordon with both lower and upper register left plain (fig. 65). Class 3's feature is similar to the previous one, with,

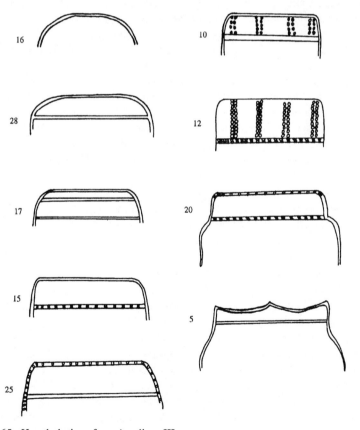

Figure 65: Hearth designs from Agedipse III

however, two horizontal and parallel appliqué cordons on the rear panel, generating three plain registers.

Category 2 consists of rectangularly features with rounded upper angles. It includes eleven specimens distributed into five classes. Class 1, the simplest, has been recorded in house 24 in the NE of the camp; it is a three-niches hearth. The rear panel has a thickened rim and is divided into symmetric plain registers by a horizontal, appliqué cordon. Class 2 includes seven specimens documented in houses 4, 7, and 8 in the W, 15 and 18 in the S and SE, and finally 23 and 27 in the NE and N. The recorded hearth is similar to specimens from class 1 but the mid-height horizontal, appliqué cordon is decorated with a double line of pinched finger impressions (fig. 65).Class 3 has a single specimen found in house 25 to the N of the camp. It has three niches, a thickened rim decorated with finger impressions, and a horizontal, appliqué cordon delineating a broader, plain upper register (fig. 65). Class 4, documented in house 17 in the SE, has a thickened perimeter and two horizontal and parallel appliqué cordons. The delineated registers are of unequal size. The upper one is a narrow, horizontal band (fig. 65); the middle one is the broadest, and the lower one corresponds to the pot-supporting devices. Finally, class 5, found in house 1 in the NW has a thickened rim panel decorated with crisscrossed horizontal and vertical appliqué cordons creating a loose checkerboard.

Category 3, with rectangular panel, and more or less right upper angles, is comprised of two specimens, found in houses 10 and 12 in the southwestern part of the camp.The simplest variant, recorded in house 10, is a three-niches feature with the panel divided into symmetric registers by a plain, horizontal, appliqué cordon. The lower register is plain. The upper one is filled with more or less equidistant sets of vertical double-finger impression lines (fig. 65). The other variant, found in house 12, has four pot-supporting devices. Its rear panel is divided into two registers by a horizontal, appliqué cordon decorated with pinched finger impressions. The lower one corresponds to the height of the pot-supporting devices. The upper one, much broader, is filled with four more or less equidistant sets of vertical double-finger impression lines perpendicular to the cordon (fig. 65).

Categories 4 and 5 have low lateral walls. The former includes three Kotoko-made portable hearths, and the latter has two additional clay "hearthstones." Category 4 hearths are rectangular in shape with rounded upper angles and square low lateral walls (fig. 65). Two such specimens have been recorded, in house 20 in the E and 26 in the N. The panel is divided into two by a horizontal, appliqué cordon situated at mid-height. Both registers are plain. The panel's upper side and the cordon are decorated; the former with a simple and the latter with a double horizontal line of pinched finger impressions (fig. 65). Category 5, with a bi-concave upper side and triangular low lateral wall, is documented by a single occurrence from house 5 to the W of the camp. A horizontal, appliqué cordon divides the panel into two registers. The upper one is a plain narrow band. The lower, much broader, has four equidistant, vertical, and elongated clay bumps (fig. 65).

Appliqué cordons with or without finger impressions are the only decorative

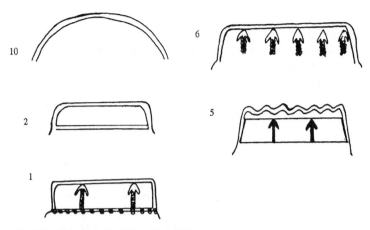

Figure 66: Hearth designs from Agedipse IV

elements used by the inhabitants of the Agedipse III camp. However, the shapes represented are surprisingly diverse for a dry-season camp.

Seven out of nine hearths have been recorded from the Agedipse IV camp, inhabited by family groups from Tumam. The documented hearths can be partitioned into three categories with one to three specimens each (fig. 66). Category 1, with convex-shaped features, includes a single occurrence from house 10 to the E of the camp. The hearth's panel has a thickened rim and five equidistant, vertical, and elongated clay bumps in its lower half (fig. 66). Category 2, rectangular with rounded upper angles, includes five specimens distributed into three classes. Three specimens from house 2 in the N, 4 in the W, and 8 in the S belong to class 1. The panel with a thickened outline is divided into two registers by a horizontal, appliqué cordon. The upper half is plain and the lower has three equidistant, vertical, and elongated clay bumps (fig. 66). Classes 2 and 3 have one specimen each. The former was recorded in house 1, to the N of the camp, and the latter in house 6, in the opposite S side. House 1's hearth has low lateral walls and a two-register panel. The horizontal, appliqué cordon is decorated with pinched finger impressions; the register below is filled with four more or less equidistant, vertical, and elongated clay bumps. The upper one has two upward-oriented appliqué arrows also decorated with pinched finger impressions (fig. 66). House 6's specimen also has low, rectangular, lateral walls but three additional hearthstones. The panel is decorated with five equidistant, vertical, and elongated clay bumps located in the lower half, each attached in the upper half to an upward-oriented appliqué arrow decorated with pinched finger impressions (fig. 66). Finally, category 3 is a trapeze-shaped crenellated feature (fig. 66) found in house 5 to the S of the camp. The documented hearth has two hearthstones, low lateral walls, and a two-register panel. The lower register has three equidistant, vertical, and elongated clay bumps. The upper one has a trapezoidal, framed space delimited by appliqué cordons. The delineated area is filled with two upward-oriented arrows. And finally, the panel's upper side is crenellated. There is no discernible spatial patterning in the overall distribution of hearths' shapes and decorative motifs in the case of Agedipse IV. In fact, each of the camps presents a peculiar case.

The Language of Hearths

If read from Wobst's (1977) perspective on stylistic behavior and information exchange, Shuwa-Arab hearths are flagrantly paradoxical and redundant. They are located in the inner sanctum of the house, accessible to a limited range of individuals, relatives, and very close family friends. They are self-signaling (Sterner 1987).When interviewed and asked about the meanings of the design and design elements used for hearth decoration, all the informants displayed an identical sequence of reactions. They were first surprised by such a question. Then, they smiled, more or less, and said there is no meaning at all. And finally, they specified that the decoration is basically for aesthetic purposes. However, they agree that one design element, the upward-oriented arrow, carries meaning. It represents the "cooking stick," a crafted wood piece used to stir the staple dish made of sorghum, millet, or maize flour. The selection, combination, and patterning of design elements, thus, seem to derive from each married woman's creativity. It can be argued that the very fact of the subject's freedom does not rule out the existence of some relationship with prior experience, as, subliminally, the newlywed may rely on the pool of design elements she was familiar with in her childhood.

The general patterning of hearth decoration at intra- as well as inter-site levels will now be scrutinized to address the issue just outlined above. The questions to be addressed can be framed as follows: What design element in which combination is found where? Are there site-specific patterns? If not, what is the nature of the regional patterns of distribution?

At a relatively general level, variations in shape and decoration were used to organize the documented features into categories and classes (table 40). The number of hearths' categories varies from one to five among the tested settlements, with the notable exception of Gobrem. This pattern of variation is, however, more instructive if considered at the level of settlement groups.

Sites from the Early Group are poorly represented, with a hearth frequency per site ranging from 1 (Ngumati) to 5 (Ndom). The recorded hearths are divided into three categories (table 40) with 1 to 3 classes. In this group, hearth diversity is equal to the sample size, and varies from 1 to 5.

In the Middle Group settlements (table 40), the frequency of recorded hearths varies from 7 (Mishiskwa) to 33 (Abuzrega). The ratio of undecorated to decorated features fluctuates between 1:6 (Mishiskwa) and 16:15 (Abuzrega). Three hearths' categories are represented in all four permanent villages. With a total of 64 hearths ranging from 4 (Djidat I) to 29 (Abuzrega), category 1 (rectangularly shaped with rounded upper angles) is largely predominant. It is followed by category 3 (rectangular with pointing tips) with 33 ranging from 2 (Abuzrega and Marafaine) to 15 (Djidat II), and finally, category 2 (rectangular with right upper angles) with 14, varying from 2 (Abuzrega) to 5 (Djidat I). Abuzrega, Marafaine, and Mishiskwa are linked by the prevalence of hearth category 1. Djidat I and II belong clearly to the other pole, with predominantly category 3 hearths.The number of classes per hearth category ranges from 2 to 11 in category 1, 2 to 4 in category 2, and finally, 2 to 8 in category 3. Hearth diversity, the number of hearths classes represented in each site, thus varies from a minimum of 6 at Mishiskwa to a maximum of 21 at Djidat II.

Three to nineteen hearths have been documented from the Late Group settlements, at Bawara and Ngada II, respectively (table 40). They are divided into four categories, with the ratio of undecorated to decorated features varying from 0:3 at Bawara to 4:9 at Ngada I. Category 1 hearths are largely predominant even if they are absent from Bawara. Their frequency ranges from a minimum of 5 at Bilbede to a maximum of 11 at Ngada II and IV, with the number of classes varying from 4 (Ngada IV) to 8 (Ngada II). Category 2 hearths are absent from Gallis and Ngada III; their frequency fluctuates between 1 (Bawara, Bilbede, and Ngada IV) and 3 (Ngada I and II) for 1 to 3 classes. One (Bilbede) to 5 (Ngada III) category 3 hearths are recorded. They are absent from Gallis and Ngada II and are distributed into 1 to 5 classes (table 40). Finally, category 4 hearths are absent from Bawara, Bilbede, and Ngada III. They are documented in the four remaining settlements with frequency ranging from 1 (Gallis and Ngada I) to 4 (Ngada II) for 1 to 3 classes in each.The overall diversity of the recorded hearths ranges from a minimum of 3 at Bawara to a maximum of 13 at Ngada II.There is a significant split of settlements into two groups, one with a relatively low diversity (3 to 7) at Bawara, Bilbede, and Gallis, and the other a relatively high one (9 to 13) at Ngada I–IV. Population size partly explains the patterning, but the position of Gallis within this divide is certainly due to the partial recording of its hearths.

A relatively large sample has been recorded from the dry-season camps. It amounts to 98 specimens divided into 47 undecorated hearths and 51 decorated hearths (table 40). There are interesting variations between both camps' clusters. In the Amachita cluster, the number of hearths varies within a narrow range of 5 to 8. The ratio of undecorated to decorated features fluctuates between 6:0 (Amachita IV) and 2:6 (Amachita III). Category 4 of convex-shaped hearths with 24 specimens is predominant, followed by category 1 with 19. Categories 2 and 3, with 1 and 3 hearths, respectively, are marginal. The frequency per site of category IV hearths range broadly from 1 (Amachita II) to 7 (Amachita V), for 1 (Amachita I, II, and IV) to 3 (Amachita III and VI) classes, and that from category 1 from 1 (Amachita V and VI) to 6 (Amachita VII) for 1 (Amachita V and VI) to 4

(Amachita VII) classes.The overall diversity of the recorded hearths fluctuates between 1 (Amachita IV) to 7 (Amachita III).

There is more variation among the features documented in the Agedipse cluster (table 40). The frequency of hearths per site varies from a minimum of 6 at Agedipse II to a maximum of 21 at Agedipse III. The ratio of plain to decorated features shifts from 4:3 at Agedipse IV to 7:14 at Agedipse III. Three to five hearth categories have been documented. Categories 1 to 3 are found in all the tested camps, and 4 and 5 exclusively at Agedipse III. More precisely, 24 hearths distributed into 2 (Agedipse II) to 5 (Agedipse III) classes belong to category I. The sample from category 3, the second largest, amounts to 16 partitioned into 1 (Agedipse II and IV) to 6 (Agedipse I) classes. And finally, category 2, the third in size, has 9 specimens distributed into 1 (Agedipse I and IV) to 3 (Agedipse II) classes. Categories 4 and 5 are represented by 2 and 1 specimens from a single class in both cases. The overall diversity of the Agedipse camps' clusters ranges from 5 (Agedipse IV) to 12 (Agedipse III).

Settlements from the Middle Group present the largest sample size as well as the greatest diversity of hearths documented in the study area. With significant overlap, the recorded diversity decreases along the settlement's gradient, from the permanent villages to the semipermanent one, and then the dry-season camps, with the situation of the Early Group sites undecidable. It ranges from 6 to 21 with the Middle Group, from 3 to 13 in the Late group, and from 1 to 13 for the dry-season camps. Diversity thus seems to be population dependent. A larger pool of married women, relying on their creative drive combined to their learned "heritage," generates a multiplicity of design patterns.

Surprisingly, the design elements used for the decorations of hearths are few. They include: arrows, finger impressions (single or pinched), circles, and squares. Appliqué cordons are structuring elements used to create registers and especially framed spaces. The sample from the Early Group is too small to allow any farther discussion (table 41). Clearly, the material from the Middle Group includes the largest design spectrum, with upward-oriented arrows predominant with 51 occurrences, followed by finger impressions with 22, then squares with 8, others with 3, and finally circles with 3 (table 41). The frequency of upward-oriented arrows ranges from 3 (Mishiskwa) to 16 (Djidat I), and that of finger impressions from 2 (Abuzrega) to 7 (Djidat II). Fifty-eight hearths out of a total of 112, slightly more than 50 percent, have appliqué cordons. This figure shifts to 89.61 percent for the Late Group sites hearths with appliqué cordons on 69 specimens out of a total of 77. There is one case of square design found at Bawara. All the design elements used in Late Group settlements revolve around upward-oriented arrows and finger impressions. In this case, however, finger impression is by far the predominant motif documented in 49 occurrences out of 77. The frequency per site varies from a minimum of 2 at Bawara to a maximum of 13 at Ngada II. Arrows' frequency varies within a narrower range, from a minimum of 1 at Bawara, Gallis, Ngada I, and Ngada III, to a maximum of 5 at Ngada IV. A similar pattern of strong predominance

Table 41: Frequency distribution of hearth design elements

Settlement Group	Arrow	Cordon	Finger's impression	Circle	Square	Others
Early Group						
Danguerchem	2	2	—	—	—	—
Gobrem	—	—	—	—	—	—
Ndom	2	4	2	—	—	1
Ngumati	—	1	1	—	—	—
Total	4	7	3	—	—	1
Middle Group						
Abuzrega	9	11	2	1	1	—
Djidat I	16	8	4	—	2	1
Djidat II	13	24	7	—	2	—
Marafaine	10	8	3	—	3	1
Mishiskwa	3	7	6	1	—	1
Total	51	58	22	2	8	3
Late Group						
Bawara	1	3	2	—	1	—
Bilbede	2	7	4	—	—	—
Gallis	1	7	5	—	—	—
Ngada I	1	11	8	—	—	—
Ngada II	4	15	13	—	—	—
Ngada III	1	10	7	—	—	—
Ngada IV	5	16	10	—	—	—
Total	15	69	49	—	—	—
Dry-Season Camps						
Amachita I	3	4	—	—	—	—
Amachita II	2	4	3	—	—	—
Amachita III	1	6	5	—	—	—
Amachita IV	—	—	—	—	—	—
Amachita V	—	2	2	—	—	—
Amachita VI	—	4	1	—	—	—
Amachita VII	—	4	2	—	—	—
Agedipse I	4	6	7	—	—	—
Agedipse II	2	1	2	3	—	—
Agedipse III	—	10	11	—	—	—
Agedipse IV	3	4	2	—	—	—
Total	15	45	35	3	—	—

of finger impressions followed by upward-oriented arrows is documented for the dry-season camps, with, however, lower figures. Appliqué cordons are found on 45 hearths out of a total of 98, slightly less than 50 percent. finger impressions are recorded on 35 specimens and upward-oriented arrow on 15.

The material discussed in this chapter can be used to address research issues framed at three hierarchical levels: (1) as identity-markers in a multiethnic area; (2) as an indicator of intra-tribal matrimonial networks; (3) as free but patterned creations of each individual married woman.The studied hearths are specific to the Shuwa-Arab; as such they can be considered as identity markers. They are, however, not displayed to the outside world and are, accordingly, self-signaling. There is no evidence suggesting any link between clan affiliation, matrimonial networks, and patterns of postmarital residence. There is a slight preference for lateral cross-cousin marriage, but according to informants, the system is practically undifferentiated, without any exogamic prescription. All the Shuwa-Arab groups from the study area belong to the Banu Salamat but are divided into two major tribes: the Essala and the Ulad Daoud. There is, nonetheless, a preferential clustering of upward-oriented arrows with Essala permanent villages, at Abuzrega, Djidat I and II, and Marafaine.This predominance is apparent at the Amachita I dry-season camp, settled by family groups originating from Djidat. Ngada II, Ngada III, and Amachita III belong to the Ulad Jubara; but they share very few clues beyond the frequent use of pinched finger impressions. Amachita VI and Amachita VII were settled by family groups originating from Alaya I and Mahanna, both settlements belonging to the Ulad Abdallah, as is the case for Gallis and Bilbede. Their hearths do not show any preferential design arrangement that may be indicative of an identical clan affiliation.The same applies to Ngada I and Ngada IV, both inhabited by the Ulad Fokhara. Bawara belong to the Ulad Yesiye, Mishiskwa to the Ulad Migebil, and Ndom to the Ulad Ukhura. In fact, an important fact emerges from the discussion conducted all along this chapter, and it is the fact that the decorative repertoire depends on the decision of each individual married woman. Even in this case, however, there are some significant intra- and extra-site patterns outlined in different parts of this chapter.

Chapter 14

Patterns of Subsistence

Introduction

The term *production,* as used in this chapter, refers to different aspects of craft specialization and intensification involved in the process of making a certain range of goods available. Subsistence, on the other hand, refers to all techniques and practices instrumental in the procurement of food resources. In both cases, however, the analysis is based exclusively on the material record documented from the sample of studied settlements.

Crafts and Specialized Occupations

A narrow array of crafts and occupational specialization are represented in the material record from the tested settlements. At one extreme, one may mention the Imam [Marabout], the Muslim scholar in charge of the Friday Mosque and the "boarding" Koranic school of Djidat II. One may add the operator of the engine-pulled mill also located Djidat II; he is, unfortunately, not a resident from that settlement and commutes from Houlouf everyday. Blacksmith installations or products have been found at two settlements: in shelter 75A at Djidat II and Amachita V. The former consists of a blacksmith workshop with its furnace, bellows, blow-pipes, as well as a supply of scrap metal. In the latter, two freshly made pieces of equipment, an iron axe and a socketed adze, were lost in the dry-season camp. A shoe-polisher's box was found in house 35 at Ngada IV suggesting that the house's owner may have been involved in part-time work in the nearby towns, Kusseri in Cameroon or Ndjamena, the capital of the Chad Republic, on the opposite river bank. And finally, a reed-mat weaving workshop was recorded in house 26 at Ngada IV. There is a high demand for such mats in villages and cities during the dry seasons, when they are used to build open shelters in courtyards.

Patterns of Intensification

The concept of intensification is used here in a strictly relational perspective. It aims to single out any significant difference in output well beyond local subsistence needs. Production intensification seems to be driven by the combination of a few independent forces: the constant pressure exerted on all adult males older than eighteen years of age to raise cash to pay for the annual per capita tax; the proximity of large markets from nearby towns; and, for the younger segment of the population, the appeal and desire to access certain sides of mass consumption. There are a few indications of production intensification in two components of the production-subsistence continuum alluded to in chapter 12. One involves poultry and the other goats.

The first one is documented in the settlement layouts by the presence of sets of chicken coops. They are found in Middle and Late Groups sites. In the former settlement group, the variation recorded between sites, all of them permanent villages, is confined within a narrow range of 5–9. In fact, localities such as Abuzrega and Djidat II that are devoid of milking installations have the highest number of chicken coops, 8 and 9 respectively. In the latter Late Group sites, chicken coops are recorded in four villages out of seven with frequencies varying from 1 to 27. Two of the villages, Bilbede and Ngada IV, with 22 and 27 chicken coops, respectively, stand out as poultry production localities.

The second component of the production-subsistence continuum subject to intensification revolves around the production of goat milk. It is indicated in site layouts by the presence of milking stations. Dairy products are an essential component of the herders' diets, and each family owning cattle or sheep/goats, or both, collect a certain amount of milk for household consumption during the adequate period of the year. This household milking is carried out without special installations. The documented milking stations, exclusively for goats, are special purpose features consisting of a series of equidistant wooden poles set in pens, round huts, courtyards, and even along walls. They are used to streamline the milking process. As far as the social division of labor is concerned, milking operations, transportation, as well as market transactions are carried out by females. Milking stations have been recorded at two permanent villages, Djidat I and Marafaine, with, respectively, 10 and 5 occurrences. The former village is clearly specialized in animal products, with seven chicken coops and ten milking stations for eleven households. The latter has five milking stations and five chicken coops for ten households.

Patterns of Subsistence

Shuwa-Arab subsistence systems include grain agriculture and livestock husbandry in all the cases. But the balance, in terms of labor investment and social values, varies according to local situations and historical circumstances. A third element, fishing, can be added to that fundamental pair, but its position within the systems is slightly ambiguous as most of the catches are sold in the town markets as sun-dried fish. Fish is, nonetheless, an important component of the Shuwa-Arab diet.

Fishing

For the study area, fishing is a strictly seasonal activity confined to the flood period (September–November) when the Yaere is transformed into a continuous water body. The productivity of fishing expeditions that settle in camps on available higher ground is, however, low at the peak of the flood period because of the dispersion of fish populations. It is higher at the onset of the flood and during the receding phase (Blache 1964; Blache and Miton 1962; Laure 1974). Different tools are part of the fishermen's gear; they include dugouts, nets, batteries of fish hooks, as well as a range of cutting tools. Fishing parties generally consist of young adult males (fig. 67). They settle in fishing camps for several weeks in a row during the optimal season and process their catch on a daily basis. Two complementary techniques are used: sun-drying for small fish, and smoking for the larger specimens. Sun-drying on a woven reed mat does not require any special installation and is, as such, archaeologically invisible. Smoking is performed in specially built features

Figure 67: Late season net fishing in the Yaere

Figure 68: Fish-smoking features

(fig. 68). The specimens recorded near the Amachita camps' cluster, on a low archaeological mound (Holl 2002), are elongated and horseshoe shaped. They consist of a low mud wall, 0.20 to 0.30 m in height. Wooden twigs are set on top of the
substructure thus created, and the fish to be smoked is emptied and laid flat above.
The hollow space underneath the feature is filled with slow-burning and thick
smoke-producing fuel, generally a combination of partly dry and wet wood, leaves,
and grass. Depending on the size of the catch, quantities of both sun-dried and
smoked fish are transported to the markets, or the whole production is stored in
the fishing station for the whole season.

Agriculture

All the communities from the study are involved in agricultural production; the
levels of involvement, however, vary from one set of groups to another. It is minimal for some of the groups inhabiting semipermanent villages, and much more
important for the those living in permanent settlements. The documented agricultural activities are divided into two main components: grain agriculture devoted to
the cultivation of sorghum and maize for the production of the staple food, on the
one hand, and on the other, intensive gardening geared toward the production of
green vegetables (lettuces, cucumbers, tomatoes) sold in the nearby town markets.

Figure 69: Gardens in the Yaere

Intensive gardening is carried out during the first half of the dry season. It is a labor-intensive production process involving frequent watering of the carefully designed green vegetable plots (fig. 69). Green vegetable production general starts with the receding of the flood and last, as long as the water table is high enough to allow optimal access to water. The gardens are located on the northern edge of the Yaere, approximately 1 kilometer S of the settlement of Madaf. It is, predominantly, a young adult male activity, from which they raise some cash. Plots are owned by individuals, close kin, or friends, and labor cooperation seems to be minimal. Finally, besides its cash value, the contribution of intensive gardening to the villagers' diets is negligible.

The bulk of agricultural production revolves around the cultivation of sorghum and maize. Red sorghum is preferentially cultivated by the inhabitants of semi-permanent settlements. They provide some explanations for their choice: (1) red sorghum's growth and maturation cycle is shorter, and consequently, it can be sown after the beginning of the receding flood and harvested just in time for the move to the dry-season camping area; (2) it does not attract birds, so the amount of loss to natural competitors is minimal; (3) it is tastier and much more nutritious. White sorghum is preferentially grown by the inhabitants of permanent villages; its output per acreage is higher, but it is the favorite target of birds. Different bird-scaring devices are developed to protect the harvest; they include classic scarecrows, noisemaking devices, as well as active involvement of children stationed on elevated platforms with their stone-throwers. The proportion of maize in the local agricultural output is still minute; Bilbede appears to be an interesting case of a shift from sorghum to maize production, if judged by the large amount of corncobs found on the site.

There are no differences in tools or field preparation techniques used in the cultivation of both red and white sorghum and maize. In most of the cases, settlements are surrounded by one or several rings of fenced, cultivated plots. That is unfortunately not the case for Danguerchem, Gobrem, and Ngumati, three out of the four Early Group settlements. All these sites were abandoned at the time of fieldwork; the absence of evidence for cultivated plots is certainly due to poor preservation. Ndom, the remaining Early Group site, has six fenced fields for six households, ranging in size from 65 m × 30 m for the largest to 30 m × 25 m for the smallest.

The situation is radically different for the Middle Group settlements. All the studied sites are surrounded by several rings of cultivated fields. Mishiskwa is located on a shallow mound; the rings of fenced fields are not attached to rest of the village features. They are also comparatively narrow, stretched on less than 500 m outward. Abuzrega, Djidat I, Djidat II, and Marafaine have more complex catchment areas stretched on a radius of 2 to 3 kilometers. In fact, the whole central-western part of the study area has a dense pattern of dendritic field systems visible on low altitude aerial photographs. The shift toward a heavier reliance on agricultural production, already suggested with the high average frequency of storage platforms, is clearly visible in the landscape.

Late Group settlements present a more diverse picture as far as the nature, distribution, and size of cultivated fields are concerned. The frequency of cultivated plots per site varies from a maximum of 10 at Bilbede to a minimum of 2 at Bawara.There are three settlements, Bawara, Ngada II, and Ngada I, with two to four cultivated plots. In the first site, with two fields for seven household units, the recorded plots measure 48 m × 37 m for the larger specimen, and 17 m × 14 m for the smaller. At Ngada II, the second site, with three fields for eight household units, two of the cultivated plots, measuring 40 m × 30 m for the larger and 15 m × 12 m for the smaller, are devoted to sorghum, and the last one, 25 m × 17 m, to maize. And finally, at Ngada I, the third site, with four plots for nine household units, two of the largest plots, measuring 22–23 m × 25 m, are devoted to the cultivation of gourds for calabashes and a kind of herbal tea. The smaller specimens, 20 m × 18 m and 15 m × 7 m, are sorghum fields.

Bilbede, Gallis, Ngada III, and Ngada IV have six to ten cultivated plots. Gallis has six fields for nine household units, ranging in size from 58 m × 40 m for the largest specimen to 28 m × 25 m for the smallest one. Both Ngada III and Ngada IV have nine fields each, for fourteen and twelve household units, respectively. In the former, the largest cultivated plot measures 44 m × 34 m, and the smallest, 13 m × 10 m. In the latter, they measure, respectively, 37 m × 25 m and

20 m × 13 m. Finally, Bilbede has the highest number of cultivated plots, ten for nine household units, as well as a large enough threshing area. They vary in size from 60 m × 40 m for the largest to 16 m × 16 m for the smallest.

If measured by the number of cultivated plots documented, the involvement of Late Group settlements' inhabitants in agriculture appears to be extremely variable. With the number of cultivated fields systematically lower than the number of documented household units, some family groups may have pooled their plots or, quite unlikely, relied on exchange for their supply of agricultural products.

Livestock

Evidence for livestock husbandry was found in all the tested settlements. Their nature and frequency vary from village to village. In general, however, they include cattle corrals, sheep/goat pens, livestock houses, tethering as well as milking poles, and milking stations. All such features have been described in their relevant context, in dry-season camps, and semipermanent and permanent villages. A more straightforward archaeological approach to the analysis of subsistence patterns is adopted here. Faunal samples have always played an important, if ambiguous role in the identification of past socioeconomic systems (Cribb 1991; Sadr 1991; Smith 1992). "Traditionally, sites with a predominance of domestic animals in the faunal remains have been attributed to pastoralists. In some instances, researchers have tried to go farther, to infer milk, meat, or wool production from the age and sex profile of the domestic animals remains . . . But faunal samples, so easily distorted by taphonomic processes, are rarely representative enough to allow such studies . . . Furthermore, most interpretations of animal mortality curves are based on a tentative model . . . the validity of which has been challenged" (Sadr 1991:13). Sadr's critique of faunal remains analyses is unfortunately not backed by useful suggestions on how to extract good information from archaeological faunal samples.

Animal bones were not collected from all four permanent villages because of an overall extremely low density. The faunal samples considered in this discussion have been collected from the semipermanent sites and dry-season camps, systematically within the confines of each of the investigated settlements. The sampling universe was delimited by the outer perimeter of houses. Visible animal bones were hand picked by a working crew of fifteen workmen from 2-m-wide transects. It was thus possible to collect the maximum accessible faunal material. The sampling techniques used in this case favor large bones. Not surprisingly, despite the well-known high consumption of fish among Shuwa-Arabs from the study area, fish bones are literally absent from the collected samples. Two dense bones scatters were found and mapped; one was discovered a few hundred meters E of Gobrem, on the right bank of the Abani, the seasonal stream, and the other at less than 100 m S of Ngada IV.

The Bones Scatters

The bones scatter from Ngada IV consists of the carcass of a calf that died two years prior to the 1989 field season. The cause of death was not made explicit to the field crew. The bulk of the calf remains, with most of the bones contained within a dry and parched skin, is located in squares C11–C12 and D11–D12. With the exception of three goat scapulas, found in square A3, C5, and C7, all the remaining 128 mapped bones result from the dismemberment and scattering of the calf's skeleton by dogs. Gnawing marks were found on a left patella recorded in square A4. Limb bones, head bones, and cervical as well as part of lumbar vertebras were found widely scattered around the rib cage, which was still preserved in the dried skin.The set of processes leading to the formation of the described bones scatter are almost straightforward. On the one hand, a dead calf was abandoned at some distance of the village; it is not known if the young animal died in the village with the carcass transported later at an acceptable distance. On the other hand, domestic dogs, which are scarcely fed in the African countryside, took the opportunity to feed on the available meat, scattering most of the limb bones away from the axial skeleton, and, at the same time, bringing in a few sheep and goat bones. The recorded bones scatter is comprised exclusively of domestic animal remains; however, it does not provide crucial information on the settlement-subsistence status of the village's inhabitants. By itself, it does not help discriminate between a dry-season camp, a semipermanent village, and a permanent settlement.

The Gobrem bones scatter is, in fact, located on the spot of a vanished twin site on the right bank of the Abani seasonal stream. It is spread over 395.20 square meters and divided into four subcomponents, termed BS I to IV. All the 237 recorded bones belong to cattle, with densities varying from 0.75/square meters to 0.38/sq.m. Bone scatter (BS) I is found at the northwestern end of the grid sample. It contains 76 bones, 28 from the appendicular and 48 from the axial skeleton. Jaws and cranium bones are rare, with two cases of left and right mandibles, the latter with fully erupted M3. Two individuals are represented in the studied sample, a mature and a juvenile animal. All anatomical elements, from head to hooves, are represented, suggesting that both animals were probably discarded carcasses later fed upon by domestic dogs and scavengers like golden jackals. Fifteen bones out of a total of 76 present evidence of gnawing by carnivores. Interestingly enough, all the bones with gnawing marks belong to the axial skeleton: cervical, thoracic, and lumbar vertebras, suggesting a late access to the carcass. This is generally the case when an animal dies during the flood season in a riverbed, with the carcass accessible after the receding of water. BS II is located a few meters SE of BS I. Ninety-four cattle bones have been recorded, 49 from the axial skeleton, and 45 from the limbs. Gnawing marks are documented on 30 out of 94 bones. Most of these marks are found on vertebras, mandibles, and cranial bones. However, 5 limb bones: scapula, pelvis, tibia, and tarsal were found with tooth marks. BS III is located 13 m SE of BS II. The recording grid measures 10 m in length and 8 m in width. Thirty-one cattle have been mapped. Twenty-two belong to the axial skeleton and nine to the appendicular one. The sample represents a single individual with gnawing marks found on five bones: the proximal end of the left and right femurs, both left and right sides of the pelvis, and the sacrum sides. The pattern of tooth marks suggests the scavenger to have fed on the upper part of the rear limbs. Finally, BS IV, the remaining subcomponent, is spread over 91.20 square meters E of the three previous ones. It measures 15.20 m in length and 6 m in width and includes 36 cattle bones, 20 from the axial skeleton and 12 from the limbs. The scatter seems to be comprised of the skeleton of two individuals. In order to clarify that issue, the sampled area was divided into four equal units, quadrant I to IV (Q-I to Q-IV). Ten bones were recorded from Q-I; they include the sacrum gnawed on its edge, two left scapulas both with gnawing marks, one proximal and one distal femur, a left humerus, one specimen each of cervical, thoracic, and lumbar vertebras, and finally, a right pelvis fragment. The subset consists of elements of the upper limbs and the backbone, with gnawing marks found on seven out of ten bones. Ten bones have also been recorded in Q-II; there are four vertebras, one cervical and two thoracic, two proximal ends of ribs, a left femur proximal, a right humerus proximal, and two tarsals. Five of the bones have gnawing marks. Q-III has seven bones, with, this time, a complete cranium of a young mature cow with well-preserved horn-cores. Interestingly enough, the specimen has extensive gnawing marks, and dried jackal's feces were found on the cranium. The rest of the sample includes a left ulna, a proximal right humerus, a distal left femur, a cervical vertebra, a rib fragment, and a tarsal bone. Gnawing marks are rare on the rest of the sample, suggesting the scavenger to have focused on the cranium. Finally, Q-IV, with nine bones, mostly includes elements of the axial skeleton. There are four vertebras, three cervical and one lumbar, two mandibles, left and right, one proximal left femur, one scapula blade, and a tarsal bone. Gnawing marks are found on two bones, the scapula blade and the lumbar vertebra. The Gobrem bones scatters appear to have resulted from the dismemberment of dead animals by scavengers.

In both Ngada IV and Gobrem cases, there is no human contribution to the scatter of domestic animal bones described above. The strong predominance of cattle can easily lead any archaeologist to infer the existence of a livestock husbandry system. But the material at hand does not allow us to move farther.

Faunal Remains from Semipermanent Settlements

Faunal remains have been collected from three groups of settlements, the Early and Late Groups, as well as dry-season camps. The amount of bones varies significantly from site to site, with, in general, low figures for Early Group settlements (table 42).

The number of animal bones collected from Early Group sites varies from a minimum of 7 pieces at Danguerchem to a maximum of 231 at Gobrem, with the frequency of undetermined elements ranging from 4 (Danguerchem) to 54 (Ndom). The documented faunal spectra are comprised of one to seven taxa. They can easily be partitioned into food and non-food species; horses, donkeys, and dogs are not

Table 42: Faunal remains from the Early Group settlements

Site	Danguerchem		Gobrem		Ndom		Ngumati	
	n	percent	n	percent	n	percent	n	percent
Bos taurus	3	42.85	176	76.19	65	31.70	24	44.44
Ovis/Capra	—	—	24	10.38	47	22.92	4	7.40
Bovidae sp.	—	—	13	5.62	20	9.75	8	14.81
Equus caballus	—	—	—	—	—	—	4	7.40
Equus asinus	—	—	4	1.73	12	5.85	1	1.85
Equus sp.	—	—	—	—	6	2.92	5	9.25
Gazella sp.	—	—	—	—	1	0.45	—	—
Loxodonta afri	—	—	—	—	1	0.45	—	—
Undetermined	4	57.14	14	6.06	54	26.34	8	14.81
Total	7		231		206		54	

food items for the Shuwa-Arab of the study area. As such, they are not by-products of subsistence decisions and have to be held out of consideration when issues of strict food intake are raised. They are nonetheless critical elements of the pastoral ways of life and, in this regard, deserve full consideration. Danguerchem has the poorest collected sample. Three of the bones belong to cattle, and the remaining four are undetermined fragments. Gobrem has the largest sample of the group. Fourteen out 231 bones are undetermined. The bulk of the sample belongs to cattle, sheep/goat (10.38 percent), *Bovidae* sp. (5.62 percent), and donkey (1.73 percent). Cattle, representing 76.19 percent of the faunal sample, is the predominant species (table 42). Ndom, with 206 collected pieces, has the second largest sample of the group. The number of undetermined elements, amounting to 54, is significantly higher. The remaining portion of the sample includes bones of seven taxa. Cattle, represented by 65 bones (31.70 percent), is dominant, followed by sheep/goat with 47 pieces (22.92 percent), and *Bovidae* sp. with 20 bones (9.75 percent). Wild mammals are represented by two bones, one of a gazelle (*Gazella rufifrons*) and the other of an elephant (*Loxodonta africana*). Donkey and equid bones with, respectively, 12 (5.85 percent) and 6 bones (2.92 percent) are well represented in the sample. Finally, six taxa have been determined from the Ngumati sample, which amounts to 54 bones, with 8 undetermined fragments. Cattle bones are predominant with 24 pieces (44.44 percent). Eight (14.81 percent) bones belong to unspecified bovids and 4 (7.40 percent) to sheep/goats as well as a horse. The rest of the sample includes 5 (9.25 percent) equid bones and 1 (1.85 percent) donkey bone.

Samples from Late Group settlements are larger on average. The recorded amount of bones varies from a minimum of 87 at Bawara to a maximum of 795 at Gallis (table 43). The number of undetermined pieces is high on average, ranging from 31.13 percent (27 bones) at Bawara to 45.37 percent (275 pieces) at Ngada III.

Table 43: Faunal remains from the Late Group settlements

Taxa	Bawara		Bilbede		Gallis		Ngada I		Ngada II		Ngada III		Ngada IV	
	n	%	n	%	n	%	n	%	n	%	n	%	n	%
Domestic Animals														
Bos taurus	24	27.58	174	29.19	307	38.61	150	27.17	98	27.45	210	34.65	185	40.65
Ovis/Capra	7	8.04	55	9.22	88	11.06	61	11.05	29	8.12	43	7.09	46	10.10
Bovidae sp.	15	17.24	84	14.09	110	13.83	76	13.76	54	15.12	44	7.26	44	9.67
Equus caballus	—	—	1	0.16	—	—	1	0.18	7	1.96	—	—	—	—
Equus asinus	9	10.34	4	0.57	7	0.88	3	0.54	9	2.52	15	2.47	3	0.65
Equus sp.	4	4.59	14	2.34	15	1.88	15	2.71	7	1.96	14	2.31	3	0.65
Gallus sp.	—	—	18	3.02	—	—	2	0.32	20	5.60	5	0.82	—	—
Canis sp.	—	—	—	—	—	—	—	—	4	1.12	—	—	3	0.65
Wild animals														
Gazella sp.	1	1.14	—	—	3	0.37	—	—	—	—	—	—	—	—
Loxodonta africana	—	—	—	—	3	0.37	—	—	—	—	—	—	—	—
Lepus capensis	—	—	—	—	3	0.37	—	—	—	—	—	—	—	—
Fish	—	—	—	—	—	—	1	0.18	—	—	—	—	—	—
Undetermined	27	31.03	246	41.27	259	32.57	243	44.02	129	36.13	275	45.37	171	37.58
TOTAL	87		596		795		552		357		606		445	

Two sites samples, Bawara and Gallis include remains of wild animals. In the former, there is a single gazelle bone among 24 (27.58 percent) cattle, 15 (17.24 percent) *Bovidae* sp., 9 (10.34 percent) donkey, 7 (8.04 percent) sheep/goat, and 4 (4.59 percent) *Equus* sp. ones. In the latter, there are three animal species, gazelle, elephant, and hare, represented by three bones each (table 43). The rest of the sample is divided into two groups of domestic animals: bovids and equids. The former is comprised of cattle and sheep/goat with respectively 307 (38.61 percent) and 88 (11.06 percent) skeletal remains, with, in addition, 110 (13.83 percent) bones of unspecified *Bovidae* sp. And the latter consist of 7 (0.88 percent) bones of donkey and 15 (1.88 percent) *Equus* sp.

The bones' sample from Bilbede, with a relatively important proportion of chicken skeletal remains, supports the impression gained from the recorded high frequency of chicken coops. Chicken bones amount to 18 remains representing 3.02 percent of the sample. Cattle largely predominant with 174 pieces (29.19 percent), followed by *Bovidae* sp. with 84 (14.09 percent), and sheep/goat with 55 (9.22 percent). Horse and donkey are represented by 1 (0.16 percent) and 4 (0.57 percent) bones, and unspecified equids by 14 (2.34 percent).

The Ngada sites cluster presents the broadest range in variation in terms of represented taxa. The recorded faunal spectra range from six (Ngada III and Ngada IV) to eight taxa (Ngada I and Ngada II). Despite the persistent predominance of cattle, with proportion, varying from 40.65 percent to 27.17 percent, each of the settlement has a specific combination of species. Ngada I's sample includes, in addition to the 150 (27.17 percent) cattle remains, 76 (13.76 percent) *Bovidae* sp., 61 (11.05 percent) sheep/goat, 15 (2.71 percent) *Equus* sp., 3 (0.54 percent) donkey, 2 (0.32 percent) chicken, and finally, 1 (0.18 percent) each for horse and fish (table 43). Ngada II has the largest proportion of chicken bones, with 20 (5.60 percent) remains, as well as domestic dog bones. The rest of the sample consists of cattle (98, 27.45 percent), *Bovidae* sp., (54, 15.12 percent), sheep/goat (29, 8.12 percent), donkey (9, 2.52 percent), and finally, horse and *Equus* sp. (7, 1.96 percent each). Ngada III's sample includes a few chicken bones (5, 0.82 percent) in addition to the standard domestic animals, strongly dominated by cattle with 210 (34.65 percent) skeletal remains. Finally, Ngada IV has a handful of remains of dog, with 3 (0.65 percent) bones. The rest of the sample with cattle largely predominant (185, 40.65 percent), is divided into sheep/goat, *Bovidae* sp., donkey, and *Equus* sp., with proportion, varying from 10.10 percent to 0.65 percent.

Faunal Remains from the Dry-Season Camps

The animal bones collected from the sampled dry-season camps provide a desperately monotonous picture of the represented faunal spectra that is, nonetheless, the most accurate indication of pastoralism (table 44). The samples are small, in general, with frequencies varying from a maximum of 65 at Amachita VI to a minimum of 10 at Agedipse IV. Two species, cattle and sheep/goat, are represented, with a few specimens of snail's shells. The *Limicolaria* sp. shells recorded

Table 44: Faunal remains from the dry-season camps

Site	Bos taurus	Ovis/capra	Others	Undetermined	Total
Amachita Camps' cluster					
Amachita I	3	55	—	—	58
Amachita II	27	7	2 limicolaria sp.	20	56
Amachita III	24	11	2 limicolaria sp.; 1 Equus sp.	8	46
Amachita IV	37	14	6 limicolaria sp.	—	57
Amachita V	10	3	2 limicolaria sp.	—	15
Amachita VI	62	—	3 limicolaria sp.	—	65
Amachita VII	15	2	2 limicolaria sp.	—	19
Agedipse Camps' cluster					
Agedipse I	19	4	—	—	23
Agedipse II	60	9	—	—	69
Agedipse III	43	13	—	—	56
Agedipse IV	7	2	1 limicolaria sp.	—	10

are not food refuse. They result from the natural death of snails that fed on the camps refuse.

The small size of all the collected samples offers the opportunity to address interesting issues revolving around the management of animal products. The represented body parts and the relative age of the animals can be used to tackle this issue.

In the Amachita camps' cluster, the amount of collected faunal remains varies from 65 at Amachita VI to 15 at Amachita V. Snail shells are more frequent, ranging from two to six specimens. A single donkey bone was found at Amachita III (table 44).

Amachita I is a four-household camp inhabited by people from Djidat. The faunal material includes 3 cattle and 55 sheep/goat bones. All cattle bones belong to an adult animal represented by two mesial humerus fragments and an additional scapula. It is clearly part of a share of meat chopped from the animal's upper front limb and brought to the dry-season camp. The rest of the sample consists of goat bones. They are partitioned into 3 cranium fragments with horn-cores, 6 jawbone fragments, 11 ribs, and a set of bones representing the lower limbs. They include, two tibia distal end, one belonging to a younger animal, three tarsal bones, an ulna fragment, and finally, 29 chopped and undetermined bones. With the exception of one tibia piece, all the goat bones belong to adult animals. The striking absence of vertebras and upper limb bones suggest that sun-dried goat meat may have also been brought to the camp.

Amachita II, with six household units, was settled by the families from Magourde. The animal bones sample consists of 56 remains, 27 for cattle, 7 for goat, and 2 snail shells, as well as 20 undetermined pieces. The recorded goat bones include one cranium, four jawbones, a left pelvis fragment, and a distal tibia with attached astragalus. A large proportion of the recorded cattle bones, 20 out of 27, belong to calf. They are comprised of 4 crania, three of them horn-less, 4 right and 3 left mandibles, 2 pelvis fragments, 1 right scapula, 1 right and 2 left humerus, 1 right radio-ulna, 1 right tibia, and 1 left metacarpus. The presence of a sacrum fragment with an attached left pelvis half suggests that at least one of the calf carcasses was not butchered. Its bones were scattered after death and abandonment. Adult cattle are represented by two radio-ulna (right and left), two metacarpus (right and left), and finally, a complete right hind-limb with the femur, tibia, calcaneum, and astragalus in anatomic connection. This set of bones also suggests the adult animal skeleton to have been scattered after death and abandonment. Paradoxically enough, the cattle bones from Amachita II do not seem to have resulted from meat consumption, but more likely from a post-abandonment scattering of dead animal skeletons.

Amachita III is an eight-household units camp inhabited by people from Chaouram. The faunal sample includes eight undetermined fragments, 2 *Limicolaria* sp. shells, a third phalanx of donkey, as well as 24 cattle and 11 sheep/goat bones. Seven of the cattle bones are from calf; they are distributed into a cranium, a cranium fragment, a jawbone, a jawbone fragment, a radius, a right tibia, and a metacarpus. Adult cattle bones are comprised of a right horn-core, 2 molar teeth, 1 cervical vertebra, 2 pelvis fragments, 1 femur proximal, 1, right radio-ulna, 2 distal radio-ulna, 1 right tibia, 4 carpals, and finally, 1 astragalus and 1 tarsal. The uncovered goat remains belong to an adult animal that appears to have been butchered. They consist of 1 cranium and 1 cranium fragment, 1 molar, 1 rib fragment, 1 sacrum fragment, 2 humerus (left and right), 2 radio-ulna (left and right), 1 mandible, and 1 proximal metacarpus. The faunal assemblage thus seems to be comprised of the remains of three animals, one calf, one adult cow and one goat.

Amachita IV, a nine-household units camp, was settled by families from Bam Kala. The collected faunal material consists of 57 pieces divided into 6 *Limicolaria* sp. shells, 14 sheep/goat bones, and 37 cattle bones. The goat bones belong to a single adult animal and are represented by six fragments, 4 ribs, one complete and two mandible fragments, and finally, a cranium. Cattle bones belong predominantly to calves, with 29 pieces out of a total of 37. Adult cattle are represented by lower limb bones, 1 ulna proximal, and 7 phalanx, 5 first, one second, and one third. Calf are represented by three complete skulls, 1 occipital, 1 complete vertebral column from the atlas to the sacrum, 1 earbone, 2 mandibles (left and right), 4 jaw fragments, and 1 molar for the axial skeleton. The limb bones include 1 complete and 5 mesial portions of humerus, 1 left femur, 1 radio-ulna, 1 left tibia, 2 complete and 2 proximal ends of metacarpus, and finally, 3 metatarsus. The presence of a complete vertebral column strongly suggests that at least one of the calf died with its bones scattered later. The adult cattle bones, as well as those from the goat, side more than less with food refuse.

Amachita V is a seven-household units camp. The amount of animal bones collected from the site is surprisingly small, with a total of 15 pieces divided into 2 snail shells, and 3 sheep/goat and 10 cattle bones. Sheep/goat bones are limited to 2 ribs and one femur of an adult animal. Two individuals, one adult and a calf, are represented among the cattle remains. One skull fragment, 1 molar, and 1 second phalanx belong to a calf, with the adult bones consisting of 3 fragments and 1 distal end of humerus, and 2 proximal and 1 distal end of radius. The eclectic representation of anatomic elements seems to suggest that the Amachita V faunal remains resulted from food consumption.

Amachita VI was settled by eight families from the semipermanent village of Alaya I. The faunal sample collected from the camp is comprised of 65 pieces, with 3 snail shells, and 62 cattle bones belonging to calf and adult animals (table 43). Calf are represented by 2 skulls, 4 occipital fragments, 1 horn, 2 jaw fragments, 1 atlas, 1 sacrum, 1 complete pelvis, 2 right scapulas, 1 rib fragment, 1 right humerus, 2 femurs (right and left), 1 proximal femur, 1 radio-ulna, 1 left tibia, 1 metacarpus, 1 metatarsus, and finally, 1 calcaneum. Adult cattle are attested by 3 mandibles (2 right and 1 left), a jaw fragment, 5 lumbar vertebrae, 1 pelvis, 1 right femur, 2 distal humerus (left and right), 1 right radio-ulna, 2 tibia (1 complete right and 1 distal left), 2 right metacarpus, 1 metatarsus, 2 astragalus, and finally, 2 tarsals. The bones sample seems to include the remains of at least four animals, two calf and two adult individuals.The absence of any anatomic connection between the recorded pieces, and the breakage of some marrow-rich long bones suggest the animal to have been butchered.

Amachita VII, the remaining site from the camps' cluster was settled by seven households originating from Mahanna. The bones sample is small in size, amounting to 19 pieces distributed into two snail shells, and two sheep/goat and 15 cattle bones. Sheep/goats are represented by 2 lumbar vertebras of a mature animal. The collected cattle bones are those of an adult individual. They are comprised of 1 left mandible, 1 sacrum fragment, 2 scapula proximal ends, 8 radio-ulna fragments, 1 right radius distal, 1 right ulna proximal, and finally, 1 tibia proximal. The sample seems to have resulted from the consumption of small shares of meat that may have been brought from the main village.

Four faunal samples were collected from the Agedipse camps' cluster. They range in size from a minimum of 10 pieces found at Agedipse IV to a maximum of 69 from Agedipse II. The frequency of snails, with a single piece found at Agedipse IV, is negligible if compared to the Amachita cluster. Cattle bones are predominant in all the cases, with frequencies varying from a minimum of 7 at Agedipse IV to a maximum of 60 at Agedipse II. The proportion of sheep/goat bones is surprisingly low; it varies from 2 pieces recorded at Agedipse IV to 13 found at Agedipse III (table 44).

Agedipse I was settled by eight household units from the village of Kulkule. The collected faunal remains amount to 23 pieces divided into 19 cattle and 4 sheep/goat bones. The sheep/goat bones belong to an adult individual. They are represented by 1 mandible fragment, 1 right radio-ulna, 1 right scapula, and 1 left humerus. The recorded cattle bones belong to three distinct individuals, a calf, and a young and an adult animal. The calf is represented by 2 mandibles (left and right), 1 complete right humerus, and 1 mesial humerus. The young animal is attested by, 1 cranium, 1 mandible fragment, 1 atlas fragment, 2 scapulas (right and left), 2 humerus (left and right), 1 right femur, 1 right tibia, 2 radio-ulna (left and right), and finally, 1 left metatarsal. The adult individual is represented by 2 left calcaneum fragments and 1 second phalanx. Elements of the axial skeleton, amounting to five, are poorly represented.The skewed distribution of anatomical parts, with limb bones largely predominant, may have resulted from the transfer in the site of meat shares brought from outside. Alternatively, it can be suggested that calf or very young animals in poor health during the peak of the dry season may have been butchered and shared with the inhabitants of nearby settlements.

Agedipse II was settled by five family groups originating from Magourde, a mixed farming community. The collected faunal material amounts to 69 pieces divided into 60 cattle bones and 9 sheep/goat bones. Sheep/goats are represented by 2 skulls, 2 horns, 2 mandibles (left and right), 2 vertebras, and 1 astragalus, all from adult animals. The cattle bones belong to at least four individuals, one calf and three adults. The calf is represented by 1 skull, 1 horn, 1 tibia proximal, 1 metacarpal, and 1 metatarsal. Adult animals are attested by 3 skulls, 2 mandibles, 5 mandible fragments, 17 vertebras, 1 sacrum, 1 complete and 4 scapula fragments, 5 pelvis fragments, 5 rib fragments, 2 humerus (left and right), 2 femurs (left and right), 1 right radio-ulna, 5 metacarpals, 4 metatarsals, and finally, 3 phalanxes. The interpretation of Agedipse II's faunal sample is particularly delicate; it is the smallest camp of the whole cluster with the largest sample of animal bones. All the collected bones were found without anatomic connection, a feature that indicates abandoned dead animals. The material at hand thus seems to have resulted from deliberate food consumption and refuse disposal.

Agedipse III, the largest camp from the cluster, was settled by sixteen households from the village of Hinduk. The faunal sample is comprised of 56 animal bones, 13 from sheep/goats, and 43 from cattle. The sheep/goat bones belong to two adult animals, as suggested by the two recorded skulls, one of a ewe and the other of a he-goat. The remaining pieces include 2 jaw fragments, 1 left pelvis fragment, 2 metacarpals (right and left), and 6 phalanxes.The recorded cattle bones are those of at least three individuals, two adult and one young. The young animal is attested by a scapula and a complete metacarpal. The adults bones consist of 2 scapula, one complete and the other fragmented, 4 femurs (2 left and right), 4 humerus (2 left and 2 right), 4 tibia (2 left and 2 right), 4 radio-ulna (2 right and 2 left), 2 metacarpals, 5 astragalus, 5 calcaneum, 5 tarsals, and finally, six carpals. There is an interesting difference between the patterning of sheep/goat and that of cattle bones. Elements from the axial skeleton are absent from the sample of the latter and more or less well represented in the assemblage of the former. The ewe and the he-goat appear to have been butchered in the dry-season camp and probably shared. Cattle appears to have been brought to the camps as meat pieces from limbs, as if specially processed to be carried away.

Agedipse IV, the remaining camp of the cluster, was settled by five family groups originating from Tumam. The sample of faunal material is the smallest of all the documented cases with only 10 pieces: 1 snail shell, 2 sheep/goat and 7 cattle bones. All the collected bones are part of the axial skeleton, two jaw fragments for the represented sheep/goat, one skull, one skull fragment, one jaw fragment, and three vertebra fragments for the attested calf. The interpretation of the faunal assemblage is particularly difficult. No gnawing marks have been observed on the studied bones, but the selective representation of head bones suggest the activity of scavengers after the abandonment of the camp.

Conclusion

Subsistence activities and a certain but narrow range of more specialized crafts are carried out in many of the settlements investigated in this project. In terms of diversity, intensity, and frequency according to settlement categories, permanent villages easily rank first, followed by semipermanent villages, and finally, dry-season camps.With a single exception represented by iron artifacts lost by a blacksmith at Amachita VI, livestock husbandry is the key activity performed in all the dry-season camps. The analysis of animal bones brings to light interesting results. Sophisticated quantitative analyses of faunal remains can be applied to a very narrow range of settlements, namely short-term single occupation sites, as is the case for the tested dry-season camps that were settled between February and May 1990. In this case, and only in this one, it is possible to address issues concerning the number of animals represented in the sample (MNI), the body parts introduced in the site, as well as patterns of meat consumption with an accurate control of the evidence. In all other cases, from the semipermanent as well as permanent villages, the palimpsest nature of the faunal assemblages precludes any reasonable assessment of such variables as the number of butchered animals. What can be done, at best, is the proportional analysis of different parameters from faunal remains based on the crudest yardstick, the number of rests (NR).

Finally, the distributional pattern of species in each of the investigated faunal assemblages alone is not discriminant enough to allow for a subtle differentiation between distinct degrees of reliance on livestock products.

Conclusion

Toward a Shuwa-Arab Polity?

From their remote ancestry in the eastern part of the Nile Delta to their present-day life in the Chadian plain, Arab communities, later called Shuwa in the Chad basin because of their "eastern origins" in contrast to those from the N via the Sahara, have managed to survive in different ethnic milieus and political circumstances. They adjusted to different environments and sociopolitical contexts, and they adopted different subsistence systems and even different architectural styles. This long process of ethnogenesis involved migrations, cooperation and conflict with established authorities, and an intriguing resistance/avoidance of assimilation. In most of the cases, in Bagirmi, Kanem, Bornu, and Kotoko chiefdoms, they were dominated by local aristocracies and involved in multiple and constraining tributary relationships. For some short time segments, sociopolitical circumstances shifted slightly, relieving the pressure of local rulers. This was partly the case during the rule of the El Kanemiyyin dynasty in nineteenth-century Bornu when some Shuwa-Arab families were part of the ruling elite; during the short period of Rabbeh domination at the very end of the century; and finally, during the first few years of the French colonial regime. The pendulum swung back after the failure of the new territorial organization engineered by the French Colonial administration and anchored on an appointed Shuwa-Arab Sultan. The material documented from the Shuwa-Arab settlements of the study area is part of the contemporary fringe of the long-term processes alluded to above.

Settlement Dynamics

Three settlement variants, the dry-season camps, and the semipermanent and permanent villages, have been documented.They can be arranged along a mobility continuum, with the intermittent camps at one end and the sedentary communities at the other, and can be used to address the issue of the sedentarization of pastoral-nomads. They are, in fact, part of a settlement triad.The inhabitants of semipermanent as well as permanent villages use the dry-season camping area and settle in camps. Most, if not all of the inhabitants of semipermanent villages live in dry-season camps once a year for a few months; a smaller portion of those from the permanent villages do. And those who move generally belong to two generation cohorts, the young adults on the one hand and the elders on the other. These are special-purpose sites devoted to livestock husbandry. Key site facilities, livestock pens and corrals, wells and watering installations are communal, built and maintained by the whole group. Livestock pens are located at the center of the settlement and surrounded by houses.

Semipermanent villages have a higher density of features on average, and the number of household units varies from 5 to 7 in the Early Group and 7 to 12 in the Late Group.The number of units involved in community decision-making is a critical parameter in the operations of the collectivity (Johnson 1982, 1983). Growth in the number of what Johnson (1983:177) called "information sources" within an integrated system increases the probability of either systemic collapse (fission) or an increase in organizational complexity. The maintenance of non-hierarchical structure is associated with declining group-decision performance in groups of size six and greater on the one hand, and increasing group-decision performance in groups of size five and fewer, on the other. A nucleation process, involving the fencing of household complexes and the building of distinct cattle corrals, is well attested in almost all the Late Group villages, with the exception of Bawara and Ngada II, as well as in two Early Group settlements, Gobrem and Ngumati. The former village is an interesting case (Holl 1993). The site patterning appears to indicate declining group decision performance that seems to have shifted from the community to the individual household level. With seven "information sources." the village layout shows trends toward nucleation. Five out of seven households have built their own livestock facilities, signaling the collapse of the former collective herding system. Traces of large, central cattle corrals are still visible on the site. Although a fine-grained chronology of the events is lacking, and based on a comparison of livestock features' state of preservation, it seems that the central enclosures were no longer in use at the time of the site's abandonment, when systemic collapse occurred. Some of the inhabitants founded a new settlement at Alaya II, at approximately 4 to 5 kilometers W; other, left for the nearby town of Kusseri, or settled in another village as is the case for the headman (Bilama) of Mishiskwa.

Permanent villages are, on average, larger and have the highest density and diversity of settlement facilities.The most significant difference is found in the architecture, with the adoption of mud-brick and the construction of flat-roof, rectilinear buildings. The circular arrangement of houses on the perimeter of the settlement is still visible in all the tested villages. It is, however, progressively blurred at Djidat II, with the addition of an increasing number of houses in the inner-part of the village.The changes in architectural styles and building materials signal important transformations of the social systems under investigation, and different explanations have been suggested (Agorsah 1985, 1993; Bar-Yosef, 1995; Holl 1987; McGuire and Schiffer 1983). The shift from round to rectilinear architectural features has been recorded in the Pre-Pottery-Neolithic-B (PPNB) sites in the Levant during the Early Holocene. "Domestic architecture in PPNB sites reflects a major change in both house plan and building techniques. Rounded structures are replaced by rectangular or squarish buildings in sites that can be interpreted as farming communities" (Bar Yosef 1995: 193). As suggested by Bar-Yosef, these changes are driven by a shift from hunting-gathering to food-producing ways of life. Agorsah (1985: 114) offers another interesting suggestion; he argues that circular houses are more often than not arranged in fenced compounds and that the circular arrangement is not very flexible and cannot be easily combined with other forms to determine a variety of spaces. Quadrangular buildings are open-ended, more flexible, and can be used in combination with other geometric configurations to enclose a wide range of spaces. According to McGuire and Schiffer (1983:28(3), the main factors that influence the relative weighting of production and maintenance of dwelling structure costs are residential mobility, on both household and community levels, and settlement longevity. These factors, they convincingly argue, in part determine a structure's anticipated uselife; accordingly, the anticipated uselife is the critical variable that links social and adaptive factors in the decision-making process. The longer the expected uselife, the more benefits obtained from a greater investment in production (Holl 1987: 147). Changes in architecture are sensitive material fingerprints of important socioeconomic transformations. As documented with the data from the permanent villages, "habitation complexes" are consistently larger and tend to shelter multigenerational, extended families. The impact of sedentarization is far reaching even if it is more pronounced in the east and northeastern part of the study area, an area predominantly inhabited by the *Essala* tribal unit. The W is the domain of the *Beni Hassan,* and the S that of the *Yesiye.*

Djidat I–II is today a service provider and hub in the Shuwa-Arab landscape of the study area. It has a Friday Mosque and a Koranic school with students in residence; two operating blacksmiths workshops; two "retail shops"; an engine-pulled and a hand-operated mill; and an "intensive" goat milk production.

If the tested sites are arranged according to the rank/size rationale, there are three overlapping sets, with permanent villages at the top end, semipermanent sites at intermediate position, and dry-season camps at the bottom end. In the permanent village category, Djidat I and II are distinct parts of the same settlement, measuring at least 6.5 hectares in size. It is located almost at the gravity center of most densely settled part of the study area. Abuzrega, with 4.15 hectares in size, is the second largest village, followed by Marafaine (2.01 hectares). Semipermanent villages range in size from 3.36 to 0.54 hectares. Ngada I, the largest of the category, measures 3.36 hectares. It is followed in decreasing order by Gallis (3.20 hectares), Ngada IV (2.03 hectares), Ngada III (2.00 hectares), then Gobrem (1.20 hectares) and Mishiskwa (1.05 hectares), and finally, Bawara (0.78 hectares),

Bilbede (0.67 hectares), Ndom (0.63 hectares), Ngada II (0.60 hectares), Ngumati (0.59 hectares), and Danguerchem (0.54 hectares). Dry-season camp sizes vary from 1.76 hectares for the largest Agedipse III site to 0.25 hectares for the smallest Amachita II one. In the Amachita camps' cluster includes settlements of small size on average, ranging from 0.40 to 0.25 hectares. The range is broader in the Agedipse case and varies from 1.76 to 0.38 hectares.

Djidat I-II is thus the leading settlement, an activity hub in an emerging Shuwa-Arab polity. Census figures, discussed at length in chapter 2, show the Shuwa-Arab to be the fastest growing population in Northern Cameroon and the overwhelming majority in the study area. The dynamics outlined above set the stage for a political crisis that happened in the 1980s.

The Political Crisis: 1984–1991

The first half of the eighties was a period of significant, and at the same time tragic, events in the Cameroons. The one-party system collapsed. A new president was sworn in office. A feverish and extensive experimentation with political democracy was launched. It was stopped short by an attempted military coup from the Republican Guard. The coup failed after three days of total war in the capital city. The new regime decided to back up, but it was too late. The second half of the eighties was marked by the persistent attempt of the then threatened regime to regain control of the process. Two aspects of the Cameroonian national politics collided and had a lasting consequence on the study area: the creation of a myriad of political parties and the decision to transform the positions of authority at the local level into elective offices. More specifically, traditional chiefs have to be elected in free elections. The Kotoko political system was summarized in chapter 2 (Lebeuf 1969, Holl, in press). The office of Sultan [*Miarre*] is transmitted within the same family from one generation to the next along the male line, but not necessarily primogeniture. The oral and "constitutional" history of each of the fortified Kotoko towns is anchored to the dynastic list of its rulers. Elaborate rituals and complex ceremonies mark the enthronement of a new Miarre in paramount chiefdoms or principalities (Lebeuf 1969). The King to be has to disappear for forty days and live in a secluded mud-brick hut. The rationale is a simple one: he has to die as human to be reborn as king. Before colonial encroachment and takeover, the Miarre lived a secluded life in his palace, had to be concealed by curtains, and addressed the audience through a speaker (Denham et al 1828; Barth 1965; Holl 2000; Lebeuf 1969; Nachtigal 1980). The details of the ceremonies performed for access to sultanship in lower level centers such as Houlouf are not known. Some elders informants claim them to have been similar all over the Kotokoland, with differences in scale and not nature. After the death of May Hassana, the new Sultan had to be selected according to the new democratic system, through elections.

For Houlouf inhabitants, and the Kotoko population at large, such an eventuality was simply "unthinkable" and the outcome obvious: a Shuwa-Arab elected as Sultan and moving in the palace at the center of the town. In 1988, Sultan Mahamat Bahr accepted to share his thinking with the author in his Logone-Birni palace. He considered all the facets of the problem and exclaimed in complete despair: "only Allah can solve this problem." Shuwa-Arab and Kotoko joined different political coalitions with several clashes in towns demonstration. May Hassana, the venerable and respected Sultan of Houlouf, died in 1984. This death initiated a political crisis that lasted from 1984 to 1990; a crisis the author was able to observe year after year up to its surprising denouement in 1991. The office of Houlouf sultan remained vacant for six years. The Galadima, the second in the local political system, was the person in charge during that unusual interreignum. The lower level sultanship was steadily emptied of all its effectiveness during the colonial period, a process amplified after independence. The Sultan was now a mere tax collector but the prestige of the office was still palpable.

According to the regulations, the sultan has to be elected by an "electoral college" of all the villages' headmen of the El-Birke canton. Houlouf is the canton's unique Kotoko settlement. Each winter, generally in February, all the village headmen from the canton gathered at the Galadima's residence to work out a solution to the crisis. The author, as the guest of the Galadima and sharing his compound, could hear the discussions conducted late at night up to the early hours of the morning. According to Galadima's summary, right from the beginning there were three options: (1) the Houlouf inhabitants suggested to ignore the new rules and appoint the legitimate heir to sultanship; (2) Shuwa-Arab headmen, the overwhelming majority of the "electoral college," favored the strict implementation of the new rules; (3) The appointment of Galadima himself to the office of Sultan.

The third option was offered as a balanced solution by a significant group of older Shuwa-Arab village headmen. Their decision was based on personal relationships. The Galadima is, in fact, one the wealthiest men in the area. He owns a large herd of cattle, divided into smaller sets, distributed among several Shuwa-Arab villages. From time to time, he takes his horse, and with some of his friends, spends a few days visiting his Shuwa-Arab peers. Their decision was based on trust. They know the man. But the Galadima was as old as the deceased May-Hassana, about eighty-five years old when this crisis began, and was not interested in becoming a Sultan. During the Galadima *interregnum,* the paramount Sultan from Logone-Birni devised a general tax-collection tour of his jurisdiction, moving from one centrally located village to the next with an armed escort. The system worked smoothly. The discussion on the succession took place as usual, once a year in February in the Galadima's compound, and people started to get used to a vacant sultan office. Suddenly, in 1990, there was an injunction from the *Prefet,* the top-ranked official representing the Cameroonian government. The El-Birke canton headmen were summoned to elect their sultan within the next few months with a deadline. A Shuwa Arab, the headman from El-Birke, was elected. The Houlouf inhabitants were outraged, expressed their anger, and declared the new sultan persona non grata in their town. Reminded of the Kotoko fame for witchcraft, the newly elected chief fled from his village and settled in the anonymity of Kusseri, a large nearby city. The Houlouf inhabitants seceded from the canton and appointed the designated heir to sultanship.

Clash of Legitimacies

The sequence of events summarized above outlines a genuine clash of legitimacies, that of the Kotoko city dwellers on the one hand, and that of the Shuwa Arab on the other hand. Both have different historical trajectories. The Kotoko are speakers of central Chadic languages. Their remote ancestors initiated the colonization of the southern part of the Chadian plain in the very beginning of the second millennium BC (Holl 1995, 1997, 2002). In the Houlouf region precisely, the settlement patterns changed several times during the 4,000 years of their existence. The Houlouf chiefdom emerged in the second part of the first half of the second millennium AD during the Ble phase B (1200–1400 AD) to be absorbed into the Lagwan (Logone-Birni) kingdom later during the Houlouf phase B (1600–1800 AD) (Holl 2002). The expansion of the Lagwan kingdom was partially linked to the rise to regional supremacy of the Bornu empire (Holl 2000; 2002). It was within the strategic move to secure the northern border of the Lagwan kingdom that the Houlouf chiefdom was annexed. Groups of Shuwa-Arab probably entered the study area during the Houlouf phase B. Since they have been submitted to a broad range of tribute payments in order to live on the land, have access to fishing grounds, and graze their livestock. They did not create overarching political structures above the settlement level. At the end of the nineteenth century, and for less than ten years, Rabbeh, the conqueror of Bornu, welcomed as a liberator, created the short-lived *Lawan* system. The system was intended to bring all the dispersed members of Shuwa-Arab tribes under a coherent administration of their own. Theoretically, and as described in chapter 1, each tribe was put under the umbrella of a Lawan assisted by a number of sheikhs. Rabbeh's Kotoko policy was characteristically based on threat, violence, and brutality. The paramount Sultan of Logone-Birni was murdered, and a significant proportion of the adult male population of Houlouf was deported. Rabbeh's rule widened the already existing mistrust. At the beginning of the twentieth century, the scramble for territories, with a triangular competition between the British, French, and Germans, probably worsened the situation by relying on one cultural/linguistic entity or another to achieve their aims. As far as the study area is concerned, half a century of colonial administration, French, then German, and French again, resulted in the progressive erosion of local power structures without altering the tributary relationship between Shuwa Arab and their Kotoko "overlords." This was done later by the government of the independent state of Cameroon. The opening of local positions of authority to elective appointment empowered the Shuwa Arab and provided them with a legitimacy they had been deprived of for many generations. This final step thus seems to seal the paradoxical collapse of the Houlouf chiefdom, and maybe signal the emergence of a "Shuwa-Arab polity."

References

Abadie, J.-C., and F. Abadie, *Sahara-Tchad (1898–1900): Carnet de Route de Prosper Haller, Médecin de la Mission Foureau-Lamy*. Paris: L'Harmattan, 1989.

Agorsah, E. K., "Archaeological implications of Traditional House Construction among the Nchumuru of Northern Ghana." *Current Anthropology* 26 (1985): 103–115.

————. "Ethnoarchaeology: The Search for a Self Corrective Approach to the Study of Past Human Behaviour." *African Archaeological Review* 8(1990): 189–208.

————. "Archaeological Considerations on Social Dynamics and Spatial Pattern Development of Traditional Settlements." In *Spatial Boundaries and Social Dynamics* edited by A. Holl and T.E. Levy, 7–24. Ann Arbor, Mich. : International Monographs in Prehistory, 1993.

Atherton, J., "Ethnoarchaeology in Africa". *The African Archaeological Review* 1 (1983): 75–104.

Bar-Yosef, O.,"Earliest Food Froducers—Pre Pottery Neolithic (8000–5500)." In *The Archaeology of Society in the Holy Land,* edited by T. E. Levy, 190–204. London: Leicester University Press.

Barth, H., *Travels and Discoveries in North and Central Africa (Vol. II).* London: Frank Cass, 1965.

Bianquis, T., "L'Egypte depuis la conquête Arabe jusqu'à la fin de l'empire Fatimide (1171). In *Histoire Générale de l'Afrique Vol. III,* edited by M. el Fasi and I. Hrbek, 189–220. Paris: UNESCO and Nouvelles Editions Africaines, 1990.

Binford, L. R., *Nunamiut Ethnoarchaeology.* New York: Academic Press, 1978.

Blache, J., *Les Poissons du bassin du Tchad et du bassin adjacent du Mayo Kebbi: Etude Systematique et Biologique.* Paris: Editions ORSTOM, 1964.

Blache, J., and F. Miton, *Premiere Contribution a la Connaissance de la Peche dans le Bassin hydrographique Logone-Chari lac Tchad.* Paris: Editions ORSTOM, 1962

Clark, J. D., "Studies of Hunter-Gatherers as an Aid to the Interpretation of Prehistoric Societies." In *Man the Hunter,* Edited by R.B. Lee and I DeVore, 276–280. Chicago: Aldine, 1968.

Conte, E., "Entrer dans le sang: Perceptions Arabes des origines." In *Al-Ansâb, la Quête des Origines: Anthropologie Historique de la Société Arabe Tribale,* edited by P. Bonte,

E. Conte, C. Hames and A. Wedoud Ould Cheikh, 55–100. Paris: Editions de la Maison des Sciences de l'Homme, 1991.

Conte, E., and F. Hagenbucher-Sacripanti, "Habitation et vie quotidienne chez les Arabes de la rive sud du lac Tchad." *Cahiers ORSTOM-Sciences Humaines* 14(3) (1977): 289–323.

Cribb, R., *Nomads in Archaeology.* Cambridge: Cambridge University Press, 1991.

Cunnison, I., *Bagara Arabs.* Oxford: Clarendon Press, 1966.

David, N, and C. Kramer, *Ethnoarchaeology in Action.* Cambridge: Cambridge University Press, 2001.

David, N., J. Sterner, and K. Gavua, "Why are Pots Decorated?" *Current Anthropology* 29 (1988): 365–389.

Denham, F. R. S., H. Clapperton, and Dr. Oudney, *Narrative of Travels and Discoveries in Northern and Central Africa in the Years 1822, 1823 and 1824.* Vol. 2. London: John Murray, 1828.

Emberling, G., "Ethnicity in Complex Societies: Archaeological Perspectives." *Journal of Archaeological Research* 5 (1997): 295–344

Fisher, H. J., "The Central Sahara and Sudan." In *The Cambridge History of Africa Vol. 4,* edited by R. Gray, 58–141. Cambridge: Cambridge University Press, 1975.

———. "The Eastern Magrib and the Central Sudan." In *The Cambridge History of Africa Vol. 3,* edited by R. Oliver, 232–330. Cambridge: Cambridge University Press, 1977.

Frantz, C., "Fulbe Continuity and Change under Five Flags atop West Africa: Territoriality, Ethnicity, Stratification and National Integration." In *Change and Development in Nomadic and Pastoral Societies,* edited by J.G. Galaty and P.C. Salzman, 89–114. Leiden: E.J. Brill, 1981.

Gallay, A., E. Huysecom, A. Mayor, and G. de Ceuninck, eds., *Hier et Aujourd'hui: Des Poteries et des Femmes. Ceramiques Traditionnelles du Mali.* Geneve: Universite de Geneve, 1996.

Garcin, J. C., "L'Egypte et le monde musulman (du XIIè au début du XVIè siècle)." In *Histoire Générale de l'Afrique Vol. IV,* edited by D.T. Niane, 405–432. Paris: UNESCO and Nouvelles Editions Africaines, 1985.

Gould, R. A. ed., *Explorations in Ethnoarchaeology.* Albuquerque: University of New Mexico Press, 1978.

———. *Living Archaeology.* New York: Cambridge University Press, 1980.

Hagenbucher-Sacripanti, F., "Les Arabes dit *"Suwa"* du Nord-Cameroun." *Cahiers ORSTOM-Sciences Humaines* 14 1977): 223–249.

———. "Eléments de magie et de sorcellerie chez les Arabes d'Afrique Centrale." *Cahiers ORSTOM-Sciences Humaines* 14 (1977): 251–288.

Hasan, Y. F., *The Arabs and the Sudan.* Khartoum: Khartoum University Press, 1973.

Hiskett, M., "The Nineteenth Century Jihads in West Africa." In *The Cambridge History of Africa Vol 5,* edited by J.E. Flint, 125–169. Cambridge: Cambridge University Press, 1976.

———. *The Course of Islam in Africa.* Edinburgh: Edinburgh University Press, 1994.

Hodder, I., *Symbols in Action.* Cambridge: Cambridge University Press, 1982.

Holl, A., "Mound Formation Processes and Societal Transformations: A Case Study from the Perichadian Plain." *Journal of Anthropological Archaeology* 61987): 122–158.

———. "Community Interaction and Settlement Patterning in Northern Cameroon." In *Spatial Boundaries and Social Dynamics,* edited by A. Holl and T.E. Levy, 39–61. Ann Arbor, Mich.: International Monographs in Prehistory, 1993.

———. "Settlement Types and Late Stone Age Colonization of the Chadian Plain." In *The Epistemology of West African Settlements,* edited by B. W. Andah, Special Issue, *West African Journal of Archaeology* 25(1995): 33–73.

———. "Holocene settlement expansion in the Chadian Plain." In *Dynamics of Populations, Movements and Responses to climatic Change in Africa,* edited by B.E. Barich and M.C. Gatto, 28–41. Rome: Bonsignore Editore, 1997.

———. *The Diwan Revisited: Literacy, State Formation, and the Rise of Kanuri Domination (AD 1200–1600).* London: Kegan Paul International, 2000.

———. *The Land of Houlouf: Genesis of a Chadic Polity (BC 1900–AD 1800).* Ann Arbor: The University of Michigan Museum of Anthropology, 2002.

Holl, A., T. E. Levy, C. Lechevalier and A. Bridault, "Of Men, Mounds and Cattle: Archaeology and Ethnoarchaeology in the Houlouf Region (Northern Cameroon)." *West African Journal of Archaeology* 21 (1991): 6–36.

Holl, A. F. C. and T.E. Levy, "From the Nile Valley to the Chad Basin: Ethnoiarchaeology of Shuwa-Arab settlements." *Biblical Archaeologist* 561993): 166–179.

Hrbek, I., "Egypt, Nubia and the Eastern Deserts." In *The Cambridge History of Africa Vol. 3,* edited by R. Oliver, 10–98. Cambridge: Cambridge University Press, 1977.

Insoll, T., "The Archaeology of Islam in Sub-Saharan Africa: A Review." *Journal of World Prehistory* 10 (1996): 439–504.

Johnson, G. A., "Organizational Structure and Scalar Stress." In *Theory and Explanation in Archaeology,* edited by C. Renfrew. M.J. Rowlands and B.A. Segraves, 389–421. London: Academic Press, 1982.

———. "Decision-making Organization and Pastoral-nomad Camp Size." *Human Ecology* 11(1983): 175–199.

Kramer, C., ed., *Ethnoarchaeology: Implications of Ethnography for Archaeology.* New York; Columbia University Press, 1979.

———. *Village Ethnoarchaeology.* New York: Academic Press, 1982.

Kropacek, L., "La Nubie de la Fin du XIIè Siècle à la Conquête par les Funj au Début du XVIè Siècle." In *Histoire Générale de l'Afrique Vol. IV* edited by D. T. Niane, 433–459. Paris: UNESCO and Nouvelles Editions Africaines, 1985.

Lange, D., *Chronologie et Histoire d'un Royaume Africain.* Wiesbaden: Fr. Steiner Verlag, 1977.

———. *A Sudanic Chronicle: the Borno Expeditions of Idris Alauma (1564–1576).* Wiesbaden: Fr. Steiner Verlag, 1987.

Laure, J., *Valeur nutritionnelle des Produits de la Peche conserves artisanalement au Cameroun et au Tchad.* Paris: Editions ORSTOM, 1974.

Lebeuf, A. M. D., *Les Principautés Kotoko: essai sur le caractère sacré de l'autorité.* Paris: CNRS, 1969.

———. "Le Royaume du Bagirmi". In *Princes et Serviteurs du Royaume* edited by C. Tardits, 171–225. Paris: Société d'ethnographie, 1987.

Levtzion, N., and J. F. P. Hopkins, eds., *Corpus of Early Arabic Sources for West African History*. Cambridge: Cambridge University Press, 1981.

Longacre, W. A., and J. M. Skibo, eds., *Kalinga Ethnoarchaeology: Expanding Archaeological Method and Theory*. Washington D.C.: Smithsonian Institution Press, 1994.

MacEachern, S., "Foreign Countries: The Development of Ethnoarchaeology in Sub-Saharan Africa." *Journal of World Prehistory* 10(1996): 243–304.

MacMichael, H. A., *A History of the Arabs in the Sudan*. Cambridge: Cambridge University Press, 1922.

McGuire, H. R. and M. B. Schiffer, "A Theory of Architectural Design." *Journal of Anthropological Archaeology* 2(1983): 277–303.

Miller, D., *Artefacts as Categories*. Cambridge: Cambridge University Press, 1985.

Mohammed, I. M., *The Archaeology of Central Darfur (Sudan) in the Ist Millennium A.D.*. Oxford: British Archaeological Reports, 1986.

Nachtigal, G., *Sahara and Sudan (Vol. III): The Chad Basin and Bagirmi*. Translated and annotted by A. G. B. Fisher and H. J. Fisher. London: C. Hurst, 1987.

———. *Voyages et Explorations (1869–1875): Tome I: Au Tibesti, du Bornu an Bagirmi; Tome II: Au Ouadaï*. Paris: Centre d'études sur l'histoire du Sahara, 1987.

Podlewski, A.-M., La dynamique des principales populations du Nord-Cameroun I (entre Bénoué et lac Tchad). *Cahiers ORSTOM-Sciences Humaines* 3 (special issue, 1966).

———. La dynamique des principales populations du Nord-Cameroun II "Piémont et plateau de l'Adamaoua. *Cahiers ORSTOM-Sciences Humaines* 8 (special issue, 1971).

Rackham, J., *Animal Bones*. London: British Museum Press, 1994.

Reyna, S.P., *Wars Without End: The Political Economy of a Precolonial African State*. Hanover, NH.: University Press of New England, 1990.

Sadr, K., *The Development of Nomadism in Ancient NE Africa*. Philadelphia: University of Pennsylvania Press, 1991.

Smith, A., "The Early states of the Central Sudan." In *History of West Africa* edited by J.F.A. Ajayi and M. Crowder, 152–195. London: Longman, 1976.

Smith, A.B., *Pastoralism in Africa: Origins and Development Ecology*. London: Hurst and Co., 1992.

Sterner, J., "Who is signalling whom? Ceramic Style among the Sirak Bulahay." Paper presented at the Annual Meeting of the Canadian Archaeological Association, Calgary, April 22–26, 1987.

Tijani, K., "The Shuwa-Arab." In *Pastoralists of the West African Savanna,* edited by M. Adamu and A.H.M. Kirk-Greene, 62–73. Manchester: Manchester University Press, 1986.

Wobst, M., "Stylistic behavior and information exchange." In *For the Director: in Honor of J.B. Griffin* edited by C. Clelland, 317–342. Anthropological Papers 61. The University of Michigan Museum of Anthropology, 1977.

Yellen, J., *Archaeological Approaches to the Present*. New York: Academic Press, 1977.

Zeltner, J. C., *Histoire des Arabes sur les rives du Lac Tchad. Annales de l'Université d'Abidjan* 2, 1970.

———. *Les Arabes dans la région du Tchad: Problèmes d'origine et de chronologie.* Sarh: Centre d'études Linguistiques, 1979.

———. *Pages d'histoire du Kanem: Pays Tchadien.* Paris: L'Harmattan, 1980.

———. *Les Pays du Tchad dans la tourmente 1880–1903.* Paris: L'Harmattan, 1988.

Index

About the Author

Augustin F. C. Holl is professor of anthropology and Afroamerican & African Studies at the University of Michigan and a curator at the University of Michigan's Museum of Anthropology. He is the author of *The Diwan Revisited: Literacy, State Formation, and the Rise of Kanuri Domination (AD 1200–1600)* (2000) and (with M. S. Bisson, S. T. Childs, and P. de Barros) *Ancient African Metallurgy: The Sociocultural Context* (AltaMira, 2000).